Praise for *Angel in t...*

"Bobrick has studied his subject deeply and writes about it w... ...
and verve . . . [his] narrative entertainingly but authoritatively lays out the texture
of life at the time, with all the necessary sense of how people lived and thought.
And it covers the war in satisfying detail without ever losing momentum. . . . The
American Revolution is full of amazing characters and stories . . . what it has
needed in recent years is a storyteller fit to get it between two covers. Now it has
found one."　　　　　　*—The New York Times Book Review*

"Extraordinarily well-researched and gracefully written . . . a fascinating story that
is as intriguing and certainly more exciting than many works of fiction today . . .
and what an excellent work it is, filled with human interest, information on the
hows and whys of the conflict, and out-of-the-way details that fill in the picture.
All are interwoven masterfully, providing a history that is pleasing and informative
to both the lay reader and the specialist."
　　　　　　—The Virginian Pilot

"Engaging . . . Thoroughly enjoyable . . . Vivid and lively."
　　　　　　—The Boston Globe

"A stirring account of the American Revolution, well-written and well-balanced
. . . a story so compellingly told that it will appeal to every kind of reader."
　　　　　　—Asa Briggs, *The Washington Times*

"Bobrick offers an accessible history of this nation's founding."
　　　　　　—USA Today

"The author blends the political, military, cultural, and philosophical into a continuously exciting narrative. . . . Fewer books by far are written nowadays about
the Revolutionary War than about most of America's other conflicts. *Angel in the
Whirlwind* makes one wonder why this should be so, for it tells a dramatic and
surprisingly suspenseful story filled with memorable characters."
　　　　　　—Parade

"A sweeping grand narrative of the Revolutionary War, this book is equal in
stature to the events it describes. . . . No reader who starts at Lexington Green will
stop before Cornwallis hoists the white flag at Yorktown."
　　　　　　—Booklist

"A wonderful one-volume history of the war . . . Entertaining and inspiring . . .
This is a very human history of the war, full of sex, booze, treachery, derring-do,
and horror."　　　　　　*—The San Diego Union Tribune*

"A superb dramatic narrative."
　　　　　　—Library Journal

"Written with lucidity and analytical savvy. It now stands as the most accessible
single-volume narrative of the American Revolution available. A must read!"
　　　　　　—Douglas Brinkley, Director, The Eisenhower Center for
　　　　　　American Studies, University of New Orleans

"A highly impressive show of exhaustive research and engaging storytelling."
　　　　　　—Publishers Weekly

PENGUIN BOOKS

ANGEL IN THE WHIRLWIND

Benson Bobrick earned his doctorate at Columbia University. He is the author of several distinguished works of history, among them *East of the Sun*, an acclaimed narrative of the conquest and settlement of Siberia, and *Fearful Majesty: The Life and Reign of Ivan the Terrible*. He lives and teaches in Vermont.

ANGEL in the WHIRLWIND

THE TRIUMPH OF THE AMERICAN REVOLUTION

Benson Bobrick

PENGUIN BOOKS

PENGUIN BOOKS
Published by the Penguin Group
Penguin Putnam Inc., 375 Hudson Street,
New York, New York 10014, U.S.A.
Penguin Books Ltd, 27 Wrights Lane, London W8 5TZ, England
Penguin Books Australia Ltd, Ringwood, Victoria, Australia
Penguin Books Canada Ltd, 10 Alcorn Avenue,
Toronto, Ontario, Canada M4V 3B2
Penguin Books (N.Z.) Ltd, 182–190 Wairau Road,
Auckland 10, New Zealand

Penguin Books Ltd, Registered Offices:
Harmondsworth, Middlesex, England

First published in the United States of America by Simon & Schuster Inc. 1997
Published in Penguin Books 1998

1 3 5 7 9 10 8 6 4 2

THE LIBRARY OF CONGRESS HAS CATALOGUED THE HARDCOVER AS FOLLOWS:
Bobrick, Benson, date.
Angel in the whirlwind: the triumph of the American Revolution / Benson Bobrick.
p. cm.
ISBN 0-684-81060-3 (hc.)
ISBN 0 14 02.7500 2 (pbk.)
Includes bibliographical references and index.
1. United States—History—Revolution, 1775–1783. I. Title.
E208.B683 1997
973.3—dc21   97–11320

Printed in the United States of America
Set in Garamond Light
Designed by Karolina Harris
Maps by Jeffrey L. Ward

To my brother, Peter,
and to all my forebears,
patriot and loyalist,
who fought and died on both sides
of the Revolutionary War

CONTENTS

We know the Race is not to the swift nor the Battle to the Strong. Do you not think an Angel rides in the Whirlwind and directs this Storm?

—JOHN PAGE TO THOMAS JEFFERSON (JULY 20, 1776)

PREFACE

A G R E A T many books have been written on the American Revolution and quite a few of them are good. I have not written mine to try to supersede them, or out of some general dissatisfaction with the canon, but—hearkening to the voice of my own ancestral heritage—to retell the story in my own way. It is such a remarkable story that to do so scarcely needs excuse; yet it made a difference to me in the writing that I was bound by lineage to the tale.

My colonial forebears (English, French Huguenot, and Dutch) had fought and died on both sides of the war. The English, stem and branch, were the "Bakers" (my middle name is Baker); the Dutch, the "Bensons"; the French Huguenots, the "Valleaus." Some had been in America since 1649, had settled New Amsterdam and New Rochelle, served for three quarters of a century in the king's American wars (one perished in the Schenectady Massacre of 1690), but when the Revolution came were divided against themselves. The Bakers, as far as I know, were all staunch patriots. But within the Benson and Valleau families, brother stood against brother, father against son. At least two served in the Continental Army, three in loyalist troops. One of the patriots (Isaiah Valleau) was captured by the British, imprisoned in the Sugarhouse (a major site of incarceration) in New York City, and there succumbed to starvation and disease. His younger brother Peter remained a loyalist to the end. One of the loyalists (Matthew Benson, an officer in the King's Orange Rangers) had his property expropriated by his brother, John, who became a patriot judge. Matthew's eldest son was killed by patriots in battle; John's son witnessed the execution of Major John André (Benedict Arnold's coconspirator) at Tappan.

At the conclusion of the war, Matthew Benson and Peter Valleau were both exiled with many other loyalists to the Cataraqui area of Canada West, north of Lake Ontario. Matthew sailed on July 4, 1783, with his wife and surviving children from New York City on the British transport *Hope,* wintered with some four hundred other refugees in canvas tents at Sorel northeast of Montréal, and in the spring of 1784 proceeded by bateaux up the St. Lawrence River, dragging the boats by hand up numerous rapids to Adolphustown on the Bay of Quinte, where they arrived on June 16, 1784. In the beginning, Matthew worked as a mill hand and during the "Hungry Years" survived in part on flour dust swept up from the floor.

Peter Valleau also settled in the Cataraqui region and there in 1801 his daughter married Matthew's son.

In the historic White Chapel graveyard outside Picton, Ontario, every third or fourth headstone bears the Benson family name.

Meanwhile, the Bakers had remained in the States, were eventually joined by marriage to the Valleau-Benson line—a reconciliation in my blood—and came down squarely on one side of the second great American divide. My great-grandfather Benjamin W. Baker stood in the audience of one of the Lincoln-Douglas debates, and at age eighteen, at the beginning of the Civil War, answered Abraham Lincoln's first call for volunteers. He served in the Union Army until the war's end, was wounded three times (once severely), and after one battle (Chickamauga, I believe) buried his younger brother, who had fought and died beside him, on the battlefield. After the war, he became a Methodist minister. His son (my grandfather) became a bishop of the Methodist Church, and as chairman of the International Missionary Council was authorized by President Truman at the end of World War II to undertake a goodwill mission to Japan. Received by General MacArthur on October 26, 1945, he was the first American civilian after the surrender to set foot on Japanese soil. President Eisenhower also valued his counsel, but such are history's long divisions that his son-in-law (my father) ended up on Nixon's "Enemies List." Were Nixon's loyalists all patriots? One may doubt it. But these are changeable terms. And so I trust my loyalist forebears will forgive my own patriot bias in what follows, though I have tried not to slight their point of view. If I have, I may be guilty not so much of disloyalty as of some lapse in my patriot strain.

W O R K S of history have a lineage, too, and I am respectfully bound to numerous others who have gone before me and tilled the common ground. Some part of my debt is recorded in the Bibliography, but I am also obliged to the resources and staffs of the New York Public Library, the New-York Historical Society, the Virginia Historical Society, the Massachusetts Historical Society, the Library of Congress, the libraries of Columbia University, the David Library of the American Revolution, and the United Empire Loyalist Archives in Picton and Adolphustown, Ontario, Canada.

My original editor, Elaine Pfefferblit, did much to foster the idea for this book at the outset; Bob Bender, her successor, saw to it that it was completely and fervently sustained. His assistant, Johanna Li, helped smooth the process of production. Ruth Benson, Elizabeth Bobrick, Ako Po Darling, Michael Duzynski, Vicki Glasgow, Jeannie Goldstein, Malcolm Lister, Kenneth MacWilliams, Henry Marcus, Lucy Prospect, Graydon Rhodes, Vivienne Shaffer, Jane Siebert, Sarah Stern, Pat Troy, and Leslie Walsh all contributed something of value along the way.

Only Hilary knows the full extent of my loving gratitude for her support.

My brother, Peter, who preceded me into some areas of family history, will appreciate why the book is dedicated to him.

PART
ONE

1. Patriots defeat British at Lexington and Concord. April 19, 1775.

2. Arnold and Allen capture Fort Ticonderoga. May 10, 1775.

3. Battle of Bunker Hill. June 17, 1775.

4. British burn Falmouth, Maine. October 18, 1775.

5. Montgomery and Arnold repulsed. January 1, 1776.

6. Howe defeats Washington, Battle of Long Island. August 27, 1776.

7. Arnold and Carleton fight Battle of Lake Champlain. October 11, 1776.

8. British occupy Newport, Rhode Island. December 8, 1776.

9. Washington surprises the Hessians at Trenton. December 26, 1776.

10. Washington's winter quarters. 1777–1778.

11. Battle of Princeton. January 3, 1777.

12. Washington's winter quarters. 1777 and 1779.

13. British raid Danbury. April 26, 1777.

14. Burgoyne captures Fort Ticonderoga. July 6, 1777.

15. Herkimer ambushed. August 6, 1777.

16. Battle of Bennington. August 16, 1777.

17. St. Leger abandons siege of Fort Stanwix. August 22, 1777.

18. Washington defeated by Howe. September 11, 1777.

19. Wayne surprised and defeated at Paoli. September 21, 1777.

20. Battle of Germantown. October 4, 1777.

21. Burgoyne surrenders to Gates. October 17, 1777.

22. Battle of Monmouth Courthouse. June 28, 1778.

23. Cherry Valley raided by Tories and Indians. July 1–5, 1778.

24. Wayne takes Stony Point. July 16, 1779.

25. Arnold attacks New London. September 6, 1781.

The
AMERICAN REVOLUTION
in the NORTH

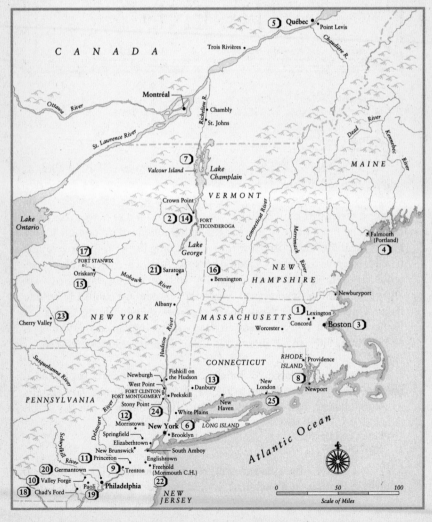

Scale of Miles

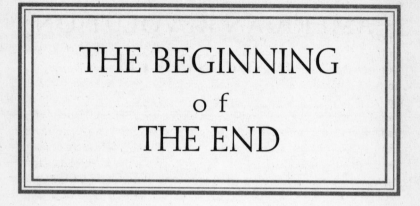

CHAPTER ONE

THE BEGINNING
o f
THE END

On July 4, 1754, a young major adjutant general in the Virginia militia retreated through mud and rain along a forest path as the defeated remnants of his expeditionary force staggered under the weight of the sick and wounded on their backs. A month and a half before, they had crossed the main ridge of the Allegheny Mountains to do battle with the French; and they had lost. Now they were going back. In the developing frontier struggle for the domination of North America, this critical reversal would cost the English such credibility with their long-standing Indian allies that in the following year, when the smoldering conflict burst into flame, "nearly all the western tribes drew their scalping-knives for France." For the Virginia major, it was perhaps the darkest day thus far of his young life, and it threatened an early and inglorious end to his career.

That major was George Washington, who was twenty-two years old at the time. But Providence had assigned him a very different fate and, by its adumbrations, had foreshadowed his later triumph in the day of his defeat.

S I N C E 1690, there had been three wars between the French and English in Europe, and each had rippled outward to the contested margins of their empires. In America, the cycle of violence had begun on February 9, 1690, when French soldiers and Indians, sweeping out of the forest, had fallen on the sleeping village of Schenectady, New York, and massacred the inhabitants. At the time, the French claimed almost the whole of North America, from the Alleghenies to the Rocky Mountains and from Mexico and Florida to the North Pole. These vast regions, with adjacent islands, they had grandly christened New France. The English, rather more modestly, claimed a string of colonial holdings on the Atlantic seaboard; but these they convincingly held. Most of the French settlers (about seventy-five thousand in all) were trappers and traders, who operated along the Mississippi and Saint Lawrence Rivers and seldom ventured to the farthest reaches of their theoretical domain; the English, on the other hand, had more than a million colonists, farming and creating growing towns and communities from Georgia to Maine.

Geography protracted the contest. In Canada and the American interior, it was hard to maneuver with decisive force and speed through forests or marshes, across mountains, or down rapids or streams choked with fallen trees. To some extent such terrain also rendered the numerical superiority of the English unavailing, since in actual encounters the numerical advantage often lay with the French. Moreover, the inability of the colonies to unite on almost any issue made it difficult for them to coordinate their efforts at defense. One Swedish visitor remarked, "It happens that in time of war things go on very slowly and irregularly here; for not only the opinion of one province is sometimes directly opposite to that of another, but frequently the views of the governor and those of the assembly of the same province are quite different; so it is easy to see that, while the people are quarrelling about the best and cheapest manner of carrying on the war, an enemy has it in his power to take one place after another!"

King William's War (begun by the Schenectady Massacre) came to an end in 1697 and, after five years of an uneasy peace, was followed by Queen Anne's War in 1702. That lasted until 1713. It was succeeded in turn by King George's War, from 1744 to 1748.

Nothing had been settled. The French remained entrenched in the vast interior, where they fortified their positions, consolidated their alliances with various Indian tribes, and at strategic points along the main tributaries of the Ohio River sank or buried engraved lead plates claiming the territory for France. By 1753, they had begun to link French Louisiana with Canada by a chain of forts in a strategy designed to prevent the English from extending their settlements westward beyond the mountains and thus to hem them in between the mountains and the sea.

The English viewed these encroachments with some apprehension, but in the international rivalry between the two empires, the development of sea power and the promotion of commerce assumed priority over all other concerns. Both France and Britain had established trading posts and ports of call in India, along the African coast, and in the West Indies in an effort to control both the slave trade and the European traffic in oriental goods. They valued their North American possessions primarily for what they could harvest or produce: fish, fur, and naval stores from the North; tobacco, sugar, rice, and indigo from the South. Sea power was essential to protect the distant trade routes, which meant not only the expansion of their respective navies but the establishment of naval stations at strategic locations like Gibraltar on the Mediterranean or Louisburg on the Canadian coast.

In North America, French and British commercial interests confronted each other on the seaboard of Acadia (extending from Nova Scotia northwestward to the Saint Lawrence basin); the area about Lake George and Lake Champlain along the Hudson–Saint Lawrence river route between New York and Montreal; the Great Lakes basin; and the Ohio Valley, which Virginia claimed even as the French moved to secure their access from the north. Late in 1753, in response, the royal governor of Virginia dispatched Major George Washington with a diplomatic protest to the French regional military commander at Fort Le Boeuf. When the French refused to withdraw, he sent Washington back early in the following year with militia and a company of British regulars to evict them.

This was the beginning of the French and Indian War.

By this time, the French were securely ensconced at Fort Duquesne on the site of modern Pittsburgh. Near Great Meadows—a level tract of grass bordered by wooded hills—Washington surprised a party of Frenchmen and opened fire, killing the French commanding officer and twenty men. Shortly thereafter, the French surrounded him in a hastily constructed log stockade, appropriately dubbed Fort Necessity, and on July 4, 1754, they forced him to capitulate.

Washington could scarcely be blamed entirely for the defeat. Promised reinforcements from North Carolina had never arrived, and those from New York, arriving late, had "crawled towards the scene of action with thin ranks, bad discipline, thirty women and children, no tents, no blankets, no knapsacks, and for munitions one barrel of spoiled gunpowder." Over the next several months, in the face of colonial inaction, the French gathered "like so many locusts" in pockets of the contested terrain.

France and Britain now poured in regular troops and roused their respective colonists and Indian allies. The Five Nations, or Iroquois tribal confederation, cast in their lot with the English, the Algonquin tribes with the French. New Englanders "rallied creditably to the side of the king's troops, but contributions from the middle and southern colonies, which had the most to gain, were negligible in proportion to their population." From the Ohio Valley the war rolled northward—at first primarily as a counter against French aggressions—but eventually amid the great lakes and wooded mountains of New England and western New York and on the wild coasts of Nova Scotia, it evolved into a contest for Canada as well.

The British went on the offensive and in February 1755 disembarked two regiments of regulars at Hampton, Virginia, under the command of General Edward Braddock of the Coldstream Guards. He proceeded up the Potomac to Alexandria, where together with several colonial governors he mapped out a campaign. The French were to be attacked at four points at once: two British regiments and a force of about 450 Virginia militia were to advance on Fort Duquesne (near the confluence of the Monongahela and Allegheny Rivers); two provincial regiments to reduce Fort Niagara (in western New York); a combined body of provincials from New England, New York, and New Jersey to seize the stronghold at Crown Point (at the southern end of Lake Champlain); and another body of New Englanders to capture Beauséjour and bring Acadia (in Canada) into subjection.

Braddock himself was to lead the expedition against Fort Duquesne, but despite his enthusiasm (and his record of success in fighting clansmen in the Scottish Highlands), he was not the right man. Benjamin Franklin, who was assigned the logistical task of rounding up wagons and packhorses for the march, wrote, "Braddock might probably have made a good figure in some European war. But he had too much self-confidence; too high an opinion of the validity of regular troops; too mean a one of both Americans and Indians." In this, he was typical of the British officer corps.

He also thought the campaign would be easy. "I shall hardly need to stop more than three or four days at Fort Duquesne; then I shall march on to Niagara, and from there to Frontenac," he told Franklin. When the latter tactfully warned him of the danger of ambush, as "the slender line, near four miles long, which your army must make, may . . . be cut like a thread into several pieces," Braddock replied with a smile, "These savages may, indeed, be a formidable enemy to your raw American militia, but upon the king's regular and disciplined troops, sir, it is impossible they should make any impression."

Braddock also paid little heed to the seasoned frontier advice of Washington, now a colonel, who accompanied his expedition as an aide-de-camp. "He looks upon the country, I believe, as void of honor or honesty," Washington wrote at the time. "We have frequent disputes on this head, which are maintained with warmth on both sides, especially on his, as he is incapable of arguing without it, or giving up any point he asserts, be it ever so incompatible with reason or common sense."

Washington already had plenty of firsthand experience with the presumptions of the king's men. When he had been trapped at Fort Necessity, reinforcements had arrived under a Captain Mackay, bearing a royal commission. Mackay, however, in a fatal separation of their forces, had refused to acknowledge Washington as his superior in command.

On the tenth of June, Braddock set off from Virginia's Fort Cumberland on his march over the mountains. His heavily laden wagons were dragged with difficulty up the steep and rugged roads, and his supply train, extending for three or four miles, contained many "articles of artificial necessity" inappropriate to a backwoods campaign. One packhorse, for example, typically carried six pounds of loaf sugar, a pound of green tea, a pound of bohea tea, six pounds of ground coffee, six pounds of chocolate, a half chest of white biscuit, a half pound of pepper, a quart of white vinegar, two dozen bottles of old Madeira wine, two gallons of "Jamaica spirits" (rum), one bottle of powdered mustard, two "well-cured hams," a dozen cured tongues, six pounds of rice, six pounds of raisins, twenty pounds of butter, and one Gloucester cheese. A full month was thus consumed in marching about a hundred miles—which slowness evoked the irrepressible sarcasm of Horace Walpole, who wrote, "General Braddock does not march as if he is at all impatient to be scalped." Meanwhile, most of the hundred or so Indians he had taken with him as scouts had deserted in the face of his abuse.

Washington advised Braddock to divide his forces, leaving one part to come on with the army's stores, baggage, and more cumbersome appurtenances, and with the other (light artillery and his elite troops) to advance rapidly on Fort Duquesne before it could be reinforced. Twelve hundred men were selected for the attack, but "I found," wrote Washington, "that instead of pushing on with vigor, disregarding a little rough road, they were halting to level every molehill and to erect bridges over every brook, by which means we were four days in getting twelve miles."

On July 9, Braddock at last crossed the Monongahela River, about ten miles from where Fort Duquesne stood.

A rough path led before them over open, level ground until it curved along the base of a line of steep, forested hills. On either side of the path were thickly wooded ravines. Braddock neglected to send out scouting parties well in advance of his soldiers to reconnoiter the flanks, but instead advanced through the clearing in the greatest order with his whole force, their bayonets fixed, colors flying, and drums and fifes beating and playing—"as if in a review in St. James's Park."

At two o'clock, French and Indians rose out of the woods. The Virginia troops immediately scattered and took up positions behind bushes and trees, in a skirmishing style of fighting with which they might have held their own; but Braddock absurdly ordered them back into line and formed his regulars into platoons.

Thus arrayed as easy targets but unable to see the enemy themselves, they wasted their ammunition while enemy bullets poured with impunity into their lines. Even more terribly, many of the Virginians were slain by the blind British fire. At length the regulars lost their nerve completely and began rushing frantically about. "When we endeavoured to rally them," recalled Washington, "it was with as much success as if we had attempted to stop wild bears."

Braddock rode back and forth in the thick of it all on his charger and, after four horses were shot under him, mounted a fifth. Washington was no less brave. Indeed, his coolness, courage, and knowledge of Indian warfare were chiefly responsible for the preservation of the surviving troops. Though he escaped unhurt, two horses were also killed under him, and four bullets pierced his clothes.

Retreat alone spared their forces absolute annihilation. When the battle was over, 750, or two thirds of the British and American contingent (including three quarters of its officers), lay dead or wounded, while the Indians and French had lost just 51. Braddock himself had taken a bullet in the lungs.

To expedite the long march back to Fort Cumberland, much of the baggage train, including cannon, munitions, and equipment, was discarded or destroyed. Provisions were scattered through the woods and swamps. Indians afterward gathered up much of the equipment—grenadiers' caps, canteens, bayonets, and so on—and as they drifted in to Fort Duquesne toward nightfall, one eyewitness remembered, "it seemed to me that almost everyone of them was carrying scalps."

Braddock, failing fast, was silent throughout the first day of the retreat and at night said only, "Who would have thought it?" On the following day, he said merely, "We shall better know how to deal with them another time." Then he expired. He was deliberately buried in an unmarked grave in the road so that all his men, horses, and wagons would pass over the spot, "effacing every sign of it, lest the Indians should find and mutilate his corpse."

Washington's subsequent account of the debacle was scathing: "The dastardly behaviour of the English soldiers exposed all those who were inclined to do their duty to almost certain death." Years afterward, Benjamin Franklin remarked facetiously, "[this battle] gave us the first suspicion that our exalted ideas of the prowess of British regular troops had not been well founded."

Of the three other British campaigns of 1755, only the attack on Fort Beauséjour in Acadia was successful. But it had little strategic bearing on the war.

BRADDOCK'S defeat left the long frontier from Maryland to Pennsylvania exposed, and, with the encouragement of the French, the western tribes now attacked the border settlements with seeming impunity. "No road is safe," wrote Washington as scalping parties came to within fifty miles of Philadelphia. Not far from the Moravian town of Bethlehem, Indians fell on the village of Gnadenhutten and massacred the inhabitants. By fall, the whole frontier was in a panic, and the French commandant at Fort Duquesne was exulting that "prisoners of every age and sex" were being held by his Indian allies. The fate of many captives and other settlers was cruel. "The [Indians] kill all they meet," admitted one French priest, "and after having abused the women and maidens, kill them and scalp the children alive."

Meanwhile, on August 14, the Virginia Assembly had appointed Washington its commander in chief of militia, and in that capacity he undertook the almost impossible task of defending a 350-mile-long frontier. At his disposal he had just 1,500 men, and the insufficiency of this force drove him almost to despair. "The supplicating tears of the women and moving petitions of the men," he wrote, "melt me into such deadly sorrow, that I solemnly declare, if I know my own mind, I could offer myself a willing sacrifice to the butchering enemy, provided that would contribute to the people's ease."

By 1756, the conflict which had begun in the backwoods of America had spread to the rest of the world. In May and June, England and France formally declared war on each other and, in what came to be known as the Seven Years' War, allied themselves to various other European powers. They preyed upon one another's shipping, clashed directly or through surrogates on the European mainland, and met directly in India and North Africa and on islands of the sea. In the wilderness of North America, it was "an abominable kind of war," wrote one Frenchman, in which "insensibility and hardness" seemed "to infect the very air one breathed." In addition to the British regulars that came over in waves, some 20,000 Americans took part in the fighting, including a special corps of American rangers made up of independent frontiersmen of particular toughness, daring, and skill. As they prowled the woodlands, "summer and winter, day and night, were alike to them," wrote the great historian Francis Parkman:

> Embarked in whaleboats or birch-canoes, they glided under the silent moon, or in the languid glare of a breathless August day, when islands floated in a dreamy-haze, and the hot air was thick with odors of the pines. They were there in bright October, when the jay screamed from the woods, or squirrels gathered their winter hoard, and in the tomb-like silence of the winter forest, with breath frozen on his beard, the ranger strode on snow-shoes over the spotless drifts; and, like Durer's knight, a ghastly death stalked ever at his side.

For two years, the British commanders—first John Campbell, the Scottish earl of Loudoun, and his successor, James Abercrombie—proved ineffectual, while the French found strength and assurance in their brilliant general, the marquis de Montcalm. Montcalm took Fort Oswego on the south shore of Lake Ontario, the most important of the English outposts, and a year later destroyed Fort William Henry at the southern end of Lake George. For his part, Abercrombie led an army of nearly 15,000 British regulars and colonial militia to ignominious defeat at Fort Ticonderoga, where, on July 5, 1758, he allowed almost his whole force to be cut to pieces by Montcalm before the fortress walls.

Then the tide turned. William Pitt was appointed the British war minister, eliminated incompetents from the general staff, and chose Jeffrey Amherst and James Wolfe for his American command. Before the end of 1758, Louisbourg, Fort Frontenac (which controlled Lake Ontario), and Fort Duquesne had fallen to their troops.

In the advance on Fort Duquesne, Brigadier General John Forbes made his way (like Braddock before him) with difficulty over the mountains, divided his force and, with 2,500 picked men, pushed on for the assault. Washington led the vanguard and (unlike Braddock) made extensive use of scouting parties, but this time there was nothing to fear. The French commander had already abandoned the stronghold, blowing up his magazines and retreating down the Ohio River by the light of the flames. On the twenty-eighth, the British-American forces marched in. The fortress was refortified and garrisoned, its name was changed to Fort Pitt (in honor of William Pitt), and it became the nucleus of the future community of Pittsburgh.

So ended the campaign of 1758. The French had held their own at Ticonderoga, but their left and right flanks had been forced back. Time for them was running out. At the end of July 1759, Fort Niagara on New York's western frontier was captured by Sir William Johnson and his Iroquois allies, and the French bastions at Crown Point and Ticonderoga finally fell to Lord Amherst, which opened the way northward to the French provincial capital of Québec.

The battle for Québec was the decisive battle of the war. The city, an almost impregnable stronghold, was the "Gibraltar of America." Standing upon the crest of a monumental headland that thrust out into the Saint Lawrence River, it had an upper city, naturally defended by steep bluffs, and a lower city, ringed by forts. Below the town lay the Saint Charles River, considered unfordable and defended by a bridgehead. A boom of logs obstructed the river's mouth, and this boom in turn was guarded by a battery of heavy guns resting on three sunken ships. Earthworks had also been thrown up along the shore on either side.

On June 26, a fleet bearing a British army of 9,000 men under General Wolfe anchored just south of Québec City. The French general Montcalm, in charge of the city's defense, had at his disposal 7,000 troops, mostly Canadian militia, as well as Indian auxiliaries. But he not unreasonably expected that if Wolfe dared to attack, it would be through the lower city. And so that was where he kept his main force.

Wolfe laid siege but from the end of June to the twelfth of September made little headway. He bombarded the French from his frigates and islands in the stream and managed to run several vessels past the French artillery that swept the riverfront. But when he attempted to attack the French left, he was repulsed with heavy losses. One afternoon, however, he spied through his telescope a goat trail leading up to the Plains of Abraham, the heights above the town. The trail was defended by about 100 men, an adequate force for such a narrow defile. But early in the morning of September 13, 24 British commandos caught them napping. Within a few hours, 3,200 British soldiers had clambered up to the heights, dragging a cannon after them. To face them, Montcalm brought out two cannon and 5,000 men.

The day before, an ailing Wolfe had told his doctor, "I know perfectly well you cannot cure me, but pray make me up so that I may be without pain for a few days, and able to do my duty; that is all I want." As he had come down the river on the ebb tide to the path up to the heights, he had recited Thomas Gray's *Elegy in a Country Churchyard:* one way or another, he knew he was going to die.

The plains were a level tract of grass commanding the town and at the place Wolfe chose for his battlefield, less than a mile wide. Between the plains and Québec itself was a wooded hill. The first French soldiers appeared on its summit at about six o'clock.

The British were in line and waiting. At Wolfe's command, each soldier loaded his musket with two balls. The French charged—the British came forward as if to meet them, then halted and stood still. When the French had come to within forty yards, the British fired. The French line broke; the British charged and drove them back in a rout. Both Wolfe and Montcalm were mortally wounded in the action, which was remarkably brief. As Wolfe lay dying, an aide exclaimed, "They run; see how they run!" "Who run?" Wolfe asked in a daze. "The enemy, sir. They give way everywhere." Wolfe whispered, "God be praised, I will die in peace." His equally gallant adversary was laid to rest in a rough coffin lowered into a crater made by a British shell.

The remnants of the French army abandoned Québec and fell back to Montreal, where they held out for another year. But in August 1760, Lord Amherst brought an overpowering army to its gates, and on September 7 he received the garrison's unconditional surrender. Meanwhile, in the wider sphere of action, the English had driven the French from all of their East Indian possessions and part of their North African claims; had captured Grenada, Guadeloupe, Dominica, Martinique, Saint Lucia, and Saint Vincent in the West Indies; and had devastated the French merchant marine. Spain, out of fear of English domination, had entered the war on the side of France in 1761, but at great cost to herself and too late to rescue her ally. In 1762, Spanish Cuba and the Philippines fell to British troops.

Peace negotiations were opened in Paris, and on February 10, 1763, Canada and its dependencies passed by the stroke of a pen to the British Crown. The British returned the West Indian islands of Saint Lucia, Martinique, and Guadeloupe but kept the rest that they had captured. Spain agreed to cede Florida but recovered Cuba and the Philippines in a similar exchange. Nothing remained of the great French dominion in North America but a pair of little islands off the coast of Newfoundland where French fishermen could dry their nets.

All this made England preeminent among the maritime and colonial powers. David Garrick, the noted actor, rejoiced in a celebratory masque:

> Great Britain shall triumph, her ships plough the sea;
> Her standard is Justice; her watchword "Be free!"
> Then cheer up, my lads, with one heart let us sing,
> Our soldiers, our sailors, our statesmen, our King.

> Heart of oak are our ships, Jolly tars are our men,
> We always are ready,
> Steady, boys, steady!
> We'll fight and we'll conquer
> Again and again.

Yet there were intimations of mortality in the way the deal had been cut. Many Britons were unhappy with the territorial swap and thought England had needlessly relinquished many gains. "We retain nothing," exclaimed Pitt with considerable exaggeration, "although we have conquered everything. . . . By our concessions . . . we have given [France] the means of recovering her prodigious losses and of becoming once more formidable to us at sea." In this he would turn out to be right. At the same time (but with less perspicacity) a surprising number were in favor of returning Canada (which they regarded as a wintry wasteland) to France in exchange for the tiny but sugar-rich island of Guadeloupe. Before long, Garrick's proud and optimistic chant was drowned out by verses like these:

> *Britannia,* MISTRESS OF THE WORLD NO MORE
> By foes deluded, by false friends betray'd,
> And rifled of the spoils her conquests made;
> Curs'd with a treaty, whose unequal terms
> Check in mid-progress her victorious arms . . .

But in the American colonies, there were no such misgivings. From New England to the Carolinas, Americans lit bonfires, rang bells, fired off their guns in celebration, threw festive banquets, and marched in parades. Protestant clergymen joined in the rejoicing but also looked upon the French defeat in biblical terms: "God has given us to sing this day the downfall of New France, the North American Babylon, New England's rival," proclaimed Eli Forbes to his congregation in Brookfield, Massachusetts. "Methinks I see towns enlarged, settlements increased, and this howling wilderness become a fruitful field which the Lord hath blessed; and, to complete the scene, I see churches rise and flourish in every Christian grace where has been the seat of Satan and Indian idolatry."

European diplomats saw something else: that the completeness of the British victory carried with it the germs of the disintegration of the king's empire in America. As long as France had threatened the colonies, they had looked to the mother country for support and leadership, being unable to muster themselves to a common defense. But once the threat was past, what was to prevent them from going their own way? Montcalm himself, before the Battle of Quebec, had predicted not only his own defeat but its great aftermath in colonial rebellion. "I console myself," he said, "that in my defeat and in her conquest, England will find a tomb." And far away in Constantinople, the comte de Vergennes, then French ambassador to the court of the Ottoman Turks, wrote with remarkable prescience, "The colonies will no longer need Britain's protection. She will call on them to contribute toward supporting the burdens they have helped to bring on her, and they will answer by striking off their chains." Twelve years later, as French foreign minister, Vergennes would emerge as the architect of his government's pro-American policy during the Revolutionary War.

Whether the colonists themselves clearly understood their own situation is a question. Benjamin Franklin (the most worldly wise of them, perhaps) believed—or affected to believe—that the colonies were so jealous of one another that they would never unite against their mother country: "If they could not agree to unite against the French and Indians, can it reasonably be supposed that there is any danger of their uniting against their own nation, which it is well known they all love much more than they love one another? I will venture to say union amongst them for such a purpose is not merely improbable, it is impossible"—unless, he added, they are made to feel "the most grievous tyranny and oppression."

CHAPTER TWO

THE COLONIAL WORLD

It was a commonplace of the discourse of Empire to speak of Britain as the "mother country" and of her colonies as "children." And this had been the case for some time. For the most part, such familial language was used with affection, but beginning in 1765 a satirical or recalcitrant vein crept in, as in a ballad written by Benjamin Franklin himself called "The Mother Country":

> We have an old Mother that peevish is grown,
> She snubs us like Children that scarce walk alone;
> She forgets we're grown up and have Sense of our own;
>> *Which nobody can deny, deny, which nobody can deny.*
>
> If we don't obey Orders, whatever the Case;
> She frowns, and she chides, and she loses all Pati-
> Ence, and sometimes she hits us a Slap in the Face,
>> *Which nobody can deny, &c.*
>
> Her Orders so odd are, we often suspect
> That Age has impaired her sound Intellect:
> But still an old Mother should have due Respect,
>> *Which nobody can deny, &c.*

Let's bear with her Humours as well as we can:
But why should we bear the Abuse of her Man?
When Servants make Mischief; they earn the Rattan,
    Which nobody can deny, &c.

Know too, ye bad Neighbours, who aim to divide
The Sons from the Mother, that still she's our Pride;
And if ye attack her we're all of her side,
    Which nobody can deny, &c.

We'll join in her Lawsuits, to baffle all those,
Who, to get what she has, will be often her Foes:
For we know it must all be our own, when she goes,
    Which nobody can deny, deny, which nobody can deny.

Franklin's ballad expressed a conditionally defiant but still loyal attitude to England, with a clear warning to the French. Nevertheless, it also seemed to predict a time of independence, when the colonies (like children upon the demise of their parents) would claim their just inheritance. Two years later, Pennsylvania lawyer John Dickinson, in one of his famous "Letters from a Pennsylvania Farmer," more sheepishly advised his compatriots, "Let us behave like dutiful children who have received unmerited blows from a beloved parent. Let us complain to our parent; but let our complaints speak at the same time the language of affection and veneration." English statesmen favored the same metaphor, for example, Lord Chatham, William Pitt: "I love the Americans because they love liberty, and I love them for the noble efforts they made in the last war . . . [but] they must be subordinate. In all laws relating to trade and navigation especially, this is the mother country, they are the children; they must obey and we prescribe."

Almost no one in America at the end of the French and Indian War would have disagreed, despite some grumbling. The colonies were joined to Britain "in a triple kinship of laws, language, and blood," as Francis Parkman put it, and it would be only after a decade of intermittent but escalating disagreement that Americans would come to believe that a "most grievous tyranny and oppression" had descended upon their lives.

B Y the time the British had prevailed over the French, English settlement in America was almost two hundred years old. In 1585, Sir Walter Raleigh had started a colony on Roanoke Island off the North Carolina coast, but it had ended mysteriously when 150 colonists had disappeared without a trace, leaving nothing but the word CROATAN (the name of a local Indian tribe) carved on a tree. In April 1607, Captain John Smith had sailed into Hampton Roads and founded Jamestown, Virginia, with a fort, a storehouse, a row of huts, and a church. For the last, he vividly tells us, "Wee did hang an awning, which is an old saile, to three or foure trees to shadow us from the Sunne; our walls were railes of wood; our seates unhewed trees till we cut plankes; our Pulpit a bar of wood nailed to two neighbouring trees. In foul weather we shifted into an old rotten tent. . . . This was our Church till we built a homely thing like a barne." Thirteen years later, in December 1620, two hundred English settlers disembarked from the *Mayflower* on the Massachusetts coast at Plymouth Rock. They clung with tenacity to their rockbound shore, building a fort and a watchtower on Burial Hill. Though more than half died of cold and scurvy that first winter, the settlement survived and grew.

Since that time, thirteen colonies had been established in America (most during the seventeenth century but the latest, Georgia, in 1732), with 2.5 to 3 million inhabitants, including 500,000 African slaves. On the whole, they formed a diverse group of political, ethnic, and religious entities that occupied the length of the eastern seaboard with settlements extending westward to the Appalachian Mountains. Although all to varying degrees had representative governments and subscribed to English law—in most instances there was a royal governor (appointed by the Crown), an upper (nominated) House, and an elected Assembly representing the various districts and towns—their political evolution (as derived from the dates and circumstances of their origin) had followed various courses. In New England and Virginia, for example, the representative assemblies were more powerful and fully constitutional (as a counterweight to the governor's royal prerogative) than in Maryland, Georgia, and the Carolinas, where such institutions were incomplete.

Both the New England colonies and Pennsylvania had been founded by those seeking religious freedom; others had developed from strategic ventures or proprietary grants. New York (originally New Netherlands) had begun primarily as a commercial enterprise launched by the Dutch West India Company in 1623; Maryland had been founded in 1632 in part as a refuge for Catholics; Georgia a century later as a repository for convicts and debtors but also as a buffer between South Carolina and the Spanish settlements in Florida. Nevertheless, over time the colonies had more or less associated themselves into three groups: the New England colonies (Massachusetts, Connecticut, Rhode Island, and New Hampshire, with the still-unincorporated territories of Vermont and Maine); the middle colonies (New York, New Jersey, Delaware, and

Pennsylvania); and the southern colonies (Virginia, Maryland, North and South Carolina, and Georgia). There was little commerce or communication among them, and regional differences, conflicting economic interests, and boundary disputes kept them apart.

The New England economies were based on farming, coastal fishing, some manufacturing (such as shipbuilding), and seaborne trade. The middle colonies depended primarily on farming and cottage industries, especially Old World crafts; while the economic life of the South revolved around large cash crops such as tobacco in Virginia and Maryland and rice in the Carolinas. Proportionately more productive and profitable per acre than maize, wheat, or oats (the major grains), tobacco had come to predominate even in Georgia, where the intention of the original colonists had been to cultivate silkworms and grapes.

Intercolony trade was modest, but the foreign trade carried on by some of the colonies was fairly large. By 1700, Virginia and Maryland were exporting annually more than £300,000 worth of tobacco to England, as well as a good deal of sugar and rice, while New England had begun to develop strong trading ties with southern Europe and the West Indies. Pennsylvania, in turn, carried on a "surprisingly extensive" trade, wrote Andrew Burnaby, a young English candidate for holy orders who traveled through the colonies in 1759–1760, "to Great Britain, the West Indies, every part of North America, the Madeiras, Lisbon, Cádiz, Holland, Africa, the Spanish Main, and several other places, exclusive of what is illicitly carried on to Cape François, and Monte Cristo." By the 1760s, the colonies accounted for close to 12 percent of British imports, a quarter of her domestic exports, and a tenth of her reexports to other lands. Imports were mostly items manufactured in England, "with the superfluities and luxuries of life."

There was competition among the great cities. Boston's fleet of seagoing vessels ranked third in the English-speaking world, exceeded only by those of London and Bristol, but by the time of the Revolution, Philadelphia had surpassed Boston in size and, after London, was the second city of the empire. On the other hand, New York was considered the geographical and military fulcrum of British colonial power. Bostonians regarded their own town as the most civilized of the great ports, or at least as more civil than Philadelphia or New York. New Yorkers (then as now) tended to talk "very loud, very fast, and all together," complained one Bostonian, who also wrote that Philadelphia, for all its grandeur, lacked taste and style and was governed by inferior laws.

Philadelphia's grandeur was all its own. William Penn had conceived it as a "greene countrie towne which may never be burnt" and had laid it out in a grid, with each house placed in the middle of a large lot so as to leave ground on either side for gardens or orchards or fields. It had neat, wide, tree-lined streets that were "straight as a string," with wide sidewalks for pedestrians and many fine brick houses, some with handsome painted awnings and second-story balconies "where oftentimes the men sit in a cool habit and smoke."

Many of the streets were paved (and diligently cleaned by a sanitation department that carted away the refuse); at night they were lit by streetlamps and patrolled by constables. By the end of the colonial period, Philadelphia had 40,000 inhabitants, almost twice the number of New York.

New York, the next in size with a population of 25,000, occupied the southern end of Manhattan Island and in 1770 extended only to about Catherine and Reade Streets. At the island's southern tip stood the main battery, a great half-moon or semicircular rampart facing out upon the water and mounted with fifty-six great guns. At the opposite end of town was the common. Connecting the two was the wide, paved central thoroughfare of Broadway, lined on both sides with regularly spaced young poplars and elms. To the north lay farmlands, marshes, and woods.

Most of the side streets were narrow, meandering, and poorly paved, leading to the Hudson or East Rivers, but there were sidewalks as far as Vesey Street, and a few streetlamps on posts had recently been installed. Most areas of New York, however, were required to have a lantern and candle hung on a pole from every seventh house. The watchman repeatedly called out, "Lanthorn, and a whole can-dell-light. Hang out your lights." He was also an auxiliary policeman, or rattle-watch, so called because he carried a large rattle, or "klopper," which he would strike to frighten thieves away. All night long he announced the hour and the weather: "One o'clock and fair winds" or "Five o'clock and cloudy skies." Regular policemen, or constables, carried black staves six feet long, tipped with brass.

Unlike in Philadelphia, many of the houses in New York were set wall to wall like tenements, without a surrounding firebreak, and as yet the city had no system of water supply, though a large public well was being built at Broadway and Chambers Street from which an engine was to pump water to residents through wooden pipes. There was also no fire department, but in New York as well as Boston, each family owned fire buckets made of heavy leather and embossed with the owner's name, which were kept in a nearby church. When a fire broke out, local residents would form a double line to the nearest river and pass the buckets to and from the blaze.

• • •

I N one way or another the colonies had been trying to unite since 1643, when the four New England colonies had signed articles for mutual defense against invasion by Indians or any other hostile force. In 1696, William Penn had suggested the formation of a colonial congress with a commissioner appointed by the king as executive officer. Five years later, three regional confederations had also been proposed, but without result.

Although the British often complained of the lack of coordination among the colonies in such matters as defense, they also discouraged concerted effort out of fear that some "dangerous union" (as one royal governor of Pennsylvania put it) be formed. In 1754, however, the British authorities, as represented by the London Board of Trade, called a conference at Albany, New York, to try to get the colonies to unite at least on their Indian affairs. Benjamin Franklin, who went as a delegate, was an ardent champion of the idea. Three years before, he had told a friend that he found it "a very strange thing, if six Nations of ignorant Savages [meaning the Iroquois confederacy] should be capable of forming a Scheme for such an Union," yet "a like Union should be impracticable for ten or a Dozen English Colonies." In May 1754, the *Pennsylvania Gazette* had printed his famous woodcut of a snake broken into eight pieces, each piece labeled with initials: N.E., N Y, N J., P., M., V., N.C., S.C., with the caption JOIN OR DIE. "Every Body cries, a Union is absolutely necessary," he wrote, "but when they come to the Manner and Form of the Union, their weak Noddles are presently distracted. So if ever there be an Union it must be form'd at home by the Ministry and Parliament." A month later, he set off for the Albany conference, where he presented a plan that guaranteed local self-government to each colony and provided for a federal council of representatives chosen by the colonial assemblies under a governor-general with executive powers appointed by the Crown.

The conference endorsed it, but in the end it found favor with neither the colonial assemblies to which it was submitted (which were jealous of their own independence) nor the officials in London (who preferred a union of a less popular sort). As Franklin later noted in his *Autobiography,* had the colonies been allowed to unite, they could have defended themselves and "there would then have been no need of troops from England." When the troops came, they furnished the reason or pretext for the taxes against which the colonists rebelled.

• • •

EARLY propaganda designed to promote settlement in the New World had encouraged great expectations. One pamphlet published in London in 1670 described New York as a kind of Eden where every crop of grain had a "very good increase" and "all other Fruits and Herbs common in England besides." The woods were said to abound with game and the waters off Long Island to teem with fish, seals, walrus, and whales. Local medicinal plants offered the immigrant a complete therapeutic range: "Many are of the opinion, and the Natives do affirm, that there is no disease common to the Countrey, but may be cured." As for the Indians, there was nothing to fear. "There are now but few upon the Island, and it hath been generally observed," claimed the pamphlet with a terrible condescension, "that where the English come to setle, a Divine Hand makes way for them, by removing or cutting off the Indians, either by Wars one with the other, or by some raging mortal Disease." Those that remained were said to be harmless gamblers or drunks.

Other colonies lured newcomers with a similar pitch. Georgia was said to be such a land as "Nature has not bless'd the World with any Tract, which can be preferable to it, that Paradise with all her Virgin Beauties, may be modestly suppos'd at most but equal to its Native Excellencies"; and those interested in settling in South Carolina were assured in 1733 that "all things will undoubtedly thrive there"—where wild game already flourished and the woodlands were bursting with succulent fruit.

As extravagant or mythologized as such claims appear, immigrants were not always disappointed. For those who carved out a place for themselves even in the wilderness were usually better off than in the country from which they'd come. The Scotch-Irishman's backwoods log cabin, for instance, was a vast improvement on rural housing in Ulster, "the most miserable Huts you can imagine, of Mud and Straw, much worse than Indian Wig Wams." Food was better and more abundant, and though work was hard, the virgin soil generally gave a good return. So did cottage industry and trade. One Dutch baker in Germantown, Pennsylvania, for example, enthusiastically wrote home after a year that he had already acquired a Negro slave, a cow, a horse, pigs, chickens, geese, a garden, "and next year . . . an orchard . . . and I have no rent or excise to pay."

Bounty abounded. Visitors to a Dutch village on Long Island in 1679, for example, were served "a full pail of Gowanus oysters . . . best in the country . . . as good as those of England [thrown on the fire to roast] . . . some not less than a foot long. . . . We had for supper a roasted haunch of venison, which weighed thirty pounds and was exceedingly good and tender. Also turkey and wild goose." Three quarters of a century later, a

Swedish traveler noted in his journal, "Every countryman, even the poorest peasant, has an orchard with apples, peaches, chestnuts, walnuts, cherries, quinces and such fruits, and sometimes we saw vines climbing in them. The valleys were frequently blessed with little brooks of crystal-clear water. The fields by the sides of the road were almost all mown."

It was a land of opportunity. In 1767, George Washington could rejoice in the rich possibilities "in the back country for adventurers, where . . . an enterprising man with very little money may lay the foundation of a noble estate." One traveler to the Wyoming Valley of Pennsylvania in the mid-1770s noted "the prodigious number of houses rearing up, fields cultivating, the great extent of industry open'd to a bold indefatigable enterprising people." French diplomat François de Barbé-Marbois, another relatively impartial observer, was likewise in awe of the overall prosperity he found. The land, he wrote, "repays a moderate degree of labor very generously," and he asserted that in a journey of 150 leagues, he did not meet a single peasant "who was not well dressed and who did not have a good wagon or at least a good horse. The best of our kings was satisfied to wish that each peasant might have every Sunday a hen in his pot. Here, we have not entered a single dwelling in the morning without finding there a kettle in which was cooking a good fowl, or a piece of beef, or mutton with a piece of bacon; and a great abundance of vegetables; bread, cider, things from the dairy, a profusion of firewood; clean furniture, a good bed, and often a newspaper."

Although some European visitors noted with repugnance the emphasis (particularly in New England) on commerce and advantage—they try to "cheat [a stranger] if they can," wrote one in a typical complaint—Americans had also not yet begun to rationalize differences between the classes in disparagement of the poor. Begging and homelessness were almost unknown in the colonies, and most towns had hostels subsidized by the community which took in old people or those unable to work. As for the unemployed, "care is taken," one traveler noted with admiration, "that they lack neither work nor food." The poorhouse and hospital he visited were nothing like the sad establishments of the kind he was acquainted with in France. They were orderly, neat, and clean and appeared "the work of enlightened and compassionate humanity."

ALTHOUGH colonial society was hierarchical, with a relatively leisured elite, there was a good deal of social mobility and class distinctions were not fixed. In major towns and cities (such as Boston, Providence, and Newport) there was a substantial merchant class, and the more prosperous formed a kind of local aristocracy, as did the great landowners and merchants in the South; but there was no titled nobility, and the typical farmer owned, rather than rented, his land. The artisan, though distinguishable from his superior by his rougher garb, also had the given right to discard it. Except for slaves and indentured servants, most Americans also had a life in local politics. Generally speaking, only those with property were allowed to vote, but by property was often meant, as defined by the Virginia legislature in 1670, "such as by their estates real or personal, have interest enough to tye them to the endeavor of the public good." In America, there were few without some property in that sense. Royal officials complained of "town meetings" where "the lowest Mechanics" could discuss "the most important points of government, with the utmost freedom." Or, as a less hostile observer remarked, "Each individual has an equal liberty of delivering his opinion, and is not liable to be silenced or browbeaten by a richer or greater townsman than himself; and each vote weighs equally whether that of the highest or lowest inhabitant."

Nevertheless, some were more equal than others, and the practice of democracy was more evident in the North (and the middle colonies) than the South. In the North, there were few great landowners and therefore nothing like the clear disparity of wealth and social division that existed in Virginia and Maryland, for example, between laborers and the stupendously propertied manorial lords. The inhabitants of New Jersey were said to enjoy a "near equality of Wealth" because most townships "divided, & then again subdivided [their land] into two & three Hundred Separate, proper, creditable estates." Moreover, northern gentlemen "in the first rank of Dignity & Quality . . . associate freely & commonly with Farmers & Mechanicks tho' they be poor & industrious." In such a milieu, "Ingenuity & industry" were "the Strongest, & most approved recommendations to a Man." Foreigners, indeed, were struck by the dignity of labor—that is, by the respect in which laborers were held. "No form of activity is considered ignoble here," wrote a visitor, "as long as it is useful to society." In the North, master and servant often ate at the same table, shared each other's conversation and society in the parlor of the home, and (the "Gentlemen setting a laborious example to their Domesticks") often worked beside them in the fields. By contrast, in Virginia, observed a contemporary, "such amazing property . . . blows up the owners to an imagination . . . that they are exalted as much above other Men in worth & precedency, as blind stupid fortune has made a difference in their property."

Yet considering what that difference was, some owners might have been excused for the illusion of their exaltation. "The house that we reside in," wrote a guest at one such mansion in Albemarle County, Virginia,

> is situated upon an eminence, commanding a prospect of nearly thirty miles around it, and the face of the country appears as an immense forest, interspersed with various plantations, four or five miles distant from each other; on these there is a dwelling-house in the center, with kitchens, smoke-house, and out-houses detached, and from the various buildings, each plantation has the appearance of a small village; at some little distance from the houses, are peach and apple orchards, &c. and scattered over the plantations are the negroes huts and tobacco-houses, which are largely built of wood.

Slavery as a supplement to white labor was the mainstay of the southern economy, but it infected all the colonies to some degree. Blacks were bought on the coast of Africa by New England sea captains with barrels of New England rum, then carried on slave ships to the West Indies, where they were sold to planters and slave dealers for molasses. Between 5,000 and 15,000 a year were conveyed to the New World in this way. By 1775, the number of slaves below the Mason-Dixon Line exceeded 450,000; above it, 60,000—about a fifth of the total population of the land. Blacks made up one third of the population of Maryland and half that of Virginia and in South Carolina outnumbered whites.

Above the Chesapeake, the heaviest concentrations were in Rhode Island, New Jersey, and New York, where they worked under less oppressive conditions as farmhands, coachmen, butlers, maids, and so on, more as indentured servants than as slaves. "They are assiduously cared for when they are sick," wrote one European traveler, giving their situation an overly domestic cast, "and they are well fed and clothed. They attach themselves to their masters, whose children they regard as their own. . . . While traveling, I have often happened to spend the night in the houses of Dutch or Germans. In the morning the negro wakes them, crying, 'Get up, master, it is time for us to go to work.' The master gets up, they eat a light breakfast, work together, and dine together like equals. They are clothed in the same way, and the slave can be recognized only by his color." Yet this same visitor also reported that some freed blacks had established their own slave plantations, which they administered with considerable cruelty. "It would seem that having gone through the miseries of slavery, they should be more humane. But as they have known the depravity of the human heart in this deplorable condition, they realize that slavery can be maintained only by severity."

Perhaps the most celebrated black person in America during the revolutionary period was the "Boston Negress" Phillis Wheatley, who had been born in Africa and brought to Boston at the age of ten. At seventeen, she had emerged as an accomplished poet, demonstrating, to the surprise of many, that Africans were capable of education and refinement. In her autobiographical verses, she interpreted her own unlikely story as a blessing in disguise:

> 'Twas mercy brought me from my Pagan Land,
> Taught my benighted Soul to understand,
> That there's a God; that there's a Saviour too;
> Once I Redemption neither sought nor knew,
> Some view our sable Race with scornful Eye,
> "Their Colour is a diabolic Dye."
> Remember, christians, Negroes, black as Cain,
> May be refin'd, & join the Angelic Train.

And she was proof of it, so many thought. Nevertheless, when her poems were first gathered into a volume, it was deemed necessary to print certificates of authenticity in front of the book, testifying to her authorship.

N E X T to the English, black Africans were the largest ethnic group in America, which displayed great cultural diversity and a tremendous immigrant mix. The white populaton of Virginia was mainly of unalloyed English stock, save for the Scotch-Irish belt along its western mountain borders; but within the first few years of Pennsylvania's founding, for example, Scots, Ulstermen, German and Dutch Pietists, Swiss Mennonites, and French Huguenots poured in. (Some of the "Germans" were actually Dutch but had emigrated from German territory; others, conversely, were "Pennsylvania Dutch," that is "Deutsch.")

By the middle of the eighteenth century, the tide of European immigration had become a flood. At least fourteen different languages were spoken on the streets of New York, and at a tavern in Philadelphia, one Scottish visitor found himself in "very mixed company. . . . There were Scots, English, Dutch, Germans, and Irish; there were Roman Catholicks, Church men, Presbyterians, Quakers, Newlightmen, Methodists, Seventh day men, Moravians, Anabaptists, and one Jew. The whole company consisted of 25 planted round an oblong table in a great hall and divided into committees in conversation; the prevailing topick was politicks and conjectures of a French war. A knott of Quakers there talked only about selling of flower [flour] and the low price it bore." According to Bernard Bailyn new settlers included more than 55,000 Protestant Irish, more than 40,000 Scots, and more than 30,000 Englishmen—125,000 from the British Isles alone. Some British officials even feared that "the mass exodus to America would in time depopulate their realm."

Some German princes might have had the same concerns. About 10 percent of the colonial population was German-speaking, the first wave of German immigrants having disembarked at Philadelphia in August 1683. They proved to be skillful farmers and artisans and thrived at a host of cottage industries: weaving, shoemaking, wood carving, cabinet-making, leather-craft work, pottery, and so on. In 1690, they built the first paper mill in America, and the Bible was printed in America in German before it was printed in English.

The colonies were also religiously diverse, with a kind of egalitarian dispersion of faiths. New England was adamantly Congregationalist, Maryland substantially Roman Catholic, New York and Virginia Anglican, Pennsylvania largely Quaker, Rhode Island Baptist, yet all mingled with Huguenots, Lutherans, Moravians, and other sects to some degree. America also had about 2,500 Jews, mostly refugees from religious persecution in Germany, Portugal, and Spain. The first to arrive—twenty-three on a French ship in 1654—had disembarked at New Amsterdam (later, New York) after being expelled by the Portuguese from Brazil. In New York they established a congregation for worship and in 1730 built Shearith Israel, America's first synagogue, on Mill Street. In 1744, the synagogue had about fifty regular members. According to a Swedish visitor, Jews enjoyed "all the privileges common to the other inhabitants of this town and province" except the right to vote. The Jewish congregation in New-port, Rhode Island, also thrived, and its synagogue was regarded as the finest house of worship in the town.

There was, of course, some intolerance. The Puritans of New England were unalterably hostile to Quakers, the Catholics distrustful of Anglicans (though near to them in faith), and the Anglicans of New York tried unsuccessfully to establish themselves as the official church by legislative act in 1693. This did not sit well with the colony's resident Calvinists, Puritans, French Huguenots, Presbyterians, Reformed Dutch, Catholics, and Jews. On the other hand, the Anglican Church in Virginia was less dogmatic and more tolerant than most of the dissenting sects.

The ethnic religious mix in Pennsylvania was particularly volatile be-cause the militant Scotch-Irish (who began to arrive in great numbers after 1728 and numbered 100,000 by 1754) despised the pacifist Quakers and German Pietists. From their Calvinist doctrine of predestination they derived their right to appropriate the land of the Indian by force; but "whatever they lacked in sweet reasonableness," writes one historian, "they made up in strength of character and vigor of mind."

Another notable group, the Moravians, were Czech Protestants (originally the followers of Jan Hus), who settled primarily in Georgia, the Carolinas, and Pennsylvania after the 1730s and, like the Quakers, held pacifist views. Their frontier communities were decent, upright, and industrious, distinguished by their emphasis on education and renowned for silversmithing, cabinetry, and other crafts. Their municipal water supply system of wooden conduits was the first such engineering in the New World. Music was also strong in their daily life: drums and flutes accompanied the reapers into the fields, and trumpet fanfares crowned the raising of a house. At the Moravians' Bethlehem settlement in 1756, Benjamin Franklin heard "good Musick, the Organ being accompanied with Violins, Hautboys, Flutes, Clarinets, etc." Other instruments common to their communities were the bassoon, harp, harpsichord, clavichord, and even trombone. The "Father of Chamber Music" in America was Johann Friedrich Peter, a Moravian composer of string quartets.

A M E R I C A was just beginning to come into her own in the sciences and arts. The first poetry written in America had been a translation into English of Ovid's *Metamorphoses* by George Sandys, treasurer of Virginia, in 1623. Within a century, native talent had begun to bloom, and by 1743 "the first Drudgery of Settling new Colonies, which confines the Attention of People to mere Necessaries," wrote Franklin, was "pretty well over; and . . . many in every Province [had] leisure to cultivate" more intellectual and artistic pursuits.

America's two most famous scientists at the time were Franklin himself and David Rittenhouse—both "naturals" with little formal education. Rittenhouse, whose great-grandfather had built the first paper mill in America, showed a precocious aptitude for mathematics as a boy, became a skilled surveyor (helping, in 1764, to determine the Mason-Dixon Line), made new and improved mathematical instruments of his own devising, and was the first to use crosshairs (for which he adapted spiderwebs) in the focus of a telescope. In 1770, he completed his celebrated "orrery," a planetarium or mechanical model of the solar system. Thomas Jefferson esteemed him "second to no astronomer living" and a mechanical genius. He went on to become a military engineer for Washington's Continental Army and, after the war, the first director of the U.S. Mint.

But Franklin was the man everybody knew. Even before the Revolution, he was already America's elder statesman, and it is fitting to pause for a moment to give some account of his astounding life.

The tenth son of seventeen children of a soap- and candlemaker, Franklin was born in Boston in 1706. His formal schooling abruptly ended at the age of ten, and at twelve he was apprenticed to his brother, a printer, even as he continued to study on his own. Inclined to poetry, he composed two occasional ballads in his youth, one about a shipwreck, the other about Blackbeard, the pirate, but "they were wretched stuff," he later recalled, "in street-ballad style. The first sold prodigiously, [which] . . . flattered my vanity; but my father discouraged me by criticizing my performances, and telling me verse-makers were generally beggars." Franklin took the admonition to heart. At the age of seventeen, he left home and made his way first to New York, then to Philadelphia, where he became a typographer's assistant. Six years later (such was his enterprise), he became the printer of paper currency of his adoptive state.

Meanwhile, as he tells us in his *Autobiography,* he had conceived the

arduous project of arriving at *moral perfection.* I wished to live without committing any fault at any time, and to conquer all that either natural inclination, custom, or company might lead me into. As I knew, or thought I knew, what was right and wrong, I did not see why I might not *always* do the one and avoid the other. But I soon found I had undertaken a task of more difficulty than I had imagined. While my attention was taken up, and employed in guarding against one fault, I was often surprised by another; habit took the advantage of inattention; inclination was sometimes too strong for reason. I concluded, at length, that the mere speculative conviction that it was our interest to be completely virtuous, was not sufficient to prevent our slipping; and that the contrary habits must be broken, and good ones acquired and established, before we can have any dependence on a steady, uniform rectitude of conduct.

Accordingly, he drew up a list of thirteen cardinal virtues, with an instructive precept annexed to each:

1. *Temperance.*—Eat not to dullness; drink not to elevation.
2. *Silence.*—Speak not but what may benefit others or yourself; avoid trifling conversation.
3. *Order.*—Let all your things have their places; let each part of your business have its time.

4. *Resolution.*—Resolve to perform what you ought; perform without fail what you resolve.

5. *Frugality.*—Make no expense but to do good to others or yourself; that is, waste nothing.

6. *Industry.*—Lose no time; be always employed in something useful; cut off all unnecessary actions.

7. *Sincerity.*—Use no hurtful deceit; think innocently and justly; and, if you speak, speak accordingly.

8. *Justice.*—Wrong none by doing injuries, or omitting the benefits that are your duty.

9. *Moderation.*—Avoid extremes; forbear resenting injuries so much as you think they deserve.

10. *Cleanliness.*—Tolerate no uncleanliness in body, clothes, or habitation.

11. *Tranquillity.*—Be not disturbed at trifles, or at accidents common or unavoidable.

12. *Chastity* . . . . . .

13. *Humility.*—Imitate Jesus and Socrates.

In this gently self-mocking recollection of his program, he notably omitted any edifying precept to help him with "chastity," with which he had trouble all his life. Franklin's sexual appetite drove him repeatedly to Philadelphia's brothels in his youth, produced an illegitimate son, William (who became the last royal governor of New Jersey), and later led to a number of somewhat scandalous love affairs in his old age. When he was still in his forties, he told his son that it seemed to him a miracle that he had escaped the scourge ("which of all things I dreaded") of venereal disease.

Franklin set out to master one virtue at a time and made himself a little book to chronicle the effort. To each virtue he allotted a page, which he ruled with red ink into seven columns (one for each day of the week), crossed by thirteen lines. "In its proper column," he tells us, "I might [therefore] mark, by a little black spot, every fault I found upon examination to have been committed respecting that virtue upon that day."

Franklin failed in his endeavor, of course, but it helped him to a certain rectitude and more obviously bore fruit in the witty, entertaining, and often wise proverbs and maxims, designed to inculcate industry and frugality, scattered through the pages of his enormously popular *Poor Richard's Almanac,* which he had begun to publish in 1732. Meanwhile, he had assumed publication of the *Pennsylvania Gazette* in 1729, had undertaken to learn French, Italian, Spanish, and Latin, began to involve himself more directly in public service, and after 1748 decided to devote himself to science. Four years later, his electrical experiments made him a scientist of international renown.

One day in June 1752, it had occurred to Franklin, who was convinced that lightning was a form of electricity, "that by means of a common kite he could have better access to the regions of thunder." As soon as a thunderstorm arose, he walked out into a field with his son, William, let a kite fly with a key attached to the string, and at length observed that some of the string's loose threads had begun "to stand erect, and to avoid one another just as if they had been suspended on a common conductor." He immediately touched his knuckle to the key and saw a spark.

In 1757, Franklin went to London, where he remained almost continuously as the agent for Pennsylvania and a number of the other colonies until the Revolution began.

Franklin was also a literary figure of note (his *Autobiography* would become a classic), was competent at drawing and engraving, and possessed musical imagination and skill. In his person he seemed to embody the emerging diversity of America's new cultural world.

Several outstanding artists had recently stepped to the fore. America's two leading portrait painters were John Singleton Copley and Charles Willson Peale. Copley, a master of realistic detail, rendered facial warts as minutely as a lady's gown (and no one painted a lady's gown more beautifully), but his realism also "raised blemishes above 'likeness,' " wrote a cultural historian, "and made them a Puritan *memento mori,* an intimation of mortality and corruption." One of Copley's more celebrated paintings was that of Epes Sargent, Sr. (1760), an elderly merchant with gnarled and wrinkled hands. "Prick that hand," said Gilbert Stuart, his fellow artist, "and blood will spurt out." Charles Willson Peale (who had begun his formal study under Copley) was less accomplished, but his honest if crude coloring and stiff but dignified portraits of revolutionary officers (including many portraits of Washington) made him a great artistic celebrity of the day.

Another outstanding artist was Benjamin West, who had started life as a farm boy. Like Franklin and Rittenhouse, West was a kind of "natural." He made his first brush out of a cat's tail and, from the Indians, learned how to make colored paints from roots, herbs, and bark. Ultimately he achieved fame as a sophisticated "history painter" whose most famous work depicted the death of General Wolfe on the Plains of Abraham.

Music shops were stocked with classical standards—works by Corelli, Vivaldi, Handel, Pergolesi, Scarlatti, and Thomas Arne—but America had also produced a notable composer in William Billings, whose *New-England Psalm-Singer* (1770) was the first published collection of all-American music as well as the first tunebook produced by an American composer. The most popular instruments in the colonies were the harpsichord, flute, guitar, and violin, and knowledge of the violin or "fiddle" was expected of any young southern gentleman along with proficiency at dancing, boxing, fencing, and cards. Patrick Henry reportedly played the lute, flute, violin, harpsichord, and pianoforte; Thomas Jefferson was an exceptional violinist; and Robert Carter of Nomini Hall possessed "a good ear for Music, a vastly delicate Taste and . . . good instruments," including a variety of German flutes and an organ "built in part according to his own design." He also played the "armonica," or "musical glasses" (an instrument invented by Benjamin Franklin in 1763), which rotated glass bowls of various sizes on a horizontal spindle in water so that, when rubbed, the rims produced "a soft, warbling sound." Often used as a showpiece in parlor demonstrations, it eventually found its way into compositions by a number of great composers, including Mozart and Beethoven.

New York, Boston, Philadelphia, and Charleston all had subscription concerts, fortnightly concert socials, and chamber music soirees. Outdoor concerts of vocal music also drew large, festive crowds with picnic baskets to the town common or park. Singing masters traveled from town to town, tutoring individuals or choirs at "congregation" schools, and singing had begun to find acceptance in New England churches. John Adams described with a kind of awe a choir he heard in Middletown, Connecticut: "the finest Singing that ever I heard in my Life. The front and side Galleries were crowded with Rows of Lads and Lasses, who performed all the Parts in the Utmost Perfection. I thought I was wrapped up. A Row of Women all standing up, and playing their Parts with perfect Skill and Judgment, added a Sweetness and Sprightliness to the whole which absolutely charmed me."

Not much attention was yet paid to Native American music, but a sociological interest was taken in some of the instruments slaves had brought from Africa, such as the "banjor" (banjo), the "barrafou" (which resembled a xylophone), and the "quaqua" (a kind of drum).

No American writer had yet come to prominence (although some, such as Anne Bradstreet, Jonathan Edwards, and Cotton Mather, would afterward be recognized as great), but there were innumerable scribblers churning out pamphlets, broadsides, drinking songs, satires, and all sorts of occasional verse.

The literacy rate in America was extraordinarily high. Although there was no public education system as such, almost every community had a church or parish school, and most towns had elementary schools for those of artisan stock, who attended until the age of thirteen, when their apprenticeship began. Those destined for higher education usually attended Latin or grammar schools, which could be found in every sizable town throughout New England. Private tutors were also engaged by the well-to-do for most levels of instruction, particularly in the rural South. Many colonists sent their sons to Britain for university training—to Scottish universities for medicine, to the Inns of Court for law, to Oxford or Cambridge for mathematics, rhetoric, philosophy, and languages; but America had a number of outstanding universities of her own—Harvard, Yale, and William and Mary being the oldest.

At Harvard and other universities, class rank was determined by social standing, and students from less prosperous families had to perform menial chores (such as waiting on tables); otherwise all followed the same routine. At Harvard, for example, that meant dawn rising, morning prayers, and a long day of classes and study until the evening closed with lights-out at nine. The basic curriculum included Latin, Greek, logic, rhetoric, physics, natural philosophy, moral philosophy, metaphysics, geography, mathematics, geometry, modern languages, government, and history. In the study of government, the basic texts were by Hugo Grotius and Samuel von Pufendorf, whose theories were predicated on the doctrines of the social compact and natural law. In history the student began with the views set forth in Bishop Jacques Bossuet's *Discourse on Universal History,* which defined government as the necessary restraint on mankind's evil passions and its best form as absolute monarchy tempered by reason and justice.

Almost everyone in America read a newspaper. In 1725, there were only two or three in the country, including the *New England Courant,* founded in 1721 in Boston by Benjamin Franklin's older brother James. In the beginning, they printed little more than advertisements, bits of local gossip called "Remarkables," and the arrival and departure times of ships. The *New England Courant,* however, broke ranks to comment on public issues, and in 1735, John Peter Zenger, a Palatine German who had begun the *New York Weekly Journal* two years before, won a landmark court case against the royal governor that helped establish freedom of the press. By the time of the Revolution, the colonies had twenty-five papers or more.

Bookshops also multiplied. Until the 1730s, at least, almost all books were obtained from England, as there was "not a good bookseller's shop," according to Benjamin Franklin, "south of Boston." By 1771, however, Boston had at least ten and Philadelphia fifty, and by the Revolution, both Boston and New York had twenty and Philadelphia seventy-five. Most, in addition, carried stationery and contemporary prints and engravings—by Piranesi, Hogarth, and others—portraits of prominent historical figures, neoclassical landscapes, and "history paintings," or pictures on historical, biblical, and mythological themes.

Along with bookselling, a library system had also grown up. The first subscription library in America emerged out of "a club for mutual improvement" formed by Benjamin Franklin, which met at a Philadelphia alehouse every Friday evening. Aside from Franklin, the original members included a well-read scrivener with a talent for verse; a self-taught mathematician, "great in his own way," who later became a notable inventor: a merchant with an interest in philosophy; and so on. "The rules that I drew up," Franklin tells us, "required that every member, in his turn, should produce one or more queries on any point of Morals, Politics, or Natural Philosophy, to be discussed by the company; and once in three months produce and read an essay of his own writing, on any subject he pleased. Our debates were to be . . . conducted in the sincere spirit of inquiry after truth, without fondness for dispute, or desire of victory."

In time, the little group hired a room to meet in and Franklin proposed that each member of the group lodge his books there, where they could be consulted and borrowed by all. It then occurred to him, in 1731, to start a public library with subscribers whereby members paid an entrance fee plus annual dues. The monies went toward enlarging the collection or paying rent on the room or rooms where the books were kept.

In Franklin's initial trial, fifty people were found willing to give 40 shillings each plus 10 shilliings per year for the purchase of books. Their first order included the works of Homer, Plutarch, Xenophon, and Tacitus; modern histories, grammars, dictionaries, and encyclopedias; treatises on mathematics, chemistry, physics, astronomy, botany, natural history, architecture, farming, and surveying; *The Complete Tradesman* (a popular book on commerce); and the works of Dryden, Addison, and Steele—a pretty good nucleus on which to build.

The ideas soon spread, and by 1775 perhaps seventy such libraries had been formed throughout the colonies. "These libraries," wrote Franklin, "have improved the general conversation of the Americans, made the common tradesmen and farmers as intelligent as most gentlemen from other countries, and contributed in some degree" by such enlightenment (he ventured) to the determination of Americans to stand up for their rights.

Some private libraries were also substantial. In the great manor houses of the South, a prosperous planter might accumulate up to four thousand volumes. English and continental "courtesy" and "conduct" books, such as Henry Peacham's *The Compleat Gentleman* or the works of Castiglione, were on every gentleman's shelves, along with sermons and theological treatises, books on politics and statecraft, military manuals, treatises on animal husbandry, farming, gardening, surveying, and engineering, handbooks of architecture, works of literature, books on medicine and surgery, and commentaries on the law. Some of the libraries owned by prominent divines were still larger, and the largest and most impressive of these by far was that begun by Cotton Mather, who had collected as many as eight thousand volumes. Inherited by his family, it was not inappropriately compared by one bibliophile for its rarities to the Bodleian Library at Oxford and the Vatican Library in Rome.

The development of literacy was furthermore accelerated by the growth of a postal service by which the colonies were joined. The postman in those days was required to be "active, stout, indefatigable, and honest" and was expected to report on the condition of all ferries, fords, and roads along his route. He delivered his mail to the local inn, which served as a post office where people came to look over all the letters and parcels that came in. Eventually, "mile-stones" were set at mile-long intervals along all the principal post roads to measure the distance from town to town. The ubiquitously useful Benjamin Franklin started this by traveling from Boston to Philadelphia in a chaise with a kind of cyclometer of his own invention attached to it that measured the miles as he rode. At every mile, he unloaded a milestone from a cart, which was driven alongside. In 1753, he also established the penny post in Philadelphia; this later expanded into a system that stretched from the Carolinas to Maine.

The broad literacy and political involvement of the people in their democratic institutions helped turn the average American into a kind of citizen-lawyer. "In no country perhaps in the world," Edmund Burke observed in his speech *On Conciliation with the American Colonies* (1775), "is the law so general a study . . . all who read, and most do read, endeavor to obtain some smattering in that science." Judges themselves, not incidentally, were inclined to decide cases, when possible, in a manner that eschewed the law's arcane minutia and held to the basic issue in question, consistent with "natural judgment," or common sense.

Although Americans had no professional theater of their own and few playwrights, various troupes occasionally toured the colonies, which led to the establishment of theaters in some of the principal towns. A number of the stagings required an orchestra (generally made up of five to ten musicians), and in the lobby one could buy the sheet music for the performance and, at intermission, snack food (such as apples, raisins, and peanuts) as well as brandy or gin.

No playwright was more popular than William Shakespeare. At least fourteen of his plays were regularly performed, and the most popular of these were *The Tempest* and *Romeo and Juliet*. Other favorites were George Farquhar's *The Beaux' Stratagem* and John Gay's *The Beggar's Opera*. The first English play actually printed in America—in Boston in 1767—was Joseph Addison's *Cato*. This overtly political drama, known to colonial audiences since 1735, had tremendous resonance for the contemporary scene. The setting was classical, like much of colonial political theory, and told the story of a self-sacrificing republican martyr who perished in his opposition to Roman tyrannical rule. By the 1760s, it seemed to hold up a mirror to the developing struggle between British imperial prerogative and colonial rights. The language of the play became part of the language of political debate, and some of the mighty affirmations of the heroes of the Revolution were inspired by its lines. "Gods, can a Roman senate long debate / Which of the two to choose, slavery or death!" (II, i) anticipated Patrick Henry's famous speech ("Give me liberty, or give me death!") delivered on March 23, 1775; and "What pity is it / That we can die but once to serve our country!" (IV, iv) helped give immortal voice to Nathan Hale in the final moments of his martyred life.

Although actors in South Carolina and Virginia generally drew sizable crowds, in New England and Pennsylvania they had to contend with the animosity of those who believed their profession "lured people from their work, induced them to squander their money, deluded young women, and gave a false picture of life." Shakespeare was not exempt from such strictures. In 1761, *Othello* had to be promoted as "Moral Dialogues in Five Parts, depicting the evil effects of jealousy . . . and proving that happiness can only spring from the pursuit of Virtue." Still, Philadelphians had come a long way since 1682, when the Pennsylvania Assembly had passed a law imposing a fine and ten days' imprisonment with hard labor on "whosoever shall introduce into this Province, or frequent such rude and riotous sports and practices as prizes, stageplays, revels and masques."

Some of the plays were decidedly risqué. The same year *Cato* was published in America, the first American comic opera, *The Disappointment,* was produced. Written by a Philadelphia merchant named Andrew Barton, the opera ridiculed a recent local obsession with buried pirate

treasure and mixed raunchy language with racial stereotypes. Its characters included an elderly black man (of the Amos 'n' Andy type fully
formed) whose lover is a prostitute, to whom he sings a song to the
"Yankee Doodle" tune:

> O! how joyful shall I be,
>   When I get de money,
> I will bring it all to dee;
>   O! my diddling honey.

What would one day become the quintessential tune of patriot soldiers
in the Revolutionary War oddly debuted as the serenade to a whore.

There was plenty of other common entertainment to be had. Puppe-
teers, acrobats, and stunt artists performed on town street corners; traveling showmen exhibited exotic animals on village greens—a lion, an
orangutan, an alligator, or a camel—and circuslike oddities such as a
"sapient" dog that could talk or a pickled pirate's head in a jar. In August
1771, one newspaper, the *Massachusetts Spy*, advertised "a Maiden
Dwarf, who is fifty-three years old and of but twenty-two inches in
stature . . . she is willing to exhibit herself as a shew to such Gentlemen
and Ladies as are desirous to gratify their curiosity, for one shilling each."
In Albany, one tourist was entertained by a virtuoso fiddler who accompanied his playing with singing so high that "the whole company were
amazed that any person but a woman or eunuch could have such a
pipe." When they questioned his virility, he offered to show them his
testicles—"a couple of witnesses as good as any man might wear." He
then imitated the sounds of various creatures, including a cat, a dog, a
horse, a cow, and a chicken, "all to perfection." Also in Albany, the
tourist met a seventy-five-year-old man who could jump "half a foot high
upon his bum without touching the floor with any other part of his body
. . . the same upon his belly, and stand upright upon his head." Later, at
a book fair in Boston, he was introduced to a lady who kept a white
monkey as a pet. The monkey was just eighteen inches long, had a little
white, downy beard, and "laugh'd and grinned like any Christian. It was
exceedingly fond of its mistress, bussing her and handling her bubbies
just like an old rake. One might well envy the brute," he tells us, "for the
lady was very handsome; so that it would have been no disagreeable
thing for a man to have been in this monkey's place."

In the way of popular pastimes and sports, there was also horse racing,
cockfighting, bull baiting (in which a bull tied to a stake was assailed by

powerful dogs), hare and fox hunts, and the tracking of opossums—the last "perform'd afoot with small dogs in the night by the light of the moon or stars."

Then as now, darts and billboards were popular tavern games, along with backgammon, chess, and card games such as whist and loo (the eighteenth-century equivalent of poker). Though Boston "set its face sternly against cards and dice," the South favored both, as well as horseshoe pitching, skittles (ninepins), and bowling on the green.

Colonial Americans also liked to drink. Taverns were their universal haunt, in part because the tavern was not only a taproom, or bar, but the usual lodging place for travelers, as well as a meetinghouse, post office, mail drop, and clearinghouse for news.

The inevitable talk was of politics, religion, and trade. Some of the denizens talked "tolerably well," remarked one visitor who made the rounds of such establishments in 1744, and displayed "that curiosity which was a characteristic of the American rustic everywhere." In one New Jersey tavern, he overheard a discussion about physics; in another, an argument about sacred history between two Irishmen, a Scot, and a French Jew. At Saybrook Ferry, Connecticut, some "country rabble" came in and, to his surprise, began talking theology—"so pointedly, in fact, about justification, sanctification, adoption, regeneration, repentance, free grace, original sin and a thousand other such pretty chimerical knick-knacks one would have thought they had done nothing but study divinity all their lives."

Such uncommon learning, of course, mingled always with the common habits of tavern life. "Here the time, the money, the health and the modesty of most that are young and of many that are old, are wasted," wrote John Adams, in one of his more morose moods. "Here diseases, vicious habits, bastards and legislators are frequently begotten." But in any given locale (even in Puritan New England) there were often more taverns than churches—thirty, for example, in Providence alone. They went by such names as "The Sign of the Wheat Sheaf," "The Sign of the Black Lyon," and "The Sign of the White Horse." One poignant sign outside Cambridge, Massachusetts, which showed the round earth with a man crawling through it, bore the legend OH, HOW SHALL I GET THROUGH THIS WORLD? Some of the taverns resembled fancy hotels, such as Baltimore's luxurious Indian Queen, which had two hundred guest rooms and "a bell in every room." Others (such as the Sign of the Half Moon in Newport, Rhode Island) were dives. In remote areas, the tavern was often just a simple log cabin in which a rum keg and tumbler in the corner served as a bar. Their usual sign out front was an earthenware jug suspended by its handle from a pole. Although drinking establishments of any sort were scarce in the deep South, from Maryland to Georgia travelers might depend on a bibulous welcome at private homes. Some planters were so eager for company and news that they stationed servants along roads to invite wayfarers to stop over for the night.

Perhaps the most famous tavern of all was The Raleigh in Williamsburg, Virginia, which had a lead bust of Sir Walter Raleigh above the door. Its accommodations included a parlor, a bar, gaming and dining rooms, and several public or common rooms, including the Apollo, which took its name from a room in the Devil's Tavern in London, where Raleigh, Ben Jonson, and other literary figures had once slaked their thirst. Carved above its mantel in richly gilded letters was the motto HILARITAS SAPIENTIAE ET BONAE VITAE PROLES—"Jollity is the offspring of wisdom and living well."

Drinking was copious among both high and low, and "as much liquor was consumed," it was said, "in the ordination of a New England minister as at a barbecue in the South." Even Philadelphia, for all its Quaker restraint, rolled up an enviable reputation for public tippling. At the Red Lion Tavern on Elbow Lane, on February 2, 1736 (according to the *Philadelphia Mercury*), one regular "laid a wager of Half a Crown that he could drink a Gallon of Cyder Royall within the space of one hour and a half; which he had no sooner accomplished and said 'I have finished,' then he fell down dead." Although drunken and disorderly conduct was prohibited, the owner of a tavern could also be fined if he refused to permit a customer to drink all he could hold. To drink oneself drunk was, in a manner of speaking, the first of the natural rights the colonists upheld.

French and Madeira wines graced the tables of the gentry; at taverns, the usual fare was beer, cider, black-strap, and metheglin (made from fermented honey and rum). Rum and cider were the preferred drinks in New England; beer and various brandies (distilled from cherries, plums, persimmons, peaches, or pears) in the middle colonies and the South. Black-strap was mainly a concoction of rum and molasses; "mumbo," of rum, water, and sugar—called a "toddy" when hot and stirred with a stick which had a knob on one end for crushing sugar lumps. (Without sugar, it was called "grog.") In New Jersey, homemade applejack was consumed straight or as "Scotchem" (with hot water and a dash of mustard); another favorite was "Creaming Flip," compounded of strong beer, New England rum, dried pumpkin, and sugar or molasses. Once the mix was concocted, a red-hot poker or loggerhead was thrust into it to make it bubble and foam. Its burnt taste was said to be the "joy of connoisseurs."

Each tavern came up with its own brew. The famous Fish House

Punch of Philadelphia was so prized that even after the Revolutionary War it was said to be held "in almost the same regard as the Liberty Bell."

Always to be had was rum from Barbados and Jamaica—"a hot, hellish, and terrible liquor" called "Kill Devil" by the Dutch. Rum "does more mischief to people's industry than anything except gin and the Pope," exclaimed one colonist. "My dear countrymen are fonder of it than they are of their wives and children, for they often sell the bread out of their mouths to buy rum to put in their own." The same could be said for gin, for which "Strip and Go Naked" was a popular epithet, and those partial to the succor of brandy called a bottle of it, rather quaintly, "a Breast of Milk."

Major breweries were established by the Dutch at Albany and New York, and even the straitlaced Moravians of Old Salem, North Carolina, operated their own distillery. One inventory of their church-owned tavern showed 924 gallons of whiskey, 455 of apple and peach brandy, 137 of rum, and 30 of "coniac," 8 barrels of cider, and 60 gallons of Madeira wine.

For abstemious souls who wanted a nonalcoholic but still tavernlike drink, there was always "health beer," a spring tonic concocted from pine chips, pine bark, hemlock, roasted corn, dried apple skin, sassafras root, and bran mixed with hops and malt.

A L C O H O L as a solvent of sorrows and other ills was regarded by many colonists as more reliably therapeutic than what their doctor might prescribe.

Colonial medicine was a typical eighteenth-century compound of "new science," occult doctrine, and home remedies. Among doctors, there were plenty of quacks. A certain Dr. Thomas Wise, for example, blithely advertised in Philadelphia, in 1767, his ability to cure, "with small expense and pain to the Patient, cancers and wens without cutting them, the King's Evil, venereal disorders without Sallivation, Rupture, Strangury and Stone." Town apothecaries and peddlers also hawked or supplied pills and other specifics—Turlington's Balsam, Stoughton's Elixir, Lockyer's Pills, Walker's Jesuit Drops, and Swinsen's Electuary— of indeterminate brew. Some were of use. On Braddock's campaign, George Washington was cured of a persistent fever by something called "Dr. James' Powders"—"one of the most excellent medicines in the world," he declared after it brought him "immediate relief."

On the whole, however, laymen tended to rely on home remedies concocted from various plants and herbs according to traditional recipes.

They read medical guides such as *Every Man His Own Doctor*—
"for Those who can't afford to dye by the Hand of a Doctor"—by John
Tennent, a Virginia physician, which had gone into its fourth edition by
1736, and every autumn they would organize an expedition into the
woods to replenish the family medicine chest.

Tea brewed from catnip was taken for chest ailments; cough syrup
was made from the roots of the spikenard; a cold was treated with honey
and rum. A salve made of lard, resin, and beeswax was used to soothe
burns; smartweed steeped in vinegar was applied to bruises; lard mixed
with the leaves of the green bean yielded an ointment for open sores.
Saltpeter was administered in various concentrations to treat measles,
colic, sciatica, headache, giddiness, and other ailments. Nervous disorders (rather too obviously) were thought to be alleviated by chewing the
roots of the nerve vine and kidney stones by eating kidney beans. And
there were those, of course, who relied outright on sympathetic magic.
Some midwives, for example, believed that labor pains were "cut" by
placing a sharp knife under the bed or that a difficult delivery could be
facilitated by opening chests, cupboards, windows, and doors. Inhaling
cedarwood smoke was said to make a woman abort. Southernwood was
inhaled to cure "vanityes of the head" and, when made into powder
mixed with the "oyle of radishes," was thought to cure baldness when
applied to the scalp. "Great experiences" were also promised from its
use as a love charm, when a sprig was placed in a lover's shoe.

Spices such as nutmeg, cinnamon, and cloves were the ingredients of
many medicaments, along with rhubarb and ginseng, two of the pana-
ceas of the day. Ginseng was hard to come by. In 1738, it was supposedly
discovered growing near the Susquehanna River, but "Tis as easy to
propagate Chastity in a great city as it is ginseng in a garden," wrote one
doctor in pharmacological despair.

The common rhubarb, or pieplant, on the other hand, was common
in America, but it was not used medicinally. *That* rhubarb was the Chinese or Turkish rhubarb *(Rheum palmatum)*, which was ground to a
powder and administered for the relief of diarrhea, gonorrhea, jaundice,
liver disease, and other maladies. One species of it grew in the East
Indies, from where it was imported by the Dutch, but the more coveted
variety grew in Mongolia and Tibet. The Chinese shipped it to Europe
from Canton or through Russia, which endeavored to monopolize the
trade. By the early 1760s, small homegrown crops of it had begun to
appear in gardens in England and Scotland, but long after its cultivation
in America, colonists still relied on shipments from abroad. Sassafras,
too, was regarded as a kind of miracle herb:

In the spring of the year,
    When the blood is too thick,
There is nothing so rare
    As the sassafras stick.
It cleans up the liver,
    It strengthens the heart,
And to the whole system
    New life doth impart.
Sassafras, oh, sassafras!
    Thou art the stuff for me!
And in the spring I love to sing
    Sweet sassafras! of thee.

There were several antidotes to snakebite, such as the juice of hore-hound and plantain ingested together, or a potion made of powdered rattlesnake mixed with wine or rum. Without access to such specifics, victims did the best they could—like one Joseph Breintnall who, according to the *Pennsylvania Magazine* of February 10, 1746, improvised remarkably after a rattlesnake bit him on the hand. First, we are told, "he took a chicken, ripped up its belly and put it on his hand to suck the poison out. Immediately the chicken swelled, grew black and stunk. Breintnall kept his elbow bent and his fingers up. He bound his arm in a plaster made of turmeric roots. To let out the 'bad' blood, he slit his fingers with a razor and cupped the back of his hand. Three days later he applied ashes of white ash and vinegar made into a poultice. He became delirious. His arm swelled, gathered and burst—and he recovered."

Breintnall's procedure was dramatic, but medicines (including strong poultices such as vinegar and white ash) were often not administered until a patient had been "evacuated" (as he had evacuated himself)—by either bleeding or purging—to remove "morbific matter." Nevertheless, American physicians were less likely to rely on emetics, purges, bleeding, and other drastic remedies than were their European confreres. The compartmentalization or tripartite specialization of European medical practice into physician, surgeon, and apothecary also did not hold up in the colonies, where pioneering conditions obliged the local doctor to assume all three roles. One French nobleman who visited America during the Revolutionary War remarked, "The distinction of surgeon and physician is as little known in the army of Washington as in that of Agamemnon. We read in Homer, that the physician Macaon himself dressed the wounds. . . . The Americans conform to the ancient custom and it answers very well."

Nothing, however, seemed to be of much help in the treatment of bad teeth. A remarkable number of Americans were nearly toothless by middle age, including George Washington, who by the time he was forty-five had only one good tooth left. Everyone had his own theory about it. One visiting Scottish physician attributed the condition to "a constant diet of salt provisions"; others blamed it on "sweet-meats" or (like Benjamin Franklin) on a winter diet of frozen apples and hot soup. Still others ascribed it to the tremendous consumption of tea, which in those days was often drunk by sucking it through a sugar lump.

Toothaches were relieved by applying the hot, aromatic, and astringent leaves of witch hazel (the "tooth-ache tree") to the teeth and gums or by applying a hot compress of animal fat and powdered corn.

Contemporary dentistry offered scant relief. Fillings were made of wax (lead and gold did not come in until after the Revolution), and in their clumsy extractions, dentists sometimes broke not only the patient's tooth but his jaw. False teeth or dentures were carved from elephant or hippopotamus tusks or constructed from the teeth of animals such as sheep. These were fastened to their neighbors with silk thread or gold or silver wire. The choice to some degree was a matter of style—a reminder that colonial America, despite our Puritan ideas of it, was mindful of fashion and not particularly dour.

Typical garb for a man was a shirt and doublet, knee breeches, and stockings; for a woman, a shift or full-length sleeved garment like a nightgown, and a petticoat or skirt. But many southern and some New England ladies favored silk, embroidery, slashed garments, and lace. There was also a style of dress called a "trollope," which had stiff stays and hoops so large that the wearer was obliged to wiggle, bend, and point to maneuver herself sideways through a door. But North and South, it was not uncommon to see colonial ladies of fashion go about in long-armed kid gloves, high-heeled shoes, elegant bonnets, and leather pumps. Their male counterparts, not to be outdone, wore stiff silk coats lined with buckram, sleeves with long cuffs weighted down with bits of lead, white silk stockings, lace pumps fastened with silver buckles, and long queues or hairpieces tied up behind.

Such hairpieces varied a good deal in style, being curled, braided, or turned under in heavy rolls. Full-fledged wigs, which were less common, were often bound and braided with colored ribbon. Some colonials, such as George Washington, powdered their natural hair after soaking it first in oil or pomatum to make the powder stick.

The backwoods dandy made the best of his situation, with Indian-style moccasins heavily decorated with colored beads, thigh-length deerskin leggings fringed at the seams, a long loose deerskin hunting shirt, and a coonskin cap with a dangling tail.

In relations between the sexes, the women of Boston were said to be more sociable than those of Philadelphia, "free and affable as well as pritty," rarely prudish, often gay. The "pritty, frank girls" of Rhode Island were even freer, and premarital sex was not uncommon. "If a young couple spent the night with friends," the estimable Esther Forbes tells us in her biography of Paul Revere, "no questions would be asked. Strict chaperonage was unheard of, and young people . . . were allowed a freedom not to be known again in this country until the rise of the automobile." There were so many illegitimate births, in fact, that in June 1765 the Church fathers of New England issued a "seven months' ruling" that gave couples a two-month grace period to get married once the woman conceived. That spared their offspring the stigma of being bastards.

Prostitutes abounded in the major seaports, and the old riverbank caves of Philadelphia, where the early settlers found shelter, became a warren of brothel-like haunts. In New York, customers went down to the Battery. A visitor to the city in 1744 was told by his guide "that to walk out after dusk upon this platform was a good way for a stranger to fit himself with a courtezan, for that place was the generall rendezvous of the fair sex of that profession after sun set [with] a good choice of pritty lasses among them, both English and Dutch." In the early 1770s, some five hundred prostitutes were settled on land sarcastically called thereafter "the Holy Ground," because it was adjacent to (and owned by) Trinity Church.

At the end of the colonial period, the growing social freedom had clearly begun to mix uneasily with former ways.

The religious life of America was also, of course, by no means uniform. The Sabbath, beginning on Saturday (being measured from sunset to sunset—"for the evening and the morning were the first day")—was strictly observed in New England, where citizens were forbidden to work or play, or even ride (except to church). In Boston persons caught walking about on a Sunday were liable to arrest. One French visitor remarked, "One meets nobody on the streets, and if you happen on some one you dare not stop and talk with him. You cannot go into a house without finding everyone reading the Bible." But when Sunday evening arrived, children rushed out to see if three stars could be seen distinctly in the night sky—the traditional sign the Sabbath was at an end. Then late-night socializing often began, people were "Merry and Vain," and some, we are told, were "guilty of more Sin that Night than on any other Night" of the week. Connecticut fathers were so shocked at the way their young people behaved that they banned their Sunday-evening gatherings altogether, and New York Quakers were likewise appalled at the degree to which their youth lacked the "Primitive Zeal, Piety and Heat found in the Harts of their parents."

In the South, observance of the Sabbath was often quite lax. The population there was far more widely dispersed, and for a gentleman to attend church sometimes required considerable time and effort. When he did, it was perhaps as much to relieve his loneliness as to be edified. "The Gentlemen go to Church to be sure," wrote Philip Fithian, scholarly young tutor to a wealthy Virginia family, "but they make that itself a matter of convenience, & account the Church a useful weekly resort to do Business . . . giving and receiving letters . . . reading advertisements, consulting about the price of Tobacco, Grain, &c., & settling . . . the lineage, age or qualities of favorite Horses." The parson often delivered a perfunctory sermon above the murmur of conversation, followed by "pray'rs read over in Haste," while people chatted sociably with one another in the pews. After the service, they spent time "strolling around" or at cards and dice, horse racing, "folly with the negroes," and so on, before going their separate ways.

From time to time, the religious life of America was shaken by evangelicals, most notably in the mid-1730s and 1740s, when a fundamentalist revival—marked by prayer meetings, confessions, repentances, and hysterical conversions—swept through the colonies north and south. Patrick Henry's uncle, the Anglican minister of a Virginia parish, vividly recorded what their preaching was like:

They thunder out in awful words, and new coin'd phrases, what they call the terrors of the law, cursing & scolding, calling the old people, Grey-headed Devils, and all promiscuously, Damn'd double damn'd, whose [souls] are in hell though they are alive on earth, Lumps of hell-fire, incarnate Devils, 1000 times worse than Devils &c and all the while the Preacher exalts his voice puts himself into a violent agitation, stamping and beating his Desk unmercifully until the weaker sort of his hearers being scar'd, cry out, fall down & work like people in convulsion fits, to the amazement of spectators, and if a few only are thus brought down, the Preacher gets into a violent passion again, Calling out Will no more of you come to Christ? . . . and these things are extoll'd by the Preachers as the mighty power of God's grace in their hearts.

Perhaps the most charismatic of the "New Light" evangelicals was George Whitefield, a follower of John Wesley, who challenged his listeners to awake to the requirements of a spiritual life. He emphasized personal accountability as well as a more passionate communion with God, carrying his message into cities, towns, and remote frontier areas where not only whites but blacks were caught up in the fervor and responded to his call. According to Jonathan Edwards, the great Northampton preacher who was second only to Whitefield in contemporary fame, many blacks were "truly born again" in "this late remarkable season," and indeed the conversion of black slaves to Christianity in large numbers dates from this time.

Wherever he went, Whitefield attracted substantial crowds. Nathan Cole, a Connecticut farmer, remembered that as he set out one morning in October 1740 to hear Whitefield preach at the old meetinghouse in Middletown, he saw in the distance a great mist rising like a gathering cloud. "I thought at first," he wrote,

> it came from the great river—the Connecticut—but as I came nearer the road I heard the noise of horses' feet coming down the road, and this cloud was a cloud of dust made by the horses' feet. . . . I could see men and horses slipping along in the cloud like shadows, and as I drew nearer it seemed like a steady stream of horses and their riders, scarcely a horse more than his length behind another, all of a lather with foam and sweat, their breath rolling out of their nostrils every jump. Every horse seemed to go with all his might to hear news from heaven for the saving of souls.

When Cole got to Middletown, he turned, looked toward the river, and saw boats carrying believers across in such multitudes that the embankments "looked black with people and horses. All along the twelve miles, I saw no man at work in his field, but all seemed to be gone." When the assembly had gathered, Whitefield mounted a platform erected for him in the open air, and "he looked almost angelical; a young, slim, slender youth, before some thousands of people with a bold undaunted countenance. And my hearing how God was with him everywhere as he came along, it solemnized my mind and put me in a trembling fear before he began to preach; for he looked as though he was clothed with authority from the great God, and a sweet solemn solemnity sat upon his brow."

Even the worldly wise Benjamin Franklin was so moved by Whitefield's oratory on one occasion that, he tells us in his *Autobiography,* "I emptied my pocket wholly, gold and all, into the collector's dish."

People of all sects and denominations were held in thrall. And despite excesses that repelled Church authorities (and elicited censure from the faculties of Harvard and Yale), the Great Awakening helped bind Americans together with a shared sense of their spirituality as a people and, perhaps, "prepared them," in the words of one historian, "for the coming ordeal of sacrifice and war."

FRANKLIN and his compatriots were not so moved when, in the mid-1760s, the king and Parliament began to preach their own requirements and to pass the collection plate around for themselves. But they were preaching to the unconverted, and when donations did not come willingly, attempts were made to exact them by force.

Britain's power, and in particular the naval strength which had made the empire supreme, were based upon her wealth derived from trade. That trade was managed by a complex but coherent system of imperial regulation, and on the whole the colonies had prospered by their means. In the current mercantilist thinking of the time, it was axiomatic that colonies were to provide raw materials to the mother country and in turn serve as a market for her manufactured goods. Accordingly, no foreign ships were permitted to enter colonial harbors; all imported goods had to be shipped from a British port, regardless of their place of origin; and certain enumerated exports had to be shipped first to England, regardless of their destination. In short, by her Trade and Navigation Acts England sought to engross not only the carrying trade but the general trade of her colonies and to exclude them from the markets of the world. At the same time, she afforded them the best of markets, especially for the cash crops of the South and the timber and marine stores of New England. This worked well enough for more than a century, and almost no one complained.

One of those who appreciated the symbiotic character of the relationship was John Dickinson, the Pennsylvania lawyer, who in his *Essay on the Constitutional Power of Great Britain* (1774) wrote:

If an archangel had planned the connexion between Great Britain and her colonies, he could not have fixed it on a more lasting and beneficial foundation, unless he could have changed human nature. A mighty naval power at the head of the whole—that power, a parent state with all the endearing sentiments attending to the relationship—that could never disoblige, but with design—the dependent states more apt to have feuds among themselves—she the umpire and controuler—those states producing every article neccesary to her greatness—their interest, that she should continue free and flourishing—their ability to throw a considerable weight in the scale, should her government get unduly poised—she and all those states Protestant—are some of the circumstances, that delineated by the masterly hand of a Beccaria, would exhibit a plan, vindicating the ways of heaven and demonstrating, that humanity and policy are nearly related.

Yet it was not a little ironic that the plan had worked in part because the Navigation Acts which governed it were largely ignored. The colonial economy, in fact, benefited for so long from their indifferent enforcement that smuggling was almost a hereditary practice in American commercial life. As early as 1699, William Byrd of Virginia had remarked in a report to the London Board of Trade that Pennsylvania, for example, was "not precise in consulting what trade is lawful and what is not." The same could have been said for most of the other colonies from that time up until the Revolution began. One observer noted that customs collectors "dare not exercise their office for fear of the fury and unruliness of the people" and that Virginians as well as New Englanders were "haughty and jealous of their liberties, impatient of restraint, and can scarcely bear the thought of being controlled by any superior power."

Indeed, Americans in general embraced a notion of liberty that was already an almost occult compound of messianic, historical, and rationalist ideas. Even before the ouster of the French from Canada, New England clerics conjured up the vision of a mighty new North American empire "in numbers little inferior perhaps to the greatest in Europe," as one of them predicted, "and in felicity to none." He foresaw "a great and flourishing kingdom" with cities "rising on every hill . . . happy fields and villages . . . [and] religion professed and practiced through-out this spacious kingdom in far greater purity and perfection than since the times of the apostles." The language of American politicians and statesmen echoed the theme. "The liberties of mankind and the glory of human nature is in our keeping," John Adams wrote in 1765. "America was designed by Providence for the theatre on which man was to make his true figure, on which science, virtue, liberty, happiness, and glory were to exist in peace."

Some of these ideas were associated with covenant theology—in particular, with the Puritan idea that "the colonization of America had been an event designed by the hand of God to satisfy his ultimate aims"—but they were linked in a coordinate (or blended) way with political ideas of the Enlightenment and idealized conceptions of the democratic republics of Greece and Rome. The history of those republics, which had been suppressed by tyrants and supplanted by corrupt imperial regimes, was viewed by Americans (steeped by their own education in the classical world) as a warning and example to the times. By analogy, they regarded their own provincial virtues—frugality, industry, fortitude, and temperance, for example—as menaced by the degeneracy and corruption of imperial power in London. The most popular play in America (as previously noted) was *Cato*, which dramatized the martyrdom of a hero of republican liberty, and almost everyone read Charles Rollins's *Ancient History*, which traced the sad story of that liberty's demise. As a law student abroad in England, John Dickinson had compared "the most unbounded licentiousness and utter disregard of virtue" which he found in London to that of imperial Rome. More than £1 million, he reported, had been expended to buy votes in the recent general election, in which, with equal "impudence and villainy," an effort had also been made to get members of the opposition electorate so drunk they could not vote at all. "Few people can refrain from laughing," he added, when members of Parliament took their solemn oaths of office, which included a promise not to engage in electoral fraud.

"Liberty can no more exist without virtue and independence than the body can live and move without a soul," declared John Adams in a kindred spirit about the corruption of English politics, where "luxury, effeminacy, and venality are arrived at such a shocking pitch." Or as his wife, Abigail, put it more succinctly, "A true patriot must be a religious man."

Religion and politics were entwined. The so-called Liberty Tree (in Boston and elsewhere, a great elm on the common where protesters met) was Roman in origin and (in American revolutionary symbolism) related to the liberty pole or pike topped with a cap held by the figure of Libertas in the Temple of Liberty established in Rome in 135 B.C. These symbols had appeared on Roman coins, in Dutch and French prints of the sixteenth century, and in English prints during the French and Indian War. In America, they turned up in the illustrations of patriotic pamphlets, and when Charles Willson Peale later painted his portrait of William Pitt (to the colonists, a hero of enlightened government), he depicted the British statesman in the attitude and garb of a Roman orator, Magna Carta in hand, pointing to a figure of Britannia holding a liberty pole.

Ideas and attitudes associated with the Enlightenment gave the idea of *libertas* a rational and contemporary context. American writers cited Locke, Hobbes, and Montesquieu on natural rights and almost ritualistically invoked Locke's trinity of life, liberty, and property as the precious and inherited natural rights of all free men. They believed that political authority was, or should be, derived from the consent of the governed and that its goal was the general good. Moreover, they believed they shared in a unique political inheritance. It was their historical understanding (based on the writings of Samuel von Pufendorf and Hugo

Grotius) that the rights they claimed by way of the English could be traced back to the Anglo-Saxons (as depicted by Tacitus in his *Germania*), who had curbed royal power by introducing a measure of representative government. That had ultimately led to England's unique unwritten constitution, from which (in Daniel Boorstin's summary) trial by jury, due process of law, representation before taxation, habeas corpus, freedom from attainder, the independence of the judiciary, and the rights of free speech were all derived. As described by John Adams, the English constitution was "the most perfect combination of human powers in society which finite wisdom has yet contrived and reduced to practice for the preservation of liberty and the production of happiness." Whether it could really be traced, historically, to the Anglo-Saxons or not, everyone knew that in March 1628 the House of Commons had, in its Petition of Right, sought royal recognition of four principles—no taxation without the consent of Parliament, no imprisonment without cause, no quartering of soldiers on subjects, and no martial law in peacetime. And to these the king had been obliged to consent. It is therefore not surprising that even on the threshold of the Revolution, Thomas Jefferson could declare, "I would rather be in dependence on Great Britain, properly limited, than on any nation upon earth, or on no nation," as the fateful choice was framed.

A DECADE and a half after Wolfe had fallen in the capture of Québec, vastly increasing the size of the British Empire, the king and Parliament decided to erect a heroic monument to his memory. The winning design depicted the dying commander at the moment of his death supported by an English soldier pointing to a figure representing Victory. In one hand, the figure held a palm branch, the emblem of peace; in the other, the wreath of immortality. Lines on an oval tablet proclaimed that by his triumph Wolfe had "surmounted by Ability & valour All Obstacles of Art & Nature."

But the time of that glory was already past. Art and Nature had both brought about changes which neither imperial ability nor valor could withstand.

CHAPTER THREE

KING, PARLIAMENT,
and
INHERITED RIGHTS

JOHN Adams once said that "the opening gun of the Revolution" was fired in January 1750, when Jonathan Mayhew, minister of Boston's West Church, favorably commemorated in his sermons the centennial of the execution of Charles I. In the town cemetery of New Haven stood the tomb of one of the judges who had condemned the king to death, and after the Revolution began, Americans went there on pilgrimage (wrote a visiting French diplomat) "as to the tomb of their apostle."

Years later Adams wrote, "What do we mean by the American Revolution? Do we mean the American war? The Revolution was effected before the war commenced. The Revolution was in the minds and hearts of the people; a change in their religious sentiments of their duties and obligations." However, over time, there was a change in that change. For the most part, the upheaval was not a social revolution, undertaken to destroy or even substantially alter the established order of society. It was (or arose from) an argument over rights that evolved into a struggle for power—the power of each party to assert its rights as it understood them, then afterward a struggle for empire as Americans began to conceive a more ambitious and independent course for themselves. At the outset, the dissidents argued from the privileges enshrined in colonial charters, the rights of British subjects, and the unwritten British constitution, understood as a splendid accumulation of civil liberties; but before the final break came they had also begun to invoke universal principles of natural law. By then, George III, to whom Americans had repeatedly appealed as to a benevolent but misguided monarch, was made personally responsible for Britain's misrule.

Yet from the beginning the most extreme ground was laid. Jonathan Mayhew's famous *Discourse Concerning Unlimited Submission* of 1750 had, in a manner of speaking, justified regicide as well as revolution as an obligation of the soul. In the absence of good government, he wrote,

> a regard to the public welfare ought to make us withhold from our rulers that obedience and subjection which it would, otherwise, be our duty to render to them. . . .
>
> For a nation thus abused to arise unanimously and to resist their prince, even to dethroning him, is not criminal, but a reasonable way of vindicating their liberties and just rights. . . . And it would be highly criminal in them not to make use of this means. . . . And in such a case it would, of the two, be more rational to suppose that they that did NOT *resist* [rather] than that they who did, would receive to themselves damnation.

The same notion was more neatly stated in Thomas Jefferson's motto (borrowed from Benjamin Franklin), "Rebellion to tyrants is obedience to God." But such a broad principle, which gave theological sanction to resistance to oppression, would have been just as applicable to another time and place. The subtlety of the colonial situation was more aptly expressed by Edmund Burke, who warned, "The forms of a free and the ends of an arbitrary government are things not altogether incompatible." Few have paid attention to that paradox, before or since: but in the America of 1776, they did. And revolution was the result.

T H E confrontation between England and the colonies coincided with the rise of the lower houses of provincial assemblies. Since their beginnings in the seventeenth century, the American colonies had enjoyed a considerable measure of self-government while ceding to Great Britain all matters having to do with commercial regulation and the conduct of foreign affairs. But in a number of colonies—especially Virginia, Massachusetts, and New York—members were "tenacious in the Opinion that the Inhabitants . . . are entitled to all the Privileges of *Englishmen*" and "have a Right to participate in the legislative Power," as one New Yorker wrote about the representatives of his own state. The assemblies, which patterned themselves upon the House of Commons, claimed for their members the same rights of free speech, freedom from arrest, and control of the purse. In so doing, they often found themselves in conflict with the royal governors, who operated on the assumption that the assemblies existed by the sufferance of the Crown. Moreover, though some of the American assemblies thought of themselves as coequal in all but antiquity with the British Parliament itself, in London they were considered subordinate bodies, subject to both Parliament and the royal will. And this was so, even though, as Burke pointed out, they "answered in the main all the purposes necessary to the internal economy of a free people, and provided for all the exigencies of government which arose amongst themselves. In the midst of that happy enjoyment, they never thought of critically settling the exact limits of a power, which was necessary to their union, their safety, their equality, and even their liberty." However, when their own rights were formally challenged, they began to consider, critically, what the limits of that power might be.

The traditions of independence, after all, were strong. Although Massachusetts professed allegiance to the Crown, she had long borne herself, in the summary of one historian, as an almost sovereign commonwealth. She had made war and peace, taxed herself, coined her own money (the pine-tree shilling), and (with the English common law as a basis) had framed her own code of laws, including that of capital punishment. When the royal government from time to time tried to enforce obedience, "the colonists met it with diplomacy and procrastination, fortified by fasting and prayer." Their distance from England also justified their assumption of a degree of military discretion. "If we in America," said John Winthrop of Massachusetts in the early years of the colony, "should forbear to unite for offence and defence . . . till we have leave from England, our throats might all be cut before the messenger could be half seas through." Animated by a similarly independent spirit, the New England colonies of Rhode Island, Connecticut, and New Hampshire also managed to negotiate a measure of autonomy for themselves.

The New England colonies, in short, were nascent republics. By contrast, Virginia, "after some fluctuation between chartered self-government and viceregal rule," became a kind of colonial monarchy after the English pattern. It had a governor who in his authority more truly resembled the king; a council, nominated by the governor, analogous to the House of Lords; and a representative assembly analogous to the House of Commons. The assembly (dominated by the planters) enjoyed, as in New England, the mighty power of the purse, which made the governor in some things subject to the popular will; but the will of the "people" assumed a different form. In a territory where there were villages and hamlets but very few towns, there was nothing like the local township politics that characterized New England life. In the shires and colossal parishes to which they belonged, the great planters therefore enjoyed a kind of eminent domain. And there, with considerable independence in their authority, they administered local government and justice. Yet despite the oligarchical cast of their political life, they were also, no less than their New England compatriots, "tenacious of their constitutional rights as Englishmen and [they] maintained them proudly against the governor, as the barons of old had maintained them against the king." Thus, in their own way they, too, had undergone a kind of preparation for the revolt that was to come.

A T the end of the French and Indian War, seventeen regiments, or 8,000 to 10,000 soldiers, were stationed in America to secure Britain's expanded empire and to patrol the wilderness frontiers. The expense of the war had put a heavy strain on the British taxpayer, and the imperial administration decided it was not unreasonable for Americans, who had benefited and prospered as a result of British victories, to help defray the cost. The colonial assemblies, however, were slow to contribute, prompting Parliament to contemplate levying taxes to compel support of this standing force. Resistance arose. To begin with, with regard to the war itself, the colonists felt they had done their part: they had furnished their quotas of money and troops, had fought faithfully, and in some battles had even carried the day. Nearly 25,000 Americans had served— "a number equal to those sent from Great Britain, and far beyond their proportion," as Benjamin Franklin pointed out. Moreover, the colonies had incurred war debts of their own, "and all their estates and taxes are mortgaged for many years to come." Finally, contrary to the traditions of English constitutional government, the new taxes were to be levied by a Parliament in which they were not directly represented, or had an elected voice.

Eighteenth-century Americans realistically regarded their rights to life and liberty as dependent upon their right to property, because the latter gave them a measure of economic independence and the right to vote. Taxes imposed against their property or holdings on which their independence relied by an assembly in which they were not represented was, to many of them, incipient tyranny, clear and plain.

British politicians considered the Americans' reaction irrational. In their view, the cornerstone of liberty, as protected by the British constitution, was the supremacy of Parliament, which, as the contemporary jurist William Blackstone put it in his *Laws of England,* "hath sovereign and uncontrolable authority in making, confirming, enlarging, restraining, abrogating, repealing, reviving, and expounding of laws." Since the power to tax was "a necessary part of every supreme legislative authority," if Parliament "have not that power over America they have none, and then America is at once a kingdom of itself." Americans, on the other hand, believed that the legality of all parliamentary statutes was to be measured against the constitution; on that basis, being unrepresented in Parliament, they denied the right of that body to tax them directly according to the principles of constitutional law. As historian Daniel Boorstin has remarked, the United States "was born in an atmosphere of legal rather than philosophical debate."

I N April 1763, just three years after the accession of George III, Sir George Grenville, succeeding the earl of Bute, became prime minister. Although he remained in power for just two years, he cut a broad path by his initiatives for the demise of colonial power in America. With shocking haste, he implemented Bute's decision to place a large garrison of British troops on the North American continent; compelled the colonists, by a Quartering Act, to furnish them with lodging, transportation, and supplies; revived previously unenforced trade and navigation laws; authorized search warrants by customs agents; imposed, by a Sugar Act, stiffer penalties for smuggling sugar and molasses from the islands; attempted to curb the westward expansion of colonial settlements; gave greater authority over Indian affairs to British officials; sought to restrain American seaborne trade; restricted, by a Currency Act, the printing of paper money in America to ensure that British merchants would not be paid in a depreciated currency; and concomitant with the above, assessed taxes upon the colonists for the defense of the empire. All this, in the words of New Haven lawyer Jared Ingersoll, was like "burning down a barn to roast an egg."

The Revenue, or Sugar, Act of 1764, which was a principal component of Grenville's program, sought to monopolize the sugar trade for British merchants by banning foreign imports and by imposing or raising taxes on a wide variety of consumer goods. Most of the colonial supply of sugar and molasses (essential ingredients of rum) was obtained from the British West Indies in exchange for food, livestock, lumber, barrel staves, and naval stores. Americans, however, had long traded illegally with non-British territories—in particular, with islands controlled by the Spanish, Dutch, and French—because without that trade they could not acquire the hard currency they needed to pay for British manufactured goods. Since their own manufacturing was restrained and they were prohibited from obtaining finished goods from other lands, it was more galling still to have new restrictions imposed on their own production of such basic items as cloth and iron. Meanwhile, London added coffee, raw silk, hides, and potash, among other products, to the list of "enumerated" items which could not be exported to foreign ports. "Our whole Wealth centers finally among the Merchants and Inhabitants of Great Britain," complained Benjamin Franklin. The colonists, he said, had "risked their lives and fortunes" in war for the sake of "extending the Dominion and increasing the Commerce for their Mother Nation," only to find that they had somehow "forfeited the native Rights of Britons," for their pains.

A fleet of eight warships and twelve armed sloops was anchored at Halifax, Nova Scotia, to assist British officials in the enforcement of the Navigation Acts, and in the new crackdown on smuggling customs agents were authorized by means of search warrants, or "writs of assistance," to break, by force if necessary, into any ship, warehouse, dwelling, or store. "Our houses, and even our bedchambers, are exposed to be ransacked," complained one Bostonian, "our boxes, trunks, and chests broke open, ravaged and plundered by wretches whom no prudent man would venture to employ."

Such unwelcome strictness in the new British trade and monetary policies coincided with other heavy-handed and suspicious measures, including new regulations with regard to Indian affairs. The end of the French and Indian War had not made peace between the colonists and the Indians, and in the summer of 1763 there was a general uprising, known as Pontiac's Rebellion, in which the western tribes attacked the English on a long front from Detroit to Fort Pitt. Although those two posts held out, during May and June every other garrison west of Niagara was surprised and massacred.

Pontiac, an Ottaway chief, concentrated his power on the northern lakes and hoped, as he eloquently put it, "by one year's war, well pushed, to drive the English into the sea." But after a series of fierce battles, his situation deteriorated to the point of hopelessness and he appealed for a truce. Meanwhile, the ministry in London, fearful that westward migration would plunge the colonists into still more costly Indian wars, drew a long "Proclamation Line" along the ridge of the Appalachian Mountains and declared that the territory west of it belonged to the Ottaway and other tribes, according to prior treaty commitments made to them during the French and Indian War. This all but closed the trans-Appalachian region except to licensed traders, prohibited settlement and land grants west of the mountains without the express approval of the Crown, and thwarted the ambitions of colonial land buyers. If the Indians stood to benefit from this apparently enlightened directive, its principal and overriding purpose was to keep the commerce of the westward-moving population (which threatened to move out of reach) "in just subordination to and dependence upon this kingdom," as one minister remarked.

Scarcely had these measures been authorized than Parliament drafted its notorious Stamp Act, which imposed a stamp tax ranging from 1 shilling to £6 on various commercial and legal documents such as wills, mortgages, and college degrees, as well as on newspapers, almanacs, calendars, pamphlets, playing cards, and dice. Although such a surcharge had long been common in England, and a decade earlier three of the colonies—Massachusetts, New York, and Maryland—had themselves levied a stamp tax to help support the burdens of the French and Indian War, the new measure led to a storm of protest even before its enactment.

In a celebrated pamphlet (*Rights of the British Colonies Asserted and Proved*), James Otis, a classical scholar educated at Harvard and the former advocate general of Massachusetts, declared that the tax was unconstitutional and invalid and "absolutely irreconcileable" with the "rights of the colonists as British subjects and as men."

In May 1764, Boston held a town meeting during which Samuel Adams drew up a series of resolutions which contained the first formal and public denial of the right of Parliament to tax the colonies without their consent. These resolutions were adopted by the Massachusetts Assembly, while a circular letter was sent to the other colonies, setting forth the need for concerted action. In response, the assemblies of Connecticut, New York, Pennsylvania, Virginia, and South Carolina joined with Massachusetts in protesting the proposed act.

Since the Americans were already contributing substantially to the imperial coffers through British control of their trade (and were not unwilling to contribute something more, provided it be done on their own terms), Grenville, before putting the Stamp Act through the House of Commons, had felt constrained to ask the colonial assemblies to suggest alternative methods of securing a steady revenue. "I am not set upon this tax," he told Franklin. "If the Americans dislike it, and prefer any other method, I shall be content . . . provided the money be but raised." At the same time he privately dismissed the idea that the colonies would, of their own volition, raise the monies required. Nevertheless, he told Franklin (then in London) that he wanted the act to be "as little inconvenient and disagreeable to the Americans as possible," and would therefore arrange for the tax commissioners to be appointed from among the colonists themselves. Franklin thought this wise and recommended a number of friends (Jared Ingersoll among them) for the post. But Ingersoll himself warned that any internal tax "other than such as shall be laid by the legislative bodies here . . . would go down with the people like chopped hay." And Franklin was mistaken to suppose his compatriots could be so mollified.

Why? Because a parliamentary revenue raised in America but determined in England would make the governors and their appointees independent of local pressure (or accountability), completely beholden to the Crown, and more faithful in the enforcement of British statutes, from revenue legislation to the Trade and Navigation Acts. The Stamp Act was therefore viewed as a harbinger of other measures that would ultimately lead to complete oppression. As John Dickinson wrote, "Nothing is wanted at home but a PRECEDENT, the force of which shall be established by the tacit submission of the colonies. . . . If the Parliament succeeds in this attempt, other statutes will impose other duties, and thus the Parliament will levy upon us such sums of money as they choose to take, *without any other* LIMITATION *than their* PLEASURE."

Many Americans also now insisted upon a distinction (which the British regarded as a sophistry) between external taxes (such as customs duties), which Parliament had a right to impose as part of the regulation of trade, and an internal tax (such as the stamp tax), which was devised to raise revenue. This was understood by some better than others. When the act (with scarcely a dissenting vote) became law, Franklin wrote from London to a fellow Philadelphian, "We might as well have hindered the sun's setting. That we could not do. But since 'tis down, my friend, and it may be long before it rises again, let us make as good a night of it as we can. We may still light candles."

His witty but not quite wise acquiescence was not shared by his countrymen. On May 29, 1765, Patrick Henry rose in the Virginia House of Burgesses to introduce a series of momentous resolutions which he had hastily drafted on a blank leaf of an old law book:

> *Whereas,* the honorable House of Commons in England have of late drawn into question how far the General Assembly of this colony hath power to enact laws for laying taxes and imposing duties, payable by the people of this, his majesty's most ancient colony: for settling and ascertain-

ing the same to all future times, the House of Burgesses of this present General Assembly have come to the following resolves:

1. *Resolved,* That the first adventurers and settlers of this, his majesty's colony and dominion, brought with them and transmitted to their prosperity, and all other his majesty's subjects, since inhabiting in this, his majesty's said colony, all the privileges, franchises, and immunities that have at any time been held, enjoyed, and possessed, by the people of Great Britain.

2. *Resolved,* That by two royal charters, granted by king James the First, the colonists aforesaid are declared entitled to all the privileges, liberties, and immunities of denizens and natural born subjects, to all intents and purposes, as if they had been abiding and born within the realm of England.

3. *Resolved,* That the taxation of the people by themselves or by persons chosen by themselves to represent them, who can only know what taxes the people are able to bear, and the easiest mode of raising them, and are equally affected by such taxes themselves, is the distinguishing characteristic of British freedom, and without which the ancient constitution cannot subsist.

4. *Resolved,* That his majesty's liege people of this most ancient colony have uninterruptedly enjoyed the right of being thus governed by their own Assembly in the article of their taxes and internal police, and that the same hath never been forfeited, or any other way given up, but hath been constantly recognized by the kings and people of Great Britain.

5. *Resolved,* therefore, That the General Assembly of this colony have the only and sole exclusive right and power to lay taxes and impositions upon the inhabitants of this colony; and that every attempt to vest such power in any person or persons whatsoever, other than the General Assembly aforesaid, has a manifest tendency to destroy British as well as American freedom.

Henry accompanied these resolutions with a fiery speech given the next day in which he concluded, "Caesar had his Brutus, Charles the First his Cromwell and George the Third"—amid cries of "Treason" that arose from all sides of the room—"and George the Third," he continued artfully, "may profit by their example. If this be treason, make the most of it!"

Thomas Jefferson, then a student at the College of William and Mary, was standing in the doorway and heard Henry speak. "I well remember the cry of treason," Jefferson wrote afterward, "the pause of Mr. Henry at the name of George III., and the presence of mind with which he closed his sentence, and baffled the charge vociferated."

Despite conservative opposition, the resolutions passed; and though the offending fifth resolution was later struck from the records—

and the Assembly dissolved by the governor—Henry had formulated the legal battle cry of the revolt: "Taxation without representation is tyranny."

To Jefferson it seemed as if Henry "spoke as Homer wrote." But it would not be the last time Henry would articulate the collective patriot mind. He had eloquence in his blood: his uncle was a brilliant Anglican preacher, and he himself was the third cousin of Lord Brougham, an English advocate and parliamentary firebrand of renown. Although he later liked to portray himself, in the great American political tradition, as a "regular guy," he was scarcely so, though some political enemies took advantage of the image to portray him as an unlettered rustic. One biographer tells us that as an adolescent, he had been "indolent, dreamy, frolicsome, with a mortal enmity to books . . . disorderly in dress, slouching, vagrant, unambitious; a roamer in woods, a loiterer on river-banks . . . giving no hint or token, by work or act, of the possession of any intellectual gift." In fact, he had been thoroughly tutored at home in the classics, and his oratorical manner was a deliberate stylistic blend of the studied and learned Anglican preaching favored by his uncle and the evangelical oratory of George Whitefield and other preachers of the Great Awakening.

At age twenty-four, after failed attempts to make his living as a farmer and a shopkeeper, he had decided to become a lawyer. His father, a judge, evidently gave him the benefit of his tutelage, and Henry passed his bar examination after only a month of preparation. Three years later he won a celebrated and complicated case known as the "Parson's Cause." In its wake he was elected to the Virginia Assembly, and just ten days after taking his seat, on May 29, 1765 (his twenty-ninth birthday), he introduced the series of resolutions which established his name.

Copies were widely circulated, published in newspapers throughout the land, and regarded as an open declaration of resistance against the British government.

Franklin was amazed at their rashness. He wrote to a friend, "A firm loyalty to the Crown and faithful adherence to the government of this nation, which it is the safety as well as honour of the colonies to be connected with, will always be the wisest course for you and I to take, whatever may be the madness of the populace or their blind leaders, who can only bring themselves and country into trouble and draw on greater burthens by acts of rebellious tendency." But he was out of touch. The colonial reaction to the stamp tax was virtually unanimous.

Toward the end of the summer, riots broke out in Rhode Island, Maryland, New Jersey, Pennsylvania, Connecticut, and New Hampshire as increasing numbers pledged to resist the new British measures, seize and destroy the stamped paper, and force the stamp commissioners to resign. In mid-August, in Boston, various appointed officials were hanged in effigy from the Liberty Tree on the common, with a boot (to represent the late prime minister, Lord Bute) suspended nearby. From the top of the boot a grotesque horned head protruded, representing the Devil. That evening, the figures were cut down and burned in front of the local stamp commissioner's house. Twelve days later, the home of the lieutenant governor, Thomas Hutchinson, was ransacked by a mob and his valuable library destroyed. Franklin's friend Jared Ingersoll (who had been appointed a commissioner) was also burned and hanged in effigy in Connecticut, where, according to the *Connecticut Gazette,* "people of all professions and denominations" joined the cheering crowd. In New Jersey, lawyers were pressured to boycott the courts; in New York, the Stamp Act was reprinted with a death's-head affixed to it in place of the royal arms, and the lieutenant governor, faced with violence, had to surrender all the stamps in his keeping to the city council. The property of other officials was also attacked or destroyed.

Meanwhile, the Massachusetts Assembly had drawn up a paper that declared, "The Stamp Act wholly cancels the very conditions upon which our ancestors, with much toil and blood, and at their sole expense, settled this country and enlarged his majesty's dominions." If Americans, it warned, were not governed "according to the known and stated rules of the constitution," their minds might become "disaffected"—that is, inclined to revolt.

The result of all the protest was the resignation of stamp commissioners throughout the colonies and the complete inability of the British government to enforce the law.

Amid the turmoil, Henry's was not the only eloquent (and learned) voice. At the height of the crisis, John Adams published in the *Boston Gazette* "A Dissertation on Canon and Feudal Law." "It has been said by the British," he wrote,

> that . . . the King, his ministry, and Parliament, will not endure to hear the Americans talk of their *rights.* But Americans will not endure in silence the slow erosion of those freedoms which make them proud of the name of Englishmen. . . . Let it be known that British liberties are not the grants of princes or parliaments, but the original rights, conditions of original contracts, coequal with prerogative and coeval with government; that many of our rights are inherent and essential, agreed on as maxims and established as preliminaries, even before a Parliament existed.

The appeal to the British constitution was beginning to yield, tentatively, to the larger concepts of natural law.

At the same time, the practicalities of the protest were no more clearly and forcefully expressed than in a letter George Washington wrote to an in-law in London:

> The stamp act engrosses the conversation of the speculative part of the colonists, who look upon this unconstitutional method of taxation as a direful attack upon their liberties and loudly exclaim against the violation. What may be the result of this and of some other (I think I may add ill-judged) measures, I will not undertake to determine; but this I may venture to affirm, that the advantage accruing to the mother country will fall greatly short of the expectation of the ministry; for certain it is that our whole substance already in a manner flows to Great Britain and that whatsoever contributes to lessen our importations must be hurtful to her manufactures. The eyes of our people already begin to be opened, and they will perceive that many luxuries for which we lavish our substance in Great Britain can well be dispensed with. This, consequently, will introduce frugality and be a necessary incitement to industry.

Homespun cloth and simple living became the hallmarks of patriotism. There was a general movement toward the boycott of English goods (especially cloth, a staple of the British economy), and items of conspicuous luxury were forsworn. The first graduating class of Rhode Island College—now Brown University—clothed themselves in homespun fabrics, and from Massachusetts to South Carolina women banded together in patriotic societies called "Daughters of Liberty" and agreed to wear only garments of local manufacture. In many New England towns they gathered together to spin: "And all the women that were wise-hearted did spin with their hands" (Exodus 35:25). Secret societies calling themselves the "Sons of Liberty" (after a phrase used in a ringing speech made against the Stamp Act in the House of Commons by Colonel Isaac Barre) also arose and pledged themselves to resist any illegitimate parliamentary act or law.

Meanwhile, in June 1765, the Massachusetts Assembly sent a circular letter to the other colonies calling for a general congress to coordinate resistance to the new tax. The Stamp Act Congress, as it was called, attended by the representatives of nine colonies, convened in October in New York and framed resolutions of "rights and grievances" as well as a petition to the king and Parliament for repeal of the measures opposed. Most of the delegates were moderates and "speculative" men (to use Washington's term), but they were adamant and angry enough to assert "that it is inseparable to the freedom of a people, and the un-doubted right of Englishmen, that no taxes should be imposed upon them, but with their own consent, given personally, or by their represen-tatives" and that the Stamp Act had "a manifest tendency to subvert the rights and liberties of the colonists." John Adams concisely stated what had already become the universal opinion among patriotic Americans: "It is inconsistent with the spirit of the common law and of the essential fundamental principles of the British constitution that we should be subject to any tax imposed by the British Parliament; because we are not represented in that assembly in any sense."

Such views were not the province only of those conversant with legal and political theory. They had filtered down into the body politic and were everywhere shared. Paul Revere, a master craftsman but not an intellectual, later summarized the dispute this way in a letter to a cousin in France:

> The [British] covenanted with the first settlers of this country, that we should enjoy all the Libertys of free natural born subjects of Great Britain. They were not contented to have all the benefits of our trade, in short to have all our earnings, but they wanted to make us hewers of wood and drawers of water. Their Parliament have declared that they will have a right to tax us & Legislate for us, in all cases whatever—now certainly if they have a right to take one shilling from us without our consent, they have a right to all we possess; for it is the birthright of an Englishman, not to be taxed without consent of himself, or Representatives.

One ingenious English argument, in contravention of these views, was that the colonists, like "nine tenths of the people of Britain" (most of them unpropertied) who did not choose their own representatives, were in effect represented in Parliament by those elected. For the right to vote was not inextricably bound up with representation. In Parliament, "none are actually, all are virtually represented," explained one English polemi-cist, for "every Member sits in the House not as representative of his own constituents but as one of that august assembly by which all the com-mons of *Great Britain* are represented. Their rights and their interests, however his own borough may be affected by general dispositions, ought to be the great objects of his attention and the only rules for his conduct, and to sacrifice these to a partial advantage in favor of the place where he was chosen would be a departure from his duty." This ideal-ized conception of public service and political virtue (of which the members of Parliament gave scant proof) was met with considerable skepticism. By such a notion (that is, virtual representation), wrote James Otis, you could "as well prove that the British House of Commons in fact represent all the people of the globe."

To resolve the problem, either the colonies would have to be allowed to elect representatives to the British Parliament in some equitable way proportionate to their size, which seemed improbable, or the right to levy local taxes reserved to their provincial assemblies. But this the king and Parliament had already disallowed. It was also apparent that Americans could not be represented in Parliament in numbers sufficient to give them a controlling voice in their own affairs. And token representation would be worse than none.

The impasse hardened and as a result "the Colonies," wrote one New York royalist in dismay, "are universally agitated by Suspicion, Fear and Disgust." At the Stamp Act Congress a notable solidarity emerged. As Dr. Joseph Warren, a Massachusetts delegate, remarked, "Until now the Colonies were ever at variance and foolishly jealous of each other. Now they are . . . united . . . nor will they soon forget the weight which this close union gives them."

Meanwhile, in July, the king had dismissed Grenville as prime minister, appointing the marquis of Rockingham in his place. The following January, the Stamp Act came up for review. William Pitt called for its repeal; Grenville, its adamant author, wanted it imposed by force and opposed him in parliamentary debate.

Pitt compared the growing colonial unrest to England's own Glorious Revolution. It was, he said, "a subject of greater importance than ever engaged the attention of this House, that subject only excepted, when, near a century ago, it was the question whether you yourselves were to be bound or free!" He called the Stamp Act "impolitic, arbitrary, oppressive, and unconstitutional," and reminded the House of Commons that when it had been passed, he had been ill in bed; but "if I could have endured to be carried . . . I would have solicited some kind hand to have laid me down on this floor to have borne my testimony against it. . . . This kingdom has no right to lay a tax upon the colonies. . . . The Americans are the sons, not the bastards of England." As subjects, he concluded, they were "equally entitled to all the natural rights of mankind and the peculiar rights of Englishmen."

Grenville, rising to reply, said, "When I proposed to tax America, I asked the House if any man would object to the right; I repeatedly asked it, and no man would attempt to deny it. . . . America is bound to yield obedience. If not, tell me when the Americans were emancipated?"

Pitt answered, "I rejoice that America has resisted. . . . The gentleman asks, When were the colonists emancipated? I desire to know when they were made slaves. . . . Three millions of people, so dead to all feelings of liberty as voluntarily to submit to be slaves, would be fit instruments to make slaves of all the rest of us."

Yet in a politic and conciliatory way, Pitt also moved in conclusion toward a compromise stance: "Let the Stamp Act be repealed. . . . At the same time let the sovereign authority of this country over the colonies be asserted in as strong terms as can be devised, and be made to extend to every point of legislation that we may bind their trade, confine their manufactures, and exercise every power whatever, except that of taking their money out of their pockets without their consent."

His advice was ignored. On February 3, five resolutions were introduced into the House of Commons in which the authority of Parliament was upheld and the disturbances in the colonies denounced. Edmund Burke spoke against them, and Colonel Isaac Barre, who had served in the colonies, warned that America was a sleeping giant and ought not to be provoked. "All colonies have their date of independence," he declared. "If we act injudiciously, this point may be reached in the life of many members of this House."

Others could see no chance of accommodation. Those aligned with Grenville professed themselves unable to understand, for example, the alleged difference between external and internal taxes. "It is said that they will not submit to the Stamp Act," declared Lord Lyttelton when the resolutions were taken up on February 10 in the House of Lords,

as it lays an internal tax; if this be admitted, the same reasoning extends to all acts of Parliament. The Americans will find themselves crampt by the act of Navigation and oppose that too. . . . The only question . . . is whether the American colonies are a part of the dominions of Great Britain? If not, the Parliament has no jurisdiction, if they are . . . they must be proper objects of our legislature: and by declaring them exempt from one statute or law, you declare them no longer subjects of Great Britain, and make them small independent communities not entitled to your protection.

Benjamin Franklin was present during many of these debates and was himself summoned to testify for three hours before the House of Commons concerning the American reaction to the Stamp Act. Though a bit chastened by developments, his performance was superb.

"What," he was asked (by Grey Cooper, secretary to the Treasury), "was the temper of America towards Great Britain before the year 1763?"

"The best in the world," replied Franklin. "They submitted willingly to the government of the crown and paid, in all their courts, obedience to the acts of Parliament. Numerous as the people are in the several old provinces, they cost you nothing in forts, citadels, garrisons or armies to keep them in subjection. They were governed by this country at the expense only of a little pen and ink and paper. They were led by a thread. They had not only a respect but an affection for Great Britain, for its laws, its customs and manners, and even a fondness for its fashions, that greatly increased the commerce. Natives of Great Britain were always treated with particular regard. To be an Old-England man was of itself a character of some respect and gave a kind of rank among us."

"And what is their temper now?"

"Oh! Very much altered."

"If the act is not repealed, what do you think will be the consequences?"

"A total loss of the respect and affection the people of America bear to this country, and of all the commerce that depends on that respect and affection."

"Do you think the people of America would submit to pay the stamp duty if it was moderated?"

"No, never, unless compelled by force of arms."

The distinction between internal and external taxes also came up. Grenville asked him what the difference was between a duty on the importation of goods and an excise on their consumption. Franklin explained the matter this way: "An external tax is a duty laid on commodities imported; that duty is added to the first cost and other charges on the commodity, and, when it is offered to sale, makes a part of the price. If the people do not like it at that price, they refuse it; they are not obliged to pay it. But an internal tax is forced from the people without their consent, if not laid by their own representatives." When asked whether the colonists might not object "by the same interpretation . . . to Parliament's right of external taxation," Franklin adroitly replied, "Many arguments have been lately used here to show them that there is no difference, and that if you have no right to tax them internally, you have none to tax them externally or make any other law to bind them. At present they do not reason so; but in time they may possibly be convinced by these arguments."

Like Franklin himself, however, most members of Parliament doubted this, and in March the Stamp Act was repealed. Lamps were lit in countless American homes in celebration, fireworks blazed above the town commons, and in an act of mercy reflecting the universal relief, debtors were even released from jail. In New York, a lead statue of George III was erected on Bowling Green. In Boston, celebrants carried an enormous transparent obelisk of oiled paper illuminated from within (like a Japanese lantern) by three hundred lamps and covered with symbolic pictures and patriotic verse.

Although King George III afterward repented of the act's repeal—as a "fatal compliance to public demand"—in America, wrote John Adams, it quieted the public uproar and "composed every wave of popular disorder into a smooth and peaceful calm."

Yet a dragon seed had been sown. To ensure enough votes for the repeal, the Rockingham administration had felt obliged to precede it with a Declaratory Act, which reasserted the imperial right of taxation anywhere in the empire and affirmed the legislative supremacy of Parliament "to make laws and statutes of sufficient force and vitality to bind the colonies and people of America . . . in all cases whatsoever."

A few months later, in July, the Rockingham administration fell, succeeded by an administration dominated by Charles Townshend, the new chancellor of the Exchequer. Townshend had opposed repeal of the Stamp Act and, even more determinedly than Grenville, undertook after a brief interlude to oblige the colonists to yield. When a colleague warned him in Parliament not to introduce yet another tax, Townshend reputedly "stamped his foot petulantly and cried, 'I will, I will!' " Turning a debating point into a policy, he seized on the distinction made by the colonists between direct and indirect taxation and proposed indirect taxes in the form of duties on tea and various other British imports, such as lead, paper, and glass. These were incorporated into a parliamentary bill in June–July 1767, which also reaffirmed the legality of writs of assistance, established new viceadmiralty courts for adjudicating violations of the Navigation Acts without benefit of trial by jury, and set up a Board of Customs Commissioners in Boston responsible directly to the British Treasury. As the legal basis for all this, he gave the Declaratory Act. Meanwhile, since New York had refused to provide for the British soldiers sent there by the Quartering Act of 1765, Townshend brought in a measure to suspend the New York Assembly until the soldiers' requirements were met.

The Townshend Acts were expressly intended to raise money for the support of Crown officials in America, thereby making them independent of the assemblies, which had previously controlled their salaries. They had nothing to do with the regulation of trade and everything to do with asserting Britain's supremacy over the colonies at the expense of their political freedom. And so, though they were introduced in the guise of external taxes, it was obvious to vigilant patriots that these were new revenue taxes, imposed without their consent to put them under arbitrary rule.

Opposition to the new measures began with an attempt to revive the boycott of English goods. In October 1767, Massachusetts singled out such luxury items as ribbons, laces, and tea, as well as cloth, and by winter other colonies had followed suit. Newspapers also published the first of John Dickinson's vastly influential *Letters from a Pennsylvania Farmer,* which warned, "A free people can never be too quick in observing, nor too firm in opposing the beginnings of alteration either in form or reality, respecting institutions formed for their security. . . . Servitude may be slipped upon us, under the sanction of usual and respectable terms." There were, he said, three kinds of taxes: internal, for revenue; external, for revenue; and external, for the regulation of commerce. The Townshend duties were external taxes for revenue, clear and plain. They were therefore just as unconstitutional as the Stamp Tax.

The New York Assembly had been dissolved for refusing to comply with a quartering act; the Massachusetts legislature, now controlled by radicals, suffered a like fate when, early in 1768, it sent to the other colonies a circular letter, drawn up by Samuel Adams, which urged united action against the Townshend duties and the defense of colonial rights. The British government demanded that the Massachusetts Assembly rescind its action or be dissolved, and the governors of the other colonies were likewise directed to dissolve their assemblies if they responded favorably to the Massachusetts appeal. The Massachusetts Assembly refused—"We are asked to rescind," said Otis. "Let Britain rescind her measures or the colonies are lost to her forever."

Virginia took its place beside Massachusetts as the Virginia House of Burgesses passed resolutions of its own solemnly declaring that the people of the colony could be taxed only by their representatives and that it was both lawful and just for the colonies to unite in protest against violations of their rights. This Assembly, too, was dissolved, but it did not disperse. The next day twenty-eight of its members, including George Washington, Thomas Jefferson, Patrick Henry, and Richard Henry Lee, reconvened as the "late representatives of the people" in the Apollo Room of the Raleigh Tavern, where they adopted a series of resolutions prepared by Washington in which, as a continuation of the policy of nonimportation, they pledged not to purchase any taxed merchandise except paper so long as the Townshend duties remained.

Threats of violence in New York and Boston against customs agents and other government officials heightened tensions. After John Hancock's sloop *Liberty* was seized on a charge of smuggling, the royal governor of Massachusetts, Francis Bernard, appealed for armed protection. Meanwhile, General Thomas Gage, the British commander in America, then stationed in New York, had written confidentially to the British secretary of war that "the colonists are taking large strides toward independency; and it concerns Great Britain by a speedy and spirited conduct to shew them that these colonies are British colonies dependent on her, and that they are not independent states." His letter, and Bernard's appeal, were both alarmist; but the government responded in proportion to its fears. And so on September 30, 1768, "the ships of war arrived [in Boston], schooners transports etc., came up the harbour," in the words of Paul Revere, "and anchored round the Town; their cannons loaded, a spring on their cables, as for a regular siege. At noon on Saturday the fourteenth and twenty-nineth regements and a detachment from the 59th regement, and a train of artillery landed on Long Wharf; there Formed and Marched with insolent Parade, Drums beatting, Fifes playing, up King Street, Each soldeir having received sixteen rounds of Powder and Ball."

According to the royal governor, the troops from Halifax had come as a police force "to rescue the Government from the hands of a trained mob and to restore the activity of the Civil power."

Boston engaged in passive resistance. The city refused them barracks; few residents opened their homes. In the beginning they therefore had to camp out on the common or in Faneuil Hall. But by November, they were quartered all over town in distilleries, sugar houses, warehouses, sail lofts, and so on, but all rented at His Majesty's expense. The Massachusetts Assembly (now meeting under its own authority) petitioned the king for a redress of grievances, to have the troops withdrawn; and in Philadelphia, John Dickinson composed a "Liberty Song" with rousing verses (set to the tune of an old English drinking ballad) that were soon being sung in taverns throughout the land:

> COME join Hand in Hand, brave AMERICANS all,
> And rouse your bold Hearts at fair LIBERTY's Call;
> No *tyrannous Acts* shall suppress your *just Claim,*
> Or stain with *Dishonor* AMERICA's Name—

This was followed by the chorus:

> In freedom we're born and in freedom we'll live,
> Our right arms are ready,
> Steady, men, steady.
> Not as slaves but as freemen, our lives we will give.

Yet there seemed little chance that the imperial authorities would be moved. Meanwhile, Townshend's premature death brought in Frederick, Lord North, "a man thoroughly in accord" with the king's determination.

At the opening of Parliament, North referred to Boston as "in a state of disobedience to all law and government" and expressed his intention of bringing "turbulent and seditious persons" to terms. Both Houses declared the actions of the Massachusetts Assembly unconstitutional and revived an obsolete statute of Henry VIII authorizing the trial in England of persons who had committed crimes outside the "realm." This was aimed chiefly at the Massachusetts leaders—the "chief instigators of the late disorders"—who were to be transported to England and arraigned "for condign punishment."

In *The Causes of the Present Distractions in America Explained: in Two Letters to a Merchant in London,* Franklin set out the situation at the crossroads:

> America, an immense territory, favoured by nature with all advantages of climate, soil, great navigable rivers, and lakes, etc., must become a great country, populous and mighty; and will, in a less time than is generally conceived, be able to shake off shackles that may be imposed on her and perhaps place them on the imposers. In the meantime, every act of oppression will sour their tempers, lessen greatly—if not annihilate—the profits of your commerce with them, and hasten their final revolt; for the seeds of liberty are universally found there, and nothing can eradicate them. And yet there remains among that people so much respect, veneration, and affection for Britain that, if cultivated prudently, with kind usage and tenderness for their privileges, they might be easily governed still for ages, without force or any considerable expense. But I do not see here a sufficient quantity of the wisdom that is necessary to produce such a conduct, and I lament the want of it.

Though Americans were loyal, "a new kind of loyalty seems to be required of us," said Franklin, "a loyalty to Parliament; a loyalty that is to extend, it seems, to a surrender of all our properties, whenever a House of Commons, in which there is not a single member of our choosing, shall think fit to grant them away without our consent. . . . This unhappy new system of politics tends to dissolve those bands of union and to sever us for ever."

Washington, however, was of less sorrowful mind. On April 5, 1769, he wrote to his friend George Mason:

> At a time when our lordly masters in Great Britain will be satisfied with nothing less than the deprivation of American freedom, it seems highly necessary that something should be done to avert the stroke and maintain the liberty which we have derived from our ancestors. But the manner of doing it, to answer the purpose effectually, is the point in question. That

no man should scruple or hesitate a moment in defense of so valuable a blessing is clearly my opinion; yet arms should be the last resource—the *dernier ressort.* We have already, it is said, proved the inefficiency of addresses to the throne and remonstrances to Parliament. How far their attention to our rights and interests is to be awakened or alarmed by starving their trade and manufactures remains to be tried.

The northern colonies, it appears, are endeavoring to adopt this scheme. In my opinion it is a good one.

Our all is at stake, and the little conveniences and comforts of life, when set in competition with our liberty, ought to be rejected, not with reluctance but with pleasure.

General Thomas Gage was as reluctant as Washington to see a recourse to arms. The two men, in fact, were not unacquainted, for as a lieutenant colonel in 1754 Gage had led the advance guard on the field of Braddock's defeat. He had since had a sterling career. He had fought with Wolfe in the decisive battle for Québec, where directly after the war, in 1760, he had been made military governor; in 1761, he had been promoted to major general; two years later he succeeded Jeffrey Amherst as commander in chief of the British forces in America. As such, he was responsible for more than fifty garrisons and stations stretching from Newfoundland to Florida and from Bermuda to the Mississippi. He showed some tact and diplomacy in handling Indian relations and disputes over western boundaries but utterly failed to take the pulse of the independence movement, and his animosity toward patriots influenced imperial policy in tragic ways. "It is somewhat strange," wrote one militia colonel (and British ex-captain) to Edmund Burke, "that this gentleman should reside so many years in America, and yet be as ignorant of the dispositions of the people as he is of those in the moon; indeed, he took all possible means of shutting up the avenues of truth. At New York he never conversed, as I can find, with any but place and contract hunters, the staff officers and his own family; and when he was sent to Boston with express orders to inform himself of the cause of the disturbances, he applied to the very men, and those only, from whom these disturbances were said to flow." Nevertheless, he was well mannered and respectful, had an American wife, and at the time seemed a good choice to navigate the troubled waters of British-American relations. But he had an impossible task.

"There was one thing," Esther Forbes wrote in her biography of Paul Revere,

that must have been apparent to every thoughtful man who watched the unloading of troops and their "insolent parade." You cannot quarter troops on a resentful town and not have fracases. A sentry, with his face cut by an oyster shell, is going to beat up the nearest urchin and hope he has caught the right one. And the urchin's screams bring his mother and hers bring the town. . . . Women jostled in dark alleys are going to be yelling rape. Inebriated young officers are going to ride their horses into people's parlors to get them out of the rain. Eventually—it might be this hour, it might be next week, next month, next year, but surely sometime—the inhabitants who now stood watching sullenly and doing nothing would anger the soldiers and the soldiers would fire.

All this came to pass. There were nightly tavern brawls; soldiers were "accidentally" jostled off bridges and wharves or followed by small boys chanting "Bloody-backs" and "Lobsters for sale" in ridicule of their red uniforms; many girls were seduced (some quite easily, it seems), but a few were forced. One British officer predicted this "Yankey war, contrary to all others, will produce more births than burials." On Sundays, soldiers would race horses on the common or play military marches outside church doors during services. In September 1769, patriot James Otis was badly beaten up in a coffee shop by a customs agent and some soldiers. And, of course, every British transgression, however obnoxious, was also exaggerated by propaganda—as orchestrated in particular by Samuel Adams, who predicted blood would spill. And as a means of uniting the population against the occupation, there were those who were willing (even eager) to see that day come.

On the evening of March 5, 1770, it came when an angry crowd of Bostonians taunted a group of eight armed soldiers standing sentry before the Customs House. Some threw garbage and oyster shells at them, others threatened them with sticks; still others, it is said, pressing up to the muzzles of their guns, threw snow into their faces and dared them to fire. This went on for some time, until at last the frightened soldiers, believing their lives in jeopardy, suddenly did, killing five people. Crispus Attucks, a black sailor and former slave, was the first to fall. Their martyrdom was inaccurately recorded in an inflammatory engraving by Paul Revere which portrayed the incident as a massacre; and to help restore calm, the royal governor, Thomas Hutchinson, arrested the soldiers and promised to bring them to trial. The next morning, a town meeting was held at Old South Church to demand that all troops be withdrawn from Boston. Hutchinson reluctantly complied, removing both regiments to Castle William, a harbor fort. At the same time, in an attempt on the part of the protest movement to demonstrate its own commitment to the rule of law, John Adams and Josiah Quincy, both radicals, stepped forward to defend the soldiers at their trial. Adams said later that he and his fellow counsel in consequence "heard our names execrated in the most opprobrious terms whenever we appeared in the streets." Nevertheless, "I had no hesitation in answering, that counsel ought to be the very last thing that an accused person should want in a free country; that the bar ought, in my opinion, to be independent and impartial, at all times and in every circumstance, and that persons whose lives were at stake ought to have the counsel they prefer."

At the trial, held that fall, the prosecution produced witnesses who testified that the soldiers had fired into a peaceful assembly. Adams conjured up for the jury instead "a motley rabble of saucy boys, Negroes, and mulattoes, Irish teagues and outlandish jack tars . . . shouting and hazzaing and threatening life . . . whistling, screaming and rending an Indian yell . . . throwing every species of rubbish they could pick up in the street." Would you expect, he asked each member of the jury, that a soldier so provoked would "behave like a stoic philosopher"? His co-counsel, Josiah Quincy, also warned the jury not to be prejudiced by "the prints exhibited in our houses" (i.e., Revere's drawing), which had added "wings to fancy" in distortion of the facts.

Adams and Quincy prevailed. They won an acquittal for six of the eight defendants; the other two, convicted of manslaughter, were branded on the thumbs and released.

B a c k in England, Lord North realized that the Townshend duties were costing more than they brought into the Treasury and were also unsound as a commercial measure since they imposed duties on British manufactures. And so, by coincidence, on the very day the "Boston Massacre" occurred, Parliament at his behest yielded to pressure from London merchants and voted to abolish them all, except for a symbolic tax on tea. That tax, which was miniscule, remained, in part, as an affirmation of Parliament's prerogative. "The properest time to exert our right to taxation," said North, "is when the right is refused. To temporize is to yield. And the authority of the mother country, if it is now unsupported, will be relinquished forever: a total repeal cannot be thought of till America is prostrate at our feet." This brought the eloquent Isaac Barre to retort:

> To effect this is not so easy. The Americans are a numerous, a respectable, a hardy, a free people. But were it ever so easy, does any friend to his country really wish to see America thus humbled? In such a situation, she

would serve only as a monument of your arrogance and your folly. For my part, the America I wish to see is America increasing and prospering, raising her head in graceful dignity . . . vindicating her liberties . . . and conscious of her merit. This is the America that will have spirit to fight your battles, to sustain you when hard pushed by some prevailing foe, and by her industry will be able to consume your manufactures, support your trade, and pour wealth and splendour into your towns and cities. If we do not change our conduct towards her, America will be torn from our side.

But for the time being, the repeal of the Townshend duties created a lull in revolutionary activity, as many American merchants lost their enthusiasm for continued opposition and in one colony after another the boycott of English goods was relaxed. In England, "a deadness and vapidity," according to Edmund Burke, settled over the Whigs, or liberals, sympathetic to the patriots' cause. Then, in April 1773, Parliament passed a new measure, known as the Tea Act, which rallied the disaffected and brought moderates and radicals together once again. In addition to reaffirming Parliament's prerogative to tax, the Tea Act was an effort to forestall the collapse of the East India Company, which controlled the Asiatic tea trade and had huge stocks of unsold tea in its warehouses along the Thames. The company was given a monopoly in the American market, and the new tax, to be paid in London as a surcharge, would be invisible in the colonial price. That is, without lowering the duty paid in America, the government arranged to refund to the company all import duties collected in England on teas afterward shipped to the colonies. That meant a drop in the price to American consumers and made company tea even cheaper than the contraband Dutch tea it had to compete against. Although the government anticipated some resistance, it assured itself—and the members of Parliament —that "mankind are in general governed by interest" and the Americans, being great consumers of tea, would not let the bargain pass.

But it was the principle of the thing that could not be borne. Americans at once recognized the impost as a subterfuge—in fact, a bribe—to induce them to pay an unconstitutional tax, and it remains a noble feature of the whole confrontation that immediate economic interest did not determine their response.

To flout the new duty, many colonists abstained from drinking tea, drank contraband stock, or brewed tea from local herbs. In October, at a concert at Faneuil Hall, a performance of Handel's *Messiah* concluded with the chorus singing Dickinson's "Liberty Song."

During the fall, agitation mounted. Tea-laden ships were sent to Boston, New York, Philadelphia, and Charleston, but in every case except one, popular demonstrations prevented the landing of their cargo or obliged it to be shut up in warehouses with the duty unpaid. At Charleston, the tea was deliberately sequestered in moldy vaults to rot. At New York, a fortuitous storm drove the ship back out to sea. At Philadelphia, no one would help the captain pilot his vessel into port. The local patriot committee indeed warned him of a confrontation should he try. Meanwhile, Pennsylvania's Joseph Reed (then a revolutionary moderate, later a firebrand) prophetically wrote to the earl of Dartmouth:

> Any further attempt to enforce this act, I am humbly of opinion, must end in blood. We are sensible of our inability to contend with the mother country by force, but we are hastening fast to desperate resolutions, and unless internal peace is speedily settled, our most wise and sensible citizens dread the anarchy and confusion that must follow. This city has been distinguished by its peaceful and regular demeanor, nor has it departed from it on the present occasion, as there have been no mobs, no insults to individuals, no injury to private property; but the frequent appeals to the people must in time occasion a change, and we every day perceive it more and more difficult to repress the rising spirit.

Boston, of course, as implied by Reed's civic contrast, was a town with a different demeanor, and on November 17, as if to live up to its reputation, the home of the principal Boston agent for the East India Company was vandalized. Ten days later, the *Dartmouth,* the first of three tea-laden ships, sailed into port.

Broadsides were immediately distributed all over town proclaiming, "Friends! Brethren! Countrymen! That worst of plagues, the detested TEA . . . is now arrived in this harbor. The hour of destruction, or manly opposition to the machinations of tyranny, stares you in the face. Every friend to his country, to himself and posterity, is now called upon , . . to make a united and successful resistance to this last, worst, and most destructive measure of administration." A town meeting at Faneuil Hall unanimously agreed that the duty not be paid, and after the other two tea ships arrived, armed groups were appointed to keep the vessels under surveillance and riders made ready to warn neighboring towns of any effort to land the tea along the coast. Altogether the three ships, anchored alongside Griffin's Wharf, carried forty-five tons of tea worth £8,000.

Another meeting was called for December 16, this time at Old South Church. When the gathering was told that the governor had refused to allow the *Dartmouth* to leave until her cargo was unloaded, Samuel Adams mounted the pulpit and declared, "This meeting can do nothing more to save the country." A short time later, a company of men, poorly disguised as Mohawk Indians, emerged from hiding and made their way to Griffin's Wharf. One of them proudly recalled, "We wore ragged clothes and disfigured ourselves, smeared our faces with grease and soot or lampblack . . . and we surely resembled devils . . . rather than men." At the wharf, they divided into three groups, boarded the ships, chopped open the chests, and dumped the tea into the harbor. About two hundred in all took part, including Thomas Melville (Herman Melville's grandfather), Samuel Adams, and Paul Revere. When the tide rose, "there was a windrow of tea from Boston all the way to Dorchester."

The whole affair lasted three hours and was carried out with the utmost discipline. "Not the least insult was offer'd to any person," wrote one eyewitness, and care was taken that no one disgrace the protest by taking tea for himself. When it was over, the men marched away to the music of a fife. The British squadron, riding at anchor less than a quarter mile away, made no effort to intervene. In fact, the British admiral in charge watched the entire incident from the house of a friend near the docks. When the rebels marched by, he threw open an upstairs window, stuck out his head, and shouted, "Well, boys, you have had a fine, pleasant evening for your Indian caper—haven't you? But mind, you have got to pay the fiddler yet."

The caper had been such a bold one, that even patriots, at first, were divided in their reaction. Franklin considered the Boston Tea Party, as it was called, "an act of violent injustice" for which the town should make reparation. "I suppose," he said, "we never had, since we were a people, so few friends in Britain." But John Adams was convinced that to have let the tea be landed would have ratified Parliament's unconstitutional acts. In somewhat overwrought words, he expressed the fear that it might have "subject[ed] ourselves and our posterity forever to Egyptian taskmasters; to burthens, indignities, to ignominy, reproach and contempt, to desolation and oppression, to poverty and servitude." But he read the significance of the incident aright. The next day he wrote in his diary, "There is a Dignity, a Majesty, a Sublimity, in this last Effort of the Patriots, that I greatly admire. The People should never rise, without doing something to be remembered—something notable and striking. This Destruction of the Tea is so bold, so daring, so firm, intrepid and inflexible, and it must have important Consequences, and so lasting, that I cant but consider it as an Epocha in History."

The British government, of course, could not but regard the Tea Party as an act of insurrection. Addressing Parliament in early March 1774, the king called for swift retribution. After describing the "unwarrantable practices" of American patriots and especially "the violent and outrageous proceedings" in Boston, he said, "We must master them or totally leave them alone." Lord North declared either the colonies were colonies of Great Britain or they were not. Parliament therefore decided to make an example of Massachusetts, and rapidly approved by large majorities four punitive, retaliatory measures which: closed the port of Boston until restitution was made for the destroyed tea; abrogated the colony's charter of 1691; substituted a military governor for its democratic institutions; exempted royal officials charged with capital offenses from the jurisdiction of colonial courts; and revived the Quartering Act, which had been allowed to expire in 1770.

But Burke warned, "You can't pursue this Example, if other Towns should do the like. Have you considered what to do if this Example should not operate as you wish? Would you put a total proscription to the whole Trade of America?" That possibility was just over the horizon. Indeed, these Coercive, or "Intolerable," Acts, as they came to be called, had the unintended effect of radicalizing much of the colonial public that had not yet cast its lot with the patriot cause. Until the Boston Tea Party —or rather the vehemence of the British reaction to it—the protest movement had languished. Now Washington could write to a friend in England, "Does it not appear as clear as the sun in its meridian brightness that there is a regular, systematic plan to fix the right and practice of taxation upon us? . . . Ought we not, then, to put our virtue and fortitude to the severest tests?"

Meanwhile, in addition to the punitive legislation, Parliament had passed a measure known as the Québec Act, which extended the boundaries of Québec south to the Ohio and west to the Mississippi, and established French civil law and the Roman Catholic religion (both deemed hostile to American liberty) in the area.

Thus, by the conjunction of two sets of parliamentary acts, the issues of freedom of religion and taxation without representation became entwined. As John Adams put it, "If Parliament could tax us, they could establish the Church of England [i.e., a state religion] with all its creeds, articles, tests, ceremonies, and tithes, and prohibit all other churches," if they so desired.

In response to the growing concern, a network of Committees of Correspondence—radical organizations established in each colony to keep one another informed—now began to operate throughout the country.

When the news of the bill closing the port of Boston reached the town early in May, even the royal governor, Thomas Hutchinson, was "dismayed by its severity." Hutchinson was recalled, and on May 13, 1774, General Gage arrived with four regiments of troops to act as military governor. His instructions were to bring the colony to its knees. In addition to closing the port of Boston, he was to suppress town meetings, take over the judiciary, and, if he chose, transport Americans charged with capital crimes to England or Nova Scotia for trial. British troops were also to be quartered on the town. Marblehead was made the colony's new port of entry; Salem, its new capital.

Gage distributed his frigates, armed schooners, and ships of war to strategic stations and prohibited even the ferries from Boston to Charlestown to make their customary runs. When he appealed for 5,000 more troops, or eleven British regiments, they were sent. The Quartering Act also gave him the right to billet troops in anyone's house.

The patriot propaganda heated up. By the abrogation of the charter of Massachusetts, every colony was made to feel its chartered rights imperiled. The *New-York Journal,* adapting Franklin's famous 1754 engraving, printed on its masthead in June a snake severed into nine parts with the motto "Unite or Die"; in another inflammatory engraving by Paul Revere, entitled *Swallowing the Bitter Draught,* America was pictured as a woman—breasts exposed, clothes in disarray—being pinned by imperial agents on the ground as one of them poured a pot of tea down her throat and another looked under her dress. Meanwhile, on May 23, in Chestertown, Maryland, residents had their own Tea Party in emulation of that carried out in Boston when they boarded the *Geddes,* a brigantine loaded with tea anchored in the river, and dumped the cargo overboard.

Even before the Port Bill was to take effect on June 1, Massachusetts called on the other colonies for aid. They responded with alacrity. South Carolina sent rice; Virginia, flour; Maryland, rye and bread; Connecticut, sheep. Emergency relief funds were raised in Wilmington, North Carolina; Rhode Island undertook to give work to unemployed Boston carpenters. Some of the inhabitants of Quebec shipped more than a thousand barrels of wheat. Marblehead, refusing to take advantage of Boston's predicament, offered Boston merchants the use of her harbor facilities for the loading and unloading of goods.

On May 24, the Virginia Assembly expressed its solidarity with Massachusetts (which it called its "sister colony") and asked that the first of June be set aside as a day of fasting, humiliation, and prayer, "devoutly to implore the Divine interposition for averting the heavy calamity which threatens destruction to our civil rights, and the evils of civil war." Two days later, Virginia's royal governor, Lord Dunmore, dissolved the Assembly for having expressed itself "in such terms as reflect highly on His Majesty and the Parliament," but, as before, a number of its members promptly reconvened in the Apollo Room of the Raleigh Tavern. There they pronounced an attack on one of the colonies an attack on all, entered into a nonimportation agreement with respect to British goods, and urged that arrangements be made, through the Committees of Correspondence, for representatives of each colony to meet in early September 1774 in Philadelphia as a Continental Congress. By August, all thirteen colonies except Georgia had named delegates to attend.

George Washington was one of the delegates chosen. At the Virginia Convention in August, he had declared, "If need be, I will raise one thousand men, subsist them at my own expense, and march myself at their head for the relief of Boston." On August 31, accompanied by Patrick Henry and Edmund Pendleton, he set out on horseback for Philadelphia. Washington's wife, Martha, stood in the doorway that morning and said, "God be with you, gentleman!" Wrote Pendleton afterward to a friend, "She seemed ready to make any sacrifice, and was very cheerful, though I know she felt very anxious. She talked like a Spartan mother to her son on going to battle. 'I hope you will all stand firm—I know George will.' " To a concerned relative, Martha confided, "Yes; I foresee consequences; dark days and darker nights; domestic happiness suspended; social enjoyments abandoned; property of every kind put in jeopardy by war, perhaps; neighbors and friends at variance, and eternal separations on earth possible. But what are all these evils when compared with the fate of which the Port Bill may be only a threat? My mind is made up; my heart is in the cause. George is right; he is always right. God has promised to protect the righteous, and I will trust him."

Fifty-five delegates in all gathered at Philadelphia. Deliberately spurning the assembly room of the State House as representing the political establishment, they met in a large room in Carpenter's Hall—a sort of union or guild hall—on Monday, September 5. Yet despite British fears, they had come together not so much to plan for independence as to unite, if possible, upon the most effective measures for defending what they considered to be their common rights. The letter of instructions given to the Virginia delegation, for example, was conciliatory, almost apologetic, in tone, expressing allegiance to the king, supporting "all his just rights and prerogatives," and affirming a desire for a continued "constitutional connection" with Great Britain and "a return of that intercourse of affection and commercial connection that formerly united both countries; which can only be effected by a removal of those causes of discontent which have of late unhappily divided us." Most realized that excessive accommodation was also dangerous, and the clear-eyed Abigail Adams, writing to her husband, John, succinctly moralized what was at stake:

Did ever any kingdom or state regain its liberty, when once it was invaded, without bloodshed? I cannot think of it without horror. Yet we are told that the misfortunes of Sparta were occasioned by their too great solicitude for present tranquillity, and, from an excessive love of peace, they neglected the means of making it sure and lasting. They ought to have reflected, says Polybius, that, as there is nothing more desirable or advantageous than peace, when founded in justice and honors so there is nothing more shameful, and at the same time more pernicious, when attained by bad measures and purchased at the price of liberty.

In Boston, Gage had begun to fortify Charlestown Neck with entrenchments and breastworks so as to close the only approach to the city by land; he seized three hundred barrels of powder from the city arsenal and was about to mount cannon on Beacon Hill.

AT the Congress, despite sectional differences which might have divided the delegates along regional lines, there was an urgent solidarity. Patrick Henry set the tone. "All America," he said, "is thrown into one mass. Where are your landmarks—your boundaries of colonies? They are all thrown down. The distinctions between Virginians, Pennsylvanians, New Yorkers and New Englanders are no more. I am not a Virginian, but an American." After some debate, it was decided that each colony should have one vote, irrespective of the number of its delegates, and that the deliberations would be secret and nothing published but the resolves. To give proper dignity and solemnity to the proceedings, it was also proposed that they be opened each morning by prayer. That at first ran upon the rock of religious diversity. Some of those in attendance were Episcopalians, others Quakers, Anabaptists, Presbyterians, Congregationalists, and so on. It was supposed that "we could not join in the same act of worship," recalled John Adams. Then Samuel Adams rose and said that he was no bigot and could "hear a prayer from a gentleman of piety and virtue [whatever his faith or denomination], who was at the same time a friend to his country." Although a Puritan himself, he suggested that the Reverend Jacob Duche, an Episcopal minister, offer the benediction the following morning. The suggestion was adopted, and Duche read the Thirty-fifth Psalm.

Although it was hoped the delegates would represent "the united wisdom of North America," John Adams at first thought they might not be equal to their task. In his diary, he wrote, "I wander alone, and ponder.—I muse, I mope, I ruminate.—We have not Men, fit for the Times. We are deficient in Genius, in Education, in Travel, in Fortune—in every Thing. I feel unutterable Anxiety.—God grant us Wisdom, and Fortitude! Should the Opposition be suppressed, should this Country submit, what Infamy and Ruin! God forbid. Death in any Form is less terrible." But three days after the Congress began, he was of a different mind: "There is in the Congress a collection of the greatest men upon this continent in point of abilities, virtues, and fortunes. The magnanimity and public spirit which I see here make me blush for the sordid, venal herd."

Although outstanding figures may occasionally emerge in response to a historical crisis, those who arose to lead the Revolution surpassed all that might have been hoped for or have since been seen. Surely this is so in the aggregate: George Washington, Thomas Jefferson, Patrick Henry, George Wythe, George Mason, Edmund Randolph, and the Lee family of Virginia; Samuel and John Adams and John Hancock of Massachusetts; Benjamin Franklin, John Dickinson, and Robert Morris of Pennsylvania; John Jay, James Duane, and Gouverneur Morris of New York; John Rutledge and Edward Rutledge of South Carolina; and more, with Alexander Hamilton, James Madison, and others beginning to step forth into the light. Generally speaking, they were men of wealth or professional distinction, socially staid, not likely to be rebels, and belonged to an intellectual elite. About a third were lawyers, and most held university degrees. They were "gentlemen" in the old-fashioned sense of the word, which, wrote Esther Forbes, "implied lace ruffles, clean hands, and a knowledge of Latin and Greek."

Some were conservatives, some moderates, some radicals. None openly advocated independence; none openly favored obedience to Britain at any price. Nearly all desired some honorable accommodation that would have allowed them to remain within the empire. A few wrote down their first impressions of one another. John Adams thought John Alsop of New York "a soft, sweet man," and Alsop's fellow delegate James Duane "very sensible" and "very artful" despite "a sly, surveying eye." Silas Deane of Connecticut found Roger Sherman (also of Connecticut) "clever in private" but as unsuited by his countrified manner and talk to the august assembly as "a chestnut-burr for an eye-stone." Joseph Galloway, the suave speaker of the Pennsylvania Assembly and a Philadelphia aristocrat, regarded Samuel Adams with distaste as a revolutionary fanatic and demagogue who "eats little, drinks little, sleeps little, thinks much, and is most decisive and indefatigable in the pursuit of his objects." To many, Adams's lifelong radicalism was, indeed, suspect. At Harvard, he had written his master's thesis on "Whether it be lawful to resist the Supreme Magistrate [i.e., the king] if the Commonwealth cannot otherwise be preserved"—and had argued, of course, that it was. That argument became his life. But his cousin John later remarked, with awe at his perseverance, that he had been "born and tempered a wedge of steel to split the knot of *lignum vitae,* which tied North America to Great Britain." And his adherents esteemed him incorruptible and completely selfless in his dedication to republican ideals.

Patrick Henry's reputation as a colorful orator had preceded him, so the flamboyant Silas Deane was disappointed to find him as plain as "a Presbyterian clergyman" in simple gray garb. But the judgment of most may be summed up in that of a later colleague: "He had a fine blue eye and an earnest manner which made it impossible not to attend to him. In his speaking . . . he had a happy articulation, and a clear, distinct, strong voice; every syllable was distinctly uttered. He was very unassuming as to himself, amounting almost to humility, and very respectable towards his competitor . . . great at a reply, and greater in proportion to the pressure which was bearing upon him."

Perhaps the most enigmatic figure was George Washington, who was reserved in his manner almost to silence but with a magnetic presence that obliged everyone to attend to his counsel, and to turn and regard him when he walked into a room. "He is a soldier, a warrior," one delegate noted, yet "a modest man; sensible; speaks little—in action cool, like a bishop at his prayers."

Many reputations would wax and wane over the years, and some fade entirely, but after Washington's the most abiding would belong to Jefferson and John Adams—"the odd couple," as some have said, of the Revolution. Adams was short, stout, temperamental, voluble, and testy; Jefferson, calm, reserved, taciturn, tall, and thin as a reed. Eventually, when the struggle was over, they disagreed on almost every important public issue, and Adams himself remarked in his old age that for most of their lives they had "look'd at the world through different ends of the telescope." But during the Revolution, at least, they generally saw eye to eye. Although Jefferson was not a delegate to the First Continental Congress, his presence was felt by way of his leadership in the House of Burgesses and by his polemical writing. And so it may not be amiss to give some account of both men here.

• • •

B O R N on October 30, 1735, at Braintree (later Quincy), Massachusetts, Adams, by his own description, spent a carefree youth shirking
schoolwork to enjoy the pleasures of the out of doors. He wrestled,
swam, skated, and hunted with his rifle in the woods, and, due to "an
amourous disposition" from the age of ten until he entered college, spent
as much time as he could in the flirtatious company of girls.

Nevertheless, he was something of an invalid. "My constitution is a
glass bubble," he once complained, and he suffered all his life from
headaches, chest pains, poor vision, and, like all his contemporaries, bad
teeth. By his early twenties, his constitution had been further impaired
(so a doctor told him) by too much study, which "had corrupted the
whole mass of my blood and juices."

It has always been hard to picture the short, plump, physically fragile
Adams as a romantic playmate or outdoorsman, and it may be that his
autobiographical portrait was (in the great tradition of political auto-
biographies) an attempt to endow himself with a lusty, rugged manli-
ness he did not possess. In any case, he was careful to add that he
had never engaged in premarital sex, in part out of fear of contracting
venereal disease. "No virgin or matron ever had cause to blush at the
sight of me, or to regret her acquaintance with me," he boasted from
the perspective of old age. "No father, brother, son or friend ever had
cause of grief or resentment for any intercourse between me and any
daughter, sister, mother, or any other relation of the female sex. My
children may be assured that no illegitimate brother or sister exists or
ever existed."

One may believe him. Whatever his teenage escapades, at Harvard he
became quite serious, studied Latin, Greek, logic, rhetoric, philosophy,
metaphysics, physics, geography, mathematics, geometry, and theology
(according to the standard curriculum), and soon conceived "a love of
Books and a fondness for study, which dissipated all my inclination for
sports, and even for the society of the ladies." Math and philosophy were
his favorite subjects, but he eventually assembled a famously large library
in several languages, and in his old age he regretted he had not had
enough time to learn Hebrew and Chinese.

Adams began his professional life as a schoolmaster and, not unlike
Franklin, attempted to perfect himself. "Oh!" he wrote in his diary, "that
I could wear out of my mind every mean and base affectation; conquer
my natural pride and self conceit, expect no more deference from my
fellows than I deserve, acquire that meekness and humility which are
the sure mark and characters of a great and generous soul, and subdue
every unworthy passion." He resolved "to rise with the sun," study the
Scriptures four mornings a week, "some Latin author" the other three,

and devote the rest of his days to English literature. "This is my fixed determination." But the day after he wrote this, instead of rising at four to study Saint James's Epistle, he lay in bed till seven and lamented his own indolence. In his diary, he noted despondently, "This is the usual fate of my resolutions."

After a few years he also began to study for the law. In November 1758, he was admitted to the Massachusetts bar, steadily enlarged his practice by following up writs for small fees, and, in his first notable case, succeeded in having charges dropped against John Hancock for smuggling wine into the port of Boston. But his real fame began as counsel for the defense in the Boston Massacre case. The fairness he exhibited on that occasion was reflected elsewhere in his conduct in public life. At one Boston town meeting, when a Tory merchant, whose store had been vandalized by creditors trying to use the political situation to evade their debt, was shouted down by the majority, Adams rebuked the crowd with lines from Milton's Sonnet XII: "I did but prompt the age to quit their clogs / By the known rules of ancient liberty, / When straight a barbarous noise environs me / Of owls and cuckoos, asses, apes, and dogs." Though he himself believed the British occupation of Boston had corrupted local morals—on July 5, 1774, he complained in a letter to Abigail of "the universal spirit of debauchery, dissipation, luxury, effeminacy and gaming . . . profaneness, lewdness, intemperance, etc. . . . which the late ministerial measures have introduced"—he was unwilling to condone lawless action. "These tarrings and featherings, this breaking open houses by rude and insolent rabble in resentment for private wrongs, or in pursuance of private prejudices and passions," he wrote, "must be discountenanced."

By the time the First Continental Congress had convened, Adams had immersed himself in the study of political theory for more than a decade. "Aim at an exact Knowledge of the Nature, End, and Means of Government," he exhorted himself in his diary. "Compare the different forms of it with each other and each of them with their Effects on the public and private Happiness. Study Seneca, Cicero and all other good moral Writers. Study Montesque, Bolinbroke." By such application, he became a brilliant and thoroughly disciplined political thinker who worked as hard as any of the Founding Fathers to realize, in practical terms, their great revolutionary ideals.

But he was also a difficult man. "There are few people in this world with whom I can converse," he once said pretentiously. "I can treat all with decency and civility, and converse with them, when it is necessary, on points of business. But I am never happy in their company." Ambitious of fame, he chafed at public criticism, but when glory did come, he felt that his accomplishments received less than their due measure of applause.

In religion, Adams was a Congregationalist of the Unitarian school and as such lacked an aptitude for paradox. Toward the end of his days, he offered a rather plain and direct explanation of his faith. "My religion is founded on the love of God and my neighbor," he said, "on the hope of pardon for my offenses; upon contrition; upon the duty as well as necessity of supporting with patience the inevitable evils of life; in the duty of doing no wrong, but all the good I can."

JEFFERSON'S own profound skepticism had something in common with Adams's practical faith, but in most respects they were very different men. Born into prosperous circumstances on April 13, 1743, in Albemarle County, Virginia, Jefferson attended local grammar and upper schools, where he received a classical education, and in 1760 he enrolled at the College of William and Mary in Williamsburg, where he studied science, mathematics, rhetoric, philosophy, and literature under Dr. William Small. Small, he later said, "probably fixed the destinies of my life. . . . He was profound in most of the useful branches of science with a happy talent for communication, correct and gentlemanly manners, and an enlarged and liberal mind. He made me his daily companion when not engaged in the school; and from his conversation I got my first views of the expanse of science and of the system of things in which we are placed." Through Small he also met the great George Wythe, the first American professor of law, and Francis Fauquier, the elegant and accomplished lieutenant governor of the colony. The four often dined together, and at that table Jefferson recalled, "I heard more good sense, more rational and philosophical conversation than in all my life besides."

Jefferson was an ardent and indefatigable student who often studied fifteen hours a day. According to his usual regimen, he rose at five A.M. and applied himself to botany, agriculture, zoology, chemistry, anatomy, and religion till eight. From eight to noon, he read law; from noon to one P.M., politics; for the rest of the afternoon, history; and in the evenings, rhetoric, languages, and literature. In this way, he became competent in Latin, Greek, and French; familiar with the classics—Cicero, Demosthenes, Epictetus, and Plato, among others; and most of the prominent figures of English literature, including Shakespeare, Milton, Dryden, Pope, Swift, Addison, Steele, Fielding, Smollett, and Sterne. He read them all with a moral eye, out of a conviction that "everything is useful which contributes to fix in the mind principles and practices of virtue."

In his study of the law, Jefferson was tutored by George Wythe, who later taught John Marshall and Henry Clay. His own compact literary style was directly influenced by Wythe's lectures and conversation, for the latter had a very economical way of expressing himself and "in pleading," said Jefferson, "never indulged himself with a useless or a declamatory word." Jefferson himself developed the habit of abridging everything he read and urged every law student to keep a commonplace book in which "every case of value [was] condensed into the narrowest possible compass." This, he thought, would not only oblige the student "to seek out the pith of the case" but "habituate him to a condensation of thought and to an acquisition of the most valuable of all the talents, that of never using two words when one will do."

In 1767, he was admitted to the bar and entered upon a large and lucrative practice. Two years later he was elected to the House of Burgesses, where he was a leading voice among the younger, more radical members, who felt (in Jefferson's words) that some of the older members were not "up to the point of forwardness & zeal which the times required."

Jefferson was tall and thin with light gray eyes, sharp features, reddish hair, and a long, gangly physique. Though his shoulders were broad, he was slovenly in carriage and dress, and his shyness, indistinct public delivery, habitual reserve, and disinclination to look people in the eye were sometimes mistaken for a lack of candor. But among close friends he could be vivacious. Although one recent biographer has endeavored to rescue Jefferson from his long-standing reputation as a passionless man by claiming illegitimate children for him by a slave, reserve itself, of course, has nothing to do with a lack of passion but often expresses powerful emotion in restraint. And that was so in his case.

In religion, Jefferson was a deist and relied on reason, not revelation; but his intellectual curiosity knew no bounds. He mastered aspects of music, biblical criticism, linguistics, architecture, botany, landscape design, animal husbandry, cartography, meteorology, and mechanical engineering, among other disciplines, as well as political theory, of course, and law; designed his own home at Monticello; and invented all sorts of ingenious and laborsaving devices, such as retractable beds, an indoor-outdoor weather vane, the swivel chair, an adjustable tilt-top table, and the "polygraph," as he called it, which connected two pens by flexible rods and enabled him to write a letter and make a copy of it at the same time. When the First Continental Congress met, Jefferson's reputation was primarily literary. He had just published a polemical tract entitled *A Summary View of the Rights of British America,* which in clear, cogent, and elegantly written prose set forth the patriot point of view. "Americans wish for the preservation of harmony between America and the Empire," he explained in one passage. "It is neither our wish nor our interest to separate from her. We are willing, on our part, to sacrifice everything which reason can ask, for the restoration of that tranquillity for which we all wish." Nevertheless, "Single acts of tyranny may be ascribed to the accidental opinion of a day, but a series of oppressions, pursued unalterably through every change of Ministers, too plainly prove a deliberate, systematic plan for reducing us to slavery."

I N the colonies the word "slavery" had a power of suggestion all its own. By 1774, it seemed to the leaders of the revolutionary movement that there was "a settled, fixed plan for *enslaving* the colonies, or bringing them under arbitrary government." John Dickinson had written, *"Those who are taxed* without their consent . . . are *slaves."* And Josiah Quincy exclaimed, "I speak it with grief—I speak it with anguish— Britons are our oppressors . . . *we are slaves."* George Washington similarly expressed his conviction that the English government was "endeavoring by every piece or art and despotism to fix the shackles of slavery upon us," and so on. In a manner of speaking, the patriots spoke with a single metaphorical voice.

It was, however, a delicate matter for colonists to accuse the British of trying to enslave them, because abject slavery was such a prominent feature of colonial life. This was noted with irony, of course, in England, where Dr. Samuel Johnson, for example, asked, "How is it that the loudest yelps for liberty come from the drivers of slaves?" And Horace Walpole remarked, "I should think the souls of the Africans would sit heavy on the swords of the Americans." On this point, too, John Wesley, the founder of Methodism, was a prolific pamphleteer for the imperial point of view. "The Negroes in America are slaves," he wrote, "the whites enjoy liberty. Is not then all this outcry about Liberty and Slavery mere rant, and playing upon words?"

The issue was hotly discussed. James Otis, holding that "by the law of nature" all men were "free born," wrote, "Does it follow that 'tis right to enslave a man because he is black? Will short curled hair like wool instead of Christian hair . . . help the argument? Can any logical inference in favor of slavery be drawn from a flat nose, a long or short face? Nothing better [than this] can be said in favor of a trade that is the most shocking violation of the law of nature, has a direct tendency to diminish the idea of the inestimable value of liberty, and makes every dealer in it a tyrant."

In Massachusetts, recent legislative efforts to abolish the slave trade had been blocked by the governor, but at the Harvard commencement of 1773, students had debated the issue, and many southerners were adamantly opposed to the practice and would have shed it had a majority been prepared to go along. It would be Jefferson's own tendentious argument, in the first draft of the Declaration of Independence, that the practice had been forced on the colonies by the British and perniciously bred into their economic life. The First Continental Congress, however, pledged itself to oppose the slave trade generally; Rhode Island, noting that "those who are desirous of enjoying all the advantages of liberty themselves should be willing to extend personal liberty to others," ruled that slaves imported into the colony would thereafter be freed. Connecticut followed suit; Delaware prohibited the importation of slaves; and Pennsylvania taxed the trade so heavily as almost to extinguish it there. Abigail Adams spoke for many when she wrote on September 24, 1774, "I wish most sincerely there was not a slave in the province. It always appeared a most iniquitous scheme to me—to fight ourselves for what we are daily robbing and plundering from those who have as good a right to freedom as we have."

Conversely, the rhetoric of slavery had done much to arouse anti-British feeling, especially in the South, where white colonists had but to behold the degraded condition of their own blacks to imagine themselves in a related plight. "English oppression" through taxes and trade regulations, of course, could not possibly have rendered them so abject, but the *idea* of it did much to influence their apprehensions.

Yet at the time of the Revolution, black and white might have been identified as one. In colonial America, any slave who rose against and killed his master was condemned for treason as well as murder, and in a famous Massachusetts case, two slaves—Mark and his wife, Phillis— were so charged and executed, even though evidence emerged that their master had abused them. As a gruesome admonition to other blacks of insubordinate mind, Mark's body was "hung in chains" on Charlestown Common for twenty years (eventually "shrivelling up into some sort of mummy"), and Paul Revere, mindful of his own treason and potential fate, would mournfully note the spot as he passed on his famous ride.

T H E delegates to the First Continental Congress worked hard, disputed their differences, and found points of agreement and sometimes broad common ground. Occasionally they made their task harder than it might have been. Given the vast array of talent assembled, it was inevitable that some of them would give themselves up to displays of rhetoric and knowledge beyond the point at hand. "The consequence of this," complained John Adams, "is that business is drawn and spun out to an immeasurable length. I believe if it was moved and seconded that we should come to a resolution that three and two make five, we should be entertained with logic and rhetoric, law, history, politics, and mathematics, and then—we should pass the resolution unanimously." Yet at the end of the day, the delegates also knew how to unwind, and on the whole they savored the diversity of the company they were in and marveled at the cause that had made them one. A typical session met from nine until three, after which, wrote Adams, "we are unable to do anything but eat and drink." "I shall be killed with kindness in this place," he told his wife, as his abstemious diet (as prescribed by his doctors) was soon forgotten in "sinful feasts" of "everything which could delight the eye or allure the taste; curds and creams, jellies, sweetmeats of various sorts, twenty sorts of tarts, fools, trifles, floating islands, whipped syllabubs . . . Parmesan cheese, punch, wine, porter, beer, etc." "[We] go home fatigued to death with business, company, and care. Yet I hold out surprisingly."

On September 16, the Congress received a copy of the Suffolk County Resolves, framed by the Massachusetts revolutionary leader, Dr. Joseph Warren. Under the leadership of Boston, the towns of Suffolk County had worked out an organized plan of resistance. Warren, something of a firebrand, had once delivered an oration on the anniversary of the Boston Massacre dressed in a Ciceronian toga, and the language of the resolves was also oratorical in the extreme. "If we arrest the hand which would ransack our pockets," read the preamble, "if we disarm the parricide which points the dagger to our bosoms . . . if we successfully resist that unparalleled usurpation of unconstitutional power, whereby our capital is robbed of the means of life; whereby the streets of Boston are thronged with military executioners . . . the torrent of panegyrists will roll our reputations to that latest period, when the streams of time shall be absorbed in the abyss of eternity." After condemning the Coercive Acts and urging a boycott of English goods, he warned, "As men and Protestant Christians, we are indispensably obliged to take all the measures for our security . . . to acquaint ourselves with the art of war as soon as possible."

King George was of no more moderate mind: "The dye is now cast," he declared, "the colonies must either submit or triumph. I do not wish to come to severer measures, but we must not retreat."

Although the Suffolk County Resolves as a whole went considerably further than the conservatives in Congress meant to go, a motion endorsing them passed on September 18. That evening John Adams wrote in his diary, "This was one of the happiest days of my life. . . . This day convinced me that America will support Massachusetts or perish with her."

Yet there is no doubt that the overwhelming majority still hoped for reconciliation with the Crown. Many at first rallied around a proposal put forth on September 28 by Joseph Galloway of Pennsylvania. Galloway, a loyalist at heart, saw the delegates as divided into two camps: one ("men of property") standing for American rights, seeking a remedy of wrongs but intent on avoiding sedition and violence; the other ("Congregational and Presbyterian republicans, or men of bankrupt fortunes, overwhelmed in debt to the British merchants") bent on independence.

He questioned any appeal to natural law—that is, of the right of a people by natural law to constitute a government—because "the colonies from the earliest settlement had been politically organized societies, rather than having emerged from a state of nature." Therefore, he said, "only the constitutional history of England could provide a credible explanation of colonial rights. The essence of the constitution was the parliamentary representation of landed proprietors and their consent to legislation binding the inhabitants." Since there was no representation in Parliament, he acknowledged, colonial opposition to British policy was not unjustified. At the same time, "the first inhabitants of the colonies had accepted parliamentary supervision. The constitutional solution was therefore for Parliament to introduce some form of representation." "Parliament ought not, *as the Colonies are at present circumstanced,* to bind them by its Legislative Authority," he declared, and he recommended mild defiance "accompanied with an express desire of establishing a political *Union* with the *Mother Country.*" Specifically, he proposed a form of home rule, based on colonial confederation, with an American parliament to be elected every three years by the legislatures of the colonies, with a governor-general appointed by the Crown. This American parliament, with jurisdiction over all colonial legislation, would exercise "all the like rights, liberties and privileges as are held and exercised by and in the House of Commons of Great Britain" but still be "an inferior and distinct branch of the British legislature, united and incorporated with each having a veto power over the acts of the other."

Galloway's compromise Plan of Union bore some resemblance to the Albany Plan of Union drafted by Benjamin Franklin in 1754, but Franklin, when he heard about it, disowned the connection. The time for legislative union with the Parliament, he said, was past. "When I consider the extreme corruption prevalent among all orders of men in this old, rotten state"—Franklin was still in London—"and the glorious public virtue so predominant in our rising country, I cannot but apprehend more mischief than benefit from a closer union. . . . It seems like Mezentius' coupling and binding together the living and the dead." Nevertheless, Galloway's plan had enormous appeal, not only to loyalists or Tories but to men like John Jay and Edward Rutledge, and after much heated debate, it was defeated by just one vote. (Galloway himself was so embittered by the outcome that he eventually went over to the British side.)

The Congress remained in session fifty-one days. Every subject, according to John Adams, was discussed "with a moderation, an acuteness and a minuteness equal to that of Queen Elizabeth's privy council." Although unfortunately no verbatim record exists of its deliberations, before adjourning the Congress condemned the Coercive Acts as unconstitutional and tyrannical, along with thirteen other statutes enacted since 1763 which were said to violate colonial rights; countenanced the resistance of Massachusetts; approved the arming of local militia and other defense measures; and, on October 20, adopted the Continental Association, which was a nonimportation, nonexportation, nonconsumption agreement (to be superintended and enforced by local Committees of Inspection) aimed at British trade.

The underground revolutionary network spread. Whereas the earlier Committees of Correspondence had served primarily as channels for the spread of information, the committees of the Continental Association, elected by the community and operating in every county, city, and town, were charged with enforcing the resolutions of the Congress.

The power of these committees "was unlimited," writes one historian. "They walked into the stores of the merchants and forced them to show their books, and woe to the wite thus betrayed by his ledger. When merchants took advantage of the scarcity to increase prices, they were taken roughly in hand. When charges were brought against alleged violators of the agreement, they were summoned summarily before the committee to exonerate themselves or stand condemned. If condemned, they were denounced and advertised as enemies of their country."

The delegates also adopted a Declaration of Rights and Grievances addressed to the people of Great Britain and approved direct appeals to the people of Québec and "the Inhabitants of the Several American Colonies," as well as a petition to the king. "You have been told that we are impatient of government and desirous of independency," read the petition:

These are calumnies. Permit us to be as free as yourselves, and we shall ever esteem a union with you to be our greatest glory and our greatest happiness. But if you are determined that your ministers shall wantonly sport with the rights of mankind; if neither the voice of justice, the dictates of law, the principles of the constitution, or the suggestions of humanity, can restrain your hands from shedding human blood in such an impious cause, we must then tell you that we will never submit to be hewers of wood or drawers of water for any ministry or nation in the world.

With that, the Congress adjourned on October 26, agreeing to meet again if necessary the following May.

In the preparation of all these documents, a regional and philosophical balance was scrupulously maintained: John Dickinson of Philadelphia (a moderate) drafted the petition and the appeal to the Canadians; John Jay of New York (a conservative) the address to the people of Great Britain; and Richard Henry Lee of Virginia (a radical) that to the colonists themselves. Yet all were masterly state papers and so recognized abroad. William Pitt, now Lord Chatham, in a speech before the House of Lords, went out of his way to praise them: "When your lordships look at the papers transmitted to us from America; when you consider their decency, firmness and wisdom, you cannot but respect their cause and wish to make it your own. For myself, I must declare and avow that in the master states of the world I know not the people or senate who, in such a complication of difficult circumstances, can stand in preference to the delegates of America assembled in General Congress at Philadelphia."

Many men had distinguished themselves—Dickinson, Lee, Jay, Henry, John and Samuel Adams, Roger Sherman, and Edward Rutledge, among others—but when Henry, on his return home, was asked whom he considered to be the foremost man in the Congress, he replied, "If you speak of eloquence, Mr. Rutledge of South Carolina is by far the greatest orator; but if you speak of solid information and sound judgment, Colonel Washington is unquestionably the greatest man on that floor."

Washington was not one of the voluble orators John Adams had complained of, and, though a "moderate," his moderation on the issue of resistance has sometimes been overstressed. In a letter written at this time to a British captain, Robert Mackenzie, who had served with him during the French and Indian War but was now with Gage, he wrote with stinging rhetorical force:

Permit me with the freedom of a friend (for you know I always esteemed you), to express my sorrow that fortune should place you in a service that must fix curses to the latest posterity upon the contrivers and, if success (which by and by, is impossible) accompanies it, execrations upon all those who have been instrumental in the execution. . . . When you condemn the conduct of the Massachusetts people you reason from effects, not causes, otherwise you would not wonder at a people who are every day receiving fresh proofs of a systematic assertion of an arbitrary power, deeply planned to overturn the laws and constitution of their country and to violate the most essential and valuable rights of mankind, being irritated, and with difficulty restrained from acts of the greatest violence and intemperance. . . .

It is not the wish or interest of that government or any other upon this continent, separately or collectively, to set up for independence; but as you may at the same time rely on, that none of them will ever submit to the loss of their valuable rights and privileges, which are essential to the happiness of every free state and without which life, liberty and property are rendered totally insecure.

After Congress disbanded, John Adams took Patrick Henry aside and told him he thought all their "resolves, declarations of rights, enumeration of wrongs, petitions, remonstrances, and addresses, associations, and non-importation agreements . . . would be but waste paper [to the government] in England." Henry agreed and said the best they could hope for was that their efforts might help sway English public opinion to their side. Adams then rather daringly showed Henry a letter from a militia major in Massachusetts that concluded, "After all, we must fight." At those words, according to Adams, Henry "raised his head, and with an energy and vehemence that I can never forget, broke out with: 'By God, I am of that man's mind!'"

After so many years of colonial disunity, the British had hardly expected the solidarity that emerged. "It is surprising," wrote General Gage, "that so many of the other provinces interest themselves so much in this [the occupation of Boston]. They [the Bostonians] have some warm friends in New York, and I learn that the people of Charleston, South Carolina, are as mad as they are here."

Franklin, still viewing the situation from a distance, imagined that a general boycott of British manufactures "would in a peaceable and justifiable way do everything for us that we can wish." His main fear was that with British soldiers once again mixing with an agitated population, hotheads on both sides might precipitate "such a carnage . . . as to make a breach that can never afterwards be healed." The British authorities entertained such fears, too, even as they felt the colonies slipping from their grasp. At this juncture, Rear Admiral Lord Richard Howe, whose eldest brother had been killed by the French on Lake George during the French and Indian War (Massachusetts had erected a memorial to him in Westminster Abbey), invited Franklin to confer about the crisis with him at his home.

Franklin called on Christmas Day. "[Miss Howe] told me, as soon as I came in," he recalled, "that her brother, Lord Howe, wished to be acquainted with me; that he was a very good man, and she was sure we should like each other. I said I had always heard a good character of Lord Howe and should be proud of the honour of being known to him. 'He is but just by,' says she; 'will you give me leave to send for him?' 'By all means, Madam, if you think proper.' She rang for a servant, wrote a note, and Lord H. came in a few minutes." Howe offered to act as an intermediary between the colonies and the government and invited Franklin to draw up a set of terms on the basis of which a reconciliation might take place.

The next day Franklin went to see Lord Chatham. "He received me with an affectionate kind of respect that from so great a man was extremely engaging; but the opinion he expressed of the Congress was still more so. They had acted, he said, with so much temper, moderation, and wisdom that he thought it the most honourable assembly of statesmen since those of the ancient Greeks and Romans, in the most virtuous times." But Chatham also expressed his concern that some of the protestations of loyalty coming from the colonies might actually disguise an independence movement that no form of accommodation could appease. Franklin told him that he had never heard anyone in America, "drunk or sober," express the desire for a complete break.

When Chatham next spoke in Parliament on the subject, he tried to save the day. "You might destroy their towns and cut them off from the superfluities, perhaps the conveniences of life," he said, but they would "despise your power, and would not lament their loss while they have —what, my lords?—their woods and liberty. Let this distinction, then, remain forever ascertained; taxation is theirs; commercial regulation is ours. As an American, I would recognize to England her supreme right of regulating commerce and navigation; as an Englishman by birth and principles, I recognize to the Americans their supreme inalienable right to their property; a right which they are justified in the defense of, to the last extremity." Chatham's bill, wrote Franklin, "though on so important a subject, and offered by so great a character, and supported by such able and learned speakers, was treated with as much contempt as they could have shown to a ballad offered by a drunken porter." As such, it was overwhelmingly defeated by 68 votes to 18.

A great opportunity had been lost. Jefferson wrote his former teacher Doctor Small, then in Scotland, "When I saw Lord Chatham's bill, I entertained high hopes that a reconciliation could have been brought about. The differences between his terms and those offered by our Congress might have been accommodated if entered on by both parties with a disposition to accommodate. But the dignity of Parliament, it seems, can brook no opposition to its power." Indeed, the day after Chatham's bill went down to defeat, Lord North proceeded to his measures for suppressing the "rebellion" and authorized the dispatch to Boston of 6,000 more troops.

The delegates to the First Continental Congress had already forewarned their fellow citizens of what might lie ahead. "We think ourselves bound in duty to observe to you," they had declared on October 21, "that you should extend your views to mournful events, and be in all respects prepared for every emergency." A few days later, John Dickinson advised a friend in England, "The first act of violence on the part of administration in America, or the attempt to reinforce General Gage this winter or next year, will put the whole continent in arms, from Nova Scotia to Georgia." In fact, Virginia, Rhode Island, Maryland, Connecticut, and Pennsylvania were already mustering soldiers, following the lead of Massachusetts, and Virginia's Charles Lee (soon to be a general in the Continental Army) was predicting that "unless the banditti at Westminster speedily undo everything they have done, their royal paymaster will hear of reviews and manoeuvres not quite so entertaining as those he is presented with in Wimbledon Common and Hyde Park." In Portsmouth, New Hampshire, patriots seized the arms, powder, and shot kept at the harbor fort and hid them in a pit under the pulpit of the Durham meetinghouse. In Newport, Rhode Island, they carried off forty-four cannon to prevent them from falling into the hands of British marines. In Maryland, where new militia companies were also being formed, the Assembly sarcastically declared, "Such militia will relieve our mother country from any expense in our protection and defence, will obviate the pretence of a necessity for taxing us on that account, and render it unnecessary to keep any standing army—ever dangerous to liberty—in this province."

In the meantime, in Virginia, the royal governor, Lord Dunmore, alarmed by the military preparations in his own province, wrote the earl of Dartmouth that it seemed to him that every county was "now arming a company of men . . . to be employed against the government, if occasion require."

Toward the end of March, leaders of the resistance in Virginia held a convention at Saint John's Church in Richmond to discuss the establishment of a revolutionary government and the military preparations that were rapidly taking place. Some of the delegates were alarmed at the pace of the developments. On March 23, Patrick Henry took the floor. Speaking extemporaneously (or so it seemed), he repeated almost verbatim the Maryland justification for mustering provincial troops, reviewed successive acts against the colonies, warned that further delay in making a strong response might find a "British guard stationed in every house," and concluded with this impassioned plea:

> It is in vain, Sir, to extenuate the matter. Gentlemen may cry peace, peace, but there is no peace. The war is actually begun! The next gale that sweeps from the north will bring to our ears the clash of resounding arms! Our brethren are already in the field! Why stand we here idle? What is it that gentlemen wish? what would they have? Is life so dear, or peace so sweet, as to be purchased at the price of chains and slavery? Forbid it, Almighty God! I know not what course others may take, but as for me, give me liberty, or give me death!

He delivered those words with a kind of wild theatricality. According to one account, "an unearthly fire burned in his eye" and "the tendons of his neck stood out white and rigid like whipcords. His voice rose louder and louder, until the walls of the building, and all within them, seemed to shake and rock in its tremendous vibrations." When he spoke of chains and slavery, he "stood in the attitude of a condemned galley slave, loaded with fetters, awaiting his doom. His form was bowed; his wrists were crossed; his manacles were almost visible." But when he exclaimed, "Give me liberty, or give me death!" he flung his arms wide as though shattering his bonds and struck the left side of his chest with a clenched fist as though driving a dagger into his heart.

A little over a month later, Lord Dunmore seized the cache of gunpowder at Williamsburg, and Patrick Henry led an armed force of several thousand to compel him to return it. "It was their Resolution to seize upon, or massacre me," complained Dunmore afterward, "and every Person found giving me Assistance if I refused." Ultimately, he agreed to pay for it in full, but on June 8, in the hours before dawn, he fled from the governor's mansion and took refuge on board a British man-of-war in the harbor. Some days later a party of colonists forced their way into his residence and carried off three hundred guns.

By then, just as Henry had predicted, the next gale sweeping from the north had brought the clash of arms.

REVOLT

UPON the dissolution of the Massachusetts Assembly, its members had secretly reconvened at Concord and resolved themselves into a Provincial Congress. They appointed committees of "safety" and "supply" and voted to raise and organize a militia of 12,000 men. A quarter of the militia, under the direction of the Committee of Public Safety, were to serve as Minutemen—organized into fifty-man "minute companies" to be ready for action at a moment's notice. Military stores and ammunition (twenty field guns, four mortars, twenty tons of grape and round shot, and five thousand muskets and bayonets) were also to be purchased and magazines to hold them established at various locales. Before long, patriot militia were drilling on every village green.

Upon assuming command in Boston, General Gage had urged London to act with more decision—to break up the revolutionary committees, arrest the radical leaders, and take them to London in irons to be tried for high treason. As for forces, "If you think ten thousand men sufficient, send twenty. A large force will terrify, and engage many to join you; a middling one will encourage resistance, and gain no friends." In February 1775, he further advised the ministry, "To keep quiet in the Town of Boston only, will not terminate affairs. The troops must march into the Country.... The eyes of all are turned upon Great Britain, waiting for her determination." London followed his advice. The militant administration of Lord North rejected talk of a negotiated settlement and ultimately persuaded Parliament to go along with stern measures that brought the crisis to a head. The colonies were declared in rebellion, New England trade was further curtailed, and Gage was authorized to extend his operations into the countryside and to arrest and punish the "ringleaders of the riots at Boston" as well as "the destroyers of the tea."

By the spring of 1775, everybody's mind, according to the recollection of one Connecticut youngster, was filled with the "expectation of some fatal event." As the revolutionary fervor grew, the British authorities in Massachusetts moved to arrest Samuel Adams and John Hancock, whom they identified as the leaders of the resistance. "Sam Adams writes the letters and John Hancock pays the postage," it was said at the time, and it was true. Hancock had inherited a large fortune from his uncle, had greatly enlarged it by trading, and at the age of thirty-eight was the wealthiest merchant by far in Massachusetts Bay. Like every great American merchant at the time, smuggling accounted for part of his livelihood, and he had strenuously objected to British enforcement of the Navigation Acts and to all the newfangled taxes imposed by Townshend and North. He had also been chairman of the Boston town committee formed after the Boston Massacre in 1770 to demand the removal of British troops; president of the new Provincial Congress; and chairman of its Committee of Public Safety. Together with Samuel Adams, he had just been elected as a delegate to the Second Continental Congress, which was scheduled to meet in Philadelphia in May. Adams, by contrast, was a failed businessman, but he had been in the forefront of the protest movement from the start, beginning with his denunciation of the Sugar Act of 1764. He was a vociferous propagandist and a skilled organizer of street demonstrations, not all of them peaceful; at the First Continental Congress he had allied himself with the radical fringe. The British saw him as some historians have seen him since—"as a demagogue of the extreme type," in the words of one of them, "well-equipped for the part by a narrow experience, an incapacity for business, and a vitriolic facility of tongue and pen. . . . Though he had never been twenty miles from Boston, he depicted in newspaper articles and on the stump fantastic and coarse pictures of the English king and the governing classes. These travesties delighted the mobs he harangued." In fact, as historian Pauline Maier has shown, such a portrait is a caricature, and Adams did not actually become an advocate of outright independence until 1775. But he had certainly stirred things up, and in early April, after it became known that Gage had ordered their arrest, he and Hancock both had taken refuge at the parsonage of Jonas Clarke, who was married to Hancock's sister, in Lexington.

While Gage was attempting to track them down, he also laid plans for the confiscation of the large cache of munitions which had recently been collected at nearby Concord.

Before detaching troops for this purpose, he arranged for two British soldiers—one a colonel, the other a private—disguised as Yankee workmen to walk from Boston to Concord to spy out the way. Everywhere they went they found people on the lookout for British agents, and the colonel, in fact, was soon recognized and had to turn back. The private, who was much more resourceful, passed himself off as a gunsmith "eager to fix guns for the fight soon to come." That gave him a glimpse of what the British were in for once the fighting began. "Everyone was determined to be free or die," he noted afterward. Young and old were taking target practice with their squirrel guns, fowling pieces, and muskets, and he particularly remembered one seventy-seven-year-old man at Lexington whom he paused to talk to while he cleaned his gun. "I asked him what he was going to kill. He said there was a flock of redcoats at Boston . . . [and] he expected they would make very good marks. . . . I asked him how he expected to fight. He said, open field fighting or any other way." Hoping to obtain some unguarded information from a Negro fishing off a bridge, he discovered the man was actually a rebel agent who had taken up his rustic station as dutifully as a sentinel at his post. At a wayside tavern, he met a waitress who was just as vigilant and, upon returning to Boston, fearfully predicted in his report that even if the British were to march out with "10,000 regulars and a train of artillery . . . not one of them would get back alive."

Gage didn't believe him, and early on the morning of April 19, he dispatched 800 troops under Colonel Francis Smith and Major John Pitcairn to capture Adams and Hancock and seize the rebels' stores. Yet he was wary enough to take "every imaginable precaution to prevent a discovery," according to one British soldier, and had posted officers on all the roads leading from Boston to prevent word of the expedition from getting out. The soldiers themselves were not briefed on their mission until they were awakened by their sergeants, who conducted them in the utmost silence by a back way out of the barracks and through the streets. From a deserted stretch of beach, they were ferried across Boston Harbor to Lechmere Point in Cambridge in boats worked with muffled oars.

From Lechmere Point, they slogged through marshes before emerging onto a side road to Lexington; but they had scarcely gone more than a few miles when alarm guns sounded through the night air and a distant clamor of village bells told them that word of their mission had already spread. Colonel Smith sent back to General Gage for reinforcements and pressed on.

T H E resistance had a good network of spies. In Massachusetts, the rebel intelligence service was run by Joseph Warren, who sat on the Committee of Public Safety and who, as mentioned, had drafted the Suffolk County Resolves. From time to time his committee would meet at Boston's Green Dragon Tavern, where the members, sworn to secrecy, assessed information gathered from their dispersed personnel. These included household servants, dockhands, tradesmen, doctors, lawyers, prostitutes, and even (it is suspected) General Gage's own American-born wife, who may have tipped off the committee about Gage's plans. Yet it would have been fairly obvious to anyone alert to such things that the British were up to something when, a few days before, they had launched a flotilla of rowboats from their men-of-war. In any case, in anticipation of the British move, Warren and Paul Revere, a member of the committee, had arranged for twin signal lanterns to be placed in the lofty belfry of Old North Church, to alert patriots on the far side of the Charles River as to how the British, when they came, were coming—"one if by land, two if by sea." By land meant by way of Boston Neck; by sea, across Back Bay.

Well before the lanterns flashed, Revere set off on his famous ride. Leaving his house accompanied by his dog, he had linked up with two colleagues who had agreed to row him across the river. En route to a sequestered mooring, however, he suddenly realized he had forgotten his spurs and some cloth with which to quiet the oarlocks of the boat. They detoured to where the girlfriend of one of them lived, and at a whistle she came to the window. They told her they needed some cloth. She wiggled and shook a little, this way and that, then tossed down her flannel underwear, "still warm from her body," as Revere liked to recall. Still lacking his spurs (the story goes) he wrote a note to his wife, tied it to his dog's collar, and sent him home. Before long the dog reappeared with the spurs in its place.

Revere made his way past the sixty-four-gun warship *Somerset* unde- tected and, about eleven o'clock, disembarked at Charlestown, where fellow patriots (alerted by the lanterns) were waiting for him with Brown Beauty, a swift and trusty horse. On horseback, he began to pick his way carefully toward the Medford-Lexington road. The Charles River was on his left, the Mystic on his right. "The moon shone bright," he remembered. "I had got almost over Charlestown Common to Cambridge when I saw two Officers on Horseback, standing under the shade of a Tree. . . . I was near enough to see their Holsters & cockades. One of them started his horse towards me and the other up the road, as I supposed to head me [off]." Revere turned about sharply and galloped for a road that ran along the Mystic. One of the officers pursued but immediately became mired in a clay pond. A short time later, Revere crossed a plank bridge that took him into Medford, where "I awaked the Captain of the minute men: and after that I alarumed almost every house —shouting 'The regulars are out!'—till I got to Lexington." At Lexington, about midnight, he went straight to the local parsonage, where he knew Samuel Adams and Hancock were staying. There he found the house guarded by eight Minutemen, who tried to turn him away. Their sergeant warned him not to make noise and awaken the residents. "Noise!" cried Revere. "You'll have noise enough before long. The regulars are out." He pushed past them, shouting, and began pounding on the door.

Hancock, who was still awake, recognized his voice and let him in. Adams and Hancock heard his report; then, in a blustery show of martial ardor, Hancock declared himself ready to face the regulars on Lexington Green. But without too much difficulty Adams convinced him he would be of no use if he were caught or killed. A carriage was brought, and they prepared to make their escape.

Revere was now joined by two other rebels, William Dawes and Dr. Samuel Prescott, who undertook to help spread the alarm. Together the three set out for Concord, but they had not gone far before they were accosted by several British officers posted, like those before, in ambush. Dawes and Prescott managed to elude them, but this time Revere was cut off as he rode for a nearby clump of woods. The officers, he recalled, "siesed my bridle, put their pistols to my Breast, and ordered me to dismount." When they asked him where he was going, he defiantly admitted his errand, at which "they threatened to blow my brains out." But he also told them that hundreds of Minutemen were assembling nearby. In their haste to get safely back to their own regiment, they cut the bridle of his mount and let him go. Revere returned to Lexington through the woods on foot, but by then so many other riders had joined in spreading the word in every direction that, according to one British soldier, "claiming to be a patriot express was the best alibi a British spy could have."

Back at Lexington, about seventy-seven Minutemen, roused earlier by Revere's alarm, had gathered at Buckman's Tavern, where on ordinary days they were accustomed to relax after their drill. Now under their captain, John Parker, a former Indian fighter, they formed into two thin lines on the triangular green as the British advance guard swung into view. Just outside town, the redcoats had paused to load their muskets, and they were testy: they had been on the march since ten the previous evening, had waded through the swampy banks of the Charles River, at times up to their waists in mud, and had stood around wet and cold without having been given breakfast before marching on to Lexington, where they knew they were hated and despised. The morning sun was just breaking over the horizon, and as they doubled their ranks and marched up at quickstep, their leader, Major Pitcairn of the Royal Marines, called out, "Lay down your arms, you damned rebels, and disperse!" Parker had told his men earlier, "Stand your ground. Don't fire unless fired upon. But if they want to have a war, let it begin here." Now, as if in shock, the Minutemen began to move away slowly, still holding their guns.

All might yet have ended without bloodshed. And it is not at all clear who fired the first shot. But as the Minutemen moved off, someone did fire, and the British responded with a volley directly into their ranks. Eighteen fell, eight of them dead or dying; then the British came on with their bayonets.

Most of the Minutemen at Lexington were family men over thirty. A few were much older: one was sixty-three. Twelve teenagers were also there, and eight fathers had sons by their side. Adams and Hancock, hastening away to safety in their carriage, heard the firing. Adams, transported with visions of America's predestined greatness, exclaimed: "O! What a glorious morning is this!" But his words would not have swelled the breasts of any of those then holding fallen loved ones in their arms.

The sun was now fully up. As the Americans scattered, there was a victory volley from the British, followed by three jubilant cheers. With music playing, the redcoats now set out with a kind of surreal confidence for Concord. Yet with every step they took, the patriot alarm was being carried still deeper into the countryside. Men were roused from their beds in Lynn, Danvers, Tewksbury, Reading, Woburn, Acton, Bedford, Essex, Marblehead, Salem, and Andover as church bells relayed the message across the whole of Massachusetts Bay.

Dr. Prescott, who earlier had made good his escape by jumping his horse over a stone wall, had taken the alarm to Concord, where three companies of Minutemen turned out. By the time the British arrived, the cache of arms and munitions they had hoped to capture had been resequestered in covered pits dug in a field. Flints, balls, and cartridges had also been thrown into barrels or stored away in attics under feather piles. The church silver (a presumed object of British plunder) had been dropped into a barrel of soft soap.

Yet as the militia took up their positions on the high ground above the village, there were bizarre incongruities in the scene. They knew the British were coming, but not yet what they had done. And so some of the Americans, as the British columns approached, "good-naturedly" marched in front of them to the sound of their own fifes and drums. The British, not to be outdone, also began to play, as if they had all been banded together in one great festive parade.

At Concord, moreover, the British at first behaved with great civility, and the Americans responded in kind. They "set out chairs on green lawns, under blossoming cherry trees for officers to rest in," while the soldiers began a house-to-house search for military stores. But finding none, they soon became frustrated, then vindictive. They set fire to the Concord courthouse and cut down the Liberty Pole. Meanwhile, British detachments had also been sent forward to seize two bridges over the Concord River. At North Bridge, about nine that morning, they fired on a company of Minutemen blocking their way, killing two. The Americans fired back, killing three and wounding nine. The British retreated, and the Minutemen pursued.

Ralph Waldo Emerson later wrote the famous lines now inscribed on a monument at the site:

> By the rude bridge that arched the flood,
> Their flag to freedom's breeze unfurled,
> Here once the embattled farmers stood
> And fired the shot heard 'round the world.

Not simple embattled farmers, of course, spontaneously aroused, but local militia trained in advance to defend their communities. Yet they belonged, after all, to the people in the larger sense meant by Emerson's lines.

After the skirmish, it was said that two British privates left behind by their comrades had been scalped. According to Nathaniel Hawthorne, who had the story secondhand, a youth chopping wood nearby heard the shooting and ran to the bridge, still holding his ax. By the time he arrived, the British had retreated, but two soldiers lay on the ground. As the youth approached, one of them suddenly "raised himself painfully upon his hands and knees and gave a ghastly stare into his face." The startled boy, thinking himself about to be attacked, struck at his head with the ax. Later, when another British party passed by, they saw his mutilated brow and thought he had been scalped. Subsequently, the *London Gazette* reported, "Such was the cruelty and barbarity of the rebels that they scalped and cut off the ears of some of our wounded men."

The British began to withdraw from Concord about noon, along the same road by which they had come. By then everyone knew what had happened earlier that morning at Lexington, as well as at North Bridge, and they were bent on revenge. The British sensed an enveloping disaster as whole companies of militia hovered upon their flanks. Every stand of trees and every bit of rising ground seemed to give potential shelter to hostile fire. The sniping began, then steadily increased from behind bushes, stone walls, trees, fences, and barns—as the Americans turned the British march back to Boston into a bloody and disorderly retreat. Soon "a grait many Lay dead and the Road was bloddy," wrote a British corporal, and a British lieutenant recalled, "We were fired on from all sides, but mostly from the rear, where people hid themselves in houses till we had passed. . . . The country was an amazing strong one, full of hills, woods, stone walls, etc., which the rebels did not fail to take advantage of. . . . Their numbers [were] increasing from all parts, while ours [were] reducing by deaths, wounds, and fatigue; and we were totally surrounded with such an incessant fire as it's impossible to conceive; our ammunition was likely near expended." The British were caught in one ambush at Meriam's Corner and another at Lincoln township; by the time they passed back through Lexington, they were in a near rout. Colonel Smith, wounded in the leg, reportedly would have surrendered if only he could have found someone of rank to whom he could offer his sword.

About two o'clock, his battered command was finally rescued from annihilation by a relief party of about a thousand men with field artillery who had arrived in response to his earlier request for help. The reinforcements formed themselves into a hollow square, enclosing their beleaguered comrades, some of whom, recalled one British colonel, immediately collapsed, "their tongues hanging out of their mouths, like those of dogs after a chase." After about an hour, the British continued their withdrawal but now in revenge for their own losses burned and looted houses and killed men they happened upon along the way. Among the American casualties was a fifty-eight-year-old cripple named Jason Russell, who was impaled on a bayonet in the doorway of his home. In another house, belonging to a local deacon (who hid himself in the barn under a pile of hay), the redcoats ousted his sick wife, Hannah, from her bed and set the house ablaze. In Menotomy (now

Arlington), the combat was particularly fierce: forty patriots and forty British soldiers died fighting hand to hand.

At length, the British crossed Charlestown Neck to safety under the cover of their ships, and as evening fell, sprawled in the darkness over the side of Bunker Hill.

Some 3,700 patriots from twenty-three townships had taken part in the action against 1,800 regulars, and by the end of the day the British had lost 273 dead and wounded, 18 officers among them, and the Americans 95. Wrote Washington afterward, "If the retreat had not been as precipitate as it was—and God knows it could not well have been more so—the ministerial troops must have surrendered or been totally cut off."

The men who had chased the redcoats back to Boston now settled down before it, and the formation of an army began. From far and near, armed companies of patriots set out to join them, as riders galloped from farm to farm and the white, spare-spired New England churches rang their bells to call the men to arms. Farmers left their fields, where they had been plodding sturdily behind their plows; veterans took down their long guns with powder and horn. They made their way to the outskirts of Boston from Connecticut, Rhode Island, and New Hampshire, as well as Massachusetts—in such numbers that within a few days Gage found himself invested by a motley patriot army of more than 10,000 men.

On April 20, General Artemas Ward of Massachusetts took charge of the gathering force and, at a council of war made up of himself and other New England militia officers, established a plan of guard posts, fortifications, and earthworks to blockade the roads out of Boston and imprison the British in place. Within a few days, troops had been distributed among encampments that extended from Dorchester through Roxbury, Brookline, Cambridge, and Charlestown, down to the Mystic River in a semicircular line. Ward established his headquarters at Cambridge, where some of the Harvard College buildings were turned into barracks and the kitchen furnished pots, kettles, and other cooking utensils for the general staff.

For his part, Gage hurried defensive measures to prevent "some desperate attempt on the town. The numbers which are assembled round it," wrote one of his officers, "and their violent and determined spirit make it prudent to guard against what they may do."

Those of a loyalist persuasion were horrified at the new developments. They regarded the revolutionaries (as Galloway had regarded Samuel Adams) as people of bankrupt fortune, devoid of morals, social misfits, and worse. In New York, rebels paraded through the streets "with drums beating and colours flying (attended by a mob of negroes, boys, sailors, and pickpockets), inviting all mankind to take up arms in defence of the 'injured rights and liberties of America,' " according to Judge Thomas Jones, a staunch loyalist from Long Island. In the afternoon, the marchers seized the cargo of a sloop bound for Boston, and that evening broke into the city arsenal, carried off a thousand stand of arms, and distributed them "to the rabble to be used as the demagogues of rebellion should direct."

Others were less disdainful. "Whoever looks upon [the rebels] as an irregular mob will find himself much mistaken," wrote General Earl Percy, who had headed the relief column that had rescued Smith's command. "They have men amongst them who know very well what they are about, having been employed as Rangers against the Indians and Canadians, and this country being much covered with wood and hilly is very advantageous for their method of fighting. Nor are several of their men void of a spirit of [courage]. . . . You may depend upon it, that as the rebels have now had time to prepare, they are determined to go through with it, nor will the insurrection here turn out so despicable as it is perhaps imagined at home." When John Singleton Copley, the Boston painter who was then in England, heard a report of the fighting, he wrote to his brother, "The flame of civil war is now broke out in America, and I have not the least doubt it will rage with a violence equal to what it has ever done in any other country at any time. . . . Oceans of blood will be shed to humble a people which they never will subdue."

The preparations for battle went far beyond New England. "The whole country became as it were electrified," recalled John Adlum, a sixteen-year-old volunteer Pennsylvania militiaman, "and almost every one young and old were formed into companies." Organizers took advantage of the moment, for there was tremendous pressure to enlist. One Milford, Connecticut, farm boy recalled, "I was ploughing in the field about half a mile from home, about the twenty-first day of April, when all of a sudden the bells fell to ringing and three guns were repeatedly fired in succession." He went to see what was up and found most of the men of the village gathered together, infuriated at the British, and eager to fight. Every time the recruiter deposited a dollar on the drumhead (according to the procedure), it was promptly taken up.

Like many young men, the farm boy felt he already had "pretty correct ideas of the contest" from listening to his elders, and once the issue was joined, it didn't seem right to him to go back to working in the fields.

In Charleston, South Carolina, patriot authorities began to fortify the harbor against a possible British siege, and in Williamsburg members of the Virginia House of Burgesses clothed themselves in homespun garments with the words LIBERTY OR DEATH stitched across their coats. In Philadelphia, "every man . . . even the Quakers" was "learning the use of arms," and when the Second Continental Congress convened in early May, delegate Silas Deane of Connecticut wrote home to his wife that some thirty armed companies had already been raised. Each man wore a small hat encircled with colored ribbon, coded according to battalion, with a tuft of deer fur "made to resemble a buck's tail" sticking out. On their cartridge boxes, the word LIBERTY was painted in large block letters in white.

Light infantry units were also being formed, as well as a body of irregulars or riflemen dressed in long belted frocks "the shade of a dry or fading leaf"—not unlike modern army fatigues. The lightweight hunting rifle they carried was nothing like the hefty conventional smoothbore musket used by European regulars (and most militiamen) but had a long barrel, with a spiral groove in the bore, of "great exactness" for a long shot. Its effective range was double that of the musket, and it was said to be able to "split a squirrel" at three hundred yards. But the bullet, being fitted more tightly to the bore, took more time to ram home. Most of the marksmen were rugged frontiersmen from the western margins of Virginia and Pennsylvania. They wanted "nothing to preserve their health and courage," wrote one admirer, "but water from the spring, with a little parched corn. . . . The shade of a tree [was all they required] for their covering, and the earth for their bed."

Exhibitions of their skill were held on Cambridge Common to strike fear into the hearts of the British—for spies could be counted on to carry the word back to Gage's camp—and Washington later encouraged even some of his regular soldiers to wear "Hunting Shirts, with long breeches made of the same Cloth" as "a dress justly supposed to carry no small terror to the enemy, who think every such person a Marksman."

I N the midst of the crisis, the Second Continental Congress assembled on May 10 at Philadelphia, but in confirmation of its more official status, it now sat in the State House rather than in Carpenter's Hall. John Hancock of Massachusetts was elected to succeed Peyton Randolph of Virginia (president of the First Congress) in deliberate defiance of the British, who had "proscribed" him. As Virginia's Benjamin Harrison conducted Hancock to the chair, he said, "We will show Great Britain how much we value her proscriptions." Nevertheless, it was by no means certain that all of the other colonies would come to Massachusetts's defense. Most delegates were in a quandary as to what to do. The impulse toward independence, coupled with a growing experience of self-government, competed powerfully with the long-standing ties that still bound the colonies to the Crown. And hopes for reconciliation remained in the air.

John and Samuel Adams, John Dickinson, Richard Henry Lee, and other prominent figures from the First Congress had returned, but there were important new members, including Benjamin Franklin, who had at last come home from England and sat as a member of the Pennsylvania delegation. Though nearly a septuagenarian, he was constant in attendance, attentive, "composed and grave," and surprised John Adams by his radical views. "He does not hesitate at our boldest measures," wrote Adams, "but rather seems to think us too irresolute and backward . . . he thinks that we shall soon assume a character more decisive. He thinks that we have the power of preserving ourselves and that even if . . . driven to . . . independence and to set up a separate state, we can maintain it." He had changed.

Thomas Jefferson had also taken his seat as a Virginia representative, and George Washington now appeared on the floor of the Congress dressed in military uniform. This was not theatrical ostentation on his part but a sober reminder to the others of the gravity of the consequences of their deliberations, which might mean war. It was also a reminder of the best way he thought he could serve. Although many of the delegates were as voluble and "tedious" in their debates as ever, neither Washington nor Franklin, Jefferson later recalled, ever spoke more than "ten minutes at a time. . . . They laid their shoulders to the great points, knowing that the little ones would follow of themselves." Jefferson himself exhibited a similar succinctness and reserve.

To Washington, the choice before them suddenly seemed stark: "Unhappy it is to reflect that a brother's sword has been sheathed in a brother's breast and that the once happy and peaceful plains of America are to be either drenched with blood or inhabited by slaves. Sad alternative! But can a virtuous man hesitate in his choice?" Yet many did hesitate. Among other things, there was great apprehension of a North-South split, and if such an alignment were superimposed on the even more fundamental split between moderate or conservative and radical, Congress might easily become paralyzed. The southern landholding aristocracy was loath to make common cause with the leveling political spirit of New England. Or, as Patrick Henry candidly remarked to John Adams, "There is among most of our opulent families a strong bias to aristocracy." As a result, the New England representatives (and those from Massachusetts in particular) "were heard in Congress with great caution," wrote Adams, as covert advocates of "designs of independency; an American republic; Presbyterian principles, and twenty other things." Indeed, for the first month the delegates were so preoccupied with whether to send a second "humble" petition to the king that the rest of their business was suspended. There were "motions and debates without end for appointing committees to draw up a declaration of the causes, motives, and objects of taking arms, or with a view to obtaining decisive declarations against independence, etc." Yet the longer the Congress sat, the more apparent it was to most of its members that "vigorous measures" were needed to counter Britain's hostile designs.

Meanwhile, on May 16, the Massachusetts Provincial Congress had appealed to Congress to assume charge of the force outside Boston. On June 14, it at last responded and adopted the New England troops as "the American continental army." That same day, it also authorized the formation of ten companies of riflemen—eight in Pennsylvania and two in Maryland—and two companies in Virginia to be raised as a light infantry, and agreed to appropriate $2 million for the army's support. On June 15, it named George Washington of Virginia general and commander in chief of the Continental troops.

He was not at first a unanimous choice. The army outside Boston was still made up entirely of New England men with a general of their own whom they liked: Artemas Ward. But the point was forcefully made behind the scenes that a national army ought not to have a provincial cast. A consensus began to emerge for a southern general. Still, there were other candidates. According to Adams, "Hancock himself had an ambition to be appointed commander-in-chief. Whether he thought an election a compliment due to him, and intended to have the honor of declining it, or whether he would have accepted, I know not. To the compliment he had some pretensions. . . . But the delicacy of his health, and his entire want of experience in actual service, though an excellent militia officer, were decisive objections to him in my mind."

Early one day, Adams took a walk with his cousin Samuel in the State House yard and gave vent to his anxieties. Samuel asked him, "What shall we do?" John told him he had decided to nominate Washington, around whom many of the "staunchest men" in Congress had now coalesced.

And so it was that when the delegates gathered on the morning of June 14, John Adams rose in his place. He saluted Washington as "a gentleman whose skill and experience as an officer, whose independent fortune, great talents and excellent universal character would command the approbation of all America and unite the cordial exertions of all the

colonies better than any other person in the Union." Yet he had not yet
mentioned the Virginian by name, and Hancock, thinking himself the
object of the praise, listened "with visible pleasure." But when Adams
pointed out Washington as the man, "a sudden and striking change"
came over Hancock's countenance. "Mortification and resentment were
expressed as forcibly as his face could exhibit them." Washington, on
the other hand, who was sitting near the door, "as [soon as] he heard me
allude to him, from his usual modesty darted into the library-room."

The following day, Washington was again nominated—this time by a
delegate from Maryland to complement the previous nomination by a
New Englander—and unanimously approved.

In truth, there was no one more qualified. Washington was not only
America's foremost soldier but, by the time the First Continental Congress
had convened, one of its principal political figures, having been promi-
nent in the political life of Virginia for sixteen years. After the campaign
against Fort Duquesne in the French and Indian War, he had returned to
Williamsburg, settled all his public accounts, and, in the last week of
December 1758, taken his seat as an elected representative in the Virginia
Assembly. In the mid-1760s, as a planter and holder of western lands, he
had emerged in the vanguard of those protesting Britain's new policies.
After the Assembly had been dissolved by the royal governor in 1769, he
had joined other rebel members to form the association that orchestrated
the boycott of English goods. In 1774, after learning of the Boston Port
Bill, he had offered (as noted above) to raise a thousand men at his own
expense and march them to Boston. In the spring of 1775, when Virginia
had begun to organize military companies at the county level, Washington had been placed at the head of seven of them—a collective trust
granted to no other man. Moreover, as a delegate to the First and now
the Second Continental Congresses, he had served on various military
preparedness committees and was chairman of the committee to consider ways of raising arms and ammunition for the conflict, should it
begin.

In short, he had considerable military experience as well as proven
political leadership and skill. And as a Virginian, his appearance at the
head of an army to liberate Boston would symbolize colonial unity—a
bringing together of North and South, that would dispel any impression
that the Revolution was simply a New England war.

In a brief acceptance speech, Washington expressed his high and
grateful sense of the honor conferred upon him and his sincere devotion
to the cause. "But," he added, "lest some unlucky event should happen
unfavorable to my reputation, I beg it may be remembered by every

gentleman in the room, that I this day declare, with the utmost sincerity, I do not think myself equal to the command." He declined remuneration, saying that payment would not have tempted him to forgo "domestic ease and happiness" for such "arduous employment," and asked only to have his expenses reimbursed.

A few years later, delegate Eliphalet Dyer of Connecticut touched on the politics of it all in a letter home: "[Washington] is a Gent. highly Esteemed by those acquainted with him tho I don't believe as to his Military for real service he knows more than some of ours [i.e., New England officers] but so it removes all jealousies, more firmly Cements the Southern to the Northern. . . . He is Clever, and if any thing too modest. he seems discreet and Virtuous, no harum Starum ranting fellow but Sober, steady and Calm." No ranting fellow, to be sure, but most of all (added Dyer, repeating southern fears) not a New England general whose New England army, if victorious, might threaten to impose its egalitarian will on the other states.

To assuage local pride, other New England delegates likewise felt they had some explaining to do. Hancock wrote to Joseph Warren, "Washington . . . is a Gentleman you will all like. I submit to you the propriety of providing a suitable place for his Residence and the mode of his Reception." And John Adams informed Abigail, "The modest, virtuous, the amiable, generous, and brave George Washington, Esquire," has been appointed commander in chief, to "cement and secure the union of these colonies." When Abigail met Washington soon thereafter, she was captivated: "You had prepared me to entertain a favorable opinion of him," she wrote, "but I thought the half was not told me. Dignity with ease and complacency, the gentleman and the soldier look agreeably blended in him. Modesty marks every line and feature of his face."

Who was this singular personage who had suddenly emerged from a crowd of singular men?

In his person, Washington was a large, well-proportioned man, six feet, two inches tall, big-boned and stalwart, with broad shoulders and an erect but easy bearing with a soldier-like air. His face was handsome with aquiline features, but somewhat pitted from a youthful bout with smallpox. His hair was auburn; his eyes, wide-spaced and a light blue-gray. On formal occasions he powdered his hair and tied it back in a queue. Like many of his contemporaries', most of his teeth had fallen to pyorrhea by early manhood, and at various times he was fitted with bridgework or dentures fashioned from lead, ivory, and the teeth of animals, including cows.

He had an interesting pedigree. On his father's side, he was descended from William de Hertburn, an English knight, who had owned the village of Wessyngton in Durham County (from which the family name was derived), and during the English Civil War the Washingtons had taken the royalist side. One relation had served as an officer in the king's army; George's great-great-granduncle, Sir William Washington of Kent, had married the half sister of the duke of Buckingham, the favorite of Charles I.

But (so story had it) in Washington's blood there also mingled an opposite strain. On his mother's side, he was reputedly descended from John Ball, the famous radical medieval preacher who had advocated a classless society. "My good friends, things cannot go well in England, nor ever will," Ball had proclaimed on one occasion, "until everything shall be held in common; when there shall neither be vassal nor lord, and all distinctions levelled; when the lords shall be no more masters than ourselves. . . . Are we not all descended from the same parents, Adam and Eve? And what can they show, or what reasons give, why they should be more the masters than ourselves?" For such talk, Ball was excommunicated by the Church in 1366 and imprisoned by the arch-bishop of Canterbury. His rebellious disciples, led by Wat Tyler and Jack Straw, broke into the dungeon and freed him, and after plundering the archbishop's palace they marched on London. Richard II promised re-dress of grievances, but Wat Tyler and thousands of others remained encamped to ensure that the king's pledges were kept. In the ensuing confrontation, Ball was captured, tried, and hanged. Afterward, his head was stuck on a pike on London Bridge. In this gruesome way, the first great popular rebellion in English history came to an end. But its legacy was long. And it has sometimes been said that in the preaching of John Ball, England first heard the declaration of the rights of man.

As for the Washingtons, in the aftermath of the English Civil War—that is, after the beheading of Charles I and the accession of Cromwell—George's great-grandfather John emigrated to Virginia, where he pros-pered as a farmer. His son and his grandson Augustine, George's father, also fared well, with the latter—by the acquisition of land, mills, iron mines, and so on—showing exceptional enterprise. Augustine married twice, and on February 22, 1732, in Westmoreland County, Virginia, George was born to his second wife, Mary Ball.

George's father died when he was eleven, whereupon he became the ward of his eldest half brother, Lawrence. Lawrence was a man such as George aspired to be. A battle-scarred veteran of British campaigns against the Spanish in Panama and Colombia, he was also a member of the House of Burgesses and adjutant general (with the rank of major) of the militia in his district, and he had married into the family of Lord Edward Fairfax, one of the chief proprietors of the region. Through Lawrence, George was introduced to Virginia high society at its most genteel, in which "frankness and rural simplicity were united with European refinement." By the time he was sixteen, George appeared in every respect an adult—tall, athletic, and manly, with a precocious gravity and decision to his conduct that inspired respect. He was commissioned by the Fairfax family to survey some of their unsettled holdings beyond the Blue Ridge Mountains, and in May 1748 set out with several companions for the Shenandoah Valley, the "valley of the stars." They roughed it for a couple of weeks, camped out in the open, lived on wild game, slept, as he put it, under "one thread Bear blanket with double its Weight of Vermin such as Lice, Fleas, &c," and met up with a war party of thirty Indians bearing a scalp. Washington handled the whole assignment so tactfully and well that upon his return he was appointed public surveyor for the whole of Culpeper County, a post he held for three years. In the course of his responsibilities, he traveled far beyond the tidewater region into the western wilderness and came to know the land in all its aspects, even as his physical constitution and stamina were strengthened by many days of hard riding and the rugged outdoor life.

Lawrence, however, was tubercular and, in the winter of 1751, asked George to accompany him to the West Indies, where he hoped to regain his health. For a time they lived together in Barbados, where George contracted smallpox, but the following summer, Lawrence died. Shortly thereafter, George inherited Mount Vernon, his brother's large estate. Coincident with this, though only nineteen, he was appointed adjutant of the southern military district, with a major's commission, and, regarding it as no sinecure, set out to make himself worthy of the trust. He sought out veterans of earlier English campaigns who could teach him swordsmanship and other military skills and pored over treatises on military tactics, from which he acquired basic ideas of the evolution of formations in the field. Before long, he was called upon to prove himself in battle, as we have seen, and as a young man he earned a solid reputation for courage, prudence, and tactical skill in the French and Indian War. Promoted to colonel, he resigned his commission at war's end and on January 6, 1759, married Martha Dandridge, a widow with two children and the proprietress of a large estate. For the next fifteen years or so he settled down to being a gentleman farmer, attending to the rotation of his crops, the fertilization of the soil, and the management of livestock. Of farming, he said, "It is honorable, it is amusing, and, with superior judgment, it is profitable." He experimented with cattle breeding; maintained a peach and apple orchard and an extensive fishery; and established a flour mill, blacksmith shop, brick and charcoal kilns, and other industries on his property. He had coopers, weavers, shoemakers, and so on in his employ, making Mount Vernon almost a self-sufficient community.

In 1758, he was elected to the Virginia House of Burgesses. He also served as a justice of the peace for Fairfax County, and played a prominent role in the social life of the tidewater region. The elite, to which he belonged, visited one another in a regular round of entertainments, picnics, house parties, and afternoon teas; relaxed at billiards and cards; went to the theater; rode out on fox hunts; attended horse races; or celebrated their own pedigree at balls in Alexandria, where Washington, who enjoyed all these pastimes, was often an exquisitely graceful and indefatigable partner for the belles.

Like all Virginia planters, Washington also owned slaves; to his credit, he never sold any he had acquired or broke up their families. "I am principled against this kind of traffic in the human species," he once said, and it may be noted that he was the only slaveholding Founding Father to free his slaves upon his death.

Perhaps something of Washington's martial prowess derived from his great-grandfather John, who was said to have been a great Indian fighter. But in many respects he was his mother's son. A playmate from his youth recalled, "Of the mother I was ten times more afraid than I ever was of my own parents . . . whoever has seen the awe-inspiring air and manner so characteristic of the Father of His Country will remember the mother as she appeared as the presiding genius of her well-ordered household, commanding and being obeyed." If Washington inherited from his mother a spirit of command, a hot temper had also come with it that was hard for him to control. "He is subject to attacks of anger on provocation, sometimes without just cause," wrote Thomas, Lord Fairfax, to Washington's mother in 1748, when he was sixteen. But Fairfax also predicted he would discipline himself in this, for he is "a man who will go to school all his life." Nothing could have been more true. As the great historian Francis Parkman once remarked, Washington eventually achieved "the kind of mastery over others which begins with mastery over self."

Washington's consistent dignity, appropriate reserve, high-mindedness, steady decency, and meticulous tact have irritated those biographers looking for weakness, pettiness, faltering, or other evidence of shortcomings redolent of the "real" man. Yet how much more interesting and moving is the process of self-development that enabled him to achieve so many victories, in so many trying circumstances, over himself.

The idea that Washington artificially smoothed out his rusticity by studying a self-help manual in his adolescence remains a commonplace, along with such corollaries as that he had a rudimentary education, little interest in high culture or philosophical ideas, and was of a basically practical bent. These are all half-truths. And it is worth remembering that character and the evolution of knowledge are only tangentially connected with formal education or learning in the true sense. From a comparatively early age, in fact, his conduct and expression reflected a thoughtful acquaintance with law, politics, and history and a classical literary style.

As a boy, Washington had been taught by the sexton of the local parish. Afterward, he attended a "superior," or high, school where he studied mathematics, trigonometry, geography, English composition, history, and possibly Latin. He supplemented these studies with a determination to become proficient in other fields. Some of them were practical. Before he was thirteen, for example, he had taught himself bookkeeping and had copied into a notebook the forms for various kinds of mercantile and legal papers—bills of exchange, notes of hand, deeds, bonds, and so on. These, as Washington Irving remarks, "gave him throughout life a lawyer's skill in drafting documents and a merchant's exactness in keeping accounts, so that all the concerns of his various estates, his dealings with his domestic stewards and foreign agents, his accounts with government and all his financial transactions are to this day to be seen posted up in books in his own handwriting, monuments of his method and unwearied accuracy."

Like any normal boy, he was also drawn to the literature of adventure, and read *The Adventures of Peregrine Pickle* by Roderick Random, for example, and *The Travels of Cyrus* by Chevalier Ramsay, to which was appended a "Discourse Upon the Theology and Mythology of the Pagans." At the same time, he studied courtesy books, pored over Seneca's *Dialogues* emphasizing Stoic fortitude in the face of adversity, and at the age of fourteen copied out 110 "Rules of Civility and Decent Behaviour in Company and Conversation," which somewhat foreshadowed the high principles which regulated his conduct in mature life. He also transcribed a charming little verse entitled *True Happiness:*

> These are the things which once possessed
> Will make a life that's truly blessed;
> A good estate on healthy soil
> Not got by vice, nor yet by toil;
> Round a warm fire, a pleasant joke,
> With chimney ever free from smoke:

> A strength entire, a sparkling bowl,
> A quiet wife, a quiet soul.

It was just such a life that Washington eventually attempted to create for himself as a refuge and consolation from the worlds of politics and war.

He kept himself fit. His body was lean and hard, and he maintained it by regular exercise and a modest and abstemious diet which favored pineapples, Brazil nuts, and Saturday dinners of salt cod. If something rich was offered him, his usual remark was "That is too good for me." One glass of wine during dinner and another afterward, or a glass of beer, was all the liquor he allowed himself each day.

In his youth, he had excelled at a number of sports; he could ride, shoot, and swim and had a tremendous arm. "I have several times heard him say," wrote David Humphreys, his earliest biographer, "that he never met any man who could throw a stone to so great a distance as himself; and that when standing in the valley beneath the Natural Bridge in Virginia, he has thrown one up to that stupendous arch." During the war, he sometimes liked to relax with his officers by throwing a ball back and forth for hours at a time. He was also a superb horseman and broke his own colts.

All together, Washington's program of self-development compares favorably with Benjamin Franklin's early attempt at self-perfection, John Adams's determination to rid himself of every base inclination, and Thomas Jefferson's legendary fifteen hours of study every day. For the rest (to adapt a phrase from Herman Melville), the western wilderness was his Harvard and his Yale. "He learned early to read the motives of the French scouts sent out to harass an English scouting party," wrote one biographer, "or a too silent Indian guide leading him toward possible ambush. . . . At an astonishingly early age he could ford a river, clothe a regiment, and chart a mountain road."

The great portrait painter Gilbert Stuart, who knew him well, once said that Washington was a natural warrior whose face bore the lineaments of every savage passion composed and held in perfect civilized restraint. Indeed, the social graces were naturalized in him to an extraordinary degree. Jefferson once remarked that Washington was the best dancer in Virginia, and Mercy Warren, a New England poet and the daughter of James Otis, the revolutionary theorist and pamphleteer, considered Washington "the most amiable and accomplished gentleman both in person, mind and manners that I ever met."

He also read far more widely than is generally supposed, and he understood what he read. In the course of refurbishing Mount Vernon after his marriage, he had ordered from England plaster-cast busts of eminent military men, including Alexander the Great, Julius Caesar, Charles XII of Sweden, and Frederick the Great of Prussia. But his factor explained in a letter that these were not available and instead suggested busts of Homer, Virgil, Horace, Cicero, Plato, Aristotle, Seneca, Galen, Chaucer, Spenser, Jonson, Shakespeare, Beaumont, Fletcher, Milton, Prior, Pope, Congreve, Swift, Addison, Dryden, Locke, and Newton. That might seem a bit literary for a provincial colonel, yet an inventory of his library after his death revealed that in addition to sundry political tracts, sermons, and orations, books on gardening, horses, fortifications, artillery, and so on, he owned works by a number of these men.

His own literary style showed extraordinary nuance and tact. And if his sentences seem to lack something of Jefferson's rhetorical flair, they yet reflect, in ways perhaps more satisfying, the remarkably careful circumspection and beautiful firmness of his thought.

In his everyday relations, Washington was reserved but not unapproachable. Abigail Adams remarked after first meeting him, "He has a dignity which forbids familiarity mixed with an easy affability which creates love and reverence." And it is interesting to compare the impression he made on others with the advice he imparted himself. He once told a young colonel, "Be easy and condescending [i.e., natural] in your deportment to your [junior] officers, but not too familiar, lest you subject yourself to a want of that respect which is necessary to support a proper command." He was careful of his friendships. "True friendship," he counseled a nephew, "is a plant of slow growth and must undergo and withstand the shocks of adversity before it is entitled to the appellation."

For all his accomplishments, authority, and aura of command, Washington remained an extremely bashful man. In 1759, when he first took his seat in the House of Burgesses, the speaker thanked him on behalf of the colony for his "brave and steady Behaviour" and the distinguished military services he had rendered "from the first Encroachments and Hostilities of the French." Washington rose to reply, "blushed, stammered, trembled," and could not utter a word. "Sit down, Mr. Washington," said the speaker with a smile. "Your modesty is equal to your valour; and that surpasses the power of any language I possess." It was equally so in private. He was not the sort to tell war stories—indeed, "he allways avoided saying anything," according to the portrait painter Charles Willson Peale, who admired him for it, "of the actions in which he [had been] Engaged." And when John Adams nominated him for commander in chief, we may remember, he rushed in embarrassment from the room.

John Marshall, his friend and sometime biographer (and later chief justice of the United States), said of him that he had an "innate and unassuming modesty" that was "happily blended with a high and correct sense of personal dignity, and with a just consciousness of the respect which is due to station. Endowed by nature with a sound judgment, and an accurate and discriminating mind, he . . . was guided by an unvarying sense of moral right, which would tolerate the employment only of those means that would bear the most rigid examination."

The myth is that there is a myth about him. And those looking to tear down an idol in order to find the "real" man will, as they find him, have to build him back up. George Washington gave America, by his life and example, an idea of itself which has endured as an inspiration to the people ever since. By his own conduct during the Revolution—his civility, integrity, tact, and martial ardor allied to compassion and self-restraint—he showed those struggling to be free how to be worthy of their aspirations.

Yet it all might not have been. Washington regarded his elevation to commander in chief as a cross. He wrote to Patrick Henry, "From the day I enter upon the command of the American armies, I date my fall and the ruin of my reputation." And to his brother John Augustine he wrote privately, "I am embarked on a wide ocean, boundless in its prospect and in which, perhaps, no safe harbor is to be found. . . . I have been called upon by the unanimous Voice of the Colonies to take the Command of the Continental Army—an honour I neither sought after, nor desired, as I am thoroughly convinced that it requires greater abilities, and more experience, than I am Master of . . . ; but the partiality of the Congress, joined to a political motive, really left me without a choice."

Such were the sentiments that resonated in a poignant way through the letter of June 18 he wrote to his wife, Martha, in affectionate farewell:

> My Dearest:
>
> I now sit down to write to you on a subject which fills me with inexpressible concern, and this concern is greatly aggravated and increased when I reflect upon the uneasiness I know it will give you. It has been determined in Congress that the whole army raised for the defence of the American cause shall be put under my care, and that it is necessary for me to proceed immediately to Boston to take upon me the command of it.
>
> You may believe me, my dear Patsy, when I assure you, in the most solemn manner, that, so far from seeking this appointment, I have used every endeavour in my power to avoid it, not only from my unwillingness to part with you and the family, but from a consciousness of its being a

trust too great for my capacity, and that I should enjoy more real happiness in one month with you at home than I have the most distant prospect of finding abroad, if my stay were to be seven times seven years. But as it has been a kind of destiny that has thrown me upon this service, I shall hope that my undertaking is designed to answer some good purpose. You might, and I suppose did perceive, from the tenor of my letters, that I was apprehensive I could not avoid this appointment, as I did not pretend to intimate when I should return. That was the case. It was utterly out of my power to refuse this appointment without exposing my character to such censures as would have reflected dishonour upon myself and given pain to my friends. This, I am sure, would not and ought not to be pleasing to you, and must have lessened me considerably in my own esteem. I shall rely, therefore, confidently on that Providence which has heretofore preserved and been bountiful to me, not doubting but that I shall return safe to you in the fall.

After exhorting her to fortitude, he enclosed his will.

His wished-for homecoming proved a long way off. From that time on until the end of the Revolutionary War (eight years later, in 1783), he managed to return to Mount Vernon only briefly twice.

M O S T of the American officers who arose to serve and lead the revolutionary army were not homegrown soldiers but men who had served as company captains, rangers, supply officers, and so on during the French and Indian War. They knew what war was and in one capacity or another had distinguished themselves in it. In the ensuing years, they would often find themselves facing men who had been their former commanders or comrades in arms. This was so of the four major generals appointed under Washington—Artemas Ward of Massachusetts, Charles Lee of Virginia, Philip Schuyler of New York, and Israel Putnam of Connecticut—and of all but one of the eight brigadiers—Seth Pomeroy, Richard Montgomery, David Wooster, William Heath, Joseph Spencer, John Thomas, John Sullivan, and Nathanael Greene. At Washington's request, Major Horatio Gates, with whom he had served under Braddock and who was then absent at his Virginia estate, was appointed adjutant general, also with the rank of brigadier.

On June 10, in Philadelphia, 2,000 light infantrymen, grenadiers, riflemen, light horse, and artillerymen, all in uniform, went through the manual of arms and close-order drill in a public display, conducting their maneuvers, wrote John Adams, with "remarkable dexterity . . . so sudden a formation of an army never took place anywhere."

On the morning of the twenty-third, Washington, with a cavalry escort, accompanied by his aide-de-camp, Major Thomas Mifflin, his military secretary, Joseph Reed, and Generals Lee and Schuyler, set out by horseback for Cambridge in a light rain. A military band was playing, and admiring crowds lined the streets. As John Adams watched the troop go by, a kind of romantic envy got the better of him: "Oh that I were a soldier! I will be," he proclaimed in a letter to his wife; in another, with a touch of bitterness, he wrote, "Such is the pride and pomp of war. I, poor creature, worn out with scribbling for my bread and my liberty, low in spirits and weak in health, must leave others to wear the laurels which I have sown; others to eat the bread which I have earned; a common case." Yet it would not be long before he had occasion to revel, as the foremost man in Congress, in the immensity of the task destiny had placed in his hands.

"The business I have had upon my mind," he wrote with pride to Abigail a month later, on July 24, "has been as great and important as can be entrusted to man, and the difficulty and intricacy of it prodigious. When fifty or sixty men have a Constitution to form for a great empire, at the same time that they have a country of fifteen hundred miles in extent to fortify, millions to arm and train, a naval power to begin, an extensive commerce to regulate, numerous tribes of Indians to negotiate with, a standing army of twenty-seven thousand men to raise, pay, victual, and officer, I really shall pity those fifty or sixty men."

E V E N T S threatened to outpace the political deliberations. On the morning Congress had opened, Benedict Arnold and Ethan Allen, the latter with a band of his resolute Green Mountain Boys, had captured the British fortress at Ticonderoga on Lake Champlain.

Although the name of Benedict Arnold today is synonymous with "traitor," in May 1775 he was still a patriot, and much would transpire to his honor before his disgrace.

Born in Norwich, Connecticut, in 1741, Arnold had been a raucous adolescent—we might even call him a juvenile delinquent—prone to theft and other mischief, such as tying tin buckets to the tails of cows. He had physical strength beyond his years and daring, and at the age of twelve once challenged the local constable to a fight. On another occasion, he acquired a measure of local renown by clinging with his hands and feet to the waterwheel of a mill, which lifted him high into the air and then plunged him down into the rumbling depths of the race. At the same time, he was intelligent and could be studious, and after he was apprenticed to an apothecary at age thirteen, applied himself in earnest to the trade. Eight years later, he went into business on his own. He hung out a sign which read "B. ARNOLD, Druggist, Bookseller, &c., from London, *Sibi totique"* ("For himself and for everybody") and stocked his shop with a variety of potions, elixirs, tinctures, surgical instruments, cosmetics, jewelry, stationery supplies, pictures, prints, maps, and an assortment of books from the Old Testament in Hebrew to *Tom Jones.*

With prosperous enterprise, he expanded his little outlet in New Haven into a major concern, sailed on business to Canada and the West Indies, invested in horses, exchanged them for molasses, and engaged in various other speculative ventures beyond his shop. In time he acquired the honorific title of "Captain" and, with his commercial success, several vessels, warehouses, and a fine mansion on Water Street. Some of his commercial traffic was contraband, but in those days it was no mark of dishonor to be a smuggler. So when a sailor turned him in, Arnold banded together with several other merchants to make the man recant: "I, Peter Boles, not having the fear of God before my eyes, but being instigated by the Devil, did on the 24th instant [January 24, 1766], make information or endeavor to do the same, to one of the Custom House Officers for the port of New Haven, against Benedict Arnold, for importing contraband goods. I do hereby acknowledge I justly deserve a halter for my malicious and cruel intentions. I do solemnly swear I will never hereafter make information, directly or indirectly . . . against any person or persons whatever, for importing contraband or other goods into this Colony or any part of America."

Arnold was active in the local chapter of the Sons of Liberty, readily adopted their argument that the new British trade and tax policies tended to deny Americans their inherited rights, and denounced the Boston Massacre as "Cruel, Wanton & Inhuman Murders" deserving of revenge. "Good God, are the Americans all asleep & tamely giving up their glorious liberties," he wrote to a friend on June 9, 1770, from the West Indies, "or, are they all turned Philosophers that they don't take immediate vengeance on such miscreants; I am afraid of the latter and that we shall all see ourselves as poor and as much oppressed as ever heathen Philosopher was."

Arnold himself had little use for philosophy—or any of the humanities—as tending to ungainful employment, but he had a martial ardor which fitted him for the art of war. As a boy, he had tried to run away twice to join campaigns against the French and Indians, and in the winter of 1775 he helped organize a patriot militia unit, about sixty strong, in New Haven. They elected him their captain, and, like many citizen officers of the time, he did his best to absorb the standard military texts—

Caesar's commentaries on the Gallic Wars, accounts of Marshal Saxe's campaigns during the War of the Austrian Succession (1740–1748), the lives of Hannibal and Alexander the Great, and so on. When he learned of the bloodshed at Lexington and Concord, Arnold summoned his company to the public square and declared his willingness to lead them to Boston. They responded with a rousing cheer and raised their flag, which bore three grapevines on a yellow field and the motto QUI TRANSTULIT SUSTINET ("He who transplanted still sustains"). Under that enigmatic motto, they proceeded to Cambridge, smartly dressed in scarlet, white, and black—"the best drilled and the only perfectly uniformed and equipped company in the camp."

That made an impression. It gave Arnold credibility as an officer and access to the Cambridge military command. He met with the Massachusetts Committee of Public Safety, chaired by Joseph Warren, and proposed an expedition to seize the forts of Ticonderoga and Crown Point on Lake Champlain. These once mighty strongholds were known to be in dispair, moldering, and weakly garrisoned, yet equipped with enough cannon, shot, and other munitions to enable the Americans at Cambridge to maintain their siege. (Arnold estimated that there were "eighty pieces of heavy cannon, twenty brass guns, from four to eighteen pounders, and ten to twelve large mortars" at Ticonderoga alone.) Their strategic importance was also great: they commanded the northern approaches to the Hudson River and would be indispensable either in preparing an assault into Canada against the British or in thwarting any advance by British forces operating from a Canadian base. Arnold, who had occasionally traveled to Canada on business, accurately described the vulnerabilities of the forts, and told the committee he was certain that Fort Ticonderoga was defended by "not more than fifty men at the most. . . . The place could not hold out an hour against a vigorous onset." Warren, conferring with General Ward, endorsed the plan, and a few days later Arnold had a colonel's commission and authorization to recruit 400 men from among the settlements of the Berkshire Hills. He rode out of camp on May 3, but three days later, at Stockbridge, learned to his chagrin that he had been anticipated in the enterprise by Colonel Ethan Allen of Vermont, who held a parallel commission from Connecticut and who had started out at the head of 130 or so Green Mountain Boys.

The Green Mountain Boys belonged to an association of Vermont settlers formed for the purpose of ensuring their independence from New York. Allen was a kind of Vermont "nationalist" and a leader in the struggle to uphold the settlers' claims. He had been a farmer, a miner, and a land speculator and had fought as a ranger in the French and

Indian War. Physically powerful, impetuous, and unruly, with a kind of natural eloquence that blended folksy language and biblical quotes in an ornate and energetic style, he had "an original something in him," Washington later remarked, "that command[ed] admiration."

Arnold soon caught up with Allen at a tavern in Castleton, Vermont, where, after disputing each other's authority, they uneasily settled on a joint command. In a swift campaign, they made a forced march directly northwest and, on the evening of May 9, emerged onto the lakeshore opposite the fort. Having only one boat with which to effect their crossing, by dawn they had brought over just eighty-three of their two hundred or so men but decided to attack anyway while they still had the advantage of surprise. With Allen and Arnold at their head, the men rushed up a narrow path into the arched shadow of a port in the south wall, surprised a dozing sentry, and chased him through a covered way into the fort. The garrison's muskets, neatly stacked in the courtyard, were seized instantly, while another sentry led Allen to where the fort's commander slept. Allen summoned him at once, upon pain of losing his entire garrison. The officer immediately came to the door with his breeches in his hands. When Allen demanded the surrender of the fort, the officer asked by what authority. Allen replied: "In the name of the great Jehovah and the Continental Congress." Flabbergasted, the Englishman did not at first reply. Then Arnold added more intelligibly, "Give up your arms and you'll be treated like gentlemen." With that he obliged, and his garrison of forty men marched out. Stock was promptly taken of the captured arsenal, which amply answered all expectations and included a hundred pieces of artillery and some swivel guns, as well as many small arms.

"The sun seemed to rise that morning with a superior luster," recalled Allen in his memoirs. "Ticonderoga and its dependencies smiled on its conquerors, who tossed round the flowing bowl, and wished success to Congress and the liberty and freedom of America." Their cups overflowed. A number of the men raided a liquor cellar, where they found ninety gallons of rum, and, according to one of the British officers, there now followed a general "plunder."

On May 12, Crown Point, garrisoned by just thirteen British soldiers, in turn fell without resistance, yielding more arms and supplies. Five days later, Arnold himself armed a schooner and with fifty men surprised the equally small garrison at Saint Johns, eighty miles to the north. "Upon our briskly marching up in their faces," he wrote, "they retired within, left their arms, and resigned themselves into our hands. We took fourteen prisoners, fourteen stands of arms, and some small stores. We also took the King's sloop, two fine brass field-pieces, and four boats. We destroyed five boats more, lest they should be made use of against us." Though he had hoped to hold the post, he learned from his prisoners that British reinforcements were on their way and therefore prudently withdrew, but the three easy conquests (despite the misgivings of some in Congress) created a sensation that gave the rebellion tremendous confidence and heart.

CHAPTER FIVE

BOSTON

WHILE the Continental Congress had been trying to decide on a commander in chief to face the king's troops, the king had sent more troops to Boston, increasing their number to 10,000. On May 25, they disembarked under Generals William Howe, Henry Clinton, and John Burgoyne, who arrived on the warship *Cerberus*. Named for the three-headed canine monster of the underworld, the *Cerberus* (which had carried Wolfe to Québec in 1759 and had borne his body home to England after Québec fell) was supposed to connote invincibility. But one patriot rhyme mocked the three new generals as mere pups:

> Behold the *Cerberus* the Atlantic plough.
> Her precious cargo, Burgoyne, Clinton, Howe.
>   Bow, wow, wow.

The triumvirate's credentials, however, were not insubstantial. Howe, second in command to Gage, had fought in Flanders; America, during the French and Indian War; Cuba; and France. His older brother was the same Admiral Lord Richard Howe who had received Benjamin Franklin so cordially in London. Clinton and Burgoyne had both served with distinction in the Seven Years' War on the continent—Clinton in Brunswick, Burgoyne in Portugal. As the *Cerberus* cast anchor, Burgoyne reportedly exclaimed; "What! Ten thousand King's troops shut up? Well, let us get in, and we'll soon find elbow room."

The tactical options for both sides were fairly plain. Boston was dominated by high ground to the north and southeast. On Charlestown Neck to the north were two mounds, Bunker Hill and Breed's Hill, which lay half a mile across the estuary of the Charles River opposite Copp's Hill at the tip of the Boston peninsula. To the southeast, Dorchester Heights adjoined the harbor opposite Boston Neck.

On the same day Washington received his appointment, the Boston Committee of Public Safety had learned that General Gage planned to seize the high ground at Dorchester, to better defend his position and perhaps bombard the American camp. A few days before, on June 12, Gage had issued a proclamation promising to pardon all rebels—except Samuel Adams and John Hancock, who were said to deserve "condign punishment"—willing to lay down their arms. Those who retained their weapons were promised "fulness of Chastisement." But his offer fell on deaf ears.

Gage's overall plan (according to a letter written by Howe to his brother on the same day) was, first, to occupy and fortify Dorchester Heights and then, if possible, to advance across Roxbury to secure Boston from that side. From Roxbury, the British were to march to Charlestown and "attack the Rebels at Cambridge from the heights."

The rebel command got wind of the plan a few days in advance and in a preemptive strike moved at once to occupy Bunker Hill (actually Breed's Hill, an adjacent mound, afterward renamed) on the Charlestown Neck. On the night of June 16, 1,200 Massachusetts militiamen under the command of Colonel William Prescott established themselves on its summit and began erecting fortifications. As they worked through the night on a redoubt, parapet, and ditch, they could hear the sentinels on the British men-of-war crying "All's well." By daybreak they were so well entrenched that they had gained the advantage Gage had thought to have for himself. Looking at the hill through his spyglass, he asked an aide, "Who is that officer commanding?" The man recognized Colonel Prescott, who happened to be his brother-in-law. "Well, will he fight?" asked Gage. "Yes, Sir, depend upon it, to the last drop of blood in him, but I cannot answer for his men." His men would answer for themselves. At five-thirty in the morning, with their fort but half done, the British artillery opened up. The fire came primarily from three men-of-war, a number of floating batteries, and a fortification on Copp's Hill in Boston directly opposite the redoubt. "These," recalled an eyewitness, "kept up an incessant shower of shot and bombs" until about two in the afternoon, when ships anchored in the ferryway added their ordnance to the barrage. The intensity of the shelling reflected Gage's frustration and rage, but it was largely ineffectual, since the naval guns were direct-fire weapons and could not be elevated sufficiently to hit their mark. Yet a few shots, bounding or scudding up the slope, found their way into the fort. Colonel Prescott remembered the first man hit, who was decapitated: "He was so near me that my clothes were besmeared with his blood and brains, which I wiped off, in some degree, with a handful of fresh earth. The sight was so shocking to many of the men that they left their posts and ran to view him. I ordered them back, but in vain. I then ordered him to be buried instantly" to prevent the others from losing heart.

The cannonade let up about three P.M., but as the smoke cleared, the Americans beheld some forty barges of regulars crossing over with 1,550 men and a reserve of 700 under General Howe. Meanwhile, the defenders (still without sleep, exhausted from their all-night labors, and having had "little victuals," wrote a private, "and no drink but rum") continued to fortify, extending an earthwork to the left of their redoubt for about a hundred yards and breastworks, built up of fencing, bushes, and hay, almost to the Mystic River.

Spectators thronged to every elevated point which afforded a view of the scene—to Copp's Hill, rooftops, church steeples, the masts of vessels anchored at the wharves. They so far outnumbered the combatants that the whole area appeared "like unto an amphitheatre in which the battle was being staged." Everyone seemed to realize that it was not only a battle but the beginning of a war.

As the British troops disembarked, the fleet and the Copp's Hill battery redoubled their fire to cover the landing. Meanwhile, fresh rebel troops under Colonel John Stark of New Hampshire came marching up to the tune of "Yankee Doodle," increasing the strength of the defenders to 1,600 men. The lead pipes of the organ of Christ's Church, Cambridge, had been melted down to furnish them with bullets, but due to inadequate supply the men had guns of every possible caliber, so each had to hammer the balls given him into the appropriate shape. Others charged their muskets with angular pieces of iron and old nails. Those on the front line were now exhorted by their officers "to be cool" and to reserve their fire until the enemy "were near enough for us to see the whites of their eyes." General Israel Putnam of Connecticut went along the line, saying, "Fire low—take aim at the waistbands—pick off the commanders—aim at the handsome coats."

The carnage began. Gage could have landed his troops near the

Charlestown Neck causeway to Prescott's rear and, with the help of the great guns of his fleet, have completely cut off an American retreat. But unaccountably, or in a fatuous effort to prove the superior manhood of the British regulars, he decided on a frontal attack. The British advanced in two parties, one toward the rail fence, the other toward the redoubt. It was a blazing hot summer's day, and the troops were absurdly encumbered with blankets, knapsacks, and provisions, altogether weighing about 125 pounds per man. This was particularly fatiguing for those obliged to march up the hill's steep slope through the tall thick summer grass. Nevertheless, both columns advanced at first "with great confidence, expecting an easy victory" (wrote one British officer), until at forty yards' distance they were suddenly staggered, then ripped apart by "an incessant stream of fire poured from the rebel lines. It seemed a continued sheet of fire for near thirty minutes. . . . Most of our Grenadiers and Light Infantry the moment of presenting themselves lost three-fourths, and many nine-tenths, of their men. Some had only eight and nine men in a company left, some only three, four, and five."

"So precise and fatal was our fire," rejoiced an American, "that, in . . . a short time, they gave way and retired, leaving many wounded and killed."

At the bottom of the hill, opposite the rail fence, the British columns regrouped, advanced, fell back, and then advanced again. For two and a half hours the battle raged. Meanwhile, in response to sniper fire from Charlestown, where patriot marksmen had also taken post, the British bombarded the town with red-hot cannon balls and set its four hundred houses ablaze.

Burgoyne, viewing the battle from afar, found the spectacle unforgettable and afterward depicted it in a letter back home with almost cinematic detail:

> Now ensued one of the greatest scenes of war that can be conceived. If we look to the height, Howe's corps ascending the hill in the face of the entrenchments and in a very disadvantageous ground was much engaged. To the left the enemy pouring in fresh troops by thousands [actually hundreds] over the land, and in the arm of the sea our ships and floating batteries cannonading them. Straight before us, a large and noble town [Charlestown] in one great blaze. The church steeples being of timber were great pyramids of fire above the rest. Behind us, the church steeples and heights of our own camp [and] . . . the hills round the country covered with spectators. The enemy all in anxious suspense. The roar of cannon, mortars, and musketry, the crash of [Charlestown's] churches, ships upon the stocks, and whole streets falling together in ruins to fill the ear; the storm

of the redoubts with the objects above described to fill the eye, and the
reflection that perhaps a defeat would be a final loss to the British Empire
in America to fill the mind, made the whole a picture and a complication
of horror and importance beyond anything that ever came to my lot to be
witness to.

Howe's first and second assaults had been thrown back with equal
slaughter, and he experienced, he said, *"a moment that I never felt
before"* as he glimpsed what failure might mean. With a kind of stunned
simplicity, he said to his officers, "To be forced to give up Boston would,
gentlemen, be very disagreeable to us all."

Once more he formed his troops, brought cannon to bear so as to rake
the inside of the rebel breastwork, and made one final effort to storm it
as the British bombardment from the ships and batteries increased. Just
at this juncture, American ammunition gave out. Most of the men had
begun the battle with only about fifteen cartridges apiece. Many had
only two or three left. As the British surged up the slope, they were met
by two tremendous volleys. But then, as they came on, there was only
scattered shot. Yet the defenders, with incredible bravery, kept up what
fire they could until the British were upon them with their bayonets.
One British officer recalled, "There are few instances of regular troops
defending a redoubt till the enemy were in the very ditch of it, and [yet]
I myself saw several pop their heads up and fire even after some of our
men were upon the berm."

Ultimately the British prevailed, but not before they had lost a thousand of their own men (including ninety-two officers), or one-third of
the troops engaged. "The dead," said John Stark, "lay as thick as sheep
in a fold." American casualties (about half what the British suffered)
were also not inconsiderable, "but upon the whole," wrote General
Nathanael Greene of Rhode Island, "I think we have little reason to
complain. . . . I wish we could sell them another hill at the same price."
The most celebrated of the Americans to fall was Joseph Warren, author
of the Suffolk County Resolves, who had barely escaped death at Lexington two months before when a musket ball had taken off a lock of his
hair (rolled and pinned after the fashion of the day) close to his ear. At
Bunker Hill he had shown up as a volunteer soldier and, being among
the last to hold out, was felled with a point-blank shot to the back of his
head. It was afterward reported by Abigail Adams and others that he had
been decapitated by British officers, who carried his head "in triumph"
to General Gage.

Bunker Hill became sacred ground. Almost from the sunset of that day, it would be associated in human memory with Marathon and Plataea, and all the mighty struggles of determined free men.

As for General Gage, he soberly admonished the ministry back in London, "The rebels are not the despicable rabble too many have supposed them to be."

A s Washington rode north with Lee and Schuyler on June 23, a courier met them with a dispatch describing the battle. Washington wanted to know how the militia had fought. When he was told they had shown courage and even, at close quarters, had taken careful aim and withstood the enemy's fire, "it seemed as if a weight of doubt and solicitude was lifted from his heart. 'The liberties of the country, he exclaimed, are safe!' "

On July 2, Washington reached the camp at Cambridge and formally took command of the Continental Army before the Harvard College walls. Two days later, on July 4, he announced:

> The Continental Congress having now taken all the Troops of the several Colonies which have been raised, or which may be hereafter raised for the support and defence of the Liberties of America; into their Pay and Service. They are now the Troops of the UNITED PROVINCES of North America; and it is hoped that all Distinctions of Colonies will be laid aside; so that one and the same Spirit may animate the whole, and the only Contest be, who shall render, on this great and trying occasion, the most essential service to the great and common cause in which we are all engaged.

Gage now organized Boston to withstand a general siege. As patriot refugees streamed out, Tories, or loyalists, streamed in. Before long, most of the original inhabitants of Boston had left, replaced by about 5,000 British sympathizers and 14,000 enemy troops. The city became an armed camp. Although the British controlled the harbor, they were largely cut off from supplies of fuel and food and forced to subsist on beans and salt pork. "The rebels certainly block up our town and cut off our good beef and mutton," complained one British captain. "At present we are completely blockaded and subsisting almost on salt provisions."

Gage declared martial law with a ten P.M. curfew, and, according to Abigail Adams, "no man dared to be seen talking to his friend in the street." On July 25, in a fit of paranoia, he also made it a crime for anyone to be seen "to wipe his face with a white handkerchief," which he took to be "a signal of mutiny."

In the patriot army, the four original contingents had come from Massachusetts, Rhode Island, Connecticut, and New Hampshire, under the command, respectively, of Generals Artemas Ward, Nathanael Greene, Israel Putnam, and Colonel John Stark. Some of the troops had served in the French and Indian War or had skirmished with Indians on the frontier, "but none," wrote Washington Irving, "were acquainted with regular service or the discipline of European armies. . . . Most of them were hasty levies of yeomanry, some of whom had seized their rifles and fowling-pieces and turned out in their working-clothes and homespun country garbs. It was an army of volunteers." Powder and shot were scarce (the Massachusetts Congress had failed to obtain the arms it had hoped to buy), and all the artillery was light—nine fieldpieces and no heavy guns. Although some of the men carried a powder horn, ammunition pouch, and knapsack (and a wooden bottle for rum), they lacked basic provisions of all kinds, from cartridges to blankets to kitchen utensils to tents. Their motley encampments, spread over an area ten to twelve miles in diameter, were made up of improvised dwellings—sailcloth tents, board hovels, stone, and turf.

In the hectic command structure, such as it was, under Ward, the Massachusetts Committee of Public Safety had been heavily involved in intelligence and military planning, while rank and commissions for the junior officers at first depended chiefly on the number of soldiers they could bring in. Under such an ad hoc corps, men often went their own way and "frowned on all notions of discipline because they spoiled the fun of soldiering."

Thus far the men had done remarkably well, but as historian Edmund Morgan points out, the rout of the British on the way back from Concord, together with the Battle of Bunker Hill, had given many patriots "an over-confidence in the prowess of militia against regular troops."

Now Washington proceeded to give to the assembled multitude the form and discipline of a regular force.

He first tackled the issue of rank. Jealous enmities had been aroused as a result of the hierarchy created by Congress, and it was incumbent upon him to see these breaches were repaired at once. General Spencer, for example, had outranked General Putnam in the Connecticut service but was now, for no reason he could comprehend, his subordinate in the Continental Army. General John Thomas likewise declared himself unwilling to accept the seniority of General William Heath. Washington smoothed and conciliated egos, exalted all to a patriotic forbearance and solidarity, and showed favor by personal deference to those who earned his respect.

But overall his task was an unpleasant one. In New England, wrote Joseph Reed, his military secretary, "where the principles of democracy so universally prevail, where so great an equality and so thorough a leveling spirit predominates," anyone laying down the law "must become odious and detestable." Washington accepted the onus and "there was a great overturning," at every level, wrote one army chaplain, "as to order and regularity. New lords, new laws. . . . New orders from his Excellency are read to the respective regiments every morning after prayers. The strictest government is taking place and great distinction is made between officers and soldiers. Everyone is made to know his place and keep in it, or be immediately tied up, and receive not one but thirty or forty lashes according to his crime. Thousands are at work every day from four till eleven o'clock in the morning. It is surprising the work that has been done." Court-martials became common—for disorderly conduct, insubordination, theft, drunkenness, and other transgressions —and there was a new emphasis on religious observance in camp. In this, Washington was not only following his own inclination but executing the will of Congress, as laid out in the sixty-nine articles of war drawn up by one of its committees and approved on June 30 for the regulation of the new force. One of the articles "earnestly recommended to all officers and soldiers, diligently to attend Divine Service" and imposed severe penalties on those who behaved "indecently or irreverently at any place" where divine worship was held.

Under Washington, a commissariat was established; work crews were detailed to pluck fruit from surrounding orchards and harvest fields of corn; trees were cut down for fortifications, firewood, and other purposes; and every day carts rumbled into Cambridge bringing food, clothing, and medicine from the Merrimac and Connecticut River valleys and the Berkshire Hills.

In all this Washington scarcely missed a beat, except in one respect. In his correspondence, yielding to a certain aristocratic bias, he carelessly disparaged the New England troops. He wrote to his cousin Lund Washington:

They are the most indifferent kind of people I ever saw. . . . I have already broke one colonel and five captains for cowardice and for drawing more pay and provisions than they had men in their companies. There are two more colonels now under arrest and to be tried for the same offenses. In short, they are by no means such troops, in any respect, as you are led to believe of them from the accounts which are published, but I need not make myself enemies among them by this declaration, although it is consistent with truth. I daresay the men would fight very well (if properly Officered) although they are an exceedingly dirty and nasty people.

This kind of talk, even in confidence, soon got Washington into trouble. John Adams, in recommending Washington to his Massachusetts compatriots, had previously said, "I hope the people of our province will treat the General with all that confidence and affection, that politeness and respect, which is due to one of the most important characters in the world. The liberties of America depend upon him, in a great degree." But when he got wind of these aspersions, he sternly admonished the commander in chief indirectly in a letter to his artillery commander, Henry Knox: "Pray tell me, Colonel Knox, does every man to the southward of Hudson's River behave like a hero, and every man to the northward of it like a poltroon, or not? . . . I must say that your amiable general gives too much occasion for these reports by his letters, in which he often mentions things to the disadvantage of some part of New England, but seldom any thing of the kind about any other part of the continent." He might have added that Washington owed his appointment to an effort to unite North and South and to banish the sectional prejudice that existed between them even then.

To his credit, Washington took the rebuke to heart. His staff appointments thereafter, and all his public remarks, were almost religiously balanced by region, and there would be times during the war when he would bend so far over backwards not to single out southern troops for praise as to seem almost prejudiced in reverse.

John Adams, not incidentally, privately acknowledged the poor impression New Englanders might make. "My countrymen want art and address," he said. "They want knowledge of the world. They want the exterior and superficial accomplishment of gentlemen, upon which the world has set so high a value." Yet "in solid abilities and real virtues," he added, "they vastly excel any people upon this continent"—thereby making himself guilty of the very bias he'd condemned.

Nathanael Greene more truly recognized Washington's opinions for what they were:

His Excellency . . . has not had time to make himself acquainted with the genius of this people. They are naturally as brave and spirited as the peasantry of any other country, but you cannot expect veterans of a raw militia of only a few months' service. The common people are exceedingly avaricious; the genius of the people is commercial from their long intercourse with trade. The sentiment of honor, the true characteristic of a soldier, has not yet got the better of interest. His Excellency has been taught to believe the people here a superior race of mortals, and finding them of the same temper and disposition, passions and prejudices, virtues and vices of the common people of other governments, they sink in his esteem.

Nevertheless, regional tensions sometimes got the upper hand. The student dorms at Harvard had been turned into barracks, and in Harvard Yard one day a snowball fight that began with some bantering between Virginia riflemen and troops from Marblehead, Massachusetts (chiefly fishermen and sailors), turned into a free-for-all fistfight in which as many as a thousand took part. According to one eyewitness, Washington soon appeared, dismounted, and "rushing into the thickest of the melee, seized two tall brawny riflemen by the throat" and shook them vigorously to break it up.

Unity was all. At Cambridge, the first Continental flag was unfurled, with thirteen alternating red and white stripes (though the British Union Jack remained in its upper-left-hand corner), and the lyrics for the tune of "Yankee Doodle" emerged in substantially the version everybody knows:

> Yankey doodle keep it up,
> Yankey doodle dandy,
> Mind the music and the step,
> And with the girls be handy.

Originally a British marching tune with words dating back to the French and Indian War, it had appeared (as noted earlier) in Andrew Barton's comic opera *The Disappointment,* with bawdy, punning lyrics about the manic quest by some Philadelphians for Blackbeard's buried treasure. As a marching tune, its lyrics had expressed "contempt for provincial rusticity," and British reinforcements had sung the song on their way to Lexington on April 19. But after they had been mauled on the way back, the song became the patriots' own. Soon thereafter, it was published as "Yenkee Doodle, or The Lexington March," in mockery of the British defeat.

I F Washington demanded much of others, he expected much of himself. Expectations were also great upon him, and he understood the symbolic importance of a commander in chief appearing grand. But he was not greatly pleased at some of the extravagant conceptions of him, for ballad makers had already gone to work to frame their songs of praise:

> We have a bold commander, who fears not sword nor gun,
> The second Alexander—his name is Washington.
> His men are all collected, and ready for the fray.
> To fight they are directed—for North Americay.

In a similar vein, the poet Philip Freneau apostrophized him as "a second Diomede," "whose actions might have aw'd / A Roman Hero, or a Grecian God." Freneau also reminded the soldiers at Cambridge that "like ancient Romans, you / At once are soldiers, and are farmers too." And he contrasted the effete British officer with his American counterpart:

> No fop in arms, no feather on his head,
> No glittering toys the manly warrior had,
> His auburne face the least employ'd his care,
> He left it to the females to be fair. . . .

From the beginning, the drama was played out in the American mind as a morality play of Virtue against Vice. The theme had long been a commonplace of the patriotic literature, and Washington's legendary integrity of character accorded with it well. So did the story told of General Israel Putnam, for example, the farmer-soldier par excellence, who reportedly first learned of the Battle of Lexington as he was following his horse-drawn plow. General Burgoyne, on the other hand, was said to have been in a brothel when he received word of his American command. Another story told of Putnam came out of the French and Indian War, in which he had commanded a body of provincial troops. Like Washington, he had had to put up with the disdainful disregard of British officers, and one day one of them had challenged him to a duel. It was Putnam's privilege to choose the weapons, and he chose to have each of them sit on a keg of gunpowder furnished with a slow-burning fuse. The first man to be blown up would lose. The kegs were brought and the matches lit. Putnam sat with folded arms, his nose in the air, his hat cocked over one eye, his heels casually kicking the barrel staves. The Englishman, or the other hand, "disturbed by the approach of the flame and his unusual situation," suddenly jumped off the barrel and withdrew to a safe distance in disgrace.

By the end of July, Washington had his army organized. Thirty-five infantry battalions (18,538 enlisted men and 1,109 officers) had been grouped into regiments, in turn gathered into brigades. Whenever possible, units from the same colony had also been brigaded together for morale. But to create the appearance of a truly national army, these regiments were also given numerical (rather than provincial) titles—for example, the 1st Continental Regiment (which was made up of Pennsylvanians) or the 14th Continental Regiment (made up of Massachusetts men). By late August, Washington had also completed his defense lines, which extended from Cambridge to the Mystic River, and he could therefore report, "We [have] nothing more, in my opinion, to fear from the enemy, provided we can keep our men to their duty and make them watchful and vigilant."

The right wing of the army was stationed on the heights of Roxbury under Generals Ward, Spencer, and Thomas; the left wing at Prospect Hill under Generals Lee, Sullivan, and Greene; the center at Cambridge under Generals Putnam and Heath.

Military talent arose in unexpected places. There was, for example, Henry Knox, a portly, personable young man who had run the London Bookshop in Boston, where British officers often liked to browse. Knox had had quite a few books on the art of war and was himself particularly interested in the deployment of artillery, having joined an artillery company in his youth as a volunteer. He had discussed the subject avidly with the officers who came by and had emerged from his informal tutelage an expert on ordnance upon whom Washington could rely. Washington (who never had occasion to regret it) made Knox his captain of artillery and ultimately a general. After the Revolution, he would become America's first secretary of war.

Another American original was Brigadier General Nathanael Greene, a Quaker who had been expelled from the Society of Friends for supporting armed resistance to England. Raised to run the family gristmill and ironworks, he had taught himself mathematics, history, and political theory and was apparently a good Latinist as well. As a member of the Rhode Island Assembly, he had been prominent in the organization of the state militia and in May had led three Rhode Island regiments to assist the siege of Boston. But like many other such officers, his military rank primarily reflected his civic stature rather than his experience of war. Henry Knox later said of him, "His knowledge was intuitive. He came to us the rawest and most untutored being I ever met with; but in less than twelve months he was equal in military knowledge to any general officer in the army, and very superior to most." Washington came to regard him as his most capable general and the one best suited to succeed him in the command.

At the beginning of the war, however, the presumptive heir was Charles Lee. Born in Wales, Lee had come to America in 1756 as a captain of grenadiers. He had fought in Braddock's disastrous campaign, where he had first met Washington and Horatio Gates, and had been severely wounded in the failed British attempt under Abercrombie to take Fort Ticonderoga from the French. While in America, he became interested in Indian affairs, was adopted into the Mohawk tribe of the Bear, and took an Indian wife. He wrote his sister with a kind of quaint frankness, "My wife is daughter to the famous White Thunder who is Belt of Wampum to the Senakas—which is in fact their Lord Treasurer. She is a very great beauty, and is more like your friend Mrs. Griffith than anybody I know. I shall say nothing of her accomplishments, for you must be certain that a woman of her fashion cannot be without many . . . if you will allow good breeding to consist in a constant desire to do everything that will please you, and a strict carefulness not to say or do anything that may offend you." Subsequently, having left his Indian wife behind, he served gallantly in Portugal under Burgoyne, but a few years later, frustrated by his lack of advancement, he left England for Poland, where he held the rank of major general in the army of the king. As a soldier of fortune, he traveled all over Europe, fighting for various princes, and engaged in several duels. In one of them, in Italy, he lost two fingers of one hand in a sword fight, whereupon recourse was had to pistols and he shot his opponent dead.

Lee was learned, bookish, something of a linguist, with competence in Italian, Spanish, German, and French, and perhaps a capable officer. He was the most widely read if not wisest member of Washington's staff but he was also a disagreeable character, slovenly, profane, "plain in his person even to ugliness" (wrote Mercy Warren), morose, testy, cynical, licentious, and rude. The Mohawks, in acknowledgment of his irascible temperament, had given him the nickname "Boiling Water," and a surgeon who successfully treated his wounds after one battle later tried to kill him in revenge for his spiteful abuse. Ambitious of fame, he was without the dignity to support it, and he lacked the broader understanding or wisdom that alone makes accomplishments worthwhile. Perhaps his most conspicuous eccentricity was a "remarkable partiality for dogs." Two or three accompanied him wherever he went—even into the parlors and salons of elegant homes—where they squatted on chairs beside him at dinner and "lapped up the food from plates." One of them, a huge Pomeranian, was said to resemble a bear. When Abigail Adams met

Lee at a reception at headquarters, he was "determined that I should not only be acquainted with him but with his companions too and therefore placed a chair before me, into which he ordered Mr. Spada (his dog) to mount and present his paw."

With ambiguous disparagement, given his predilection, Lee sometimes called Washington's aides "puppies"—but that was when he and the commander in chief got along.

W H I L E Washington was laboring in the siege lines outside Boston, the Second Continental Congress in Philadelphia was demonstrating a comparable industry on the political front. John Adams had laid out its incredibly ambitious agenda, and to meet its imperatives, the delegates kept long hours. There were committees to promote the manufacture of saltpeter for gunpowder, to locate and mine lead and other ores, to arrange for the printing of paper money, to deal with Indian affairs, to organize a postal service, to regulate American trade, and so on. John Adams wrote to Abigail, "The whole Congress is taken up, almost, in different committees from seven to ten in the morning. From ten to four or sometimes five, we are in Congress, and from six to ten, in committees again. I don't mention this to make you think me a man of importance, because it is not I alone, but the whole Congress is thus employed, but to apologize for not writing to you oftener."

"My time was never more fully employed," wrote Benjamin Franklin to a friend in England. "In the morning at six, I am at the [Pennsylvania] Committee of Safety, appointed by the Assembly to put the province in a state of defence; which committee holds till near nine, when I am at the Congress, and that sits till after four in the afternoon. . . . It will scarce be credited in Britain, that men can be as diligent with us from zeal in the public good, as with you for thousands per annum. Such is the difference between uncorrupted new states, and corrupted old ones."

Franklin also sat on the new Committee of Secret Correspondence (forerunner of the Department of State), which was said, disingenuously, to have been created "for the sole purpose of corresponding with our friends in Great Britain, Ireland and other parts of the world."

The monetary requirements of the Revolution were considerable, and without money of its own or any authority to raise it directly, the Congress decided it might have to print it. At the same time, it called on each colony to make such appropriations, including by taxation, as would "sink its proportion of the bills ordered to be emitted by this Congress" in contribution to the common cause. As the nonimportation feature of the Continental Association had actually hurt America more than Britain, by causing shortages and inflation and preventing the acquisition of gunpowder and other war matériel, Congress decided to authorize trade in military stores.

But, perhaps inevitably, the assembly often seemed to move without the requisite dispatch. As Adams explained to his wife, "America is a great, unwieldy body. Its progress must be slow. It is like a large fleet sailing under convoy. The fleetest sailers must wait for the dullest and slowest. Like a coach and six, the swiftest horses must be slackened, and the slowest quickened, that all may keep an even pace."

In contrast to the lavish feasts of the first Congress, there was more dietary restraint. "Let us eat potatoes and drink water," Adams exhorted his fellow delegates (in his diary). "Let us wear canvas, and undressed sheepskins, rather than submit to the unrighteous and ignominious domination that is prepared for us."

Yet it remained their convivial habit to meet after hours and socialize at taverns, where they shared more than politics in their cups. In a way, it was a setting in which the life of culture bloomed. John Adams has left us a charming picture of the meetings of the first Naval Committee at the waterfront Tun Tavern in Philadelphia. At the time, the committee was made up of seven men, including Adams, Stephen Hopkins, Christopher Gadsden, and Richard Henry Lee. "Mr. Lee, Mr. Gadsden, were sensible men, and very cheerful," recalled Adams,

> but Governor Hopkins of Rhode Island, above seventy years of age, kept us all alive. Upon business, his experience and judgment were very useful. But when the business of the evening was over, he kept us in conversation till eleven, and sometimes twelve o'clock. His custom was to drink nothing all day, nor till eight o'clock in the evening, and then his beverage was Jamaica spirit and water. It gave him wit, humor, anecdotes, science and learning. He had read Greek, Roman, and British history, and was familiar with English poetry, particularly Pope, Thomson, and Milton, and the flow of his soul made all his reading our own, and seemed to bring to recollection in all of us, all we had ever read. . . . Hopkins never drank to excess, but all he drank was immediately not only converted into wit, sense, knowledge, and good humor, but inspired us with similar qualities.

During the Second Continental Congress, John Dickinson, who had formerly stood in the vanguard of the antitax revolt, emerged as leader of the moderate conservative faction. His was to be the insistent voice of conciliation. But he was not a covert loyalist, and in collaboration with

Jefferson he drew up a militant "Declaration of the Causes for Taking Up Arms":

> We are reduced to the alternative of chusing between an unconditional submission to the tyranny of irritated ministers, or resistance by force. The latter is our choice. We have counted the cost of this contest, and find nothing so dreadful as voluntary slavery. . . . Our cause is just. Our union is perfect. Our internal resources are great, and, if necessary, foreign assistance is undoubtedly attainable. . . . The arms we have been compelled by our enemies to assume, we will, in defiance of every hazard, with unabating firmness and perseverance, employ for the preservation of our liberties; being with one mind resolved to dye Freemen rather than live Slaves.

This document, threatening war (but not independence), was adopted by Congress on July 6, and on the tenth it was artfully coupled with a second petition to the king. The latter, also drafted by Dickinson—both out of deference to him and as "signal proof," explained Jefferson, "of . . . their [collective] desire not to go too fast for any respectable part of our body"—assured the monarch that if only the causes of disagreement could be removed, he would find his "faithful subjects on this continent ready and willing at all times, as they ever have been, with their lives and fortunes, to assert and maintain the rights and interests of your Majesty, and of our Mother country."

In approving this petition, many delegates had to suppress the discomfort they felt. Although there was still resistance to a formal break with Britain, more had now come around to the revolutionary point of view. Among the latter was George Wythe, Jefferson's law professor, who had been among those to shout "Treason" in interrupting Patrick Henry's famous speech at Saint John's, Richmond, in 1765. He now took his stand "against the supine and futile policy of sending abject petitions to a monarch indifferent to colonial rights." John Adams wrote, harshly, "This measure of imbecility will find many admirers among the ladies and fine gentlemen, but it will not be to my taste." Nevertheless, most (such as Charles Thomson of Pennsylvania) saw it as tactically wise, "else it would have been impossible to convince the bulk of the people of Pennsylvania that an humble petition . . . would not have met with a favorable reception and produced the desired effect."

In the end, a modest majority—eight of the thirteen delegations (New York, New Jersey, Pennsylvania, Delaware, Maryland, North Carolina, South Carolina, and Georgia)—voted to adopt it. Wrote Franklin, "We have . . . give[n] Britain one more chance, one opportunity more, of recovering the friendship of the colonies; which, however, I think she has not sense enough to embrace, and so I conclude she has lost them for ever."

Meanwhile, the congressional debate had been devisive and nasty and had led to a bitter rift between Dickinson and Adams, who had ridiculed Dickinson behind his back. In a letter to a friend in Boston Adams had referred to him as "a piddling genius" who had "given a silly cast to our whole doings," but the missive was intercepted by the British and promptly published in the Tory *Massachusetts Gazette*. Alongside it appeared a forged addition to another letter that had been intercepted from Virginia delegate Benjamin Harrison to Washington, suggesting that the commander in chief was a libertine. "As I was in the pleasing task of writing to you," Harrison supposedly wrote,

a little noise occasioned me to turn my head around and who should appear but pretty little Kate, the washerwoman's Daughter over the way, clean, trim and rosy as the morning. I snatched the golden glorious Opportunity, and but for that cursed Antidote to Love, Sukey [some intruder], I had fitted her for my General against his return. We were obliged to part, but not until we had contrived to meet again; if she keeps the appointment I shall relish a week's longer stay. I give you now and then some of these adventures to amuse you and unbend your mind from the cares of War.

The *London Gazette* expanded upon the theme:

Mr. Benj. Harrison exhibits to us a picture of American hypocrisy . . . ; for while he and his rebel brethren of the Congress are incessantly clamoring [virtue] . . . he is at the same time debauching all the pretty girls in his neighborhood on purpose to raise a squadron of whores to keep his old General warm during the winter quarters. . . . It has become fashionable in America for the Saints to have their procurers and their Delilahs. Whilst the General is fighting the Lord's battles in Massachusetts, his procurer, the holy Mr. Benj. Harrison, is fitting pretty little Kate, his washerwoman's daughter, for the Lord's General. Even Hancock, who presides over and directs the collective wisdom and virtue of all America, travels with a vestal in his train.

These slanders were disregarded; but the letter from Adams was real. Not long afterward, Adams passed Dickinson on the street "near enough to have touched elbows," but Dickinson passed him by "without moving his hat or head or hand." Whereupon Adams then decided, a bit childishly, that in the future he would refuse to acknowledge him, too.

The divisive petition proved in vain. Congress learned that King George had contemptuously refused even to read it and on August 23 had already declared, by royal proclamation, that the American rebels were to be put down by force. On October 26, he had told Parliament, "The authors and promoters of this desperate conspiracy . . . meant only to amuse, by vague expressions of attachment to the parent state and the strongest protestations of loyalty to me, whilst they were preparing for a general revolt. . . . The rebellious war now levied is . . . manifestly carried on for the purpose of establishing an independent empire." To Lord North he declared, "I am unalterably determined at every hazard and at every risk of every consequence to compel the colonies to absolute submission," since "it would be better totally to abandon them than to admit a single shadow of their doctrines."

M E A N W H I L E , at the end of September, Brigadier General Nathanael Greene had called at headquarters with information that would identify Dr. Benjamin Church, a member of the innermost circle of patriot leaders and the army's surgeon general, as a British spy. During prerevolutionary days, Church had socialized with British officers, ostensibly to extract information from them but in fact to disclose patriot secrets in return for cash. As in later instances of such treason, there had been plenty of signs. One of Church's medical assistants, for example, later recalled that on some days Church "seemed to have no money by him, then all at once he had several hundred new British guineas in hand."

Educated at the Boston Latin School and Harvard, Church had studied medicine in London but upon returning to Boston plunged into revolutionary politics. He was one of the civic leaders to protest the Boston Massacre in 1770, later giving a physician's expert deposition at the trial; wrote patriotic poems and satires; delivered a fiery oration on the third anniversary of the Boston Massacre; and had served on the Boston Committee of Correspondence, as a delegate to the Massachusetts Provincial Congress in 1774, and on its Committee of Public Safety in 1775. Revere later remembered that he had run into him in Cambridge the day after Lexington and Concord, and that he had pointed to blood on his stocking, claiming it had come from a man killed by his side.

His appointment as surgeon general had come at the end of July. No one knows when he first ended up on the British payroll, but he had evidently been transmitting top secret information to the enemy for some time.

In August, Church had entrusted a letter, written in cipher, to a Boston prostitute to convey to British lines. The woman, who was his mistress and then pregnant with his child, had sought out a former customer to obtain his help. But the man became uneasy at her furtive manner. He accepted the letter and took it to a local schoolmaster, who promptly broke the seal. The two of them saw that it was in code and turned it over to the revolutionary authorities. The letter made its way from one official to another until it lay on Washington's desk.

The prostitute was brought in and under questioning revealed that the letter had been given to her by Church. Church was sent for and acknowledged the letter but claimed it contained nothing incriminating and had been intended for his brother, who was still in Boston. Yet he declined to render it into English. Washington's cryptographers managed to do that soon enough and found that it described the strength and equipment of the Continental forces, divulged a plan then being drawn up for commissioning privateers, and alluded to another top secret Canadian operation under discussion. The letter concluded, "Make use of every precaution or I perish."

When John Adams heard the news, he wrote, "I stand astonished. A Man of genius, of Learning, of Family, of Character, a Writer of Liberty Songs and good ones, too, a speaker of liberty orations. . . . Good God! What shall we say of human nature? What shall we say of American patriots?" Another delegate exclaimed, "Who could have thought or even suspected it, a man who seemed to be all animation in the cause of his Country, highly caressed, employed in several very honorable and lucrative departments, and in full possession of the confidence of his country, what a complication of madness and wickedness must a soul be filled with to be capable of such Perfidy! What punishment can equal such horrid crimes?"

None dire but what his own conscience might have imposed. Although tried, convicted, and imprisoned for several months in Norwich, Connecticut, under a special guard, Church was released due to ill health in the spring of 1776 and eventually allowed to embark for the West Indies. The vessel he sailed on disappeared without a trace.

C H U R C H had betrayed not only secrets of military planning but (potentially more damaging) facts about the real condition of the Continental troops. From the beginning, Washington had tried to project his force as a strong one, but in fact it lacked many necessities, including adequate munitions, food, clothing, and other supplies. Clothing was not easy to come by since the production of cloth had long been willfully suppressed and potential competition from the colonies had been re-garded in Britain with jealous eyes. As early as 1699, the Crown had banned the exportation to England of American wool or woolen materi-als and remained wary of the development of any local expertise. In 1705, Lord Cornbury, the transvestite governor of New York, had warned that he had seen serge made on Long Island "that any man might wear; they make very good linen for common use; as for Woollen I think they have brought that to too great perfection." Nevertheless, every farmer grew flax, and sheep were prized above all other domestic animals for their wool, to be spun into thread and yarn, then knitted or woven into cloth. Spinning wheels and hand looms were fixtures in every home, and major towns occasionally held spinning contests—for example, at the fourth anniversary of the Boston Society for Promoting Industry and Frugality, when three hundred young spinsters assembled on Boston Common with their wheels. But the relatively coarse homespun gar-ments of the colonists, such as had been worn in protest during the tax revolt, could not compare to what was being turned out by the English in their factories near the Malvern Hills.

In August, the Massachusetts Provincial Congress, foreseeing that the siege of Boston would continue into the winter months, had made a general appeal on behalf of the army for thirteen thousand winter coats. The country responded. That fall, in virtually every colony, women worked their wool wheels and hand looms to make them; inside each coat, they sewed their own name and the name of the town in which they lived. Any soldier volunteering for eight months' service received one as a bounty, and it was a grudging tribute to their fame that the English sneeringly began to call Washington's army "Homespuns" in the first days of the war.

The troops also needed gunpowder, which few Americans knew how to make. There were times when the only powder the army had was in the powder horns carried by the men, and in August, Washington had confided to a correspondent that he had "but 32 barrels" in his maga-zines. At one time the Continental Congress had even discussed a scheme to arm American infantrymen with pikes (in lieu of British bayo-nets) and bows and arrows, due to the lack of powder and shot. In June, Abigail Adams, writing to John from their "yet quiet cottage" in Weymouth, had put it succinctly: "We live in continual expectation of alarms. Courage I know we have in abundance; conduct I hope we shall not want; but powder,—where shall we get a sufficient supply?"

At the time, the manufacture of gunpowder was something of a closely guarded secret. Saltpeter, its indispensable ingredient, was procured pri-marily from the East Indies or Persia, and numerous trade regulations controlled its conveyance and supply. But several powder mills had been established in the colonies during the French and Indian War, and after Paul Revere toured one facility near Philadelphia, taking careful notes on its operation, other mills were hurriedly built at Andover and Canton, Massachusetts.

The need for cannon foundries was also acute, and eventually, in the winter of 1776, Louis de Maresquelle, a French artillery captain, arrived to help show the rebels how to mix their ores with minerals for casting and how to bore their cannon after they were cast.

BUNKER Hill had been followed by months of static confrontations, with the two sides occasionally clashing on patrol or when American working parties approached too near the British lines. The occasional cannonades by the British were incredibly ineffectual. One Saturday, for example, according to Henry Knox, "they fired one hundred and four cannon-shot at our works, at not a greater distance than half pointblank shot,—and did what? Why, scratched a man's face with the splinters of a rail fence!" But Congress eventually grew impatient with the situation and in a secret resolution passed at the end of November urged an all-out attack (should Washington and his council think it advisable), "notwithstanding the town and property be destroyed."

At his headquarters in Cambridge, Washington pored over maps and intelligence reports, looking for vulnerabilities in the British land defenses while reportedly leaving one road out of Boston deliberately unimpeded to entice the British out. At the same time, he armed coastal schooners to interdict supplies coming to the British by sea. These vessels operated off the New England coast during the fall and winter and captured many prizes, including, in mid-December, a British ordnance ship laden with several tons of ammunition and two thousand muskets.

The British in turn made attempts to draw off Washington's army by attacking along the coast. But Washington was onto their game. When various settlements appealed for his protection, he was constrained to note that every part of the coast exposed to such depredations had "an equal claim" upon his army and that it would be futile—indeed, self-destructive—to break up his force into numerous coastal patrols. "The great advantage the enemy have of transporting troops by being masters of the sea will enable them to harass us by diversions of this kind," he explained, and no matter what he could do, "a great part of the coast must still be left unprotected." To try to protect it all "would amount to a dissolution of the army."

As it was, the army was held together by a thread. More than any lack of money, clothing, or arms, the greatest threat to its viability was the terms of enlistment by which the recruits came in. Most had enlisted for the short term, and for all New England troops that term was due to expire by December 31.

In October, Franklin had gone to Cambridge to consult with Washington on his ideas for the reorganization of the army, including his request that 20,000 men be enlisted for at least a year. On November 4, Congress endeavored to comply, resolving that the Continental forces be grouped into twenty-six infantry regiments (each having eight companies, or 728 men), one rifle regiment, and one artillery regiment, effective January 1. Endeavoring to reconstitute his army before it disintegrated, Washington had launched a recruiting drive in October, hoping especially to persuade veterans to remain. But the results had been disappointing. Patriotic enthusiasm among many of the troops had subsided, "a casualty, perhaps, of the new military discipline and the boredom of siege life." Yet it is not surprising that so many of these men—local fishermen and farmers among them—wished to "retire into a chimney-corner," as Washington put it, since the New England winters were hard, in camp were bound to be harder, and such suffering, "almost within sight of the smoke of their own firesides," seemed too much to bear. By November 28, only 2,540 men, or a fraction more than 10 percent of the projected number, had signed up.

A few days later, Washington wrote to Joseph Reed, who had returned to Philadelphia, "After the last of this month, our lines will be so weakened that the minutemen and militia must be called in for their defense; these being under no kind of government themselves will destroy the little subordination I have been laboring to establish and run me into one evil, whilst I am endeavoring to avoid another." By January, only 12,649 Continentals had enlisted, but that was not nearly enough, and he was obliged to call out 7,000 militia to help man his lines. "Search the vast volumes of history through," he wrote,

> and I much question whether a case similar to ours is to be found; to wit to maintain a post against the flower of the British troops for six months together, without powder, and at the end of them to have one army disbanded and another to raise within the same distance of a reinforced enemy. What may be the issue of the last manoeuvre, time only can unfold. . . . How it will end, God, in his great goodness, will direct. I am thankful for his protection to this time. We are told that we shall soon get the army completed but I have been told so many things which have never come to pass that I distrust everything.

His predicament gave him many sleepless nights. "I have oftentimes thought how much happier I should have been," he claimed,

> if, instead of accepting the command under such circumstances, I had taken my musket on my shoulder and entered the ranks; or, if I could have justified the measure to posterity and my own conscience, had retired to the back country and lived in a wigwam. If I shall be able to rise superior to these and many other difficulties which might be enumerated, I shall most religiously believe that the finger of Providence is in it to blind the eyes of our enemies, for surely if we get well through this month it must be for want of their knowing the disadvantages which we labor under.

Such disadvantages had obliged him to turn a siege into a mere blockade and had made him uneasy about seeking a general engagement. But the public (and many in Congress) faulted him for this, being under the impression that his army had been increased, according to quota, to the authorized strength of 20,000 well-armed men. In fact, he had less than half that number, "including sick, furloughed and on command, and those neither armed nor clothed as they should be. In short," he confided to Reed on February 10, "my situation has been such that I have been obliged to use art to conceal it from my own officers." Nor, in order to justify himself, was he willing to give aid and comfort to the enemy by revealing the truth.

This discrepancy between his real and imagined strength at times made him appear almost negligently passive (rather than cautious) and would often be repeated and haunt him through the war.

W H I L E the blockade of Boston continued, the British tried to incite a slave insurrection in the South. At the time, blacks made up about a sixth of the total population of America and could not be ignored once hostilities broke out. Many rebels in the South, of course, despite their rhetoric of rights and freedom, were committed to slavery, which enabled the British, with much cynical insincerity, to entice blacks to their side with promises of emancipation. The result was a constant, uneasy dread of slave revolt. Throughout the fall of 1775, British ships began "plying the Rivers, plundering plantations and using every Art to seduce the Negroes," which aroused fears among slave owners that thousands might rise up.

John Adams noted in his diary on September 24, 1775, the speculation "that if 1,000 [British] regulars should land in Georgia and their commander be provided with Arms and Cloaths enough, and proclaim Freedom to all the Negroes who would join his Camp . . . 20,000 would join it from the two Provinces [Georgia and South Carolina] in a fortnight. . . . The Negroes," he added, "have a wonderful Art of communicating Intelligence among themselves."

On November 7, Lord Dunmore, the last royal governor of Virginia, called upon slaves and indentured servants alike to rebel, and eight hundred immediately responded, making their way to Norfolk, a temporary British base. These were enrolled under Dunmore's banner as the "Loyal Ethiopian Regiment" and wore shirts with the inscription LIBERTY TO SLAVES stitched across the front. "If [Dunmore] is not crushed before spring," Washington wrote, "he will become the most formidable enemy America has. His strength will increase as a snowball."

Although congressional policy had originally prohibited the enlistment of blacks into the army, in January 1776, Congress began to allow free blacks into the ranks. Ultimately, about 5,000 served (more, incidentally, than fought for the British) and did their part, often as unarmed auxiliaries—guides, drivers, road builders, and so on—in almost every major battle of the war.

Meanwhile, Dunmore had undertaken marauding expeditions along the shores of the Chesapeake Bay and the Potomac and Rappahannock Rivers. At first he tried to turn Norfolk into a loyalist stronghold, but after the patriot militia's victory on December 9 over his forces in a skirmish at the Great Bridge (a causeway linking two Virginia counties), he retaliated on New Year's Day, 1776, by bombarding Norfolk from the sea, igniting a blaze that burned it to the ground.

Since warships of large draft could ascend the Potomac as far as Alexandria, nine miles from Mount Vernon, it was also feared Dunmore would sail up the river, take Martha Washington hostage, and ransack the estate. Partly to forestall such a scheme, she had set out in mid-November to join her husband at Cambridge, leaving their property in the care of Washington's cousin Lund. "Let the hospitality of the house, with respect to the poor, be kept up," Washington told Lund in his instructions. "Let no one go away hungry. If any of this kind of people should be in want of corn, supply their necessities, provided it does not encourage idleness." Lund packed up the Washingtons' china and glass in barrels, bundled other possessions into chests and trunks, and hoped for the best. The militia were called out, but, wrote Lund, they "are not in arms, for indeed they have none, or at least very few," and many of Alexandria's residents fled out of reach of the enemy's guns.

Lord Dunmore's assault up the Potomac finally came in July 1776. After being dislodged from Gwynn's Island in Chesapeake Bay, he led his little flotilla of gunboats up the river, intent on ravaging farms and plantations along its shores. Near Mount Vernon, he destroyed a number of flour mills but was prevented by a storm from doing more damage. Pursued downstream, he ultimately sought to make a profit from his plunder and sailed to the West Indies, where his cargo, including a thousand black slaves who had flocked to his banner in expectation of being freed, was sold.

Not incidentally, Dunmore's ability to prey upon the Virginia coast with relative impunity had demonstrated the folly of appointing a civilian of influence to a top field command. Though John Hancock and John Adams had been thwarted in their romantic yearnings for military rank, Patrick Henry had not. As commander in chief in Virginia, he had failed to organize the state's militia, and Washington wrote, "I think my countrymen made a capital mistake when they took Henry out of the senate to place him in the field; and pity it is that he does not see this, and remove every difficulty by a voluntary resignation." By March, Henry had seen it plain, and resigned.

I N Boston, the British reshuffled their command. Gage departed, and General Howe assumed his place. He fortified the works on Bunker Hill, cleared away houses, threw up redoubts on eminences within the town, and otherwise strengthened his defenses in the hope of holding out through the winter until reinforcements could arrive from Halifax and Ireland in the spring. The largely refugee population was organized into work details, and the men's spirits were kept up with amateur theatricals and other events. "We have plays, assemblys, and balls and live as if we were in a place of plenty," wrote one officer. "Burgoyne is our Garrick." Burgoyne, in fact, was a playwright, and David Garrick was just then staging his *Maid of the Oaks* in London in Drury Lane. A later play by Burgoyne, *The Heiress,* would prove one of the most popular in England toward the end of the century.

Since Boston did not have a theater, Faneuil Hall, "where [the radicals] used to hold yr [their] Cabals" in the sneering words of one British lieutenant, was converted into a playhouse. Various contemporary plays then popular in London were staged, as well as satirical skits that made fun of the American army. The most famous of these, *The Blockade of Boston*, written by Burgoyne, made its debut on January 8, 1776. According to a Boston diarist, it ridiculed the hypocritical morals of Bostonians and represented Washington "as an uncouth countryman; dressed shabbily, with large wig and long rusty sword."

As it happened, on opening night the play had a rude interruption.

The Americans knew exactly when the performance was to begin, and they attacked the mill at Charlestown just as the curtain went up. Art and life traded places in a superior farce. As the introductory skit was ending, one of the actors, wrote an eyewitness, came onstage from the wings

> dressed in the character of a Yankee sergeant (which character he was to play) desired silence, and informed the audience . . . that the rebels had attacked Charlestown, and were at it tooth and nail. The audience thinking this the opening of the new piece, clapped prodigiously; but soon finding their mistake, a general scene of confusion ensued. They immediately hurried out of the house to their alarm posts; some skipping over the orchestra, trampling on the fiddles, and every one making his most speedy retreat, the actors (who were all officers) calling out for water to wash the smut and paint from off their faces; women fainting, and, in short, the whole house was nothing but one scene of confusion, terror, and tumult.

Back in London, Lord North remained unaccountably optimistic. He wrote to General Burgoyne, "I cannot help thinking that many of the principal persons in North America will, with the calmness of the winter, be disposed to bring forward a reconciliation. Now they are too angry, too suspicious and too much under the guidance of factious leaders." But Britain had done nothing to allay that anger and suspicion and everything to ensure that the "principal persons" would remain defiant to the end. Such a muddled policy, which absurdly imagined the revolutionary leaders (despite all their learned and eloquent state papers) as driven primarily by emotion, was doomed—and soon to be humbled by force.

P U B L I C expectations and his own desire for action led Washington in mid-February to consider plans for an assault across the ice of Massachusetts Bay. But in council "the enterprise was thought too dangerous," according to Washington, and instead it was agreed that they try to seize Dorchester Heights with the artillery they had captured at Ticonderoga and Crown Point in May.

Knox, who had been appointed colonel commandant of artillery by Washington in November, had exerted himself to the utmost to bring this ordnance, more than 120 guns, to Cambridge. In November, he had left for Ticonderoga, where the guns had to be first dismounted, then floated in scows and boats down Lake George. After that, they had to be drawn by ox teams on sleds three hundred miles across the Berkshire Mountains. By mid-December, he had gotten the cannon down the lake and had hauled them as far as Springfield, Massachusetts, "where," he wrote Washington, "I shall get fresh cattle to carry them to camp." If all went well, he hoped "in sixteen or seventeen days' time to present your Excellency a noble train of artillery." It took him a bit longer than that as he worked his way through the woods and heavy snows, but on January 24 he had entered Cambridge at last with the cannon, mortars, and howitzers Washington had been so anxious to obtain. Throughout February, they were repaired, made serviceable, and furnished with adequate shot.

On the night of March 4, Washington rapidly mounted the artillery on Dorchester Heights, putting him into a position to destroy Boston and its British garrison. The swift fortification that had earlier marked the occupation of Bunker (Breed's) Hill was, in a manner, repeated. Thousands of boards and other materials for earthworks had been assembled, and two nights before, on March 2, Washington had begun a diversionary bombardment of British positions that continued with increasing ferocity for three nights straight. Under its cover, an advance guard of 800 men quietly ascended the heights, followed by 1,200 more under General John Thomas. Behind them came carts with entrenching tools and a train of three hundred wagons laden with fascines, gabions, and huge bundles of hay. The moon was shining brightly in a clear night sky, but "the flash and roar of cannonry from opposite points and the bursting of bombshells high in the air so engaged and diverted the attention of the enemy that the detachment had reached the summit about eight o'clock without being heard or perceived."

In the course of the night, four redoubts went up, two on Dorchester Point and two smaller ones on their flanks. "Perhaps," wrote the American general Heath, "there never was so much work done in so short a space of time." As part of the American defense works, rows of barrels filled with earth had also been placed as a frontline bulwark, to be rolled down the hill in case of an infantry attack. When General Howe the next morning saw through his spyglass what the rebels had accomplished, he exclaimed in astonishment, "My God! these fellows have done more work in one night than I could make my army do in three months."

Howe began a cannonade from his warships and Boston batteries in preparation for an intended assault the following morning, but, like all his officers, was profoundly ambivalent about carrying it forward at the risk of repeating the carnage and humiliations of Bunker Hill. Nevertheless, throughout the day, as the bombardment continued, troops embarked from various wharves on ships, and toward sunset, wrote an

American soldier, they "hauled off in succession and anchored in a line in our front." A British landing on Dorchester peninsula was set for that night. However, a violent storm arose which broke up the fleet's formation, "driving the ships foul of each other, and from their anchors in utter confusion." The storm continued all the next day and, as Howe later explained to the ministry, that "gave the enemy time to improve their works . . . and to put themselves into such a state of defence that I could promise myself little success."

Indeed the Americans feeling their strength began making conspicuous preparations for an amphibious landing and assault across the Charles River.

On March 8, Howe sent out a flag of truce. The best he could now hope for was an honorable evacuation, and to that end he assured Washington he would not attempt to devastate the city in retreat, provided his own troops were not molested as they left. Washington agreed, and on Sunday, March 17, the British sailed away. A fleet of 170 vessels had been assembled for the evacuation, including 78 ships and transports, 3 men-of-war, and scores of schooners carrying 12,000 soldiers and sailors and 3,000 loyalist refugees.

An American advance guard entered on their heels, and three days later the main body of the Continental Army marched in. Boston was at once regarrisoned with five regiments of American troops under Israel Putnam, while the rest of the army decamped for New York and its vicinity, where Washington expected the British to strike next. Indeed, he had already sent General Lee south to New York in January to begin preparations for the city's defense.

In Boston, the Americans rejoiced. "The more I think of [it]," wrote Abigail Adams, "the more amazed I am that they should leave such a harbor, such fortifications, such intrenchments, and that we should be in peaceable possession of a town which we expected would cost us a river of blood." In the House of Lords, the duke of Manchester summed up the humiliation of the hour: "The army of Britain, equipped with every possible essential of war; a chosen army, with chosen officers, backed by the power of a mighty fleet, sent to correct revolted subjects; sent to chastise a resisting city; sent to assert Britain's authority, [was] . . . imprisoned within that town by the provincial army, who, their watchful guards, permitted them no inlet to the country; who braved all their efforts and defied all that their skill and ability in war could ever attempt."

The Americans saw their victory as heroic, too, and their confidence was high. In answer to *The Blockade of Boston*, staged by the British during the siege, they put on their own farce, *The Blockheads: or, the*

Affrighted Officers, which portrayed the British as cowards and rather unpleasantly mocked the scarcities the blockade had obliged them to endure. In it, General Shallow (Howe) complained, "My teeth are worn to stumps, and my lips are swell'd like a blubber-mouth negro's, by thumping hard bones against them; my jaw bone has been set a dozen times, dislocated by chewing hard pork, as tough as an old swine's ass."

True to his word, Howe had made no attempt to destroy the town, but Americans found that many of the houses had been vandalized or pillaged and the furniture broken and destroyed. Old South Church, singled out for desecration because it had been a radical meetingplace, had been gutted to serve the British as a riding school. The floor of the nave had been spread with tanbark and one of its beautiful old carved pews used as a hog trough. The rest of the woodwork had all been cut to pieces and carried off for fuel. On the other hand, Hancock's stately mansion, which General Clinton had occupied, was missing only a backgammon board. And rather remarkably, though the British had blown up Castle William in the harbor, they had left behind a substantial cache of military stores—more than two hundred cannon and mortars, shot, shells, tons of powder and lead, thousands of muskets, small arms, and so on—with many of their own batteries and redoubts intact. All this helped make Boston secure from attack for the remainder of the war.

W H E N the British had first occupied Boston, a number of their officers had expected the war to be short and, when it was over, to settle on confiscated land. One of them had brought with him a twig from a famed weeping willow near Alexander Pope's villa at Twickenham, England, carefully preserved in a case of oiled silk. But as the siege went on and the British position began to deteriorate, he gave up on the idea of ever planting the twig on his American estate. Instead, he gave it to Custis Warren, one of Washington's occasional emissaries to the enemy camp, who planted it near his own house in Abingdon, Virginia. There, as a kind of emblem of the fratricidal sorrows of the war, it took root and grew, and it was said that all the weeping willows of the United States were descended from that stem.

CHAPTER SIX

QUEBEC

During the previous winter, while the British were testing slave support in the South, Congress had turned its eyes to the Canadian north. Although the daring actions of Allen and Arnold had originally met with an ambivalent response by the Congress (not all the delegates being yet ready to wage an offensive war), the mood had changed. And before the summer was over, they had approved another, more ambitious Canadian campaign. Its object was nothing less than to wrest the entire territory from British control.

The time to attempt it seemed opportune. Despite the fall of Ticonderoga and Crown Point, the British had failed to strengthen Canada's other principal towns and forts, and it was widely supposed that the French-speaking part of the population would rally behind an American invasion if it were prosecuted with sufficient force. The Canadian governor-general, Sir Guy Carleton, despite the popularity of his Québec Act, himself doubted the loyalty of his French subjects, since, in his judgment, they had already "imbibed too much of the American spirit of Licentiousness and Independence." So it is not surprising that a force of 2,000 men was thought to be enough to take both Montréal and Québec and all their dependent garrisons and annex Canada to the union being formed.

In the heady days of confidence that followed the Battle of Bunker

Hill, Benedict Arnold had lobbied hard and persuasively for such a venture and volunteered "to carry the plan into execution . . . and, with the smiles of Heaven, answer for the success of it." The command, however, was given to Major General Philip Schuyler, a Dutch landholder of prominence and the New York State commander, and secondarily to Brigadier General Richard Montgomery, an ex–British captain and veteran of Wolfe's assault on Québec. Montgomery had a refined, elegant manner and an "easy, graceful, manly address," according to a fellow officer, as well as "the voluntary esteem of the whole army." But Arnold was also the natural choice for a subordinate command. He had proven his enterprise and familiarity with Canadian conditions, and as a trader he knew the characters of and approaches to the various forts and towns.

The main expeditionary force was to assemble at Fort Ticonderoga, proceed north on Lake Champlain, capture Saint John's, which commanded the approach to Montreal, then take Montreal itself, before moving on to Québec. Arnold was to cooperate by leading a second force up the Kennebec River through the wilderness of Maine, across "a treacherous tangle of lake, mountain, and morass" northwestward to the Dead River. He was then to advance westward to Canada's Lake Megantic and by a hundred miles of boiling rapids down the Chaudière ("Cauldron") River to join Schuyler and Montgomery before Québec's walls.

As the expedition was about to set out, Washington composed an address to the people of Canada, calling upon them to rebel: "Come then, ye generous citizens, range yourselves under the standard of General Liberty, against which all the force and artifice of tyranny will never be able to prevail." He told Arnold, "Use all possible expedition, as the winter season is now advancing. Upon the success of this enterprise, under God . . . the safety and welfare of the whole continent may depend." The prospects of success seemed excellent. As Washington explained the matter to Congress, Carleton, having stripped his own command of troops to reinforce Gage in Boston, would be unable to defend both ends of his domain at once: if he reinforced Québec, Montreal would fall to Schuyler; if Montreal, Québec could be taken, cutting Carleton off from the sea.

Although Schuyler lacked combat experience—his main service had been as a supply officer in the French and Indian War—he was a capable general but at the time of his appointment was ill and without the requisite energy and enterprise. He lingered overlong at Fort Ticonderoga, where, in a desultory or perhaps too thorough fashion, he made his preparations, and after he returned to Albany for a conference on Indian affairs, Montgomery, growing impatient, decided to start on his own. On

August 28, he embarked on Lake Champlain with 1,200 men and wrote to Schuyler, "Let me entreat you (if you possibly can) to follow us in a whaleboat, leaving someone to bring forward the troops and artillery." Schuyler soon joined him with reinforcements, and together they proceeded to the Richelieu River, where, with 2,000 men, they laid siege to Fort Saint John's. The garrison was strong—700 men had been gathered for its defense, three quarters of them British regulars under Major Charles Preston—and the Americans fared badly in skirmishes as they approached the fort. In other respects, too, they had an unexpectedly hard time. The defenders had created a formidable abatis around the stronghold, and torrential rains turned the siege lines to mire. "Whenever we attempt to raise batteries, the water follows in the ditch," complained one American in his diary. Montgomery wrote in a dispatch, "We have been like half-drowned rats crawling through a swamp." Schuyler, meanwhile, had turned back due to illness, and in the end it would take fifty-five days of bombardment and assault for Montgomery to subdue the post—and then only after he offered the starving garrison generous capitulation terms. Meanwhile, Ethan Allen had been captured earlier in a premature and quixotic attempt to take Montreal himself. From Saint John's, Montgomery marched straight on to Montreal, where Carleton, who had been unable to assemble much of a defense, considered his own position hopeless and prudently withdrew to the more formidable stronghold of Québec. Disguised as a farmer, he hurried downstream to the city in a little boat, his garrison coming on behind in scattered groups.

Nevertheless, the British had bought valuable time at Saint John's, delaying the American siege of Québec into the winter months, while Allen's unauthorized action had serious repercussions of its own. Its failure heartened the loyal Canadians and discouraged those who might have joined Montgomery otherwise. Washington, looking for some saving grace to the affair, told Schuyler he hoped "Allen's misfortune" would "teach a lesson of prudence and subordination to others who may be too ambitious to outshine their general officers."

MEANWHILE, Arnold's force had set out from Cambridge on September 13, marched to Newburyport, and from there sailed to the mouth of the Kennebec River. His men were all volunteers, many of them (as he had requested) "active woodsmen, well acquainted with batteaux." Seven hundred and fifty were from New England; 250 others, formed into three companies, were Virginia and Pennsylvania riflemen —"beautiful boys," one of their leaders called them, "who know how to shoot." They wore buckskin breeches, leggings and moccasins decorated with colored beads, and a long, loose hunting shirt fringed and belted at the waist. Across the front of their shirts, or along the band of their broad-brimmed hats, were stitched the words LIBERTY OR DEATH. At their head was Daniel Morgan, a tall, powerfully built, deep-voiced Virginian who had been a teamster in Braddock's ill-fated campaign and had once been given five hundred lashes for striking a British officer. He had led a rifle company to Cambridge before being assigned to the Canadian expedition, and he was a born leader. His imposing presence, wrote a young Pennsylvania marksman, "gave the idea history has left us of Belisarius." Before the war's end, he would become one of Washington's most imaginative, capable, and best-loved generals.

Aaron Burr, then nineteen, and a few other adventurous young gentlemen were allowed to join the expedition at their own expense. Burr took with him a nineteen-year-old Abenaki Indian princess, Jacatacqua, whom the men called "Golden Thighs." Two surgeons and their assistants, a chaplain, two quartermasters, four drummers, two fifers, and a private secretary completed the entourage.

From the Kennebec River, Arnold's force plunged into the Maine woods. As a result of using a faulty map, Arnold had miscalculated the distance to Québec as 180 miles, not the 360 it actually was (by the route he took), and by the time he had gotten halfway, his men were exhausted, wracked by nausea and diarrhea from contaminated water, and their provisions were running out. To sustain themselves, they boiled and ate candles and butchered and "instantly devoured" a dog brought along as a mascot. "Nor," wrote an army doctor, "did the shaving soap, pomatum, and even the lip salve, shoe leather, cartridge boxes, etc., share any better fate." On October 25, a third of the men, under Colonel Roger Enos, turned back. The rest pressed on, their only nourishment now "water stiffened with flour in imitation of shoemaker's paste." That caused a constipation as deleterious as the diarrhea had before.

By November 2, two hundred had perished and the remainder, wrote one of the soldiers in his diary, "were so weak that they could hardly stand on their legs. . . . I passed by many sitting wholly drowned in sorrow. . . . Such pity-asking countenances I never before beheld. My heart was ready to burst."

That day was also the day of their reprieve. As they proceeded down the Chaudière River, they suddenly came upon a French Canadian settlement, where they were charitably received and fed fresh vegetables and beef. "We sat down," the doctor recalled, "ate our rations, and blessed our stars."

As soon as his men had recovered their strength, Arnold continued on to Québec, where, on November 15, he occupied the Plains of Abraham and tried unsuccessfully to bluff the garrison into surrendering by parading his troops. He could do little more without artillery and, being wary of coming under attack himself, soon hastily withdrew to Point aux Trembles, twenty miles to the west. There, on December 2, Montgomery linked up with him, bringing fresh clothes, captured at Montreal, for his men, as well as artillery, ammunition, and provisions of various kinds.

Montgomery reviewed the ranks and in "a short, energetic but elegant speech" praised their spirit and perseverance. He was also genuinely impressed by Arnold's character as an officer. "His corps is an exceedingly fine one," he wrote to Schuyler, "inured to fatigue and well-accustomed to cannon shot, and he himself is active, intelligent and enterprising—with a style of discipline much superior to what I have been used to see in this campaign."

The siege they were about to undertake would test their mettle to the full.

Carleton had been Wolfe's quartermaster general and confidential adviser during the climactic campaign of the French and Indian War, and behind the walls of Québec, he now presided with constructive vigilance over the city he had helped to win for the empire. He was a capable commander, had ruled the French Canadians with much fairness and consideration, inspiring loyalty and respect, and knew what had to be done for Québec to hold out. He reinforced the fortifications with palisades and blockhouses, walled up the windows of buildings in exposed places, leaving only loopholes for muskets, and mounted 150 cannon on the fortress walls. Westward from Cape Diamond, to protect the upper town from a land attack from the rear, he had strengthened a line of stone bastions thirty feet high. By December 1, he had a force of 1,600 men in arms, not counting a few hundred French volunteers, against the 2,000 maneuvering against them outside the walls.

General Montgomery was also a man of capacity, but he lacked Carleton's means. Carleton had detailed information on the numbers and condition of the Americans and even their plans, thanks to spies disguised as countryfolk who took provisions to their camp. But his own principal advantage lay in the great triangular stone citadel itself—and in the inevitable toll winter must take on the besieging troops.

On December 5, the Americans moved toward Québec, making their way through a fresh snowfall in sealskin moccasins, worn deliberately large and stuffed with hay or leaves to keep their feet warm and dry. Arnold's troops took up quarters in homes to the north of Québec City in the suburbs; Montgomery pitched his camp to the west on the Plains of Abraham.

Montgomery knew his ammunition and supplies would not last long enough to starve Québec into submission, which in any case was out of the question, because when the ice in the Saint Lawrence River broke in the spring, British reinforcements were sure to arrive. So he sent a peasant woman into the fort with an ultimatum for its surrender. Carleton received the woman in silence and had a drummer boy take the letter from her hands with a set of tongs and place it, unread, in the fire. Montgomery sent in a second letter, but it was derisively "drummed out of town." Thereafter, the patriots had to reconcile themselves to shooting their communications, tied to arrows, over the walls.

American sharpshooters picked off sentries in exposed positions, but attempts to throw up earthworks to raise a battery of guns against the fort failed miserably, since the frozen soil was too hard for the entrenching tools. Instead, by painful night labor in the bitter cold, the besiegers, on a stretch of rising ground, created an "ice fort." They built this up gradually by compacting snow around a wooden framework and from time to time drenched it with water, which instantly froze. On December 15, the American cannon (six nine-pounders and a howitzer, all light artillery) were mounted on its ramparts, but in the artillery duel which followed, the ice fort was smashed to smithereens.

Only an outright assault on the town could hope to win the day, and it could not be delayed, as the enlistment periods of most of the men were about to expire. Patriotic fervor had given way before the austerity of winter and nostalgia for home. Only the rifle corps apparently remained eager, "yet this example," wrote one, "had no manner of influence on the generality." Moreover, the British had sent a number of women infected with smallpox into the camp, and the disease had begun to gnaw through the ranks. Preparations were rushed. Montgomery announced that he would eat his Christmas dinner in Québec and issued a proclamation to inspire his troops: "The [Americans], flushed with continual Success, confident of the Justice of their cause, and relying on that Providence which has uniformly protected them, will advance with alacrity to attack the works incapable of being defended by the wretched Garrison behind them." As an incentive to their will, he promised to let them plunder the town if they got in.

With unaccustomed ardor, his troops now hammered together scaling ladders, attaching strong iron hooks to hold them to the stones, and, in expectation of hand-to-hand combat, furnished themselves with hatchets and spears. The final plan called for a feint against Cape Diamond and a full assault on the lower town. If that could be taken, the British garrison would be marooned on its lofty rock and cut off from the sea.

Carleton, of course, knew an attack was coming and night after night kept flares burning along the fortress walls.

Christmas passed in waiting; at last, on the night of December 30, Montgomery got the heavy snowfall he needed to cover his approach.

At about four in the morning, the Americans—all with scraps of white paper fastened to their caps bearing the motto LIBERTY OR DEATH—began their approach. A party of a hundred took part in the feint against Cape Diamond, while two other companies made simultaneous feints against gates to the east and west. Meanwhile, Montgomery and Arnold, with the main force divided between them, advanced on opposite ends of the lower town. They hurried forward in single file at a run, making and compacting a path in the snow as they went, their heads held low against the blizzard, covering the locks of their guns with the lappets of their coats. Behind them came an artillery unit dragging brass six-pounders on sleds.

Making his way along the northern shore of the Saint Lawrence, Montgomery encountered a fortified house. He charged against it along a narrow street, but the advance guard unit he led was spotted and met by a devastating blast of musket and cannon fire. Montgomery was killed instantly, and most of his companions were mowed down as with a scythe. At the spectacle, the rest of his soldiers retreated in dismay. Meanwhile, Arnold's division approached the Palace Gate, whereupon all the bells of the city began to ring. Their deafening clamor was almost immediately followed, wrote one soldier, by "a horrible roar of cannon" that likewise thinned their ranks. Once the Americans got in under the guns, the fighting in the lower town was house to house. But the Americans got the worst of it. They were outmatched and outnumbered, and in between the buildings, which were often many yards apart, they were caught in a galling cross fire from the ramparts above. Nearly every American field officer was killed, wounded, or captured including Daniel Morgan; 426 American soldiers were taken prisoner and about 60 killed. Montgomery's body was later reputedly found by a loyalist drummer boy "searching for souvenirs." Arnold was also hit, his lower left leg shattered by a musket ball.

While this desperate action was taking place, others far away had already blithely assumed its success. General Lee told Robert Morris of Pennsylvania early in December, "We now, my friend, sail triumphantly before the wind, the reduction of Canada, for I suppose it is reduced, gives the Coup de grace to the hellish junk. Montgomery and Arnold deserve statues of gold, and I hope the Congress will erect 'em." Washington, more cautiously, expected a brave attempt and thought Arnold might be the man to carry it off. "The merit of this gentleman," he wrote to Schuyler, "is certainly great, and I heartily wish that fortune may distinguish him as one of her favorites. I am convinced that he will do everything that his prudence and valor shall suggest to add to the success of our arms."

He could only hope so, for the price of failure would be dear. Morris wrote to General Horatio Gates, "[Canada] must be ours . . . shou'd it fall into the hands of the Enemy they will soon raise a Nest of Hornets at our backs that will sting us to the quick." By that he meant, as John Adams put it in a letter to his friend James Warren, "all the Indians upon the Continent," who might be induced "to take up the Hatchet and commit their Robberies and Murders upon the Frontiers."

After Montgomery's death, Arnold, recuperating in a field hospital, assumed command of the troops and attempted to maintain the blockade. "I have no thought," he wrote his sister, "of leaving this proud town, until I first enter it in triumph." He pulled his forces together, tried to check the flight of deserters to Montreal, and implored General David Wooster, who was now in command there, "for God's sake, to order as many men down as you can possibly spare, consistent with the safety of Montreal, and all the mortars, howitzers, and shells that you can possibly bring." Carleton, meanwhile, bided his time through the winter while cold and sickness reduced the American force. Congress, in recognition of Arnold's efforts, made him a brigadier general, but a month later, confessing himself "at a loss how to conduct matters," he asked for "some experienced officer" to take command. On April 1, Wooster finally arrived with reinforcements and heavy artillery, but his generalship was lacking. A rather fussy old man with an enormous periwig, he was said to be able to boast of "thirty years of honorable service and no immediate accomplishment." Delegate Silas Deane of Connecticut, Wooster's home state, compared him (in objecting to his Montreal appointment) to "an old woman," and Washington himself more tactfully told Joseph Reed, "I have no opinion at all of Wooster's enterprising genius." Their doubts were justified. His poor management of the garrison at Montreal had brought disarray, and his bigoted refusal to consider priests as anything better than idolaters had been a diplomatic disaster in the campaign for the hearts and minds of French Canadians.

Toward the end of March, Congress sent Benjamin Franklin, Samuel Chase, and Charles Carroll to Canada to see for themselves whether the Canadian campaign could be sustained. Franklin was chosen, according to Adams, because of his "masterly acquaintance with the French language . . . his great Experience in Life, his Wisdom, Prudence, Caution; his engaging Address"; Chase because of his knowledge of the details of the expedition; and Carroll, of Carrollton, Maryland, because he was a Roman Catholic like the Québec French. His brother John, a priest and later the first American Catholic archbishop of Baltimore, also went along.

After an exhausting journey by sloop and rowboat up the Hudson, the travelers embarked in open flatboats upon Lake George and Lake Champlain. On April 29, they finally reached Montreal. Although still hoping (according to their brief) "to promote or to form a union between the United Colonies and the people of Canada," they quickly discovered "the utter hopelessness of the situation." Early in June they returned and reported, as John Hancock conveyed the gist of it to Washington, that "our army in that quarter is almost ruined for Want of Discipline, and every Thing else necessary to constitute an Army." Chase and Carroll described the force as "disheartened, half of it under inoculation, or under other diseases; soldiers without pay, without discipline, and altogether reduced to live from hand to mouth." Nevertheless, Congress, having replaced Wooster with General John Thomas on May 1, had already belatedly decided to send several regiments of reinforcements northward to see what they could do. But upon arrival Thomas almost immediately found himself in retreat as the British, bolstered from the sea by a mighty army of 13,000 men—eight British regiments, 2,000 German mercenaries, and a formidable artillery train under General Burgoyne—carried the campaign into the field. "In the most helter skelter manner we raised the siege," wrote an army doctor, "leaving everything: all the camp equipage, ammunition, and even our clothing, except what little we happened to have on us. . . . Most of our sick fell into their hands."

The Americans tried to pull themselves together at Sorel (where General Thomas, succumbing to smallpox, was replaced by General John Sullivan) and briefly considered making a stand at Montreal. But Arnold wrote to Schuyler, "The junction of the Canadians with the Colonies— an object which brought us into this country—is at an end. Let us quit then and secure our own country before it is too late. There will be more honor in making a safe retreat than hazarding a battle against such superiority which will doubtless be attended with the loss of our men and artillery. . . . These arguments are not urged by fear for my personal safety. I am content to be the last man who quits the country."

Arnold was as good as his word. He assumed charge of the rear guard as the retreating soldiers crowded into boats at Saint John's to take them south to Isle aux Noix. According to one of his aides, Arnold waited until the British vanguard came into view before spurring his horse to the water's edge, where he drew his pistol, shot it and, as the sun was setting, pushed off in a boat.

On the thirty-first of May, Arnold wrote to Horatio Gates from Chambly:

> My Dear General:
> I am a thousand times obliged to you for your kind letter of the 3rd of April, of which I have a most grateful sense. I shall be ever happy in your friendship and society; and hope, with you, that our next winter-quarters will be more agreeable, though I must doubt it if affairs go as ill with you as here. . . . My whole thoughts are now bent on making a safe retreat out of this country; however, I hope we shall not be obliged to leave it until we have had one more bout for the honour of America. I think we can make a last stand at Isle-aux-Noix, and keep the lake this summer from an invasion that way. We have little to fear; But I am heartily chagrined to think that we have lost in one month all the immortal Montgomery was a whole campaign in gaining, together with our credit, and as many men, and an amazing sum of money. The Commissioners this day leave us, as our good fortune has long since; but as Miss, like most other Misses, is fickle, and often changes, I still hope for her favours again; and that we shall have the pleasure of dying or living happy together.
> In every vicissitude of fortune, believe me, with great esteem and friendship, my dear General, your obedient humble servant,
> Benedict Arnold.

At Isle aux Noix, the Americans had 8,000 troops, but the majority were demoralized and disabled by exhaustion and disease. It is unlikely they could have withstood any kind of British attack, even by a much smaller force, so they soon retreated farther to Crown Point, from which the conquest of Canada had been launched ten months before.

I N the Canadian campaign, Arnold had shown undoubted courage, but another side of the man had begun more plainly to emerge. During and after the siege of Québec, he got into a number of disputes with other officers, which to some degree recapitulated the squabble, marked by charges and countercharges, between himself and Ethan Allen the year before. One of his antagonists was Colonel Moses Hazen, a Canadian who had made a distinguished place for himself in the service of the colonies and had played a positive role in the military government of Montreal. On the eve of the evacuation of Montreal in June, Arnold had ordered all sorts of merchandise, including silks "and other goods of value but of no use to the army," seized from various commercial establishments. Hazen suspected this was plunder for personal gain. So when the goods were sent to Chambly, on the line of retreat, and Hazen was ordered to receive and store them, he refused. They remained unguarded on the riverbank for a while, and a considerable portion disappeared. The pilfered merchants, following the army in hope of compensation, raised a clamor against Arnold, who tried to pass the blame on to Hazen, whom he accused of insubordination. Hazen demanded a court-martial, got his wish, and was exonerated. Arnold rejected the ruling and challenged the judges to a duel.

The judges protested to General Gates, commanding at Ticonderoga, and demanded Arnold's arrest. But Gates, anticipating a new British offensive, dissolved the court in the interest of retaining Arnold's skills. "The warmth of General Arnold's temper," he explained to the Congress, "might possibly lead him a little farther than is marked by the precise line of decorum to be observed towards a court martial," but "the United States must not be deprived of that excellent officer's services at this important time."

CHAPTER SEVEN

THE DECLARATION
o f
INDEPENDENCE

I<small>N</small> general, Britain's strategy in the war as it developed was to use its army to divide the various colonies from one another to prevent their collaboration, blockade the coast, interdict supplies coming in by sea, and destroy any organized armies the colonists might form. The linchpin of this strategy was the occupation of New York City, which became the headquarters of the British campaign. The plan was then to secure the line of the Hudson Valley all the way to Canada in order to isolate New England, "the hot-bed of sedition," as the British Ministry saw it, from the colonies to the south. South of New York the strategic position eventually became the Chesapeake Bay, with positions in Maryland and Virginia to divide the middle and southern colonies from each other.

The American plan was defensive: to hold fast the line of the Hudson and otherwise evade destruction by the superior British force. Each side understood the other; there was no mystery as to the other's intentions. And so the war became a battle of wits and of limited resources—America with an improvised and uncertain army, Britain contending with the logistical problems of fighting a war three thousand miles from home. Moreover, though the British Ministry was hawkish, the British public was divided, as were the colonists themselves. The British were therefore under some pressure to prevail quickly, without much bloodshed. Washington, of course, understood this and believed that by avoiding a decisive, open field engagement, he had time on his side.

Among British officers, no one seems to have understood the situation more clearly (in his own case by bitter experience) than General Thomas Gage. From the beginning of the conflict, the British government had entertained a low opinion of the ability of the colonies to act together effectively on military matters, based on its own experience with American legislative assemblies during the French and Indian War. But after the Battle of Bunker Hill and before his recall from Boston, Gage had written the British secretary of war:

These people show a spirit and conduct against us they never showed against the French. . . .

They are now spirited up by a rage and enthusiasm as great as ever people were possessed of, and you must proceed in earnest or give the business up. A small body acting in one spot will not avail. You must have large armies, making diversions on different sides, to divide their force.

The loss we have sustained is greater than we can bear; small armies can't afford such losses, especially when the advantage gained tends to little more than the gaining of a post—a material one indeed, as our own security depended on it. The troops were sent out too late. The rebels were at least two months before-hand with us, and your Lordship would be astonished to see the tract of country they have entrenched and fortified. Their number is great, so many hands have been employed.

I have before wrote to your Lordship my opinion, that a large army must at length be employed to reduce these people and mentioned the hiring of foreign troops. I fear it must come to that, or else to avoid a land war and make use only of your fleet. I don't find one province in appearance better disposed than another, though I think if this army was in New York that we should find many friends and be able to raise forces in that province on the side of government.

The British Ministry, even while repudiating Gage's generalship, took his advice to heart. Large armies, diversions on different sides, foreign troops, and so on now formed part of an overall strategy as the British prepared to strike both North and South at once, at Charleston, South Carolina, and New York.

General Lee had been dispatched to New York to plan and lay out its defenses which, after his hasty departure for Charleston to take charge of that city in turn, were left to be completed by Israel Putnam, who succeeded him in the command. Meanwhile, Washington sent twelve battalions south through Connecticut to New York at the end of March with the rest of the army to "immediately follow in divisions," according to his directive, "leaving only a convenient space between each to prevent confusion, and want of accomodation on their march." Washington himself, deeming a British attack imminent, came on by way of Providence, Norwich, and New London, expediting the embarkation of troops from these posts, and arrived at New York on April 13. He took possession of a spacious three-story brick mansion on Pearl Street and reviewed the defensive preparations begun by Lee.

He had a little more time than he realized, but not much. Instead of sailing directly to New York, Howe had withdrawn to Halifax, where he had landed his loyalist supercargo, refurbished his ships, and awaited massive reinforcements from England. These soon arrived under Admiral Lord Richard Howe (General Howe's brother) "to chastise the miscreant and perverse rebels to their king."

Washington dispersed his forces in and around the city; on Long Island, Governors Island, and Brooklyn Heights, and also along the New Jersey shore. "New York, in ev'ry Street, was Fortify'd," wrote one eyewitness. "Numbers upon each Green, & Dock beside: The Island's width, & length, full fourteen Miles Was full of Ditches, Forts, Redoubts, & Piles: And still beyond."

Toward the end of May, Washington left for Philadelphia to confer with Congress about ways in which to strengthen the army, and it was unanimously agreed to extend the term of enlistment for each recruit to three years. Each soldier was also to be paid a bounty of $10 as an incentive to enlist. For the defense of New York itself, Congress promised to raise 13,800 militia and, since the Americans lacked a navy of their own, authorized the construction of gondolas and fire rafts to be used against enemy ships.

Meanwhile, on June 28, a large British land and sea force prepared to besiege Charleston, the chief city and principal seaport of the South. In the spring, General Henry Clinton had linked up with Admiral Sir Peter Parker and General Charles, Lord Cornwallis, off Cape Fear, North Carolina, and in early June their combined fleet of fifty ships moved to attack the port. Charleston was not unready for them. "All the mechanics and laborers about the town," wrote Colonel William Moultrie, who had been diligent for some time in strengthening the defenses, "were employed, and a great number of negroes brought down from the country and put upon the works." Lead used in the windows of churches and houses had been melted down and cast into musket balls, and a hundred cannon mounted on batteries in the harbor forts. The principal bastion was a fort on Sullivan's Island, chiefly constructed of palmetto logs and furnished with twenty-five or thirty guns.

Lee, coming south to take charge of the preparations, "hurried about to view the different works, and gave orders," recalled Moultrie, "for such things to be done as he thought necessary. He was every day and every hour of the day on horseback, or in boats viewing our situation and directing small works to be thrown up at different places. When he came to Sullivan's Island, he did not like that post at all. He said there was no way to retreat, that the garrison would be sacrificed. Nay, he called it a 'slaughter pen,' and wished to withdraw the garrison and give up the post." Others, led by Moultrie, objected, and the sagacious colonel had his way. Stormy weather delayed the British attack and gave the defenders more time to strengthen their positions, but it was widely expected that the fort would be flattened quickly—"They will knock it down in half an hour," one officer predicted—by the British naval guns.

The British attacked on the morning of June 28. Clinton landed 3,000 men on a sandbank just off Sullivan's Island but found the shoals too deep to ford. While his men were thus marooned (and under attack by swarms of mosquitoes), the British ship *Thunder* made a direct assault on the fort. Its ordnance was so well aimed that most of the shells fell into the very middle of the complex, but there "we had a morass," recalled Moultrie with amusement, "that swallowed them up instantly, and those that fell in the sand, in and about the fort, were immediately buried, so that very few of them burst amongst us." Nor could the other warships seem to have any impact on the bastion's walls, which were sixteen feet thick and filled in with earth. During the twelve-hour engagement, the fort withstood repeated cannonades and in fact grew stronger with each barrage as the soft and spongy palmetto logs absorbed the British shot, which became embedded in its walls. By the end of the battle, they were veritable walls of iron. Meanwhile, some of the British ships, having drawn closer, received terrible damage from the fort's ordnance and Parker's own flagship was completely wrecked by devastating fire.

Indian attacks, principally by the Creeks and Cherokees on border settlements in the Carolinas, Georgia, and Virginia, were to have been coordinated with the Charleston assault, but they had been poorly planned, and after Charleston held out, many Creek and Cherokee villages were exterminated in revenge.

The American victory at Charleston appeared as the harbinger of an even greater act of defiance when, six days later, the Declaration of Independence, the Magna Carta of American liberty—which elevated the rebellion into a revolution—was adopted and made public by the Congress of the United States.

• • •

T H E congress had approached its declaration with great trepidation, as a moment of awesome significance. Even among radicals such as John Adams—if not his cousin Sam—there was a great inward circumspection and reluctance to sever forever the maternal bond. Until the ultimate break, a majority still longed for some kind of reconciliation, and as late as December 1775, while rejecting the authority of Parliament, Congress had declared its continued allegiance to the Crown. In a somewhat anguished and nostalgic petition, it asserted that "the union between our mother country and these colonies, and the energy of mild and just government, produced benefits so remarkably important, and afforded such assurance of their permanency and increase that the wonder and envy of other nations was excited, while they beheld Great Britain rising to a power the most extraordinary the world had ever known." It had gone on to assure the king that the colonists were "attached to your Majesty's person, family, and government, with all the devotion that principle and affection can inspire . . . [and] not only most ardently desire that the former harmony between [Great Britain] . . . and these colonies may be restored, but that a concord may be established between them upon so firm a basis as to perpetuate its blessings."

But Britain's willingness to expand the conflict changed many wavering minds. In October 1775, King George III had told Parliament that the rebellion "is become more general and is manifestly carried on for the purpose of establishing an independent empire. . . . It is now become the part of wisdom . . . to put a speedy end to these disorders by the most decisive exertions." Falmouth (now Portland), Maine, had been burned on October 17 by British sailors, and on January 1, 1776, Norfolk, Virginia, was bombarded and set ablaze. While the British hung on to Boston, there had been attempts, as noted, in the South to incite Indian attacks on border settlements, as well as to foment slave revolt, and Congress also learned that the king was canvassing the petty German courts for mercenaries for his army, and impressing men into service and releasing others from prison if they agreed to fight in his American war. Step by step, Britain seemed to be forcing the delegates' hands.

On January 2, 1776, they had therefore condemned "the execrable barbarity, with which this unhappy war has been conducted on the part of our enemies, such as burning our defenceless towns and villages, exposing their inhabitants, without regard to age and sex, to all the miseries which loss of property, the rigor of the season and inhuman devastation can inflict, exciting domestic insurrections and murders, bribing the savages, to desolate our frontiers, and casting such of us as the fortune of war has put into their power, into gaols, there to languish in irons and in want." Some patriots were even convinced that British bullets were "poisoned" (since at Bunker Hill the American wounded had seemed, for no clear reason, to "die very fast"), and it was known that during the siege of Boston, one frustrated British general had proposed that arrows infected with smallpox be used against the patriot troops. Though the form of the proposal had been rejected, the idea had not, as the British afterward sent prostitutes and runaway slaves with the infection into the Cambridge camp. Washington, in a letter of December 10, 1775, wrote, "The information I received that the enemy intended spreading the smallpox amongst us, I could not suppose them capable of. I must now give some credit to it, as it has made its appearance on several of those who came out of Boston."

In the wake of British atrocities, both real and imagined, the ambient rhetoric heated up. Jonas Clark, pastor of the First Parish Church of Lexington, Massachusetts, was a fair representative of New England's patriotic Church Militant. For some time he had been delivering sermons on such matters as "The Importance of Military Skill, Measures for Defense, and a Martial Spirit in a Time of Peace." In commemoration of the killing on Lexington Green, he now thundered out a homily about "The Fate of Blood Thirsty Oppressors and God's Tender Care of His Distressed People" with such resonant authority that cows were said to have been "startled into attendance" in pastures nearby. British soldiers, he declared, were "more like *murderers* and *cutthroats* than the troops of a *Christian king,*" and he assured his congregation that they had a right to retaliate—that the blood of their slain brethren "does . . . cry unto God for vengeance from the ground!"

From the backwoods of North Carolina, a community of Presbyterians of Scotch-Irish descent—who "feared the Lord, but kept their powder dry"—sent to Congress a manifesto which read, "If no pacific measures shall be proposed or adopted by Great Britain, and our enemies attempt to dragoon us out of those inestimable privileges which we are entitled to as subjects, and reduce us to slavery, we declare that we are deliberately and resolutely determined never to surrender them to any power upon earth but at the expense of our lives. These are our real, though unpolished, sentiments of liberty and loyalty, and in them we are resolved to live and die."

No voice, however, was more eloquent (or influential) than that of Thomas Paine, an English-born radical then living in Philadelphia, who on January 10 published a pamphlet called *Common Sense,* which effectively unraveled the fabric of emotions that had formerly been woven around the symbols of monarchy, allegiance, and empire.

Born in 1737 in Thetford, England, Paine had received little formal education and at age sixteen had run away to sea on a privateer. When he returned to London, he went from one subsistence job to another, read widely, pored over maps and globes, attended philosophical and scientific lectures, and involved himself in discussions on such subjects as slavery, women's rights, and prison reform. In April 1759, he established himself as a master corsetmaker (his father's trade), and in 1761, he became a "supernumerary officer," or customs official of excise. Four years later, he was dismissed for negligent fraud. Though reinstated, he considered his prospects for advancement at an end. Soon thereafter, he became involved in politics, and when the excisemen lobbied Parliament for a salary increase, Paine emerged as their spokesman. He wrote a pamphlet on their behalf, taking great pains with its composition, but it failed to win them the requisite support.

In 1772, thirty-five and broke, Paine began dealing in smuggled tobacco on the side. Once again he left his excise duties unattended, and on April 8, 1774, he was fired. To avoid debtors' prison, he had to auction off all his worldly goods. Meanwhile, his own fellow excisemen accused him of embezzling upward of £30 for his own use from a fund established to manage their petition to Parliament. Even Paine's own mother disowned him as a disgrace. For a man of real capacity, with a scientific intelligence (he later designed a remarkable iron bridge) as well as literary aptitude and ability, it had been a dismal life.

Then he met Benjamin Franklin in London. Franklin, who liked his politics and recognized his talents, advised him to seek out new opportunities in the New World. Paine took his advice and embarked for America in October 1774.

Franklin had given him a letter of introduction to his son-in-law, describing him as "very well recommended to me as an ingenious worthy young man. He goes to Pennsylvania with a view of settling there. . . . If you can put him in a way of obtaining employment as a clerk, or assistant tutor in a school, or assistant surveyor, of all of which I think him very capable, so that he may procure a subsistence at least till he can make acquaintance and obtain a knowledge of the country, you will do well, and much oblige your affectionate father."

Things began to look up for him. Although a British intelligence report described him as "naturally indolent; must be driven to work; and led by his passions," three months after his arrival, he could report to Franklin, on March 4, 1775, "Your countenancing me has obtained for me many friends and much reputation, for which please accept my sincere thanks. I have been applied to by several gentlemen to instruct their sons on very advantageous terms to myself, and a printer and bookseller here, a man of reputation and property, Robert Aitkin, has lately attempted a magazine, but having little or no turn that way himself, he has applied to me for assistance. He had not above six hundred subscribers when I first assisted him. We have now upwards of fifteen hundred, and daily increasing."

Paine had become a journalist. One day in Aitkin's bookstore he met Dr. Benjamin Rush, a prominent Philadelphia patriot. "We conversed a few minutes," Rush later recalled, "and I left him. Soon afterwards I read a short essay [published on March 8, 1775] with which I was much pleased . . . against the slavery of the Africans in our country, and which I was informed was written by Mr. Paine. This excited my desire to be better acquainted with him." Meanwhile, Paine had become the editor of Aitkin's *Pennsylvania Magazine,* with a salary of £50 a year. In emulation of Franklin's eclectic style, he wrote polemical and scientific articles, as well as numerous short items of an anecdotal kind—about Alexander the Great, for example, or a piece entitled "Reflections on Unhappy Marriages," evidently based on his own experience: "As extasy abates coolness succeeds, which often makes way for indifference, and that for neglect. Sure of each other by the nuptial bond, they no longer take any pains to be mutually agreeable. Careless if they displease, and yet angry if reproached; with so little relish for each other's company that anybody else's is more welcome, and more entertaining."

One month after Paine became editor of Aitkin's magazine, blood was shed at Lexington and Concord, and his next issue contained a notable summary of Lord Chatham's great parliamentary speech in which he warned that the crown of the British Empire would lose its luster if "robbed of so principal a jewel as America." In a footnote implying his own hatred of George III, Paine remarked, "The principal jewel of the crown actually dropt out at the coronation."

Paine's antipathy to the monarchy, of course, did not derive from his American experience. He was an alienated intellectual who for thirty-seven years had lived in impecunious obscurity at odds with the British establishment. Yet even as a child he seems to have had some strange intimation of the variability of the fortunes of empires, as suggested by an epitaph he wrote for a crow he buried in his yard:

> Here lies the body of John Crow,
> Who once was high, but now is low;
> Ye brother Crows take warning all,
> For as you rise, so must you fall.

Paine was understandably concerned at first that the outbreak of fighting would disrupt his new livelihood. He wrote to Franklin, "I thought it very hard to have the country set on fire about my ears almost the moment I got into it."

But then he grabbed a torch. Throughout the fall of 1775, he worked on his celebrated pamphlet, which "burst" upon the new year, wrote Benjamin Rush, "with an effect which has rarely been produced by types and paper." In a kind of eloquent but sloganeering style "hitherto unknown on this side of the Atlantic . . . it insinuated itself into the hearts of the people," wrote Edmund Randolph of Virginia, by arguing for independence in a way that the man in the street could understand. Many thousands of copies were printed—120,000 by the end of the year: in proportion to the population, still the greatest best-seller in American history—and by April 1 it had already begun, in Washington's words, to work "a wonderful change in the minds of many men."

Paine reminded the colonists that their cause was "not the affair of a City, a County, a Province, or a Kingdom; but of a *Continent*—of one-eighth part of the habitable Globe. 'Tis not the concern of a day, a year, or an age; posterity are virtually involved in the contest, and will be more or less affected even to the end of time, by the proceedings now." Therefore, "The cause of America is . . . the cause of all mankind." The issue was not only natural rights but oppressive government:

> Society is produced by our wants and government by our wickedness; the former promotes our happiness *positively* by uniting our affections, the latter *negatively* by restraining our vices. . . . Society in every state is a blessing, but government even in its best state is but a necessary evil; in its worst state an intolerable one; for when we suffer, or are exposed to the same miseries by *a government,* which we might expect in a country *without government,* our calamity is heightened by reflecting that we furnish the means by which we suffer. Government, like dress, is the badge of lost innocence; the palaces of kings are built on the ruins of the bowers of paradise.

Paine's attack on the British establishment was somewhat crude. Repudiating the divine right of kings (which he incorrectly traced in England to William the Conqueror), he wrote, "A French bastard landing with an armed Banditti and establishing himself king of England against the consent of the natives, is in plain terms a very paltry rascally original. It certainly hath no divinity in it."

With mockery and contempt he also repudiated the institution of royalty:

Male and female are the distinctions of nature, good and bad the distinction of heaven; but how a race of men came into the world so exalted above the rest, and distinguished like some new species, is worth enquiring into, and whether they are the means of happiness or of misery to mankind. . . . In England a King hath little more to do than to make war and give away places; which, in plain terms, is to empoverish the nation and set it together by the ears. A pretty business indeed for a man to be allowed eight hundred thousand sterling a year for, and worshipped into the bargain. Of more worth is one honest man to society, and in the sight of God, than all the crowned ruffians that ever lived.

In this way (a rather typical mix) he combined dubious analysis with indubitable truths.

While upholding natural rights, Paine's most appealing argument was perhaps that the dependence of America on Britain had become an unnatural bond:

I have heard it asserted by some, that as America hath flourished under her former connexion with Great Britain, that the same connexion is necessary towards her future happiness, and will always have the same effect. Nothing can be more fallacious than this kind of argument. We may as well assert that because a child has thriven upon milk, that it is never to have meat. . . . We have boasted the protection of Great Britain, without considering that her motive was *interest* not *attachment;* that she did not protect us from our *enemies* on *our account,* but from *her enemies* on *her own account,* from those who had no quarrel with us on any *other account,* and who will always be our enemies on the *same account.* Let Britain waive her pretensions to the continent, or the continent throw off the dependence, and we should be at peace with France and Spain.

This, of course, was naïve, since France and Spain had their own interests, which did not necessarily agree with those of the colonies. But Paine's arguments were coupled with a strong emotional appeal:

Every thing that is right or natural pleads for separation. The blood of the slain, the weeping voice of nature cries, 'TIS TIME TO PART. Even the distance at which the Almighty hath placed England and America, is a strong and natural proof, that the authority of the one, over the other, was never the design of Heaven. . . .

Small islands, not capable of protecting themselves, are the proper objects for kingdoms to take under their care; but there is something very absurd in supposing a continent to be perpetually governed by an island. In no instance hath nature made the satellite larger than its primary planet.

But where; say some, is the King of America? I'll tell you, Friend, he reigns above.

Admiration of Paine was not universal. Some of the Founding Fathers abhorred him as a kind of creeping anarchist. Although the majority may have believed in natural rights, not all believed in the natural goodness of man, since most (if not all) believed in Original Sin. One preacher, speaking from the meetinghouse pulpit at Cambridge, was not being particularly old-fashioned when he quoted a predecessor as saying, "Every natural man is born full of sin, as full as a toad is of poison, as full as ever his skin can hold." And Gouverneur Morris of New York sarcastically remarked, "He who wishes to enjoy natural Rights must establish himself where natural Rights are admitted. He must live alone."

Nevertheless, there was enough "sound doctrine and unanswerable reasoning," to use Washington's words, in Paine's pamphlet to lend it respectability even among the more circumspect. On March 19, John Adams wrote to Abigail from Philadelphia, "You ask what is thought of 'Common Sense.' Sensible men think there are some whims, some sophisms, some artful addresses to superstitious notions, some keen attempts upon the passions. . . . But all agree there is a great deal of good sense delivered in clear, simple, concise, and nervous style. His sentiments of the abilities of America, and of the difficulty of a reconciliation with Great Britain, are generally approved. But his notions and plans of continental government are not much applauded. Indeed, this writer has a better hand in pulling down than building up." It seemed to Adams that Paine's notion of government lacked any understanding of the need for checks and balances—"without any restraint or even an attempt at any equilibrium or counterpoise, that it must produce confusion and every evil work." (In later years, the mere mention of Paine was reputedly enough to make John Adams "foam at the mouth.")

While *Common Sense* and other righteous rhetoric worked their will upon the public, Congress received word that Parliament had declared the colonies under blockade. In April, it responded by declaring American ports open to the commerce of all countries except Great Britain. Meanwhile, rumors that the king planned to offer new terms of reconciliation had also reached the delegates, and the conservatives among them were eager to know what those terms were.

On April 6, Robert Morris of Pennsylvania wrote to General Gates, "Where the plague are those [Peace] Commissioners, if they are to come what is it that detains them: It is time we should be on a certainty and know positively whether the libertys of America can be established and

secured by reconciliation, or whether we must totally renounce connection with Great Britain and fight our way." Some delegates, such as
Carter Braxton of Virginia, seemed almost to be looking for an excuse
to give up the cause: "[Independence] is in truth a delusive Bait which
men inconsiderately catch at, without knowing the hook to which it is
affixed. . . . America is too defenceless a State for the declaration, having
no alliance with a naval Power nor as yet any Fleet of consequence of
her own to protect that trade which is so essential to the prosecution of
the War, without which I know we cannot go on much longer."

But his was a minority voice. Most of the colonies had begun drafting
resolutions and manifestos in favor of independence, and one by one
they fell into line. By May 20, John Adams could exult, "Every post and
every Day rolls in upon Us, Independence like a Torrent. . . . Here are
four colonies to the Southward who are perfectly agreed now with the
four to the Northward. Five in the middle are not quite so ripe; but they
are very near to it." And on June 7, Richard Henry Lee of Virginia rose to
offer the following resolutions on the floor:

> That these United Colonies are, and of right ought to be, free and inde-
> pendent States, that they are absolved from all allegiance to the British
> Crown and that all political connection between them and the State of
> Great Britain is, and ought to be, totally dissolved.
> That it is expedient forthwith to take the most effectual measures for
> forming foreign Alliances.
> That a plan of confederation be prepared and transmitted to the respec-
> tive Colonies for their consideration and approbation.

Lee's historic motion was promptly seconded by John Adams and
supported by seven delegations. The other six—from Pennsylvania, New
York, New Jersey, Delaware, Maryland, and South Carolina—were still
"not yet matured," said Thomas Jefferson, "for falling from the parent
stem." In order to allow them more time to confer with their state governments, Congress wisely decided to delay a vote on the resolution until
July 1, in the expectation that they could all then present a united front.
At the same time, a committee made up of Jefferson, John Adams, Benjamin Franklin, Roger Sherman, and Robert R. Livingston was appointed
to consider the proper form a declaration of independence might take.

O N the whole, the issue for most delegates was no longer whether
such a declaration was justified but whether the timing was right. As

John Adams explained the matter in a letter to Patrick Henry on June 3, "The natural course of things was this; for every colony to institute a government; for all the colonies to confederate, and define the limits of the continental Constitution; then to declare the colonies a sovereign state, or a number of confederated states; and last of all, to form treaties with foreign powers. But . . . we cannot proceed systematically, and . . . shall be obliged to declare ourselves independent States, before we confederate, and indeed before all the colonies have established their governments." Why? Because it had become painfully obvious that it would take a long time for the various states to settle on their state constitutions and, given their differences, even longer to confederate on terms acceptable to all. Moreover, a foreign alliance, specifically with France, was imperative if the war were to be prosecuted successfully. Such an alliance could not wait for confederation, but it also could not be obtained until a definite separation from England took place. That is, until independence was declared, the patriots could only be viewed officially by other monarchical powers as rebels against their king. As such, they could not hope to obtain the open support and official recognition they desired.

But not every patriot of prominence saw it that way. Edward Rutledge of South Carolina, for example, as eager for a foreign alliance as any of his colleagues, fretted in a letter to John Jay of New York that the colonies would "render themselves ridiculous in the Eyes of foreign powers by attempting to bring them into a Union with us before we had united with each other."

General Charles Lee, on the other hand, with a kind of simplistic optimism, believed, based on raw economics, that France would ally herself with the colonies at the first opportunity. "The superior commerce and marine force of England were evidently established on the monopoly of her American trade," he explained in a letter to Patrick Henry on May 7, 1776. "The inferiority of France, in these two capital points, consequently had its source in the same origin. Any deduction from this monopoly must bring down her rival in proportion to this deduction. The French are and always have been sensible of these great truths."

For his part, Patrick Henry would have preferred that a declaration be delayed not only until a confederation of the colonies could be established by written articles but until there was some guarantee of backing by foreign powers. Yet he also acknowledged, in a letter to John Adams, that the issues to be thrashed out in forming a confederation, such as equal representation, might "split and divide; certainly will delay the

French alliance, which with me is everything." And he was particularly afraid that unless the alliance could be arranged quickly, Britain, using Canada as a bargaining chip, might come to some accommodation of her own with France. "The half of our continent offered to France may induce her to aid our destruction, which she certainly has the power to accomplish. I know the free trade with all the States would be more beneficial to her than any territorial possessions she might acquire. But pressed, allured, as she will be,—above all, ignorant of the great thing we mean to offer,—may we not lose her? The consequence is dreadful."

F R A N C E was waiting. She had long coveted an American alliance and together with Spain thirsted to revenge the losses she had suffered in the Seven Years' War. No sooner had that war ended than she began assessing the prospects for American independence and the impact it would have on her military and strategic interests around the world. In the intervening years, she had rebuilt her navy, and by 1776 she had sixty-four ships of the line and thirty-six frigates afloat. To make up for her losses in the East Indies and North America, she had developed the commerce of the French Antilles—Santo Domingo, Guadeloupe, and Martinique—which poured their rich harvests into the French economy. Her power had also grown in Corsica and the Levant, and Egypt had begun to emerge as a base of French operations against British possessions in India.

As for America, the French had dispatched a number of secret agents to take the pulse of colonial discontent. One of the earliest was a military analyst, Johann de Kalb, sent "to inquire" (according to his instructions) "into the intentions of the inhabitants, of the strength of their purpose to withdraw from the English government. And he will examine their resources in troops, fortified places, and forts, and will seek to discover their plan of revolt and the leaders who are expected to direct and control it. He will also endeavor to ascertain whether they are in want of good engineers and artillery officers, or other individuals, and whether they should be supplied with them."

Kalb set out from France on May 2, 1767, and went first to Amsterdam to interview commercial agents and others who had regular dealings with the colonies. There he learned, as he put it in his first report, that notwithstanding the repeal of the Stamp Act, "the breach between the colonies and the mother country is as wide as ever." The English at the time had 20,000 troops on American soil, but "they were widely dispersed." The "Pennsylvania Dutch alone," he was told, could raise

60,000 men if fighting broke out, and the provincial assemblies were "resolved to maintain their rights by the sword."

The French Ministry told Kalb to proceed at once to America "to satisfy yourself by personal inspection . . . as to the means at our command if disposed, in case of a war with England, to make a diversion in that direction."

Kalb landed at Philadelphia on January 12, 1768. He confirmed "a general fermentation," and noted with admiration that women had also begun to take an active part in the resistance—"they deny themselves tea, they deny themselves foreign sugar, they will have no more fine linens from England, but sedulously ply their spinning-wheels to prepare them linens of their own. Silks, which they cannot yet make for themselves, they will do without." Everyone, it seemed to him, was "imbued with such a spirit of independence and freedom from control that if all the provinces can be united an independent state will certainly come forth in time." Yet he also warned that if France supported the unrest prematurely or attacked England directly, it would draw the colonists back to their former feelings of allegiance and fidelity to the British Crown.

A coherent, if cautious, French policy emerged. As the colonies' rift with Britain widened, assistance in the form of arms and money was to be given to the insurgents as far as it could be done secretly; war was to be avoided as long as possible—that is, until the Americans had given unequivocal proof of their perseverance and strength.

English statesmen recognized the peril. "You will draw a foreign force upon you," warned Burke in the House of Commons in 1774, "if you get in war with the colonies." And Lord Chatham more urgently declared, "France has her full attention upon you. War is at your doors."

But under Louis XVI, who ascended the French throne in 1774, the government's attention was at first divided. Under the influence of his finance minister, Pierre-Robert-Jacques Turgot, the young king became preoccupied with a budget deficit and with the cost of new reform measures aimed at putting the French military onto a par with Austria and Prussia. In council, Turgot also opposed aid to the colonies as a further strain on French finances, even though, as the king's war minister pointed out, if Britain consolidated her hold on America, she would likely move to oust the French completely from the West Indies, from which the French economy drew much of its strength. Turgot's influence declined, however, ending in his removal in May 1776, and the king came under the domination of his accomplished foreign minister, Charles Gravier, comte de Vergennes, in whom the policy of covert aid to America found its most adept expression.

Meanwhile, in November 1774, American agents in London had approached the French chargé d'affaires with a request for assistance. The French sent observers to America to assess the situation, and in December 1775 a secret agent, Achard Bonvouloir, to Philadelphia to consult with members of the Committee of Secret Correspondence about undercover operations for the supply of money and munitions of war. Montreal had just been taken; in Boston, the British were under siege; all signs then pointed to the capture of Québec. Bonvouloir had also been empowered to say that under no circumstances would France, as America's ally, seek to recover Canada. The committee responded well to his overtures, and Bonvouloir's reports to Vergennes—which were written in milk, as a form of invisible writing—were upbeat. Meanwhile, the committee decided to send Silas Deane, a lawyer and former Connecticut delegate, to France.

His qualifications were not of the best. He spoke no French and had no diplomatic experience. And although, in the words of John Adams, "he was a person of a plausible readiness and volubility with his tongue and pen," he was "much addicted to ostentation and expense in dress and living" and "without any deliberate forecast or reflection, solidity of judgment or real information." In short, a bon vivant. But it was just that taste for high living that the committee naïvely thought would help him to cut an acceptable figure at a European court.

Deane's instructions were to masquerade as a merchant engaged in "providing goods for the Indian [fur] trade . . . it being probable that the court of France may not like it to be known publicly that any agent from the Colonies is in that country." In conference with Vergennes, however, he was to indicate that a declaration of independence was forthcoming and offer France a full-fledged commercial alliance in exchange for 100 pieces of field artillery and arms and equipment for 25,000 men.

Deane sailed in March 1776, going by the Bermudas and Spain to escape interdiction by English cruisers. From Spain he made his way over the Pyrenees to France. On July 17, he was finally presented to Vergennes. Vergennes, however, was noncommittal. The Québec campaign had been a disaster; colonial union remained uncertain; independence (so far as he knew) had not yet been declared. Vergennes would say only that "the people of America and their cause were very respectable in the eyes of all disinterested persons." In short, he would adhere to the original scheme of "veiled and hidden aid to appear to come from Commerce" while postponing an alliance until conditions were right.

In the meantime, to facilitate the covert operation, a fictitious trading concern, Roderigue Hortalez & Company, had been established in May with a million francs under the direction of the dramatist Pierre-Augustin Caron, baron de Beaumarchais, later famous as the author of *The Marriage of Figaro* and *The Barber of Seville*. Beaumarchais (who styled himself, according to his original position, "Watchmaker to the King") had previously proved his adroitness and discretion in several delicate missions for the government, including a stint as a secret agent in London. In Paris, as a front for Hortalez & Company, he rented in the Faubourg du Temple an enormous house known as the Hôtel de Hollande, in which the Dutch ambassadors had formerly dwelt. There he installed a considerable staff of clerks and employees, and, working himself with energy and zeal, made arrangements to send munitions to Haiti and Martinique, from which American agents could transship them to the mainland. French naval squadrons were stationed in the English Channel and the French West Indies to deter the British from interfering with the operation, and efforts were made to enlist the active assistance of Spain. But the Spanish felt that if war were to be made on England, its principal object should be the acquisition of Portugal and Minorca for herself and the liberation of Ireland. Nevertheless, she was eventually willing to make common cause with France in the hope of protecting her own New World possessions from American revenge.

T H R O U G H O U T the month of June, debate over Lee's momentous resolutions went on in the Congress, while the committee to draft the declaration—"that no time be lost, in case the Congress agree"—got to work. Jefferson was not necessarily the most obvious candidate to compose the text. He had often been absent from Congress and, being naturally reserved and shy at public speaking, had said little in debate. "In fact, during the whole time I sat with him," John Adams later remarked, "I never heard him utter three sentences together." But he had acquired a certain literary reputation as a result of his articulate pamphlet *A Summary View of the Rights of British America*, published in July 1774, and his "peculiar felicity of expression" made him an appropriate choice to give the document its literary form.

Nevertheless, it seems that Jefferson initially tried to get out of the assignment and urged Adams to prepare the first draft instead. But Adams refused, and years later recalled the following exchange:

"You should do it," said Jefferson.

"Oh, no."

"Why will you not?"

"I will not."

"Why?" pressed Jefferson.

"Reasons enough," said Adams.

"What can be your reasons?"

"Reason, first, you are a Virginian and a Virginian ought to appear at the head of this business. Reason second, I am obnoxious, suspected and unpopular. You are very much otherwise. Reason third, you can write ten times better than I can."

"Well," said Jefferson, "if you are decided, I will do as well as I can."

"Very well," said Adams, "when you have drawn it up we will have a meeting."

And so, in the middle of June 1776, working chiefly in the parlor of his rented quarters on Market Street in downtown Philadelphia, Jefferson bent over his custom-made mahogany writing desk lined with green felt, and wrote the immortal text. On the morning of the nineteenth or twentieth, he showed his rough draft (copied from his original draft, which he had worked over until it was "scratched like a schoolboy's exercise") to Adams, who was "delighted" on the whole "with its high tone and the flights of oratory." He disagreed with Jefferson's portrayal of King George as a tyrant, deeming the attack "too passionate . . . too much like scolding for so grave and solemn a document." But for some reason he kept this opinion to himself. Franklin reviewed the document as well, making a handful of preliminary changes—replacing "sacred & undeniable" with "self-evident," for example—before it was submitted to Congress on June 28.

Meanwhile, in the intervening three weeks, growing popular support had enabled Virginia and New England to lead most of the doubtful middle states to assent. But the argument had now gone on for so long that the delegates were testy. Joseph Hewes of North Carolina wrote to a friend, "We do not treat each other with that decency and respect that was observed heretofore. Jealousies, ill natured observations and recriminations take the place of reason and Argument. Our Tempers are soured. Some among us urge strongly for Independence and eternal separation, others wish to wait a little longer and to have the opinion of their Constituents on that subject."

A great deal of maneuvering went on behind the scenes. "Mr. Harrison had courted Mr. Hancock," wrote John Adams,

and Mr. Hancock had courted Mr. Duane, Mr. Dickerson and their party, and leaned so partially in their favor, that Mr. Samuel Adams had become very bitter against Mr. Hancock, and spoke of him with great asperity in private circles. . . . Although Harrison was another Sir John Falstaff, excepting in his larcenies and robberies, his conversation disgusting to every man of delicacy or decorum, yet, as I saw he was to be nominated with us in business, I took no notice of his vices or follies, but treated him, and Mr. Hancock, too, with uniform politeness. I was, however, too intimate with Mr. [Richard Henry] Lee, Mr. Adams, Mr. Ward, &c. to escape jealousy and malignity of their adversaries.

In other words, Adams had to lobby for the votes of people he detested (but who he thought would go along) but was hampered by his own reputation as a radical, no matter how diplomatic he managed to appear.

Lee's resolutions on behalf of a declaration came up for renewed consideration before Congress on July 1. John Adams and John Dickinson of Pennsylvania spoke on behalf of the opposed factions in a great debate. Dickinson, "a Constitutional Whig of the English pattern," was committed to legal remedies, and his credentials were impeccable. His "Letters from a Pennsylvania Farmer," published in the *Pennsylvania Chronicle,* had set forth in a clear and measured style the grounds for the colonial protest against imperial oppression and had made him as famous in the patriot camp as Jefferson, Patrick Henry, or John Adams. He was also amiable, sincere, a dazzling conversationalist, and had a mind, wrote an admirer, that was "a rich casket of all the various knowledge which history contains." Jefferson said of him, "He was an honest man, and so able a one, that he was greatly indulged even by those who did not feel his scruples." Indeed, it was almost impossible not to give him the benefit of the doubt. Moreover, in this instance he "had prepared himself with great labor and ardent zeal," wrote John Adams with reluctant admiration, "and in a speech of great length, and with all his eloquence, he combined together all that had before been written in pamphlets and newspapers, and all that had from time to time been said in Congress by himself and others. He conducted the debate not only with great ingenuity and eloquence, but with equal politeness and candor, and was answered in the same spirit."

Yet Adams by all accounts proved the more formidable of the two. "John Adams was our Colossus on the floor," remembered Jefferson. "He was not graceful nor elegant, nor remarkably fluent but he came out occasionally with a power of thought and expression, that moved us from our seats."

On the following day, Lee's resolutions were passed with New York abstaining, Delaware divided, and Pennsylvania and South Carolina still opposed. On July 3, Pennsylvania and South Carolina agreed to go along for the sake of unanimity, and an absent Delaware delegate, Caesar Rodney, rode eighty miles through rain and thunder to break the tie in his delegation's vote.

Congress then proceeded to go through the text of the declaration itself. Jefferson had read the document aloud to Congress on June 28, but consideration of it had been tabled until the matter of independence had been resolved. Now, for almost twelve hours (in various sessions from late Tuesday, July 2, into Thursday, July 4) the delegates went over the document word by word. Justly proud of his composition, Jefferson was appalled when his colleagues began changing words and phrases and making drastic cuts. But he was also, in fact, extremely sensitive to criticism. Two years before, he had rejected various editorial improvements tactfully offered by John Dickinson to his draft of the "Declaration on the Causes and Necessity of Taking Up Arms." The committee appointed to draw up this declaration afterward rejected Jefferson's version entirely with one New Jersey delegate, William Livingston, remarking that it suffered from too much "fault-finding" and emotional "declamation." The same shortcomings were now ascribed to the Declaration of Independence. Franklin, seated beside him, noted Jefferson's discomfort and sympathetically remarked that he had made it a rule never to prepare papers to be reviewed by a public body and tried to console him with an amusing anecdote:

When I was a journeyman printer one of my companions, an apprentice hatter, having served out his time was about to open shop for himself. His first concern was to have a handsome signboard with a proper inscription. He composed it in these words: *John Thompson, hatter, makes and sells hats for ready money,* with a figure of a hat subjoined. But he thought he would submit it to his friends for their amendments. The first he showed it to thought the word "hatter" tautologous, because followed by the words "makes hats" which show he was a hatter. It was struck out. The next observed that the word "makes" might as well be omitted, because the customers would not care who made the hats. If good and to their mind, they would buy, by whomsoever made. He struck it out. A third said he thought the words "for ready money" were useless, as it was not the custom of the place to sell on credit. Everyone who purchased expected to pay. They were parted with, and the inscription now stood: "John Thompson sells hats." "Sells hats?" says his next friend. "Why, nobody will expect you to give them away. What then is the use of that word?" It was stricken out; and "hats" followed it, the rather as there was one painted on the board. So his inscription was reduced ultimately to "John Thompson" with the figure of a hat subjoined.

The declaration was not reduced so absolutely, but it was substantially pared. Most of the document consists of an enumeration of grievances against King George III, and there was much in that section (between the preamble and the resolutions declaring independence at the end) that the delegates did not approve. In one passage, for example, Jefferson excoriated the British for dispatching "foreign mercenaries to invade & destroy us." This, he said, in a poignant turn of phrase, had "given the last stab to agonizing affection, and manly spirit bids us to renounce for ever these unfeeling brethren. We must endeavor to forget our former love for them, and to hold them as we hold the rest of mankind, enemies in war, in peace friends. We might have been a free & a great people together; but a communication of grandeur & of freedom it seems is below their dignity." Congress objected to this language as an ill-advised and inappropriate attack on the British people, rather than on their government and king. Nevertheless, Jefferson resented the excision and long afterward wrote sarcastically, "The pusillanimous idea that we had friends in England worth keeping terms with, still haunted the minds of many."

In another passage, Jefferson claimed that the colonies had been settled "at the expense of our own blood and treasure, unassisted by the wealth or the strength of Great Britain," and that the colonists had never accepted, in fact or in idea, the authority of Parliament in any respect— "submission . . . was no part of our constitution"—even though they had "adopted one common king." This was not really true. And what truth there was in it was too arguable to include. A third passage, likewise rejected, accused the monarchy of imposing the slave trade upon the colonies against their will: "He [the king] has waged cruel war against human nature itself violating its most sacred rights of life & liberty in the persons of a distant people who never offended him, captivating & carrying them into slavery in another hemisphere, or to incur miserable death in their transportation thither."

Though Jefferson had imbibed some of the stereotypes about blacks current in his day, he was a reluctant slaveholder whose own domestic economy happened to be dependent upon the human property of his inheritance. He and others had been "born into mastery," but at least they had endeavored (in Virginia, for example) to prevent the importation of more slaves into the colony. The king, however, had vetoed this initiative. And Jefferson had already condemned him in nearly identical words in a draft he had been working on for a new Virginia constitution. Certainly, he would have rid the whole society of the evil of slavery if he could. In his autobiography Jefferson afterward recalled that his antislavery passage "was struck out in complaisance to South Carolina and Georgia, who had never attempted to restrain the importation of slaves. . . . Our northern brethren also, I believe, felt a little tender under those censures; for though their people had very few slaves themselves, yet they had been pretty considerable carriers of them to others."

Other charges against the king remained intact, including those that accused him of "cutting off our Trade"; "imposing Taxes on us without our Consent"; "depriving us, in many cases, of the Benefits of Trial by Jury"; "taking away our Charters, abolishing our most valuable Laws, and altering fundamentally the Forms of our Governments"; "suspending our own Legislatures"; "waging War against us"; and so on, making up "a long Train of Abuses and Usurpations" which were aimed at reducing the colonies "under absolute Despotism." All this was important. But it is the preamble of the declaration that made it the immortal document it is:

> We hold these Truths to be self-evident, that all Men are created equal, that they are endowed by their Creator with certain unalienable Rights, that among these are Life, Liberty, and the pursuit of Happiness—That to secure these Rights, Governments are instituted among Men, deriving their just Powers from the Consent of the Governed, that whenever any Form of Government becomes destructive of these Ends, it is the Right of the People to alter or to abolish it, and to institute new Government, laying its Foundation on such Principles, and organizing its Powers in such Form, as to them shall seem most likely to effect their Safety and Happiness.

Thankfully, these lines emerged from the stern editorial scrutiny of the delegates unchanged.

Nevertheless, Jefferson remained indignant about the revisions for the rest of his life. In all, close to a hundred changes were made and the text cut by about a fourth. Adams himself believed that Congress, while making some judicious emendations, had also "obliterated some of the best of it." Richard Henry Lee was likewise sorry to see many of the phrases go. "I wish sincerely, as well for the honor of Congress, as for that of the States," he later wrote Jefferson, "that the Ms. had not been mangled as it is. However, the Thing in its nature is so good that no cookery can spoil the dish for the palates of freemen."

And who would deny it?

In the declaration, Jefferson evidently emulated the prose he admired in the English statesman Lord Bolingbroke—"a lofty, rhythmical full-flowing eloquence, something with the elevation but not the pomp of oratory." In the formulation of his ideas, John Locke was an obvious influence, but (with a kind of startling license) Locke's classic natural-rights trinity of "life, liberty, and property" was mysteriously transmuted into "life, liberty, and the pursuit of happiness." Perhaps Jefferson was recalling a passage from one of John Dickinson's patriotic writings, in which, with almost equal grandeur, the leading opponent of the declaration had declared that neither kings nor Parliament could give "the *rights essential to happiness....* We claim them from a higher source—from the King of kings, and Lord of all the earth. They are not annexed to us by parchments and seals. They are created in us by the decrees of Providence, which establish the laws of our nature. They are born with us; exist with us; and cannot be taken from us by any human power without taking our lives. In short, they are founded on the immutable maxims of reason and justice."

Whether that echo was deliberate or not, he almost certainly borrowed from the new Virginia state constitution, for which George Mason had just proposed the following Declaration of Rights: "That all men are born equally free and independent, and have certain inherent natural Rights of which they can not by any Compact, deprive or divest their Posterity: among which are the Enjoyment of Life and Liberty, with the Means of acquiring and possessing Property, and pursuing and obtaining Happiness and Safety." Mason's Declaration of Rights had been published in the Philadelphia press on the sixth and twelfth of June.

Years later, after Adams and Jefferson had their famous falling-out, Adams wrote that there had been nothing new in Jefferson's declaration and that every idea in it had been taken from a revolutionary pamphlet by James Otis! Jefferson, apprised of these and other remarks, wrote to James Madison, "[It] may all be true. Of that I am not to be the judge. . . . I only know that I turned to neither book nor pamphlet while writing it. I did not consider it as any part of my charge to invent new ideas altogether and to offer no sentiment that had ever been expressed before." Rather, he said, his simple purpose had been "to place before mankind the common sense of the subject, in terms so plain and firm as to command their assent."

And so he did. "All honor to Jefferson," wrote Abraham Lincoln, "to the man who . . . had the coolness, forecast, and capacity to introduce into a merely revolutionary document an abstract truth, . . . and so to embalm it there, that today, and in all coming days, it shall be a rebuke and a stumbling-block to the very harbingers of reappearing tyranny and oppression."

• • •

O N the morning of July 4, Jefferson rose before dawn, and at six A.M. calmly noted that the temperature was 68 degrees Fahrenheit. The wind was southeast and the mercury soon climbed to 76. He soaked his feet in a basin of cold water (as was his morning habit), took some tea and biscuits, and proceeded to Independence Hall. By midafternoon, the collective editing of the declaration (accelerated by a plague of horseflies which had swarmed out of the stables nearby) had come to its happy end. It was voted on and adopted (New York alone abstaining), whereupon Joseph Hewes of North Carolina, who had repeatedly voted against it, "started suddenly upright, and lifting up both his Hands to Heaven as if he had been in a trance, cry'd out, 'It is done! and I will abide by it.'" An old bellman at nearby Christ's Church, waiting for the signal from a boy stationed at the State House door, suddenly heard the lad clap his hands and shout, "Ring! Ring!"

Those who afterward lined up to sign the document (on August 22) had reason to be uneasy. They knew the peril and penalty of treason and were signing, as it were, with halters about their necks. John Hancock, as president of Congress, wrote his name first. "We must be unanimous," he reportedly declared. "There must be no pulling different ways, we must all hang together." "Yes," replied Franklin, "we must indeed all hang together, or most assuredly we shall all hang separately." Behind them stood Benjamin Harrison, a large, heavy man, who nervously picked up the theme. To the diminutive Eldridge Gerry, he said, "I shall have a great advantage over you, Mr. Gerry, when we are all hung for what we are now doing. From the size and weight of my body I shall die in a few minutes, but from the lightness of your body, you will dance in the air an hour or two before you are dead."

Yet there was also an overriding and mystical feeling of providential cover to the boldness of their act. As John Page, a Virginia statesman, put it rather beautifully to Jefferson two weeks after the declaration was adopted, "God preserve the United States. We know the Race is not to the swift nor the Battle to the Strong. Do you not think an Angel rides in the Whirlwind and directs this Storm?"

Congress had copies of the declaration sent to every state Assembly and convention, to the various committees of safety, and to the commanding officers of the Continental Army to proclaim before their troops.

John Adams, writing to Abigail, was moved to prophecy by the transcendent spirit of the hour: "You will think me transported with enthusiasm, but I am not. I am well aware of the toil, and blood, and treasure that it will cost us to maintain this Declaration, and support and defend these States. Yet, through all the gloom, I can see the rays of ravishing light and glory. I can see that the end is more than worth all the means, and that posterity will triumph in that day's transaction, even though we should rue it, which I trust in God we shall not."

It seemed to him, moreover, that it was just as well consideration of the declaration (by which he meant Lee's resolutions) had taken as long as it had:

> Time has been given for the whole people maturely to consider the great question of independence, and to ripen their judgment, dissipate their fears, and allure their hopes, by discussing it in newspapers and pamphlets, by debating it in assemblies, conventions, committees of safety and inspection, in town and county meetings, as well as in private conversations, so that the whole people, in every colony of the thirteen, have now adopted it as their own act. This will cement the union, and avoid those heats, and perhaps convulsions, which might have been occasioned by such a Declaration six months ago.

With his usual prescience, he predicted the day would be "celebrated by succeeding generations as the great anniversary festival" and "solemnized with pomp and parade, with shows, games, sports, guns, bells, bonfires, and illuminations, from one end of this continent to the other, from this time forward forevermore." (The practice, of course, has been to celebrate the Fourth of July, the day on which the form of the Declaration of Independence was agreed to, rather than the second, when Lee's resolutions were adopted and which Adams actually had in mind.)

Celebrations followed in city, town, village, and country hamlet, with bell ringing, parades, bonfires, and illuminations throughout the land. In New York, after the colonial assembly "at the risque of our lives and fortunes" gave its assent on July 9, Washington had the army brigades drawn up at six P.M. to hear "the United Colonies of America" declared *"Free and Independent States."* After the text was read, he saw fit to add, "The General hopes that this important event will serve as a fresh incentive to every officer and soldier to act with fidelity and courage, as knowing that now the peace and safety of his country depend, under God, solely on the success of our arms; and that he is now in the service of a state possessed of sufficient power to reward his merit, and to advance him to the highest honors of a free country."

That evening New Yorkers toppled the lead equestrian statue of King George III (erected after repeal of the Stamp Act) from its pedestal on

Bowling Green. Eventually, its metal would be melted down and molded into 42,000 cartridges for patriot guns. Citizens in Baltimore, Savannah, and elsewhere likewise burned or buried the king in effigy and tore from their hinges all signs bearing the royal arms. In Worcester, Massachusetts, thirsty patriots repaired to a local tavern and offered toasts to the prosperity of the United States and a dozen other things, including "Perpetual itching without benefit of scratching to the enemies of America." That Sunday, Bishop William White, the patriot rector of Christ's Church in Philadelphia, omitted the usual prayers offered for the king, and one year later, as a sign that God's imprimatur was now stamped upon the radical sermons he preached, a bolt of lightning struck and shattered the Royal Crown of England affixed to the top of the spire.

In just over two years, a new nation had been born. In the early spring of 1774, rebel leaders had established their Committees of Correspondence, which had led to the election of a revolutionary Congress. That Congress (or nascent central government) had in turn established a continental economic association with committees to enforce its mandates. These committees became the nuclei of revolutionary power in each colony and dominated the colonial assemblies. The latter, now revolutionary or semirevolutionary bodies, began drafting new state constitutions to legalize their own authority. Nine months later, the delegates to the Second Continental Congress had declared the united colonies an independent state.

For radicals such as John Adams, the victory was particularly sweet. At one time kept at arm's length by his colleagues—"like a man infected with the leprosy," he claimed—he was almost unable to forbear rejoicing at the change of fortune that had brought his adversaries to inglorious defeat. "Dickinson, Morris, Alsop, all fallen, like grass before the scythe, notwithstanding all their vast advantages in point of fortune, family and abilities. I am inclined to think, however, and to wish, that these gentlemen may be restored at a fresh election, because, although mistaken in some points, they are good characters, and their great wealth and numerous connections will contribute to strengthen America and cement her union."

Adams was too wise to gloat. And if he had, he would have been shamed. Robert Morris, despite his longing for the British peace commissioners, in the end had signed the declaration; and though Dickinson had failed to, once independence was declared he laid aside his misgivings, raised a regiment of Pennsylvania militia, and rode at their head to New Jersey to oppose the enemy there. On August 7, he wrote to Charles Thomson, "The enemy are moving, and an attack on New York is quickly expected. As for myself, I can form no idea of a more noble fate than

. . . to resign my life, if Divine Providence should please so to dispose of me, for the defence and happiness of those unkind countrymen whom I cannot forbear to esteem as fellow-citizens amidst their fury against me."

Meanwhile, the issue of confederation had come up for consideration on July 12. Franklin's Albany Plan of 1754 had been the precursor of his own more ambitious Articles of Confederation and Perpetual Union, which he had laid before the Congress the previous July. That in turn helped inspire the first draft of a new Articles of Confederation now presented to Congress by the committee assigned to consider the issue. This document projected a union in which there would be a common Treasury and in which an elected assembly would have exclusive jurisdiction over foreign relations, with the power to form alliances, raise a national army (to be sustained by requisitions on the states), and make war and peace. But it would have no general authority to regulate either foreign or interstate commerce (except to a limited extent by commercial treaties), nor the power to tax.

As Congress began its long and seemingly interminable consideration of the articles, the delegates found that they could not agree on several great issues. The most important of these was the matter of representation. The question was, Should each colony have a single vote, or be represented in proportion to its size and wealth? John Witherspoon of New Jersey asked, "Is it not plausible that the small states will be oppressed by the great ones?"

And then there was the question as to "whether Congress should have the authority to limit the dimensions of each colony." Virginia, for example, claimed a western boundary reaching to the Pacific Ocean. But Samuel Chase of Maryland declared, "No colony has a right to go to the South Sea [Pacific Ocean]; they never had; they can't have. It would not be safe to the rest. It would be destructive to her sisters and to herself." James Wilson of Pennsylvania, in support of Chase, pointed out that the original colonial charters, which had imagined the Pacific Ocean to be much closer than it was, had been "based upon a mistaken idea of the geography of North America." In other boundary disputes, Virginia and Connecticut both claimed large sections of Pennsylvania; New York and New Hampshire the territory of Vermont; and so on. Such issues naturally combined with doubts in the minds of many delegates about the wisdom of uniting under a strong central government. Would the individual states retain their essential sovereignty or belong to a nation or union in which the states would be subordinate? As Patrick Henry had predicted before voting for the declaration, these matters would not be settled for a long time.

CHAPTER EIGHT

NEW YORK

Even as Congress debated the form of a future national union, the largest expeditionary force Great Britain had ever assembled gathered off the port of New York. The vanguard, under General Howe, had sailed with three ships from Halifax on June 11, and on June 25 it anchored near Sandy Hook, the peninsula guarding the southern entrance to the harbor. Within five days, 130 ships had joined it, and by July 4 there were so many sails that the bay "looked like a forest of pine trees with their branches trimmed." On July 12, William's elder brother Admiral Lord Richard Howe arrived on the flagship *Eagle,* and as many as a hundred British ships sailed up the Verrazano Narrows that day. Thirty-two thousand well-trained professional soldiers (including 8,397 Hessians), completely armed and equipped, were poised to disembark from 170 transports supported by 20 frigates and 10 ships of the line. Still more ships of war and their tenders continued to arrive, including, at the beginning of August, the squadron led by Sir Henry Clinton, recently repulsed at Charleston, with 3,000 more men. "His coming," wrote an American colonel, "was as unexpected as if he had dropped from the clouds." After Clinton's arrival, the armada numbered 427 transports and 52 ships of war.

The hiring of mercenary German troops to subdue the rebellion had outraged most Americans. Though it was not unusual for European na-

tions to supplement their own small standing armies with such soldiers
—all the great wars of Europe until the French Revolution were conducted largely in this way—the conflict was still viewed by many on
both sides of the Atlantic as a family quarrel. The king had first tried to
hire Russian shock troops, such as had recently scored victories over the
Turks, and when Catherine the Great refused his request, he appealed
to Holland, which also turned him down. Six German principalities,
however—Anhalt-Zerbst, Anspach-Bayreuth, Brunswick, Hesse-Cassel,
Hesse-Hanau, and Waldeck—readily obliged. In the course of the war,
they would contribute 30,000 men, and for their services and blood,
Britain would pay their princelings £7 million. As elector of Hanover, the
king of England was also able to assign Hanoverian troops to his garrisons at Gibraltar and Minorca, thereby releasing five well-trained battalions of infantry, or 2,365 more men, for his American war. In Parliament,
these actions were denounced by Lords Cavendish, Camden, Chatham,
Shelbourne, and others, and Paine spoke for the majority in America
when he said, "Of all the acts of transcendent folly and wickedness
perpetrated by the British Ministry, none could do more to convince
the Americans of the necessity of an immediate declaration of independence than the hiring of foreign mercenaries." In the declaration itself,
Jefferson had included the mercenaries in his list of grievances against
the king.

At the same time, Lord Howe had arrived with an "olive branch."
Though much anticipated, and widely publicized, it turned out to be
nothing more than a royal pardon for all those willing to abandon the
rebellion and "aid in restoring tranquillity." He made an effort to deliver
a copy of it to Washington and with a flag of truce sent it up the harbor
enclosed in a letter, but as the letter was addressed to "George Washington, Esq.," in deliberate neglect of his military title (which the British
were unwilling to recognize), Howe's messenger was turned away. A
week later, Howe sent it again, this time addressed to "George Washington, Esq., etc., etc." The messenger was indulged with an audience and
tried to explain that "the etceteras on the letter meant everything. 'Indeed,' said Washington, with a pleasant smile, 'they might mean
anything,' " and he returned the letter without breaking the seal.

Washington pointed out, however, that as he served under the authority of Congress, it was Congress with whom Lord Howe would have to
deal. But he doubted anything would come of it, as His Lordship seemed
empowered only to grant pardons, which the rebels didn't need as they
had committed no crime. "No doubt we all need pardon from Heaven,"
the patriot governor Jonathan Trumbull of Connecticut afterward re-

marked, "for our manifold sins and transgressions; but the American who needs the pardon of his Britannic Majesty is yet to be found."

AGAINST the assembled British force of 32,000 men, Washington had been able to marshal about 17,000, most of whom were undisciplined militia or fresh recruits. All the promised efforts of Congress to double his force had fallen short. Joseph Hewes of North Carolina sounded a refrain that would often be repeated during the war: "We resolve to raise regiments, resolve to make Cannon, resolve to make and import muskets, powder and cloathing, but it is a melancholly fact that near half of our men, Cannon, Muskets, powder, cloathes, etc., is to be found nowhere but on paper." Moreover, as summer wore on, noted one officer, it became increasingly difficult "to prevail on the people to leave their harvests"—for in revolutionary America, everything still centered around hearth and home.

One of those to answer the call was Joseph Plumb Martin, a Milford, Connecticut, farm boy who in July enlisted in a regiment of Connecticut state troops. Martin had often gone to enlistment rallies and had looked with some envy upon those, only slightly older than himself, marching off to war. At last, overcoming his own hesitations ("thought I . . . I must stick to it; ther will be no receding"), he went one evening to where the recruiter had set up in the village and found a number of other young men he knew pressing one another to join. "If you will enlist I will, says one; come, says another, you have long been talking about it—now is the time." Martin sat down at the table, "enlisting orders were immediately presented; I took up the pen, and loaded it with the fatal charge."

In the enthusiasm of his youth, Martin regarded the Americans as "invincible." He set out for war with a folding pocket sunglass and a small screwtop wooden box containing a lock of his girlfriend's hair. He professed not to be at all discouraged when he learned that the British were being reinforced by 15,000 men. "It made no alteration in my mind; I did not care if there had been fifteen times fifteen thousand, I should have gone just as soon." He boarded a troopship for New York, where he went into training; then, with several thousand others, he prepared to cross over to Brooklyn Heights. As they marched to the ferry landing at the foot of Maiden Lane, they filed past provisioning casks from which they took handfuls of "sea bread" (made of canel and peasmeal) "hard enough to break the tooth of a rat."

They crossed the East River, landed at Brooklyn Heights, and marched up to the plain. Everyone, Martin remarked, wore his own civilian clothes, and most of the officers of the new levies were distinguishable from their men only by the colored cockades of their hats.

Washington had been obliged to accept all who came. Ambrose Serle, secretary to Lord Howe, described the rebel host on the eve of battle as "the strangest that was ever collected: Old men of 60, Boys of 14, and Blacks of all ages, and ragged for the most part, compose the motley Crew."

On July 23, Congress told Washington that it had "such an entire confidence in his judgment" that he could make use of his troops in whatever way "as to him shall seem the most conducive to the public good." That did not help him much, since, given the power of the British navy and the patriots' lack of a naval force of their own, New York was almost impossible to defend. The broad, deep waters about Manhattan Island afforded easy access to the enemy fleet, which could come and go at will up the Hudson and East Rivers and interpose itself between whatever scattered positions the Americans chose to man. Nevertheless, a valiant effort was made. The shore of Manhattan Island was dotted with small forts and redoubts that had been erected by Lee in the spring, and forts were also built at the upper end of the island, on Governors Island, and at Paulus Hook (now Jersey City) on the New Jersey shore. Though obliged to divide up his forces in this way, Washington gave priority to the fortification of Brooklyn Heights, which commanded New York City (which then occupied only the lower end of Manhattan Island) in the same strategic way as Boston had been commanded by Dorchester Heights or the hills on Charlestown Neck.

W H I L E the military preparations continued, the patriot authorities also had to deal with the enemy within. Every colony had its proportion of loyalists, or Tories, who felt that the Continental Congress and the various revolutionary committees had gone too far. They were not all necessarily die-hard defenders of the British government, and some had not only opposed the Stamp Act and other measures but had done what they could to secure their repeal. But they were set against the destruction of the empire.

On the whole, the division between patriot and loyalist was principled and seldom contaminated by ethnic or racial animosities. These, in any case, were irrelevant, but there were those who occasionally tried to mix things up. One (unfortunately) was the brilliant patriot theorist James Otis. When Martin Howard, a loyalist of Newport, Rhode Island, defended the Stamp Act in 1765, Otis denounced the whole town as full of

"Turks, Jews, and other infidels with a few renegade Christians and Catholics." By "renegade Christians" Otis also meant Anglicans (which would have included George Washington, for example), and he pointedly contrasted Newport with the rest of New England for its more unblemished Puritan beliefs. In another unfortunate, if solitary, lapse, John Adams in his Boston Massacre defense had dismissed the incident as a melee between soldiers and a "motley mob of saucy boys, negroes, mulattoes, Irish teagues, and outlandish jacktars"—which not only smacked of bigotry but slighted the memory of Crispus Attucks, the first casualty of the rebellion.

For its part, the loyalist cause was also compromised by some of its allies. Lord Dunmore's mercenary behavior—bombarding Norfolk and arming a few bewildered slaves in January 1776—had discredited if not absolutely destroyed the cause in Virginia, and the following month, the loyalists in North Carolina (under Josiah Martin, the colony's last royal governor) had suffered a similar defeat. In tandem with the slave revolt plotted by Dunmore, Martin had tried to exploit some of the smoldering ethnic animosities in the region—in particular, between a second-generation settlement of Scots Highlanders (who held their lands directly from the Crown) and the more recent Lowland or Scotch-Irish immigrants, many of whom had joined the rebel cause.

On February 27, 1776, 1,200 kilted Highlanders, armed with two-handed claymores and marching to screaming bagpipes, had met a thousand Scots-Irish woodsmen in hunting shirts at Moore's Creek. The claymores were no match for the woodsmen's rifles as "the action became another Culloden, the bright kilts of the slain filling the little stream."

Yet there was nothing vindictive in the aftermath. When the captive Highlanders were removed to other colonies for the sake of public safety, the Provincial Congress declared, "We have their security in contemplation, not to make them miserable. In our power, their errors claim our pity, their situation disarms our resentment." This wasn't just talk, for commissioners were promptly appointed in six North Carolina counties to protect the Highlanders' property and to see that their families were not molested or beggared by need.

Although Boston had had its share of loyalists, pro-British sentiment was much stronger in and about New York, Long Island, Staten Island, and New Jersey. In March, a committee appointed by Congress to confer with General Lee about New York's defense had recommended "that the inhabitants of Statten Island shou'd without loss of time be disarm'd and their arms delivered to some Regiment already raising but unfornished with muskets. I do not imagine that disarming the Tories will incapacitate them from acting against us, as they can easily be supplied by the Ships. I shou'd therefore think it prudent to secure their Children as Hostages. If a measure of this kind (hard as it may appear) is not adopted, the Childrens Children of america may rue the fatal omission."

Congress found this recommendation (endorsed by General Lee) utterly uncouth, as did members of the New York Assembly, who also objected to Lee's imposition of a loyalty oath as "a Test upon the inhabitants of our Colony. . . . However salutary such a measure might be . . . we were much alarmed that it should owe its authority to any military officer, however distinguished. . . . There can be no liberty where the military is not subordinate to the civil power in everything not immediately concerned with their operations."

There was much to be concerned about in either case. While Lord Dunmore had been waging war against his former colony (and threatening Washington's Mount Vernon estate), New York's ex-governor William Tryon, then living on a warship in New York harbor, was laying plans to blow up the city arsenals and murder Washington and his staff at his headquarters at Richmond Hill. Tryon managed to bribe a member of Washington's Lifeguard, an Irishman named Thomas Hickey, who according to one account was to dispense with the commander in chief by poisoning a dish of peas. The plot was discovered, and Hickey was tried, convicted, and hanged on June 28 in a field near the Bowery, the first man in the Continental Army to be executed. New York's Tory mayor, David Mathews, was also arrested at his house in Flatbush at one o'clock in the morning and implicated in a larger plot to raise an underground loyalist force to assist in the British conquest of New York.

A crackdown followed. According to Thomas Jones, a Tory judge, "A universal hunt after Loyalists took place. Parties . . . were sent into every quarter of the county. . . . The Loyalists were pursued like wolves and bears, from swamp to swamp, from one hill to another, from dale to dale, and from one copse of wood to another. In consequence . . . numbers were taken, some were wounded, and a few murdered. The prisoners were conducted, with infamy, under a guard of rebels to New York, insulted and abused upon the road, and without a hearing ordered by a board of officers . . . to be transported into different parts of New England." Jones himself was arrested on June 27 but later released.

The British fleet moved quickly to sever river communications between New York and Albany. The Americans had artillery on either side of the lower Hudson, but in mid-July, to test the effectiveness of these batteries, the British sent the *Phoenix* of forty guns and the *Rose* of twenty, their decks bolstered with sandbags and accompanied by three tenders, boldly up the river. Despite a heavy cannonade, they passed the gun emplacements without sustaining any damage and sailed into the broad part of the river, called the Tappan Sea. On August 17, however, some of the fire rafts authorized by Congress were floated against them, burning one and obliging the other to retreat downstream.

Of more promise (if with less result), the Americans launched the *Turtle,* the first submarine in military history. Manned by a single person and somewhat resembling a tortoise, six feet in height and seven feet stem to stern, it could remain submerged for half an hour, had a hand-driven propeller, and could reach a speed of three miles an hour. On the outside it was equipped with an egg-shaped time bomb with an iron screw for penetrating the hull of an enemy ship. The pilot entered the submarine at the top, which had a bubblelike brass cover surrounded by glass and fitted with brass tubes. The tubes were "to admit fresh air when requisite," while a ventilator on the side removed air "unfit for consumption." Other equipment included a barometer to record the submarine's depth, a compass for steering (with needles of fox-fire wood that glowed in the dark), a hand-operated rudder, a sounding lead at the bow, a valve to admit water to make the submarine descend, and two brass forcing pumps to expel the water so it could rise. Three pairs of oars, each "fixed like the two opposite arms of a wind mill" and turned by foot "like a spinning wheel," enabled the navigator to maneuver in any direction—forward or backward, right or left, up or down. The time bomb (really a hollowed-out oak log filled with 150 pounds of gunpowder) was situated above the rudder to the rear and could be released by a spring. When it was, it simultaneously drew out a pin (as with a grenade), "which set the watch-work agoing, which, at a given time, springs the lock and the explosion ensues." The explosion could be set as much as twelve hours in advance.

This fantastic little craft had originally been built as a science project at college by David Bushnell, who afterward became an explosives expert in the Continental Army.

In August, in its one and only venture, it was launched in New York Harbor against the British flagship *Eagle,* the sixty-four-gun vessel commanded by Lord Howe. The pilot, First Sergeant Ezra Lee, successfully maneuvered the submarine under water to the ship's keel but was unable to attach the bomb to its copper-sheathed frame.

THROUGHOUT the summer, the battle lines were drawn. On July 3, the British landed 9,000 troops unopposed on Staten Island, and on August 22 another 15,000 to 20,000, supported by forty guns, crossed over to Gravesend, Long Island.

The defense of Brooklyn Heights was entrusted to General Nathanael Greene. He spent the summer fortifying it and had 9,000 men—or about half the patriot army—to man his lines. These extended from Wallabout to Gowanus Bay, about a mile and a half from Brooklyn Heights, and commanded all the approaches from the northern and southern shores of Manhattan Island. Red Hook and Fort Greene were connected by entrenchments, and in front of these was a range of thickly wooded hills, called the Heights of Guian, extending the length of the island. It was a formidable enough network of defenses and might have been adequate had it not been cut by roads wide enough for cavalry and artillery and manned largely by raw recruits.

On August 22, several enemy battalions under General Clinton landed with artillery near Brooklyn Ferry at Verrazano Narrows and marched across the low ground at Flatbush to within three or four miles of the American lines. As they advanced, a party of Pennsylvania troops fell back to guard the higher ground.

General Israel Putnam (replacing General Greene, who had fallen ill) placed about 4,500 men behind the line of hills and his best troops next to Red Hook, where he also constructed abatis and traps to prevent the enemy from getting through.

During the night of August 26, the British moved up to attack.

There were four ways through the hills: the coastal or shore road; the Flatbush Pass; the Bedford Pass; and the Jamaica Pass at their eastern end. General Clinton, having determined that the Jamaica Pass was weakly guarded, silently drew the van of his army off in that direction. Just before daybreak, he surprised and captured the defenders and began to move his column into the level country that led toward Brooklyn beyond. Meanwhile, the British left wing had advanced slowly along the coast so as to make a diversion in the opposite direction, and the British fleet had begun a bombardment at Red Hook. At dawn, in another feint, the Hessians began pummeling the American right wing with artillery at the Flatbush Pass. By nine o'clock, Clinton had completely turned the American left flank, gained the rear of the American lines, and fired two signal guns for an advance on all fronts.

The patriots scattered. The American left wing crumpled. The center was driven back. The right wing, stranded on the hills, withdrew through the marshes of Gowanus Creek and successfully defended its retreat by a courageous stand around the Vechte-Cortelyou courthouse, commanding the road to South Brooklyn. "The morning on which the British troops landed," remembered one sixteen-year-old Dutch girl, "was one of the loveliest we had ever seen. The sky was so clear and bright that you could scarcely think of it as a day which was to bring so much sorrow." As the British pushed toward her village, her family loaded as much of their furniture and other heavy belongings as they could onto a great farm wagon, buried valuables in the garden, hid the silver tea service under the hearthstone, and directed their "faithful old negro manservant" Caesar, with his little grandson, Cato, to drive the livestock along the farm lane to the woods beyond. Yet a kind of holiday air incongruously marked the occasion, as the door of the little red school-house opened and the children, as if on vacation, "rushed out with a shout."

But as the Americans stationed along the western shore retreated, the British burned a number of houses, including the girl's family farm. When she and others later returned, they found desolation—all the homesteads in the area ruined, fences broken, gardens trampled, crops destroyed. Elsewhere, the Hessians ransacked every dwelling they came upon and absolutely looted the more luxurious country estates—"all the Furniture, Glass, and Windows," lamented one British official, with some embarrassment, "and the very Hangings of the Rooms [were] demolished or defaced."

The rout had been both terrible and cruel. According to one British soldier, some of the Hessians and Scots Highlanders, having been told the Americans had intended to show them no mercy, had "put all to death that fell into their hands. . . . It was a fine sight," he added with malevolence, "to see with what alacrity they despatched the Rebels with their bayonets after we had surrounded them so that they could not resist." By the end of the day, the Americans had lost more than a thousand men, captured, wounded, or killed.

As night fell, it appeared the remains of the army had been trapped. Stranded within their last line of fortifications on Brooklyn Heights, they had the East River at their back. Washington came over from the city with about 2,000 reinforcements, increasing his total force to about 10,000 men, and prepared to resist a siege. But he could scarcely hope to prevail. On the evening of the twenty-eighth, the British broke ground for the erection of a battery within six hundred yards of his position and drew out their army in a semicircular line. At any moment, the British fleet might close in behind and make the trap complete.

On the night of the twenty-ninth, however, a storm with powerful winds prevented the fleet from sailing up the East River, and under cover of a heavy fog—which seemed "to settle in a peculiar manner over both encampments"—Washington, with the help of a special seafaring contingent of Cape Cod fishermen under Colonel John Glover, managed to ferry his entire army, together with its field artillery, tents, and baggage, across the river to New York.

The operation was carried out with such silence, order, and dispatch that not a single man was lost; and it is said that while the Brooklyn shore was shrouded in fog, "the atmosphere was clear on the New York side of the river. The wind, too, died away, and the river became so smooth that the row-boats could be laden almost to the gunwale, and a favoring breeze sprang up for the sail-boats, too." When later that morning the irate British climbed into the abandoned redoubts, "they could not find so much as a biscuit or a glass of rum wherewith to console themselves." Two days later, Washington abandoned Governors Island and concentrated his entire force in New York.

Afterward, General Israel Putnam said, "General Howe is either our friend or no general. He had our whole army in his power . . . and yet suffered us to escape without the least interruption. . . . Had he instantly followed up his victory, the consequence to the cause of liberty must have been dreadful." A British officer gave the reprieve a more charitable cast: "It cannot be denied but that the American army lay almost entirely at the will of the English. That they were therefore suffered to retire in safety has by some been attributed to the reluctance of the commander in chief [Howe] to shed the blood of a people so nearly allied." Even so, British propaganda reveled in the blood that had been shed. After the battle, it was reported in Britain that 3,000 rebels had been killed or taken prisoner, as against 300 Hessians and 50 English regulars; that numbers of other rebels had been drowned in their flight to New York; and that Washington's army was plagued with epidemic diseases, which had obliged British troops "to burn the [rebel] camp and all on it, on account of the dirt and infectious filth of which it was full."

Washington's escape allowed him only the briefest rest. His army had been demoralized, if not destroyed, and on September 2 he wrote to Congress, "Our situation is truly distressing. The check our detachment sustained on the 27th ultimo has dispirited too great a proportion of our troops and filled their minds with apprehension and despair. The militia, instead of calling forth their utmost efforts to a brave and manly opposition in order to repair our losses, are dismayed, intractible and impatient to return [home]. Great numbers of them have gone off; in some instances almost by whole regiments, by half ones and by companies at a time." And they were going off with the ammunition and guns. One soldier was even caught with a cannonball in his bag which, he said, he was taking home to his mother "for the purpose of pounding mustard."

General Howe took immediate possession of all the former American posts on Long Island, extending his line northward to Hell Gate. The two armies, separated only by the East River, fired upon each other from their batteries along a nine-mile front. As he prepared to attack the city, Howe sent part of the fleet around Long Island to the sound and two frigates up the East River, while keeping most of his ships at anchor near Governors Island, from which they could sail up either the East River or the Hudson, as the unfolding battle might require.

At this juncture, Admiral Lord Howe, in what appeared to be a gesture of conciliation, invited Congress to appoint some of its members to confer privately with him about finding some way to end the war. Congress declined to send any members to confer with him in their "private capacities" but appointed a committee to ascertain the extent of his authority to negotiate and "to hear any propositions that his lordship may think proper to make."

It was, on the part of Congress, a strategic move—first, to buy valuable time for the Continental Army and the militia to prepare for the impending assault and, second, to demonstrate to all that Congress was trying to find its way to an honorable peace, so that the responsibility for continuing the war would fall on Howe.

Benjamin Franklin, John Adams, and Edward Rutledge of South Carolina were selected for the mission and rode overland to the New Jersey shore. They found the roads thronged with soldiers, and the inn at New Brunswick was so crowded that Franklin and Adams had to share a bed in a tiny room with one window. "The window was open," Adams remembered, "and I, who was an invalid and afraid of the air of the night, shut it close. 'Oh!' says Franklin, 'don't shut the window; we shall be suffocated.' I answered I was afraid of the evening air. Dr. Franklin replied: 'The air within the chamber will soon be, and indeed is now, worse than that without doors. Come, open the window and come to bed, and I will convince you. I believe you are not acquainted with my theory of colds.' " Adams, who was curious about the theory, left the window open and later remembered vaguely that Franklin was still expounding upon it when he fell asleep.

On the afternoon of September 11, a barge manned by redcoats met them at Perth Amboy and ferried them across Raritan Bay to the tip of Staten Island. Lord Howe greeted them politely and escorted them up to the house "between lines of grenadiers, looking fierce as ten Furies," recalled Adams, "and making all the grimaces and gestures, and motions of their muskets, with bayonets fixed, which, I suppose, military etiquette requires." Although the house itself, formerly used to quarter guards, was "as dirty as a stable," Howe had made one large room in it inviting by spreading a carpet of moss and green sprigs across the floor. This made it appear "not only wholesome but romantically elegant; and he entertained us with good claret, good bread, cold ham, tongues and mutton."

Then the talks began.

Howe declared that he had long believed that the differences between the two countries could be reconciled. He was, as everyone knew, politically a Whig, had been supportive of Franklin in London, and was extremely grateful to the Americans for having erected the marble monument in Westminster Abbey to his eldest brother, who had been killed in the French and Indian War. He said he esteemed that honor to his family "above all things in this world." The king and Parliament, he went on, were "very favorably inclined toward redressing all grievances," including all objectionable statutes, and "very willing" to rectify "any errors that might have crept in." He said he felt for America as for a brother and would lament as for the loss of a brother if America should fall. Franklin interjected, "My lord, we will use our utmost endeavours to save your lordship that mortification."

Howe's face changed. "I suppose you will endeavour to give us employment in Europe," he said curtly, meaning by bringing France into the conflict and entangling Britain in a European war. No one said a word. Then, in a more conciliatory way, Howe added that he was sorry he had not arrived before independence had been declared, as he had no power to treat with the colonies as independent states. Since he could not acknowledge the legality of Congress because that body was not recognized by the king, he must regard its emissaries "merely as gentlemen of great ability and influence . . . now met to converse together and to try if any outline could be drawn to put a stop to the calamities of war." This threatened to put an end to the discussion, but Franklin promptly came up with a diplomatic formula that allowed them to proceed: "His lordship," he said, "might consider the gentlemen present in any view he thought proper," but "they were also at liberty to consider themselves in their real character." As "there was no necessity on this occasion to distinguish between the Congress and individuals, . . . the conversation might be held as amongst friends."

So they talked: first, about taxation. Money, said Howe, was the smallest consideration, as America could "produce more solid advantages to Great Britain" in "her commerce, her strength, her men." "Aye, my lord," said Franklin, "we have a pretty considerable manufactory of men," meaning the potential for a great army through natural reproduction.

(Franklin was an expert on this subject. In his *Observations concerning the Increase of Mankind* of 1751, he had pointed out that if America's English population continued to double every twenty-five years, it would not be long before there were more Englishmen in America than in England. And on October 3, 1775, he had written with malicious pride to his friend Joseph Priestley, a clergyman and chemist in London, "Britain, at the expense of three million pounds has killed one hundred and fifty Yankees this campaign which is twenty thousand pounds a head. . . . During the same time sixty thousand children have been born in America.")

Howe ignored Franklin's remark. "When an American falls England feels it," he said. "Is there no way of treading back this step of independency and opening the door to a full discussion?"

But the committee stood united. Franklin, according to the minutes, reminded Howe that "forces had been sent out and towns destroyed; that they could not expect happiness now under the domination of Great Britain; that all former attachment was obliterated; that America could not return again to the domination of Great Britain and therefore imagined that Great Britain meant to rest it upon force." Adams, for his part, stressed that the Declaration of Independence had been unanimous, and Rutledge claimed that even if Congress were to reverse its course, South Carolina was determined to remain an independent state.

With that the talks came to a close. Howe said he was sorry the gentlemen had come so far to so little purpose and escorted them back to his barge. Franklin, with a kind of ostentation—to suggest America's independent wealth—endeavored to tip the sailors with gold and silver coin.

I N a council of war held on September 7, the American general staff considered giving up New York. General Putnam argued that it would be impossible to defend, given the forces at Howe's disposal, and that it would be better to try to keep the army together and preserve its military stores. This was also the opinion of General Greene, who suggested that the army abandon the island and withdraw to Kingsbridge and the Westchester shore. The city and its suburbs, he said, were really a Tory stronghold, and there was no good reason to risk the army in its defense. He went further: the city should be burned to deprive the enemy of winter quarters and to reduce its usefulness as a base.

But there was no consensus on the matter, and Congress, in a resolution of September 3, had already told Washington "in case he should find it necessary to quit New York, that no damage be done to the said city by his troops, on their leaving it: The Congress having no doubt of being able to recover the same."

A middle course was adopted: 5,000 men were to be stationed in the city, 9,000 at Kingsbridge, and another 4,000 (principally militia) in between. Even so, in anticipation of the imminent attack, Washington had begun to evacuate the city with a view to massing his troops on Harlem (now Morningside) Heights, a rocky plateau north of present-day 125th Street. But before he could accomplish this, Howe, on the fifteenth, landed two divisions—one British, one Hessian—under the cover of heavy fire from his ships at Kip's Bay on Manhattan's east side. The American breastworks at that point were manned by raw recruits, who at once panicked and ran. Washington promptly came down with two New England brigades to give them mettle and, galloping on his charger to the scene, endeavored to rally the men before they completely dispersed. In a moment of rage, he dashed his hat onto the ground and exclaimed, "Are these the men with whom I am to defend America!" So heedless was he of his own safety that he might have fallen into the hands of the enemy had not an aide-de-camp seized the bridle of his horse and "absolutely hurried him away." But once again, though half of Washington's army might have been captured or annihilated, Howe failed to march across the island and make the trap complete. As a result, almost the entire New York garrison was able to escape up the island's west side.

There was little else to celebrate. "The [Americans] had intended to dispute every inch of ground," noted an observer. "In every street they had made ditches and barricades, and fortified every little eminence about the town. But when the British landed, they fled, leaving their defenses to fill up with stagnant water, damaged sauerkraut, and filth."

On the following day, Howe tried unsuccessfully to dislodge Washington from the northern area of the island at Harlem Heights; on the twentieth, a fire (possibly set by arsonists—or by "a misguided patriot," in Washington's words) broke out at a city wharf and, spreading, ultimately burned about a third of New York to the ground.

Two days later, Captain Nathan Hale, a former Connecticut schoolmaster, having been taken within the British lines on an errand for Washington, was hanged as a spy. In his final hours, with disgraceful disregard for his humanity, he was refused both a clergyman and a Bible, and the farewell letters he wrote to his mother and friends were destroyed. This was done, said the British provost marshal, "that the rebels not know they had a man who could die with so much firmness." If so, it was done in vain. For, as every schoolchild knows (or used to know), just before his execution Hale proclaimed, "I only regret that I have but one life to lose for my country."

Howe now divided his own army into three parts. The first was to guard and garrison New York City; the second, to sail up the Hudson River and prevent Washington from crossing into New Jersey; and the third (and largest) under Howe himself to land at Throgs Neck and cut off Washington's supply line, which had its base in Connecticut.

In Parliament, Edmund Burke tried to persuade the government to sue for peace:

> By [your] delay [in negotiating seriously] you drove them into the declara-
> tion of independency . . . and now they have declared it, you bring it as an
> argument to prove, that there can be no other reasoning used with them,
> but the sword. . . . In order to bring things to this unhappy situation, did
> not you pave the way, by a succession of acts of Tyranny;—for this, you
> shut up their ports;—cut off their fishery;—annihilated their charters;—
> and governed them by an army. Sir, the recollection of these things being
> the evident causes of what we have seen, is more than what ought to be
> endured.

The British resumed their offensive on October 12. Enveloped by an early-morning fog, Howe sailed up the East River and landed his forces at Throgs Neck in an attempt to encircle the American rear and cut off Washington's escape route to the north by land. Yet there was a kind of lethargy to his advance. He inexplicably allowed a small creek and a marsh to detain him almost a week, giving Washington time to withdraw his command to White Plains. Then, plodding his way with artillery through a countryside intersected by fences and stone walls, he allowed another twelve days to elapse before he finally attacked Washington's position on October 28.

Washington was encamped on high, broken ground, his main army to the north and east, a separate detachment of 1,600 to the west on Chatterton's Hill. Howe attacked the hill from two sides and once again turned the American flank. But he did it at disproportionate cost, losing 229 lives to 140 in the American camp. Two days of rain then followed, delaying a general assault. That allowed Washington to withdraw a short distance, on November 1, to a much stronger position at North Castle, beyond the Croton River. In an effort to entice Washington out, Howe moved down the east bank of the Hudson to Dobbs Ferry, from which he could attack Fort Washington in northern Manhattan or cross into New Jersey and attack Fort Lee before advancing on Philadelphia.

In response, Washington now redivided his own army. He left General Lee with 7,000 men at North Castle with standing instructions to cooperate with him promptly, as required, posted 3,000 others to guard the highlands at Peekskill, and with 5,000 more crossed the Hudson and moved down the river into New Jersey to be near Forts Washington and Lee.

Washington had been inclined to abandon these two forts as indefensible, since they had been unable to prevent the British fleet from sailing upriver, but Congress, as well as a full council of general officers, had insisted they be held. Yet it was clear to him that the British would attempt to take them before the end of their autumn campaign. He wrote to William Livingston, the new patriot governor of New Jersey, "Some suppose they are going into winter quarters and will sit down in New York. . . . I cannot subscribe wholly to this opinion myself. . . . [Howe] must attempt something on account of his reputation, for what has he done, as yet, with his great army?"

On November 16, Howe suddenly surrounded Fort Washington and captured its entire garrison of 3,000 men, the largest number of patriot soldiers taken in a single action in the North during the war. Also taken was a goodly portion of the army's cannon, powder, and shot. Two days later, on the night of the eighteenth, the enemy crossed the Hudson in two divisions (6,000 men) under Lord Cornwallis and disembarked with their cannon under the palisades at a place called Closter Dock above Fort Lee. General Nathanael Greene, commanding at the fort, saw that his position was hopeless; as Cornwallis marched down upon him, he evacuated his garrison of 2,000 men with such expedition that, it is said, "they left their very pots boiling upon the fire." He managed to gain the bridge to Hackensack, but only after discarding most of his stores.

Trying desperately to avoid encirclement, Washington joined Greene in Hackensack and slipped across the Passaic River on November 21, just as Cornwallis's advance guard came up. Washington hoped to make a stand at Newark, but instead of attracting new recruits, his already small army found itself reduced by nearly half as the soldiers' terms of enlistment expired. It was an old story. "I am wearied almost to death with the retrograde motion of things," Washington wrote to his brother Augustine, "and I solemnly protest that a pecuniary reward of twenty thousand pounds a year would not induce me to undergo what I do; and after all, perhaps to lose my character, as it is impossible, under such a variety of distressing circumstances, to conduct matters agreeably to public expectation."

By the end of November, Washington had scarcely 3,000 men under his immediate command. These were encamped in open country amid a substantially royalist population, without entrenching tools, stores, or tents to shelter them from the cold weather coming on. One division remained in the highlands for the defense of the Hudson and the mountain passes and another 5,000 to 7,000 men, partly militia, at White Plains under General Lee.

As Washington retreated through New Jersey, he briefly occupied and then abandoned Newark, New Brunswick, and Princeton in succession as the British followed at his heels. From Newark he had written candidly to General Lee that it was "more owing to the badness of the weather than to any resistance we could make" that the enemy had not caught up with him. But even as he wrote this, the enemy drew near. So rapid was the British pursuit that the rear of one army was often within sight and shot of the other's vanguard, and before Washington had completed destroying the bridge over the Raritan, Cornwallis came up to the span.

On they raced to the Delaware. At Trenton, to avoid capture, Washington secured all the boats for seventy miles up and down the river. "All the shores were lighted up with large fires," wrote the artist Charles Willson Peale, who was traveling with the army as a captain of militia. "The Boats continually passing and repassing full of men, Horses, artilery, and Camp Equipage." The rear guard had barely landed and was dragging the last of its boats up the Pennsylvania side when Cornwallis appeared "with all the pomp of war" in great expectation of crossing in his wake. Not one boat was to be found, however, so he gave up the chase and distributed his (mostly German) troops in cantonments along the left bank of the river. Only the Delaware now stood between the British and Philadelphia, and before long they expected to be able to cross the Delaware on the ice.

It was the darkest period in the history of the Revolution. Though Washington's conduct during the siege of Boston had given evidence of his virtues and capacities, after the British had swept aside his army in New York and had overrun Forts Washington and Lee, doubts had been raised. The enemy was now in possession of Long Island, New York City, Staten Island, and almost the whole of New Jersey and seemed poised to advance into Pennsylvania. In early December, Howe had also seized Newport, Rhode Island (then a haven for American privateers), as a naval station for British ships entering Long Island Sound. With winter coming on, he returned with Cornwallis to New York, where he issued a proclamation offering a full pardon to all who would take the oath of allegiance to the Crown.

"I tremble for Philadelphia," Washington wrote to his cousin Lund on

December 10. "Nothing in my opinion, but General Lee's speedy arrival, who has been long expected, though still at a distance, can save it." But Lee deliberately dragged his feet, apparently hoping, in the interest of his own advancement, to create a debacle for Washington that would lead to the commander in chief's disgrace.

Lee had returned to New York from Charleston with the aura of victory about him, and on October 14 Washington had given him command of the right wing of the army on Harlem Heights. Upon the resignation of General Artemas Ward the previous spring, Lee had become senior major general, and in the event of Washington faltering he might hope to become commander in chief. The calamitous fall of Fort Washington seemed to afford the opportunity. When Washington ordered Lee to cross the Hudson River without delay and effect a junction of their forces, Lee "pretended to regard the order in the light of a suggestion and didn't stir." As Washington fell back through New Jersey in order to avoid fighting against overwhelming odds, his messages to Lee "grew more and more peremptory, but Lee, instead of obeying, busied himself with writing letters calculated to spread and increase disaffection" with the commander in chief. Unfortunately, Lee at that moment was being extravagantly flattered by a number of colleagues, including some members of Washington's personal staff. Colonel Joseph Reed wrote confidentially to him:

> I do not mean to flatter or praise you at the expense of any other, but I do think it is entirely owing to you that this army, and the liberties of America, so far as they are dependent on it, are not entirely cut off. You have decision, a quality often wanting in minds otherwise valuable, and I ascribe to this our escape from York [Manhattan] Island, King's Bridge and the Plains. And I have no doubt, had you been here, the garrison of Mount Washington would now have composed a part of this army. And from all these circumstances, I confess, I do ardently wish to see you removed from a place where there will be so little call for your judgment and experience, to the place where they are likely to be so necessary. Nor am I singular in my opinion. Every gentleman of the family, the officers and soldiers generally, have a confidence in you. The enemy constantly inquire where you are and seem to be less confident when you are present.

Alluding directly to the fall of Fort Washington, Reed more plainly indicated that Washington had not acted decisively enough: "O general! An indecisive mind is one of the greatest misfortunes that can befall an army. How often have I lamented it this campaign. All circumstances considered, we are in a very awful and alarming situation, one that requires the utmost wisdom and firmness of mind. As soon as the season will admit, I think yourself and some others should go to Congress and form the plan of the new army. . . . I must conclude with my clear and explicit opinion that your presence is of the last importance."

Reed had written this letter on November 23. That same day, Lee himself wrote to James Bowdoin, president of the Massachusetts Committee of Public Safety, "Before the unfortunate affair at Fort Washington it was my opinion that the two armies—that on the east and that on the west side of the North River—must rest each on its own bottom; that the idea of detaching and reinforcing from one side to the other on every motion of the enemy was chimerical; but to harbor such a thought in our present circumstances is absolute insanity." The following day, he again wrote to Bowdoin, and in his letter this remarkable passage appears: "Affairs appear in so important a crisis that I think the resolves of the Congress must no longer too nicely weigh with us. We must save the community in spite of the ordinances of the Legislature. There are times when we must commit treason against the laws of the State, for the salvation of the State. The present crisis demands this brave, virtuous kind of treason." This was a man the young republic had reason to fear.

In his reply to Reed, Lee agreed with the latter's implied censure of the commander in chief: "I lament with you that fatal indecision of mind which in war is a much greater disqualification than stupidity or even want of personal courage." The letter, however, fell into Washington's hands. Supposing it to be an official dispatch, he opened it, then sent it on to Reed with the following note: "Dear Sir, The inclosed was put into my hands by an express from White Plains. Having no idea of its being a private letter, much less suspecting the tendency of the correspondence, I opened it, as I have done all other letters to you from the same place, and Peekskill, upon the business of your office, as I conceived and found them to be. This, as it is the truth, must be my excuse for seeing the contents of a letter which neither inclination nor intention would have prompted me to."

It was not until December 2 that Lee finally crossed the Hudson and began a laggard march. Washington had advised him to keep well to the west and had even indicated, when he came to the Delaware, the particular road and ferry by which he was to cross. But insubordinate now in all things, Lee instead moved slowly toward Morristown. At that moment, General Horatio Gates was making his way through northern New Jersey with seven regiments sent down by General Schuyler to Washington's assistance from Fort Ticonderoga. Lee interposed and diverted three to his own command. By then Washington had retreated beyond the Delaware, and almost everybody considered that his army was doomed. Lee's plan was to look on and see Washington defeated before striking a blow on his own account. "I am in hopes," he boasted in a letter, "to reconquer (if I may so express myself) the Jerseys." But he soon lost a portion of his own men in muddling skirmishes and managed to neglect his own security. On December 13, he was surprised *en déshabillé* by a British patrol and borne away in his dressing gown.

It was a remarkable development. The day before, Lee had decamped from Morristown. After marching just eight miles, he had left his troops in the care of a subordinate and, accompanied by a small guard, had gone off to a tavern to spend the night. According to Major James Wilkinson, on errand from General Gates, Lee lingered in bed until eight A.M., then came down half dressed, in his usual slovenly style, and lounged about for a couple of hours before sitting down to breakfast at ten. After breakfast, he decided to write a sarcastic letter about Washington to General Gates. "The ingenious maneuvre of Fort Washington," he began, "has completely unhinged the goodly fabric we had been building. There never was so damned a stroke. *Entre nous,* a certain great man is most damnably deficient."

He had just finished writing this sentence when Major Wilkinson, looking out of the window down a lane, suddenly beheld a party of British dragoons rounding the corner at full charge.

"Here, sir, are the British cavalry!" he exclaimed.

"Where?" replied Lee.

"Around the house!"

Lee cried out, "Where is the guard? Damn the guard, why don't they fire?"

But the guards, in emulation of their negligent commander, had stacked their arms and repaired to the south side of the road to sun themselves.

Dressed as he was, Lee was whisked away on Wilkinson's horse, which stood tethered by the door, "with every mark of triumph and indignity," in a great psychological blow to the cause. Since he was widely (if mistakenly) perceived as the most capable American commander, many expected the rebellion to collapse as a result.

The Continental Congress declared a day of solemn fasting and prayer "according to the custom of our pious ancestors in times of imminent dangers and difficulties . . . to implore of Almighty God the forgiveness of the many sins prevailing among all ranks, and to beg the countenance and assistance of his Providence in the prosecution of the present just and necessary war." In expectation of an enemy advance on Philadelphia, Congress fled to Baltimore.

Everyone expected the rebel capital to fall. Washington himself could see little chance of preventing a new triumph by British arms. "Happy should I be, if I could see the means," he wrote. "At present I confess I do not."

T H R O U G H O U T the fall, while Washington had been pursued by Howe and Cornwallis through New York and New Jersey, a second British army had been moving south from Canada by the Saint Lawrence River–Lake Champlain route in an effort to cut New England off from the other colonies and divide the revolt.

In all, the British had assembled some 17,000 men—soldiers, sailors, and 900 Canadians impressed into service as work crews, as well as engineers, shipwrights, carpenters, and blacksmiths—at the northern tip of the lake. By summer's end, they had been ready to descend on the sick and demoralized American rear guard at Crown Point, about seven miles north of Ticonderoga.

The thrust had been anticipated. But in the scramble to meet it, a bitter power struggle, analogous to that between Washington and Lee, developed behind the scenes. In this case, it pitted General Philip Schuyler, one of the first four major generals created by Congress and head of the Northern Department of the army, against General Horatio Gates. After the collapse of the American attempt on Quebec, Congress, unhappy with Schuyler's overall command of the Northern Army, had decided to replace him with Gates. John Adams emerged as Gate's patron and ally. He had written to him in May, "I wish you was a major general. . . . What say you to it?" Adams soon had his wish, and on June 13 Samuel Chase of Maryland told Gates, "A general is to be sent to Canada with the powers of a Roman dictator. Many of the Congress have their eyes upon you." Five days later, Adams told him, "We have ordered you to the Post of Honour, and made you Dictator in Canada for Six Months, or at least until the first of October." By "dictator," Chase and Adams both meant that he would have the authority to appoint and fire subordinates without civilian review.

As soon as Gates reached Albany, Schuyler announced that the "Canadian army" no longer existed, since the last American troops had been withdrawn from Canadian soil. There was therefore nothing Canadian for him to command. Gates viewed this as a technicality, insisting that it was obvious from his commission that Congress wanted Schuyler to step aside. Schuyler replied that that was unlikely, as he was of senior rank. Gates appealed to Congress, which, having no stomach for the quarrel, confirmed Schuyler's command.

Gates took charge of the forts at Ticonderoga and Crown Point and gave Benedict Arnold ("who is perfectly skilled in maritime affairs") command of the American "fleet" on the lake. "With infinite satisfaction I have committed the whole of that department to his care," he wrote to John Hancock on July 29. And in doing so he did not make a mistake.

There was much to be done. The old stone walls of the fortress at Crown Point were in disrepair, and the garrison, reported an American colonel, was "not an army but a mob, the shattered remains of twelve or fifteen very fine battalions, ruined by sickness, fatigue, and desertion, and void of every idea of discipline or subordination."

Gates abandoned Crown Point as indefensible and undertook to strengthen Ticonderoga as much as he could. Four thousand men were assigned to garrison it, while skilled shipbuilders were collected from New England seaports to hammer together sixteen flat-bottomed gondolas and galleys—each one partially decked, mounted with swivel guns and artillery, and fitted with oars and sails (the latest development in freshwater warfare)—as more men and supplies came in. But the main hope was not to defeat the British but to slow their advance long enough to allow the severities of winter itself to stop it and draw it out into the following year.

By early August, Arnold had put together a kind of navy, and on August 24, just as Washington was about to meet defeat on Long Island, he sailed north from Crown Point toward the Canadian frontier. Behind Arnold's flagship, the twelve-gun, two-hundred-ton *Royal Savage,* came the schooner *Revenge,* mounting eight cannon in her ports and ten swivel guns on her gunwales, followed by the eight-gun schooner *Liberty* and the ten-gun sloop *Enterprise.* These four ships were arrayed to protect the smaller square-rigged gondolas, fifty-nine feet long and each carrying forty-five men. "We begin to fear," wrote one cocky young soldier, "that they will not Darst to come and meet us."

But the British fleet assembled to oppose them was much more powerful. It included three large ships disassembled into sections, transported overland, and rebuilt on the lake; twenty gunboats; a thirty-ton gondola; a great two-masted scow; thirty longboats; and four hundred bateaux. Except for the bateaux, all bristled with cannon and howitzers of heavier caliber than any of the ordnance under Arnold's command. Behind Sir Guy Carleton's fleet, General John Burgoyne waited with the British main army, ready to invade America once Carleton had cleared a path.

Gates told Arnold to maintain a posture of defense but, if attacked, to receive the enemy "with such cool determined valour, as will give them reason to repent their temerity."

On September 19, Arnold's flotilla sought a more secure position at Saint Armand Bay north of Cumberland Head, near the long and thickly wooded island of Valcour. He deployed his sixteen ships stem to stern in a crescent across the channel just north of its southern tip, taking advantage of the island's good harbor and refuge from which he might run his fleet out to do battle on the lake.

On the morning of October 11, the black hulls and bellied canvas of His Majesty's squadron came into view. Carleton had evidently expected Arnold to meet him in Cumberland Bay or make a run for the protection of Fort Ticonderoga's guns. In either scenario, the superior British fleet could beat or overtake the Americans. When Arnold was not found waiting off Cumberland Head, Carleton continued southward down the lake, spotted the American force as he passed Valcour Island, and doubled back. Arnold (whose only previous experience in naval warfare had been confined to trading voyages between Connecticut and the West Indies) went out to meet him. The two squadrons engaged, and the battle raged all day. By nightfall, the patriot flotilla had been more or less crippled and its avenue of retreat to the south blocked by the British ships. But in the darkness, Arnold slipped through the line. The following day, Carleton pursued. He easily caught up with and sank several of the vessels, and in the end, 80 Americans were killed, 120 more taken prisoner, and two thirds of the American vessels destroyed. But for the British, though they now controlled Lake Champlain, it was a Pyrrhic victory: they had sustained losses far beyond what Arnold's flotilla might have been expected to inflict, and the season was too advanced for them to attempt to subdue Fort Ticonderoga and extend their supply lines into New York. In other words, they had lost another year.

Spared the onslaught of the British host, the garrison in the fort was ecstatic. "Great confusion was in the camp," recorded a soldier in his journal, "as strong liquor is now plenty; and this day being appointed by the Creator as a day of rest, was allowed to most of them as such: but instead of spending it as he has directed, many were using it to satisfy their brutish passions. May God Omnipotent convince us of our error, and ere it is too late deliver us from the bondage of sin and Satan." But from the bondage of the British, at least, they had been temporarily spared.

W A S H I N G T O N had been granted no such reprieve. Even with the remnants of Lee's command, which had finally reinforced his phantom army, he had no more than 5,000 to 6,000 men, and the enlistment terms of most of these were due to expire on December 31. If they all went home, he would be left with 1,400 men at most. As it was, his thinning ranks were in a terrible state, many of the soldiers, he wrote the president of Congress, "being entirely naked and most so thinly clad as to be unfit for service." In a letter of December 20 he warned, "Ten days more will put an end to the existence of our army." To his cousin Lund, he wrote, "Our only dependence now is upon the speedy enlistment of a new army. If this fails, I think the game will be pretty well up."

By all appearances, the British had won.

Admitting that little could be done to save Philadelphia, Washington asked Congress for emergency powers, so that "every self-evident matter" need not await the imprimatur of the delegates. At the same time, he assured them that he had "no lust after power, but I wish with as much fervency as any man upon this wide-extended continent for an opportunity of turning the sword into the ploughshare." The difference between Washington and Lee was that instead of seeking to supersede the authority of Congress, Washington sought Congress's authority to supersede its usual restraints.

Congress responded by bestowing sweeping powers upon him for six months. These were similar to, but more extensive than, those granted earlier to General Gates, but to say, as some have claimed, that an American "dictator" was created by the congressional resolution of December 27 is untrue. "Congress never thought of making him dictator or of giving him a sovereignty," John Adams later told his wife. "Such false news, uncontradicted, does more or less harm. Such a collection of lies would be a curiousity for posterity."

More than an imperial mandate, however, Washington needed men. Even as his army evaporated before his very eyes, Congress had also finally granted Washington's abiding request for an army of long-term regulars. Earlier in the fall, it had voted to raise eighty-eight infantry battalions to serve for three years or the duration of the war, assigning each state a quota of regiments based on population and promising recruits a $20 bounty and 100 acres of land at war's end. On December 27, Congress also authorized Washington to raise 16 additional infantry battalions, 3,000 light dragoons, 3 artillery regiments, and a corps of engineers—in all, a standing army of 76,000 men.

It was a handsome prospect, but such a mighty army never came to be. And the grandiose recruitment plans stood in stark contrast to the tiny army then under Washington's command.

Washington established his men in makeshift huts on the wooded ridges of the Pennsylvania side of the Delaware River and requisitioned several stone houses to shelter his staff. In one of them, he sat down to work out a complicated and daring plan to strike a last blow at the enemy before his army completely disappeared. It was an operation from which there could be no retreat. "Victory or Death," remembered eighteen-year-old Lieutenant James Monroe (later president of the United States), was the watchword; all hung on the operation's success.

After surveying the British positions, Washington had resolved on a surprise attack on the Hessian garrison at Trenton, where 1,500 men were stationed under Colonel Johann Rahl. Rahl had fought with distinction at White Plains, where his Hessians had turned the American flank, and at Fort Washington, where they had borne the brunt of the fighting. They were a highly drilled, disciplined corps. But Trenton was also the most exposed post in the British line. That line extended seventy-seven miles from Burlington, New Jersey, to the Hackensack River near New York, and the troops, cantoned loosely along it, could not readily be brought together on a sudden alarm. Trenton was half a day's march from Bordentown, the nearest British camp. Washington, at Newtown in Pennsylvania, was nearer, and the enemy's confidence was carelessly high. Rahl had done little to strengthen his position, either by erecting earthworks or by sending out patrols, and knowing the broken and dispirited state of the Americans, considered them incapable of any offensive enterprise. In other respects, too, he had grown quite lax. Although a good subordinate officer, it was said that when left to his own devices "safe from the gaze of superior officers, he was apt to rise late after a night's carousing and keep the guard waiting in the snow while he finished his bath."

Washington's plan was to ferry 2,400 men with eighteen guns across the Delaware about eight miles above Trenton and march upon the town in two columns from the north and west. At the town, the columns would envelop the enemy and drive it south toward Assunpink Creek. Two smaller contingents were to cross below Trenton: one to engage the Hessian brigade at Burlington as a diversion, the other to seize the bridge over Assunpink Creek to prevent the garrison's escape. "Christmas-day, at night, one hour before day, is the time fixed upon for our attempt," he wrote Colonel Joseph Reed on December 23. "For Heaven's sake keep this to yourself, as the discovery of it may prove fatal to us; our numbers, sorry I am to say, being less than I had any conception of; but necessity, dire necessity will, nay must, justify *any* attempt."

On the eve of the attack, the first of Thomas Paine's *Crisis* pamphlets was printed, and copies were distributed through the camp. It began, "These are the times that try men's souls. The Summer soldier and the sunshine Patriot will, in this crisis, shrink from the service of their country; but he that stands it *now,* deserves the love and thanks of man and woman." These electrifying words, which Paine had written on a drumhead by the light of a campfire during the New Jersey retreat, were felt and believed by the half-clad, disheartened soldiers, who were called together before the battle to hear them read aloud.

As Washington was about to draw up his men for inspection, Major James Wilkinson suddenly arrived from Philadelphia with a letter from General Gates. There was snow on the ground, and he had traced the march of the troops by the blood from their feet. He found Washington alone at his headquarters, whip in his hand, preparing to mount his horse. "As I presented the letter to him, he exclaimed with solemnity, 'What a time is this to hand me letters!' I answered that I had been charged with it by General Gates. 'By General Gates! Where is he?' 'I left him this morning in Philadelphia.' 'What was he doing there?' 'I understood that he was on his way to Congress.' He earnestly repeated, 'On his way to Congress!' then broke the seal."

There was reason for Washington's animus. Like Lee, Gates had long had a disinclination to serve immediately under Washington, and he had refused to lead a contingent in the planned attack on Trenton as he was convinced that it would fail. "While Washington was watching the enemy above Trenton," he had told Wilkinson, "they would construct bateaux, pass the Delaware in his rear and take possession of Philadelphia before he was aware." Instead of attempting to stop Howe at the Delaware, he thought Washington "ought to retire to the south of the Susquehanna and there form an army. He said it was his intention to propose this measure to Congress."

Washington's troops assembled on the banks of the river and about sunset began to cross. The current was strong, the frost sharp, and dark clouds covered the moon. Once again Washington called on the seafaring skills of Colonel John Glover's amphibious regiment of Marblehead fishermen, who battled ice floes and a sleet blizzard that began to descend as the boats pushed off. Most of the boats were not the romantic, curved whalers depicted in paintings but sturdy, flat-bottomed, shallow-draft scows formerly used to carry iron ore down the river to Philadelphia.

Getting the horses and artillery across proved especially difficult, but "perseverence accomplished what at first seemed impossible," wrote three-hundred-pound Henry Knox, who by his own extraordinary exertions (to which he lent full weight and girth) did much to accomplish it as he called out instructions with "stentorian lungs." Nevertheless, it was three in the morning before the ordnance had been landed and nearly four before the troops took up their line of march. Trenton was eight miles distant and could not be reached before dawn. Through a forest of black oak and hickory the men followed a rutted trail slippery with ice and snow. Many, lacking shoes, wore only rags wrapped around their feet. Behind them came the artillery, lit by torches that "sparkled and blazed in the storm."

The storm soon rendered many of the muskets useless. "What is to be done?" Sullivan asked Washington. He replied, "You have nothing for it but to push on and use the bayonet."

About halfway to Trenton, Washington formed the troops into two columns. The first, or left, under his own command, was to make a circuit by the upper road to the north of Trenton; the other, led by General Sullivan and including a brigade under General Arthur St. Clair, was to take the lower river road, leading to the west end of town. Sullivan's column was to halt a few minutes at a crossroad to give Washington's column time to effect its circuit, so that the attack might be simultaneous. At Trenton, they were to force the outer guards and push directly into Trenton before the enemy had time to form up.

Washington's situation was more critical than he knew. Notwithstanding the secrecy with which his plans had been conceived, Colonel Rahl had received a warning of the intended attack from his superior at Princeton. It so happened that about dusk, while Washington was preparing to cross the Delaware, there was a false alarm at the Trenton outpost. The whole garrison was immediately drawn out under arms as a local patriot band emerged from the woods and carried out a quick hit-and-run attack. Rahl had his men scour the woods and make the rounds of the outposts, but when they found nothing amiss, he supposed this to be the attack against which he had been warned. Accordingly, he relaxed into his Christmas festivities. As the night was cold and stormy, he even permitted his troops to return to their quarters and lay their arms aside.

In fact, the only guard the Hessians had that night consisted of two isolated, lightly manned picket houses about a half mile from the town.

It was about eight o'clock when Washington's column approached the outskirts of the village. The storm had kept everyone within doors, and the snow had deadened the footfalls of the troops and the rumbling of the artillery. Washington, accompanied by an artillery captain named Thomas Forrest, came to a man chopping wood by the roadside and asked him where the Hessian outposts were.

" 'I don't know,' he replied.

" 'You may speak,' said Captain Forrest, 'for that is General Washington.'

"The astonished man raised his hands to heaven and exclaimed, 'God bless and prosper you, Sir! The picket is in that house, and the sentry stands near that tree.' "

The outposts were driven in. At the same time, the right column approached from another direction and pressed into the town.

The Hessians, still drowsy from their Christmas celebrations, were completely surprised. Some engaged in wild and undirected fire from the windows of their quarters; others rushed out in confusion and attempted to form up in the main street. There they found themselves facing the field artillery of Knox. When the enemy endeavored to erect a battery themselves, Captain William Washington, cousin to the general and a superb cavalry officer, together with Lieutenant James Monroe, raced forward with the advance guard and, "taking two pieces in the act of firing, drove the artillerists from their guns."

Those Hessians captured in the town were hurried away under guard, but others began to re-form east of the town under Rahl. Rahl mounted his horse, waved his sword, and, shouting, *"Alle was meine Grenatir seyn, vorwerds!"* ("All my grenadiers, forward!"), led his men against the Americans in a suicidal charge. The Americans took cover and, being almost invisible to the enemy in the falling rain and snow, were able to pick off the grenadiers like sitting ducks. Rahl, hit twice and mortally wounded, fell from his horse and was carried into a nearby church, where he was laid out on a pew.

Within two hours, it was over. The last group of fleeing Hessians ran right into St. Clair's brigade.

In the entire action, the Americans lost only three men killed (one of whom froze to death) and six wounded, while capturing a thousand men, including twenty-three officers, six brass field pieces, and a thousand stand of arms. And this despite the fact that neither of Washington's two supporting divisions under James Ewing and John Cadwalader had been able to cross the Delaware with all their men and equipment downstream.

Washington's attack had been masterful, but a twist of fate had also played a hand. Aside from the false alarm that had made the Hessians complacent, the story goes that a loyalist spy or disgruntled farmer had appeared at Rahl's headquarters later that night to tell him that Washington was advancing on his camp. The colonel, however, had left strict orders not to be disturbed, as he wished to devote himself to liquor and cards. The informer wrote out his message, and an orderly took it in.

Rahl, preoccupied with his pleasures, put it unread into his pocket and forgot that it was there.

Washington's victory breathed new life into the American cause. And it rescued his personal reputation as commander in chief. Intent on following it up, he crossed the Delaware again and on the thirty-first reoccupied Trenton, as Cornwallis, who had been about to embark for England, hastened back from New York and assembled 8,000 troops at Princeton, just twelve miles away.

Washington took post behind nearby Assunpink Creek to await the enemy's advance. There was a narrow stone bridge across it where the water was very deep, and he placed his artillery so as to command this bridge and the fords. Meanwhile, the term of enlistment for a large part of his force was due to expire on December 31. After numerous appeals —the men being addressed by companies—about 1,300 Continentals agreed to serve for six weeks more "on receipt of ten dollars bounty." (Since they would not accept the money issued by Congress, Washington pledged his own personal fortune to maintain his army intact.) These troops, together with 3,500 Pennsylvania militia, were all he had at his command.

On January 2, 1777, Cornwallis marched quickly toward Trenton to attack. Washington sent some picked units forward to forestall his advance and placed two cannon on a hill overlooking the Princeton road. Cornwallis came on and drove the American troops before him, but some remarkably accurate or lucky firing by the two cannon "did considerable execution" when the British came within their range. Cornwallis pushed into Trenton but again suffered quite a few casualties, this time from sniper fire. The American sharpshooters were at last dislodged toward dusk, and, after a brief artillery exchange, Cornwallis extended his lines on the heights above the town. A stream and a stone bridge were all that now separated the two armies, and the ice-clogged Delaware River was at Washington's back. Cornwallis reportedly told his general officers that everything was now as he could wish it and he would bag Washington in the morning as a hunter bags a fox. Therefore, "the troops should make fires, refresh themselves and take repose." In this his staff concurred, with the signal exception of the quartermaster general, who exclaimed, "My Lord, if you trust those people tonight, you will see nothing of them in the morning!" The admonition was not heeded, and the British settled down for the night as the advance sentries of each army took up their positions only 150 yards apart.

At a council of war that night, Washington resolved to slip away quietly, circle around the enemy's rear, and make a quick strike at Princeton.

"More effectually to mask the movement," wrote Major Wilkinson, "Washington ordered the guards to be doubled, a strong fatigue party to be set to work on an intrenchment . . . within distinct hearing of the sentinels of the enemy," while American campfires were kept blazing all along the creek to make it appear as if the entire army remained in place.

At dawn, Cornwallis awoke to the sound of artillery fire to the north. At once he realized that Washington had escaped and that the three regiments he had left at Princeton were under attack. He marched quickly in that direction, concerned also for the safety of his military stores at New Brunswick. But he could not cover the ground in time. The Americans had converged on Princeton by two roads—Washington and the main column on the right, General Hugh Mercer with 400 men on the left. Mercer encountered the enemy first, arrayed his men behind a fence, and managed to get off three volleys before the British charged. Wrote Wilkinson, "The smoke from . . . the two lines mingled as it rose, and went up in one beautiful cloud." Washington sent some of his militia over to help, but they quailed before the British bayonets. He tried to rally them, placing himself in such danger that an aide could not bear the sight and covered his eyes.

The rest of the Americans now came up. Outnumbered and threatened with encirclement, the British broke and ran. "It is a fine fox chase, my boys!" cried Washington, mocking the fox-hunting bugle call sounded by the British on Long Island, as two hundred prisoners fell into his hands. In Princeton itself, some sixty enemy soldiers holed up in a stone dormitory but surrendered at once when the Americans dragged cannon into the college yard.

At this juncture, rather than risking a general engagement, Washington decided to take his army northward to Morristown, which lay on the flank of the British line of communications with New York. General Putnam advanced from Philadelphia to occupy Princeton, and within just a few days, by such maneuvering, the line of the American army had been extended from Princeton to the Hudson River and the British confined to New Jersey, Perth Amboy, New Brunswick, and Paulus Hook.

That gave Washington some breathing space. And having, in effect, saved Philadelphia, he spent the rest of the winter trying to re-create his army from its exiguous remains.

WASHINGTON'S late successes rankled, and during the winter the British took out their frustrations on American prisoners of war.

Britain's Lord Germain had taken the position at the start of hostilities that, as the Americans were rebels, they did not deserve to be treated as regular prisoners. But in the long run, the harshness of their confinement did not favor the British cause. It, in fact, stirred patriotic feeling and made American soldiers less likely to yield in combat or desert.

"I understand," Washington had written to Gage in April 1775, during the siege of Boston, "that the officers . . . who by the fortune of war have fallen into your hands, have been thrown indiscriminately into a common jail appropriated to felons, that no consideration has been had for those of the most respectable rank. My duty now makes it necessary to apprise you that for the future I shall regulate all my conduct towards those gentlemen who are or may be in our possession exactly by the rule you shall observe towards those of ours now in your custody." Washington's protest had been verbosely answered by Burgoyne. He told Washington that "Britons ever prominent in mercy have overlooked the criminal in the captive" and had shown the American officers much "care and kindness" simply by not hanging them. He also offered Washington some unctuous moral advice: "Be temperate in political disquisition; give free operation to truth; punish those who deceive and misrepresent; and not only the effects but the causes of this unhappy conflict will be removed." Washington, in any case, was too decent to follow through with his threat, and captured British officers almost always fared better than their American counterparts did in British hands.

During the winter of 1776, most American prisoners in New York were confined in the city's large Sugarhouse, in Bridewell (the city prison), and in the crypts of churches. The conditions were often horrendous. According to one eyewitness, the floors were covered with the dead and dying, mingled with their own excrement, and in the first year and a half of the war, about two thousand perished from cold, hunger, or disease. Many unseaworthy ships were also converted by the British into prisons or "hospital ships," which were really floating dungeons of despair. Among them, anchored in Wallabout Bay, was the *Jersey*, a former sixty-four-gun man-of-war on which American soldiers, sailors, and other rebel prisoners were packed below deck under locked gratings, twelve hundred or more at a time. Clad only in the clothing they had on when captured, they were given a meager diet of wormy bread, oatmeal, and beef cooked in seawater that left them unable to resist the smallpox and yellow fever that raged in their midst. One of those to survive was Thomas Dring, a Rhode Islander captured on a privateer. Dring had never had smallpox and so, surrounded by the sick and dying, decided to inoculate himself against it. With a pin, he scarified the skin between his thumb and forefinger, took some pus from the sore of a fellow inmate, applied it to the area, and bound up his hand. The next morning the wound began to fester, "a sure symptom that the application had taken effect." "Since that time," he wrote in his memoirs, "more than forty years have passed away, but the scar on my hand is still plainly to be seen. I often look upon it when alone, and it brings fresh to my recollection the fearful scene in which I was then placed."

WASHINGTON'S new position at Morristown was strong. The village was protected by forests and rugged heights, and any attack from the coast was likely to be discouraged by a chain of hills extending from Pluckamin to the vicinity of the Passaic River. Various defiles to the rear afforded a safe retreat. Morristown was also nearly equidistant from Perth Amboy, Newark, and New Brunswick, the principal enemy posts, so that any movement made from them could be met by a countermovement on Washington's part. As his troops built log huts in a sheltered, wooded valley to the southeast, he established his headquarters at the Freemason's Tavern on the north side of the village green.

Throughout the winter, Washington kept the British in a state of siege. He ambushed their foraging parties and with forays and skirmishes otherwise harassed them as he schooled and seasoned his troops. On one occasion, a British contingent trying to appropriate flour from a mill near New Brunswick was surprised and scattered as the Americans captured forty wagons, a hundred horses, and a considerable number of sheep and cattle which the British had collected on their march. Near Princeton, another foray netted ninety-six wagons laden with provisions and 150 British prisoners of war.

By degrees, Cornwallis drew in his troops, thus presenting, in the words of Alexander Hamilton, "the extraordinary spectacle of a powerful army straitened within narrow limits by the phantom of a military force and never permitted to transgress those limits with impunity." Indeed, at Morristown, a portion of Washington's army (their six-week contract extension having expired) went home. Under the circumstances, his skirmishing tactics were a tour de force. Despite his advantageous location, he had only the skeletal remnants of five regiments and "a force of 500 resolute men," writes one embittered loyalist historian, "could have demolished them." At that moment the British had 10,000 fresh troops within a day's march of Washington's camp.

By a kind of subterfuge, the British were also discouraged from attacking other American posts. On Washington's orders, it was customary for each commander to "give out your strength to be twice what it is," as he wrote to General Putnam on January 5. Putnam himself showed ingenuity in improvising on the ruse. Among the British who had been left on the field after the Battle of Princeton was a Captain McPherson, who had been shot through the lungs. He received every medical attention, but while his recovery was in doubt, the captain asked that a fellow officer be allowed to visit him and help him make out his will. At the time, Putnam had only fifty men in his Princeton camp—the remainder being out in detachments—and while he wished to oblige the dying officer, he also did not want to afford a British spy the opportunity to report on his strength. He therefore dispatched a flag of truce to New Brunswick with the captain's request but gave strict orders to the courier not to return until dark. In the evening, lights were turned on in all the rooms of the college and in every apartment of every house (though most were empty) in the town. Throughout the night, the fifty men, sometimes all together, sometimes in small detachments, were marched from different quarters past the house where McPherson lay. This created the impression of a multitude, and upon his return, McPherson's friend told Cornwallis that the rebels at Princeton were several thousand strong.

If there is an argument for the role of Providence in the emergence of the United States, it is in such unaccountably recurring circumstances as this. Nor could Washington himself understand his own immunity from attack. Everything he did was known to the British, for New Jersey was full of loyalist spies.

But Howe was happy where he was. Knighted for his victory in the Battle of Long Island and with Washington seemingly out of reach, he had settled into comfortable winter quarters in New York. And there he enjoyed himself to the hilt. From the king of Prussia he took his motto, *"Toujours de la gaieté"*; helped organize productions of Farquhar's *The Beaux' Stratagem* and Henry Fielding's *Tom Thumb;* and regaled his mistress at banquets and feasts. Later that winter, he sponsored a satirical skit entitled *The Battle of Brooklyn,* which depicted Washington as a whoremongering barbarian and demagogue whose own (imaginary) mistress charged him $30 a night.

The British army remained more or less idle through the winter. In the late spring, it carried out two raids against supply depots, one on the Hudson at Peekskill, the other at Danbury, Connecticut. By the end of May, however, Washington again had a sizable army, as 8,000 to 9,000 Continentals had enlisted—this time for three years or the duration of the war. Meanwhile, possession of the highland passes became the preoccupation of both camps. Washington had always recognized the need to hold them and had stationed a sizable force at Peekskill the previous November. In mid-June, he undertook to obstruct the river near Fort Montgomery with a great boom or chain made of sixty-pound links that extended from bank to bank. Two cables were strung in front of the chain to slow the momentum of any enemy ship, and two ships and two row galleys were positioned above it to rake it with their fire. Washington offered the highland command to Benedict Arnold, but in a kind of temper he declined.

About this time, Arnold had begun to be more troublesome. He had returned a hero from Canada, but his rash courage and impatient energy had aroused the enmity of several officers. In February 1777, Congress had created five new major generals (William Alexander, Lord Stirling; Thomas Mifflin; Arthur St. Clair; Adam Stephen; and Benjamin Lincoln), but, to everyone's surprise, had passed over Arnold. On March 3, Washington dispatched a letter to him, urging patience and expressing his own conviction that the promotion must "have been omitted through some mistake. . . . I beg you will not take any hasty steps in consequence of it, but allow proper time for recollection, which I flatter myself will remedy any error that may have been made. My endeavors to that end shall not be wanting." Washington then wrote to Richard Henry Lee to ascertain "whether General Arnold's non-promotion was owing to accident or design; and the cause of it. Surely a more active, a more spirited, and sensible officer, fills no department in the army. Not seeing him then in the list of major generals, and no mention made of him, has given me uneasiness, as it is not to be presumed (being the oldest brigadier) that he will continue in service under such a slight."

Arnold confirmed Washington's apprehensions when he wrote to him on March 12:

Congress undoubtedly have a right of promoting those whom, from their abilities, and their long and arduous services, they esteem most deserving. Their promoting junior officers to the rank of major-generals, I view as a very civil way of requesting my resignation, as qualified for the office I hold. My commission was conferred unsolicited, and received with pleasure only as a means of serving my country. With equal pleasure I resign it, when I can no longer serve my country with honor. The person who, void of the nice feelings of honor, will tamely condescend to give up his right, and retain a commission at the expense of his reputation, I hold as a disgrace to the army, and unworthy of the glorious cause in which we are engaged. When I entered the service of my country my character was unimpeached. I have sacrificed my ease, interest and happiness in her cause. It is rather a misfortune than a fault that my exertions have not been crowned with success. I am conscious of the rectitude of my intentions.

Despite this artful show of wounded pride, which he rounded off with a sentence he would often repeat, regardless of circumstance, he did not resign as he claimed his honor demanded but, so as not to be guilty, he said, of any hasty step, demanded a court of inquiry into his conduct instead. His whole purpose was to get Washington and Gates to weigh in on his side. But the episode probably marked the beginning of the end of his allegiance to the Revolution. Unappreciated by Congress and his fellow officers (as he saw it), he eventually found in his disappointed vanity an insidious rationale for treason. Two weeks later, he wrote Washington again, reiterating his complaints. Washington replied promptly on April 3 and gave him a little lesson in republican government:

It is needless for me to say much upon a subject, which must undoubtedly give you a good deal of uneasiness. I confess I was surprised, when I did not see your name in the list of major generals, and was so fully of the opinion that there was some mistake in the matter, that I (as you may recollect) desired you not take any hasty step, before the intention of Congress was fully known. The point does not now admit of a doubt, and is of so delicate a nature, that I will not even undertake to advise; your own feelings must be your guide. As no particular charge is alleged against you, I do not see upon what ground you can demand a court of inquiry. Besides, public bodies are not answerable for their actions; they place and displace at pleasure, and all the satisfaction that an individual can obtain, when he is overlooked, is, if innocent, a consciousness that he has not deserved such treatment for his honest exertions. Your determination not to quit your present command, while any danger to the public might ensue from your leaving it, deserves my thanks, and justly entitles you to the thanks of your country.

General Greene, who has lately been at Philadelphia, took occasion to inquire upon what principle the Congress proceeded in their late promotion of general officers. He was informed, that the members from each state seemed to insist upon having a proportion of general officers, adequate to the number of men which they furnish, and that as Connecticut had already two major generals, it was their full share. I confess this is a strange mode of reasoning, but it may serve to show you, that the promotion which was due to your seniority, was not overlooked for want of merit in you.

In short, it all came down to "proportionate representation," or the quotas of democratic politics.

Arnold, however, was impatient with such lessons, and while he tempered his letters to Washington with a kind of imitation of the commander in chief's own style, on March 25 he wrote with more honest vituperation to General Gates, citing some contemporary lines:

I know some Villain has been busy with my Fame—& basely slandered me.
But who will not rest in safety that has done me wrong.
By Heavens, I will have Justice
And I'm a Villain if I seek not
A Brave Revenge for injured honour.

"I cannot draw my sword," he added, "until my reputation, which is dearer than my life, is cleared."

He soon drew his sword to clear it. On April 25, 1777, William Tryon, the former royal governor of New York, landed 2,000 men near Fairfield, Connecticut, and marched them hastily north toward the rebel supply base at Danbury. The following day, before the stores could be removed, his force, which included some loyalist regiments, reached Danbury and quickly crushed a disorganized and scattered resistance. Stockpiles of cloth destined for uniforms and tents were destroyed, along with five thousand barrels of beef and pork. Three hundred puncheons of rum and fifty pipes of wine were also poured out, "chiefly down the throats of the victors, who passed the night in jubilant carousing, mere soldiers no longer, but furious heroes and eminent good fellows, shouting and singing through the darkness all night long." Toward morning, Tryon began burning rebel homes. One American soldier testified that "the town was laid in ashes" and "a number of the inhabitants murdered and cast into" the flames. "I saw the inhabitants, after the fire was out, endeavoring to find the burnt bones of their relatives amongst the rubbish. . . . The streets, in many places, were literally flooded by the fat which ran from the barrels of pork the enemy had burnt." An ad hoc force under General David Wooster began to harry the enemy's rear, and Arnold, with several hundred more, assembled to take a stand in front. Under the cover of a low-hanging mist, Wooster surprised the British sentries, broke into their camp, and took forty prisoners; Arnold, in front, arranged his men between a ledge of rocks and a farmhouse and on the twenty-eighth met Tryon in a sharp engagement at Saugatuck Bridge. As Tryon made his way westward back to his ships, he lost 10 percent of his force in killed or wounded (five times the rate of American casualties), and Arnold played a gallant part—two horses were shot from under him, and a musket ball pierced the collar of his coat.

Based on the battlefield reports, Congress relented and made Arnold a major general on May 2. But it notably failed to antedate his commission, which meant that he was still outranked by the five who had been promoted before.

Washington, anticipating his petulant response yet eager not to lose his sword, wrote to the president of Congress: "General Arnold's promotion gives me much pleasure, he has certainly discovered, in every instance where he has had an opportunity, much bravery, activity and enterprise. But what will be done about his rank? He will not act most probably under those he commanded but a few weeks ago." As a mollifying gesture of his own personal trust, he arranged for Arnold to take command at Peekskill. Perhaps that would have sufficed. But it so happened that (aggravating Arnold's wounded pride) a handbill had just been published by a fellow officer, Colonel John Brown, in which the long-standing charges against him of looting and embezzlement from the Canadian campaign were repeated and in which this prophetic sentence appeared: "Money is this man's god and to get enough of it he would sacrifice his country." On May 12, Arnold rode into Washington's headquarters in a huff and announced that he would seek an investigation into all charges against him and demand the seniority he was due. Eight days later, he wrote to Congress, "Conscious of the rectitude of my intentions . . . I must request the favor of Congress to point out some mode by which my conduct, and that of my accusers, may be inquired into, and justice done to the innocent and injured."

Is it difficult to condemn a valuable officer in wartime, but the hard evidence against him was also scant; as a result, he was exonerated of most of the charges—although the involved matter of his financial dealings was referred to a later date. As for the delicate matter of his advancement, on May 21, the Board of War heard his testimony until well past midnight. At four in the morning, John Adams wrote to his wife: "I am wearied to death with the wrangles between military officers, high and low. They quarrel like cats and dogs. They worry one another like mastiffs. Scrambling for rank and pay like apes for nuts."

CHAPTER NINE

SARATOGA

IN the summer of 1777, Howe extended his position along the Hudson and strengthened his hold on Newport, Rhode Island, and New York. Meanwhile, the colonial secretary, Lord George Germain, had financed a crack new army to be led by Major General John Burgoyne as part of a three-pronged effort to seize the Hudson Valley from rebel control. Burgoyne, with one column, was to move down from Canada by way of Lake Champlain; Howe, with another, up from New York to form a junction with Burgoyne at Albany; and a third, under Lieutenant Colonel Barrimore St. Leger, was to proceed up the Saint Lawrence, land at Oswego, capture Fort Stanwix (with the assistance of Iroquois Indians and loyalists under Sir John Johnson), and then sweep down the Mohawk Valley to join Burgoyne and Howe. By severing New England along the Hudson River–Lake Champlain Axis from the other colonies to the south, the British hoped to bring the rebellion to a close.

It was partly the enmity between Lord Germain, His Majesty's secretary of state for the American Colonies and a Tory, and Sir Guy Carleton, a Whig, that gave Burgoyne, an inferior officer, command of the southward march to glory. Carleton undoubtedly deserved the honor. Not only had he opened the way for it with his victory on Lake Champlain, but he was familiar with backwoods American warfare and knew the contested terrain. But Burgoyne thought himself the right man for the job. A general, dramatist, and leader of London fashion, he had been born into a prosperous family whose inherited property could be traced to 1387, according to the following curious deed:

> I John of Gaunt
> Do give and do graunt
> Unto Roger Burgoyne
> And the heirs of his loyne
> All Sutton and Potton
> Until the world's rotten.

His father, grandfather, and great-grandfather had all been baronets, and it was one of his many ambitions to add a knighthood to his name. As a soldier, he had served with distinction during the Seven Years' War in Europe, gaining a measure of celebrity by dashing cavalry exploits in Portugal, France, and Spain. For his civil behavior toward his troops, he earned the nickname "Gentleman Johnny," preferring, as he put it, the French system of relying upon "points of honor" in discipline to the Prussian system of "training men like spaniels by the stick." He was also a frequent and flamboyant speaker in Parliament, to which he had been elected in 1761. But his immoderate taste for the high life (which he shared with General Howe) curled a question mark over his capacities, and even in a farewell and affectionate letter to his wife before he sailed for Boston in 1775, he felt obliged, as a self-confessed libertine, to couple his declarations of everlasting love with apologies for "the levities, the inattentions, and dissipations of my common course of life."

Unlike the Howes, however, Burgoyne had little sympathy for American grievances, and after his reelection to the House of Commons in 1768, he spoke of the colonists in the most condescending way. In April 1774, when voting against repeal of the tax on tea, he said, "I look upon America as our child, which we have already spoilt by too much indulgence." For this he was rebuked by Lord Chesterfield: "For my part, I never saw a forward child mended by whipping; and I would not have the Mother Country become a step-mother"—thus predicting the familial estrangement which soon took place.

At the siege of Boston, where he served (to no particular purpose, as he complained) with Howe and Gage, he was very critical of his superiors, writing captious letters home about them when he was not staging a farce or writing one of his verbose letters to Washington or Lee. Upon his return from Boston, he found the British War Department much preoccupied with expelling the Americans from Canada and, when called in to advise, drew up a proposal (as expressed in his pamphlet *Reflections upon the War in America*) that "two armies should advance, one from the North in Canada, and one from the South, join at some given point, and cut the colonies in half."

Burgoyne had a low opinion of the American soldier and, like many in England at the time, believed that in any open confrontation the Americans would put up a poor fight. General Gage had once thought so too—"they will be lions while we are lambs," he had told the Home Office in 1775—but afterward he had been forced to absorb the sobering lessons of Bunker Hill. However, the received wisdom still dominated government thinking and had been engraved almost indelibly on the ministerial mind by the redundant pronouncements of many British heroes who had served in American wars. General James Wolfe (who was regarded almost as a military saint) had called the provincials "the dirtiest, most contemptible, cowardly dogs you can conceive. There is no depending on them in action. They fall down dead in their own dirt and desert by battalions, officers and all. Such rascals as these are rather an encumbrance than any real strength to an army." And General John Forbes, the conqueror of Fort Duquesne, had described his colonial troops as "an extream bad Collection of broken Innkeepers, Horse Jockeys, and Indian traders . . . a gathering from the scum of the worst people." Such a lack of appreciation of American mettle was of course rebuffed from time to time in Parliament, and strikingly so in a speech made in the House of Commons on March 27, 1775, by David Hartley:

Everything here asserted about America is done so to serve the present turn without the least regard for truth. I would have these matters fairly sifted out. To begin with the late war: the Americans turned the success of the war, at both ends of the line. They took Louisburg from the French, singlehanded, without any European assistance. The men themselves dragged the cannon over a morass which had always been thought impassable, and they carried the shot upon their backs. . . . Whenever Great Britain has declared war they have taken their part. . . . They have been engaged in more than one expedition to Canada, ever foremost to partake of honour and danger with the mother country. Well, Sir, what have we done for them? Have we conquered the country for them from the Indians? Have we cleared it? Have we drained it? Have we made it habitable? What have we done for them? I believe precisely nothing at all, but just keeping watch and ward over their trade, that they should receive nothing but from ourselves, and at our own price. . . . In all the wars which have been common to us and them, they have taken their full share. But in all their own dangers, in all the difficulties belonging separately to their situation,

246 ANGEL IN THE WHIRLWIND

in all the Indian wars which did not immediately concern us, we left them to themselves to struggle their way through.

Burgoyne, however, in a letter to Lord North from Boston, had suggested that Americans by nature were afraid of an open fight. Yet even he had learned a few things since. In discussing the character of the American soldier, he tried to convey some notion to the ministry of the unconventional warfare Europeans faced:

> Accustomed to felling of timber and to grubbing up trees, they are very ready at earthworks and palisading, and they will cover and entrench themselves wherever they are for a short time left unmolested with surprising alacrity. . . . Composed as the American army is, together with the strength of the country, full of woods, swamps, stone walls, and other enclosures and hiding-places, it may be said of it that every private man will in action be his own general, who will turn every tree and bush into a kind of temporary fortress, from whence, when he hath fired his shot with all the deliberation, coolness, and certainty which hidden safety inspires, he will skip as it were to the next, and so on for a long time till dislodged either by cannon or by a resolute attack of light infantry.

This picture, marred only by its condescending suggestion that the scampering Americans (depicted here almost as a species of forest animal) were brave only when fighting behind a blind, nevertheless contained important truths. Had Burgoyne extrapolated from his own observations, he might have fared better than he did.

Burgoyne's previous service in Canada as second in command to Carleton had not been satisfying. Although he had easily routed the exhausted American army before Quebec (which had merely reinforced his prejudice), he had not been allowed, given the lateness of the season, to follow up Carleton's victory on Lake Champlain. The two men were opposites, and, though they might have complemented each other, their strangeness estranged. But Burgoyne won the greater affection of the men. One officer who had served under them both remarked, "General Carleton is one of the most distant, reserved men in the world, he has a rigid strictness in his manner which is very unpleasing and which he observes even to his most particular friends and acquaintants. . . . He was far from being the favourite of the army. General Burgoyne alone engrossed their warmest attachment. From having seen a great deal of polite life, he possessed a winning manner in his appearance and address . . . which caused him to be idolized . . . his orders appearing more like recommending subordination than enforcing it."

After the Canadian campaign of 1776 came to an end, Burgoyne returned home and, at Germain's prompting, drew up some "Thoughts for Conducting the War from the Side of Canada," which laid out the campaign for the following year. He accurately predicted that Ticonderoga would be well fortified with artillery and a large garrison and that the Americans would assemble a naval force on Lake George to help with any retreat. They would also block the roads from Ticonderoga through Skenesborough to Albany by felling trees, destroying bridges, and creating other impediments, while fortifying strong positions in the hills and woods. To overcome all these obstacles, the British would have to assemble an army of at least 8,000 regulars, "having a weight of artillery with it," with a corps of sailors, 2,000 Canadians, and 1,000 or more Indians. He repeated his idea of a junction with Howe at Albany but, to draw off the Americans, recommended a diversionary expedition by Lake Ontario and Oswego to the Mohawk River.

For the British, the Mohawk Valley in New York was fertile ground. Sir William Johnson, the Indian superintendent for the northern tribes who had died in 1774, had left "an intricate network of alliances among elements of the Iroquois confederacy, local white settlers (some of them indebted to Johnson for loans and favors), wealthy New York landowners, and British officials in Quebec" who were in a position to oversee and direct loyalist efforts in the region and coordinate them with the projected campaign.

Yet from the point of view of military planning, the whole scheme of breaking up the army into three converging columns was unsound. In the first place, it assigned the two columns advancing from Canada rather long lines of march over bad roads through hostile, unfamiliar country where supplies would be hard to obtain, and it gave the Americans an opportunity to unite their forces and meet and defeat the columns one at a time—the classic advantage of "interior lines." On the other hand, the Americans remained disorganized, and that above all gave the strategy a reasonable chance.

Burgoyne's command immediately went to his head. One evening before he sailed for Quebec, he was relaxing at Arthur's, a celebrated London Club, when he happened to remark to Charles James Fox, his companion at cards as well as his foil in parliamentary debate, that he "hoped to bring America to her senses before he returned." Fox told him, "Be not over-sanguine: I believe when you next return to England you will be a prisoner on parole."

Burgoyne landed in Quebec on May 6, 1777, with 9,000 men including a large German mercenary contingent under General Baron Friedrich von Riedesel. The Germans were a motley crew. They included, in one description, "a runaway artist from Jena, a bankrupt tradesman from Vienna, a fringe-maker from Hanover, a discharged secretary from the Post Office at Gotha, a monk from Wurzburg, an upper steward from Meningen, a Prussian sergeant of Hussars, and a cashiered Hessian Major." Their equipment, wholly inappropriate for backwoods warfare, was equally bizarre: "haversacks, long skirted coats, long swords, enormous canteens, grenadier caps with heavy brass ornaments, as well as "much hair-powder and pomatum and great clumsy queues." But, like the Hessians serving with the British in New York, they were all very well trained and disciplined in the Prussian manner and tough. One loyalist recalled seeing a German corporal run the gauntlet eight times through the regiment: "he had upwards of 2,000 lashes which he bore with the greatest resolution and firmness, not a single muscle of his face discomposed all the time."

After stockpiling supplies at Crown Point, Burgoyne set out from Saint John's in mid-June with 4,000 British regulars; light infantry; grenadiers; 473 artillerymen with 130 brass guns; 500 loyalists (the Queen's Loyal Rangers and the King's Loyal Americans); more than 3,000 Germans, "trudging along in their great heavy boots, sabers rattling at their sides and plumes nodding overhead"; and 400 Indians smeared with bear's grease, their scalp locks trimmed with feathers, their bodies and faces tattooed. Behind them came a long supply train with hundreds of female camp followers as well as officers' wives.

Some idea of Burgoyne's buoyant expectation of triumphant progress is suggested by the manifold luxuries he took along, from feather beds to European culinary delicacies. In this respect, he committed the same error as Braddock had in his march across the mountains of Virginia twenty years before.

Although Carleton had originally hoped to lead the expedition—and candidly protested to Germain the "Slight, Disregard and Censure" of his demotion, which he attributed entirely to Germain's "private Enmity"—he did his utmost to support it, and six weeks later Lord North could write to him, "All the letters from General Burgoyne and the other officers of the northern army are full of the warmest acknowledgements of the cordial, zealous and effectual assistance they have received from you."

Yet all the king's horses and all the king's men could not alter the fact that the Americans knew exactly what the British plan was. In mid-May, Burgoyne had been aghast to discover "a paper handed about [Montreal] publishing the whole design of the campaign, almost as accurately as if it had been copied from the Secretary of State's letter." And Dr. James

Thacher, an American surgeon, described it precisely in his journal, kept at Ticonderoga in mid-June, just as Burgoyne was setting out:

It is . . . understood that the British government have appointed Lieutenant-General Burgoyne commander-in-chief of their army in Canada, consisting, it is said, of eight or ten thousand men. According to authentic reports, the plan of the British government for the present campaign is that General Burgoyne's army shall take possession of Ticonderoga and force his way through the country to Albany. To facilitate this event, Colonel St. Leger is to march with a party of British, Germans, Canadians and Indians to the Mohawk River and make a diversion in that quarter. The royal army at New York, under command of General Howe, is to pass up the Hudson River; and, calculating on success in all quarters, the three armies are to form a junction at Albany. Here, probably, the three commanders are to congratulate each other on their mighty achievements and the flattering prospect of crushing the rebellion. . . . [T]he communication between the southern and eastern states will be interrupted, and New England, as they suppose, may become an easy prey.

Uneasy at how carelessly the campaign had been publicized, quite a few of the Canadians assembled for it began at once to desert. Burgoyne complained to Carleton; the latter replied, "If the Government laid any great stress upon assistance from the Canadians for carrying on the present war, it surely was not upon Informattion proceeding from me. Experience might have taught them (and it did not require that to convince me), these People had been governed with too loose a Rein for many years . . . to be suddenly restored to a proper and desirable Subordination."

And so toward the end of June, as a contemporary American ballad put it:

> Burgoyne, the King's commander
>   From Canada set sail;
> With full eight thousand reg'lars
>   He thought he could not fail.
> With Indians and Canadians
>   And his cursed Tory crew
> On board his fleet of shipping
>   Up Lake Champlain he flew.

He flew up the lake, gliding smoothly over the waters: the redcoats, loyalists, and Germans in their gunboats and barges, escorted by the frigates *Inflexible* and *Royal George,* and the Indians in their birch-bark canoes. They landed at some distance from the American positions and advanced along the shores, their main body under Burgoyne on the western bank, the German reserve under Riedesel on the east.

From June 27 to 29, Burgoyne paused at Crown Point to bring up the rear of his army and establish a military hospital. On the thirtieth, he issued a general order in which he said that the army's purpose was "to vindicate the Law, and to relieve the oppressed. . . . The Services required of this particular expedition are critical and conspicuous. . . . This Army must not Retreat." By then, they had come into view of Fort Ticonderoga, now under the command of General Arthur St. Clair. The British frigates and gunboats arrived and anchored just out of reach of the American batteries, and by day's end Burgoyne was encamped four miles north of the fort and had begun to entrench.

At the time, Fort Ticonderoga was garrisoned with about 4,000 men. Although not impregnable, it had recovered remarkably from the poor state it had been in the previous spring. Many of the men then had been sick and lacked shoes, blankets, and other basic equipment, including guns. The powder magazines in the fort had rotted, and some of the barracks had collapsed.

Politics had contributed to the neglect. When, the previous March, Gates by his appointment to Ticonderoga had appeared to supersede Schuyler in the Northern Department of the war, Schuyler (it may be remembered) had appealed to Congress, which had confirmed his seniority. Gates, in a fury, had come south to appear before Congress and had appalled and embarrassed the delegates by extravagantly extolling his own virtues as a commander. Valuable time had been lost in this wrangle over precedence while the plans for the British invasion from the north were being hammered out. Moreover, since Schuyler, being a New Yorker, was unpopular with the New England troops, who favored Gates, many of them had gone home.

Meanwhile, the remnant at Ticonderoga had prepared as best they could for the impending siege. A star-shaped fort with pickets had been built upon the summit of Mount Independence, a high, circular hill opposite the fort on the eastern side of the lake: halfway down the side of the hill was a battery; and at the base were works strongly furnished with artillery. The two forts were connected by a floating bridge supported by twenty-two sunken piers in timber caissons which spanned the narrow channel at the head of the lake. Between the piers themselves were great floats, fifty feet long and twelve feet wide, yoked together by iron chains. On the north side of the bridge was a large segmented timber boom secured by riveted bolts, and beside this a double iron chain with links an inch and a half thick. In short: a boom across the channel at the head of the lake, a small fort to protect the boom along the shore, and another fort halfway up Mount Independence to protect this shore redoubt. The bridge, boom, and chains, four hundred yards in length, were designed to protect the upper part of the lake and represented a barrier under cover of the fortress guns which it was believed the British ships would be unable to break through.

However, the highest point in the area, Sugar Loaf Hill, part of a mountain bridge separating Lake Champlain from Lake George, had been left unfortified, even though the Polish-born military engineer Tadeusz Kościuszko had warned that enemy cannon on its summit would place all the other defenses at the mercy of its shot.

Kosciuszko, educated at the military academy in Warsaw and afterward in military schools in Paris and Mézières, had been recommended to Congress by Silas Deane. After planning Philadelphia's fortifications and river defenses, he had been made an engineering colonel in the Continental Army and, in the spring of 1777, had joined the staff of General Gates. Why his opinion was dismissed is not clear, since Colonel John Trumbull, sometime aide-de-camp to Washington, had also proved the preceding year how dangerously close the summit was by throwing a shot from a twelve-pounder in the fort nearly to its top. Then the ridge had been pronounced inaccessible. This Trumbull had likewise shown to be false by clambering up to the heights with Generals Arnold and Anthony Wayne. A small fort there, he said, with twenty-five heavy guns and 500 men, would be as formidable as Ticonderoga itself with one hundred guns and 10,000 men.

On July 2, Burgoyne seized a strategic outpost commanding the connection with Lake George, and General William Phillips, who commanded Burgoyne's artillery train, sent an engineer up Sugar Loaf Hill to assess its potential for the siege. "Where a goat can go, a man can go; and where a man can go he can haul up a gun," declared Phillips, no doubt alluding to the goat path that Wolfe had discovered in Quebec. The engineer promptly reported back that, indeed, a road could be cut up the rugged slope and the ground leveled for cannon at the top.

The road was cut, and ammunition and stores were conveyed up in a single night. Before morning, the summit had been prepared for the British heavy guns, which were hauled up diagonally from tree to tree by ropes.

On July 5, therefore, to their astonishment and consternation, the American garrison awoke to behold a legion of redcoats on the crest of

Sugar Loaf Hill, completing works which must soon lay their whole defenses waste.

General St. Clair surveyed the enemy position through his spyglass and said, "We must away from this, for our situation has become a desperate one." He prepared to evacuate his forces without delay that night, sending most of his troops toward Castleton, Vermont, by land and the light artillery, stores, provisions, sick and wounded, officers's wives, and so on, on two hundred bateaux escorted by galleys, to the head of the lake. From there they were to proceed to Fort Edward at the southern end of Lake George.

The evacuation went beautifully at first and was efficiently conducted in silence and with great care. The flotilla departed undiscovered and was soon gliding under the shadows of the mountain walls. But as St. Clair and the rest of the garrison crossed the makeshift bridge to the Vermont side of the lake, one of the houses within Fort Independence caught fire, suddenly illuminating his troops in full retreat. The British dashed into Fort Ticonderoga, hoisted their own flag over it, secured it as well as Fort Independence with a garrison, and pursued the American rear guard. The American vessels were also chased in gunboats and frigates, which managed to shatter the floating bridge blocking the channel with its boom and chain.

The following day, the British caught up with the flotilla at Skenesborough, blew up three of its galleys, and—the Americans having beached their boats to make a run for it—landed troops and Indians in a furious chase. The Americans retreated past Skenesborough's stockaded fort, which they set on fire, and made their way toward Fort Anne, twelve miles away. Meanwhile, St. Clair and the rest of the garrison had fled through the woods, through Castleton to Hubbardton, where the British overtook their rear guard. At sunrise, the British struck the hill where the Americans were eating breakfast, in an action that became almost a repeat of Bunker Hill. The patriots strung themselves out along the ridge of the plateau behind rocks, fences, and trees as the advancing British grenadiers, heavily laden with equipment, marched up the steep slope in dressed ranks only to be decimated by close, careful fire. This scenario was repeated until General Riedesel arrived with German reinforcements and stormed the hill. The defenders retreated, but at the end of the day, both sides had lost about 300, or a third, of their men, a casualty rate higher than that at Waterloo. The British, thus checked, gave up the chase. The Americans, without further loss, continued on to Fort Edward, where, on the twelfth, they staggered in "greatly distressed," wrote an eyewitness, "and worn down by fatigue."

Over the next several days, other beleaguered troops drifted in from the destroyed fort at Skenesborough and from Fort Anne, which had also fallen to the British on July 7.

When news of the capture of Ticonderoga reached London on August 22, King George reportedly ran into the queen's bedroom, clapping his hands and shouting, "I have beat them! beat all the Americans." And Burgoyne, writing in exultation to George Germain on July 11, did not overstate the American defeat when he said, "I have the honor to acquaint your Lordship that the enemy was dislodged from Ticonderoga and Mount Independence on the 6th instant . . . with the loss of 128 pieces of cannon, all their armed vessels and bateaux, the greatest part of their baggage and ammunition, provision and military stores to a very large amount."

The fall of Ticonderoga, which fort had been regarded by both sides as a kind of northern Gibraltar, was a great blow to the Americans. On July 30, Abigail Adams wrote to her husband, "How are all our vast magazines of cannon, powder, arms, clothing, provision, medicine, etc., to be restored to us? But, what is vastly more, how shall the disgrace be wiped away?" She wondered "if cowardice, guilt, or deceit" might have contributed to the capitulation and, if so, hoped those responsible would be punished, "howsoever high or exalted" their station might be. Indeed, there was a general demand for an accounting. John Adams was so upset that he said, "I think we shall never defend a post until we shoot a general . . . and this event in my opinion is not far off. . . . We must trifle no more. We have suffered too many disgraces to pass unexpiated." Even Washington, normally imperturbable, was astonished and appalled at the news of Ticonderoga's fall, which he first learned of in a letter from Schuyler dated July 7. In that letter he was told that General St. Clair and the better part of his army had disappeared into the woods. "The affair," wrote Washington, "is so mysterious that it baffles even conjecture." A week later he learned that the missing troops were making their way toward Fort Edward. Although pleased to hear they had not been captured, he could not forbear adding, "The evacuation of Ticonderoga and Mount Independence is an event of chagrin and surprise not apprehended, nor within the compass of my reasoning. . . . This stroke is severe indeed and has distressed us much. But . . . we should never despair. Our situation before has been unpromising and has changed for the better, so I trust it will again." As for the British, according to an observer, "they deemed their fortune and their prowess to be irresistible. They regarded their enemy with the greatest contempt and considered their own toils to be nearly at an end and Albany already in their hands."

It now appeared that all Burgoyne had to do was to float his troops, cannon, and equipment down Lake George, push through some woods, and cruise down the Hudson. On July 16, with Burgoyne just twenty miles to the north of Fort Edward, the total remaining patriot force was just 2,600 Continental troops and 2,000 militia.

The American resistance was melting away.

S o it appeared. But Gouverneur Morris, a member of the New York Committee of Safety, told his colleagues after consulting with Schuyler, who had consulted with Washington, "I will venture to say that if we lay it down as a maxim, never to contend for ground but in the last necessity, and to leave nothing but a wilderness to the enemy, their progress must be impeded by obstacles, which it is not in human nature to surmount." Burgoyne, doubting that anything could impede his progress, had written to George Germain on July 11 that "the spirit and zeal" of his troops were "sufficient to surmount" any obstacles, however "laborious." But then obstacles began to accumulate at an alarming rate. In an earlier letter to Howe (July 2) he had written, "Ticonderoga reduced, I shall leave behind me proper engineers to put it in an impregnable state, and it will be garrisoned from Canada, where all the destined supplies are safely arrived. My force therefore will be left complete for future operations." But that was not how it worked out. Carleton was unable to garrison the fort with the forces at his own command, which obliged Burgoyne to assign a thousand of his men to the task. As the length of his supply lines grew, he also found it necessary to divide up his force for foraging expeditions.

Already there was a subtle change in Washington's assessment, as the commander in chief, often wrongly faulted for a lack of strategic vision, foresaw the emerging circumstances of Burgoyne's defeat. As he explained to Schuyler, in command at Ford Edward:

> Though our affairs for some days past have worn a dark and gloomy aspect, I yet look forward to a fortunate and happy change. I trust General Burgoyne's army will meet sooner or later an effectual check and, as I suggested before, that the success he has had will precipitate his ruin. From your accounts, he appears to be pursuing that line of conduct which of all others is most favorable to us. I mean acting in detachment. This conduct will certainly give room for enterprise on our part and expose his parties to great hazard. Could we be so happy as to cut one of them off, supposing it should not exceed four, five or six hundred men, it would inspirit the people and do away with much of their present anxiety.

At the same time, consistent with the military opportunity he saw unfolding, Washington cautioned Schuyler against relying too much on fortified positions of any kind. "I begin to consider lines as a kind of trap," he wrote, "and not to answer the valuable purposes expected from them unless they are in passes which cannot be avoided by the enemy."

John Adams had the same thought. "I begin to wish there was not a fort upon the continent," he wrote to his wife from Philadelphia on July 13. "Discipline and disposition are our resource. It is our policy to draw the Enemy into the country, where we can avail ourselves of hills, woods, rivers, defiles, etc., until our soldiers are more inured to war. Howe and Burgoyne will not be able to meet this year, and if they were met, it would only be better for us, for we should draw all our forces to a point too. If they were met, they could not cut off the communication between the northern and southern States. But if the communication was cut off for a time, it would be no misfortune, for New England would defend itself, and the southern States would defend themselves." His overall assessment might have seemed too optimistic, but the army surgeon, Dr. Thacher, similarly predicted that the fall of Ticonderoga, "apparently so calamitous, will ultimately prove advantageous by drawing the British army into the heart of our country and thereby place them more immediately within our power."

Meanwhile, Congress unfairly blamed Schuyler, as the senior commander in the region, for Burgoyne's initial success. Schuyler ignored the calumnies and proceeded to act with a shrewdness and dispatch he had not been thought to possess. He asked Washington for artillery, ammunition, and all the equipment that could be spared from his own encampment and from Peekskill, even as Washington dispatched urgent communiqués to the militia in Massachusetts and Connecticut to hurry to Schuyler's aid. "I trust you will immediately upon receipt of this, if you have not done it already, march with at least one third of the militia under your command."

Meanwhile, Schuyler rallied his remaining forces to slow Burgoyne's advance, giving him time to build an army from the militia levies. He also asked Washington for generals popular with the New England troops. Washington sent him Benedict Arnold—"an active, judicious and brave officer" with a knowledge of the area—and Benjamin Lincoln.

Burgoyne had boasted that he would eat his Christmas dinner in Albany, just as Montgomery had similarly boasted two years before in front of Québec. But instead of embarking south on Lake George in boats, which might have made the dinner more palatable, he chose to make his way, with his whole swollen baggage train, through the dense northern forests of New York. As he advanced, it became more and more difficult for him to provision his army as Americans destroyed crops and other sources of supply in his path. Schuyler's wife, hearing that British soldiers were on their way to commandeer the grain harvest of their estate, set fire to the family's fields with her own hands. Ahead of Burgoyne, work crews managed to obstruct every road and stream with tree trunks and boulders so that, when added to the natural impediments of the countryside, "it was with the utmost pains and fatigue," wrote British lieutenant Thomas Anburey, that "we could work our way through them. Exclusive of these, the watery grounds and marshes were so numerous that we were under the necessity of constructing no less than forty bridges to pass them, and over one morass there was a bridge of near two miles in length." After an extraordinarily difficult march through the forest and bogs, advancing on average just one mile a day, Burgoyne finally reached and took Fort Edward on July 30, as Schuyler withdrew his forces southward along the west bank of the Hudson past Saratoga to Stillwater, near the south of the Mohawk.

The fall of Fort Edward brought Burgoyne more grief than glory. On its outskirts, some of his Indian warriors killed and scalped a young woman by the name of Jane McCrea. She happened to be a Tory sympathizer and at the time was on the way to a forest tryst with her lover, an officer in Burgoyne's loyalist auxiliary corps. As Dr. Thacher tells it, "The Indians [had] made her their prisoner; and on their return towards Burgoyne's camp a quarrel arose to decide who should hold possession of the fair prize. During the controversy one of the monsters struck his tomahawk into her skull and immediately stripped off her scalp." The name of this frontier girl became known all over England and America, and no excuse or apology could atone for the sorry episode. Not only did the British cause suffer morally, but the affair had the practical effect, despite her own Tory leanings, of arousing the countryside as militia volunteers now flocked by the hundreds, then by the thousands, to Schuyler's camp.

Burgoyne, moreover, had not helped matters much by pardoning the Indian responsible to prevent others from defecting from his ranks.

It might all have been foreseen. While it was considered legitimate to employ Indians as auxiliaries under military discipline, a century of border strife had shown that in war they could not be restrained from engaging in atrocities. In September 1774, General Gage had written from Boston to ask Sir Guy Carleton whether "a body of Canadians and Indians might be collected . . . should matters come to extremities." Burgoyne himself had recommended the "expediency" of such a measure to Lord North. Meanwhile, in April 1775, the Second Provincial Congress of Massachusetts had sent an address to "our brethren the Indians, natives of Stockbridge," urging them to "take up the hatchet in the cause of Liberty." The Stockbridge Indians answered the call and joined the patriot army at Cambridge, whereupon Gage advised Lord Dartmouth in London, "We need not be tender of calling on the savages, as the rebels have shown us the example by bringing as many Indians down against us here as they could collect." Darmouth, borrowing the rebels' own language, replied on July 24 by urging the Indian superintendent for the northern tribes "to take such steps as may induce them [the Indians] to take up the Hatchet against His Majesty's Rebellious Subjects in America."

Yet both sides had grave misgivings about carrying through with their threats. In war the Indians wanted plunder and scalps. If they got them, would the ill will sown be worth the gain? The British thought it might, since by terrorizing the frontier, the Indians could divert hundreds and perhaps thousands of militiamen to inconsequential outposts for defense. A more judicious policy had been adopted by the Continental Congress, which had urged all the tribes to remain neutral and appropriated funds for presents and bribes to try to ensure that they would. Attempts were also made to overawe them—for example, several chiefs were taken to Philadelphia to see the Continental battalions drawn out and reviewed by their commanders, "in order to give these savages," wrote Joseph Hewes of North Carolina, "some idea of our strength and importance."

Others needed little persuading. On one occasion, a congressional commission met with a number of chiefs at a German Reformed Church in Easton, Pennsylvania, to solicit their neutrality. "After shaking hands, and drinking rum, while the organ played," wrote Thomas Paine, who was secretary to the commission, "we proceeded to business. . . . The chief of the tribes, who went by the name of King 'Last-night,' because his tribe had sold their lands, had seen some English men-of-war in the waters of Canada. He was impressed by the power of such great canoes; but he also saw that the English made no progress against us by land. . . . 'The King of England,' said he, 'is like a fish. When he is in the water he can wag his tail; when he comes on land he lays down on his side.' " Although Washington himself, in July 1775 (before the congressional policy had been established), had consulted, at his Cambridge headquarters, seven sachems of the French Caughnawaga tribe living around Montreal about an alliance, in the end he wisely decided to urge the Indians to adhere to a neutral stance.

Not so Burgoyne.

On June 20, at Crown Point, as the expedition was setting out, he had issued a proclamation warning that no patriot should consider himself safe merely because of his distance "from the immediate situation of my camp. I have but to give stretch to the Indian forces under my direction (and they amount to thousands) to overtake the hardened enemies of Great Britain and America. I consider them the same wherever they may lurk." At the same time, Burgoyne fatuously attempted to get the Indians to abide by certain rules of war. He enjoined them not to attack unarmed civilians—"aged men, women, children; prisoners must be held sacred from the knife or hatchet"—but told them that "in conformity and indulgence to your customs, which have affixed an idea of honour to such badges of victory, you shall be allowed to take the scalps of the dead."

As Burke pointed out in Parliament (as reported by Horace Walpole), Burgoyne's invitation "was just as if, at a riot on Tower Hill, the keeper of the wild beasts had turned them loose, but adding, 'my gentle lions, my sentimental wolves, my tender-hearted hyenas, go forth, but take care not to hurt men, women, or children.' " Lord Chatham later wrote, "We had sullied and tarnished the arms of Britain for ever by employing savages in our service, by drawing them up in a British line, and mixing the scalping-knife and the tomahawk with the sword and the fire-lock."

Yet under Burgoyne, and not just in this instance, the Indians "were much encouraged," admitted one British officer, "as useful to the army in many particulars." They enjoyed a kind of license among the troops, "walk freely through our camp and come into our tents without the least ceremony, wanting brandy or rum, for which they would do anything." Burgoyne himself, even before the murder of Jane McCrea, had begun to fear their predations. By then he realized that his proclamation threatening the use of Indians against the settlers had served only to arouse them against him, and in a dispatch to Germain he wrote, "Were they left to themselves, enormities too horrid to think of would ensue; guilty and innocent, women and infants, would be a common prey." On the outskirts of Fort Edward it later emerged that they had also killed "a Negro man and woman" and "a family of seven and Skalped them."

B Y the time Burgoyne had reached Fort Edward, his supply line extended over 185 miles. Although he had been assured by his advisers that much of the population of New York and Vermont would welcome him, there had been no groundswell of local loyalist support. He lingered at the fort to await the arrival of artillery, ammunition, and provisions, and from the end of July to mid-August his army was continually employed in bringing bateaux forward from Fort George to the Hudson. Yet with all the efforts Burgoyne could make, his labors were inadequate for the supply of his soldiers.

Again Washington wrote to Schuyler, offering strategic advice:

> You mention their having a great number of horses, but they must nevertheless require a considerable number of wagons, as there are many things which cannot be transported on horses. They can never think of advancing without securing their rear, and the force with which they can act against you will be greatly reduced by detachments necessary for that purpose. And as they have to cut out their passage and to remove the impediments you have thrown in their way before they can proceed, this circumstance, with the encumbrance they must feel in their baggage, stores, etc., will inevitably retard their march and give you leisure and opportunity to prepare a good reception for them.

In keeping with this scenario, he endorsed Schuyler's plan of stationing some troops in the Hampshire Grants (Vermont) on Burgoyne's flank and soon thereafter, at the request of Congress, sent him Colonel Daniel Morgan with a picked corps of 500 riflemen—"selected from the army at large and well acquainted with that mode of fighting"—that is, that in which the Indians engaged.

General Lincoln was soon at Manchester and Colonel John Stark at Bennington with a New Hampshire brigade. Stark, a veteran of Rogers' Rangers (perhaps the single most effective unit in the French and Indian War) had carried out numerous raids and reconnaissance expeditions behind French lines and had led the American rangers in Wolfe's victory at Québec. More recently, he had done his part at Trenton and Princeton. Burgoyne ought to have remembered him, for he had also proved heroic at Bunker Hill.

Informed that a large quantity of arms and supplies, including horses, which he needed for his artillery, were being held at Bennington and "guarded only by militia," Burgoyne dispatched about 800 men—including 300 Queen's Loyal Rangers, 374 Germans, 50 marksmen, and about 75 Indians—under Colonel Friedrich Baum to seize the cache and "try the affections of the country."

Baum set out from Fort Anne at a lumbering pace. Each British soldier carried a knapsack, a blanket, a haversack, a canteen for water, a hatchet, a musket, and sixty rounds of ammunition—which altogether weighed about sixty pounds. The Germans, in addition, carried a broadsword

260 ANGEL IN THE WHIRLWIND

weighing about twelve pounds, a heavy carbine instead of a musket, flour with which to make bread, and wore great jackboots, stiff leather breeches, huge gauntlets, and a heavy, feathered hat. On August 15, Baum and his troops, plunging heavily through the woods accompanied by two field guns, came up against a lightly armed but mobile force of 800 Americans with field guns of their own commanded by John Stark.

Instead of waiting for Baum, who he knew was coming, Stark had marched six miles west to engage him at Walloomsac Station, across the New York line. Baum entrenched himself upon a hill and sent to Burgoyne for reinforcements. Stark rallied his men and sent to General Lincoln for Seth Warner and his Green Mountain Brigade.

On the sixteenth, Stark attacked. As he gave the word to advance, he pointed his sword at the enemy and cried, "Tonight our flag floats over yonder hill, or Molly Stark is a widow!" Moving rapidly through the woods with practiced stealth, his men surrounded the enemy position and attacked with ferocity. Both sides went at it hammer and tongs. "Such an explosion of fire," wrote one British lieutenant, "I never had any idea of before, and the heavy artillery joining in concert like great peals of thunder, assisted by the echoes of the woods, almost deafened us with the noise."

The Queen's Loyal Rangers were trapped and decimated; some of Baum's regulars—who at one point mistook informally dressed insurgents approaching from behind for local loyalists coming to their support—were surrounded almost to a man. The battle continued till sunset, when the Americans finally forced the German breastwork "at the muzzle of their guns" and captured the enemy cannon, 700 prisoners, and "207 dead on the spot. . . . Our loss was inconsiderable," wrote Stark, "about forty wounded and thirty killed."

At this juncture, the reinforcements Baum had sent for—another German contingent of 500 led by Lieutenant Colonel Francis Breymann—drew near but were intercepted by the arrival of Warner's brigade. Warner, though outnumbered, attacked at once and drove Breymann from hill to hill while parties of Americans kept circling around to his rear to cut him off.

Though Breymann himself escaped, most of his force was captured, and for days afterward the Americans kept finding dead Germans in the woods.

Though the Battle of Bennington cost Burgoyne a sixth of his force, he tried to dismiss it lightly as "a common accident of war, independent of any general action, unattended by any loss that could affect the main strength of the army, and little more than the miscarriage of a foraging party." But privately he wrote, "The New Hampshire Grants, a country unpeopled and almost unknown in the last war, now abounds in the most active and rebellious race on the continent and hangs like a gathering storm on my left."

New York, Connecticut, and Massachusetts, as well as Vermont, now poured in their militia. Counting incoming Continentals, by mid-August Schuyler, stationed at the mouth of the Mohawk, had upward of 13,000 men.

In the meantime, Lieutenant Colonel Barrimore St. Leger had advanced along the route laid down for him—up the Saint Lawrence River and across Lake Ontario to a landing at Oswego on the New York shore. Proceeding eastward toward the Mohawk Valley with 1,000 Indians and 500 regulars, he had arrived at Fort Stanwix, 110 miles from Albany, on August 3.

Fort Stanwix was the key to the valley. At the time, it was garrisoned by 750 New York militia, who were fiercely determined to resist the impending siege, though they were vastly outnumbered and had few provisions, little powder, and ammunition that did not always match their guns. Instead of a properly stitched patriot flag (according to the design adopted by Congress for the national banner in June), the garrison had pieced one together out of a white shirt, strips of red cloth from a woman's petticoat, and a commander's blue military cloak. When run up the flagstaff, it was the very first raising of the Stars and Stripes.

St. Leger summoned the commander of the post to surrender and threatened, if he refused, to unleash his Indians on the civilian population of the valley. On the following day, toward evening, the Indians spread out through the woods, encircled the stockade, and, by yelling hideously through the night, attempted to intimidate the defenders. Meanwhile, General Nicholas Herkimer, the elderly commander of the county militia, was hurrying to their relief with about 800 men. Whether he was negligent in his march or not has been debated, but on the morning of the sixth he was ambushed in a deep, wooded ravine by Indians and Tory Rangers at Oriskany, about seven miles from the fort. The militia maintained their ground with remarkable resolution, even after Herkimer fell from his horse with a wound that shattered one leg below the knee. Propped by an aide against a tree, he lit his pipe and calmly continued to issue orders as his men fought the enemy hand to hand for six long and incredibly bloody hours with bayonets, rifle butts, and knives. In the end, the Americans held the field, but each side lost almost 400 men, making it the bloodiest encounter, in proportion to the numbers engaged, of the war.

At Fort Stanwix, St. Leger had begun a scientific siege, advancing by parallels to within 150 yards of the walls. But his men grew discouraged by their own mounting casualties and by a daring sortie from the Americans that staggered his camp. After the ambush of Herkimer's reinforcements, moreover, Schuyler had detached 900 men under Benedict Arnold (who had ridden into Fort Edward on July 24) for the relief of Fort Stanwix. Arnold spread rumors of his strength through a half-witted Dutchman, Hon-Yost, revered by the Mohawks as a sort of holy fool, and they credited his report that the British main army had been decimated and that Arnold was advancing with an overwhelming force. They began to desert St. Leger in large numbers, and on August 22, shortly before Arnold arrived, St. Leger himself abandoned the siege.

A L L this time, Washington had been performing a kind of balancing act. While carefully adjusting his forces to lend the support needed to thwart Burgoyne on the upper Hudson, he had kept his eyes on Howe on the seaboard, deftly maneuvering to counter any initiative Howe might undertake.

In response to Howe's movement beyond the Raritan, Washington had shifted 8,000 men from Morristown and taken up a strong position along the heights of Middlebrook, flanking Howe's line of march. Howe made several feints as if to pass by the American camp and march to the Delaware but was unable to lure Washington into a general engagement. After two weeks he withdrew his whole army, on June 30, to Staten Island.

However, Washington assumed that at some point Howe would ascend the Hudson, try to seize the highland passes, and open the way for a junction with Burgoyne. That, of course, is what the ministry in London thought it had told him to do. But in a remarkable lapse of tactical coordination, Howe had been left some discretion by the ministry as to whether to link up with Burgoyne or not. Burgoyne did not know this (he himself had been given no discretion), and while he waited for Howe, the latter pursued other plans. Lord Germain seems to have been responsible for the confusion. He drafted his dispatch to Howe ordering him up the Hudson, then apparently put it aside and forgot all about it. Howe, who later saw a copy of the letter, said in a committee of the House of Commons, "The letter intended to have been written to me . . . and which was probably to have contained some instructions, was never sent." It later came out that Germain's negligence had been due to his haste to get out of London for a weekend in Sussex. As a result, the master plan for one of the greatest campaigns of the war collapsed.

Although Howe had some confidence in Burgoyne's abilities, he was reluctant to act in a way that might allow an officer of lesser rank to absorb all the glory of the enterprise. And since he expected Burgoyne to succeed without difficulty in the north, he took advantage of Germain's failure to send positive orders confirming what he knew was expected of him and began his glamorous but ineffectual campaign against the rebel capital.

From Staten Island, Howe made a number of feints, first up the Hudson, then into Long Island Sound, then past Sandy Hook, to keep Washington guessing as to his destination. Washington, still taking it for granted that Howe would eventually go up the Hudson in Burgoyne's support, returned to Morristown. But when Howe at last put to sea on July 23 with thirty-six British and Hessian battalions, including light infantry and grenadiers with considerable artillery, the Queen's Loyal Rangers, and a regiment of light horse—in all, about 18,000 men—he realized that Philadelphia must be his object. Accordingly, he ordered several divisions across the Hudson from Peekskill and proceeded toward the capital. When on July 31 he learned that the enemy's fleet of 260 sail had arrived the previous day at the mouth of Delaware Bay, he wrote to Schuyler that he had nothing to fear from Howe. In the meantime, he moved his own camp to Germantown, about six miles from Philadelphia, to prepare for the capital's defense. But the very next day word came that the British fleet had sailed eastward out of the capes instead of up the Delaware River.

"Where the scourge of God and the plague of mankind is going to," wrote John Adams to his wife, "no one can guess. At any rate," he continued, apparently expecting stormy seas, "he will lose all his horses." He was right about that. Storms and contrary winds delayed the expedition; several ships were struck by lightning; and by the time Howe disembarked, after forty-seven days at sea, most of his horses were dead.

Then, in the middle of August, he reappeared, heading up the Chesapeake, and on the twenty-fifth, after much tacking back and forth, he landed his army, 18,000 strong, from 160 ships at the head of the bay. This put him about fifty miles south of Philadelphia. Although he might have tried to force his way up the Delaware, the American river defenses were formidable enough to place his whole force at risk, as they included floating batteries, chevaux-de-frise, and other sunken obstructions, and two substantial forts, Fort Mifflin, on Mud Island on the Pennsylvania side, and Fort Mercer, at Red Bank on the New Jersey shore.

The day before Howe landed (at Elkton, Maryland, at the head of the Elk River), Washington had marched his whole army, 16,000 strong, through Philadelphia, taking great pains with a show of artillery, wagons, light horse (with sabers drawn), and infantry (twelve abreast)—their ranks in order, arms shouldered, stepping in time to the fife and drum—to make the display as impressive as possible. But the captious John Adams was not entirely pleased with what he saw. "Our soldiers have not yet quite the air of soldiers," he noted. "They don't step exactly in time. They don't hold up their heads quite erect, nor turn their toes so exactly as they ought. They don't cock their hats; and such as do, don't all wear them the same way."

The army crossed the Schuylkill River and continued on to Wilmington, Delaware, near Brandywine Creek. There Washington set up his headquarters and encamped his troops on the neighboring heights.

Adams thought Washington's caution extreme and longed for prompt and decisive action. "The officers drink, 'A long and moderate war,' " he wrote Abigail. "My toast is, 'A short and violent one.' " At the same time, Adams privately wondered whether it might not be better if Howe captured the capital: "1. Because there are impurities [i.e., people with loyalist sentiment] here which will never be so soon or so fully purged away as by that fire of affliction which Howe enkindles wherever he goes. 2. Because it would employ nearly the whole of his force to keep possession of this town, and the rest of the continent would be more at liberty. 3. We could counteract him here, better than in many other places. 4. He would leave New England and New York at leisure to kill or catch Burgoyne."

Washington, however, was prepared to make a stand. Expecting that the British would try to turn his right flank, he took up a position at Chad's Ford, Pennsylvania, on the east bank of Brandywine Creek, which lay directly in the enemy's line of march.

On September 8, he and another officer rode out together to reconnoiter the area between the ford and the British camp. As they emerged into a clearing to get an exact view, they came within the gun sights of four British sharpshooters concealed in the brush nearby. One of them, Major Patrick Ferguson, was among the best marksmen alive. He had once put on an amazing demonstration of his skill for King George III, and the rifle he carried, the first breech-loader made, was a deadly accurate instrument of his own invention that weighed only seven and a half pounds.

Ferguson noted Washington's buff-and-blue uniform, majestic demeanor, and "remarkably large cocked hat" but didn't know who he was. Fortunately, instead of firing, he decided to try to capture him as well as his companion. He shouted out to the latter, who was nearer, to dismount; but this man in turn called out a warning to Washington, who calmly wheeled his horse about and the two galloped off.

Several days later, while recuperating from a wound, Ferguson learned the identity of his target and remarked, "I could have lodged half a dozen balls in or about him before he was out of my reach. But it was not pleasant to fire at the back of an unoffending individual who was acquitting himself coolly of his duty, and so I left him alone." To his decent forbearance, America owes an incalculable debt.

Early on the morning of September 11, the British came on. One column of their forces, under the German general Wilhelm von Knyphausen, began to bombard the American position across the creek, as if it were to be the main point of attack, while another column, the British main army, under Howe and Cornwallis, crossed in a flanking movement seventeen miles upstream.

Misled by conflicting reports about their position, Washington was outmaneuvered and, finding that Cornwallis had gained the rear of his army, sent orders to Sullivan to oppose him with the entire right wing. In the meantime, General Anthony Wayne was to keep Knyphausen at bay with the American center at the ford, and General Greene was to hold himself ready with the reserve to give aid wherever required.

As soon as Knyphausen learned that the British flanking movement had succeeded, he made a push to cross Chad's Ford. Greene, to keep him from doing so, was about to reinforce Wayne when he was summoned by Washington to the support of the right wing, which Cornwallis seemed about to overcome.

Knyphausen, encountering a faltering resistance, surged across the Brandywine and captured the American artillery, which he promptly turned on the defenders; Cornwallis launched a bayonet attack into the gap in the American right flank. The American lines broke, and the soldiers began fleeing in the belief that no hope remained of saving the day. In the midst of this rout, General Greene, at the head of George Weedon's Virginia Brigade, having covered four miles at a run, shrewdly opened his ranks to receive them and, after their passage, closed them up so as to retire in good order, checking the enemy's pursuit with continual fire.

In the battle, Washington's army lost three hundred killed and six hundred wounded. Four hundred more were captured—in all, about double the losses the British had sustained. In its aftermath, Greene and Washington had the only altercation they reputedly ever had. In his public commendations, Washington had failed to make special mention of Weedon's brigade. Greene objected strongly, but Washington told him, "You, sir, are considered my favourite officer. Weedon's brigade, like myself, are Virginians. Should I applaud them for their achievement under your command, I shall be charged with partiality: jealousy will be excited, and the service injured." Greene replied, "In my own behalf I have nothing to ask. But do not, sir, let me entreat you, on account of the jealousy that may arise in little minds, withhold justice from the brave fellows I had the honour to command." Washington, however, stood firm, and Greene, upon reflection, apologized and accepted the judgment of his commander in chief.

No one could fault Greene for his conduct during the battle. Washington faulted himself. But public blame tended to fall on General Sullivan for having moved without skill to check Cornwallis's advance.

The Americans, having retreated to the north side of the Schuylkill River on September 12, fell back to Chester. Washington made the White Horse Tavern near Malvern his headquarters but left about 1,500 men under General Wayne on the river's south side to harass Howe's troops. Wayne encamped in the woods at Paoli, but Tories in the area divulged his whereabouts, and on September 20, in the middle of the night, three British battalions under Sir Charles Grey and Colonel Thomas Musgrave surprised and attacked the Americans with bayonets and swords. The Americans scattered "in all directions with the greatest confusion," wrote a British officer. "The light infantry bayoneted every man they came up with. The camp was immediately set on fire, and this, with the cries of the wounded, formed altogether one of the most dreadful scenes I ever beheld."

The Americans lost 450 in this carnage, many of them butchered in their beds. British casualties were less than 20 killed.

Washington's defense of Philadelphia had thus far been a catastrophe. The following day, the twenty-first, Howe made a rapid march high up the Schuylkill on the road leading to Reading, as if to capture the military stores kept there, as Washington kept pace with him on the opposite bank. But on the twenty-third, by rapid countermarching, the British managed to outmaneuver him again and cross the ford behind. That enabled them to march unimpeded toward Philadelphia. On the twenty-fifth, Howe halted at the village of Germantown, Pennsylvania, where he encamped the main body of his army while sending Lord Cornwallis on with a large force to take formal possession of the capital.

Everything about his entry was calculated to make an impression as legions of British and Hessian grenadiers, accompanied by long trains of artillery and squadrons of light dragoons, stepped to the music of a large military band playing "God Save the King." In their crisp scarlet uniforms and with their glittering arms, they presented a striking contrast to the comparatively ragged Continental troops who had recently passed through the same streets in brown linen hunting frocks and caps decorated with sprigs of evergreen. A few days before, members of Congress had been roused from their beds with word that the enemy "had it in their power," wrote John Adams, "to be in Philadelphia before morning." Before Cornwallis arrived, every one of them had fled.

Washington remained determined to undermine the British victories. More batteries were erected on the Delaware River with other obstructions to prevent passage of the British fleet, and Admiral Lord Howe, who had managed to maneuver his ships and transports around from the Chesapeake into the Delaware with supplies, was stuck above New Castle, unable to proceed upstream. Upon learning that Howe had detached some of his regiments to reduce the river fortifications, Washington decided, with reinforcements drawn from Peekskill, to fall upon the weakened British camp at Germantown.

At the time, Germantown was little more than a single main street about two miles long, flanked here and there by modest stone houses surrounded by gardens and trees. Beyond the village, about a hundred yards to the east, stood a spacious stone mansion with ornamental grounds, statues, groves, and shrubbery—the country seat of Benjamin Chew, chief justice of Pennsylvania.

On September 30, Washington's force—about 8,000 Continentals and 3,000 militia—advanced to Skippack Creek, about fourteen miles from the British position. At dusk on October 3, the troops moved out over the four main roads that converged on the village and reached its outskirts just after dawn. A mist rose with the sun, "wrapping the whole countryside in a ghostly, glowing pall."

The attack began with several columns advancing on the enemy at once. The British pickets were driven in; their infantry gave way. By nine A.M., Washington's center and left wing were in the village, and within a short time the troops stationed in the heart of it were also overpowered. "The enemy were chased quite through their camp," remembered one soldier. "They left their kettles, in which they were cooking their breakfasts, on the fires; and some of their garments were lying on the ground." Howe himself, who had reportedly been up all night gambling and had "just returned from the faro table, not having been in bed above an hour," thought all the commotion had to do with a minor hit-and-run raid. He therefore failed at first to organize a coherent defense, which allowed General Greene, his division pressing rapidly forward, to take a number of prisoners and to strike the British right wing head on. This was done with such force that so many were killed or wounded, wrote one British officer of his own battalion, that "had we not retreated at the time we did we should all have been taken and killed." The Americans, animated by "Rage and Fury" in revenge for the cruelties of the Paoli Massacre, "were not to be Restrained," wrote General Wayne, "for some time—at least not until great numbers of the Enemy fell by our Bayonets." But at the moment of triumph, six British companies sought refuge in the Chew mansion, which they barricaded and transformed into a fort. From behind its walls, they poured upon their pursuers a relentless fire.

The Americans might have passed the mansion by. Instead, a substantial force paused to lay siege to it, chiefly at the instance of General Henry Knox, who in an uncharacteristic lapse of judgment rather bookishly insisted upon the medieval military maxim that "you must never leave a castle in your rear."

A flag was sent forward with a summons to surrender, but the soldier who carried it was shot down. This so infuriated the Americans that their determination to dislodge the British overwhelmed their attention to the larger battle plan. In a vain and time-consuming effort, the house was bombarded with field artillery too light to have much effect. This was followed by an unsuccessful attempt to set the basement on fire. Time was lost, and tactical coordination, as companies became separated from one another in the dense, low-lying fog. Some of Greene's troops now also ran out of ammunition. And in the penumbral haze, one division mistook the approach of a body of their compatriots on its flank for British soldiers. As they fell back, they ran into another American division, which, in turn, made the same mistake and opened fire. In the ensuing disarray, the British were able to regroup, advance in order, and, with the help of a squadron of light horse which had just arrived from Philadelphia, compel the Americans to retreat.

In a letter to Benjamin Franklin written some months later, Thomas Paine described the American withdrawal firsthand:

> I met several of the wounded on waggons, horseback, and on foot. . . . The retreat was extraordinary. Nobody hurried themselves. Everyone marched his own pace. The Enemy kept a civil distance behind, sending every now and then a Shot after us, and receiving the same from us. That part of the Army which I was with collected and formed on the Hill on the side of the road near White Marsh Church; the Enemy came within three quarters of a mile and halted. The orders on Retreat were to assemble that night on the back of Perkiominy Creek, about 7 miles above Camp. . . . The Army had marched the preceding night 14 miles and having full 20 to march back were exceedingly fatigued. They appeared to me to be only sensible of a disappointment, not a defeat."

Indeed, contemporary opinion judged it not much of a defeat at all. "Fortune smiled on us for full three hours," wrote General Wayne afterward as he summed up the battle. "The enemy were broke, dispersed and flying in all quarters. We were in possession of their whole encampment, together with their artillery park, etc., etc. *A wind-mill* [i.e., quixotic] attack was made upon a house. . . . Our troops . . . thinking it something formidable, fell back to assist—the enemy believing it to be a retreat, followed—confusion ensued, and we ran away from the arms of victory open to receive us." Although the American losses were heavy— 150 killed, 521 wounded, and 400 taken prisoner—British casualties were comparable, and the Americans managed to carry off all their cannon and wounded, thanks to another skillful rearguard action by General Greene. "Though the event miscarried," said Virginia's George Weedon, "it was worth the undertaking"—and this was the general verdict of the time. In Europe, the battle was taken as proof of the Americans' ability to win the war. As a result, there began an inexorable shift in the policy and attitude of the European states. Congress, too, showed an understanding of the outcome—"the best designs and boldest efforts may sometimes fail by unforeseen incidents"—and there was even some grudging respect in the British camp. That evening, one British officer said to his men, drawn up to bury the mingled dead, "Dan't bury them with their faces up, and thus cast dirt in their faces. They are all mothers' sons."

A F T E R the Battle of Germantown, Howe withdrew his whole force into Philadelphia, and some of the military preparations Washington had originally undertaken to protect the capital—the Delaware forts as well as the chevaux-de-frise and gunboats in the river—now hemmed the British in. The chevaux-de-frise were dangerous to any ships that might run against them, subjected as they would be to the batteries of Fort Mifflin on one side and those of Fort Mercer at Red Bank on the New Jersey shore. Unless Howe could open the river for communications and supply, he could neither use Philadelphia to advantage nor hold it against rebel assault. Meanwhile, Washington posted his own troops on the heights of the Schuylkill and scoured the country between it and the Delaware with cavalry and light infantry to prevent the British from foraging and to deter Tories and others from conveying provisions to their camp.

On October 21, Howe sent a detachment of 2,000 men down the New Jersey shore under German colonel Carl von Donop to subdue Fort Mercer. After an artillery barrage which seemed to have some effect, they rushed across a ditch and past the outworks, which the Americans had abandoned, to the parapets of the redoubts but were unable to scale them without ladders. There, at close quarters, they were decimated by murderous fire. A second assault was also repulsed with heavy losses and after they came under coordinate fire from American gunboats to the south, they gave it all up, threw their cannon into a creek to free the gun carriages for carrying their wounded, and hurried away. Five hundred of their brethren had fallen killed or wounded, including Donop himself, who died pathetically exclaiming, "I perish the victim of my own ambition and the avarice of my prince."

The more vulnerable Fort Mifflin came under attack next. Erected on a low, reedy mud flat called Mud Island a few miles below Philadelphia, the fort was surrounded by dikes and fortified with batteries that, wrote a defender, "were nothing more than old spars and timber laid up in parallel lines and filled between with mud and dirt." Only a narrow channel separated the island from the Pennsylvania shore. Several British vessels, including four large warships, forced their way through the lower line of chevaux-de-frise and began to bombard the fort. British shore batteries soon thereafter added their pounding to the barrage. The Americans had some light artillery but only one heavy cannon—and no shot for it—in the fort. In order to obtain the cannonballs they needed, an American artillery officer offered a pint of rum for every enemy shot of the right caliber the soldiers gathered up. With a kind of wild bravado, dozens of men lined up on the parade ground "waiting with impatience" for a ball to come in. When one did, they scrambled after it with such agility that it "would often be seized before its motion had fully ceased, and conveyed off to our gun." This deadly sport did not last long. The enemy cannonade became increasingly intense as the British brought into play the batteries of several more warships, a frigate, a gunship, and an armed sloop. "I saw five artillerists belonging to one gun cut down by a single shot," wrote a defender, "and I saw men who were stooping to be protected by the works, but not stooping low enough, split like fish to be broiled."

There was some letup after the enemy was forced to engage in a duel with an American frigate and some floating batteries, but on the twentieth the bombardment was renewed with such violence that, according to one estimate, Fort Mifflin was struck by a thousand shells every twenty minutes. As night fell, "the fort exhibited a picture of desolation. The whole area was ploughed like a field. The buildings [were] hanging in broken fragments, the guns all dismounted," and a large number of the garrison lay dead. Under cover of darkness, the remainder (about 150 men) prepared to evacuate, opened the floodgates of the dikes, and slipped across to the Jersey shore.

The fall of Fort Mifflin left the British in control of the river to Red Bank. That rendered Fort Mercer untenable, and it was promptly abandoned and burned by the Americans in retreat.

I N New York, General Sir Henry Clinton had for some time been trying to decide if, given his garrison of 7,000 men, he had the means to assist Burgoyne. Howe had left him with standing instructions to do so "if circumstances warranted." Such circumstances had long since arrived.

Burgoyne, in dispatches back to London, tried to minimize the setbacks and losses he had sustained at Bennington and elsewhere, and attributed his deteriorating situation to the failure of the loyalists in the region to come to his aid. "I find daily reason to doubt the sincerity of the[ir] resolution," he complained. He also found "most embarrassing . . . the want of communication with Sir William Howe." As he made his way down the Hudson toward Albany, he still had no idea that Howe's own plans had changed and thought the reason he hadn't heard from him was that, "Of the messengers I have sent, I know of two being hanged and am ignorant whether any of the rest arrived. The same fate has probably attended those dispatched by Sir William." On or about August 20, he was astonished to learn—from a message sent by Howe written on thin strips of paper concealed in a quill pen—that "his intention is for Pennsylvania," not Albany, where all along Burgoyne had understood, according to the plan worked out in advance, the three columns of the British army were to join. Clinton (so Howe now informed him) was to remain in New York and act only as a reserve, "as occurrences might direct." Burgoyne wrote at once to Lord Germain and began to distribute the blame for his own possible failure in advance. "When I wrote more confidently," he began, "I had not foreseen that I was to be left to pursue my way through such a tract of country and hosts of foes, without any co-operation from New York. Nor did I then think the garrison[ing] of Ticonderoga would fall to my share alone. . . . I yet do not despond. Should I succeed in forcing my way to Albany, and find that country in a state to subsist my army, I shall think no more of a retreat, but, at the worst, fortify there and await Sir W. Howe's operations." In the interim, Howe had written matter-of-factly to Clinton, "If you can make any diversion in favour of General Burgoyne's approaching Albany . . . I need not point out the utility of such a measure."

Clinton took the suggestion under advisement and did nothing; but with each passing day, Burgoyne's situation continued to deteriorate, and it became harder and harder for him to provision his army. General Lincoln was hovering with militia to his rear; the main American army before him was steadily gaining strength. Reinforcements arrived from Putnam in the highlands, Morgan and his 500 sharpshooters came in, and Arnold returned from Fort Stanwix with more troops. Meanwhile, on August 4, Congress had replaced General Schuyler with General Gates, who reached Stillwater on the nineteenth.

Schuyler was caustic about his removal. "I am sensible of the indignity of being ordered from the command of the army at a time when an engagement must soon take place," he said. To Gates, he wrote, "I have done all that could be done . . . but the palm of victory is denied me, and it is left to you, General, to reap the fruits of my labors." This Gates was determined to do.

It was, in fact, the opportunity of his career. At the time, Gates was about fifty years old. Born in England, he had been educated at British military academies, commissioned lieutenant, promoted to major, and, during the French and Indian War, had commanded a company under Braddock. At war's end, he settled in America, and, at the beginning of the Revolution, was appointed adjutant general of the Continental Army with the rank of brigadier. "As Adjutant-General at Cambridge," writes one historian, "he had discovered that he knew more of the detail and routine of an army than Washington, and, having a natural ignorance of deeper qualities for action, he became strongly convinced that the Americans would find in himself the ideal commander. He was shallow and vulgar. But his shallowness could be poured out in such broad expanses of military theory and doctrine as to create a common impresson of profundity and wisdom."

His gift was for organization, not tactics or strategy, but his apparent knowledge and real conviviality had gained him a number of adherents in both Congress and the army. It was not irrelevant, of course, that Schuyler happened to be a New Yorker, and his strict discipline while in command had made him unpopular with the New England troops. But Washington had tried to stay clear of the regional animosity behind the feud and had discreetly asked "to be excused from making the appointment of an officer to command the Northern Army" shortly before Congress made its decision on August 4.

Burgoyne was falling fast. On top of all his losses and blunders, his security was lax. The baronness von Riedesel, wife of the general in command of the German troops, remembered that "the wives of all the officers belonging to the expediton knew beforehand everything that was to happen," which seemed to her extraordinary since, in her own experience in the Seven Years' War, secrecy had always been maintained. After an important tactical maneuver went awry, she exclaimed, "The Americans, as usual, were waiting for us."

Burgoyne's martial ardor also seems to have been dissipated by profligate cravings and his need to have a good time. He had a weakness for luxuries, even on campaign (thirty wagons alone being allotted to his personal effects). He enjoyed lavish dinners and spent his nights singing, drinking, gambling, and carousing with his mistress, the wife of a commisary, "who loved champagne as well as he."

Although Burgoyne's situation was not yet absolutely hopeless, he no longer had enough horses to pull his artillery and supply train, nor even grain enough to feed the horses he had. Nevertheless, he resolved to try to fight his way through. He had excellent field artillery, which gave him an advantage in any open-field engagement, and so he looked for open ground. On September 13, he crossed the Hudson on pontoon bridges to Saratoga, twelve miles north of the American entrenchments. As he drew up his ranks along the west bank of the river, he declared absurdly, "Britons never lose ground."

Indeed, the complacence of some of the British officers could only be called surreal. One of Burgoyne's aides-de-camp wrote:

> The British are equal to anything. . . . One proof of the spirit of our army, the Ladies do not mean to quit us. Lady Harriet Acland graces the advanced Corps of the Army, and Madame Riedesel the German brigades. We have frequent dinees and constantly musick; for my part . . . this campaigning is a favourite portion of Life: and none but stupid Mortals can dislike a lively Camp, good Weather, good Claret, good Musick and the enemy near. I may venture to say all this, for a little fusillade during dinner does not discompose the Nerves of even our Ladies. . . . Therefore we set our faces forward, and mean to bite hard if anything dares to show itself. As to numbers of our foes, I believe them great, mais n'importe, what are we not equal to?

By such unimportant numbers do empires rise and fall. On the nineteenth, Burgoyne moved to attack Gates's army ensconced behind fortified positions near Stillwater on Bemis Heights. For a week, 7,000 men had labored to establish the American breastworks, which spread to the west and north. Many were surrounded by abatis, fallen trees with their branches sharpened; cannon were positioned to rake the river road. In addition to sharpshooters and militia, Gates now had several battle-hardened Continental units under his command. In this forest upland, broken by hills and ravines, there was but one space of cleared land.

On the morning of September 19, "the sun burned off the mist and melted a light frost into dew as signal guns boomed in the forest," guiding the march of Burgoyne's advancing columns—General William Phillips and Riedesel following the river road, Burgoyne and General Simon Fraser, with the grenadiers and light infantry, plodding over the thickly wooded hills, advancing in an attempt to turn the American left wing.

Shortly after noon, the British vanguard reached a 350-yard clearing known as Freeman's Farm. Burgoyne took advantage of the open ground to form three regiments in line, with two others on the flanks. Gates sent Morgan's rifle corps and the light infantry of the army to stall their advance. Morgan's riflemen, many of them perched in trees, communicated with one another by wild turkey calls and aimed at the "kingbirds" (as they called the British officers) while the Continentals swept the clearing with volleys of fire. The British line crumpled and was soon blown back. Then the Americans charged, until at length they, too, were forced to retreat before withering fire. For almost four hours, the fight raged back and forth. Unable to stand in the clearing against an enemy sheltered by the woods, neither side could hold the advantage it gained. Again and again the American forces flowed up to the British cannon and uproariously claimed them for America, then once more lost their prize as the British grenadiers came on with bayonets. "In this manner did the battle fluctuate," wrote Major James Wilkinson, "like waves of a stormy sea."

In a house not far behind the British lines the baroness von Riedesel and her three small daughters had taken refuge. "I was full of care and anguish, and shivered at every shot," she wrote afterward, "for I could hear everything. I saw a great number of wounded; and what was still more harrowing, they even brought three of them into the house where I was. One of these was Major Harnage. . . . He had received a shot through the lower part of the bowels."

Meanwhile, Benedict Arnold, in charge of the American left wing, kept extending it farther into the woods, curling it uphill and around the British right flank. This forced Burgoyne to bend his own flank back to the west to avoid its being turned, which increasingly exposed the British center to fire from both sides. Burgoyne then ordered 500 Hessians under General Riedesel with light field artillery to attack the American right. The British recovered some advantage, and at dusk the Americans withdrew into the woods.

In this battle, the British lost upward of 600 men killed, wounded, or taken prisoner, a third of their regimental strength; the Americans, 381. Three quarters of Burgoyne's artillerymen also fell, and one British regiment, which had been 500 strong when it left Canada, was now reduced to 60 men. The dead lay thick in the grass, "as thick," one Yankee militiaman wrote home to his wife, "as ever I saw rock heaps lay in the field. . . . God grant I may make a wise improvement of such an awful scene." Burgoyne claimed victory, since he technically remained in possesson of the ground. But as one British lieutenant put it, "no very great advantage, honor excepted, was gained by the day."

That night Gates learned that a party of Americans had swooped down on Fort Ticonderoga, carried the outworks, and released a large number of prisoners. All but the old stone core of the fort had fallen into their hands. At the news, thirteen volleys were fired in salute in the American camp, followed by thirteen cheers. And Gates allowed one of his prisoners to escape so that Burgoyne's demoralized forces might know why.

Both sides strengthened their positions, with fieldworks and redoubts, and for two and a half weeks they remained nearly within cannon shot of each other, while Burgoyne anxiously awaited some word from New York. On September 27 and 28, he sent urgent dispatches in duplicate to Clinton, appealing for his help and direction, "To which I returned the following answer," Clinton later explained. "That not having received any instructions from the commander-in-chief [Howe] relative to the Northern Army, and [being] unacquainted even of his intentions concerning the operations of that army, excepting his wishes that they should get to Albany, [I] could not presume to give orders to General Burgoyne." Generals Riedesel and Fraser urged retreat, but Burgoyne vacillated, loath to accept the fact that the coveted knighthood he had been promised in reward for his success had all but slipped from his grasp.

The British camp stank of rotting corpses. "Many bodies," wrote a British soldier, "not buried deep enough in the ground reappeared after a great rain as the soil was a light sand." About eight hundred sick and wounded lay in tents and roughly constructed huts, while the cries of unrecovered others filled the darkness and mingled hideously with the cries of wolves who gathered to feed upon them or to scratch up the freshly buried dead.

The continuing standoff only meant depletion for Burgoyne and increasing strength for Gates. Even a band of Oneida Indians arrived and offered the Americans help. This was unwanted, but "almost daily," wrote James Wilkinson, "they presented scalps and prisoners at headquarters, and their shocking death halloo resounded through our lines."

Meanwhile, after the Battle of Freeman's Farm, as it came to be called, Gates and Benedict Arnold had had a falling-out. Gates had failed to acknowledge Arnold's contribution to the fighting in a report to Congress, and after a heated exchange Arnold had been confined to his tent. General Benjamin Lincoln was appointed to replace him as head of the American right wing, whereupon Arnold asked to leave. Gates obliged but accompanied his pass with an open letter to John Hancock, the president of Congress:

> Sir,
> Major General Arnold desired permission for himself and aide-de-camp to go to Philadelphia. I have granted his request. His reasons for asking to leave the Army at this time shall, with my answers, be transmitted to your excellency. I am sir.
> HG
> 23d Sepr 1777

Arnold returned the note with another letter the same day, demanding to know why Gates did not at least "condescend to acquaint me with the reasons which had induced you to treat me with affront and indignity." Gates declined to discuss the matter further, but other officers by their entreaties (valuing his abilities) prevailed upon Arnold to remain.

While this dispute simmered, Gates tried to anticipate Burgoyne's next move. On October 4 (the day Washington's army was meeting defeat at Brandywine), he wrote, "Perhaps his despair may dictate to him to risque all on one throw; he is an old gamester and has seen all chances in his time." On October 5, Clinton decided after all to attack up the Hudson and in three days, with 3,000 men, captured Forts Montgomery and Clinton (named for George Clinton, the patriot governor of New York) in the highlands. From there he wrote Burgoyne a letter, but it never arrived. Concealed in a hollowed-out silver musket ball, it was swallowed by its bearer when he was captured, but after a "severe dose of tartar emetic" was administered, he disgorged the following quaint communiqué:

> Fort Montgomery, October 8, 1977.
> *Nous y voici,* and nothing now between us and Gates I sincerely hope this little success of ours may facilitate your operations. In answer to your letter of the 28th September, by C.C. [Captain Campbell, who had carried it], I shall only say I cannot presume to order, or even to advise, for reasons obvious. I heartily wish you success.
> Faithfully yours,
> H. CLINTON

Had Burgoyne received this, he might have wondered whether Clinton meant to go further or was content to have created a diversion by his "little success." After it was all over, Clinton asked Burgoyne, "Could you with reason, my dear friend, expect that I should form the most distant idea of penetrating to Albany?" But that, with reason, was what Burgoyne had expected; and having received no word from Clinton, he resolved to try to break through the American lines.

On October 6, a rum ration was served out to the British troops, and on the following morning the baroness von Riedesel noticed that many of the Indians had donned their war dress and were carrying guns. "To my question where they were going, they cried out to me, 'War! War!', which meant that they were going to fight." Burgoyne had decided on a large reconnaissance force. Some 1,500 men, with ten guns, were to try "to discover whether there were any possible means of forcing a passage should it be necessary to advance."

No sooner had Burgoyne set his troops in motion than the alarm was sounded by the American advance guard. Major Wilinson rode to the top of a hill and from there got a clear view of the British column. "I returned and reported to the General [Gates], who asked me what appeared to be the intentions of the enemy.

" 'They are foraging and endeavouring to reconnoitre your left; and I think, sir, they offer you battle.'

" 'What is the nature of the ground, and what your opinion?'

" 'Their front is open and their flanks rest on woods, under cover of which they may be attacked. Their right is skirted by a lofty height. I would indulge them.'

" 'Well, then, order on Morgan to begin the game.' "

Morgan's corps, by a circuit through the woods, gained the heights on the enemy's right and from there coordinated their attack with regiments assaulting the British left. The advantage was all with the Americans. The British were driven back and retreated into their camp, the German entrenchments were carried, and some of the breastworks were stormed. Even so, at one point, Burgoyne's most capable officer, General Simon Fraser, began to rally the British left wing. Morgan called two or three of his best marksmen together and, pointing to him, said, "Do you see that gallant officer, mounted on a charger? That is General Fraser—I respect and honor him; but it is necessary that he should die." A minute later, a bullet cut the crupper of his horse; another grazed its mane. "You are singled out, general," said his aide-de-camp, "and had better shift your ground." "My duty forbids it," he replied, and a moment later he fell.

The baroness von Riedesel and other women were collected to the rear of the camp. "I heard skirmishing and firing which by degrees grew louder and louder," she recalled, "until there was a frightful noise. . . .

About 3 o'clock in the afternoon instead of the guests who were to have had dined with me they brought in poor General Fraser upon a litter. The dining-table, which had been prepared, was taken away and a bed for the General placed there instead. I sat in a corner trembling. The noise got louder and louder and I feared lest they should bring in my husband also. The General said to the surgeon, 'Do not hide anything from me. Am I going to die?' The ball had gone through his bowels.''

Arnold refused to stay out of the fray. Wrote Major Wilkinson, "It was very natural that an officer of his ambition should, on the commencement of the action, feel irritated by the humiliating situation in which he found himself. . . . He rode about the camp betraying great agitation and wrath, and . . . he was observed to drink freely." Finally, he rushed to the field of battle and by his own wildness inspired the men to equally reckless exertions, which overcame the last measure of resistance the British were able to put up. One of the soldiers said of him, with admiration, "He was a bloody fellow. . . . He didn't care for nothing; he'd ride right in. It was 'Come on, boys!' 'twasn't 'Go, boys!' . . . there wasn't any waste of timber in him." Charging across the open field of Freeman's Farm, Arnold led his men in capturing the redoubt on Burgoyne's right flank. In so doing, his horse was killed under him and he took a wound in his left leg—the same leg that had been hit during the assault on Quebec.

British casualties were heavy. Toward midnight, the body of General Fraser was laid to rest. His grave had been dug within range of the American batteries, and while the service was proceeding, a cannonball struck the ground close to the coffin and spattered the chaplain's face with dirt.

The following evening, Burgoyne began his retreat. The greatest silence was enjoined, and, in emulation of Washington's earlier ruse against Cornwallis before the Battle of Princeton, fires were kindled in every direction and many tents left standing, to make the Americans believe the camp had not been moved. Burgoyne marched all night, briefly halted to take an inventory of his artillery, but then on the ninth got mired down all day by a torrential rain. That day all of his Indian allies disappeared into the woods. Everyone was discouraged or scared out of their wits. The baroness von Riedesel recalled, "My chambermaid did nothing but curse her situation, and tore out her hair. I entreated her to compose herself, or else she would be taken for a savage. Upon this she became still more frantic and asked 'whether that would trouble me.' And when I answered 'Yes,' she tore her bonnet off her head, letting her hair hang down over her face, and said, 'You talk well! You have your husband! But we have nothing to look forward to, except dying misera- bly on the one hand, or losing all we possess on the other!' "

In the evening, the army came to Saratoga. Others wanted to keep going, but Burgoyne professed himself worn out. As the army resumed its march the following morning, "the greatest misery," wrote the baron- ess, "and the utmost disorder prevailed." The commissaries had ne- glected to distribute basic daily rations among the troops, and although "the whole army clamored" for a quicker retreat, Burgoyne vacillated between the obvious imperatives of his situation and his desire to effect a junction with Clinton—if he were near. By his indecision, she wrote, "everything was lost."

The American army, which was growing daily, now numbered 16,000. Burgoyne had fewer than 5,800 men left. At two in the afternoon, the Americans opened up with their artillery in advance of their final assault. The baroness and her children took refuge with others in the cellar of a nearby farmhouse which had been turned into a field hospital. "I laid myself down in a corner not far from the door. My children laid down on the earth with their heads upon my lap, and in this manner we passed the entire night. . . . On the following morning the cannonade again began, but from a different side. . . . Eleven cannon balls went through the house, and we could plainly hear them rolling over our heads. One poor soldier, whose leg they were about to amputate, having been laid upon a table for this purpose, had the other leg taken off by another cannon ball in the very middle of the operation."

The British camp was subjected to bombardment from batteries to the south and across the Hudson, as well as to a galling fire from Morgan's riflemen stationed on the hills to their rear. Burgoyne called a council of war and was deliberating with his officers when an eighteen-pound cannonball passed through the tent and swept across the table at which they sat.

And so the end came. After a campaign of "hard toil, incessant effort, stubborn action" (as Burgoyne would later explain it to Germain),

till disabled in the collateral branches of the army by the total defection of the Indians; the desertion or the timidity of the Canadians and Provin- cials . . . ; disappointed in the last hope of any timely cooperaton from other armies; the regular troops reduced by losses from the best parts, to 3,500 fighting men, not 2,000 of which were British; only three days provi- sions, upon short allowance, in store; invested by an army of 16,000 men, and no apparent means of retreat remaining; I called into council all the

Generals, Field-Officers, and Captains commanding corps, and by their
unanimous concurrence and advice I was induced to open a treaty with
Major-General Gates.

Negotiations were opened on the thirteenth.

The first terms offered by Gates required the enemy to surrender as
prisoners of war and ground their arms within their own entrenchments.
Burgoyne replied, "This article is inadmissible in every extremity: sooner
than this army will consent to ground their arms in their encampment,
they will rush on the enemy, determined to take no quarter"—that is, to
fight to the death. Burgoyne made counterproposals, which, to his surprise, were largely accepted, namely, that the British were to march out
of their camp, with their artillery and all the honors of war, to a fixed
place where they were to pile their arms at the command of their own
officers. They were then to be allowed free passage to Europe on condition they not serve in America again. The men were not to be separated
from their officers, and the officers were to be paroled and allowed to
retain their sidearms. No personal baggage was to be searched.

The articles were settled on October 15, but that very evening a messenger arrived from Clinton with an account of his successes and tidings
that part of his force had penetrated as far as Esopus, within fifty miles
of Burgoyne's camp. Burgoyne called another council and proposed to
break his word. He asked his officers "whether it was consistent with
public faith, and if so, expedient, to suspend the execution of the treaty
and trust to events." Again, they wisely prevailed upon him not to do so,
saying their public faith was already pledged, and "afterwards," wrote a
member of his entourage, "the Americans told us that had the capitulation been broken we would all have been killed."

The articles were therefore signed on the seventeenth, and Burgoyne's
entire army—more than 5,752 men, with 42 brass cannon, 7,000 muskets, and a great quantity of tents and other military stores—fell into
American hands. The defeated troops also took with them into captivity
"a great number of slatternly women, dogs, bears, coons, and other
objects of sentimental attachment," according to one eyewitness, and as
they marched out, an American military band struck up "Yankee Doodle," which, wrote a British officer, "it was not a little mortifying to hear
them play." The Americans drawn up to receive them were like no other
army they had ever seen. "Not one of [them] was uniformly clad," recalled a Hessian. "Each man had on the clothes he was accustomed to
wear in the field, the tavern, the church, and in everyday life. Yet no
fault could be found in their military appearance, for they stood in an

erect and soldierly attitude, and remained so perfectly quiet that we were utterly astounded. Not one of them made any attempt to speak to the man at his side; and all the men who stood in array before us were so slender, fine-looking and sinewy, that they were a pleasure to behold."

Burgoyne appeared, wearing a hat with streaming plumes. According to one of his German officers, he had "bestowed so much care on his whole toilet that he looked more like a man of fashion than a warrior." He rode toward Gates, and Major Wilkinson recorded the scene: "General Gates, advised of Burgoyne's approach, met him at the head of his camp, Burgoyne in a rich royal uniform, and Gates in a plain blue frock. When they had approached nearly within sword's length, they reined up and halted. . . . General Burgoyne, raising his hat most gracefully, said, 'The fortune of war, General Gates, has made me your prisoner;' to which the conqueror, returning a courtly salute, promptly replied, 'I shall always be ready to bear testimony that it has not been through any fault of your excellency.' " A number of the principal officers of both armies then gathered at Gates's headquarters, where at a table formed by two planks laid across two empty beef barrels, they dined rather sumptuously on ham, goose, beef, boiled mutton, and New England cider and rum.

As the baroness von Riedesel passed by, she noticed that Burgoyne and the other British officers were on an "extremely friendly footing" with Gates, which seemed to her unseemly, given their complete and humiliating defeat. General Schuyler approached and said to her, "It may be embarrassing to you to dine with all these gentlemen; come now with your children into my tent, where I will give you, it is true, a frugal meal." "You are certainly a husband and father," answered I, "since you show me so much kindness," and he served her "excellent smoked tongue, beefsteaks, potatoes, good butter, and bread."

Burgoyne and his staff had reason to be ebullient, for Gates had allowed them to surrender on remarkably generous terms—so generous, in fact, that they seemed measurably to detract from the victory. Congress decided they were generous to a fault and later abrogated them without apology. The officers were paroled, but the troops were retained as prisoners, most of them being taken to a camp near Charlottesville, Virginia.

In the interim, the terms of the capitulation had become a subject of national debate. Gates justified them on the grounds that General Clinton's threatening advance up the Hudson had made it imperative to come to terms quickly and not to be as stern as other circumstances might have allowed. As he explained the matter to Congress in a letter written by his aide James Wilkinson, now adjutant general of the Northern Army:

> Lieutenant General Burgoyne, at the time he capitulated, was strongly entrenched on a Formidable Post, with Twelve Days' Provisions: the reduction of Fort Montgomery & the Enemies consequent Progress up the Hudson's River, endangered our Arsenal at Albany: a reflection which left Him no Time to contest the Capitulation with Lt. General Burgoyne, but induced the necessity of immediately closing with his Proposals . . . this delicate situation abridged our Conquest & procured Lt. General Burgoyne the Terms he enjoys . . . had an attack been carried against Lt. General Burgoyne; the dismemberment of our Army must necessarily have been such as would have incapacitated it for further Action this Campaign.
>
> With an Army in Health, Vigour & Spirits, Major General Gates now waits the commands of the Honourable Congress.

Many accepted this explanation. Abigal Adams, for one, writing from Boston on October 25 to her husband, John, ventured that "General Gates by delaying and exacting more might have lost all. This must be said of him, that he has followed the Golden Rule, and done as he would wish himself, in like circumstances, to be dealt with."

For once, sentiment clouded her judgment. Gates had not only failed to confiscate many of the arms and supplies carried by the enemy (because he had agreed not to search their personal baggage) but more seriously, by Article II of the convention, had allowed for the "free passage" to England of Burgoyne's entire army. What did this mean? Burgoyne knew exactly what it meant and was explicit about it in a letter to Germain on October 20. After shamelessly blaming the German troops for his defeat ("Had the force been all British perhaps the perseverance had been longer"), he continued, "As it was, will it be said, my Lord, that in the exhausted situation described, and in the jaws of famine, and invested by quadruple numbers, a treaty which saves the army to the state, for the next campaign, was not more than could have been expected? I call it saving the army because, if sent home, the state is thereby enabled to send forth the troops now destined for her internal defence; if exchanged, they become a force to Sir William Howe, as effectually, as if any other junction had been made."

Washington grasped all this at once. On November 5, he wrote to a friend, "As soon as they [the prisoners] arrive [in England] they will enable the ministry to send an equal number of other troops from their different garrisons to join General Howe here, or upon any other service against the American states. . . . I think, in point of policy, we should not be anxious for their early departure." The same day, he wrote to General Heath, "I do not think it to our interest to expedite the passage of the prisoners to England; for you may depend upon it that they will immediately upon their arrival there throw them into different garrisons and bring out an equal number."

Some reason or pretext for abrogating the convention was sought, and it soon turned up in a foolish letter Burgoyne sent to Gates to complain about the shoddy accommodations his officers had to put up with in Cambridge.

The British had been escorted to Boston with many civilities, and some of the officers had even found themselves importuned by adoring girls eager to "bundle with" a Britisher. One officer, refusing to take to bed a certain Jemima, "a very pretty black-eyed girl of seventeen," found himself upbraided by her parents for his restraint: "Oh la! Mr. Ensign, you won't be the first man our Jemima has bundled with, will it, Jemima?" to which Jemima archly replied, "Not by many, but it will be with the first Britainer."

The British reached Boston at the beginning of November, and after dinner one evening Burgoyne visited Charlestown in the company of General William Heath. On their way to the ferry the streets were so crowded with people eager to catch a glimpse of him that he could hardly make his way through. Yet no one was "disrespectful by word or gesture." He turned to Heath and said, "Sir, I am astonished at the civility of your people: for, were you walking the streets of London, in my situation you would not escape insult." But at Cambridge his accommodations did not meet his expectations. On November 14, he wrote to Gates, "The officers are crowded into the barracks, six and seven in a room of about ten feet square & without distinction of rank. The General officers are not better provided for. I & Genl. Phillips after being amused with promises of quarters for eight days together, are still in a dirty miserable tavern [the Blue Anchor] lodging in a bed room together, & all the gentlemen of our suite lodge upon the floor in a chamber adjacent a good deal worse than their servants have been used to . . . the publick faith is broke."

"The publick faith is broke," declared Burgoyne, and with that phrase Congress—with a literary critic's attention to nuance—found what it was looking for: that is, by interpreting it to mean that Burgoyne himself did not intend to abide by the surrender terms. Henry Laurens of South Carolina even contended on the floor of Congress that as a result of the "pretended breach of the convention" Burgoyne meant to ship his troops directly to Delaware or New York. On January 8, 1778, Congress therefore resolved "That the embarkation of Lieut.-Gen Burgoyne and the troops under his command be suspended till a distinct and explicit ratification of the Convention of Saratoga shall be properly notified by the Court of Great Britain to Congress." To do so, of course, King George III and his ministers would have had to recognize Congress—that is, American independence—which was unthinkable. And so, though Burgoyne himself was allowed to return home on a plea of illness, his troops remained in captivity until the end of the war.

Congress was long faulted for casuistry on this matter, but in 1932, when Sir Henry Clinton's secret service papers were declassified, it was revealed that the British had indeed planned to send the surrendered troops back into active American service, as had been feared.

Washington, in any case, had anticipated the whole scenario even before Burgoyne had written his self-incriminating letter of November 14. In a letter of his own to Richard Henry Lee on October 28, the commander in chief had warned, "Unless great delicacy is used in the precautions, a plea will be given them [the British], & they will justify a breach of the Covenant on that part—do they not declare (many of them) that no faith is to be held with Rebels?"

But all this took place largely away from the public eye. The more general reality was that after the loss of Philadelphia, "the news of Burgoyne's surrender [wrote John Adams to a friend] lifted us up to the stars." Americans were roused from their despondency, and the victory had decisive long-term diplomatic and military consequences besides. It inspired European confidence in the rebellion and in the following year led directly to the coveted alliance with France.

Congress designated December 18 "for solemn thanksgiving and praise," and on that day all across America bonfires blazed, bells pealed, and in the streets and on village greens the people sang patriotic songs.

Back in London, George Germain, secretary of state for the colonies, announced to Parliament that he had "a piece of very unhappy intelligence to report." Many of the members gasped audibly at his news, and the British public, whose happy expectations, led on by the parliamentary hawks, had been seduced into a kind of inane patriotic gladness by Burgoyne's quick capture of Fort Ticonderoga and Howe's September victory at Brandywine, was stunned. In vain had Edmund Burke, at times almost a solitary voice crying in the wilderness, tried to convince his militant colleagues that such interim victories would only prove "delusive advantages which will encourage us to proceed, but will not bring matters nearer to a happy termination." On the contrary, he predicted that Britain would be lured "deeper and deeper" into a "System of endless hopes and disappointments"—only to meet defeat at the end.

As for Carleton, he said merely, "This unfortunate event, it is to be hoped, will in future prevent ministers from pretending to direct operations of war in a country at three thousand miles distance, of which they have so little knowledge as not to be able to distinguish between good, bad, or interested advice."

But of course, it did nothing of the kind.

Chapter Ten

VALLEY FORGE

At the end of 1777, the British still occupied New York City and had taken Philadelphia; Washington's army held the highland passes and the forts near West Point. By capturing Burgoyne's army when it came down from Canada, the Americans had thus prevented the British from securing control of the Hudson Valley, the main object of contention during the first three years of the war.

Outside Philadelphia, Washington prepared to make his winter quarters in a sheltered valley at White Marsh, twelve miles to the north. There he took possession of an elegant two-story brick dwelling and posted his army on the hills to the north of it—the right wing on Wissahickon Creek, the left on Sandy Run. But with every ambush and skirmish, his situation began to seem less feasible, and in mid-December he decided to move his army to a greater distance from the town. But before he could do so, and on the very night his wife, Martha, joined him there (arriving by sleigh over the snowdrifts on December 10), the British marched out to surprise the American camp. The camp was a temporary station, with hardly a breastwork thrown up to defend it, but, for reasons known only to himself, Howe hastily retreated, though he afterward claimed in a letter to Lord Germain that the camp had been "a strongly fortified place." After several unsuccessful attempts to draw Washington from his entrenchments, he finally withdrew his whole force into Phila-

VALLEY FORGE 287

delphia to establish himself in comfortable quarters and give its social life a whirl.

The encampment at White Marsh was also broken up, and Washington's suffering army prepared to march to Valley Forge. It took them a whole week to cover the thirteen miles through snow, sleet, and icy rain, and when they got there nothing but desolation met their eye. At the time, the village of Valley Forge, on the west bank of the Schuylkill, was owned by a wealthy Quaker who had built a sawmill and a gristmill on the banks of nearby Valley Creek. Steep hillsides and the swift Schuylkill River helped fortify the perimeter of the wooded plateau where the army built its huts, but it was "a dreary kind of place and uncomfortably provided," as Washington remarked. He told his soldiers, "I will share in your hardships and partake of every inconvenience," and, for the most part, he did. It was not until all the troops had some shelter of their own that he himself moved out of a tent and took up residence in a stone house on the grounds. His wife, Martha, confided to a friend, "The General is well, but much worn with fatigue and anxiety. I never knew him to be so anxious as now."

Thomas Paine was at Valley Forge as the huts went up. "The [soldiers]," he wrote, "appeared to me to be like a family of Beavers; every one busy; some carrying Logs, others Mud, and the rest fastening them together." About nine hundred were built in all, each 15 feet square and 6½ feet high. A number were set in pits or trenches, partly underground, and all were rudely chinked with mud and windowless to keep out the cold. Within, the men slept twelve to a hut on bunks made of poles and split saplings or lay on mats of straw.

Washington's army numbered about 11,000. For four months they had marched and countermarched, fought hard, and worn themselves to the bone. About a quarter of the men were unfit for duty, and a still larger proportion were half naked and starving, without breeches, shoes, stockings, or even a blanket to cover them at night. At times, according to Dr. James Thacher, the army surgeon who had served at Ticonderoga and was now at Valley Forge, there were not enough able-bodied men "to discharge the basic duties of the camp." The officers' wives, including Martha Washington, knitted socks, patched garments, and made shirts for the soldiers as best they could, but this was scarcely enough. "Our prospect was indeed dreary," recalled one private. "In our miserable condition, to go into the wild woods and build us habitations . . . in such a condition, was appalling in the highest degree. However, there was no remedy, no alternative but this or dispersion. But dispersion, I believe, was not thought of . . . we were determined to persevere." Nevertheless, he was so hungry his first night at Valley Forge that, he said, he would have taken any bit of food or drink "by force from the best friend I had on the earth." And over the next two days, all he could find to eat was half a pumpkin, which he cooked "upon a rock, the skin side up, by making a fire upon it." This was not much less palatable than their usual fare—"firecake" (patties of flour and water partially baked on hot stones) and pepper hot soup (a thin tripe broth flavored with a handful of peppercorns). Even water was not always in ample supply, despite the proximity of the Schuylkill River, since it had to be hauled up the steep slopes to the camp by hand.

Congress failed to relieve the army's plight. The delegates had fled Philadelphia for York, Pennsylvania, in the early-morning hours of September 19, and perhaps their own abrupt dislocation and relatively spartan quarters preoccupied them more than was right.

York was a farming community of some 1,800 inhabitants with 286 houses and three taverns. It was chiefly made up of Germans who attended schools "in their own language," wrote John Adams to his wife, "as well as prayers, psalms and sermons, so that multitudes are born, grow up and die here without ever learning English." Each morning the town bell summoned the delegates to a little courthouse on the square, where John Hancock, the president of Congress, and Secretary Charles Thomson sat at the judge's desk with the delegates in rows of seats before them. The assembly was warmed by an enormous wood stove with a pipe extending to the rear wall. Nearby, the Board of War, presided over by John Adams, from time to time conferred in a local law office, and the Board of Treasury, chaired by Eldridge Gerry (also of Massachusetts), met in a private home where printing presses were set up in two rooms to turn out Continental bills.

Attendance was sparse. On average, only twenty-one members gathered that winter to deliberate on the business of the nation—and often just thirteen. Sometimes only nine. And they were fractious. On one occasion, the assembly found itself unable to censure an unruly member without his own vote.

Relations between Washington and the Congress were strained. Although Washington might have withdrawn his army to more commodious winter quarters—to Lancaster, York, or Carlisle, for example—his doing so would have allowed the British a good deal of breathing room around Philadelphia and a large and fertile area in which to forage for supplies and proselytize for the king. Instead he denied them that convenience and hemmed them in.

Washington could not understand why the basic needs of the army were not being met. On December 22, he wrote to the president of Congress, "I do not know from what cause this alarming deficiency or rather total failure of supplies arises, but unless more vigorous exertions and better regulations take place in that line (the commissaries' department) immediately, the army must dissolve." And the following day: "Since the month of July we have had no assistance from the quartermaster-general"—upon which the commissary general of course largely depended—and after describing the army's stark suffering, he proceeded to take the armchair soldiers of Congress to task. The delegates listened uncomfortably as Secretary Thomson read his letter aloud. Some gentlemen, said Washington, seemed to fault the performance of the army

> as much as if they thought the soldiers were made of stocks or stones and equally insensible of frost and snow, and moreover as if they conceived it easily practicable for an inferior army, under the disadvantages I described ours to be—which are by no means exaggerated—to confine a superior one, in all respects well appointed and provided for a winter's campaign, within the city of Philadelphia, and to cover from depredation and waste the States of Pennsylvania and Jersey. . . . I can assure these Gentlemen that it is a much easier and less distressing thing to draw remonstrances in a comfortable room by a good fire side than to occupy a cold bleak hill and sleep under frost and Snow without Cloaths or Blankets; however, although they seem to have little feeling for the naked, and distressed Soldier, I feel superabundantly for them, and from my soul pity those miseries, wch. it is neither in my power to relieve or prevent.

He closed by reminding Congress that "upon the ground of safety and policy, I am obliged to conceal the true State of the Army from public view" even though it exposed him "to detraction and Calumny."

Congress at this time was not held in very high regard. After the Battle of Germantown, the Reverend Jacob Duche, who had opened the Second Continental Congress with a stirring patriotic benediction, turned apostate. Writing from behind enemy lines at Philadelphia, he called upon Washington to give up the cause and ridiculed the delegates at York. "Take an impartial view of the present Congress," he wrote. "What can you expect of them?" He singled out some of the delegates from Virginia and Pennsylvania for special disdain, and as for those from New England, "can you find one that, as a gentleman, you could wish to associate with, unless the soft and mild address of Mr. Hancock can atone for the want of every other qualification necessary for the seat he fills? . . . The few gentlemen that are now among them are well known to be on the balance and looking up to your hand to move the beam."

Gouverneur Morris, a delegate from New York, though he would happily have attended Duche's execution, did not entirely disagee with this assessment. That winter, he wrote to John Jay in New York, "The powerful American Senate is not what we have known it to be. Continental money and Congress have both depreciated." His colleague Charles Carroll of Carrollton, Maryland, empathically expressed his disgust, "The Congress do worse than ever: We murder time, and chat it away in idle impertinent talk: However, I hope the urgency of affairs will teach even that Body a little discretion."

At Valley Forge, food already scarce, grew scarcer. Salted pork was rationed and fresh meat almost unobtainable; by Christmas, there were only twenty-five barrels of flour left. At Washington's meager breakfast table, his staff learned to eat corn hoecake; Christmas dinner was served in a tent without bread, sugar, tea, coffee, or milk.

Clothing was even more difficult to obtain than food. Before the war, as noted, textiles, shoes, stockings, blankets, and almost all other manufactured articles had been obtained from England. France had secretly promised to send many of these items, but her shipments were uncertain and subject to all the hazards of the British blockade.

The various privations of the encampment soon got to Dr. Albigence Waldo, an army physician who helped to inoculate the army against smallpox. He noted in his diary:

> I am sick, discontented, and out of humor. Poor food—hard lodging—cold weather—fatigue—nasty clothes—nasty cookery—vomit half my time—smoked out of my senses—the Devil's in't—I can't endure it—why are we sent here to starve and freeze—what sweet felicities have I left at home! A charming wife—pretty children—good beds—good food—good cookery—all agreeable—all harmonious. Here all confusion—smoke and cold—hunger and filthiness—a pox on my bad luck. There comes a bowl of beef soup—full of burnt leaves and dirt, sickish enough such to make a Hector spew.

However, it was even worse to be a prisoner in Philadelphia, where the inmates suffered as badly as those incarcerated within the great black hull of the prison ship *Jersey* or in the Sugarhouse in New York. It was reported by a doctor who was allowed to visit them that "one of the poor unhappy men, driven to the last extreme by the rage of hunger, ate his own fingers up to the first joint from the hand, before he died. Others ate the clay, the lime, the stones of the prison walls. Several who died in the yard had pieces of bark, wood, clay, and stones in their mouths, which the ravings of hunger had caused them to take in for food in the last agonies of life!"

After most of the horses in Washington's camp perished from lack of forage, men had to yoke themselves to vehicles for hauling wood and provisions or bear the heavy loads on their backs. "Camp fever" (typhus) and "putrid fever" (typhoid) ravaged the army, along with smallpox. A local schoolhouse in the heart of the four-thousand-acre camp was turned into a hospital, where the diseased were unwholesomely mingled with the wounded from Paoli, Brandywine, and Germantown.

The men died by the hundreds—by winter's end, 2,500 from exposure, malnutrition, and disease. On February 16, Washington wrote to New York's patriot governor George Clinton, "For some days past there has been little less than a famine in the camp. A part of the army has been a week without any kind of flesh, and the rest three or four days. Naked and starving as they are, we cannot enough admire the incomparable patience and fidelity of the soldiery, that they have not been, ere this, excited by their sufferings to a general mutiny and desertion."

In so saying, Washington was hoping against hope. Inevitably, morale declined as Washington's men contrasted their own plight with the situation of war-wealthy profiteers and the well-supplied redcoats luxuriating in Philadelphia. Occasionally from the huts could be heard rebellious rumblings and a forlorn chanting among the men of their neglect: "No pay! no clothes! no provisions! no rum!" In addition to the 2,500 who perished, by winter's end a thousand would also desert.

Washington's own accommodations in the stone house on the grounds consisted of just two rooms, one for business (about sixteen feet square, with a large fireplace), the other a bedroom. The rest of the house was occupied by the Potts family, which owned it. Eventually, though not until March, an adjoining log cabin was built as a dining room. In such spare surroundings, the commander in chief kept his valuable papers in a secret box built into the east window casement, which had a blind trapdoor at the top.

Washington's Lifeguard was stationed near the river within sight of headquarters, and various brigades were scattered over the adjoining hillsides under the command of the general staff. Henry Knox kept his cannon ready in the artillery park on the high ground.

The British, for their part, had rendered their Philadelphia defenses next to impregnable. An abatis made of felled fruit trees extended from the Delaware to the Schuylkill, with redoubts at intervals along the line. The redoubts, along the high ground, were "framed, planked and of great thickness, and surrounded by a deep ditch inclosed and fraised."

Houses on the city's northern outskirts that might have served as cover for American snipers had been burned, as well as all the dwellings along the road to Germantown.

Yet for all its winter desolation, Valley Forge lay in the midst of a fruitful agricultural country, a land full of prosperous farmers, cattle, bread, and meat. And it was partly for that reason that Washington had chosen it, although most of the local farmers refused to accept the paper money printed by Congress and instead sent their produce to Philadelphia to be sold to the British for silver and gold. "Speculations, peculation, engrossing, forestalling," declared Washington, "afford melancholy proofs of the decay of public virtue." "The Love of country and public virtue are annihilated," asserted congressional delegate William Ellery of Rhode Island. "If Diogenes were alive and were to search America with candles, would he find an honest man?"

War profiteering and inflation combined to make the paper notes printed by Congress scarcely worth the paper they were printed on. Said delegate John Henry of Maryland, "The Avarice of our people and the extravagant prices of all commodities, joined with the imperfect management of Affairs, would expend the mines of Chile and Peru." Yet it is not surprising that the Continental money was sometimes rejected with scorn. To begin with, counterfeit bills were often printed on better paper and more professionally engraved. The thirty-dollar bills Congress churned out in February, for example, absurdly spelled Philadelphia "Philadelpkia," whereas the counterfeit version looked much smarter and got the name right. Because of the occasional confusion as to which was which, even some patriotic merchants declined payment except in coin.

By February 1778, the army was on the point of dissolution, and Congress, in a desperate measure, authorized Washington to requisition supplies. The assembly had been badgering him to do so for some time —"to subsist his army from such parts of the country as are in its vicinity" —but when Washington showed great reluctance to exercise this option, Congress actually chided him, in a resolution of December 10, for his "delicacy in exerting military authority on the citizens of these states; a delicacy, which though highly laudable in general, may, on critical exigencies, prove destructive to the army and prejudicial to the general liberties of America." That was a bit unseemly. Having failed to supply his army, the delegates were asking him to do their dirty work for them; and such work was not his way. When, out of dire necessity, he finally consented, he wrote a wise warning note to the Congress to consider more carefully the consequences of what it advised: "Such procedures may give a momentary relief but if repeated will prove of the most

pernicious consequence. Beside spreading disaffection, jealousy and fear
among the people, they never fail, even in the most veteran troops under
the most rigid and exact discipline, to raise in the soldiery a disposition to
licentiousness, to plunder and robbery, difficult to suppress afterward."

A s Washington took counsel with his general staff, one discreetly quiet
but prominent new member of it was the marquis de Lafayette, who had
come to America the previous summer and had made the cause of liberty
his own.

Lafayette, wrote the poet Alphonse Lamartine, had "an instinct for
renown." And renown was in his blood. Christened Marie-Joseph-Paul-
Yves-Roch-Gilbert du Motier, he belonged to an ancient and illustrious
house that could trace its lineage back to forebears who had fought in
the Crusades, at the Battle of Poitiers, and by the side of Joan of Arc.
One of them had been marshal of France during the reign of Charles VII.
Lafayette's father, a colonel, had died a hero in the Battle of Minden
during the Seven Years' War. Lafayette himself, commissioned cadet in
the famed regiment of the Black Musketeers, had risen to the rank of
captain by the age of eighteen. In the summer of 1775, he happened to
be stationed at Metz, where he met the duke of Gloucester, the brother
of King George III. The duke was vehemently opposed to his brother's
American policies and, at a dinner the marquis attended, denounced
them in the strongest terms. Before Lafayette left the table that evening
(so he tells us in his memoirs), he had decided to offer his services to
the Congress of the United States.

The French government officially (or publicly) opposed his intentions,
but when he embarked for America on April 20, 1777, his companion
was none other than Baron Johann de Kalb, the secret military agent
dispatched by the French government to America a decade before. They
arrived off the South Carolina coast about fifty miles south of Charleston
(then under British blockade) on June 13, and upon landing, Lafayette
dramatically raised his hand and swore to live or die by the ideals of the
rebellion.

Was he a sincere idealist? It would seem so. On board ship he had
written to his wife, "The welfare of America is intimately bound up with
the happiness of humanity. She is going to become a cherished and safe
refuge of virtue, of good character, of tolerance, of equality and of a
peaceful liberty." No one could fault his hopes.

In the tidewater region, he came upon some blacks in a large canoe
grappling for oysters. They directed him to the home of Major Benjamin

Huger, an officer in the South Carolina regiment, but it was not till about midnight that Lafayette and Kalb knocked at his door. The Huger family, having gone to bed, thought at first it was a British raid. But the situation was soon clarified (the Hugers were of French Huguenot descent and spoke French), and the two were hospitably entertained. A few days later they began to make their way slowly through the South Carolina pine barrens toward Philadelphia, 650 miles away. Arriving on July 27, they were received rather coldly by John Hancock, the president of Congress, who referred them to Robert Morris, a Pennsylvania delegate whose expertise was finance. The following day, Morris and Massachusetts delegate James Lovell, a former instructor at the Boston Latin School and now chairman of the Committee of Foreign Affairs, met Lafayette, Kalb, and their aides in front of Independence Hall. "He [Lovell] talked with us in the street, where he left us, having treated us . . . like a set of adventurers," recalled Lafayette. " 'Gentlemen,' he said, 'have you any authority from Mr. Deane? We authorized him to send us four French engineers; but, instead of that he has sent us Mr. du Coudray and some men who pretend to be engineers but are not, and some artillerists who have never seen service. We then instructed Mr. Franklin to send us four engineers and they have come. It seems that French officers have a great fancy to enter our service without being invited. It is true we were in need of officers last year, but now we have experienced men and plenty of them.' " Lovell then turned on his heel, leaving Lafayette and Kalb standing in the street.

A number of French officers (and some imposters) had indeed presented themselves to Congress in the past year, expecting to be made generals at huge salaries. "You cannot conceive what a weight these kind of people are upon the service and upon me in particular," wrote Washington. "Few of them have any knowledge of the branches which they profess to understand and those that have are entirely useless as officers from their ignorance of the English language." Although few had been accepted, even a handful of such appointments had been demoralizing to the American officers who had served without much pay from the beginning of the war.

The position of Congress in this matter was a difficult one. To ratify Deane's contracts would not only offend American officers but put some of the most important positions in the army into the hands of foreigners. On the other hand, the contracts were technically binding and having been made with agents of the French government, their annulment might imperil French aid.

In one incident (to which Lovell had referred), Tronson du Coudray, a French artillery officer of distinction, had come with a commission from

Deane promising him the rank of major general and chief of artillery. Generals Greene, Knox, and Sullivan had all sent in their resignations, to take effect if the commission were confirmed. As it happened, shortly after his arrival he accidentally drowned in the Schuylkill River, which "saved us much trouble," wrote John Adams, "and embarrassment." Lafayette's application had a different cast. The day Lovell dismissed him, Lafayette wrote Congress to say that he wished to be allowed to serve without pay, and at his own expense, as a volunteer. He had also been accompanied from Paris by one of Franklin's aides, who briefed Congress on his mission, and Deane's letter of introduction (which urged that Lafayette be granted the rank of major general) spoke of his "high birth, his alliances, the great dignities which his family hold at the French court, his considerable estates, his personal merit, his reputation, his disinterestedness, and, above all, his zeal for the liberty of our provinces." Washington likewise received a pointed letter from Franklin which drove the message home:

> The Marquis de Lafayette, a young nobleman of great family connections here and great wealth, is gone to America in a ship of his own, accompanied by some officers of distinction, in order to serve in our armies. He is exceedingly beloved, and everybody's good wishes attend him; we cannot but hope he may meet with such a reception as will make the country and his expedition agreeable to him . . . we are satisfied that the civilities and respect that may be shown him will be serviceable to our affairs here, as pleasing not only to his powerful relations and the Court but to the whole French nation.

Neither Washington nor Congress, eager for a French alliance, could easily disregard such a recommendation, and so on July 31, 1777, four days after his arrival, he received an honorary appointment as a major general in the Continental Army. In response, he donated 60,000 francs to help procure the army urgently needed supplies.

The marquis met Washington for the first time at a dinner given in the commander in chief's honor on August 1. The two took an immediate liking to each other. Washington invited him to witness a review of the troops the next day, and as the ragged and disheveled army passed by, Washington said, "We are rather embarrassed to show ourselves to an officer who has just left the army of France." "I am here, sir," replied Lafayette, "to learn and not to teach."

Although Lafayette hoped for an active command, Washington was reluctant at first to oblige him and wrote for guidance to Benjamin Harrison, chairman of the congressional Committee on Military Affairs:

What the designs of Congress respecting this gentleman were, and what line of conduct I am to pursue to comply with their designs and his expectations, I know no more than a child unborn, and beg to be instructed. If Congress meant that his rank should be unaccompanied by command, I wish it had been sufficiently explained to him. If, on the other hand, it was intended to invest him with all the powers of a major-general, why have I been led into a contrary belief, and left in the dark with respect to my conduct towards him? . . . Let me beseech you, my good Sir, to give me the sentiments of Congress on this matter, that I may endeavour, as far as it is in my power, to comply with them.

Harrison cautiously replied that Congress considered Lafayette's appointment honorary but left the rest to Washington's discretion: he could be given an active command if the commander in chief so wished.

Lafayette's youth did not of itself disqualify him, at least not in Washington's eyes; Washington himself had been a major at nineteen. Nor, of course, was he the military novice he might have seemed. On the contrary, he was a young man in the Washington mold: of precocious understanding, self-possession, and dignified reserve. There was nothing frivolous or immature about him. His manner, according to an acquaintance at the time, was grave beyond his years, and his somewhat "silent disposition" stood in "singular contrast to the petulance, the levity, and the ostentatious loquacity of persons of his own age." Gouverneur Morris, who was critical of almost everybody, wrote, "I was deeply surprised at [his] mature Judgment and solid Understanding," and Alexander Hamilton, among others, similarly expressed his esteem. In any case, the bond between Lafayette, then twenty years old, and Washington, then forty-five, was fast established, and Washington's paternal interest in and affection for him were not feigned. As for Lafayette, he was absolutely devoted to his mentor—"That inestimable man, whose talents and virtues I admire—the better I know him the more I venerate him," as he testified in a letter to his wife. "I am established in his house, and we live together like two attached brothers, with mutual confidence and cordiality."

He soon did his part. At the Battle of Brandywine, in which Washington gave him a minor command, he performed his duty with coolness and bravery, coming to within twenty yards of the enemy, and received a wound in the leg. As Washington ordered him from the field to have his wound dressed, he said to the surgeons, "Treat him as though he were my son."

The baron de Kalb, to whom Deane had also promised a commission, at first was similarly rebuffed. And in a bitter letter to John Hancock, he had given vent to his indignation: "I do not think that either my name, my services, or my person are proper objects to be trifled with or laughed at. I cannot tell you, sir, how deeply I feel the injury done to me. . . . I should be sorry to be compelled to carry my case against Mr. Deane or his successors for damages. And such an action would injure his credit and negotiations, and those of the state at Court." Kalb was not amiss to take offense. Though no baron (he was actually the son of a German peasant), he had joined a German regiment in French service during the Seven Years' War and had risen to lieutenant colonel. He had learned the art of war under Marshal Hermann Saxe—"the professor," in the words of Frederick the Great, "of all the European generals of his age"—and at the Battle of Rossbach had saved the army's rear guard from destruction. Moreover, he had been instrumental in fostering French aid to the rebellion from its very inception, through advice based on his military expertise. Congress looked more closely into his qualifications, reconsidered, and gave him the rank he sought. Again, they did not make a mistake. For he would fight—and die—most bravely in the war.

D U R I N G the fall and winter of 1777–1778, slander and intrigue compounded Washington's hardships as he weathered defeat outside Philadelphia and the bitter months at Valley Forge.

After Burgoyne's surrender at Saratoga, General Gates had acquired the glitter of a general who wins. The fact that he had taken over from Schuyler just as the British invasion began to falter was lost sight of, as was the fact that Washington's strategy and reinforcements had laid the groundwork for the victory he achieved. And so the apparent contrast between his tactical triumph in the north and Washington's evident blundering at Brandywine and Germantown aroused a good deal of discussion, and before long a faction in both the army and Congress began to seek to have Washington replaced. To history, this faction is known as the Conway Cabal.

The cabal was probably not an organized conspiracy as the word suggests—though Washington himself used the term—but rather a loose association of men who had similar, doubtful views about the way the war was going and who complained to one another behind Washington's back. Some of them, however, out of personal ambition, tried to undermine the commander in chief. One was Thomas Conway, an Irishman who had served as a colonel in the French army and had come to America for the glory and advancement he had not found in the European wars. Silas Deane had recommended him to Washington as an officer of merit, and Congress made him a brigadier general, even though a number of American colonels awaiting their own promotions were incensed. After the Battles of Brandywine and Germantown (in which Conway took part, to his own applause), he threatened to resign if he were not promoted to major general—and on December 14, with the support of Thomas Mifflin (who had also fallen out with the commander in chief), he was. Congress also made him inspector general of the army, with powers, according to John Marshall, that amounted to *"imperium in imperio"* in preparation for his assumption of a more open command. At the same time, in deference to the wishes of Gates, Wilkinson was made a brigadier by brevet as a reward for carrying the former's victory dispatch.

Nine brigadiers had objected to Conway's elevation, and Wilkinson's promotion had prompted Colonel John Laurens to declare, "There is a degradation of rank and an injustice to senior and more distinguished officers when a man is so extraordinarily advanced for riding post with good news. Let Congress reward him with a good horse for his speed, but consecrate rank to merit of another kind!" The irony is that even on that ground Wilkinson didn't deserve it, as he had made haste to Congress rather slowly, taking time to stop at Reading to visit his girlfriend before continuing on to York.

Washington had also opposed Conway's promotion as giving him unjustifiable seniority. On October 17, he wrote to Richard Henry Lee:

> Upon so interesting a subject, I must speak plainly. . . . General Conway's merit as an officer and his importance in this army exist more in his own imagination than in reality. For it is a maxim with him to leave no service of his own untold, nor to want anything which is to be obtained by importunity. . . . I would ask why the youngest brigadier in the service should be put over the heads of the oldest and thereby take rank and command of gentlemen who but yesterday were his seniors, gentlemen who, as I will be bound to say in behalf of some of them at least, are of sound judgment and unquestionable bravery. . . . This truth I am well assured of, that they will not serve under him. I leave you to guess therefore at the situation this army would be in at so important a crisis if this event should take place.

Washington's views were disregarded. At about the same time, General Gates was placed at the head of the new Board of War, to which Congress gave enlarged powers of direction and control.

Ambition had already gotten the best of Gates, before his judgment was deranged with excessive praise. He had failed to notify Washington of Burgoyne's surrender by official dispatch, though this was a duty he owed his commander in chief, and it was only after Washington received a letter from General Putnam with a copy of the capitulation terms enclosed that Washington could be sure of the event. Gates also waited unduly long to release any part of his army (for example, Morgan's rifle corps) for service elsewhere, even though he had no further need of them himself. Washington therefore sent Colonel Alexander Hamilton, his aide-de-camp, with a letter dated October 30 to Gates to find out what was going on:

> By this opportunity I do myself the pleasure to congratulate you on the signal success of the army under your command in compelling General Burgoyne and his whole force to surrender themselves prisoners of war, an event that does the highest honor to the American arms and which I hope will be attended with the most extensive and happy consequences. At the same time I cannot but regret that a matter of such magnitude and so interesting to our general operations should have reached me by report only, or through the channels of letters not bearing that authenticity which the importance of it required and which it would have received by a line under your signature stating the simple fact.

Before long, Washington became aware of the praise being heaped on Gates at his expense and of the false comparisons, based on false information, being made. James Lovell, chairman of the Committee of Foreign Affairs, for example, wrote to Gates on November 27, "We want you at different places but we want you most near Germantown. Good God! What a situation we are in! How different from what might have been justly expected! You will be astonished when you know accurately what numbers have at one time and another been collected near Philadelphia to wear out stockings, shoes and breeches." Once more, it was supposed that Washington's force was much larger than it was, yet he could not enlighten the public without giving aid and comfort to the enemy and putting his army at risk. In a letter to Patrick Henry, then governor of Virginia, he felt constrained to point out the difference between his own army and that formerly gathered against Burgoyne:

> This is only to inform you, and with great truth I can do it, strange as it may seem, that the army which I have had under my immediate command has not, at any one time since General Howe's landing at the Head of Elk, been equal in point of numbers to his. In ascertaining this I do not confine myself to continental troops but comprehend militia . . . , I was left to fight two battles in order if possible to save Philadelphia, with less numbers than

composed the army of my antagonist, whilst the world has given us at least double. This impression, though mortifying in some points of view, I have been obliged to encourage because, next to being strong, it is best to be thought so by the enemy. And to this cause, principally, I think is to be attributed the slow movements of General Howe.

How different the case in the Northern Department! There the States of New York and New England, resolving to crush Burgoyne, continued pouring in their troops till the surrender of that army, at which time not less than fourteen thousand militia, as I have been informed, were actually in General Gates's camp, and those composed for the most part of the best yeomanry in the country, well armed and in many instances supplied with provisions of their own carrying. Had the same spirit pervaded the people of this and the neighboring States, we might before this time have had General Howe nearly in the situation of General Burgoyne.

Obviously, the matter was being widely discussed, for it turns up in the diary entry for December 26 of Dr. Albigence Waldo at Valley Forge: "Many country gentlemen in the interior parts of the states, who get wrong information of the affairs and state of our camp are very much surprised at General Washington's delay to drive off the enemy, being falsely informed that his army consists of double the number of the enemy's. Such wrong information serves not to keep up the spirit of the people." The contemporary assessment of Waldo's colleague, Dr. James Thacher, more or less accords with history's longer view:

The Assembly of Pennsylvania and a certain party in our Congress entertain an idea that the royal army was permitted to take possession of Philadelphia by the timidity, or by the extreme caution, of our commander-in-chief. It is well known that from necessity he has evinced himself more the disciple of Fabius Maximus than of Marcellus. He temporizes and acts on the defensive when a superior force and the peculiar circumstances of his army compel him to adopt such conduct. But no one will deny that he has displayed the greatest courage in opposing danger, and the greatest presence of mind in retreating from it. He has perplexed the enemy by his judicious manoeuvres, and braved him frequently in his camp; and it is by his superior generalship and the unfailing resources of his mind that the enemy was not sooner in possession of Philadelphia, and that our feeble, half-starved, naked army has not been entirely destroyed.

But that was not how the matter was seen by some others, including James Lovell, who had supported Gates in opposition to Schuyler. In a remarkable letter to Gates, he wrote:

You have saved our Northern hemisphere, and in spite of consummate and repeated blundering you have changed the condition of the Southern campaign, on the part of the enemy, from offensive to defensive. . . .

We have had a noble army [i.e., Washington's] melted down by ill-judged marches, marches that disgrace the authors and directors and which have occasioned the severest and most just sarcasm and contempt of our enemies.

How much are you to be envied, my dear general! How different your conduct and your fortune!

Conway, Spotswood, Connor, Ross and Mifflin resigned, and many other brave and good officers are preparing their letters to Congress on the same subject. In short, this army will be totally lost unless you come down and collect the virtuous band who wish to fight under your banner and with their aid save the Southern Hemisphere. Prepare yourself for a jaunt to this place—Congress must send for you.

Washington was also criticized by other members of Congresss, including John Adams, who, though he had nominated him for commander in chief, subsequently began to fear that excessive reverence for him might lead to dependency and military rule. On that score, he had nothing to worry about, of course, but he could not have known that for certain at the time. After the victories at Trenton and Princeton, he had warned Congress, according to the diary of Dr. Benjamin Rush: "I have been distressed to see some members of this house disposed to idolise an image which their own hands have molten. I speak here of the superstitious veneration that is sometimes paid to Genl Washington. Altho' I honour him for his good qualities, yet in this house I feel myself his Superior. In private life I shall always acknowledge that he is mine. It becomes us to attend early to the restraining our army." After Burgoyne's surrender, he was not sorry to see Washington cut down to size. He wrote Abigail, "Congress will appoint a thanksgiving, and one cause of it ought to be that the glory of turning the tide of arms is not immediately due to the Commander-in-Chief nor to the southern troops. If it had been, idolatry and adulation would have been unbounded, so excessive as to endanger our liberties. . . . Now we can allow a certain citizen to be wise, virtuous, and good, without thinking him a deity or a savior." Throughout the war, in fact, Adams remained ambivalent about Washington's generalship. At times, he longed for more decisive, aggressive action; on other occasions, he commended Washington's more cautious approach.

Meanwhile, Gates and others, without consulting Washington, had drawn up plans for another Canadian campaign. Troops were to assemble at Albany, march north, cross the ice of Lake Champlain, burn the

British shipping at Saint John's, then press on to Montreal. Lafayette was offered the command, with Conway as his subordinate, in a flattering attempt to lure him away from the commander in chief.

Lafayette's loyalty to Washington was a problem for the Conway Cabal because of his uncertain influence on overall French policy. But the campaign collapsed almost immediately due to poor planning, and Lafayette—despite the blandishments of Conway and others—was never the faction's pawn. He saw through the intrigue and appreciated the stakes. At the beginning of 1778, he told Washington, "If you were lost for America there is nobody who could keep the army and the revolution for six months. There are often dissensions in Congress, parties who hate one another as much as the common enemy; stupid men, who without knowing a single word about war, undertake to judge you, to make ridiculous comparisons; they are infatuated with Gates, without thinking of the different circumstances, and believe that attacking is the only thing necessary to conquer."

Lafayette had also inquired into Conway's character, and "I found," he continued, "that he is an ambitious and dangerous man. He has done all in his power, by cunning maneuvers, to take off my confidence and affection for you. . . . But I am now fixed to your fate, and I shall follow it and sustain it as well by my sword as by all means in my power."

The virtual filial bond between the two men stands in striking contrast to the happenstance and fraudulent affection between General Gates and Major James Wilkinson, a member of Gates's staff. Conway had written a flattering letter to Gates (evidently one of many), which Wilkinson happened to read. One night Wilkinson got drunk at a dinner party and quoted what Conway had said: "Heaven [i.e., working through Gates] has been determined to save your country, or a weak general [Washington] and bad counsellors would have ruined it." At White Marsh on November 8, Washington heard about this from General Lord Stirling, who had been there, and sent Conway a note, which contained just these words:

> Sir: A letter which I received last night contained the following paragraph: "In a letter from General Conway to General Gates, he says, 'Heaven has determined to save your country, or a weak general and bad counsellors would have ruined it.' "
> I am, Sir, Yr. Hble Servt. George Washington.

Conway, mortified, protested that he had been misquoted but couldn't recall exactly what he'd said. He explained that in congratulating Gates on his victory over Burgoyne,

I spoke my mind freely and found fault with several measures pursued in this army, but I will venture to say that in my whole letter the paragraph of which you . . . send me a copy cannot be found. My opinion of you, sir, without flattery or envy, is . . . you are a brave man, an honest man, a patriot, and a man of great sense. Your modesty is such that although your advice in council is commonly sound and proper, you have often been influenced by men who were not equal to you in . . . experience, knowledge, or judgment. . . . I believe I can assert that the expression, weak general, has not slipped from my pen. . . . In order that the least suspicion should not remain . . . about my way of thinking, I am willing that my original letter to General Gates should be handed to you.

However, he never arranged to do this, and in the opinion of Colonel John Laurens (the son of Henry Laurens, who had recently succeeded John Hancock as president of Congress), "The perplexity of his style and evident insincerity of his compliments betray his real sentiments and expose his guilt."

When in December Conway paid a visit to Valley Forge in connection with his official duties, he was greeted with a degree of formality that made him feel shunned. He protested his "cool reception" as thwarting his commission, and Washington sent a copy of Conway's complaint to the president of Congress with some remarks: "If General Conway means . . . that I did not receive him in the language of a warm and cordial friend, I readily confess the charge. I did not, nor shall I ever, till I am capable of the arts of dissimilation. . . . At the same time, Truth authorizes me to say that he was received and treated with proper respect to his official character and that he has had no cause to justify the assertion that he could not expect any support for fulfilling the duties of his appointment." Meanwhile, Gates suspected, or affected to suspect, that someone was secretly reading and copying his correspondence and tried to find out what part of it was known. He wrote to Conway and Mifflin, asking for their help in exposing the culprit—"There is scarcely a man living who takes a greater care of his letters than I do. I never fail to lock them up, and keep the key in my pocket"—but neither they nor his own staff, including Wilkinson, admitted to knowing who it was. On December 8, casting the matter in a letter to Washington as one affecting national security, he presumed to solicit his aid: "As a public officer, I conjure your Excellency to give me all the assistance you can in tracing the author of the infidelity which put extracts from General Conway's letters to me into your hands. Those letters have been stealingly copied, but which of them, when and by whom, is to me as yet an unfathomable secret." He sent a copy of his letter to the president of Congress, which seemed to imply that Washington or a member of Washington's staff might somehow be involved. On January 4, Washington replied:

> Your letter of the 8th ultimo came to my hand a few days ago and, to my great surprise, informed me that a copy of it had been sent to Congress, for what reason I find myself unable to account. But as some end was doubtless intended to be answered by it, I am laid under the disagreeable necessity of returning my answer through the same channel lest any member of that honorable body should harbor an unfavorable suspicion of my having practised some indirect means to come at the contents of the confidential letters between you and General Conway.

> I am to inform you, then, that Colonel Wilkinson, on his way to Congress in the month of October last, fell in with Lord Stirling at Reading and, not in confidence that I ever understood, informed his aide-de-camp, Major McWilliams, that General Conway had written this to you: "Heaven has been determined to save your country, or a weak general and bad counsellors would have ruined it." Lord Stirling, from motives of friendship, transmitted the account.

Washington added (much to Gates's embarrassment, we may suppose), "I considered the [original] information as coming from yourself and given to forewarn and consequently to forearm me against a secret enemy, or in other words a dangerous incendiary, in which character, sooner or later, this country will know General Conway. But in this, as in other matters of late, I have found myself mistaken."

Upon reading this, Gates at once realized that Washington's knowledge of his correspondence with Conway was confined to a single sentence as reported secondhand. He wrote back, "The letter which I had the honor to receive yesterday from your Excellency has relieved me from unspeakable uneasiness. I now anticipate the pleasure it will give you when you discover that what has been conveyed to you for an extract of General Conway's letter to me was spurious. It was certainly fabricated to answer the most selfish and wicked purposes." Meanwhile, Washington's friend Dr. James Craik had written to him from Maryland, "The morning I left camp I was informed that a strong faction was forming against you. . . . It is said they dare not appear openly as your enemies but that the new Board of War is composed of such leading men as will throw such obstacles and difficulties in your way as to force you to resign."

Patrick Henry soon got a taste of the faction's methods when he received an anonymous letter from York dated January 12: "We have only passed the Red Sea. A dreary wilderness is still before us, and unless a

Moses or a Joshua are raised up in our behalf we must perish before we reach the promised land. . . . But is our case desperate? By no means. We have wisdom, virtue and strength enough to save us, if they could be called into action. The northern army has shown us what Americans are capable of doing with a General at their head. The spirit of the southern army is no way inferior. . . . A Gates, a Lee, or a Conway would in a few weeks render them an irresistible body of men." The author then urged Henry to destroy the letter but to publicize its contents "to awaken, enlighten, and alarm our country."

Henry promptly sent the letter, with his condemnation of it, to Washington, who recognized the handwriting as belonging to Dr. Benjamin Rush. "This man has been elaborate and studied in his professions of regard for me," Washington noted in his reply, "and long since [i.e., even after] the letter to you."

Washington also replied on February 9 to the two letters from Gates, pointing out their inconsistencies and holding up Conway to scathing ridicule. After noting that he had contributed nothing of value (despite his vaunted "rich treasuries of knowledge and experience") in councils of war, he said, "Were it necessary, more instances than one might be adduced from his behavior and conversation to manifest that he is capable of all the malignity of detraction and all the meanness of intrigue to gratify the absurd resentment of disappointed vanity or to answer the purposes of personal aggrandizement and promote the interest of faction."

Wilkinson, meanwhile, learned that Gates had identified him as the scoundrel who had betrayed his correspondence. Aghast now at his former own indiscretion, Wilkinson protested his innocence and challenged Gates to a duel. Gates accepted, and they agreed to meet with pistols at eight in the morning behind York's Anglican church. But on the morning set for their encounter, Gates went to see him, took him by the hand, led him down a side street, burst into tears, and abjectly declared that he would just as soon shoot his own son. "I was too deeply affected to speak," recalled Wilkinson, and he agreed to call the duel off.

A few days later, however, at a meeting of the Board of War, Gates was coldly civil to him, in complete contradiction of the tenderness expressed. Wilkinson rode toward Valley Forge but en route learned that his promotion to brigadier general by brevet had been remonstrated against in Congress by forty-seven colonels. This humiliation was too much for him. Having been seduced, as it were, to forego his duel with Gates, he decided to try to rescue his honor by issuing a challenge to Lord Stirling instead. But in the end he asked only that Stirling acknowledge in writing that the telltale conversation between them had been private and confidential. Stirling replied, in writing, that it had been private but not confidential. Wilkinson, forsaking his pretended honor, let the matter go.

Instead, he went to Valley Forge, where his memory suddenly improved. Afterward, he swore in a letter to Washington that Gates had lied in denying that the telltale letter from Conway had said what it had. Not long afterward, he resigned from his position as secretary of the Board of War and charged Gates with "acts of treachery and falsehood."

Conway was reassigned (that is, demoted) to Albany, which had become an insignificant post, and shortly thereafter, on April 22, sent in his resignation. He then had second thoughts, rode a horse almost to death from Albany to York to overtake the courier before his resignation was delivered, but arrived too late. Two and a half months later, because of his continuing slanders, he was challenged to a duel by General John Cadwalader. They met on July 4 and agreed that, upon the word being given, each might fire at his own discretion, either by an offhand shot or by taking deliberate aim. The moment came: Conway fired at once and missed. A gust of wind arose, and Cadwalader calmly kept his pistol down. "Why do you not fire?" exclaimed Conway. "Because," Cadwalader replied, "we came not here to trifle. Let the gale pass and I shall act my part." "You shall have a fair chance of performing it well," rejoined Conway and immediately presented a full front. Cadwalader raised his pistol, fired, and Conway fell forward on his face. His second, running to his assistance, found blood spouting from behind his neck and, lifting up the queue of his hair, saw the ball drop from it, having passed through his mouth and head. As Cadwalader stood over him, he said, "I have stopped the damned rascal's lying tongue, at any rate." Conway languished for several days and, certain he would die, wrote Washington a letter of apology: "Sir, I find myself just able to hold my pen during a few minutes, and take this opportunity of expressing my sincere grief for having done, written, or said any thing disagreeable to your Excellency. My career will soon be over. Therefore, justice and truth prompt me to declare my last sentiments. You are, in my eyes, the great and good man. May you long enjoy the love, esteem, and veneration of these states, whose liberties you have asserted by your virtues. I am, with the greatest respect, Your Exellency's Most obedient and humble servant, THS. CONWAY."

So far as it concerned himself, Washington had long since been willing to let the whole matter go. On February 24, he had written Gates, "I am as averse to controversy as any man and had I not been forced into it, you never would have had occasion to impute to me even the shadow of a disposition towards it. . . . And it is particularly my wish to avoid any personal feuds or dissentions with those who are embarked on the same great national interest with myself, as every difference of this kind must in its consequences be very injurious."

Washington did not consider himself above criticism and was ready enough to admit his faults. "But why should I expect to be exempt from censure?" he had written to Henry Laurens on January 31, 1778. "I may have been very often mistaken in my judgment of the means, and may in many instances deserve the imputation of error." At the end of the whole affair, he told Patrick Henry, "I cannot precisely mark the extent of the views [of the cabal] but . . . I have good reason to believe that their machinations have recoiled most sensibly upon themselves."

I N the campaign to defeat Burgoyne, it had become apparent to members of both Congress and the army that fortified enclaves, such as towns and citadels, were not of much use to the Americans but rather (in Washington's words) almost "a kind of trap." Indeed, John Adams was perhaps not wrong to take heart from Montesquieu's analysis of Hannibal's failure to conquer Rome. In the beginning, Hannibal had been unstoppable and had taken town after town. But then he began to garrison what he had captured, and his scattered and isolated army lost its unity and fighting edge. Whether the comforts of Philadelphia softened Howe's army much as the "delights of Capua" are said to have weakened Hannibal's may be debated. But such an outcome seems to have been anticipated by Benjamin Franklin, who, when told in Paris that Howe had taken Philadelphia, reportedly replied, "I beg your pardon, Philadelphia has taken Howe." Franklin's defensively witty yet knowing remark proved true enough. For that winter the British army indulged itself and did nothing to extend its sway.

In a reprise of their occupation of Boston, the redcoats moved into Independence Hall, took over the city's almshouses, turned churches into stables, and occupied the hospitals and jails. Also as in Boston and New York, they tried to have a good time. Taverns soon rang with "God Save the King" and "Briton Strike Home," and the officers ate well, drank much, claimed the city's finest houses for themselves, and kept themselves comfortable and warm. They met, flirted with, and conquered many a Philadelphia girl, debauched themselves in the city's riverside brothels, and enjoyed such refinements as they had known at home. The occupation newspaper, *The Royal Pennsylvania Gazette,* advertised a startling array of luxury goods—cards, cricket bats, "velverett" (cotton cloth with a velvet surface), "fashionable crooked combs," "lip salve," "purified Italian shaving powder," and so on. For diversion, there were also cockfighting, horse racing, cricket matches, and weekly subscription balls. At least fourteen plays were mounted at the local theater, including Shakespeare's *Henry IV, Part I,* John Home's *Douglas,* and Samuel Foote's *The Minor.*

In a letter to a friend, the loyalist Rebecca Franks, a young woman of legendary beauty and later the model for the heroine of Sir Walter Scott's *Ivanhoe,* described the social life of occupied Philadelphia from the point of view of a much-courted debutante: "You can have no idea of the life of continued amusement I live in. I can scarce have a moment to myself. There is a ball every Thursday, never a lack of partners, for you must know 'tis a fixed rule never to dance but two dances at a time with the same person. . . . I am engaged to seven different gentlemen."

As profligate as this may seem, even those with patriotic sympathies could not wholly condemn the youth of Philadelphia for being drawn into the social whirl. One Philadelphia lady, a bit guilty about indulging herself, insisted that "proper allowances" ought to be made while "in the bloom of life and spirits, after being so long deprived of the societies and amusements of life which their ages and spirits called for."

Howe had no such excuse but was evidently unwilling to break from his pleasures to try his hearty soldiers against Washington's starving troops. One exasperated loyalist wrote:

> Awake, awake, Sir Billy,
>   There's forage in the plain.
> Ah! leave your little filly,
>   And open the campaign.
>
> Heed not a woman's prattle
>   Which tickles in the ear,
> But give the word for battle
>   And grasp the warlike spear.

The "little filly" was Mrs. Joshua Loring, "a very handsome woman but very gay and reckless," whom Howe had first met in Boston in 1775. She had accompanied him to New York and by her extravagant living, addiction to gambling (which Howe shared), and apparent influence over his judgment and affections was known as "the Sultana" among the British officer corps. Howe made her husband, Joshua, his commissary of prisoners (at a guinea a day with all sorts of perks) in recompense for his acquiescence, but among loyalists this "illustrious courtesan" was detested as a cause of Howe's failure at arms. "Nothing seemed to engross his attentions but the faro table, the playhouse, the dancing assembly and, last but not least, Mrs. Loring," wrote Judge Thomas Jones.

Francis Hopkinson, a signer of the Declaration of Independence, also ridiculed Howe's dalliance in a popular song. This was its wildly popular refrain:

> Sir William, he, snug as a flea
> Lay all this time a-snoring;
> Nor dream'd of harm, as he lay warm
> In bed with Mrs. Loring.

The American general Charles Lee put it more crudely: "[Howe] shut his eyes, fought his battles, drunk his bottle, and had his little whore."

In Washington's camp, there was no such dalliance or abandon. Officers and their wives occasionally socialized in the evening, but these soirees s ¹ n included dancing or entertainment, except singing. Often out of co… y to the mostly French foreign officers, they were held at the quarters of General Greene, whose wife, wrote a guest, was "a handsome, elegant, and accomplished woman [who] spoke French . . . and was well versed in French literature. . . . The evening was spent in conversation over a dish of tea or coffee. . . . Every gentleman or lady who could sing was called upon in turn for a song." Some of the soldiers themselves, of course, were musicians, and one evening just before Christmas, Dr. Albigence Waldo heard in an adjacent hut a violinist "excellent . . . in the soft kind of music which is so finely adapted to stir up the tender passions." It conjured up for him "all the endearing expressions, the tender sentiments, the sympathetic friendship . . . of the tenderest of the fair. . . . I wished to have the music cease and yet dreaded its ceasing lest I should lose sight of those dear ideas which . . . gave me pain and pleasure at the same instant."

Similarly moved and astonished was a French interpreter in the camp who one morning while walking in the woods came upon "a tall Indian . . . in American regimentals with two large epaulets on his shoulders," singing an aria from a popular French opera in a "powerful yet melodious voice. I thought myself for a moment at the Comédie Italienne." The singer turned out to be a Canadian Abenaki who had converted to Catholicism under the French and had joined the Americans at the beginning of the war. He had since risen to colonel in the Continental Army.

A B O U T the only military action Howe's army engaged in that winter developed into a farce. On the night of January 4, David Bushnell, the American explosives expert who had designed the *Turtle,* mined the Delaware River with kegs of powder designed to float with the tide among the British shipping and destroy it. The tide, however, did not cooperate, and the first keg spotted was sportively pursued by two boys in a boat. It exploded on contact, disconcerting some riverfront guards, but when several other kegs appeared, an alarm immediately spread through the city, and it was rumored that some of the kegs were filled with armed rebels in a cunning infiltration of the town. The British opened fire on the kegs from their ships—"whole broadsides were poured into the Delaware"—and from batteries along the shore. "Not a wandering chip, stick, or drift log," according to a newspaper account, "but felt the vigor of British arms." This "Battle of the Kegs" as it was mockingly called, reportedly lasted the whole day, making it the longest single action of the war.

H O W E ' S lassitude and passivity merit some comment, for they have remained a puzzle of the conflict to this day. He was not a bad general. He had fought in Flanders, France, and Cuba with distinction. And when he had fought with General James Wolfe in Canada, his conduct had been brilliant and courageous. But after assuming command at Boston, with a splendid army of 10,000 British regulars against a motley aggregate of Americans, he had made almost no effort to break the siege. Like the noble duke of York in the old nursery rhyme (to whom some contemporary satirists compared him), he had 10,000 men and "marched them up to the top of the hill and marched them down again." Even the hill he had chosen was wrong. He had failed to occupy Dorchester Heights, an unmistakably strategic position commanding the town, and when, after months of waiting, the Americans put guns on them, he had evacuated Boston, leaving behind a valuable stockpile of military stores.

He was not without initiative, but his occasional tactical successes, which showed what he could do, merely served to throw his overall indolence and sloth into sharper relief. He had turned Putnam's flank on Long Island and Washington's at Brandywine (short encirclement was his favorite maneuver), but "he could probably have killed or captured every American soldier on Long Island," it is said, "and possibly ended the rebellion. Instead, he had given Washington time to escape across the East River and regroup. Again, instead of pursuing Washington's demoralized little band into New Jersey, he had followed it slowly a short way, then stopped and given it time to recruit and reorganize." Afterward, during the winter months in New York, as in Philadelphia, it was said that he had done nothing but "riot in the fleshpots and frivolities" of social life. Indeed, the apparent moral contrast between the self-indulgent Howe in Philadelphia and the spartan Washington at Valley Forge—Vice and Virtue—could not have been more pronounced.

It may be that as a Whig, sympathetic at first to the revolutionary cause, he had hoped that the colonists would come to their senses or see the hopelessness of the struggle and lay down their arms. The brothers Howe, but Sir William especially, had been reluctant warriors. Bostonians, as Lord Richard Howe had noted in his meeting with the congressional representatives in September 1776, had raised a monument to their late eldest brother, Brigadier General Lord Howe, who had fallen at Ticonderoga during the French and Indian War, and as a member of Parliament Sir William had publicly pledged to his constituents that he would not participate in crushing the rebellion. Perhaps some dutiful recollection of that pledge restrained his zeal. Howe himself protested afterward that his military conduct had merely reflected the conciliatory policy of the government at that time. "Although some persons condemn me for taking every means to prevent the destruction of the country . . . yet am I . . . satisfied to my own mind that I acted . . . for the benefit of the King's service. Ministers themselves . . . did at one time entertain a similar doctrine, and . . . it is certain that I should have had little reason to hope for support from them if I had been disposed to acts of great severity." Nevertheless, it is hard not to disregard the consistent verdict of his contemporaries that a lenient policy could not entirely account for his inaction. One German officer who served under him said, "Sir William liked to enjoy himself, so much so that he sometimes forgot his duties as a commander." And one of his own aides affirmed, "He had a dislike to business, a propensity to pleasure, and was addicted to private conviviality."

Aside from Howe's sometimes perplexing conduct, there were so many unexpected turns in the war and providential escapes that the idea took hold early on that Washington's success depended ultimately upon some supernatural blessing and the approving hand of God. Washington himself would not entirely have disagreed with that assessment and seemed often to speak as if humbly convinced of it, for he felt the Revolution had been constantly rescued by a higher power. As for his own role, he had said at the beginning that he thought "a kind of destiny" had called him to the task, and he exposed himself to danger like a man prepared to accept whatever fate decreed. At the same time, his unswerving sense of duty, patience, tact, patriotism, and tenacity held his little army together through long years of disappointment and more or less constant retreat. His occasional self-distrust was sometimes taken for indecision. But it is not at all true, as some have claimed, that he was a passive strategist or had little idea what to do with the army under his command. His attack at Trenton, subsequent escape from Cornwallis by circling back to Princeton, and his occupation of Morristown on the flank of the enemy's line of communication were brilliant strategic feats, justly compared to some of the famed maneuvers of Stonewall Jackson during the Civil War. In just a few days, with a small, ragtag force, he had recovered New Jersey from the British and thwarted a British overland advance against Philadelphia. As a result, Howe had to take his army around by sea.

Other brilliant actions would follow even as Washington began to give imaginative attention to the fighting methods of his troops. Following the Trenton-Princeton campaign, for example, Washington always attached an artillery company of two or four light guns to each of his infantry brigades and "directed his men to give their cartridges more sting by loading a few buckshot with the standard musket ball. Firing 'buck and ball' at close quarters often enabled a Continental to bring down several men with one round." In August 1777, Washington had also formed his first light infantry corps by drawing off picked men from the brigades, and eventually every regiment had its own light company. During some campaigns, these companies were combined into a separate corps.

Loyalist historians remain exasperated at the way things turned out. One writes, "No one could have foreseen that a heaven-sent general like Washington would appear. . . . Even as it was, could the Americans have hoped for such an ally as Howe in the British Commander-in-Chief? . . . But that an inexperienced colonel major with a gift for backwoods fighting, should turn out a great commander with the precise temperament needful for this difficult work; and Howe, a tried soldier, so belying his reputation as to behave like a traitor to his country and his employers, was a conjunction of circumstances utterly outside the shrewdest calculations." Judge Thomas Jones, who had very little good to say about the patriots, said of Washington, "No other person could have kept such a heterogeneous army together as he did."

CHAPTER ELEVEN

"NABOUR AGAINST NABOUR"

THROUGHOUT the war, the British were often under the impression that most Americans were against it—or supported it with so little enthusiasm that they could be coaxed, lured, or forced back into the royal fold. Howe had tempered his own efforts in part to give the rebels time to reconsider (or so he said) and to do as little damage to the country as possible, according to the unspoken policy of London; Burgoyne had expected to succeed in part through the support of the "loyal population" of upper New York and Vermont. Both had been disappointed, but not because there wasn't a reasonable basis to their plans.

The American Revolution was as much a civil and guerrilla war as a revolutionary war in the usual sense. There was no attempt to overturn the existing social order or to effect a radical redistribution of wealth and opportunity; nor, as a colonial rebellion, did it involve a subject people of different ethnic stock asserting its national identity against an alien imperial power. It was, by and large (and was so understood at the time), a civil war within the British Empire between English-speaking peoples of largely British stock who subscribed to the same legal and political traditions. Contemporaries used the term "civil war" to describe the struggle as often as "revolution," and in doing so they were not far wrong. In some respects, in fact, it was more genuinely a civil war than the Civil War fought in America a century later, since families, friends, businesses, universities, churches, legal partnerships, even marriages were sundered; the war's lines of demarcation being drawn not between regions or classes but through every class in every region to a more or less equal degree. "Nabour was against Nabour," as one contemporary put it; loyalists and patriots were divided across the board. And this remained true long after it became clear that the Revolution was also a substantial contest between the Old World empire of Britain and the "rising empire" of the new United States.

Countless prominent families were split, and those of the Founding Fathers not the least. John Hancock's brother-in-law and the father-in-law of Henry Knox were both loyalists, for example, as was the son-in-law of Henry Laurens, who succeeded Hancock as president of the Continental Congress. Benjamin Franklin's illegitimate son, William, the last royal governor of New Jersey, also refused, despite his father's admonitions and pleading, to repudiate the king. Samuel Quincy, the brilliant lawyer and solicitor general of Massachusetts, who had prosecuted British captain Preston after the Boston Massacre, became a loyalist; but his father, brother, sister, and wife stood with the patriots. The Reverend Jacob Duche of Philadelphia (brother-in-law of Francis Hopkinson) had, with his prayerful invocation at the opening of the Continental Congress, moved the delegates to tears. But when Howe occupied Philadelphia, he had second thoughts, as we have seen, urged Washington to abandon the war, and offered prayers for King George. Dr. Isaac Wilkins, the brother-in-law of Gouverneur and Lewis Morris, the latter a signer of the Declaration of Independence, turned loyalist, while a third brother, Staats Morris, became a British general and member of Parliament. Thomas Jefferson's maternal kinsman Peyton Randolph had been the first speaker of the Continental Congress, but John Randolph, a cousin to whom Jefferson was close, regarded the agitation for independence as treasonable and emigrated to England. John's own son Edmund was an ardent patriot. Indeed, John Adams was most unusual in being able to say, "I was happy that my Mother and my Wife . . . and all her near relations, as well as mine, had been uniformly of my Mind."

As with families, so with society at large, where the general schism was also reflected in most religious and ethnic groups—even among the smallest of the small, that is to say, the Jews. The Jewish population of America numbered about 3,000, less than 0.1 percent of the total population, but they pulled more than their weight. One out of every twenty-five served in the patriot military; others, such as the Gratz brothers, Bernard and Michael of Philadelphia, helped supply the army with food, clothing, and other items of need. Both had signed the Non-Importation

Agreements, and Michael Gratz handled the financial affairs of the Virginia delegation to the Continental Congress. Bernard established a courier service on which Washington relied. One of Philadelphia's most prominent Jewish financiers, Haym Salomon, also worked closely with Robert Morris, the superintendant of finance. On the other hand, David Franks, Philadelphia's leading Jewish merchant, was a die-hard loyalist whose daughter Rebecca was (as noted) the belle of the Philadelphia social scene.

Most Indian tribes tended to be loyalist not out of conviction but because they were accustomed to dealing with imperial authorities, whom they preferred to the rapacious frontiersmen threatening their lands.

In religion, Anglicans and members of the conservative branch of the Dutch Reformed Church, Catholics, and (generally speaking) traditionalists in any given denomination were likely to be loyalists; their "progressive" counterparts were in the patriot camp. Most patriot preachers, of course, thought they had God on their side. If they weren't sure, they were prepared to bargain with the Almighty, like the Reverend Israel Evans, chaplain of a Continental brigade, who before one battle declared: "O Lord of Hosts, lead forth thy servants of the American Army to battle and give them victory; or, if this be not according to Thy sovereign will, then, we pray Thee, stand neutral and let flesh and blood decide the issue." Others were more confident as to where God stood. The Reverend Judah Champion of Litchfield, Connecticut, even gave Him battle plans: "O Lord, we view with terror and dismay the approach of the enemies of Thy holy religion. Wilt Thou send a storm and tempest and scatter them to the uttermost parts of the earth. But, peradventure, should any escape Thy vengeance, collect them together again, O Lord, and let Thy lightnings play upon them in the hollow of Thy hand."

Still others directly joined the fight, such as the Reverend John Peter Gabriel Muhlenberg of Virginia, who appealed to his congregation to enlist, then suddenly shed his gown and, standing before them in a Continental uniform, buckled on a sword. The congregation rose to sing Luther's stirring "Eine feste Burg ist unser Gott" ("A Mighty Fortress Is Our God"), while outside the church, by prearrangement, the drums of an army band rolled to its strains. Within half an hour, 162 members of his flock had signed up.

With comparable drama, George Duffield, pastor of Philadelphia's Third Presbyterian Church, stepped to his pulpit one Sunday and declared, "There are too many men here this morning. I am going to the front"—and did, becoming a chaplain at Valley Forge.

Politics and religion were so commingled in some minds that one distinguished professor of natural philosophy at the College of William and Mary described the Kingdom of Heaven as "that Great Republic, where all men are free and equal and there is no distinction of rank."

A number of loyalist clerics were harassed. One in Hebron, Connecticut, was given a coat of tar and feathers as a warning; another in Amwell, New Jersey, arrived one Sunday morning at his church to find dangling over his pulpit a hangman's noose. At Redding, Connecticut, someone fired at the Reverend John Beach while he was reading a prayer for the king. The Reverend Mather Byles of Boston, though a staunch loyalist, was treated with more forbearance. He had long been a popular preacher and in 1776 was seventy years old. At the beginning of the Revolution, he had been arrested and threatened with imprisonment because he had refused to stop including the king in his public prayers. His sentence, however, was commuted to house arrest, which he mocked by marching up and down in front of his home with a gun on his shoulder, guarding himself.

Not so amused (or amusing) was the Anglican Reverend Jonathan Boucher of Virginia, a clergyman of outstanding ability who never wavered in his loyalty to the Crown. He warned that he would repel violence with violence, and for six months he kept a pair of loaded pistols on the pulpit cushion while he spoke.

Such defiance was not exceptional, and from the beginning many "refused to be coerced into supporting the patriot cause." These, according to Robert Calhoon, included the Highland Scot settlers of North Carolina; the German Pietists in Pennsylvania, North Carolina, Connecticut; poor white yeoman farmers in Maryland, Delaware, and Virginia, and so on. Indeed, passive loyalists, apathetic Whigs, and various neutrals, such as the Quakers, probably made up the "silent majority" during the war.

On the whole, the Quakers simply declined "to join in any of the prevailing seditions and tumults," as one of them put it, although the conservative Quaker leadership in Pennsylvania collaborated with the British during the occupation of Philadelphia. The Moravians, on the other hand, though they did not object to the bearing of arms, condemned it as a sin if contrary to conscience. The equally equivocal Mennonites of Pennsylvania "were willing to sell their farm produce to the Continental Army but firmly refused to take the oath prescribed by law because they would not abjure allegiance to the king." More cautious still were the Schwenkfelders, "the most apolitical and literalistic of the German Pietist sects." One of their leaders, George Kriebel, told a judge that "he could not take the oath of allegiance because the outcome of the war was still in doubt and therefore he did not yet know 'upon what side God almighty would bestow the victory.'"

Countless individuals managed to straddle the fence or changed sides with amazing alacrity. Benjamin Towne, for example, who ran the *Pennsylvania Evening Post,* a Whig paper until late 1777, hailed the British occupation of Philadelphia as "the dawn of returning Liberty." But as soon as the army marched out, King George III once again became a "tyrant" to be excoriated on every page. His Janus-faced twin in this respect was the publisher Isaiah Thomas, whose *Massachusetts Spy* was wildly radical but whose *Royal American Magazine* was almost as popular among Tories as his profligate wife, Mary Dill, who reputedly slept with the entire British officer corps.

But in truth few men at the outset were extremists, and honest disagreement explained the difference in their views. Most loyalists, or Tories, had originally opposed the British revenue measures, while many of the revolutionaries themselves had initially banished all thought of independence from their minds. This was rather dramatically displayed in the Continental Congress debates in the days leading up to the Declaration of Independence. Joseph Galloway's Plan of Union had been defeated by just one vote. In the end, a large percentage of the "loyalist" population simply recoiled before the "calamity" of "blackest rebellion . . . , the horrors of unnatural civil war."

For this reason, for example, William Allen, chief justice of Pennsylvania, was among those unwilling to take up arms against the king. So were Allen's sons, though one of them, Andrew, was a member of the First Continental Congress, and another son, James, had led the Philadelphia mob in the Stamp Act riots of 1765. Both, however, ultimately came down on the loyalist side. In July 1775, James had written in a purely patriotic strain, "The Eyes of Europe are upon us; if we fall, Liberty no longer continues an inhabitant of this Globe: for England is running fast to slavery. The King is as despotic as any prince in Europe; the only difference is the mode; and a venal parliament are as bad as a standing army." In October, he even joined a local militia unit, but then he began to have second thoughts: "My inducement principally to join them is; that a man is suspected who does not; and I chuse to have a Musket on my shoulders, to be on a par with them, and I believe discreet people mixing with them, may Keep them in Order." In other words, he thought he could have a moderating influence on potential extremists. But things were already getting out of hand. "The most insignificant now lord it with impunity and without discretion over the most respectable characters," he complained. The world was turning upside down. In March 1776, he wrote, "The plot thickens; peace is scarcely thought of—Independency predominant. Thinking people uneasy, irresolute and inactive. The Mobility [mob] triumphant. . . . I love the Cause of Liberty; but cannot heartily join in the prosecution of measures totally foreign to the original plan of Resistance. The madness of the multitude is but one degree better than submission to the Tea-Act." Before long, he decided to oppose the growing "madness" any way he could.

Similarly, only one degree of latitude separated Peter Van Schaack, a reluctant loyalist, from his close friend John Jay, a reluctant patriot of a very light stripe. Both had graduated from King's College (now Columbia University) were prosperous lawyers, and conservative in their politics. Both had also opposed British "innovations" beginning with the Stamp Act and had served on a committee formed in New York City in 1774 to help thwart Britain's attempt to close the port of Boston. Both had also supported the Continental Association to boycott British goods. But they parted company irrevocably when independence was declared.

The president of the revolutionary Stamp Act Congress in 1765, Bostonian Timothy Ruggles, also refused to cross that line.

Another halfhearted loyalist was Daniel Leonard, a member of the Massachusetts Assembly who had served on the Committee of Correspondence in 1773. At the time, according to his friend John Adams, Leonard made "the most ardent speeches that were delivered in the House against Great Britain in favor of the colonies." After the Boston Tea Party, however, he broke with the Whigs, and in 1774 and 1775, writing as "Massachusettensis," had accused his former comrades of self-interest and sophistry. Like Van Schaack, James Allen, and others, he was fundamentally afraid of anarchy and convinced (not unreasonably) that once the passions of the populace were released from the restraints of law and morality, they would know no bounds. Such a descent into barbarity was what civil war meant: "a state of war, of all against all . . . [where] might overcomes right; [and] innocence itself has no security."

In the opinion of such men, America had been "led down the fatal road to chaos and treason" by a militant minority. They had "plunged the colonies into an irrational, unjustifiable, and self-destructive war against a mother country whose benevolence, protection, aid, and commitment to constitutional liberty should have evoked gratitude rather than revolt. In the words of Leonard, who succinctly summed up this point of view, 'The annals of the world have not yet been deformed with a single instance of so unnatural, so causeless, so wanton, so wicked a rebellion.' "

A general uncertainty and ambivalence rendered the Revolution ever precarious, and it is one of the reasons why enlistment often lagged. One South Carolina loyalist wrote with disarming candor, "We are at present all Whigs until the arrival of the King's troops." Much of the population, indeed, was "inclined to acquiesce to whatever regime was best able to maintain order and security." When the state Provincial Congress learned that George Washington, the new patriot commander in chief, and William Tryon, the state's royal governor, were both expected in New York City on the same day, it judiciously dispatched a party to welcome "either the General, or Governor Tryon, whichever should arrive first."

Out of 231 male inhabitants of Poughkeepsie, New York, for example, 101 were said to be "committed patriots," 61 "staunch loyalists," 29 "occasional patriots," and 40 "occasional loyalists"—whatever such terms may mean. Some of the people, of course, couldn't have cared less. Many tradesmen were wholly preoccupied with their trades, and many farmers, as one historian puts it, were "more concerned with the soil, the weather, and the prospects for the next crop than with debating the merits of Britain's imperial administration." Washington regarded such indifference as "infinitely more to be dreaded than the whole [British] force."

As the debate in the colonies raged, "men struggled desperately," wrote Esther Forbes, "to keep some middle ground, until that ground was cut from under their feet by the rising tide of emotion, violence, and blood."

F R O M the start, there was a degree of intolerance and hooliganism on the part of the Sons of Liberty, who sometimes, "their faces blacked, with white Night caps and white Stockens on," appeared at the windows and doors of prominent Tories with "Great clubs in their hands." They shouted threats, smashed windows, and occasionally broke into and vandalized homes. Rarely, however, were people assaulted or harmed.

Aside from property damage, political harassment, and (mostly) verbal abuse, a campaign of political indoctrination was carried on aimed at swaying the uncommitted or cowing those of conservative views. After the Continental Congress had recommended that local committees enforce the provisions of the Continental Association and publicly discredit violators "as the enemies of American liberty," a network of more than seven thousand committeemen—a remarkable infrastructure of local revolutionary leadership—arose and involved local civic leaders in the association's enforcement. As the committeemen soon realized that "it would be futile to try to catch violators of non-importation red-handed" —and perhaps guided, by what one historian calls "the Manichaean language" of Congress about "enemies" and "foes to the rights of British America"—they decided to draw up lists of likely offenders. The result was that many suspected loyalists were subjected to public interrogation, and public confessions and recantations became a feature of the revolutionary scene.

At least as early as September 1774, for example, one noncompliant citizen of Haverhill, Massachusetts, was publicly obliged to acknowledge, "As My comfort in life does so much depend on the regard and good will of those among whom I live, I hereby give it Under my Hand that I will not buy or Sell Tea or Act in Any public office Contrary to the Minds of the people in General . . . and will yet hope that all My errors in Judgment or Conduct meet with their forgiveness and favour which I humbly ask." In November 1774, a village schoolmaster in Virginia was hauled before the local Committee of Inspection simply because he had written a letter to a friend in Scotland critical of the growing unrest. Under duress, he was forced to "implore the forgiveness of the country for so ungrateful a return made for the advantages I have received from it, and the bread I have earned in it, and hope, from this contrition for my offence, . . . to subsist among the people I greatly esteem." In May 1775, six men in Marblehead, Massachusetts, were forced to apologize publicly for having signed a farewell address to Thomas Hutchinson, the royal governor, and to declare that their recantation before the community was "a cleansing force."

About the same time, a young German in York County, Pennsylvania, was almost tarred and feathered for objecting to the tenor of a speech given by a militia captain at a house raising. The captain, a recruiting officer, had taken advantage of the occasion to urge everyone to join up, adding that "anyone who refused would be ranked among the Tories, as one who would not join our cause." The German, who happened to be a Mennonite, spoke against mustering on religious grounds and suggested that those who enlisted "might one day repent it." He was immediately reported as "a Tory and enemy to his country" to the local Committee of Public Safety, which arraigned, charged, and condemned him to be tarred and feathered for his remarks. A crowd gathered in front of the local courthouse, but no one stepped forward to carry out the sentence. At length he was told to "tar himself." In pathetic obedience, "the young man pulled off his shirt and put one hand in the tarbox and applied it to his shoulder," while the rest of the committee, wrote an eyewitness, "sneaked off apparently ashamed of the business and themselves." A few moments later, one of the bystanders told him to "take up his shirt and jacket and go home."

Other patriots bent on intimidation had no such qualms. As a result, some citizens of uncertain allegiance who might otherwise have quietly tended their own gardens were provoked to take up arms. One such was James Moody, a second-generation New Jersey farmer, who was more or less apolitical until he was told, as the general cry then was, to "Join or die!" As he relished neither of these alternatives, he was harassed and shot at, and his property was vandalized. In April 1777, he set out for the British lines with seventy-three other disaffected New Jerseyites whom he formed into a loyalist paramilitary band. They roamed the New Jersey and Pennsylvania countryside, carried out hit-and-run raids against the rebels, and in June of 1779 destroyed an important arms depot and captured several patriot officers, including a colonel, a lieutenant colonel, a major, two captains, and some others of lesser rank. Moody also intercepted top secret mail and once came close to capturing William Livingston, the patriot governor of New Jersey. A manhunt was launched for him, and he was finally captured by General Anthony Wayne.

Patriots made another unnecessary enemy of Christopher Sower, the young publisher of the *Germantown Gazette*. Sower, a Quaker and pacifist, had refused to join the revolutionary army. For this he was fined, even though he had already contributed money to a local revolutionary committee. Though he had previously been happy to publish the resolutions passed by Congress, he drew the line at propaganda. For this, the local Committee of Public Safety shut his paper down. Deprived of his livelihood, he defected to the British camp. Eventually, he was attached to a British regiment as a guide, but on December 5, 1777, he was captured by a patriot patrol and brought for questioning before Washington himself. "Well, Mr. Sower," said Washington, "now we will give you some sour sauce." That bit of dry humor fortunately did not augur abuse, and six weeks later, having been treated well in the interim, Sower was exchanged for George Lusk, a gunpowder manufacturer the Americans valued more. Subsequently, Sower served as a loyalist printer and as an undercover agent in the German-American community of Pennsylvania.

Although Sower was execrated as an apostate, he had certainly not lost his soul. One day he recognized, among a group of patriot prisoners huddled together on the New York City docks, the man who had arrested him at Germantown three years before. Sower asked that he be released into his custody, put him up in his own house, gave him fresh clothes and treated him with perfect consideration until arrangements could be made for his exchange.

In truth, there were many reciprocal kindnesses as well as acts of animosity and hate. One patriot who successfully made his way through Tory Long Island owed his life to the discreet sympathies or humanity of the inhabitants he chanced to meet. On one occasion, he came to a large and respectable house and asked the woman he found there for something to eat. "She made no objections, asked no questions, but promptly furnished me with the dish of food I desired. Expressing my obligations to her, I rose to depart. But going round through another room, she met me in the front entry, placed a hat on my head, put an apple pie in my hand, and said, 'You will want this before you get through the woods.' I opened my mouth to give vent to the grateful feelings with which my heart was filled. But she would not tarry to hear a word, and instantly vanished out of my sight."

It was a very confusing time. Well into the war, it was even a question exactly when the rebellion had begun. For example, at the treason trial of one Samuel Chapman in Pennsylvania, the court found itself obliged to admit that until February 11, 1777, when the state had enacted a treason statute, it was not yet technically a crime to be a loyalist, so that at the time of Chapman's alleged offense (in December 1776, when he joined a loyalist troop) "Pennsylvania was not a nation at war with another nation, but a country in a state of *civil war.*"

The patriot regime in New York was less indulgent. In early 1777, when Cadwallader Colden II, son of the colony's last royal lieutenant governor, was brought before the New York Committee for Detecting and Defeating Conspiracies, he told them that he could not in conscience renounce British authority because "he conceived the former oath of allegiance which he had taken to the King of Great Britain to be binding upon him & professed a desire on being permitted to observe a state of neutrality." The committee (after some delay) told him, "No such state of neutrality can be known." Asked to reconsider, Colden declared himself "a faithful & true Subject" of the state of New York from which he had "receiv'd protection." That wasn't acceptable either, and he was driven by denunciations into the British camp.

The extraction of loyalty oaths became common. In 1776, Massachusetts obliged all adult males to swear that they believed the rebellion to be "just and necessary" and would "do nothing to help the British." All who refused or demurred had to surrender their arms. In time, more stringent laws were passed permitting the arrest, imprisonment, and exile of Tories and the confiscation of their estates. Congress urged such measures early on "to frustrate the mischievous machinations, and restrain the wicked practices of these men" (resolution of January 2, 1776), and on November 27, 1777, it urged that the states "confiscate and make use of all the real and personal estate therein, of such of their inhabitants and other persons who have forfeited the same . . . and to invest the money ensuing from the sale in continental loan office certificates."

In October 1779, New York passed its own Law of Forfeiture, which also evicted the families of absent loyalists from their homes. Many of them were assembled in a no-man's-land near the Canadian border and transferred under a flag of truce to Nova Scotia and Quebec.

There was often more than a touch of mercenary greed or "sordid interest" in such reprisals, as Alexander Hamilton pointed out. "One [person] wishes to possess the house of some wretched Tory, another fears him as a rival in his trade or commerce"; a third, who may owe him money, wants "to get clear of his debts." Many soldiers in the patriot army did not hesitate to plunder whatever they could lay their hands on or burn and destroy whatever they could not carry away. Washington did what he could to punish and suppress this rapacity, and on September 24, 1776, even as he was retreating from Howe's onslaught, he warned Congress that "the infamous practice of plundering, if it cannot be checked, will prove fatal both to the country and the army. For, under the idea of Tory property . . . no man is secure in his effects, and scarcely in his person. . . . We have several instances of people being frightened out of their houses, under pretence of those houses being ordered to be burnt; and this is done with a view of seizing the goods. Nay, in order that the villainy may be more effectually concealed, some houses have actually been burned to cover the theft."

The term "lynch law," which at the time had nothing to do with hanging, was originally coined to describe the patriot abuse of loyalists in Virginia. There, one Judge William Lynch, a colonel in the patriot militia, used to hold informal court in his parlor and impose fines and imprisonment on suspects however he pleased.

Loyalists had few opportunities to retaliate in kind. One came, however briefly, later in the war, after the restoration of Sir James Wright as royal governor of Georgia. Upon resuming his former duties, Wright passed the Disqualifying Act, which reversed some punitive measures and allowed suits for debt to be brought against patriot estates and the sale of the estates of patriot absentees.

But by the fall of 1776, the ill will was already such that when New York fell to the British, thousands of persecuted loyalists poured into the city and its environs. "From every colony they came," writes one historian, "by boat, on foot, in carriage or on horseback, thanking God when they passed within the British lines."

Yet few on either side would probably have disagreed with the sentiments of Nicholas Cresswell, one of those refugees. In his diary for June 24, 1777, he wrote, "It brings a sadness and melancholy upon my mind to think that a set of people who three years ago were doing everything they could for the mutual assistance of each other, and both parties equally gainers, should now be cutting the throats of each other and destroying their property."

N o one knows how many Tories there were during the Revolution, but John Adams thought a third of the people at least were loyalists, and more than a hundred thousand Americans left the country during the war. Some thirty thousand others served with the British forces in one campaign or another, as loyalist troops. Much of the Carolina backcountry was strongly Tory in its sympathies, and in New York, Gouverneur Morris thought that half the colony (whose population was 180,000) was in open or secret sympathy with the king.

The first loyalist regiments were organized soon after Howe captured New York. In the beginning, they were not expected to do much serious fighting, but by 1777 they had begun to assume a more active role. Since the British were unable to dispatch troops to America in numbers large enough to occupy whole regions, a substantial loyalist collaboration became indispensable to their prospects. Up to fifty provincial regiments, as they were called, were formed, among them Sir John Johnson's Royal Yorkers, who fought in the Mohawk Valley during Burgoyne's campaign; Lieutenant Colonel John Simcoe's Queen's Rangers, an elite troop made up of loyalist volunteers and Irish and Scots regulars, who fought at Brandywine and through the southern campaigns; the Queen's Loyal Rangers, who were almost wiped out at the battle of Bennington; the King's American Regiment of North Carolina, led by David Fanning, which took part in the assaults on Forts Clinton and Montgomery and later in the battle of King's Mountain; and the New York Volunteers and De Lancey's Brigade, which were both involved in the British sweep of Long Island and later sent south. Other loyalist regiments of note were the Loyal American Regiment, recruited by Colonel Beverly Robinson; the New Jersey Volunteers, recruited by Cortlandt Skinner; the Royal Guides and Pioneers; the Pennsylvania Loyalists; the Maryland Loyalists; the American Riflemen, led by Patrick Ferguson; the Prince of Wales American Regiment; and the King's Orange Rangers.

Loyalists were also widely employed as guerrillas, propagandists, counterfeiters, spies, guides, foragers, pilots, and so on, as well as civil administrators, such as Joseph Galloway in Philadelphia, by the occupation force.

Whereas Howe believed that the population would return to their former allegiance as soon as they saw the patriot army in retreat, others, including Galloway, were convinced that they would do so only if assured of security. As superintendent of police in occupied Philadelphia, Galloway became impatient with Howe's languor and passivity and undertook himself to organize an intelligence network, a civilian commissary, a new sanitation department and involved himself in such civil functions as the issuance of tavern licenses, curfew regulations, and poor relief. At his own expense, he also organized two paramilitary companies of loyalist refugees to serve as a home guard and auxiliary police. By efficient government, he hoped to lend credibility to British rule. Isaac Ogden, who worked with Galloway in the civil administration, wrote in November 1778, "The rebellion hangs by a slender thread. The great majority of Americans are heartily tired of the war and groan under the yoke of tyranny. . . . In this situation what is necessary to crush the rebellion . . . [is] only one vigorous campaign, properly conducted. I mean by . . . a man of judgement, *spirit,* and *enterprise.*" Howe's failure to expand British authority into the countryside left Galloway and others bitterly disappointed, and Galloway later appeared as a principal witness in the parliamentary inquiry into Howe's conduct of the war.

MONMOUTH

T H E R E were three classes of American soldiers: the Continentals, the militia, and state. The Continentals were the regulars; the standing militia was a local body in which all able-bodied men between sixteen and sixty-five (with certain exceptions) were required to serve; and the state troops were volunteer levies raised mainly in the early years of the war. Washington, as mentioned, had also thought of using Indians as auxiliaries "mixed with our own Parties" and as scouts and light troops. Congress authorized him to raise four hundred, but he ultimately changed his mind.

At the beginning of the war, America had an armed citizenry, but the people abhorred the idea of a standing army. Such a professional force was thought of "as the instrument of tyrants and the enslaver of peoples," by association with the princes and monarchs of European principalities and states.

By contrast, in the militia system as established in Massachusetts and other New England colonies, the men elected their own officers, and military leadership tended to belong to the civilian leaders of the community. The militia thought of themselves primarily as an armed guard defending their homes and localities, not as manpower for wars. They did not lack zeal and as a rule were ready enough to turn out for a fight. But they objected to "campaigning"—garrison duty, marching, digging trenches, chopping wood—almost as an infringement on their rights. In the militia there was also little class distinction. As one contemporary noted, "Our inn-keeper was a captain, and there are shoemakers who are colonels." The result was an informality or familiarity in the relations between officers and soldiers which was almost incompatible with discipline. This "leveling spirit" had been exasperating to British officers in colonial days. "Our Militia is under no kind of discipline," complained one in 1754. "They are impatient under all kind of superiority and authority."

The British army, on the other hand, was recruited from the lowest rungs of English society—three British regiments in the American Revolution were composed entirely of reprieved criminals—and its heavy-handed sergeants instantly and severely disciplined insubordinates. British officers, coming largely from the upper classes, expected and got submissive respect and unquestioning obedience from their men.

Washington was not partial to the British model, but he hated the militia system, which in the beginning of the war was the foundation of his army. "The militia come in," he wrote, "you cannot tell how, go out and you cannot tell when; consume your provisions, exhaust your stores, and leave you at a critical moment." They left just as they were beginning to understand their duties—sometimes even before their term was up. Desertions were commonplace. Occasionally, it was necessary to recruit a new army even as the enemy advanced. General Richard Montgomery had felt obliged to hasten his assault on Quebec in late December 1775 because the enlistments of his New England troops were about to expire; Washington's more fortunate strike at Trenton had been influenced by the same concern. Even so, the militia did enormous service to the cause. They "patrolled the coastline, protected the countryside from British foragers and raiding parties, defended frontier settlements from Indian depredations, and on rare occasions, when they were inspired and well led, surprised their severest critics by standing fast on the battlefield. At Saratoga, a patriot army made up primarily of militiamen from New England and New York twice defeated and finally captured nearly 6,000 redcoats and Hessians, turning the tide of the war." Nevertheless, they were unreliable and never an adequate substitute for a professional fighting force.

About the time the British overran New York, Washington had written to the president of Congress:

To place any dependence upon militia is assuredly resting on a broken staff. Men, just dragged from the tender scenes of domestic life, unaccustomed to the din of arms, totally unacquainted with every kind of military skill (which is followed by a want of confidence in themselves, when opposed to troops regularly trained, disciplined, and appointed, superior in knowledge, and superior in arms), are timid, and ready to fly from their own shadows. Besides, the sudden change in their manner of living brings on an unconquerable desire to return to their homes, and produces the most shameful and scandalous desertions. Again, men accustomed to unbounded freedom, cannot brook the restraint, which is indispensably necessary to the good order and government of any army, without which licentiousness and every kind of disorder triumphantly reigns.

Creating a national, or Continental, army had been a difficult task. Washington found himself competing for men against the militias of the separate states, which in turn competed against one another to hold their own men in home guards. Although Congress periodically offered bonuses as enticements for enlistment, states also raised troops of regulars to defend their own borders, and some offered bounties larger than Congress could afford.

At the same time, given America's diversity, the Continental Army was occasionally riven by state, regional, and ethnic animosities. Southerners already called New Englanders "Yankees" with some disparagement; New Englanders and Pennsylvania Dutch found each other extremely odd. One Connecticut soldier wrote, "There was not much cordiality subsisting between us, for, to tell the sober truth, I had in those days as lief been incorporated with a tribe of Western Indians as with any of the Southern troops." Schuyler's replacement by Gates had more to do with the bias of New England troops for a commander of their own than with Schuyler's deficiencies as a general; but Washington, for one, as in his rare rebuke to Greene after the Battle of Brandywine, did his best to harness parochial pride to the common cause. "I have labored, ever since I have been in the service," he wrote at the end of 1776, "to discourage all kinds of local attachments and distinctions of country [i.e., of state], denominating the whole by the greater name of *American,* but I have found it impossible to overcome prejudices; and, under the new establishment, I conceive it best to stir up an emulation; in order to do which would it not be better for each State to furnish . . . their own brigadiers?"

The officer corps was a problem unto itself. During the colonial period, British officers had looked down upon their provincial counterparts, and it had been established policy "that all Troops serving by British commissions shall take Rank before all Troops which may serve by Commission from any of the Governors or Councils of Our Provinces in North America." In disputes over rank and precedence, British officers had prevailed over their American confreres. Such jockeying was now reenacted among the officers of the Continental line. "Not an hour passes," Washington wrote to the president of the Continental Congress on August 3, 1778, "without new applications and new complaints about rank. . . . We can scarcely form a Court Martial or parade a detachment in any instance, without a warm discussion on the subject of precedence."

Responding to an inquiry from the Congress, Washington explained, "If in all cases ours was *one* army, or *thirteen* armies allied for the common defence, there would be no difficulty in solving your question; but we are occasionally both, and . . . sometimes *neither,* but a compound of both."

After 1777, those willing to serve as regulars for the duration of the war were less often patriotic tradesmen and farmers than men from the poorer and more disadvantaged segments of American society. "They were vagrants, loafers, unemployed laborers, indentured servants, debtors, free blacks, and even slaves," writes one military historian, "desperate men who felt there was more to gain from military service than civilian life. Most were attracted by the promise of free land at war's end." Eventually, the ranks came to include ordinary criminals, enemy deserters, and prisoners of war. Tories facing execution could save themselves by enlisting, and after 1777 "a noticeable number of the 'able-bodied and effective' recruits rounded up for the Main Army were over-aged men and young boys. Many were drunk into the army by recruiting sergeants. There was room for all in the Continental Line." They endured smallpox, dysentery, boils, and yellow fever; subsisted on tripe, bits of raw beef, and "sea-bread" (hard biscuit "nearly hard enough for musket flints") and endured all the myriad hardships and privations of a soldier on the march. During the Battle of Harlem Heights, when one of the men complained of being hungry, an officer reached into his pocket and took out an ear of Indian corn burnt black as coal. "Here," he said, "eat this and learn to be a soldier."

Although Washington had a reverence for the dignity of the soul, he did not have a sentimental view of human nature. "Men may speculate as they will," he wrote, "they may talk of patriotism; they may draw a few examples from current story . . . but whoever builds upon it as a sufficient basis for conducting a long and bloody war will find themselves deceived in the end. . . . For a long time it may of itself push men to action, to bear much, to encounter difficulties, but it will not endure unassisted by Interest." His practical, but not cynical, view of the need for incentives helped him to assess from day to day what he could ask for and expect and, in the end, what was required.

Even so, the self-sacrifice of his soldiers left him amazed. "To see men without clothes to cover their nakedness," wrote Washington as the hard winter came to an end, "without blankets to lay on, without shoes, by which their marches might be traced by the blood from their feet, and almost as often without provisions as with; marching through frost and snow, and at Christmas taking up their winter quarters within a day's march of the enemy, without a house or hut to cover them till they could be built, and submitting to it without a murmur, is a mark of patience and obedience which in my opinion can scarce be paralleled."

And in that forge of misery, a tougher army was born.

T H E eighteenth century was the "Age of Limited Warfare," regulated by formal rules which tended toward an inconclusive result. "Now it is frequent," Daniel Defoe remarked, "to have armies of fifty thousand men of a side stand at bay within view of one another, and spend a whole campaign in dodging, or, as it is genteelly called, observing one another, and then march off into winter quarters. . . . The present maxims of war are—'Never fight without a manifest advantage,' and 'always encamp so as not to be forced to it.' And if two opposite generals nicely observe both these rules, it is impossible they should ever come to fight." (This was how Washington and Howe positioned their armies during the winter of 1778.)

When the enemies finally met, it was usually, writes Daniel Boorstin, "on large open fields, where the customary rules and formations could be obeyed. At the opening of a battle, the opposing forces were set up like men on a chessboard; each side usually knew what forces the other possessed, and each part of an army was expected to perform only specific maneuvers. Sneak attacks, irregular warfare, and unexpected and unheralded tactics were generally frowned on as violations of the rules."

The formal slaughter of two parading armies had its own barbarities, of course, and was the more impersonal for being so arranged. But backwoods warfare was different. The Indians fought ruthlessly as individuals or in guerrilla bands and in their disregard of European military etiquette had obliged the colonists to adopt their skirmishing techniques.

Many Americans today suppose that the colonials prevailed by their use of frontier military tactics—by shooting from behind stone walls, rocks, and trees at redcoats who mechanically advanced across open ground in dressed line formations. In fact, "linear warfare" was practiced on both sides, and while frontier fighting methods sometimes tipped the scales, in most confrontations, which way the battle went had more to do with the science of ballistics. There was little to choose from in weaponry: the British "Brown Bess" musket and the typical American musket both had an effective range of about seventy-five yards. Most of the troops on either side carried the smoothbore flintlock musket, a fairly cumbersome weapon with an unrifled bore. The musket ball was fitted loosely to the bore for easy loading and bounced along the barrel when fired. Whether or not it hit its mark "depended on the last bounce it took." One Continental soldier claimed that "at least eighty balls were fired for one that took effect," and often "but one ball in near three hundred." In that respect, the Battle of Bunker Hill was the deadliest battle ever fought up until that time, "taking into view the quantity of fire or the number of shots that were fired," since about one ball in every thirty (fired by the patriots) hit its mark.

A musket was best used by soldiers in close formation, who fired at the enemy in a volley all at once in order "to propel a wall of lead into the opposing line." Some European armies did not even train their men to aim. What counted more than marksmanship was speed—the number of volleys the troops could get off in the shortest possible time. Because the musket was rarely accurate at a distance, volleys were exchanged at close range, followed by hand-to-hand combat, in which a compact formation also proved of use.

By contrast, quite a few Continentals were armed with the American long rifle, known variously as the Pennsylvania rifle (because it was first made by German Pietists in that state) or the Kentucky rifle (after the state in which it gained its fame). Its accuracy and increased range intimidated the enemy, since an expert marksman could hit a bull's-eye repeatedly at one hundred yards. On the other hand, since the rifling in the bore resisted the passage of the charge, the rifle took much longer to load than a common musket, and it could not accommodate a bayonet. Riflemen were therefore unable to maintain their ground before a bayonet attack.

In February 1778, Friedrich Wilhelm von Steuben, a professional soldier and veteran of several European campaigns, arrived at Valley Forge. Steuben had served on the staff of Frederick the Great, and at Valley Forge, in a remarkably short time, he transformed the roughshod Continentals into an effective European-style fighting force. No matter that he passed himself off as a "baron," which he was not, and a former "lieutenant general," when he had never risen higher in the ranks than captain; Washington recognized his military ability and accepted his offer to serve without rank or pay. He wrote to Henry Laurens, the president of Congress, "[The baron] appears to be much of a gentleman and, as far as I have had an opportunity of judging, a man of military knowledge and acquainted with the world." In fact, his credentials were superb.

Born into a Prussian military family, Steuben had grown up among guns, drums, trumpets, fortifications, drills, and parades. His uncle had written one of the standard books on fortifications, and his father had been a major of military engineers. Steuben himself had served as a volunteer in the Prussian siege of Prague, had risen to first lieutenant in the army, and had commanded a regiment at the beginning of the Seven Years' War. During 1758, he had served as adjutant general to General von Mayr, from whom he had learned the management of light infantry. He was subsequently promoted to captain and served for a time on the staff of Frederick the Great.

On a visit to Paris, he became acquainted with members of the French military establishment, including the comte de Saint-Germain, the minister of war, and in May 1777 the two met and discussed what Steuben might do to assist the American cause. In America, said Saint-Germain, there was glory, fortune, and a field for applying his military knowledge such as no European war could afford. He gave him a letter of introduction to Beaumarchais, who introduced him to Silas Deane; Deane took him to see Franklin.

At the time, the French were convinced that without a reform in the organization of the American army, all the money and military stores they were providing would eventually go to waste. Steuben's mission was to make the army efficient, and to make him appear more impressive, the French concocted his rank and titles and advised him to offer himself to Congress as a volunteer.

Franklin, who understood the French concerns, cooperated in the scheme, and one suspects that Washington understood Franklin's game. "The gentleman who will have the honour of waiting on you with this letter," Franklin wrote to him on September 4, "is the Baron de Steuben, lately a lieutenant-general in the king of Prussia's service, whom he attended in all his campaigns, being his aide-de-camp, quartermaster-general, etc." On September 26, Steuben set sail for America in a warship that masqueraded as a commercial transport belonging to Beaumarchais's Rodrique Hortalez & Co. with the pretended destination of Martinique. The crossing took two months, which allowed Steuben plenty of time to occupy himself with mathematical calculations (according to his predilection), take target practice, and acquaint himself with the works of the Abbé Raynal. When his ship finally docked at Portsmouth, New Hampshire, on December 1, he was effusively welcomed by the local American commander, inspected the harbor fortifications, and dispatched a letter to Washington at Valley Forge. Briefed in advance about the political sensitivity of foreign appointments, he wrote, "My greatest ambition is to deserve the title of a citizen of America by fighting for the cause of liberty. But if the distinguished ranks in which I have served in Europe should be an obstacle, I had rather serve under your Excellency as a volunteer than to be a subject of discontent to such deserving officers as have already distinguished themselves amongst you."

From Portsmouth, he proceeded to Boston, where he was the guest of John Hancock, and then on to York, Pennsylvania, to see what Congress would do.

The journey was not without adventure. Near the Connecticut border, when his weary party sought refuge from a furious snowstorm, a Tory innkeeper refused to put him up. "I have no beds, bread, meat, drink, milk, nor eggs for you," he adamantly told them, which they could see was untrue. But repeated remonstrations did no good. "Bring me my pistols!" cried Steuben in German, and suddenly the innkeeper found a pistol at his chest. Accommodations were promptly furnished; their table lavishly spread. The following morning, after an abundant breakfast, the party resumed its journey, not forgetting to pay the innkeeper liberally with the Continental money he despised.

In Pennsylvania, where the Pennsylvania Dutch (Deutsch) community was large, he was everywhere received with both hospitality and pride. Many members of the community had portraits of Frederick the Great on their walls, and in one establishment at Manheim he almost collapsed from laughter at an engraving showing a Prussian knocking down a Frenchman, with the caption *"Ein Franzmann zum Preuszen wie eine Mücke"* ("To a Prussian a Frenchman is like a gnat").

Steuben made a favorable impression at York. Congress accepted his services, and he set out for Valley Forge. Washington met him on the outskirts of his encampment, and the very next day the troops were mustered for his review. "Never before or since, have I had such an impression of the ancient fabled God of War," wrote a young private long afterward, "as when I looked on the baron: he seemed to me a perfect personification of Mars. The trappings of his horse, the enormous holsters of his pistols, his large size, and his strikingly martial aspect, all seemed to favor the idea."

Steuben soon discovered that in the Continental Army as it existed there was little internal administration in the conventional sense. Although the number of men in a regiment or a company, for example, had been fixed by Congress, each was made up of men who had enlisted for different terms. Thus, with the uncharted comings and goings of personnel, at any given moment a company might have more men in it than a regiment and a regiment than a brigade. "The words company, regiment, brigade and division were so vague," he wrote, "that they did not convey any idea upon which to form a calculation, either of the particular corps or of the army in general. . . . I have seen a regiment consisting of thirty men, and a company of one corporal. . . . No captain kept a book." Leaves of absence and even dismissals were not always recorded, and many still on the regimental books had long since ceased to be part of the army. Army property—muskets, bayonets, clothing, and so on—was scattered everywhere, and at the end of each campaign, five thousand to eight thousand new muskets were carried off by men whose terms of enlistment had expired. There was no uniform code or system of regulations, and as for drill, "each colonel had a system of his own."

Under Steuben, all that changed. Records were scrupulously kept, and at rigorous monthly inspections, every man not present had to be accounted for, as well as every piece of equipment—every musket, flint, and cartridge box. Steuben's own methods of discipline were unfamiliar and at first met resistance: "My good republicans wanted everything in the English style; our great and good allies everything according to the French *mode*. When I presented a plate of *sauerkraut* dressed in the Prussian style, they all wanted to throw it out of the window. Nevertheless, by the force of proving by *Goddams* that my cookery was the best, I overcame their prejudices."

Americans were not accustomed to blind obedience, and Steuben recognized and respected this. The genius of the nation, he wrote, "is not in the least to be compared with that of the Prussians, Austrians or French. You say to your soldier, 'Do this,' and he doeth it, but here I am obliged to say, 'This is the reason why you ought to do that: and then he does it.' "

Steuben's genius was his ability to unite Prussian virtues to those of the American mind. He brought uniformity and order to Continental training, drilled the troops repeatedly in different formations, and taught them how to deploy quickly from column into line, fire scything volleys, and deliver and receive bayonet attacks. He also insisted that all Continental officers drill their own soldiers instead of assigning the task to a soldier of lesser rank, both to encourage greater professionalism and to promote a closer bond between the officers and men. Until his advent, troops had drilled from at least three separate manuals, so that when they were brigaded together, disarray ensued.

Steuben's new military manual, or "Blue Book," simplified and shrewdly adapted standard procedures to the particular requirements of training patriot troops. In European armies at the time, a man who had been drilled for three months was still considered a raw recruit; Steuben knew he could not always count on more than a couple of months in which to turn his American recruits into soldiers. He worked on the manual during the winter of 1779, and it was accepted by Congress on March 29, 1779, and published as *Regulations for the Order and Discipline of the Troops of the United States, Part I*. It remained the official manual of the U.S. Army until the War of 1812.

Steuben's training brought together the best of traditional military thinking and American technique. He took into account the skirmishing style colonials had developed for themselves (in loose bodies rather than in close formations), organized sharpshooters into light infantry companies with their own special discipline and drill (an American innovation afterward adopted by all European armies), taught the Continentals how to use the bayonet, and had them aim their muskets like rifles, which improved their accuracy to a considerable degree. As occasion warranted, the light companies could also be detached from their "parent" regiments, brigaded together in a separate corps, and used as shock troops or advance guards for the main army.

As an example to the other officers, Steuben also created a model company which he drilled himself. "To see a gentleman dignified with a lieutenant general's commission from the great Prussian monarch," wrote one American colonel, "condescend with a grace peculiar to himself to take under his direction a squad of ten or twelve men in the capacity of a drill sergeant, commanded the admiration of both officers and men."

Steuben had begun his task with almost no knowledge of English, and his young secretary and translator, Pierre Duponceau, remembered that "when some movement or maneuver was not performed to his mind he began to swear in German, then in French, and then in both languages together. When he had exhausted his artillery of foreign oaths, he would call to his aides, 'My dear [Captain Benjamin] Walker and my dear Duponceau, come and swear for me in English. These fellows won't do what I bid them.' A good-natured smile then went through the ranks and at last the maneuver or the movement was properly performed."

(Steuben's English steadily improved to the point where he was capable of a happy pun. Despite his parade-ground vituperations he had an elegant social manner, and on one occasion, on being presented to a beautiful Miss Sheaf, he said, "Ah, madam, I have always been cautioned to avoid *mischief*, but I never knew till today how dangerous she was.")

Not all his military exercises went as planned. One morning a mock battle was staged between two full divisions. Duponceau was sent to reconnoiter, with orders to return immediately when the enemy was in sight. About a quarter of a mile from camp, he saw a blur of red which he mistook for a body of British soldiers. He raced back with the news that the enemy really was marching on the camp. Steuben's division marched out smartly on the road Duponceau indicated and, drawing near to where the British had supposedly been seen, prepared to charge, when the red blur was discovered to be "some red petticoats hanging on a fence to dry." Duponceau's error naturally excited hilarity, to his own "utter confusion and dismay," and summoned into Washington's presence, he expected a reprimand. Instead, Washington passed around a bowl of punch to the officers present and invited Duponceau to share in the good cheer.

On March 24, Steuben put on a demonstration involving Washington's whole army. All the brigades turned out, "each regiment on its own parade," and after he took them through all the formations of their drill, he conducted maneuvers with ten and twelve battalions "with as much precision as the evolution of a single company." A new spirit had entered the army. Its encampments became more orderly, and parades, maneuvers, and reviews exhibited a harmony of movement that gave thousands of soldiers the appearance of acting as a single body under the control of a single will. On March 28, Washington officially appointed Steuben inspector general of the army "till the pleasure of Congress shall be known. . . . The Importance of establishing an uniform system of useful maneuvers, and regularity of discipline, must be obvious." On May 5, Congress ratified the appointment and gave Steuben the rank of major general in the American army.

W A S H I N G T O N ' S complaints about the inadequacies of supply had brought a congressional committee to Valley Forge at the beginning of the year to assess the situation firsthand. They found the Quartermaster Department, as lately administered by Thomas Mifflin, in a state of collapse. On March 22, 1778, Mifflin was replaced by the infinitely more capable and dedicated Nathanael Greene. In recommending his appointment, Washington told one member of Congress, "There is not an officer of the army, nor a man in America, more sincerely attached to the interests of his country. Could he best promote their interests in the character of a *corporal,* he would exchange, as I firmly believe, without a murmur, the epaulet for the knot." By the spring, the knotted supply system had been disentangled, the Quartermaster and Commissary Departments revamped. To improve morale among the officers, Congress considered a measure granting them half pay for life upon retirement with pensions for their widows. (Nathanael Greene had written Adams early in June 1776, "urging him to press upon Congress the necessity of providing pensions for soldiers who were wounded or incapacitated." This, he felt, would be "the most effective possible recruiting measure, as even a zealous patriot would hesitate to enlist if he thought a disabling wound might make him a pauper and impoverish his family.") Opponents of the bill maintained that Congress had no authority to create a peacetime establishment and that the proposal would introduce a standing army. A compromise bill changing the life payments to payments for seven years was then passed on May 15.

The long winter at Valley Forge finally came to an end. With the spring arrived provisions and clothing, including new uniforms for the summer campaign, and fresh troops marched in. Washington asked Elias Boudinot, his commissary of prisoners, to do whatever he could to obtain the exchange of General Lee. Lee, confined in New York, was to have been taken to England for trial as a deserter from the British army. Washington, however, had written Howe that he was holding five Hessian field officers as hostages for Lee's personal safety, well knowing that for Howe to disregard their welfare would risk disaffection among the German soldiers.

Lee was unworthy of such efforts on his behalf. In captivity, he had assured Howe that he had been opposed to the Declaration of Independence, and he sought to curry favor by advising the British on how to conduct their next campaign. Subsequent events suggest he may have become their man.

Boudinot succeeded, and Washington, out of deference to Lee's rank, arranged festivities to honor his return. When the day (April 5) arrived, a military band was assembled, and the entire army, including its principal officers, was drawn up to receive him. Washington rode down the road toward Philadelphia and, when Lee appeared, dismounted and greeted him, wrote Boudinot, "as if he had been his brother." Together they passed the troops in review, and afterward, at headquarters, Lee was entertained with an elegant dinner, chamber music, and song. As Washington's guest, he was given a room behind Martha Washington's sitting room, but "the next morning he lay very late and breakfast was detained for him. When he came out," wrote Boudinot, "he looked dirty, as if he had been in the street all night. Soon after I discovered that he had brought a miserable dirty hussy with him from Philadelphia (a British sergeant's wife) and had taken her into his room by a back door, and she had slept with him that night."

This affront to Washington's hospitality did not go over well. Nor had Lee learned to curb his spiteful tongue. As he rode toward York to consult with Congress, he was rash enough to tell Boudinot that in his opinion "General Washington was not fit to command a sergeant's guard."

The privations suffered by Washington's army at Valley Forge had put Congress in a penitential mood. Their guilt was transferred to the population at large when April 22 was appointed as a day of fasting and prayer on which Americans were exhorted to "confess their iniquities and transgressions, for which the land mourneth; that they may implore the mercy and forgiveness of God; and beseech him that vice, prophaneness, extortion, and every evil, may be done away; and that we may be a reformed and happy people."

On May 3, everyone's spirits were lifted by the announcement of the new treaty of alliance (concluded on February 6) between the United States and France. Three days later, the whole army gathered in grateful morning prayer, then turned out for inspection and parade. The brigades were assembled, and after the good news was proclaimed, there was a graduated firing of arms that continued until all thundered together— "swelling and rebounding from the neighboring hills and gently sweeping along the Schuylkill"—in one great triumphant salute. The men looked clean and smart, their arms in good order, polished and flashing with bayonets. As they cheered—"Long live the King of France!" "Long live the friendly European powers!" and "Long live the American States!" —their voices sounded, wrote one soldier, more musical than the most beautiful piece of music Handel ever wrote.

When it was all over, everyone applauded the commander in chief "with loud huzzas, which continued till he had proceeded a quarter of a mile, during which time," wrote an officer, "there were a thousand hats tossed in the air. His Excellency turned round with his retinue and huzzaed several times." It was a very different army from the one John Adams had dolefully watched march through Philadelphia the previous August and which Lafayette had first reviewed.

Indeed, an amazing kind of optimism now abounded in the camp. Dr. Albigence Waldo, so liable to complaint, broke into song:

> The day serene—joy sparkles round
> Camp, hills and dales with mirth resound,
> All with clean clothes and powder'd hair
> For sport or duty now appear,
> Here squads in martial exercise

There whole brigades in order rise,
With cautious steps they march and wheel.
Double—form ranks—platoons—at will.
Columns on columns justly roll,
Advance, retreat, or form one whole. . . .

Then diff'rent companies are found
Gathered on various plats of ground
Where'er the elastic ball will hop,
Or on clean, even places drop,
When the strong butt's propelling force
Mounts it in air, an oblique course,
One Choix at Fives are earnest here,
Another furious at cricket there. . . .

The improbable jollity of this idyllic scene, with the men at play or choreographed drill, spruced up, clean, and even attending to their hair, was shared by their commander in chief, who pitched ball and played at wicket with his aides.

T H E long-sought-after alliance with France had become almost inevitable. Even before the news of Burgoyne's surrender reached England—indeed, when the news of that disastrous campaign was still good—Sir William Pitt, at the opening of Parliament on November 18, had told his colleagues bluntly, "I know that the conquest of English America *is an impossibility*. You cannot, I venture to say it, *you cannot* conquer America. . . . My lords, you *cannot conquer America.*" And he left them with this thought: "If I were an American, as I am an Englishman, while a foreign troop was landed in my country, I would never lay down my arms—never—never—never!"

Two days before, Edmund Burke had introduced a "Bill for composing the present Troubles in America" and had predicted that France and Spain would eventually combine against England. "Be very sure," he declared, "this country is utterly incapable of carrying on a war with America and these powers acting in conjunction."

Meanwhile, clandestine French aid in arms, artillery, ammunition, clothing, shoes, and other supplies had been flowing into American ports since the summer of 1776, and the previous March France had contributed 3 million livres without interest for the duration of the war. "All Europe," Adams had written a colleague, "wish us well, excepting only Portugal and Russia . . . all the ports of France and Spain and Italy and all the ports in the Mediterranean, excepting Portugal, are open to our privateers and merchant ships. . . . In short, my friend, although we have many grievous things to bear, and shall have more; yet there is nothing wanting but patience." He had been right.

After news of Burgoyne's capitulation reached London on December 2, Pitt pleaded for a reconciliation with the colonies in time to prevent a French alliance from coming about. But the government moved slowly and not with a whole heart. Although rumors of negotiations between France and the colonies had tormented the cabinet for months, it was not until Lord North learned that a treaty of some sort had actually been signed in Paris that in a last desperate measure to prevent its ratification by Congress, he belatedly asked Parliament, on February 17, to repeal both the tax on tea and the Coercive Acts, and to authorize the dispatch of new peace commissioners to negotiate an end to hostilities.

The bills passed easily, but it was immediately apparent to all that North would never have framed such broad concessions, reversing the government's policy of the last three years, unless it appeared that England would soon be at war with France. When North had completed his presentation, "a dull melancholy for some time followed his speech," wrote Edmund Burke, "then Astonishment, dejection and fear overwhelmed the whole assembly."

The treaty between France and the United States bound France to help the colonies win their independence and the Americans, in turn, to help France if a war between France and Great Britain should result. Both agreed not to conclude peace with Great Britain without the other's consent. This defensive alliance was coupled with treaties of amity and commerce, which promised a special and enduring relationship between the two states.

Other European powers had begun to reconsider their positions, and in the end, the greater part of Europe, including Spain, Holland, and Prussia, followed the French example, with Russia, Denmark, and Sweden also emerging as openly hostile to British arms.

For its peace commissioners, the British chose George Johnstone, who had been governor of West Florida; William Eden, a brother of the last royal governor of Maryland; and the earl of Carlisle. Before sailing, they met with Lord North, George Germain, and other members of the British cabinet at the prime minister's residence, but "little passed between us of any real importance," recalled the earl of Carlisle later, "and I confess I came away by no means satisfied with the conversation, and not a little shocked at the slovenly manner with which an affair so serious in its nature had been dismissed."

Reports of the new British initiative soon reached America, and Congress prepared its response in advance. On April 22, it indicated a willingness to negotiate if Great Britain "as a preliminary thereto" either withdrew its forces or acknowledged "in positive and express terms" American independence. At the same time, recounting the infamies of British aggression, it warned the public against efforts to "lull you with the fallacious hopes of peace, until they can assemble new armies to prosecute their nefarious designs." The British mission was next to hopeless, and it proceeded in a way which ensured its hapless fate. In a misguided attempt to stir up old colonial animosities toward the French, the commissioners published a vitriolic attack on America's new allies and also appealed over the heads of the Congress to the population at large. The old imperial condescension also remained. On June 13, when they presented their proposals to Congress in writing, they bound them up in a packet with triple seals depicting a fond mother embracing her prodigal child.

On June 17, all thirty-one delegates to Congress as well as all thirteen states unanimously voted to reject the proposals. Afterward, Joseph Reed claimed that one of the commissioners, Johnstone, had tried to win him over with a £10,000 bribe. Before Congress, he rather grandly declared that "the king of England was not rich enough" to buy him. In any case, there was now a general conviction that, given a French alliance, the British could not win. "The subjugation of the colonies," Kalb wrote his wife, "is now out of the question." Commissioner William Eden thought so, too. "It is impossible to see even what I have seen of this magnificent country," he said with a kind of anguish on June 18, "and not to go nearly mad at the long train of misconducts and mischances by which we have lost it." Lord Carlisle diverted himself from such melancholy thoughts with a pet raccoon, which he took back to London.

The Franco-American alliance changed London's strategic thinking as the American Revolution became a world war. British ministers now had to concern themselves with securing the West Indies and their sugar plantations, the long sea route around the Cape of Good Hope, India and its wealth, the English Channel, French Canada, the neutrality of Holland, and the disposition of Spain, as well as Washington's army. France was capable of disputing Great Britain's command of the sea, and since it could not be known in advance whether the French would attack the English in America or the West Indies—or both at once—Britain decided to evacuate her forces from Philadelphia, where they were vulnerable to blockade, and concentrate them at New York. From New York, reinforcements could be expeditiously sent to wherever they were required.

In the British North American command, there had also been a change at the top. Howe had long since written to Germain to say that since it appeared to him that he no longer enjoyed the confidence of the government, it would be inappropriate for him to remain at his current post. He also declared the war hopeless unless London poured in 35,000 more troops. This discouraging letter from the general who had brought Britain her only triumphs and who had just taken the rebel capital, reached North on December 1, just one day before he learned of Burgoyne's disastrous defeat.

If Howe's lassitude infuriated and dismayed the loyalists, he had remained popular with his troops. They learned on March 27 that he was to be replaced by Sir Henry Clinton, and on May 25 they gave him a huge send-off with festivities that included a fantastic pageant worthy of that staged for the Roman emperor Claudius on the Fucine Lake. The day began with a regatta on the Delaware River involving hundreds of people in costume riding in decorated galleys and flatboats, and a barge devoted to the British army band. The regatta landed near a triumphal Doric arch, two small amphitheaters, and a carousel. In the amphitheaters were horses on parade, heralds, knights fitted out for a mock joust, and ladies, with names drawn from medieval romance, gallivanting about in lavish attire. There was a joust between the Black Knights (of the "Burning Mountain") and the White Knights (of the "Blended Rose"), followed by "a magnificent bouquet of rockets" that began with fireworks culminating in "bursting balloons." This display signaled the beginning of a banquet that was served in an enormous arcade decorated with artificial flowers, mirrors, chandeliers, and green silk festoons. When Howe entered, "twenty-four black slaves in Oriental dress with silver collars and bracelets, were ranged in two lines and bowed to the ground." At the end of the banquet, the herald of the Blended Rose, attended by his trumpeters, entered and toasted the health of the royal family, the army, navy, and their respective commanders, and the knights and their ladies, each with a musical piece. After that, everyone danced until four in the morning.

This extravagant affair—or "meschianza" (an Italian word meaning "medley"), as it was called—had been imagined, designed, and arranged by John André, an amorous and romantic captain in the British service with a taste for intrigue and a talent for theatricals, idealized portraits, and light verse.

Not all British sympathizers reveled in the spectacle, however. The loyalist Judge Thomas Jones, for example, impatient for a different kind of triumph, accurately observed, "The exhibition of this triumphal Mischianza will be handed down to posterity, in the annals of Great Britain and America, as one of the most ridiculous, undeserved and unmerited triumphs ever yet performed. Had the General been properly rewarded for his conduct while Commander-in-Chief in America, an execution and not a Mischianza would have been the consequence."

And Ambrose Serle, Howe's secretary, confided to his diary, "Our Enemies, will dwell upon the Folly and Extravagance of it with Pleasure. Every man of Sense, among ourselves, tho' not unwilling to pay a due Respect, was ashamed of this mode of doing it." Serle could only sigh at its prodigality and bad taste.

I N mid-June, Sir Henry Clinton learned that a powerful French fleet under Admiral Charles Hector, comte d'Estaing, had sailed for America from Toulon and might arrive any day and blockade the Delaware. To avoid entrapment, most of the British cavalry and artillery, two regiments of Hessians, and some 3,000 loyalists with their movable property were sent to New York by sea, while the rest of the army—9,000 strong, with a baggage train of 1,500 wagons that extended almost twelve miles—set out on a forced march across New Jersey.

In mid-May, anticipating the British evacuation, Washington had ordered out almost a third of his effective troops (2,200 men) under Lafayette to patrol the area between the Delaware and the Schuylkill "to obstruct the incursions of the enemy's parties, and to obtain intelligence of their motions and designs." Washington's letter of instructions betrayed some anxiety as to whether the marquis could handle the assignment. "You will remember that your detachment is a very valuable one," he told him, "and that any accident happening to it would be a very severe blow to this army. You will therefore use every possible precaution for its security, and to guard against a surprise." Lafayette was diligent and cautious, but the British almost caught him anyway when they brought out an overwhelming force to try to trap him between the two rivers. According to Lafayette in his *Mémoires,* Clinton was so sure of his success in advance that he invited a number of ladies and gentlemen to a party in Philadelphia where the marquis was to be the featured guest. But the British pincers did not close. On the night of May 18, the marquis discovered a ford across the Schuylkill that had escaped the notice of British topographers, and he led his detachment to safety with a trifling loss. Thanks in part to Steuben's training, he was able to do so in an orderly manner, while Washington, preparing to go to Lafayette's aid, was able in less than fifteen minutes to have his whole army under arms and ready to march.

In mid-July 1778, British forces left Philadelphia and started northward through New Jersey toward New York. Washington learned of Clinton's movement around noon on July 18 and sent a Continental brigade, a rifle corps, and New Jersey militia ahead to harass his line of march. For several days running they kept close enough to the British to reach their campgrounds an hour after they had left. He also directed six brigades under Charles Lee and Anthony Wayne to hurry in pursuit, with three more divisions to follow the next morning. Meanwhile, Clinton's progress was slow, both because of his immense baggage train and because "the rebels had taken care to break down all the bridges, blow up the causeways and fill up the wells in the route which it was supposed the British army would take." In revenge, the British vandalized the land through which they passed, killing cattle in the fields and pastures, cutting down fruit trees, filling up wells with earth.

Early in the morning of the twenty-fourth, Washington conferred with his officers and decided to force a confrontation. Lee, according to Alexander Hamilton, was "the *primum mobile*" of a more cautious plan, to "keep up a vain parade of annoying them by detachment." Washington's strategy, however, was adopted, and Lee insisted on commanding the vanguard. Afterward, he changed his mind, then changed it again twice, until Washington, weary of his vacillation, assigned it to Lafayette, with Wayne as second in command. Their object was to attack the enemy's rear at the first opportunity, with the rest of the army coming up to support the action or, if necessary, to cover the vanguard in retreat. On the face of it, the attack had few risks. The rear guard—roughly 6,000 men under Clinton and Cornwallis—would be separated from the vanguard by the baggage train, making it difficult for the van to double back; if Clinton were pinned down, he would be forced to fight the American main army, marching up to attack. On the other hand, the British rear guard was made up of elite troops, which was not the usual disposition of forces in retreat. Washington read it correctly as being a reverse vanguard intended, if necessary, to spearhead a counterattack, and he quickly reinforced his advance corps with two brigades. To appease General Lee, who was smoldering with resentment, he placed him in charge of these brigades and gave him overall authority over Lafayette. By noon on the twenty-seventh, the 5,000 men of their combined command linked up at Englishtown. There Washington conferred with Lee and ordered him to attack Clinton's column the next day, "when the front was in motion, or marched off." Lee decided, however, that it would be "better," as he put it, "to act according to circumstances." On June 28, Lee approached the British rear guard near Monmouth Court

House in Freehold, New Jersey, as Washington came forward with his main army in support. The Americans "did not need much haranguing to raise their courage," recalled one soldier, "for when the officers came to order the sick and lame to stay behind as guards, they were forced to exercise their authority to the full extent before they could make even the invalids stay."

But Lee did not take advantage of the enthusiasm. Instead, he advanced in a haphazard and disorderly fashion, changed the position of his troops two or three times by retrograde movements, which threw them into confusion, then allowed some of his units to engage the British while others stood idly by. His idea of acting according to circumstances created havoc all down the line. Without a plan of coordinated action, "individual units were left to shift for themselves." Washington sent forward an aide to Lee for an explanation. Lee replied curtly, "Tell the General I am doing well enough."

It was a blistering hot day, and some of the men began to fall from sunstroke; "it was almost impossible," recalled one soldier, "to breathe." Lee proceeded with his platoon through a deep narrow valley, covered with thick woods, and emerged onto an Indian cornfield surrounded on three sides by tall, thick trees. The men drew back into the woods a bit for shade and then, to their mortification, received orders to retreat. Washington now rode forward to see for himself what was going on. To his astonishment, he found the whole advance guard marching away from the British line.

Lafayette now witnessed the confrontation that occurred between Washington and Lee. As they came up to each other, Washington cried, "What is the meaning of this, sir? I desire to know the meaning of this disorder and confusion!" "The American troops," said Lee, "would not stand the British bayonets." "You damned poltroon," shouted Washington, "you never tried them!" Wrote Lafayette afterward, "It was the only time I ever heard General Washington swear."

It is not certain, in this famous encounter, that Washington's language was quite that temperate. General Charles Scott of Virginia, who also fought at Monmouth, claimed that Washington "swore on that day till the leaves shook on the trees." If so, Washington hardly paused long to do it, for, passing through the ranks, he at once countermanded Lee's order before dashing into the middle of the field to get a better view of the advancing enemy. "He remained there some time upon his old English charger," wrote an eyewitness, "while the shot from the British artillery were rending up the earth all around him." Then he ordered two brigades to make a stand at a fence to delay the enemy while behind them artillery was drawn up on a ridge with a detachment of troops somewhat lower down on the slope protecting it in front. The two brigades held the British at bay until they were forced to abandon the fence by an overwhelming charge. The British then set up their own artillery on the spot, and both sides exchanged cannonades.

In a striking demonstration of their training under Steuben, Lee's broken ranks now rallied and wheeled into line under heavy fire as calmly and precisely as if the battlefield had been a parade ground. Lafayette later recalled that Washington rode up and down "amid the shouts of the soldiers, cheering them by his voice and example and restoring to our standard the fortunes of the fight."

One of the artillerymen had his wife with him, and she helped him man his gun. This was Mary Ludwig Hayes, who had done equally brave service at Fort Clinton, where, in October 1777, she had actually fired the last shot before the fortress fell. At Monmouth, according to a fellow soldier, "while in the act of reaching a cartridge and having one of her feet as far before the other as she could step, a cannon shot from the enemy passed directly between her legs, without doing any other damage than carrying away all the lower part of her petticoat. Looking at it with apparent unconcern, she observed that it was lucky it did not pass a little higher, for in that case it might have carried away something else, and continued her occupation." After the battle, she did legendary service carrying water for the wounded, which earned her the nickname "Molly Pitcher," by which all such battlefield angels have since been known.

The battle continued for several hours under the broiling sun, both sides giving and taking patches of ground, but without a decisive action. Toward evening, the two armies drew off. Each had lost about 350 men, more to heat than to bullets, but the Americans looked forward to renewing the contest in the morning. The British, however, counting up their losses, slipped noiselessly away into the night and hurried toward Sandy Hook, where Lord Howe was waiting with his fleet.

Although Lee's artificially orchestrated retreat had prevented an American victory, the Continentals, as refashioned by Steuben, had fought the flower of the British forces to a draw. "Tell the Philadelphia ladies," said Wayne, "that the heavenly sweet pretty redcoats, the accomplished gentlemen of the guards and grenadiers, have humbled themselves on the fields of Monmouth."

Clinton reached Sandy Hook on July 1 and there embarked his army for New York. Washington, unable to catch up with him, crossed the Hudson River from King's Ferry near Haverstraw to Westchester County and undertook, by a cordon of military posts strung from the Delaware River to Long Island Sound, to imprison Clinton's army on Manhattan Island. As of July 1778, the two hostile armies were therefore exactly where they had been in 1776—New York and Newport being the only points the British had managed to hold. "It is not a little pleasing," observed Washington, "nor less wonderful to contemplate that [fact]."

C O N G R E S S had adjourned from York on June 27 and on July 2 reconvened in Philadelphia. Public celebrations were held on July 4, and that Sunday the delegates attended church in a body "to return thanks for the divine mercy in supporting the independence of these states."

Returning residents, however, found Philadelphia despoiled. All the fences were demolished, many houses in the suburbs had been pulled to pieces, evidently for firewood, and those in the center of the city had been left in ruins. Some of the houses had been used for stables and "holes cut in the parlor floors to clean them out." Churches had been stripped of their pews, gravestones overturned, the city's squares and commons churned to mud and littered with debris. The north side of the city was "so much altered," wrote one, "that people who were born here and have lived here all their lives are much at a loss to find out the situation of particular houses . . . the fine fertile fields are all laid waste."

The "diplomatic immunity" that, at the beginning of the war, had spared the residences of important Bostonians had not been extended to Philadelphia's patriot elite. Benjamin Franklin's house had been pillaged, and his scientific instrument collection, as well as a portion of his personal library, had been carried away by John André. Charles Thomson found his summerhouse a ruin, and John Dickinson's magnificent country estate was a scene of wanton destruction. The red-brick State House, now known as Independence Hall, had been used as a hospital and left in deplorable shape. A nauseating stench rose from a pit nearby into which corpses had been thrown, and the first meeting of Congress had to be put off until the building was cleansed.

The morals of the inhabitants were also said to have been corrupted, for "it is agreed on all hands that the British officers played the devil with the girls. The privates, I suppose, were satisfied with the *common* prostitutes." Not every American was unhappy with the change. After the Fourth of July celebration at Philadelphia's City Tavern, one officer remarked, "Here it is all gaiety and every lady and gentleman endeavors to outdo the other in splendor and show. The manners of the ladies are much changed. They have . . . lost their native innocence which formerly was their characteristic, and supplied its place with what they call an easy behavior. . . . You cannot conceive anything more elegant than the present taste."

Nevertheless, André's stupendous meschianza remained a scandal, and the returning forces lost no time in mounting a parody of it, in which "a noted strumpet," wrote an eyewitness, "was paraded through the streets with her head dressed in the modern *British* taste [an enormous headdress with a profusion of curls], to the no small amusement of a vast crowd. She acted her part well; to complete the farce, there ought to have been another lady of the same character (as General Howe had two), and somebody ought to represent a British officer."

H A R D L Y had Congress settled down to business than the French fleet of the comte d'Estaing arrived in Delaware Bay. On board was Conrad-Alexandre Gérard, the first French minister plenipotentiary to the United States. A committee met him at Chester in "a Barge with 12 Oarsmen dressed in Scarlet trimmed with Silver" and hailed him with a fifteen-gun salute. At the formal accreditation ceremony, President Henry Laurens, surrounded by the delegates, sat on a platform in a mahogany armchair before a large table covered with green cloth. Gérard addressed the assembly in French, professing his government's support for the Revolution, and after Laurens politely thanked him, everyone repaired to the City Tavern on Second Street to feast and drink. But tensions between the ambassador and some members of Congress soon ran high. Silas Deane, one of the three American commissioners to negotiate the treaty with France, had returned and was under a cloud. He was faulted for having offered lavish commissions to foreign officers and stood accused by another commissioner, Arthur Lee of Virginia, of engaging in private commercial ventures and misappropriating public funds. The principal question, however, was whether the supplies furnished to the United States by Beaumarchais prior to the alliance had constituted a debt to an individual, as Deane maintained, or a gift from France, as claimed by Lee. Beaumarchais, of course, had been acting as a secret agent for his government, but to admit this publicly would have exposed France's former neutrality as a fraud. On the other hand, to interpret the aid as a debt owed to a private person, rather than assistance from a foreign power, would inflict a financial burden on the United States greater than it could bear.

It was a matter to be settled behind closed doors. But the press became involved and, more particularly, Thomas Paine, who at the time was secretary to the congressional Committee of Foreign Affairs. In an article published in several installments in the *Pennsylvania Packet* and transparently written under the pen name "Common Sense," he asserted in January 1779 that official papers conclusively proved that the supplies furnished by Beaumarchais had been a free gift from France. Paine's divulgence of such top secret information transformed the issue from a congressional quarrel into an international incident. The French ambassador immediately called upon Congress to repudiate Paine's statement, and when the assembly took up Gérard's protest on January 7, Gouveneur Morris of New York pressed for Paine's dismissal, disparaging him as a "mere Adventurer from England, without Fortune, without Family or Connections, ignorant even of Grammar." The last was the unkindest cut of all.

T H E confrontation between Washington and Lee played itself out. Immediately after the Battle of Monmouth, Lee wrote to Washington:

Camp, English-Town, 1st July, 1778, SIR—From the knowledge that I have of your Excellency's character, I must conclude that nothing but the misinformation of some very stupid, or misrepresentation of some very wicked person, could have occasioned your making use of such very singular expressions as you did, on my coming up to the ground where you had taken post: they implied that I was guilty either of disobedience of orders, want of conduct, or want of courage. Your excellency will, therefore, infinitely oblige me by letting me know on which of these three articles you ground your charge, that I may prepare for my justification; which I have the happiness to be confident I can do to the army, to the Congress, to America, and to the world in general. Your excellency must give me leave to observe, that neither yourself, nor those about your person, could, from your situation, be in the least judges of the merits or demerits of our manoeuvres; and, to speak with a becoming pride, I can assert that to these manoeuvres the success of the day was entirely owing. I can boldly say, that had we remained on the first ground—or had we advanced—or had the retreat been conducted in a manner different from what it was, this whole army, and the interests of America, could have risked being sacrificed. I ever had, and I hope ever shall have, the greatest respect and veneration for General Washington; I think him endowed with many great and good qualities; but in this instance I must pronounce, that he has been guilty of an act of cruel injustice towards a man who had certainly some pretensions to the regard of every servant of his country; and I think, sir, I have a right to demand some reparation for the injury committed; and unless I can obtain it, I must, in justice to myself, when the campaign is closed, which I believe will close the war, retire from a service, at the head of which is placed a man capable of offering such injuries;—but at the same time, in justice to you, I must repeat that I, from my soul, believe that it was not a motion of your own breast, but instigated by some of those dirty earwigs, who will for ever insinuate themselves near persons in high office; for I am really assured that, when General Washington acts from himself, no man in his army will have reason to complain of injustice and indecorum.

I am, sir, and I hope ever shall have reason to continue, Yours, &c.
CHARLES LEE.

Washington replied:

Head-quarters, English-Town, June 28, 1778
SIR—I received your letter, dated through mistake the 1st of July, expressed, as I conceive, in terms highly improper. I am not conscious of having made use of any singular expressions at the time of my meeting you, as you intimate. What I recollect to have said was dictated by duty, and warranted by the occasion. As soon as circumstances will admit, you shall have an opportunity, either of justifying yourself to the army, to Congress, to America, and to the world in general, or of convincing them that you are guilty of a breach of orders, and of misbehaviour before the enemy on the 28th instant, in not attacking them as you had been directed, and in making an unnecessary, disorderly, and shameful retreat.

I am, sir, your most obedient servant,
G. WASHINGTON.

This was about as strong a letter as Washington ever wrote, and Lee was stunned. Whatever Washington had said on the spot, he was now saying, unmistakably, that Lee was guilty of insubordination and cowardice in action. In response, Lee foolishly challenged Washington to ask a court to judge which of them was the more capable general. ("You cannot afford me greater pleasure," Lee wrote, "than in giving me the opportunity of showing to America the sufficiency of her respective servants. I trust that the temporary power of office and the tinsel dignity attending it will not be able, by all the mists they can raise, to obfuscate the bright rays of truth. In the meantime your Excellency can have no objection to my retiring from the army.") Shortly thereafter, he asked that a court-martial decide the case.

Washington immediately placed Lee under arrest, granted his wish to be tried, and informed him of the charges: "disobedience of orders in not attacking the enemy," "misbehavior before the enemy by making an unnecessary, disorderly and shameful retreat," and "disrespect to the commander-in-chief in two letters, dated the 1st of July and the 28th of June."

A court-martial was convened and found Lee guilty on all counts (though the word "shameful" was stricken from the second charge), and he was suspended from his command. Congress approved the sentence, then dismissed him from the service altogether after he wrote the president of Congress an insulting note.

Lee remained Washington's implacable foe. In his calumnies, he seemed unable to curb his venom, and at length Colonel John Laurens, one of Washington's aides, challenged him to a duel and shot him in the side. Lee survived and retired to a secluded corner of Virginia, where he reportedly lived like a hermit in a windowless hovel, alone with his dogs. In the fall of 1782, forlorn and broken, he moved to Philadelphia, took lodgings in an ordinary tavern, the Sign of the Conestoga Wagon, and died of tuberculosis on October 2. Virtually his only attendants were two faithful dogs. In vain they attempted to awaken their dead master, lay down by his corpse, and for a long time refused to move.

Lee remained peevish to the last. He wrote in his will, "I desire most earnestly that I may not be buried in any church or church-yard, or within a mile of any Presbyterian or Anabaptist meeting house; for since I have resided in this country, I have kept so much bad company while living, that I do not choose to continue it while dead." His wishes were disregarded, and he was buried in the yard of Christ's Church in Philadelphia, though in an unmarked grave. For all that, some part of him secretly longed for the company and human warmth he pretended to scorn. His last words were "Stand by me, my brave grenadiers."

PART
TWO

1. British fleet repulsed.
June 28, 1776.

2. British capture Savannah.
December 29, 1778.

3. French and American assault repulsed.
October 9, 1779.

4. Lincoln surrenders to Clinton.
May 11, 1780.

5. Tarleton massacres Americans
at Waxhaw. May 29, 1780.

6. Gates defeated by Cornwallis.
August 16, 1780.

7. Ferguson defeated at
Kings Mountain. October 7, 1780.

8. Morgan defeats Tarleton.
January 17, 1781.

9. Greene confronts Cornwallis.
March 15, 1781.

10. Rawdon confronts Greene in Battle
of Hobkirk's Hill. April 25, 1781.

11. Rawdon abandons Fort Ninety Six.
July 3, 1781.

12. Lafayette repulsed by Cornwallis.
July 6, 1781.

13. Greene victorious at Eutaw Springs.
September 8, 1781.

14. Washington defeats Cornwallis.
October 19, 1781.

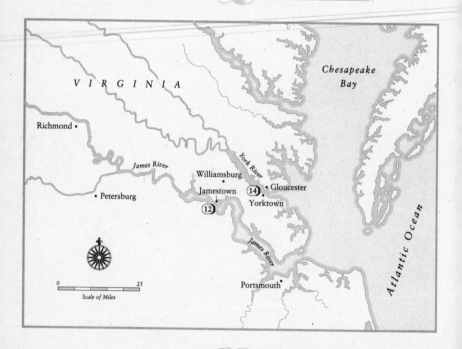

The
AMERICAN REVOLUTION
in the SOUTH

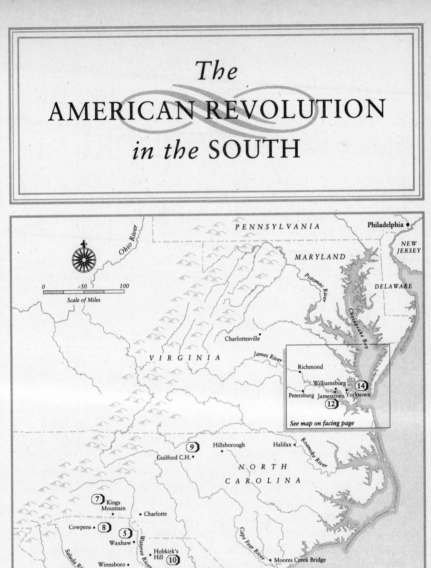

CHAPTER THIRTEEN

FROM NEWPORT
to
STONY POINT

D'ESTAING'S fleet had failed to catch Admiral Howe carrying Clinton's troops back to New York, but after Washington and d'Estaing conferred, they decided to attack the British fleet in the harbor. The French fleet was superior to that of the British and consisted of twelve ships of the line and six frigates, not counting d'Estaing's own magnificent flagship, the ninety-gun *Languedoc,* perhaps the finest fighting ship afloat. If the naval battle went well, the two armies—d'Estaing had 4,000 troops on board—were to combine in a land and amphibious attack on New York.

Having crossed the Hudson with his army at King's Ferry, Washington encamped in readiness at White Plains about the middle of July. But much to his chagrin, d'Estaing's largest ships proved of too deep draft to pass over the bar at Sandy Hook, so it was decided instead to try to dislodge or capture the British garrison at Newport, Rhode Island. For the operation, the Americans mustered about 1,500 regulars and 8,000 New England militia under General John Sullivan in a joint operation with the French.

The militia assembled were not the most fit. According to one French officer, they presented a "laughable spectacle. All the tailors and apothecaries in the country must have been called out, I should think. One could recognize them by their round wigs. They were mounted on bad nags and looked like a flock of ducks in cross-belts. The infantry was no better than the cavalry, and appeared to be cut after the same pattern."

Newport was protected by batteries, a small naval force, and about 7,000 men, most within strongly entrenched lines extending across the island three miles from town. Nevertheless, the prospects of success seemed excellent. Not all the defenders were regulars, being mixed with loyalist volunteers, and the allied numbers were objectively overwhelming. The fleet was to force its way into the harbor as the Americans approached by land, with the French troops landing from their ships on the west side of the island while the Americans landed on the east. On July 29, the French fleet appeared south of Newport, and on August 8, Sullivan occupied the island's northern end. Some 4,000 French troops disembarked on Conanicut Island to the west.

An apprehensive Admiral Lord Howe sailed out of New York to attempt battle with d'Estaing, and as his thirty vessels came into sight, the French admiral, over Sullivan's irate objections, reembarked his forces and at once gave orders to sail. His fleet passed majestically in front of the enemy's earthworks, and each vessel gave them a broadside as it passed.

There was little wind, but what there was was favorable to the French as they maneuvered for position in the open seas. But just as the two fleets were about to engage, a tremendous gale arose and both were dispersed. A number of vessels on either side were crippled by its batterings, the *Languedoc* itself was dismasted and nearly captured, and the British ship *Somerset* was shipwrecked off Cape Cod. The *Somerset*'s 480 British seamen and naval officers were also captured, along with twenty-one of its big guns which, were salvaged from the wreck. These were taken to Boston and mounted on the harbor forts.

D'Estaing struggled back to Newport and Howe to New York. Meanwhile, Sullivan, having decided not to delay his operations, had advanced his men to within two miles of the British positions. He opened siege lines and began an artillery duel but needed d'Estaing's help to prevail. The latter, however, anxious to refurbish his fleet, declined to cooperate and withdrew even the three frigates he had left behind for the Americans' support. Sullivan lost his head and denounced the French as traitors as d'Estaing set sail for Boston for repairs. There resentment against his perceived betrayal erupted into street violence when a mob, decrying "monarchy and popery," beat up several French sailors, one of whom died.

The failure of the Newport expedition was exasperating to Washington, who wrote to his brother, "If the garrison of that place . . . had been captured, as there was in appearance at least, a hundred to one in favor of it, it would have riven the finishing blow to British pretensions of sovereignty over this country and would, I am persuaded, have hastened the departure of the troops in New York as fast as their canvas wings would carry them away." Indeed, it is doubtful the British could have survived the blow of another army surrendering so soon after Saratoga, but the immediate effect of the debacle was instead to creat a serious rift between the French and American commands. In its aftermath, Washington cautioned Sullivan, "Prudence dictates that we should put the best face upon the matter." At the same time, he asked Lafayette, who had come close to challenging Sullivan to a duel, to do his utmost to "afford a healing hand to the wound that unintentionally has been made." Some successful naval action on d'Estaing's part might have added balm to the wound, but on November 4 he set sail for the West Indies, despite his instructions, which had required him, before doing so, to perform "some action advantageous to the Americans, glorious for the arms of the King, and fitted to show the protection which his Majesty extends to his allies."

ALTHOUGH the alliance with France had been a triumph of American diplomacy as well as arms, considerable delicacy and tact were needed to sustain it, as the altercation between Sullivan and d'Estaing and the furor surrounding the Silas Deane affair suggest. Among Americans in general, there was a lingering distrust of France, whose North American ambitions they had opposed for so long. Washington himself continued to wonder if France hoped to recover Canada, and when plans were occasionally submitted to him for Canadian campaigns, he suspected there might be in them "more than the disinterested zeal of allies." In any case, there was no denying that the French and their Indian proxies had probably drawn as much American blood in past fighting as the English had thus far shed in the war. But now the Americans and French were bound together in martial effort and fraternal enterprise.

Within that context, the Silas Deane affair had been an extremely delicate one involving high policy, intrigue, covert operations, and a dummy corporation, all bearing on the cultivation of a relationship critical to the success of the war. But however valuable, Deane's dealings had also aroused suspicion that he had tried to enrich himself by double billing—that is, by charging Congress for French supplies sent as "gifts." Those who took sides in the matter automatically risked their careers, and it was Thomas Paine's misfortune, as mentioned, that he not only became involved but indiscreetly leaked privileged, sensitive information entrusted to him as secretary of the Committee of Foreign Affairs. As a result, he was reduced from his lofty post to a clerkship in a local Philadelphia law office. Before long, he found himself once again in financial straits, having donated the proceeds from his pamphlets to the war.

For its first official envoys to Paris, the Continental Congress had turned to Benjamin Franklin, Thomas Jefferson, and Silas Deane. Jefferson, declining, had been replaced by Arthur Lee, but Jefferson's refusal to serve (and withdrawal from Congress) brought down upon him the muted wrath of some of his distinguished colleagues. Richard Henry Lee, when informed that Jefferson had excused himself on the grounds of "family affairs," wrote to him, "I heared with much regret that you had declined both the voyage, and your seat in Congress. No Man feels more deeply than I do, the love of, and the loss of, private enjoyments; but let attention to these be universal, and we are gone, beyond redemption lost in the deep perdition of slavery." John Adams wrote to him in a more sympathetic vein: "We want your Industry and Abilities here [in Congress] extreamly. . . . Pray come and help Us, to raise the Value of our Money, and lower the Prices of Things. . . . Your Country is not yet, quite Secure enough, to excuse your Retreat to the Delights of domestic Life. Yet, for the soul of me, when I attend to my own Feelings, I cannot blame you."

In fact, with a kind of zest and urgent enterprise, Jefferson had returned to Virginia to work on legislation to reform land tenure (still held on a somewhat feudal basis, as tied to the law of inheritance by primogeniture), extend suffrage, abolish the death penalty except for murder and treason, and put an end to the importation of slaves into the state. He did not succeed as to the last, as he later explained: "It was found that the public mind would not bear the proposition. . . . Yet the time is not distant when it must bear and adopt it, or worse will follow. . . . Nothing is more certainly written in the book of fate than that these people are to be free."

Jefferson also drafted Virginia's Statute for Religious Freedom, which promoted broad religious toleration and the separation of church and state. That statute, eventually ratified in 1786, made it law "that no man shall be compelled to frequent or support any religious worship, place of ministry whatsoever" or "suffer on account of his religious opinions or beliefs; but that all men shall be free to profess, and by argument maintain their opinions in matters of religion, and that the same shall in no wise diminish, enlarge or affect their civil character." In Virginia at the time—though such laws were rarely enforced—heresy could be punished by death, denial of the Trinity by three years in prison, and freethinkers and Unitarians could be deprived of their children because of their beliefs. But "Almighty God hath created the mind free," wrote Jefferson in his statute. "Our civil rights have no dependence on our religious opinions, any more than our opinions of physics or geometry. . . . *The opinions of men are not the object of civil government, nor under its jurisdiction.* . . . Truth is great and will prevail if left to herself. . . . She is the proper and sufficient antagonist to error, and has nothing to fear from the conflict unless by human interposition disarmed of her natural weapons, free argument and debate."

Jefferson's time in Paris would come later, after the Revolution had been won. But the delegation without him, as led by Franklin (probably the more skillful diplomat), had accomplished great things. For just that reason, when John Adams arrived in Paris in April 1778 to take Deane's place, he was aghast at the rancor he found. Arthur Lee suspected that Franklin's confidential secretary, Edward Bancroft, a Fellow of the Royal College of Physicians, was a spy (and he was right), but his own hostility to the French government opened the way for others to suspect that he himself was an Anglophile. Ironically, Lee's own secretary, whom he did not suspect, was on the British payroll. Adams tried to avoid being a partisan of either side, but he blamed most of the bad blood on Lee's "unhappy disposition" and his "prejudices and passions." "His countenance is disgusting," wrote Adams, "his air is not pleasing, his manners are not engaging, his temper is harsh, sour, and fierce, and his judgment of men and things is often wrong." Lee had been Deane's principal antagonist, but he had also been incessantly critical of Franklin, who finally told him bluntly that he had a "sick mind." And he warned him, "If you do not cure yourself of this temper, it will end in insanity."

Adams soon allowed himself to be drawn into the circle of retraction. Though he detested Lee, he also disapproved of the way Franklin lived his life, and regarded him as a kind of "indolent voluptuary who was neglecting his country's needs." "The Life of Dr. Franklin," he recalled years later, was "a Scene of continual dissipation," of late nights, amorous adventures, immoderate feasting, and audiences granted to an endless troop of supercilious admirers who came "to have the honor to see the great Franklin, and to have the pleasure of telling stories about his simplicity, his bald head and scattering straight hairs." As a result, complained Adams, he could rarely "obtain the favor of his company" in the mornings and often had to chase after him for several days to get him to sign some embassy document or other that he or Arthur Lee had drawn up.

Nevertheless, Adams was honest enough to recognize the pleasures at hand. "The delights of France are innumerable," he wrote to Abigail soon after his arrival. "The politeness, the elegance, the softness, the delicacy, are extreme. In short, stern and haughty republican as I am, I cannot help loving these people for their earnest desire and assiduity to please." Nor was he immune to their allure. Two weeks later, he confided, "If human nature could be made happy by anything that can please the eye, the ear, the taste, or any other sense, or passion, or fancy, this country would be the region for happiness. . . . To tell you the truth, I admire the ladies here. Don't be jealous. They are handsome and very well educated. Their accomplishments are exceedingly brilliant, and their knowledge of letters and arts exceed that of the English ladies, I believe." As for Franklin, he recognized that his great public stature and "character more beloved and esteemed than that of Leibniz or Newton, Frederick [the Great] or Voltaire," was of such advantage to the embassy that Adams could hardly wish him replaced. "His name was familiar to government and people, to kings, courtiers, nobility, clergy, and philosophers, as well as plebeians, to such a degree that there was scarcely a peasant or a citizen, a *valet de chambre*, coachman or footman, a lady's chambermaid or a scullion in a kitchen who was not familiar with it and who did not consider him a friend to human kind. . . . When they spoke of him they seemed to think he was to restore the golden age."

Adams therefore decided to be completely practical and concerned himself with routine consular duties and with straightening out the embassy's accounts.

All three of the original members of the embassy had run up large personal accounts that they had failed to distinguish from the public ones, and the record keeping was a mess. "Our affairs in this kingdom I find in a state of confusion and darkness," Adams wrote to his cousin Samuel. "Prodigious sums of money have been expended and large sums are yet due, but there are no books of account nor any documents from whence I have been able to learn what the United States have received as an equivalent." Deane had evidently embezzled some part of the money given or lent by European powers; while Franklin, who inhabited a covert world all his own, had deliberately kept a rather hazy and penumbral record of his own expenditures. Much later, "on having his accounts looked over by the [congressional] Committee appointed to do so," wrote a contemporary diarist, "there was found to be a deficit of 100,000 pounds. Franklin was asked how this happened. 'I was taught when a boy to read the scriptures and to attend to them,' said he very gravely, 'and it is there said: muzzle not the ox that treadeth out his master's grain.' A word to the wise, in this instance, seemed to be sufficient, and no further inquiry apparently was ever made into the deficient sum."

Franklin enjoyed a latitude granted to no other, and Congress's confidence in him seems to have been complete. Nor was it misplaced. Though an unabashed hedonist, Franklin was an incorruptible patriot, and his dissipation had nothing to do with the kind of profiteering in which Deane and others had engaged. *That* kind of selfish opportunism at the time was much discussed and was connected in the minds of Washington and others with the failure of the individual states to contribute their fair share to the war.

Although Congress could make requisitions upon the states for money or troop quotas, it had no way of enforcing its demands. In the frustrated assessment of General Greene, "The local policy of all the states is directly opposed to the great national plan; and if they continue to persevere in it, God knows what the consequences will be." He attributed the policy to "a terrible falling off in public virtue. . . . The loss of morals and the want of public spirit leaves us almost like a rope of sand," and pointed to the "luxury and dissipation" he saw around him—"the common ofspring of sudden riches"—as further evidence of the decay. Richard Henry Lee, in a letter to George Mason, similarly inveighed against "the demon of avarice, extortion, and fortune-making," and Washington wrote to Gouverneur Morris with equal disgust, "Can we carry on the war much longer? Certainly *no,* unless some measures can be devised and speedily executed to restore the credit of our currency, restrain extortion, and punish forestallers."

Toward the end of December, Washington went to Philadelphia to consult with Congress about the 1779 campaign. It was a discouraging encounter and provided an occasion for him to descant upon such themes: "If I was to be called upon to draw a picture of the times," he wrote to Benjamin Harrison,

and of the men, from what I have seen, heard, and in part know, I should in one word say that idleness, dissipation, and extravagance seem to have laid fast hold of most of them; that speculation, peculation, and an insatiable thirst for riches seems to have got the better of every other consideration and almost of every order of men; that party disputes and personal quarrels are the great business of the day whilst the momentous concerns of an empire, a great and accumulated debt, ruined finances, depreciated money, and want of credit (which in their consequences is the want of everything) are but secondary considerations. . . . I am alarmed and wish to see my Countrymen roused.

From Congress, Washington returned to his winter quarters, which he was then establishing in New Jersey, near the village of Middlebrook on the Raritan River. Seven brigades pitched their tents and built huts between the steep acclivities of the hills, while Henry Knox established his artillery park near Pluckemin, a few miles away.

The winter was an exceptionally mild one—scarcely any snow fell after January 10—and Washington's spirits seem to have revived in accord with the good cheer in his camp. Occasional soirees were held at the house occupied by the Knoxes and at the Dutch farmhouse on the banks of the Raritan occupied by the Greenes. Greene wrote to a friend, "We had a little dance at my quarters a few evenings past. His Excellency and Mrs. Greene danced upwards of three hours without sitting down. Upon the whole, we had a pretty little frisk." As for the lifestyle of the lesser officers, "We spend our time very sociably here," wrote one, "are never disturbed by the enemy, have plenty of provisions, and no want of whiskey grog. We sometimes get good spirits, punch, etc., and have Madeira sometimes. We have a variety of amusements. Last evening the tragedy of *Cato* was performed at Brunswick by officers of the army."

On February 18, the camp celebrated the first anniversary of the alliance with France. Guests arrived from all over the state, and in a kind of answer to the decadent meschianza staged by the British in Philadelphia, the occasion was marked by an impressive military review, followed by a banquet in a specially constructed "temple" designated "the Academy in the Park." The temple was supported by a colonnade with thirteen painted arches, each depicting some idea or event connected with the war. The first, inscribed "The scene opens," portrayed the start of hostilities at Lexington; the second, the burning of Charlestown, Falmouth, Norfolk, and other towns; the third, the separation of America from Britain—an arch broken in the center with the legend "BY YOUR TYRANNY to the people of America you have separated the wide arch of an EXTENDED empire." The fourth linked the fate of the British Empire to that of Babylonia, Egypt, and Rome with images of decay—a barren landscape littered with crumbling buildings, fallen spires, vultures hovering in the sky, and a gloomy setting sun. The remaining arches, by contrast, depicted an American empire on the rise. The fifth showed a bright sun beaming over a fertile land, cities emerging in the wilderness, and harbors filled with ships; the sixth featured an idealized portrait of King

Louis XVI of France as the patron of arts and letters and the benefactor of humanity; the seventh and central arch paid homage to THE FATHERS IN CONGRESS; the eighth showed Benjamin Franklin, as the American ambassador to France, extracting lightning from the clouds; the ninth and tenth, the defeat and surrender of Burgoyne; the eleventh, a naval battle between French and English ships; and the twelfth, several fallen American heroes resurrected in Elysium, where they received the thanks of Brutus, Cato, and other classical figures who had stood up to tyranny. Spanning this arch were the words THOSE WHO SHED THEIR BLOOD IN SUCH A CAUSE SHALL LIVE AND REIGN FOREVER. The thirteenth and final arch paid a hopeful homage to "Peace," which, in the figure of a woman, was shown presiding over unrestrained commerce and prosperity, with an olive branch in her right hand and the fruits of a harvest at her feet.

After the banquet, there were fireworks followed by a ball, which Washington opened by dancing a minuet with General Knox's wife.

On June 4, the army broke camp at Middlebrook and marched to the Hudson River highlands, which it appeared the British might attack. The main defenses of the highlands had been established at a narrow double bend of the river between West Point and Constitution Island, with forts on either side. The fortified heights rose as if in stories, with ancillary redoubts, in a complicated redundant defense protecting the principal fort. In addition to their ordnance, which was capable of demolishing any passing vessel with heavy fire, the Americans had stretched a huge iron chain across the river, stoutly moored to both banks. The chain rested on log pontoons just below the river's surface, and each link weighed about a hundred pounds.

Washington had also begun construction of two redoubts just below the highlands—at Stony Point on the west side of the Hudson and at Verplanck's Point on the east—to guard the mountain passes and the key crossing at King's Ferry. Both were still under construction when Clinton, intent on their capture, succeeded in routing their small garrisons before Washington could march to their aid.

Rather than attempt to retake them immediately, Washington made it his task, as he explained to a colleague, "to prevent a further progress on the river and to make the advantage of what they have now gained as limited as possible." Clinton, however, was less intent on advancing up the Hudson than in luring Washington down from his mountain fastnesses into a general engagement. Accordingly, he sent William Tryon, the last royal governor of New York, on a series of provocative raids. Tyron, operating from a fleet of warships and tenders, with 2,600 troops, plundered and ravaged a number of towns—including New

Haven, Fairfield, and Norwalk—along the Connecticut coast. Hundreds of dwellings, mills, shops, and even churches were destroyed, and on July 5 the village of Fairfield—"as large and as beautiful as any in the state"—was almost completely burned to the ground.

"The British troops were exceedingly abusive, especially to women," wrote one American colonel. "They solicited, they attempted their chastity; and though no rape was committed, yet some were forced to submit to the most indelicate and rough treatment." From Fairfield, Tryon sailed to Norwalk, which was likewise devastated, and "all the small privateers in the harbours and creeks along the Connecticut shore" were destroyed.

Congress seriously considered a scheme to hire incendiaries to burn London in retaliation, starting with the Royal Palace, but fortunately decided that would only contribute to the new ruthlessness with which the war was being carried on. The king felt no such restraint. As soon as France had entered the war, he was willing to support the sternest measures—to view the Americans, in fact, as foreigners. He also now subscribed to a kind of domino theory with respect to his colonial possessions, as he explained to a discouraged Lord North on June 11, 1779: "Should America succeed . . . the West Indies must follow them; Ireland would soon follow the plan and be a separate State . . . then this Island would be reduced to itself, and soon would be a poor Island indeed."

Meanwhile, in June, the British had begun to set up a naval base at Penobscot Bay in Maine from which to prey on American and French shipping along the New England coast. Twelve hundred militiamen were assembled to evict them, in an action to be coordinated with a fleet of nineteen armed ships with as many transports carrying 800 marines. But a quarter of these, according to an eyewitness, "appeared . . . to be small boys and old men unfit for service," and among them they had only "500 stand of arms." Nevertheless, the British position was weakly manned and poorly defended, with earthworks so low it was said "a soldier with a musket in each hand could jump over them." In the third week of July, the fleet stood off the coast and the militia landed. But when the fighting began, about a quarter of them fled. Dudley Saltonstall, the naval commander, might have moved in to destroy the two armed British sloops guarding the river, thereby giving the militia cover, but he chose not to do so, and the chance for a quick victory was lost.

The standoff lasted several days, which allowed British reinforcements to arrive from New York on four warships. They boldly went on the attack, and the American fleet scattered, some boats being beached, others set on fire. One officer wrote in his journal, "To attempt to give a description of this terrible Day is out of my Power. It would be a fit subject for some masterly hand to describe it in its true colors, to see four ships pursuing seventeen sail of our Armed Vessels, nine of which were stout Ships, Transports on fire, Men of War blowing up every kind of Stores on Shore, throwing about, and as much confusion as can possibly be conceived."

Meanwhile, instead of taking Clinton's bait, Washington had set his sights on Stony Point, which he thought might be retaken by a surprise attack. General Anthony Wayne was chosen to lead it and to use the bayonet. In this way, in commemoration of the Paoli Massacre outside Philadelphia, he was to exact a consonant revenge for that humiliating hour.

It was a perilous mission. The fort, situated on a rocky promontory, was surrounded on three sides by water and joined to the mainland by a causeway extending across a marsh. Its British garrison was 700 strong and equipped with heavy cannon behind sturdy ramparts with two rows of abatis at their base.

On the morning of July 15, Wayne, with a picked body of several hundred men, set out. He made his way around the side of Bear Mountain, then turned south along rough forest trails. In his plan of attack, he was to send his main column along a sandbar on the south side, a second up the north face, and a third along the causeway to divert the defenders from the bayonet attacks on their flanks. At about eight o'clock, he came within sight of the fort. Toward midnight, he gave each man a slip of white paper to fix in his hat as an insignia (so they could identify one another in the dark) and ordered all bayonets fixed and charges drawn. Then he exhorted them to do honor to themselves, their country, and their respective states. But he warned, "Should there be any soldier so lost to a feeling of honor as to retreat a single foot, or skulk in the face of danger, the officer next to him is immediately to put him to death that he may no longer disgrace the name of soldier, or the corps, or the state to which he belongs."

Wayne privately regarded the assault as suicidal. And he expected to die. As the men were eating their rations, he wrote to a friend to ask him to look after his family and protect his good name and reputation after his death. He dated his letter "15 July, 1779, near the hour and scene of carnage."

The troops advanced, "guided by a negro," according to Washington Irving, "who had frequently carried in fruit to the garrison and served the Americans as a spy. He led the way accompanied by two stout men disguised as farmers. The countersign was given to the first sentinel, posted on high ground west of the morass. While the negro talked with him, the men seized and gagged him. The sentinel posted at the head of the causeway was served in the same manner." The troops followed and at about one o'clock came up to the enemy pickets, who gave the alarm. Within a few moments, fire poured upon them from the fortress, but the Americans scrambled over the abatis and up the slope with such silence and speed that in just twenty minutes they had gained possession of the fort. Wayne, felled by a bullet which had grazed his skull, cried out to his aides, "Carry me up to the fort, boys! Let me die at the head of my column." But the wound turned out not to be serious, and he was soon writing to Washington with pride, "Our officers and men behaved like men who are determined to be free." Even more, they had the British at their mercy yet showed wonderful restraint. As a newspaper account put it at the time:

> Spurred on by their resentment of the former cruel bayoneting which many of them and others of our people had experienced and of the more recent and savage barbarity of plundering and burning unguarded towns, murdering old and unarmed men, abusing and forcing defenceless women, and reducing multitudes of innocent people from comfortable livings to the most distressful want, our people, deeply affected by these cruel injuries, entered the fort with the resolution of putting every man to the sword. But the cry of "Mercy! mercy! . . . quarter! Quarter!" disarmed their resentment in an instant, insomuch that even Colonel Johnson, the commandant, freely and candidly acknowledges that not a drop of blood was spilled unnecessarily. Oh, Britain, turn thy eye inward, behold and tremble at thyself.

"The humanity of our brave soldiery," wrote Wayne in his dispatch, "who scorned to take the lives of a vanquished foe . . . , reflects the highest honor on them and accounts for the few of the enemy killed." The loss to the Americans was fifteen killed and eighty-three wounded. Of the garrison, sixty-three were slain, including two officers, and 553 were made prisoners of war.

A month later, on August 19, a similar attack was made on the British outpost at Paulus Hook, a sandy spit west of the Hudson River. Like Stony Point, the hook was cut off from the mainland by salt marshes, making it accessible only at low tide, and strongly defended by a circular moat, abatis, two blockhouses, and ten cannon, all manned by a Hessian garrison of 248 men. Just before dawn on the nineteenth, a suicide squad cut through the abatis, and the men surged through the gap into the circular redoubt. Fifty Hessians fell to the American bayonets and 158 were captured, with only a handful of casualties on the American side.

Washington made no attempt to hold either post but did his best to destroy them and carry off their stores. The enemy immediately reoccupied and rebuilt them, but their losses and what was required of their efforts consumed their resources for a summer campaign.

The baron de Kalb, who served with Washington that summer in the highlands, described in letters back home what the service was like. He visited the posts and pickets of the army in the solitudes, woods, and mountains, clambering over the rocks and picking his way over rugged roads. When his horse fell lame, he had to make his way over long distances on foot, sometimes in the rain or blistering heat. On occasion, he would return from his duties without "a dry rag on me, and was so tired that I could not sleep." Yet he was unwilling to complain. "My temperate and simple habits greatly contribute to keep me in good health," he assured his wife, "and I hardly notice the annoyances of camp life. Dry bread and water make my breakfast and supper; at dinner I take some meat."

The typical repast of this major general was hardly better than that of his troops. A few days later, after a dinner of mutton and beef, he nicely conjured up from the meager circumstances of his meal the epic story of the war: "Large round crackers served as plates," he wrote, "in the absence of any kind of crockery. The scene forcibly reminded me of the conquest of Italy by Aeneas, and the words of Ascanius, when they had reached the future site of Rome. There, too, hunger compelled them to devour the cakes upon which their food had been served up, and recalled the oracle of the harpies, that they would not reach the end of their wanderings and toils, nor call Italy theirs, until they should have eaten their tables with their meals."

T H E northern theater of the war quieted down. The anticipated arrival of another French fleet and army obliged Clinton to evacuate Newport in October, bring off the garrisons from Stony Point and Verplanck's Point (which he had therefore refortified in vain), and concentrate his forces at New York. Washington made his spartan camp about West Point. There the chevalier César de la Luzerne, the new French minister plenipotentiary to the United States, paid a visit to him in the fall and was welcomed with a tremendous artillery salute. "[Washington] received us," recalled the marquis de Barbé-Marbois, secretary to the French legation, with a noble, modest, and gentle urbanity and with that graciousness which seems to be the basis of his character. He is fifty years old, well built, rather thin. He carries himself freely and with a sort of military grace. He is masculine looking, without his features' being less gentle on that account. I have never seen anyone who was more naturally and spontaneously polite. His eyes are blue and rather large, his mouth and nose are regular, and his forehead open. His uniform is exactly like that of his soldiers. Formerly, on solemn occasions, that is to say on days of battle, he wore a large blue sash, but he has given up that unrepublican distinction. I have been told that he preserves in battle the character of humanity which makes him so dear to his soldiers in camp. I have seen him for some time in the midst of his staff, and he has always appeared even-tempered, tranquil, and orderly in his occupations, and serious in his conversation. He asks few questions, listens attentively, and answers in a low tone and with few words. He is serious in business. Outside of that, he permits himself a restricted gaiety. His conversation is as simple as his habits and his appearance. He makes no pretensions, and does the honors of his house with dignity, but without pompousness or flattery. . . . He is reverent without bigotry, and abhors swearing, which he punishes with the greatest severity. As to his public conduct, ask his compatriots, and the universe. . . . His appearance and his actions reveal virtue, and he inspires it in all who surround him. . . . If you like historical parallels, I might compare him to Timoleon who freed the Sicilians from the tyranny of the Carthaginians, and who joined to his military qualities those which make up an excellent citizen, and who after having rendered his country signal services lived as a private citizen, ambitious neither of power nor honors, and was satisfied to enjoy modestly the glory of having given liberty to a powerful nation.

In so saying, Barbé-Marbois perfectly predicted Washington's retirement at the end of the war.

During their visit, Washington took the French envoys on a tour of the highland fortifications, sailing down the Hudson to West Point. "The general held the tiller, and during a little squall which required skill and practice, proved to us that this work was no less known to him than are other bits of useful knowledge." Divisions of his army were distributed among the hills in and about the forts and redoubts covering the heights. But his own headquarters were in a tent. There he and his staff entertained the guests with a modest feast, as the waves of the river, which had been driven back by the tide, "came right up to the tent-pins, where they broke with a solemn roar."

In the course of one conversation, Barbé-Marbois told Washington that Lafayette's service in America had earned him great esteem at home. "Washington," he recalled, "blushed like a fond father whose child is being praised. Tears fell from his eyes, he clasped my hand and could hardly utter the words: 'I do not know a nobler, finer soul, and I love him as my own son.' " Some months before, Lafayette had returned to France, and Washington had recently received an affectionate letter from him. "I have a wife who is in love with you," he had written, and he expressed the hope that Washington would visit France once the war was over. Washington thanked him for the invitation and replied playfully:

> Tell [your wife] . . . that I have a heart susceptible of the tenderest passion, and that it is already so strongly impressed with the most favorable ideas of her that she must be cautious of putting love's torch to it, as you must be in fanning the flame. But here, methinks, I hear you say, I am not apprehensive of danger. My wife is young, you are growing old, and the Atlantic is between you. All this is true, but know, my good friend, that no distance can keep anxious lovers long asunder and that the Wonders of former ages may be revived in this.

Then, with a touch of sadness perhaps, reflecting the weariness of war, he added, "[Still,] amidst all the wonders recorded in holy writ no instance can be produced where a young woman from real inclination has preferred an old man."

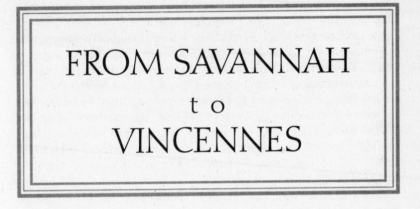

CHAPTER FOURTEEN

FROM SAVANNAH
t o
VINCENNES

Y and large, except for Lord Dunmore's early depradations, the South had been spared direct involvement in the war. After Sir Henry Clinton had been ingloriously repulsed from before Charleston in June 1776 and the Cherokees defeated on the frontier, the southern colonies had enjoyed a respite from hostilities of nearly three years, as the strength of the British had been concentrated upon the subjugation of the North. But that strategy had failed. Burgoyne had surrendered; France had entered the war; Philadelphia had been relinquished; and, although Clinton still held New York, the northern colonies remained as defiant as before. Nor were the middle colonies showing much inclination to submit. As a result, the British high command began to elaborate a scheme to conquer the American South by occupying Florida and Georgia, establishing a chain of forts across the Carolinas, and seizing Charleston, which, in the opinion of Lord Germain, would inspire the majority of the local population "to flock to the standard of the king." Indeed, British military planners saw the South as a loyalist stronghold. Once his majesty's troops moved into Virginia and Maryland, wrote Germain, perhaps "all America to the south of the Susquehanna would return to their allegiance and . . . the northern provinces might be left to their own feelings and distress to bring them back to their duty."

This was also the view of many loyalists, such as Isaac Ogden, who, it may be remembered, thought the Revolution could be crushed by one great "vigorous campaign, properly conducted. I mean by . . . a man of judgment, *spirit,* and *enterprise.*" In Clinton, the loyalists thought they had their man.

Clinton had grown up in New York, where his father had been royal governor, returned to England, entered the army, and by age eighteen had risen to lieutenant in the Coldstream Guards. By age twenty, he was a lieutenant colonel in the Grenadiers. During the Seven Years' War, he served as an aide-de-camp to Prince Ferdinand of Braunschweig, was promoted to major general in May 1772, and, after the Battle of Bunker Hill, to lieutenant general as second in command to Howe, who succeeded Gage. After his skillful performance in the Battle of Long Island and his subsequent capture of Newport, Rhode Island, he had been knighted by the king.

Clinton was cultivated and musical, sponsored concerts in occupied New York, where the works of Bach, Haydn, and Boccherini, among others, were performed; refurbished the John Street Theater (which was now renamed the Theater Royal); and financed performances of *Venice Preserved, She Stoops to Conquer, The Beaux' Strategem, Richard II, Richard III, Othello,* and the first performance in America of Sheridan's *The Rivals.*

With his American roots, he was considered a man around whom the "silent majority" of loyalists might rally. But though "gallant to a proverb and possessing great military knowledge in the field," according to William Franklin, he was also "weak, irresolute, unsteady, vain, incapable of forming any plan himself, and . . . too proud and conceited to follow that of another."

Such a combination was bound to be disastrous, since Lord Germain was careful in his instructions to absolve both himself and the king in advance of any failure in the field. He told Clinton, "I have thus stated the King's wishes and intentions, but he does not mean you to look upon them as orders, desiring . . . that you use your discretion in planning . . . all operations which shall appear the most likely means of crushing the rebellion." The plan was set, and in the fall of 1778 operations were begun.

Clinton sent a large detachment to the Caribbean to take the French island of Saint Lucia and another of 3,500 men under Scottish brigadier general Archibald Campbell to try to capture Savannah, Georgia. The main American defense line was drawn up about a half mile east of the city, and, though protected by swamps on either flank, it was poorly manned. In a swift and embarrassingly easy action, coordinated with

2,000 men who had advanced from Saint Augustine, Florida, the British landed their light infantry on December 29, swept a company of rebels off a bluff, and, wrote a British officer, "drove them instantly to the woods." A part of the British force advanced to attack the main American position straight on, while another, led by a slave named Quamimo Dolly, raced along a secret path through the swamps, circled around behind and caught the defenders unawares. The Americans scattered in retreat; 83 perished and 453 were captured, along with considerable artillery. As a result, "the capital of Georgia, the shipping in the harbor, with a large quantity of provisions, fell into our possession before it was dark." The British counted only three of their own men killed and ten wounded.

"Never was a victory of such magnitude so completely gained with so little loss," wrote an American major, and after the British moved inland and captured Augusta on January 29, 1779, Georgia was in their hands. In February, the Americans struck back when Brigadier General William Moultrie attacked a British detachment at Beaufort, South Carolina. He forced the British to retreat but then ran out of ammunition before he could pursue. A month later, Colonel Andrew Pickens of South Carolina defeated a band of Tories at Kettle Creek, Georgia, northwest of Augusta, but was then outflanked and defeated at Briar Creek on March 3.

After Savannah and Augusta had fallen to British troops, one of Clinton's officers laid before him some further thoughts for the prosecution of the war. Once the rebels realized that they could not drive the British from Georgia, he explained, "and the French fleet departed American waters, Britain would be free to undertake a campaign of retribution, 'distressing the countryside,' seizing and punishing rebel leaders, and 'living off of plunder.' Washington would have to do battle or suffer a humiliating retreat, the currency would collapse, Congress would lose all ability to punish deserters, and the people would 'see no end of their fruitless sufferings.' That is, by carrying the war to the whole society, by using plunder and destruction as psychological weapons—in short, by threatening to precipitate complete social chaos—Britain could convert dispirited rebels into desperate and disillusioned advocates of peace and submission."

One Virginia loyalist, subscribing to this doctrine, proposed a pincer attack on Williamsburg, "the metropolis of infamy." "I know the Virginians," he explained, and

An example of devastation would have a good effect, the minds of the people struck with a panic would expect the whole country to share the same fate. Offer rewards for bringing to justice the active rebels, let them be proportioned to their rank and consequence . . . , make proper examples, countenance and protect the inoffensive and honest farmers. This done, every rebel will suspect his neighbor, all confidence will cease, the guilty will retire in crowds to the back country without a possibility of removing provisions for their subsistence, hunger will make them desperate and open their eyes, they will fall on their destructive leaders, peace and submission, of course, must follow.

The danger was real, and Major General Benjamin Lincoln of Massachusetts was hurriedly dispatched to oppose the British advance.

It was also part of Clinton's strategy to launch attacks from the west, that is, from the northwest forts at Niagara and Detroit acquired from France in 1763. Acting at times through their Indian allies, the British in the summer and fall of 1778 had sponsored raids on outlying villages along the western borders of Pennsylvania and New York while marshaling a number of the southern tribes.

Perhaps the most savage raids of the war were those carried out by Tories and Indians against the Wyoming Valley settlements in northern Pennsylvania at the beginning of July 1778, and against those in New York's Cherry Valley on November 11 to 12. The loyalists afterward claimed the raids were provoked, because the local Committee of Public Safety had rounded up Tory males in the area and exposed their families to insult. But it is only the massacres that are remembered now.

In July 1778, Colonel John Butler, with 400 Tories and 500 Seneca and Delaware Indians, swept down from Fort Niagara upon the Susquehanna River settlements of the Wyoming Valley, overran three stockaded blockhouses, butchered their militia defenders, destroyed a thousand homes, took at least 227 scalps, and left the once beautiful and picturesquely settled valley a vale of tears. The garrison of the fort at Wilkes-Barre, lured out of their stronghold, were pursued "with the fury of devils," wrote the *New York Journal,* and, according to J. Hector St. John Crèvecoeur, "for a long time afterward the carcasses [of the slain] floated, and infested the border of the Susquehanna as low as Shamokin." Four months later, in November, 200 Tory Rangers and 500 Indians under Joseph Brant carried out similar depredations on Cherry Valley, about fifty miles west of Albany. There (according to the *New Jersey Gazette*):

the enemy killed, scalped and most barbarously murdered thirty-two inhabitants, chiefly women and children; also Colonel Alden and . . . [ten] soldiers of his regiment. . . . [Five] officers were taken prisoners . . . [as were] thirteen privates. [They] burnt twenty-four houses with all the grain, etc.;

took above sixty inhabitants prisoners . . . committed the most inhuman barbarities on most of the dead. Robert Henderson's head was cut off; his skull bone was cut out with the scalp. Mr. Willis' sister was ripped up; a child of Mr. Willis', two months old, scalped and arm cut off; the clergyman's wife's leg and arm cut off, and many others as cruelly treated.

At the behest of Congress, Washington organized a punitive expedition against the Six Nations and their white allies and offered the command to Gates. Washington meant no insult by the offer, but Gates declined in a reply that reflected the suspicion he still entertained toward his commander in chief: "The man who undertakes the Indian service should enjoy youth and strength, requisites I do not possess. It, therefore, grieves me that your Excellency should offer me the only command to which I am entirely unequal." By "only" he clearly implied that he was entirely capable of assuming the position held by Washington himself. Washington ignored Gates's letter and offered the command to General Sullivan.

Washington's instructions were harsh: Sullivan was to attack with "impetuosity," "ruin" the Indian crops, "prevent their planting more," and take as many hostages as possible. As insurance against future attacks, their settlements were to be not "merely overrun but destroyed." Although Americans today tend to think of all Indian communities as having been primitive, the settlements of the Six Nations, which ranged from the Catskill Mountains to Lake Erie, were substantial—not clusters of tepees but villages of wood and stone houses surrounded by beautiful orchards and cultivated fields. Joseph Brant, the Iroquois leader, had been educated at a church school in Connecticut, was a friend of James Boswell, the biographer of Samuel Johnson, a Freemason, and a member of the Anglican Church. He was also a savage partisan in the war.

In mid-May, Washington invited a number of Oneida Indian chiefs —hereditary foes of the Mohawk—from western Pennsylvania to his Middlebrook headquarters to enlist their support, and they rode along the line with him on their saddleless horses, wearing headdresses of eagle plumes, strings of bear claws, and large pendants dangling from their noses and ears. To Washington's wife, Martha, they looked "like cutthroats, all."

In July, Sullivan advanced with 4,000 men divided into two columns, one moving up the Susquehanna River, the other up the Mohawk Valley to Canajoharie. Twelve hundred packhorses were loaded with baggage, and 120 boats embarked up the river with artillery and stores. His progress, however, was slower than Washington had anticipated, and on July

29 the commander in chief wrote to him, "I cannot but repeat my entreaties that you will hasten your operations with all possible dispatch; and that you will disencumber yourself of every article of baggage and stores which is not necessary. . . . 'Tis a kind of service in which both officers and men must expect to dispense with conveniences and endure hardships."

Although the British were aware of Sullivan's coming, they doubted the field reports of the size of his force and therefore did almost nothing to protect their Indian allies. As a result, Sullivan had almost a free hand. In a monthlong campaign, he burned upward of forty Indian settlements —Newton, Catherineton, Kendaia, Canadosaga, and Genesee, among others—while laying waste hundreds of acres of orchards and cultivated fields. Genesee had 128 houses, some "very large and elegant," in Sullivan's own description, "beautifully situated and almost encircled with a clear flat extending for a number of miles." It grieved even him to make a desert of the land.

Indeed, however provoked, the campaign was a tragedy and did the Revolution little good. For it made the Indians even more dependent on the British (indeed, for their very survival) and sharpened their thirst for revenge.

LIKE the Iroquois in the North, the Cherokee, Creek, Choctaw, Chickasaw, and other tribes of the South and West allied themselves with the king's men. British agents furnished them with blankets, guns, powder, lead, tomahawks, and even rouge war paint—the Choctaw and Chickasaw being supplied from Mobile, the Indians north of the Ohio River (Shawnee, Miami, Wyandot, and Ottawa) from stockpiles at Fort Detroit. Detroit in turn was supplied by the British by way of the Saint Lawrence River, Lake Ontario, and Lake Erie. It was a long supply line. But the new villages and hamlets in Kentucky—and all along the southern bank of the Ohio River from Pittsburgh to Louisville—were shaken again and again by Indian attacks. Many of these raids were sponsored by British lieutenant colonel Henry Hamilton, known as the "Hair Buyer" because he promised rewards to his Indians for American scalps.

In response to such predations, George Rogers Clark, a Virginia militia officer who had spent his youth in the Kentucky and Ohio Valleys, raised a regiment to protect the western settlements. With 200 frontiersmen, he set out in flatboats down the Ohio River for Kaskaskia, an old French settlement ruled by the English with 250 houses and a stone fort, reached the town on July 4 and took it without firing a shot. He then divided his force into two. One party advanced on Cahokia on the Mississippi, the other on Vincennes on the Wabash River. Hamilton reacted vigorously and set out from Fort Detroit for Vincennes with 600 British regulars and several hundred Indian allies. From there he was to move against the other settlements Clark had captured, but because of his passion for scalps, he halted at Vincennes to allow the Indians to gather from among the white settlers of the area as many such trophies as they pleased. This savage indulgence on his part scattered and reduced his contingent and proved his undoing in the end.

Clark had been prepared to defend Kaskaskia, but when he learned that Hamilton had no more than eighty men in his garrison, he decided to attack. It was the depth of winter, and a number of the icy rivers had overflowed their banks. Clark knew that Hamilton could hardly suppose the Americans would be "so mad as to attempt to march eighty leagues through a drowned country" in that season and "would not even think it worth while to keep out spies."

In February 1779, he sent forty-six men on a large row galley armed with six light guns up the Ohio and Wabash Rivers to a point below Vincennes and, with 170 others, half of them French volunteers, set out overland toward the British post. He had four rivers and more than two hundred miles to cross, and the going was rough. To divert themselves from their daily sufferings, the men shot game, held Indian feasts by their campfires in the evenings, and ran splashing and hollering through the mud and water like the wildest of men. "Thus insensibly without a murmur," wrote Clark, did he lead his company on "through incredible difficulties far surpassing anything any of us had ever experienced before."

The area around Vincennes was inundated, but having made it thus far and overcome so much, the men had come to think of themselves as superior to other mortals and that nothing could keep them from their goal. Following Clark's example, they blackened their faces with powder and with war whoops plunged into the icy water, which at times rose up to their chests.

On February 23, they at last came within sight of the settlement, where Hamilton and his garrison were holed up in a stockade. After parading his troops around and around behind hills to give the impression of a thousand men, he marched into the village "with colors flying and drums brassed" in two columns just as evening fell. That night, almost all of Hamilton's artillerymen were picked off by American marksmen shooting through the loopholes of the fort.

Shortly after dawn, Clark called upon Hamilton to surrender. Hamilton refused, but during that afternoon a party of Indians allied to the British were captured with scalps while returning from a raid. Clark had them bound, taken to a clearing, and horribly executed within sight of the garrison. "One of them was tomahawked immediately," according to Hamilton. "The rest, sitting on the ground in a ring, seeing by the fate of their comrade what they had to expect," began to sing their death songs. "The chief of this party, after having the hatchet stuck in his head, took it out himself and delivered it to the inhuman monster who struck him first, who repeated his stroke a second and a third time, after which [he] ...was dragged by the rope around his neck to the river [and] thrown in."

When Hamilton's Indian allies saw that the British could not protect them and the British themselves saw what they might expect from Clark's men, they decided to capitulate. As the two commanders met to discuss the terms on the esplanade before the fort gate, Clark, according to Hamilton, "spoke with rapture of his late achievements while he washed the blood from his hands."

A F T E R the British had overrun a large part of Georgia and defeated the Americans at Briar Creek, they tried to advance against Charleston but were repulsed at Stone Ferry and driven back to Savannah, where, with the aid of d'Estaing's fleet, General Lincoln laid siege.

Although the comte d'Estaing had suffered a devastating defeat in his attempt to retake the West Indian island of Saint Lucia from the British in December 1778, he had captured the British islands of Saint Vincent's and Grenada the following July and in August (after receiving an urgent message from the Americans when he docked at Santo Domingo) had made for the Georgia coast. General Lincoln and South Carolina governor John Rutledge there prevailed upon him to join in a coordinated attempt to retake Savannah. On September 8, he came to the mouth of the Savannah River with twenty-two warships and ten frigates carrying 4,000 troops, took Tybee Island, and on the thirteenth landed his men at Beaulieu to prepare for the siege. Meanwhile, Lincoln had banded his troops back into their regiments and called out the Continentals from the Charleston forts. The French army lay before Savannah; Lincoln's army (1,350 strong, including a cavalry legion commanded by the Polish Count Kazimierz Pułaski) approached. On September 16, d'Estaing, having blockaded the river, demanded the surrender of the garrison, but General Augustin Prévost asked for twenty-four hours to consider. This was granted, and in that time Prévost strengthened his defenses while 1,800 British reinforcements also arrived.

Prévost was now determined to fight. Trenches were opened, and at midnight on October 3, the siege began.

Savannah was encircled by creeks, streams, and marshes, and some of the French ships ran aground. The French naval guns let loose a furious bombardment, but at two o'clock it was discovered, to d'Estaing's mortification, that a number of the shells had fallen onto the French army's own entrenchments after being "misdirected" by drunken cannoneers. At four o'clock, the suspended firing was resumed, but still "with more vivacity than precision. . . . Besides," wrote an attacker, "our projectiles did little damage to works which were low and constructed of sand."

This pathetic situation was all the more annoying to d'Estaing, who had hoped by the capture of Savannah to rehabilitate his tarnished reputation after his previous failure at Newport. And he grew impatient. "Having been now a month on our coast," recalled General Moultrie, "his officers remonstrated to him the dangerous situation the fleet was in and the hazards they ran of being attacked by the British fleet whilst theirs was in a bad condition and a great many of their officers and men on shore." D'Estaing consulted with his engineers, who told him it would take them at least ten more days to work their entrenchments into the enemy's lines. That seemed too long to him, and he decided to try to carry the works prematurely by storm. General Lincoln counseled forbearance, but d'Estaing threatened to abandon the operation if the Americans wouldn't go along.

Just before daybreak on October 9, the allies began their attack, as a force of 3,500 French troops, 600 Continentals, and 350 militia advanced across a swamp. They had counted on surprise, but the enemy were awake and waiting with their muskets cocked.

Among those most conspicuous for valor in the action that followed was Kazimierz Pułaski, who returned repeatedly to the assault in a vain attempt to charge through an opening in the enemy's lines. Within an hour, the whole area about the defenses, wrote a British officer, "was filled with mangled bodies, and the ditch filled with the dead." The French lost upward of 600 men, the Americans about 400. D'Estaing himself was among the wounded and Count Pułaski among the slain. British losses were 150 at most.

D'Estaing refused to cooperate further, and on the eighteenth the siege was raised. He retrieved what he could of his cannon and stores and returned to the West Indies, while Lincoln retreated to Charleston, which he was soon obliged to fortify against attack.

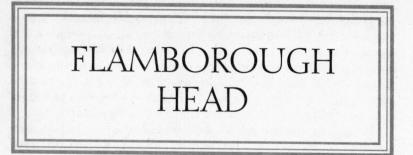

FLAMBOROUGH HEAD

As long as England controlled the seas, she could hope to be triumphant. But now France contested her hegemony in American waters and gave the fledgling Continental Navy—in the beginning, hardly more than a haphazard collection of converted merchant ships—a vicarious might. This was already so despite d'Estaing's failure to turn his fleet to account. For the very threat of his coming had obliged the British to evacuate Philadelphia out of fear of blockade. Nevertheless, his ineffectual collaboration had been discouraging, and his departure not only crippled all hope of retaking Savannah but for the moment allowed Britain to regain command.

In the Continental Congress, the need for a regular navy (an enormously expensive proposition) had been the subject of heated debate. "It is the maddest idea in the world to think of building an American fleet . . . we should mortgage the whole Continent," declared Samuel Chase of Maryland in late August 1775. But to this Virginia's George Wythe replied, "Why should not America have a navy? No maritime power near the sea-coast can be safe without it. It is no chimera. The Romans suddenly built one in their Carthaginian war. Why may we not lay a foundation for it? We abound with firs, iron ore, tar, pitch, turpentine; we have all the materials for its construction." And he hoped "that America *inter nabila condit*"—could build in time of tribulation, as the Romans had.

The Roman model was a tantalizing one, given the Founding Fathers' predilection for classical precedents. But, with John Adams as its practical advocate, the program undertaken was on a far more modest scale. By the end of October 1775, Congress had overcome its qualms enough to form a Naval Committee which rented a room at a waterfront tavern and was authorized to purchase and arm four ships "for the protection and defense of the United Colonies." The United States Navy was born. On November 10, Congress created the Marine Corps, and on the twenty-eighth it adopted "Rules for the Regulation of the Navy of the United Colonies of North America."

By Christmas, the Naval, or Marine, Committee had purchased and begun to fit out eleven vessels, including three merchantmen, to be converted into warships for its first fleet and had ambitiously undertaken to construct thirteen frigates, 115 to 160 feet long, with twenty-four to fifty guns each. Only two were completed and launched, however—the others being variously bottled up at their building yards by the British or, to avoid capture, deliberately destroyed on the stocks. Most of the American warships that eventually saw action were of smaller make: sloops of war, 80 to 120 feet long, with 6 to 20 guns; converted merchantmen; armed schooners; and so on, such as were used on the Delaware for the defense of Philadelphia or assembled by Benedict Arnold against Carleton on Lake Champlain. Only one ship of the line (the colonial equivalent of the modern battleship)—the *America,* 175 feet long and mounting 74 guns—would be built during the war.

Congress also acquired some foreign-built vessels, but in the end it was not a regular navy but some 800 privateers—armed private vessels that fought for plunder—that sailed the seas. They preyed on British commerce, captured supplies for the American army, and made fortunes for themselves. They struck at British merchantmen laden with West India sugar and rum, English woolens and Irish linens bound for the Continent, furs and stores from Quebec and Hudson Bay, and intercepted British military transports, exacting losses of up to £2 million a year. As many as 20,000 Americans manned such piratical vessels, captured or destroyed at least 600 British merchant ships and overall took 2,000 prizes as well as thousands of prisoners of war.

Many of the American privateers absolutely bristled with guns—not only with captured cannon but with musketry on their quarterdecks and tops—so that "in action," wrote one mariner of his own vessel, the *Fair American,* "she was a complete flame of fire."

France gave refuge to privateers at L'Orient, Brest, Bordeaux, and other ports, where the captured contraband could also be sold or exchanged, and it was not uncommon for Frenchmen to fill out American crews.

In time, however, these commerce-destroying vessels, though approved by Congress in March 1776—"That the inhabitants of these Colonies be permitted to fit out armed vessels, to cruise on the enemies of these United Colonies"—became rivals rather than associates of the navy. To begin with, service on board a privateer was more carefree and democratic, safer (since a privateer was generally "so heavily sparred," writes one historian, "that she could outsail a more powerful vessel"), and more lucrative. "Prizes are taken in no small numbers," wrote John Adams on August 12, 1776. "Thousands of schemes for privateering are afloat." Indeed, the lure of prizes and great takings was such that they proved a manpower drain on the Continental Army, which could offer nothing to compare to the promised gain. Farmers and laborers left their fields and trades to try their luck at such high-seas adventure, while the competition for seamen to man the vessels was as intense as the scrimmage for the prize. Steuben, in fact, had been unable to get his new army manual printed promptly in Philadelphia because almost all the local typesetters had gone off to serve on privateers.

With regard to the prize money, the navy simply failed to compete. In the beginning Congress allowed Continental crews a third to a half the value of the vessel taken, the balance going to the public treasury. Privateers took all.

The first commodore of the Continental Navy was Esek Hopkins of Rhode Island, an elderly merchant skipper who had commanded privateers in the French and Indian War. Hopkins was an old-fashioned salthorse sailor—an "antique character," said General Knox—and in the navy's first expedition, in January 1776, was supposed to take a fleet of four warships into the Chesapeake Bay to ascertain "the Enemie's Situation and Strength." Whatever enemy ships he found, he was to "attack, take and destroy." Ice, however, prevented him from dropping down Delaware Bay, and so instead (having been given great latitude in his operations) he decided to make a surprise attack on New Providence in the Bahamas and capture gunpowder and arms.

At the time, New Providence was defended by two stone forts manned only by civilian volunteers. The Americans landed unopposed, occupied the nearest stone fort, marched on the town the next morning (March 4), and obtained the keys to the second fortress from the astonished British governor. Hopkins loaded his fleet with the captured equipment and stores, including 88 cannon, 15 brass mortars, 5,458 shells, 11,077 cannonballs, a number of gun carriages, and 24 casks of powder. In terms of the take, his booty compared with that seized by Arnold and Allen at Forts Ticonderoga and Crown Point.

A number of other skippers were incredibly daring and successful—for example, Gustavus Conyngham, Nathaniel Fanning, and John Paul Jones. Conyngham, sailing in the *Revenge*, a little fourteen-gun Continental cutter, took no fewer than sixty merchant vessels in eighteen months of patrolling the waters off the West Indies and the Atlantic coast. Fanning, a sometime naval officer, became a "pirate," and one of his more dashing escapades came late in the war as captain of the privateer *Eclipse*.

At the time, Fanning, flying French colors, was cruising about in the English Channel when he was chased by three British ships. A fourth, a large cutter with fourteen guns, steered right into his path to prevent his escape. Fanning shot past her with a crippling broadside, "which carried away her topmast, jib tack, and peak tye," and continued on his course. Before long, he had outsailed all but the fifty-gun ship, when he espied ahead of him the entire English Channel fleet, including twenty-eight ships of the line (several of which were three-deckers), and a number of frigates, sloops of war, and cutters, extending in a line southward for about nine miles from the Isle of Wight.

There appeared to be no alternative but to run directly through their ranks. He ran up an English flag, and since his own cutter, having been built in England, was painted exactly like those of the king (and most of his officers and crew were dressed like Englishmen), he approached the English fleet with boldness, entered the center of their line, and passed through. As he did so, he was hailed: "What cutter is that?" Fanning mischievously replied, "His Majesty's cutter *Surprize.*" They continued to hail him and then "hallooed us to bring to. We answered, 'Ay, ay,' but notwithstanding kept on our course." The English quickly realized that they had been duped, and the center of their line exploded with fire. The shot, however, flew over the Americans' heads. Three of the frigates, a sloop of war, and a cutter now gave chase. At the same time, the fifty-gun ship which had been pursuing Fanning all along also reached and passed through the line. As Fanning maneuvered to escape, the sails of his ship were shot full of holes—750 (as he meticulously counted them later) piercing the mainsail alone. Nevertheless, by a kind of miracle, not a bit of rigging had been severed by the fire.

On another occasion, this time in the privateer *Ranger,* Fanning managed to wreak some havoc on another British fleet. Sailing from Dunkirk for the Downs on the English coast, he suddenly found himself among sixty-odd sail not far from Dover. He immediately covered his guns with light sails, unshipped and stowed his swivels, and hoisted an English flag. Most of the men were ordered below, and in the guise of an English coasting sloop, he fell in with the fleet and sailed with it to the west.

On the third night, a storm arose and the ships scattered for shelter. This gave Fanning his chance to seek out prey. He readied his men for boarding and in the evening ran under the lee of a large ship. Most of the English crew were upon the yards, reefing the topsails, as the Americans leapt on board. A couple of pistol shots were all that was required, and the crew were methodically seized as they came down from the yards. Fanning put his first lieutenant and ten men in charge of the ship and sent it on its way to the nearest French port.

Under cover of darkness, he next ran alongside a large brigantine and boarded and took her in a similar manner, discovering to his delight that it mounted four carriage guns and was laden with sheathing copper for the navy. He turned this vessel over to another of his officers with a crew of six and in turn sent it on its way. Before the night was over, he had also captured a large sloop laden with sea coal, dry goods, and lead— and with that he headed home.

Other American captains might boast notable exploits, but no career was more celebrated than that of John Paul Jones. Born in Scotland, Jones had first come to America as a cabin boy on a merchant ship. From the age of twelve, when he was apprenticed to a shipowner in Whitehaven, his life as a sailor was set. By the age of nineteen he had worked his way up to first mate on a slaver that traded between Jamaica and the coast of Guinea, and by twenty-one he was master of a ship. In 1774, however, he killed a mutinous member of his crew in the West Indies, fled to America, and thereafter was wanted in England for murder. When the Revolutionary War broke out, he was commissioned a first lieutenant in the Continental Navy.

Between August and October 1776, as captain of the sloop *Providence,* he ranged over the Atlantic from Bermuda to Nova Scotia, with authorization "to Seize, take, Sink, Burn or destroy" any enemy ship. Twice eluding British frigates, he took eight vessels in a voyage of forty-nine days, including the whaling brigantine *Britannia* and a merchant ship, *Sea Nymph,* bound from Barbados to London with a cargo of rum, sugar, ginger, oil, and Madeira wine. He might have taken more, but by late October he found himself shorthanded, having had to assign most of his crew to manning the prizes he had seized.

Upon his return, Jones wrote Robert Morris, who sat on the Marine Committee, that it would soon be almost impossible to engage seamen for the fleet because privateers offered them the full value of prizes they took, while the navy generally offered its crews one third. Unless "the private Emoluments of individuals in our Navy is made superiour to that in Privateers it never can become respectable. . . . And without a Respectable Navy—alas America! . . . If our Enemies, with the best established and most formadable Navy in the Universe, have found it expedient to assign all Prizes to the Captors—how much more is such policy essential to our infant Fleet."

Congress took heed: on October 30, 1776, it increased the captors' share of all nonmilitary vessels to one half their value and allowed them the entire value of a privateer or man-of-war. That helped, but it did not go far enough, and the following summer one congressman complained that unless the navy made itself more competitive, it would soon be "officered by Tinkers, Shoemakers, & Horse Jockeys, and no Gentleman worth employing will accept a Commission."

Jones next sailed from Providence, Rhode Island, on October 27, 1776, in the *Alfred,* and was scarcely out of port before he took a 350-ton armed transport carrying a cargo of winter uniforms and other supplies to Quebec for the British army. Over the next few weeks, he burned a British supply ship, captured three colliers from Sydney bound for New York as part of the fleet Howe depended upon for fuel for his army, a small schooner, and an armed merchant vessel before heading home unscathed.

In all, during the last six months of 1776, Jones had captured or destroyed five transports, two ships, six schooners, seven brigantines, one sloop, and a sixteen-gun privateer.

At the beginning of 1777, the strategy of the Continental Navy changed. Up until then, its mission had been to prowl the eastern seaboard. But as "our Infant fleet cannot protect our own Coasts," wrote Robert Morris, "the only effectual relief it can afford us is to attack the enemies' defenceless places and thereby oblige them to station more of their Ships in their own Countries, or to keep them employed in following ours, and either way we are relieved." Commerce destroying was now to be left to privateers, while the navy engaged in surprise attacks. Jones wholeheartedly supported this approach. "It appears to me to be the province of our . . . Navy to Surprise and spread Alarm," he remarked, "with fast sailing ships. When we grow stronger we can meet their Fleets and dispute with them the Sovereignty of the Ocean."

In February 1777, he was given a squadron of five ships with which to seize the British sugar island of Saint Kitts. "I fancy you will make a considerable booty," Robert Morris told him. From Saint Kitts he was to proceed to Pensacola on the Gulf of Mexico, capture some British sloops of war (primarily for their ordnance), give the British "an alarm at St.

Augustine," show the flag in Georgia and the Carolinas, and sail either for the West African coast or to Barbados to capture British slave ships bound for the West Indies.

Jones might have accomplished all of this, but in June he was instead sent across the Atlantic in the *Ranger,* a sloop of war with eighteen nine-pound guns. In the *Ranger* Jones cruised through the Irish Sea; captured the 250-ton ship *Lord Chatham* of Dublin without a fight; sank a Scots coasting schooner loaded with oats and barley and took her crew prisoner; and, in the only American operation of the war conducted on English soil, terrorized the English coast with a series of audacious hit-and-run raids. Following one daring attack on Whitehaven, in which he spiked the guns of the two harbor forts and tried to burn the shipping, the landing party headed straight for the nearest pub and "made very free with the liquor." Four days later, he outfought the British sloop of war *Drake* and took her as a prize.

On another raid farther up the coast, Jones's men boldly approached the mansion of the Countess, Lady Selkirk, who had just finished break-fast when some "horrid-looking wretches" armed to the teeth sur-rounded the house. Taking them for pirates, she sent the women and children of the house to the top story while she remained with the butler below. Two American officers entered, identified themselves, and explained that they had been ordered to confiscate her household silver. They promised not to molest her household in any way if she complied, and she quickly decided that she had better do as they wished, since she had nobody to defend her. Afterward, Jones felt that the whole venture had been lacking in a certain etiquette, even though Lady Selkirk herself reported that his men had "behaved with great civility." Indeed, one of Jones's lieutenants had even left a receipt. In any case, Jones wrote the "Amiable Countess" a remarkable letter of apology:

Tho' I have drawn my Sword in the present generous Struggle for the rights of Men; yet I am not in Arms as an American, nor am I in pursuit of Riches. My Fortune is liberal enough, having no Wife nor Family, and having lived long enough to know that Riches cannot ensure Happiness. I profess myself a Citizen of the World, totally unfettered by the little mean distinctions of Climate or of Country, which diminish the benevolence of the Heart and set bounds to Philanthropy. Before this War began I had at an early time of Life, withdrawn from the Sea service, in favor of calm contemplation and Poetic ease. I have sacrificed not only my favorite scheme of Life, but the *softer Affections of the Heart* and my prospects of Domestic Happiness:—And I am ready to sacrifice Life also with cheer-fulness—if that forfeiture could restore Peace and Goodwill among man-kind.

As the feelings of your gentle Bosom cannot but be congenial with mine let me entreat you Madam to use your soft persuasive Arts with your Husband [an influential aristocrat] to endeavor to stop this cruel and destructive War, in which Britain can never succeed. Heaven can never countenance the barbarous and unmanly Practices of the Britons in America, which Savages would blush at; and which if not discontinued will soon be retaliated in Britain by a justly enraged People.—Should you fail in this, (for I am persuaded you will attempt it; and who can resist the power of such an Advocate?) Your endeavours to effect a general Exchange of Prisoners, will be an Act of Humanity, which will afford you Golden feelings on a Death bed.

He also promised to return her silver after the war—and did.

Meanwhile, the maraudings were having their effect. On March 8, 1778, a frustrated Lord Germain told Sir Henry Clinton that if he could not soon bring Washington to a decisive engagement, he was to organize an amphibious operation "to attack the Ports on the Coast, from New York to Nova Scotia, and to seize or destroy every Ship or Vessel in the different Creeks or Harbors, wherever it is found practicalle to penetrate, as also to destroy all Wharfs and Stores, and Materials for Ship-Building, so as to incapacitate them from raising a Marine, or continuing their Depredations upon the Trade of this Kingdom."

F o r all his hard fighting and intrepid boldness on the high seas, Jones, in his person (as his letter to the Lady Selkirk might suggest) made a more ambiguous impression, exuding a kind of romantic vulnerability that contributed to his social conquests and made him quite a ladies' man.

"His voice is soft and still and small," wrote John Adams, who got to know him, "his eye has keeness and Wildness and softness in it." Abigail nicely filled the portrait out:

From the intrepid character he justly supported in the American Navy, I expected to have seen a rough, stout, warlike Roman—instead of that I should sooner think of wrapping him up in cotton wool, and putting him in my pocket, than sending him to contend with cannon-balls. He is small of stature, well proportioned, soft in his speech, easy in his address, polite in his manners, vastly civil, understands all the etiquette of a lady's toilette as perfectly as he does the mast, sails and rigging of his ship . . . he is said to be a man of gallantry and a favorite amongst the French ladies, whom he is frequently commending for the neatness of their persons, their easy manners and their taste in dress. He knows how often the ladies use the baths, what color best suits a lady's complexion, what cosmetics are most favorable to the skin.

Benjamin Franklin once told Jones that the best way to learn French was to find a "sleeping dictionary" (that is, a French mistress). In passing on the advice, Jones gave it an elegant twist. At a dinner given by him at L'Orient, which John Adams attended, the problem of learning a foreign language came up for discussion. Said Jones, there were two good ways of learning French: to "take a Mistress or go to the Comédie Française." Someone impertinently asked Adams which way he thought best. He replied, "Perhaps both would teach it soonest; to be sure, sooner than either. But the language is nowhere better spoken than at the Comédie."

Despite a voluptous strain, Jones was moderate in his tastes, lean and fit, never drank hard liquor, and only occasionally allowed himself two or three glasses of wine. His usual drink was lemonade—lime juice and water, "with a little sugar to make it the more palatable"—as an antidote to scurvy.

Though often exposed to enemy fire, Jones, like Washington, was never hit, and he once gallantly remarked to a lady that he had been wounded "only with arrows that no enemy discharged."

I N August 1779, Jones took command of the *Bonhomme Richard,* a converted French warship of forty guns that had been renamed in honor of the "Poor Richard" of Franklin's celebrated almanac. Accompanied by four small ships, he circled the British Isles, captured merchant vessels and men-of-war within sight of their harbors, sailed into numerous bays, and even approached the Thames. Every coastal city pleaded with the king for protection. Then, on September 23, he engaged in the greatest —or most celebrated—naval battle of the war when he met the HMS *Serapis,* a new and more powerful frigate of fifty guns commanded by Captain Richard Pearson, off the great chalk cliffs of Flamborough Head.

At the time, the *Serapis* was escorting a Baltic convoy of merchant ships, which, as the battle was about to begin, raced for the protection of the batteries on shore.

The *Richard* and the *Serapis* approached each other "just as the moon was rising," recalled Nathaniel Fanning, then a midshipman under Jones. The weather was clear, the surface of the sea "perfectly smooth, even as in a millpond." Captain Pearson hailed, "What ship is that?" And Jones, according to Fanning, shouted, "Come a little nearer and I will tell you." Pearson then asked, "What are you laden with?" To which Jones replied,

"Round, grape, and double-headed shot!" Instantly he ran up the American flag, and the two ships let loose their broadsides.

"The battle being thus begin," Jones wrote afterward, "was Continued with Unremitting fury. Every method was practiced on both sides to gain an advantage, and rake each other; and I must confess that the enemy's ship, being much more manageable than the *Richard,* gained thereby several times an advantageous situation in spite of my best endeavors to prevent it."

At length the two ships collided bow to stern, locked in a kind of fatal dance. The *Serapis* had thrust the tip end of her bowsprit right into the *Richard's* mizzen shrouds, so that the wind acting on the sails of both ships at once caused them to pivot together stern to bow. Their topsides were also clapped together "such that the muzzles of their guns actually touched." Captain Pearson called out, "Has your ship struck?" to which Jones immortally replied, "I have not yet begun to fight!"

It was now between eight and eight-thirty in the evening, the battle lit by a harvest moon. For two long hours, the *Richard* and the *Serapis* were thus so completely entwined that the gunners had to thrust their staves into the enemy's gun ports in order to load and ram their charges home.

All this while, the cannon of the *Serapis* below deck kept firing, her eighteen-pound shot, wrote Fanning, going "through and through our ship . . . she made dreadful havock among our crew." By ten o'clock the situation of the *Richard* seemed hopeless as only a few stanchions prevented the quarterdeck from falling into the gunroom or the main deck from crashing into the hold. The rest of the *Richard* was a mass of flaming fragments, and she was starting to go down. The *Serapis,* however, was also in deplorable shape. Her spars, sails, and rigging were destroyed, and the dead and dying scattered about her deck. At length, when the mainmast of the *Serapis* began to topple, Captain Pearson, who before the engagement had nailed his flag to the mast and had vehemently sworn that he would never strike, "lost his nerve" and struck. To compound his humiliation, none of his men dared expose themselves to American marksmen, so he had to ascend the quarterdeck himself and haul his standard down.

Conducted on board the victorious vessel, he offered Jones his sword. "It is with the greatest reluctance," he said, "that I am now obliged to resign you this, for it is painful to me, more particularly at this time, when compelled to deliver up my sword to a man who may be said to fight with a halter around his neck!" But Jones magnanimously replied, "Sir, you have fought like a hero, and I make no doubt but your sover-

390 ANGEL IN THE WHIRLWIND

eign will reward you in a most ample manner for it." Pearson then asked
Jones the nationality of his crew. "Americans," said Jones. "Very well,"
said Pearson, "it has been 'diamond cut diamond' with us"—in disparagement of the French. Jones ignored the remark, politely returned his
sword, and invited him below into his cabin to drink a glass of wine.

In the three-and-a-half-hour battle, each side lost about 150 men, and
both vessels were utterly destroyed. In the end, it was not the *Serapis*
but the *Richard* that went down, and Jones had to transfer his flag and
crew to the defeated ship. "A person must have been an Eye Witness to
form a Just idea of this tremendous scene of Carneg, Wreck and ruin that
Every Where appeared," wrote Jones. "Humanity cannot but recoil from
the prospect of such finished horror, and lament that which should produce such fatal consequences." The tangle of mangled corpses was
enough, wrote Fanning, "to appall the stoutest heart. . . . Upon the
whole, I think this battle and every circumstance attending it minutely
considered, may be ranked with propriety the most bloody, the hardest
fought, and the greatest scene of carnage on both sides, ever fought
between two ships of war of any nation under heaven."

News of the victory electrified France. "Scarce anything [has been]
talked of at Paris and Versailles," wrote Franklin to Jones, "but your cool
Conduct & persevering Bravery." And John Adams a bit mischievously
remarked, "The cry of Versailles and the Clamour of Paris became as
loud in the favour of Monsieur Jones as of Monsieur Franklin, and the
inclination of the Ladies to embrace him almost as fashionable and as
strong."

The engagement off Flamborough Head had taken place at a time
when Britain was also at risk of invasion by France and Spain. Spain had
moved more slowly than France toward an American alliance and with
different designs. Having important American colonies herself—Louisiana as a buffer province between the United States and Mexico and, so
she claimed, the Mississippi River as well as territory along its east bank
—she had remained apprehensive of the territorial ambitions of a new
United States. In Europe, Spain desired above all things to recover and
control Gibraltar. During 1778, she had made diplomatic efforts to persuade England to give up Gibraltar as the price of Spanish neutrality.
England refused, and on June 21, 1779, Spain entered the fray. Within a
month, 50,000 French and Spanish troops had gathered at Saint-Malo
and Le Havre. Lafayette, who had returned to France the previous winter,
was sent to Le Havre to assist in the preparations and asked Vergennes if
he might be allowed to lead the invasion. "Judge if I ought not to be
impatient to know if I am destined to be the first to arrive on that coast

and to plant the first flag in the midst of that insolent nation!" He was especially enthusiastic about the idea of a full-fledged amphibious assault on a major seaport such as Liverpool. He discussed the operation with Franklin, but the latter thought John Paul Jones the proper man to lead it. Lafayette, acquiescing, in turn wrote to Jones that he would be happy to divide with him "whatever share of glory may await us."

By the end of July, a combined fleet of sixty-four French and Spanish ships of the line with 4,774 guns, not counting frigates, corvettes, and smaller craft, had assembled to sail against the English Channel fleet of thirty-eight ships of the line with 2,968 guns. The whole scheme, however, depended not on Lafayette's ardor but on the cooperation of Spain, and Spain, after considerable vacillation and debate (in which the fate of her armada in Elizabethan times was troublingly recalled) declined to go along, at least to the extent originally planned. By then the opportunity had been lost. On August 16, the combined fleet sailed to Plymouth, but the British wisely declined to engage. Meanwhile, the French crews were suffering from smallpox, scurvy, and typhus, and as water and food began to run short, the number of sick among the Spanish also grew. In the end, the allied force broke up, not without some mutual recriminations, as the French and Spanish sailed home to their respective ports.

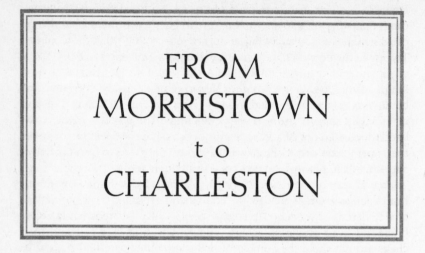

CHAPTER SIXTEEN

FROM MORRISTOWN to CHARLESTON

THE war had been fought to a standstill in the North. As the winter of 1779–1780 approached, Washington divided his army, placing one division in the Hudson highlands under General Heath for the protection of West Point and the surrounding posts while he again established his own winter quarters in New Jersey, this time at Morristown.

Morristown's strategic location had served Washington well before. Ironworking furnaces and forges indispensable to the army could be found nearby, along with gristmills, sawmills, and ample wood for shelters and fuel. For his own quarters, he chose a house belonging to a Mrs. Jacob Ford, the widow of a New Jersey militia officer. In the meadow to the southeast, about fifty log huts were built for his guard. The main body of the army was bivouacked on a mountain plateau about two miles away.

The dreary encampment at Valley Forge has become proverbial for its hardships, yet they were scarcely more trying than those suffered by Washington's army at Morristown that winter, which was incredibly severe. A three-day blizzard struck in January, before the troops had erected all their huts. Roads and fences were completely obliterated, and the men were actually buried in their tents. One severe snowstorm followed another—twenty-eight snowfalls in all that season—and on one occasion it snowed for four days straight. The mercury remained below freezing for weeks. The Passaic and Delaware Rivers, and even the mighty Hudson, froze solid from bank to bank. The ice in New York Bay was so thick that regiments of troops in close order with heavy cannon could pass over it from New York City to Staten Island, a distance of six miles. Around the American camp the snow lay up to six feet deep. The soldiers, miserably clad and grumbling for their arrears, were short of provisions and were obliged to eat, as Washington confessed, "every kind of horse food but hay." Recalled one soldier stationed near Elizabethtown, "We were absolutely, literally starved. I did not put a single morsel into my mouth for several days, except for a little black birch bark which I gnawed off a stick of wood. . . . I saw several of the men roast their old shoes and eat them, and I was afterwards informed that some of the officers killed and ate a favorite little dog."

The frontier self-sufficiency of early Americans, so often lauded in history books was, among New Englanders at least, already a thing of the past. "Yankees [are] as ignorant of making meal or flour into bread as a wild Indian would be of making pound cake," a Connecticut corporal said of his confreres. "All we had any idea of doing with it was to make it into hasty pudding, and sometimes, though very rarely, we would chance to get a little milk, or, perhaps, a little cider, or some such thing to wash it down with; and when we could get nothing to qualify it, we ate it as it was . . . as clammy as glue, and as insipid as starch."

Yet the core of the little army held on. "I cherish," wrote the young and chivalrous Colonel John Laurens, "those dear, ragged Continentals, whose patience will be the admiration of future ages."

The British, frozen in themselves, refrained from attacking, but there were occasional skirmishes that kept both camps alert. On January 18, 1780, an American expeditionary force on sleighs was sent against a British position on Staten Island, but the enemy got wind of it and the Americans lost the advantage of surprise. Exasperated, they blew up an armed enemy brigantine trapped in the ice not far from shore, then pitched their camp nearby "upon a bare bleak hill, in full rake of the northwest wind, with no other covering or shelter than the canopy of the heavens, and no fuel but some old rotten rails which we dug up in the snow."

Now and then British patrols also threatened the outskirts of Washington's camp. On such occasions, Washington's guard would immediately take up positions around his residence, barricade the doors, and station five soldiers at each window with their muskets cocked until troops from the main camp arrived. Such alarms were rather uncomfortable for the ladies—that is, Mrs. Washington and Mrs. Ford—who were compelled to remain in bed, sometimes for hours at a time, with their room full of soldiers.

Yet no one ever heard Martha Washington complain. By all accounts, she was a most pleasant and unassuming woman and a devoted wife. Mercy Warren, her friend and an early historian of the Revolution, described her as "affable, candid and gentle," ideally suited to "soften the hours of private life" and "smooth the rugged cares of War." Her attire was extremely plain, typically a homespun gown, a "neat cap," and a white kerchief covering her neck and chest. The only jewelry she wore was a plain gold wedding ring. Fond of knitting, she did so even when entertaining and was known to greet her guests, however illustrious, with a ball of yarn protruding from an outside pocket and some half-knit stocking in her left hand as she extended her right. This was in keeping with her frugality, which her husband much admired. During the war, for example, she unraveled all her worn silk gowns and rewound the redyed threads on bobbins, to weave them into covers for cushions and chairs. And there was a red-and-white-striped dress she evidently favored that had been woven in part from some old stockings her husband had worn. One society matron who went to see her at the Morristown headquarters wrote afterward to a friend, "We expected to find the wealthy wife of the great general elegantly dressed, for the time of our visit had been fixed; but, instead, she was neatly attired in a plain brown habit. Her gracious and cheerful manners delighted us all, but we felt rebuked by the plainness of her apparel and her example of persistent industry, while we were extravagantly dressed idlers. . . . She talked much of the sufferings of the poor soldiers, especially of the sick ones. Her heart seemed to be full of compassion for them."

Washington struggled to feed and clothe his men, keep a close watch on the enemy, and keep his army intact. Many of the men were still serving on short terms of enlistment, but there was no money available to pay them a bonus to remain. At the same time, some of the seasoned veterans who had sustained the struggle for years felt obliged to return home to their families and tend their neglected farms. In an attempt to rebuild his army, Washington dispatched recruiters and wrote to Congress repeatedly for funds. But there was no relief in sight. The currency having depreciated, the commissaries found it difficult to purchase supplies for the immediate wants of the army and impossible to provide any stores in advance. They were left destitute of resources, and the public credit was prostrated by accumulating debts.

One of the emerging lessons of the war was the need for a strong central government. "Certain I am," wrote Washington on May 31, unless Congress speak in a more decisive tone, unless they are invested with powers by the several States competent to the great purposes of the war, or assume them as a matter of right, and they and the States respectively act with more energy than they hitherto have done, that our cause is lost. . . . One State will comply with a requisition of Congress, another neglects to do it; a third executes it by halves; and all differ either in the manner, the matter, or so much in point of time, that we are always working up hill; and, while such a system as the present one or rather want of one prevails, we shall ever be unable to apply our strength or resources to any advantage.

Since Congress could not, and the states would not, impose taxes sufficient to finance a revolution that had sprung from a resistance to taxation, the Continental troops were largely supported by the states to which they belonged. Some states gave more support than others, but the troops, being paid in paper money at its nominal value, found in general that the four months' pay of a private soldier was not enough to buy a single bushel of wheat, nor the pay of a colonel oats enough for his horse. It cost four hundred Continental dollars to buy a pair of boots or a hat.

In one of the most vehement letters he ever wrote, Washington gave vent to his hatred of big-time war profiteers—the "monopolizers, forestallers, and engrossers of condign punishment. . . . It is much to be lamented that each state, long ere this, has not hunted them down as the pests of society and the greatest enemies we have to the happiness of America. I would to God that one of the most atrocious in each state was hung in gibbets upon a gallows five times as high as the one prepared by Hamen. No punishment, in my opinion, is too great for the man who can build his greatness upon his country's ruin."

The army that remained was at risk of revolt. On May 28, Washington wrote to Joseph Reed, "I assure you, every idea you can form of our distresses will fall short of the reality. There is such a combination of circumstances to exhaust the patience of the soldiery that it begins at length to be worn out, and we see in every line of the army the most serious features of mutiny and sedition."

Indeed, a few days before, two regiments of the Connecticut line had paraded without their officers and resolved to march into the country to provision themselves and supply their neglected wants. Only after a tense standoff did the two regiments return to their barracks, but few could entirely fault their discontent. As Dr. Thacher put it at the time, "Their complaints are that . . . their sufferings are insupportable, that their pay is five months in arrear and that it is of no value when received. These circumstances are known to be substantially true."

The mutiny had ended without violence, but on the following day it so happened that eleven men were scheduled to be executed for other crimes. Three received pardons in advance. The rest, according to Dr. Thacher, "were brought in carts to the place of execution . . . and placed side by side on the scaffold with halters round their necks, their coffins before their eyes, their graves open to their view, and thousands of spectators bemoaning their awful doom." After they were blindfolded and had audibly begun to pray, an officer suddenly advanced and read a reprieve for seven of the eight. The remaining criminal (guilty of having forged more than a hundred discharge papers, including one for himself) turned out to be in his own way—at least in his final hour—a remarkable man. "He appeared penitent," wrote Thacher,

and behaved with uncommon fortitude and resolution. He addressed the soldiers, desired them to be faithful to their country and obedient to their officers, and advised the officers to be punctual in all their engagements to the soldiers and give them no cause to desert. He examined the halter and told the hangman the knot was not made right and that the rope was not strong enough, as he was a heavy man. Having adjusted the knot and fixed it round his own neck, he was swung off instantly. The rope broke and he fell to the ground, by which he was very much bruised. He calmly reascended the ladder and said, "I told you the rope was not strong enough! Do get a stronger one!" Another being procured, he was launched into eternity.

As preparations were made for the summer campaign, Congress optimistically promised the French ambassador, Luzerne, that it would raise 35,000 Continental troops. But as always the states failed to fill their quotas, even as two new loyalist brigades in New York were ready to take the field. At Morristown, Washington, had fewer than 5,000 effectives left under his immediate command. "I have almost ceased to hope," he wrote. "The country is in such a state of insensibility and indifference to its interests that I dare not flatter myself with any change for the better." And he warned that the French might even reconsider their alliance if they thought they were making more of an effort than the Americans themselves:

The present juncture is so interesting that if it does not produce corresponding exertions it will be a proof that motives of honor, public good and even self-preservation have lost their influence on our minds. This is a decisive moment; one of the most, I will go further and say *the* most important America has seen. The court of France has made a glorious effort for our deliverance, and if we disappoint its intentions by our supineness, we must become contemptible in the eyes of all mankind, nor can we after that venture to confide that our allies will persist.

Perhaps the one consolation of the hour was that the British economy was also failing. British agents had been obliged to seek new loans in Europe at high interest rates, adding to a national debt of £200 million, while hostilities with France and Spain had led to a rise in unemployment and the decay of trade. In the gloating words of the *Pennsylvania Packet,* "Britain's boasted wealth and grandeur are crumbling to pieces, never again to be united . . . and, if she persists in her present self-destroying systems, there will be a time when scarcely a monument of her former glory will remain. The fragments of her empire, and its history, will then be of little other use to mankind, but, like a ruined tower on a dreary coast, to serve as a landmark to warn against the shoals on which her political navigators had ship-wrecked that infatuated nation." Britain's needs as well as its desire to cripple the American economy had been principal factors in shaping the new southern strategy—as explained to Clinton by Lord Germain: by the conquest of the South "a very valuable branch of commerce would be restored to this country and the rebels deprived of a principal resource for the support of their foreign credit and of paying for the supplies they stand in need of, as the product of these provinces make a considerable part of their remittance to Europe."

Britain's southern strategy continued to harvest victories for the king. While Washington was braving the bitter winter at Morristown, Sir Henry Clinton, leaving his New York garrison under the command of General Wilhelm von Knyphausen, had embarked 7,500 men on board transports, ships of the line, and frigates for Charleston, South Carolina, on December 26, 1779. After a difficult five-week voyage which ought to have taken him eleven days, in which he lost most of his heavy ordnance, all his cavalry horses, and much basic equipment besides, he dropped anchor off John's Island, thirty miles below Charleston, on February 11. He sent part of his fleet around at once to blockade the harbor but delayed an assault until the end of March, by which time he had obtained artillery and powder from the Bahamas and had reinforced his army with 1,500 troops from Savannah and 2,500 under Lord Francis Rawdon from New York. That gave him a total strength of 11,500 men.

Charleston, defended by General Lincoln, was located at the tip of a narrow peninsula bounded by the Ashley and Cooper Rivers. To prevent British warships from entering the latter, the Americans had sunk some of their own vessels at the river's mouth. Eighty cannon and mortars had been mounted on the city's ramparts; Fort Moultrie on Sullivan Island in the harbor, which had done so much to repulse Clinton's siege three years before, had been refortified; and a body of 500 cavalry and militia had been positioned thirty miles to the north at Monck's Corner to guard an escape route for the garrison if the American defenses were overrun.

The defenses were not inconsiderable, but, given the size of Clinton's army and fleet, it might have been more prudent for Lincoln to abandon Charleston and retreat into the countryside, as Washington had done when Howe landed at New York. Instead he tried to make a stand. He had several thousand troops—including 1,450 Continentals and 2,500 militia—under his command, bolstered by about 2,000 enlisted from the North Carolina countryside. But he was unable to get the local white population, fearful of a slave revolt on their own plantations and farms, to turn out.

On March 29, Clinton sent picked troops in flatboats across the Ashley River to occupy part of the peninsula on which Charleston sat, thus closing off any retreat to the west. Eight British frigates also sailed past Fort Moultrie—this time declining to engage in a costly attack—and anchored within sight of the Charleston docks. The city was thus hemmed in by the enemy on three sides.

On April 10, Clinton called upon Lincoln to surrender. Lincoln refused, threatening "to hold out to the last extremity." Four days later cavalry commanded by British lieutenant colonel Banastre Tarleton surprised and routed the Americans at Moncks Corner, cutting off their only escape route and capturing fifty supply wagons and a hundred men. By then, a steady British bombardment had begun to smash many of Lincoln's defenses, and enemy entrenchments had advanced to within 250 yards of the American lines. Fort Moultrie capitulated on May 6, after British marines, landing on Sullivan Island, surrounded its garrison; on the eighth, the two sides opened talks. The following evening, they broke down. Each side then waited tensely for the other to renew the battle, and at length the Americans fired the first gun. There immediately followed "a tremendous cannonade," recalled William Moultrie,

and the mortars from both sides threw out an immense number of shells. It was a glorious sight to see them like meteors crossing each other and bursting in the air. It appeared as if the stars were tumbling down. The fire was incessant almost the whole night, cannon balls whizzing and shells hissing continually amongst us, ammunition chests and temporary magazines blowing up, great guns bursting, and wounded men groaning along the lines. It was a dreadful night! It was our last great effort, but it availed us nothing. After this, our military ardor was much abated. We began to cool, and we cooled gradually, and on the eleventh of May, we capitulated.

Lincoln's entire remaining army of 5,400 men, with all its weaponry and supplies, including 376 barrels of gunpowder, fell into British hands. To make the humiliation complete, by the terms of their surrender, the Americans were refused the usual dignity of parading with the honors of war.

Two and a half weeks later, a retreating column of 350 Virginians under Colonel Abraham Buford, who had marched for the relief of Charleston but was now making his way toward Hillsboro, was overtaken and butchered by Tarleton's Legion at Waxhaw, a pastoral village near the North Carolina border bounded by a creek. On the afternoon of the twenty-ninth, Buford's men were passing through a sparse wood when the British, "with the horrid yells of infuriated demons," suddenly attacked. The Virginians resisted stoutly but, recalled an American doctor who was with them, soon "perceiving that further resistance was hopeless, ordered a flag to be hoisted and the arms to be grounded, expecting the usual treatment sanctioned by civilized warfare. This, however, made no part of Tarleton's creed. His ostensible pretext for the relentless barbarity that ensued was that his horse was killed under him, just as the flag was raised. The demand for quarter, seldom refused to a vanquished foe, was at once found to be in vain. Not a man was spared, and it was the concurrent testimony of all the survivors that for fifteen minutes after every man was prostrate, they went over the ground, plunging their bayonets into everyone that exhibited any signs of life." "One hundred and thirteen were killed on the spot," wrote Charles Stedman, a British officer, "and . . . one hundred and fifty were badly wounded. . . . The King's troops were entitled to great commendation for their activity and ardour . . . but the virtue of humanity was totally forgot." British casualties amounted to just nineteen.

The fall of Charleston decided the fate of South Carolina. With the city as his base, Clinton dispatched three expeditions into the interior—one to reoccupy Augusta, another to overrun and subdue the country around Fort Ninety-six, and the third and largest, under Lord Cornwallis, to disperse patriot militia reportedly assembling to the north. The three were then to unite and carry the war into North Carolina and Virginia and eventually, it was hoped, by effecting a connection with New York, subdue the country south of the Hudson.

At first, all went spectacularly well. The whole of South Carolina, from the seacoast to the mountains, was rapidly conquered, and everywhere the people submitted with embarrassing alacrity. Tories, of which the country was full, flocked to the royal standard in great numbers and increased the British strength. Small bands of patriots who had remained in arms after the fall of Charleston were soon cut to pieces or took refuge under such daring partisan leaders as Thomas Sumter and Francis Marion in swamps and forests across the North Carolina line. In South Carolina itself, only a few hundred patriot militia, their headquarters on the Broad River at the Cherokee Ford, remained.

Thus the whole of Georgia and South Carolina lay prostrate at the feet of the invader. Colonel Robert Gray, a South Carolina loyalist provincial officer and backcountry native, wrote of his home state:

> The conquest of the province was complete; the loyal inhabitants readily took up arms to maintain the British government and others enrolled themselves in the [loyalist] militia, partly because they believed the war to be at an end in the southern provinces and partly to ingratiate themselves with the conquerors. They fondly hoped they would enjoy a respite from the calamities of war and that the restoration of the King's government would restore to them the happiness they enjoyed before the war began. With these views on both sides, the Whigs and Tories seemed to vie with each other in giving proof of the sincerity of their submission.

On July 5, Clinton embarked for New York, leaving to Lord Cornwallis the task of extending British control throughout the South. How he was to do this was largely left to his own discretion, but in general, he was expected to hold on to the British gains and strike north into North Carolina while Clinton sent raiding parties into Virginia to prevent troops from that state from coming to North Carolina's aid.

Forty-two years old at the time, Cornwallis had begun his military career as an ensign in the Grenadier Guards. Like Clinton he had served under Prince Ferdinand of Braunschweig in the Seven Years' War, had risen to lieutenant colonel and commander of the British Twelfth Regiment and then, in 1775, to major general. Meanwhile, in 1762, he had succeeded his father in the House of Lords. As a member of Parliament, he had voted against taxation of the colonies; but once sent against them (he had participated in the battles of Long Island, Trenton, Brandywine, and Germantown) proved zealous at his task. To oppose him Congress now turned to General Gates, who on June 13 was appointed supreme commander of the American forces in the South.

Gates hastened to the trust, and at first the arrival of an officer of such exalted reputation lifted the spirits of the troops. With a kind of sympathetic condescension, he commiserated with General Lincoln about the late failures of his own command:

> The series of misfortunes you have experienced, since you were doomed to the command of the Southern Department, has affected me exceedingly. I feel for you most sensibly. I feel for myself, who am to succeed to what? To the command of an army without strength—a military chest without money, a department apparently deficient in public spirit and a climate that increases despondency instead of animating the soldier's arm. . . . You will oblige me very much by communicating any hints or information which you think will be useful to me. . . . You know that I am not above advice, especially where it comes from a good head and a sincere heart.

Gates needed more advice than he realized but failed to heed the better part of what he got. On July 16, the baron de Kalb, who had temporarily assumed command of the southern army after the fall of Charleston, received him at Wilcox's Mills on the Deep River in North Carolina. Gates paid him the compliment of confirming his standing orders but then startled everyone by ordering the men to prepare to march toward Camden, then held by the British, the following day. At the time, the soldiers were suffering from general shortages and wracked by dysentery. Nevertheless, Gates announced that they were to proceed through a wilderness of pine barrens, even though all the leading officers signed a remonstrance pointing out that the army would not be able to provision itself. Gates assured them that supplies were on the way from the North.

The disastrous march began. Disease, hunger, and a terrible summer heat steadily thinned the ranks; men deserted; mutiny was "twice at the door." The promised supplies never came. To slake their thirst, the men found only brackish water in the barren and, in the absence of bread, ate unripened corn and peaches still half green. On August 13, they reached Clermont, within thirteen miles of the enemy. Two days later, plans were drawn up for an attack. Although Gates had 7,000 men in his command, fewer than half were in any condition to fight. And two thirds of these were raw recruits. At a council of war, most of the officers favored fortifying the position they held—Clermont being a place "strong by nature and capable of being made stronger by art." "We have Cornwallis against us!" exclaimed one colonel. Replied an offended Gates, "He will not dare to look me in the face."

At ten that evening, the tents were struck. The sky was clear and the stars shone brightly, but the air remained sultry from the day's burning heat. Underfoot, deep sand deadened the rumble of the American artillery and the heavy tread of the troops.

Every now and then men sickened and fell out of the ranks. Earlier that evening, instead of handing out rum, as was the usual custom before battle, Gates (lacking liquor) had issued extra rations of molasses, which had a crippling laxative effect. Meanwhile by coincidence Lord Cornwallis, with a force that included Tarleton's Legion and Lord Rawdon's Volunteers of Ireland, was advancing toward Clermont at the head of some 3,000 men. Thus the two armies were fast approaching each other in the dark. At two in the morning, their vanguards collided in a glade in the pine forest, and after a brief skirmish, filled with cries of astonishment, both drew back.

At daybreak, the general battle began. It was fought on a narrow stretch of ground with swamps on either side, and as soon as the two armies engaged, the militia from Virginia and North Carolina threw down their arms and fled without firing a shot. The remainder crumbled before the British onslaught in the most devastating defeat of the war. "The impetuosity with which the [British] advanced," wrote an American officer, "*firing* and *huzzaing,* threw the whole body of the militia into . . . the utmost consternation." Their rout was absolute and irretrievable. In vain did Gates attempt to rally them (though he didn't do so for long) as he spurred after them, not stopping, however, till he had reached Charlotte, ahead of his scattered army, sixty miles away. Alexander Hamilton expressed the general public disgust when he asked, "Was there ever such an instance of a general running away . . . from his whole army? And was there ever so precipitous a flight?"

The impression was all the more shameful because other officers had remained and fought to the death. Kalb was one of them. Three times he led his men forward through the glade; three times superior numbers forced him back. His horse was shot from under him; his scalp was laid open by a saber stroke. An aide bound up the wound with a scarf and begged him to withdraw, but he returned to the fray and led the charge on foot. At last he fell, riddled with eleven wounds.

Cornwallis and his suite rode up. "I regret to see you so badly wounded, but am glad to have defeated you," said the British general, and gave orders that Kalb be cared for; but he died.

Several days later, at Hillsboro, 180 miles away, Gates collected the fragments of his army around him. A bit disingenuously, he tried to put the best face on things in a letter to his commander in chief: "The victory is far from bloodless on the part of the foe. . . . I shall continue my unwearied endeavors . . . to recommence an offensive war, and recover all our losses in the southern states. But if being unfortunate is solely reason sufficient for removing me from command, I shall most cheerfully submit to the orders of Congress and resign an office few generals would be anxious to possess and where the utmost skill and fortitude are subject to be baffled by the difficulties which must for a time surround the chief in command here."

Washington, while not excusing Gates's behavior, also lamented the contribution the militia had made to the defeat. "I solemnly declare," he said, "I have found them useful as light Parties to skirmish in the woods, but incapable of making or sustaining a serious attack. . . . The Militia fled at the first fire, and left the Continental Troops surrounded on every side, and over-powered."

Gates marched to Charlotte, which he made his new base, but the tide of his popularity ebbed as fast as it had flowed. A court of inquiry was ordered to look into his conduct, and on October 14 Congress replaced him with Nathanael Greene. Although ultimately acquitted of all charges (partly in deference to his former laurels), he resigned in the shadow of disgrace.

MEANWHILE, all had not been quiet on the Northern front. On June 6, General Wilhelm von Knyphausen, commanding in New York in Clinton's absence, had brought 5,000 British and Hessian troops across from Staten Island into New Jersey. They burned several houses in Elizabethtown but, encountering stiff resistance from the local militia, retreated to the coast. In the third week of July, after Clinton had returned from the South, Knyphausen advanced again, hoping not merely to destroy the military depot at Morristown but to seize the heights where Washington was encamped. This time he was effectively opposed at Springfield by a detachment of Continentals and, after burning the village, beat a second, more costly, retreat. The British were disappointed, though not discouraged: too much was going their way.

Yet imperceptibly the tide of the war had already begun to change. After the plans for an invasion of England had collapsed, France decided to send a powerful fleet—five frigates and five ships of the line—and an army of 5,500 under the comte de Rochambeau to America. Lafayette had been sent on ahead as the herald to announce their coming, and on July 10, after a voyage of seventy days by way of the Azores and around Bermuda, to avoid enemy interdiction, the French fleet docked at Newport. Another French squadron was also expected from Brest.

On September 21, Washington, accompanied by Knox and Lafayette, the latter acting as interpreter, met with Rochambeau at Hartford, Connecticut. The two commanders were "quite charmed with one another," according to a French officer, but failed to make any definite plans for their cooperation in a campaign. "We could only combine possible plans on the supposition of possible events," wrote Washington, though it was generally agreed that if the rest of the French fleet arrived before late fall, an attempt might be made against New York. Otherwise, a combined operation might be considered to dislodge the British from the South.

Washington left Hartford on the twenty-third, paused at Peekskill to visit with the French minister, Luzerne, and on the twenty-fifth went on to West Point, where Benedict Arnold was in command.

There he discovered "treason of the blackest dye."

CHAPTER SEVENTEEN

WEST POINT

FROM the beginning of the war, Benedict Arnold's leadership, initiative, and daring as an officer had almost always been shadowed by some kind of questionable dealing or practice involving money or goods acquired for his own aggrandizement. Some of the charges may have been unfair, but as early as the siege of Boston there was something discernibly opportunistic about him which John Trumbull, one of Washington's young aides, had glimpsed when he described him as an "inveterate schemer." During the Quebec campaign, the young Aaron Burr had a more particular impression. Though he admired Arnold's martial readiness "for any deeds of valor," he also doubted that Arnold had "a particle of moral courage. He is utterly unprincipled and has no love of country or self-respect to guide him. He is not to be trusted anywhere but under the eye of a superior." Colonel John Brown more forcefully asserted, "Money is this man's god, and to get enough of it he would sacrifice his country."

Those were prophetic words.

Though regularly (and rapidly) promoted, Arnold, in his own eyes, had been insufficiently appreciated and not always given an appropriate command. At Saratoga, such feelings had inspired his defiance of Gates. For the extremity of his insubordination, another officer might have been dismissed or even shot. But Arnold had been indulged—and would continue to be—by the commander in chief, out of respect for his services and popularity. It was, in fact, his private ingratitude combined with public betrayal that made his treason complete.

We must go back a bit in time. Despite all the turmoil associated with his career, in the spring of 1778 Arnold was still an officer in good standing as he made his way to Washington's headquarters at Valley Forge. Although eager for a new appointment, he was also a widower soon to turn forty with a bad leg. And his mind was partly on romance. Arnold had recently met the wealthy daughter of a prominent Tory, Miss Elizabeth "Betsy" DeBlois, age seventeen, and sought to win her over with elaborately formulated letters of conventional supplication, mixing affectionate accusation with protestations of despair:

April 8th 1778
Dear Madam,
Twenty times have I taken up my pen to write to you, and as often has my trembling hand refused to obey the dictates of my heart. A heart which has often been calm and serene amidst the clashing of Arms, and all the din and horrors of Warr, trembles with diffidence and the fear of giving offence when it attempts to address you on a subject so Important to its happiness. Long have I struggled to erase your heavenly Image from it. Neither time, absence, misfortunes, nor your cruel Indifference have been able to efface the deep impression your Charms have made, and will you doom a heart so true, so faithfull to languish in dispair? Shall I expect no returns to the most sincere, ardent, and disinterested passion? Dear Betsy, suffer that heavenly Bosom (which surely cannot know itself the cause of misfortune without a sympathetic pang) to expand with Friendship at last and let me know my Fate. If a happy one no man will strive more to deserve it; if on the contrary I am doom'd to dispair, my latest breath will be to implore the blessing of Heaven on the Idol, & only wish of my soul.

Arnold's appeal made Betsy most uncomfortable. She told him so and made it plain that she was not romantically attracted to him. Nevertheless, in a letter of April 26, Arnold pressed his suit:

Had I imagined my letter would have occasioned you a moment's uneasiness, I never should forgive myself for writing it,—You intreat me to solicit no further for your affections; Consider Dear Madam when you urge impossibilities I cannot Obey; as well might you wish me to exist without breathing as cease to love you, and wish for a return of affection.—As your intreaty does not amount to a positive Injunction and you have not forbid me to hope, how can I decline soliciting your particular affections, on which the whole happiness of my Life depends:

A union of hearts I acknowledge is necessary to happiness, but give me leave to observe that true and permanent happiness is seldom the effect of an alliance form'd on a romantick passion when Fancy governs more than Judgement.

Friendship and esteem founded on the Merit of the object is the most certain basis to build a lasting happiness upon, and when there is a Tender and Ardent passion on one side, and Friendship and esteem on the other, the heart must be callous to every tender sentiment if the taper of Love is not lighted up at the Flame, which a series of reciprocal kindness and attention will never suffer to expire.

If Fame allows me any share of Merit, I am in a great measure indebted for it to the Pure and exalted passion your Charms have Inspired me with, which cannot admit of an unworthy thought or action,—A passion productive of good and Injurious to no one you must approve, and suffer me to indulge.

Pardon me Dear Betsy if I called you Cruel. If the eyes are an Index to the Heart Love and Harmony must banish every Irregular passion from your Heavenly Bosom.

Arnold continued to beseech and implore her, but she refused to see him again.

A month later, on May 20, Arnold rode into Valley Forge to consult with Washington on how he might best continue to serve the Revolution. He suggested that Washington make him military governor of Philadelphia, to take effect immediately after the British evacuation. Washington agreed.

On June 19, with a regiment of Massachusetts Continentals, Arnold took control of the city, set up a new administration, and, in accordance with a resolve of Congress, ordered that an inventory of all merchandise be taken and its owners identified before public trade resumed.

With all trade but his own prohibited, Arnold evidently took advantage of his position to make wholesale purchases at low prices, ostensibly for the army but in fact in part for himself, and later sold through middlemen a portion of what he had acquired at a large profit for personal gain. Meanwhile, he had established himself in the finest mansion in town, a spacious brick building with a walled garden, coach house, stable, and warehouse that had recently served as the headquarters of General Howe.

Arnold made useful mercantile connections, and his dealings soon brought him into association with the wealthy (and largely Tory) local aristocracy. In their company, his already resentful allegiance to the Revolution began to wane. Tory sentiment in the city remained shockingly high. The French minister, Gérard, confided to his government, "Scarcely one quarter of the ordinary inhabitants of Philadelphia now here favour the cause of [independence]. Commercial and family ties, together with an aversion to popular government, seem to account for this. The same feeling exists in New York and Boston, which is not the case in the rural districts." "Even our military gentlemen," wrote one socialite to a friend, "are too liberal to make any distinction between Whig and Tory Ladyes. If they make any, it is in favour of the latter. Such, strange as it may seem, is the way those things are conducted at present in this city. It originates at headquarters, and that I may make some apology for such strange conduct, I must tell you that Cupid has given our little General a more mortal wound than all the hosts of Britons could—Miss Peggy Shippen is the fair one."

The "little General" was Arnold and his "fair one," Margaret "Peggy" Shippen, then eighteen, a true femme fatale. As with the former object of his affections, Betsy DeBlois, her family was Tory, but Arnold thought Peggy even more fetching, with "a slim and graceful figure, and a very pretty, submissive face, crowned by a fortune in carefully nurtured yellow curls." Unlike Betsy, however, she was nothing if not flattered by Arnold's courtship and dazzled to be desired by this battle-scarred hero, "with a warmly florid face, domineering chin and brow, rich, persuasive lips and the boldest eyes that she had ever seen: a forceful, commanding lover, and a great man."

In appealing for her affections, Arnold resurrected his two earlier letters to Betsy and more or less blended them into one:

> Twenty times have I taken up my pen to write to you, and as often has my trembling hand refused to obey the tates of my heart—a heart which, though calm and serene amid the clashing of arms and all the din and horrors of war, trembles with diffidence and the fear of giving offence when it attempts to address you on a subject so important to its happiness. Dear Madam, your charms have lighted up a flame in my bosom which can never be extinguished; your heavenly image is too deeply impressed ever to be effaced. My passion is not founded on personal charms only: that sweetness of disposition and goodness of heart—that sentiment and sensibility which so strongly mark the character of the lovely Miss P. Shippen—render her amiable beyond expression, and will ever retain the heart he has once captivated.
>
> On you alone my happiness depends. And will you doom me to languish in despair? Shall I expect no return to the most sincere, ardent and disinterested passion? Do you feel no pity in your gentle bosom for the man who would die to make you happy? May I presume to hope it is not impossible

I may make a favorable impression on your heart? Friendship and esteem you acknowledge. Dear Peggy! suffer that heavenly bosom (which cannot know itself the cause of pain without a sympathetic pang) to expand with a sensation more oft, more tender than friendship. A union of hearts is undoubtedly necessary to happiness. But give me leave to observe that true and permanent happiness is seldom the effect of an alliance founded on a romantic passion, where fancy governs more than judgment. Friendship and esteem, founded on the merit of the object, is the most certain basis to found a lasting happiness upon. And when there is a tender and ardent passion on one side, and friendship and esteem on the other, the heart (unlike yours) must be callous to every tender sentiment if the taper of love is not lighted up at the flame. . . .

Suffer me to hope for your approbation. Consider before you doom me to misery, which I have not deserved but by loving you too extravagantly. Consult your own happiness, and, if incompatible, forget there is so unhappy a wretch, for may I perish if I would give you one moment's inquietude to purchase the greatest possible felicity to myself! Whatever my fate may be, my most ardent wish is for your happiness, and my latest breath will be to implore the blessings of Heaven on the idol and only wish of my soul.

The interchangeability in the language of his affection, regardless of its romantic object, oddly parallels (and perhaps predicted) the interchangeability of his allegiance in the war.

Peggy's parents had misgivings and cautioned her against being too impulsive, but she was quite overwhelmed by Arnold's advances and responded to her family's resistance with hysterical fits.

Meanwhile, Arnold found himself at odds with the patriot camp. A good deal of Philadelphia, of course, did not belong to the social circle in which he moved, and the frivolities (if not license) which had characterized life during the occupation led to something of a backlash. At a time when the suffering public looked to their leaders to inspire them with "the proper attitude of self-sacrificing devotion," Arnold's administration and his opportunistic dealings were seen as the worst possible example to set.

There was also a desire for retribution against the Tory population. Congressman Gouverneur Morris of New York, primarily concerned with replenishing the Continental treasury, urged that all citizens at first be confined to their houses and forced to pay a collective tribute of £100,000, the individual amounts to be determined by their wealth and degree of collaboration with the British; Congressman Joseph Reed of Pennsylvania, Washington's former military secretary, more harshly suggested that about 500 Tories of all ranks and stations be hanged for treason and their property seized. Arnold's policy, which was more indulgent, proceeded under cover of the instructions he had received from his commander in chief. "You will take every prudent step in your power," Washington had told him on June 19, "to preserve tranquility and order in the city and give security to individuals of every class and description; restraining, as far as possible, till the restoration of civil government, every species of persecution, insult or abuse, either from the soldiery to the inhabitants or among each other." Arnold did so, but the suspicion soon arose that his show of impartiality disguised Tory affinities, which his style of living (including a coach and four and expensive entertainments at his mansion) seemed to bear out.

"You must know," Samuel Adams wrote, "that in humble imitation, as it would seem, of the example of the British Army, some of the Officers of ours have condescended to act on the Stage; which others, and one of Superior Rank, were pleased to countenance with their Presence." He meant, of course, Arnold, who seemed to be trying to recapture the gaieties of the occupation days. Congress, however, missed the point and, with a kind of prudish futility, introduced unenforceable legislation "to suppress stage playing, horse racing, gaming, and such kinds of diversions, as are productive of Vice, Idleness, Dissipation and a general Depravity of Principals and manners." Attitudes grew more severe, especially after Joseph Reed was elected president of the Supreme Executive Council of Pennsylvania. In his campaign to ferret out Tories of every stripe, he suggested (through a local newspaper) "that the right hand and right side of the face of every Tory be dyed black, that his neighbors might know him." Hundreds were prosecuted in the courts, and several Quaker collaborators were publicly hanged.

At the beginning of February 1779, Arnold, under pressure, resigned as military governor, and the Supreme Executive Council promptly charged him with eight counts of misconduct and abuse of power. The charges were published in the newspapers and sent to the legislatures of the thirteen states. A joint committee of Congress and the council met and, on April 3, recommended a court-martial on the first, second, third, and fifth charges, having to do with profiteering and the use of public property for private ends.

Arnold now hastened toward his fateful date with corrupted connubial bliss and infamy. On April 10, he married Peggy Shippen, and about the same time, under the code name Gustavus, he made contact with British agents in New York. As he sent his three children from his first marriage off to a Maryland school, he told their tutor to concentrate on practical subjects and not to bother with the humanities. "I wish their education to be useful rather than learned," he explained. "Life is too short & uncertain to throw away in speculations upon subjects that perhaps only one man in ten thousand has a genius to make a figure in."

In a letter of May 5 to Washington he wrote, "I little expected to meet the ungrateful returns I have received from my countrymen; but as Congress have stamped ingratitude as a current coin I must take it. I wish your Excellency, for your long and eminent services, may not be paid in the same coin."

On May 14, with his court-martial pending, Arnold wrote to Washington again, asking for an opportunity "to render my country every service in my power at this critical time, for though I have been ungratefully treated, I do not consider it as from my countrymen in general but from a set of men who, void of principle, are governed entirely by the private interest. The interest I have in the welfare and happiness of my country, which I have ever evinced when in my power, will, I hope, always overcome my personal resentment for any injury I can possibly receive from individuals." In remarkably similar (shall we say interchangeable?) language he had written to Gates two years before, in August 1777, that "no public or private injury or insult shall prevail on me to forsake the cause of my injured and oppressed country until I see peace and liberty restored or nobly die in the attempt."

It was not to be so. In striking back at those who he believed had failed to appreciate his services or had publicly besmirched his honor or done him other wrongs, he was also prepared to sacrifice others, including Washington himself, who had done all they could on this behalf. On May 21, exactly one week after he wrote this letter—expressing just those noble sentiments which might have enabled him to surmount his temptations—he disclosed troop movements and other top secret information in his first coded message to the enemy.

In his initial contacts with the British, Arnold kept his own identity secret but described himself as a high-ranking officer and hinted at a willingness to defect. He offered bits of valuable information, and Clinton turned the negotiations over to his adjutant general, Major John André, who had recently been appointed to run Clinton's network of spies. André was a clever and cultivated man but to some degree without scruples. During the occupation, he had lived in Benjamin Franklin's house, and upon departing (as noted earlier) he had made off with most of Franklin's treasured collection of books. He had also been one of Peggy Shippen's admirers and the architect of Howe's farewell meschianza bash.

André detailed the information Arnold might provide: the names of American agents, the number and position of troops and reinforcements, the location of American supply depots, the contents of top secret dispatches, and so on. These were to be conveyed by letter in a correspondence ostensibly conducted between Arnold's wife, Peggy, and one of her friends in New York, with Arnold writing his secret messages to André in code or between the lines in invisible ink. Such letters could be read either by holding them over a candle until the interlineations became legible or by brushing the entire page with acid to make the hidden writing emerge. The code was to be made up of three-number groups— the first number indicating the page number in Blackstone's *Commentary on the Laws of England;* the second, the line on that page; the third, the word itself. (Arnold, however, finding Blackstone's *Commentary* too cumbersome, arranged instead to key his messages to a contemporary dictionary.)

Arnold claimed to be disenchanted with America's new alliance with the French. He was also, he said, out of sympathy with the Declaration of Independence, which he considered a document drafted by extremists, and he declared his intention of coming over to the British in a way most advantageous to the Crown. But he wanted to be indemnified for all the losses his magnanimous defection would cause him—in short, he wanted a lot of money in the deal. John André, writing transparently under the name of John Anderson, pretended to take his correspondent's political opinions seriously and by flattery moved Arnold to hope that he might yet be esteemed a man of honor and repute. At the same time, he made the business plain: "Accept a command," he told him, "be surprised, be cut off: these things may happen in the course of maneuver, nor can you be censured or suspected. A complete service of this nature involving a corps of five or six thousand men would be rewarded with twice as many thousand guineas."

The letters went back and forth, carried by various go-betweens, sometimes erroneously dated or in cipher. Through an intermediary, Arnold demanded £20,000. André offered half that sum.

After the date for his court-martial was set, Arnold traveled to Washington's camp, then at Middlebrook, New Jersey. At headquarters, he tried to clear his name. He "self-invited some civilities," wrote Washington afterward, "I never meant to show him, or any officer in arrest, and he received a rebuke before I could convince him of the impropriety of his entering upon a justification of his conduct in my presence."

When the court-martial convened on December 19, 1779, Arnold called the charges against him "false, malicious, and scandalous." "Mr. President and gentlemen of this honorable court," he began,

I appear before you to answer charges brought against me by the supreme executive council of the commonwealth of Pennsylvania. It is disagreeable to be accused, but when an accusation is made, I feel it is a great source of consolation to have an opportunity of being tried by gentlemen whose delicate and refined sensations of honor will lead them to entertain similar sentiments concerning those who accuse unjustly and those who are justly accused. . . .

When the present necessary war against Great Britain commenced, I was in easy circumstances and enjoyed a fair prospect of improving them. I was happy in domestic connections and blessed with a rising family, who claimed my care and attention. The liberties of my country were in danger. The voice of my country called upon all her faithful sons to join in her defense. With cheerfulness, I obeyed the call. I sacrificed domestic ease and happiness to the service of my country, and in her service have I sacrificed a great part of a handsome fortune. I was one of the first who appeared in the field and, from that time to the present hour, have not abandoned her service.

He reminded the court in detail of his tremendous contribution to the war and of the many commendations he had received. And he portrayed the charges against him as a methodical attempt at character assassination conducted by Reed. Since Reed's malice was manifest and his penchant for intrigue, which Washington himself had experienced, widely known, Arnold was able to mount a plausible defense. In the end, the case against him could not be proved conclusively, and, being found guilty of two minor charges, he merely received a reprimand from the commander in chief. Tactful as always, Washington mixed praise with blame, casting his reprimand as a necessary but reluctant act:

Our profession is the chastest of all; even the shadow of a fault tarnishes the lustre of our finest achievements. The least inadvertence may rob us of the public favor, so hard to be acquired. I reprimand you for having forgotten that in proportion as you have rendered yourself formidable to our enemies, you should have been guarded and temperate in your deportment towards your fellow-citizens. Exhibit anew those noble qualities which have placed you on the list of our most valued commanders. I will myself furnish you, as far as it may be in my power, with opportunities for regaining the esteem of your country.

This gesture of trust, and the implied promise of a new command, might have inspired enormous gratitude and zeal in a man of higher principle. Instead, Arnold sought to take advantage of Washington's goodwill.

At first he hoped for the independent command of an army, so that he could offer it as a chip to the enemy in return for a higher price. Early in

April 1780, he met with Philip Schuyler, who agreed to speak to Washington on his behalf. On June 2, Schuyler told Arnold that Washington had expressed great appreciation for his abilities, merits, and sufferings and seemed eager to appoint him either to an important post or to a top field command. At this juncture, on the pretext that his crippled left leg rendered him incapable of active service, Arnold began to maneuver in earnest for jurisdiction over the critical fortress and surrounding defenses of West Point. These had been improved in the previous year to thwart any new British thrust southward from Canada or northward from New York.

In mid-June, he got word to the British of his prospects and gave them an account of the vulnerabilities of the defenses that he hoped would soon be in his charge. West Point, a complex of seven different forts, could not, he said, hold out against a British siege. The garrison was inadequate to man the works, provisions were low, and though scores of cannon in the forts were positioned to fire on any ships which tried to break through the chain blocking the channel, "I am convinced the boom or chain," wrote Arnold, "cannot be depended upon. . . . A single ship, large and heavy-loaded with a strong wind and tide would break it."

The appointment was confirmed and at the end of July, Arnold established his headquarters at Beverley, a country estate a little below West Point, on the other side of the river. There he was joined by his wife and newborn son.

With no apparent or immediate threat to the fortifications, the garrison was relaxed. "We make ourselves very Merry at this place," a soldier wrote in his diary. "As there aren't many women around, we enjoy ourselves without them. [Last] evening several of us dressed in women's clothes and had a genteel Country Dance—spent the evening in great glee."

Arnold spent most of his time hobbling about headquarters on his cane or riding over the hills to inspect the works. But all his thought was now on how to betray his men. He weakened the defenses, redistributed the garrison in such a way as to make it easier to be overcome or captured, and ordered that the great chain across the river be repaired. In the process, one link was surreptitiously weakened and the ends so loosely bound together that a vessel could easily break through.

His spirits rose as American fortunes fell. Gates, whom he hated, had been defeated in the South in mid-August; the French fleet was bottled up at Newport; inflation continued to rise. On September 16, he received a letter from Washington: "I shall be at Peekskill on Sunday evening, on my way to Hartford to meet the French admiral and general. You will be pleased to send down a guard of a captain and 50 at that time, and direct the quartermaster to have a night's forage for about 40 horses. You will keep this to yourself, as I want to make my journey a secret." Two days later, Arnold met Washington at King's Ferry and accompanied him across the Hudson to Peekskill. Washington asked Arnold for an up-to-date report on the state of the West Point defenses. Arnold assured him that all was secure.

The British planned to take West Point within the week. There seemed little to prevent them, and, on the night of the nineteenth, Clinton and his staff threw a banquet in anticipation of success. In the middle of dinner, André, who had been promised a promotion and the hereditary title of baronet if all went well, stood up to sing a song sung by British soldiers on the eve of their great victory at Quebec:

> Why, soldiers, why,
> Should we be melancholy, boys,
> Whose business 'tis to die?
> For should next campaign
> Send us to Him who made us, boys,
> We're free from pain.
> But should we remain,
> A bottle and kind landlady
> Makes all well again.

Two days later, the British sloop of war the *Vulture* sailed up the Hudson River into the highlands and anchored in Haverstraw Bay, four miles south of Stony Point. Near midnight, one Joshua Hett Smith, who had agreed to act as Arnold's agent, rowed out to the *Vulture* and met with Colonel Beverly Robinson, a loyalist officer who owned the farmhouse in which Arnold now lived, and John André. André put on a long blue coat to cover his uniform, climbed down into the boat, and was rowed by Smith to the western shore. There he was led into a fir grove, where Arnold awaited him. They consulted until about four A.M., then retired to an upper room in Smith's stone house nearby and consolidated their plans. André was given six documents, which he hid in his stockings, and after Arnold left, André and Smith waited until the following evening before setting out upon the highway to the south. They crossed the river at King's Ferry, were briefly questioned by a patriot patrol, slept at a farmhouse nearby, and in the morning rode on. Up until then, André had been a sullen companion. He now became more loquacious. "I found him highly entertaining," recalled Smith. "He was not only well informed in general history but well acquainted with that of America . . . he conversed freely on the belles-lettres. Music, painting and poetry seemed to be his delight. He displayed a judicious taste in the choice of the authors he had read, possessed great elegance of sentiment and a most pleasing manner of conveying his ideas by adopting the flowery colouring of poetical imagery. He lamented the causes which gave birth to and continued the war." After a few miles, Smith turned back, leaving André with some twenty miles of neutral ground to traverse before he was in the clear. This no-man's-land between the British and American positions was often roamed by bandits—those with patriot leanings were called "Skinners," those with Tory affiliation, "Cowboys" or "Refugees."

Near Tarrytown, three men suddenly stepped out of the woods and ordered him to halt. One grabbed the bridle of his horse. "I hope, gentlemen," said André, "you belong to the lower party," meaning those allied to the British "lower" down the river in New York.

"We do."

"So do I. I am a British officer on business of importance and must not be detained."

Then he realized his mistake. He was ordered into the woods, stripped and searched, and the telltale documents were found. One of his captors recalled, "You never saw such an alteration in any man's face. Only a few moments before, he was uncommonly gay in his looks, but after we made him prisoner, you could read in his face that he thought it was all over with him. After traveling one or two miles, he said, 'I would to God you had blown my brains out when you stopped me!' " They briefly considered holding him for ransom, but thought better of it and conducted him to Lieutenant Colonel John Jameson, in command at North Castle.

The following morning, as Arnold anxiously awaited word of the impending British attack, he learned that Washington himself was on his way to West Point. After meeting with Rochambeau at Hartford, Washington had decided to inspect his fortifications along the Hudson and, with Lafayette, Hamilton, Knox, and other members of his staff, had left Hartford on September 23. Two of Washington's aides preceded him and were at breakfast at Arnold's table when a letter suddenly arrived announcing that an enemy officer calling himself John Anderson and carrying incriminating papers had been captured in disguise. Arnold, visibly distressed, excused himself without explanation and went upstairs to explain the situation to Peggy, who paled and fainted in his arms. Then, he called for a horse, rode down to the water's edge, where a barge lay moored, and had the men at the oars push off for the *Vulture,* promising each two gallons of rum for his pains.

Meanwhile, Washington had crossed the river earlier that morning, expecting Arnold to be on hand with an appropriate honor guard. "The impropriety of his conduct when he knew I was to be there struck me very forcibly," said Washington afterward, "and my mind misgave me, but I had not the least idea of the real cause."

Washington spent the next several hours inspecting the lower fortifications, which he was appalled to find in such disrepair—breaches in the walls, guns out of commission, and so on—and as he approached headquarters, he learned of Arnold's hasty and mysterious departure. Then a messenger arrived with the incriminating papers, which Alexander Hamilton, Washington's aide, was the first to read. They included a pass for Anderson, dated September 22; an overall estimate of the current strength of the Continental Army; and an account of the West Point defenses, including the usual arrangements for the disposition of the troops and artillery in case of an attack. Hamilton hurried to Washington, who looked the papers over, recognized Arnold's hand, and saw that his signature was on Anderson's pass. Yet another document revealed that Anderson was Major John André, adjutant general in the British army. As Washington confided this information to Lafayette and Knox, "he looked at them with imploring eyes, and said, 'Whom can we trust now?'"

Upstairs, Peggy lay unconscious; when she awoke, she began to rant and rave, "her clothing in disarray, her hair hanging about her shoulders and over her face." She began crying hysterically, and the commander in chief, whose compassionate nature asserted itself even at this bitter hour, sat beside her to comfort and assure her that no one, as she seemed wildly to believe, would harm her child. He then arranged for Peggy and her son to be escorted safely to Philadelphia.

Within the hour, Washington also acted to strengthen West Point and its satellite forts and to redeploy the garrison in a more secure defense. "The enemy," he warned, "may have it in contemplation to attempt some enterprise, even tonight, against these posts." Two regiments of the Pennsylvania Line were ordered up from Fishkill to fill out the garrison, and General Greene, with a division, was summoned to King's Ferry. "Transactions of a most interesting nature," Washington wrote to him, "and such as will astonish you have been just discovered." On the morning of the twenty-sixth, the following statement, composed by Greene, was read to the army:

Treason of the blackest dye was yesterday discovered. General Arnold, who commanded at West Point, lost to every sentiment of honor, of private and public obligation, was about to deliver up that important post into the hands of the enemy. Such an event must have given the American cause a dangerous, if not a fatal wound. Happily the treason has been timely discovered to prevent the fatal misfortune. The providential train of circumstances which led to it affords the most convincing proofs that the liberties of America are the object of divine protection. . . . Great honor is due to the American army that this is the first instance of treason of the kind, where many were to be expected from the nature of our dispute.

Meanwhile, Washington had received a letter from Arnold which must have made his ears burn:

On Board the Vulture, Sept 25th, 1780. Sir,—

The heart which is conscious of its own rectitude, cannot attempt to palliate a step which the world may censure as wrong; I have ever acted upon the principle of love to my country, since the commencement of the present unhappy contest between Great Britain and the Colonies. The same principle of love to my country actuates my present conduct, however it may appear inconsistent to the world, who very seldom judge right of a man's actions.

I have no favor to ask for myself; I have too often experienced the ingratitude of my country to attempt it; but from the known humanity of your Excellency I am induced to ask your protection for Mrs. Arnold, from every insult and injury that the mistaken vengeance of my country may expose her to. It ought to fall only on me. She is as good and as innocent as an angel and is incapable of doing wrong. I beg she may be permitted to return to her friends in Philadelphia or to come to me, as she may choose; from your Excellency I have no fears on her account, but she may suffer from the mistaken fury of the country.

I have to request that the enclosed letter may be delivered to Mrs. Arnold, and she permitted to write to me.

I have also to ask that my clothes and baggage which are of little consequence may be sent to me. If required, their value shall be paid in money. I have the honor to be

With great regard and esteem,

Your Excellency's most obedient humble servant

B. Arnold.

Arnold had nothing to worry about. And he was safe, but the life of his accomplice, André, was in the gravest jeopardy. In the custody of Major Benjamin Tallmadge himself, the British "Prince of Spies" was taken to Tappan. As they rode along, André "became very inquisitive to know my opinion as to the result of his capture," recalled Tallmadge.

> When I could no longer evade his importunity, I remarked to him as follows: "I had a much-loved classmate in Yale College by the name of [Captain Nathan] Hale, who entered the army in 1775. Immediately after the Battle of Long Island, Washington wanted information respecting the strength of the enemy. Hale tendered his services, went over to Brooklyn, and was taken just as he was passing the outposts of the enemy on his return." Said I with emphasis, "Do you remember the sequel of the story?"
> "Yes," said André. "He was hanged as a spy. But you surely do not consider his case and mine alike!"
> I replied, "Yes, precisely similar; and similar will be your fate."

At his trial, held on September 29 in the old Dutch Church at Orangetown, New Jersey, and presided over by General Greene, André frankly confessed everything but scrupulously refused to implicate others, which the court could not but admire. It unanimously agreed that he must die but ambivalently considered his last request, that he be shot and not, like a common felon, hanged. In this regard, he made a powerful and pathetic direct appeal to Washington, who was "staggered in his resolution." The commander in chief referred the matter to his general officers, who, with one exception, were inclined to indulge André's request.

The exception was General Greene, who thus stated his dissent. "Andre," he said,

> is either a spy or an innocent man. If the latter, to execute him in any way will be murder: if the former, the mode of his death is prescribed by law. . . . Nor is this all. At the present alarming crisis of our affairs, the public safety calls for a solemn and impressive example. Nothing can satisfy it short of the execution of the prisoner as a common spy. . . . Besides, if you shoot the prisoner, instead of hanging him, you will excite suspicion which you will be unable to allay. Notwithstanding all your efforts to the contrary, you will awaken public compassion, and the belief will become general, that, in the case of Major Andre, there were exculpatory circumstances, entitling him to lenity, beyond what he received—perhaps entitling him to pardon. Hang him, therefore, or set him free.

Clinton appealed for André's life and offered to free any prisoner of war Washington might name. Washington wanted Arnold, but this Clinton could not do. Arnold himself wrote to dissuade Washington from carrying out the sentence but failed to offer himself in return. Expressing superfluous fears that harm might come to his family, he warned, "Remember, I will revenge their wrongs in a deluge of American blood."

In contrast to Arnold's savage blusterings, André faced his end with uncommon self-possession and fortitude. "When the hour of his execution was announced to him in the morning [of October 2]," relates Dr. Thacher,

> he received it without emotion, and while all present were affected with silent gloom, he retained a firm countenance, with calmness and composure of mind. His breakfast being sent to him from the table of General Washington, which had been done every day of his confinement, he partook of it as usual, and having shaved and dressed himself he . . . cheerfully said to the guard officers, "I am ready at any moment, gentlemen, to wait on you. . . ."
>
> The fatal hour having arrived, a large detachment of troops was paraded, and an immense concourse of people assembled. Almost all our general and field officers, excepting his Excellency and his staff, were present on horse-back. Melancholy and gloom pervaded all ranks. . . .
>
> Major Andre walked from the stone house in which he had been confined between two of our subaltern officers, arm and arm.

When he came in sight of the gallows he "involuntarily started backward" but, recovering himself, said, "I am reconciled to my death, though I detest the mode." By the scaffold, he nervously rolled a stone over with his foot and choked a little in his throat, "as if attempting to swallow," but as soon as he saw that everything was ready, "stepped quickly into the wagon and, . . . elevating his head with firmness, he said, 'It will be but a momentary pang.' " He then placed the noose over his own head with the knot directly under his right ear and, taking a handkerchief from his own pocket, tied it over his eyes. One of the subalterns tied his arms behind his back.

After the death sentence was read aloud, André was asked whether he had any last words. "I pray you to bear me witness," was the answer, "that I meet my fate like a brave man."

Washington made no unseemly attempt to disparage André's courage. On the contrary, he paid handsome tribute to it at Arnold's expense: "Andre has met his fate," he wrote, "with that fortitude which was to be expected from an accomplished man and a gallant officer. But I mistake if Arnold at this time is undergoing the torments of a mental Hell. He wants feeling. From some traits of his character which have lately come to my knowledge, he seems to have been so hacknied in crime, so lost to all sense of honor and shame, that while his faculties still enable him to continue his sordid pursuits there will be no time for remorse."

Arnold appealed to the king for a pardon for himself and published an address to the inhabitants of America in which he endeavored to vindicate his conduct. He said he had originally taken up arms against Great Britain for a redress of grievances but had considered the Declaration of Independence precipitate. He also claimed that, so far as he could tell, all grievances had been adequately redressed by the offers made by the peace commissioners during the previous year. Nevertheless, Congress, he said, had allied itself with France, the enemy of the Protestant faith and all liberty. As for those who condemned him, "They may be assured that, conscious of the rectitude of my intentions, I shall treat their malice and calumnies with contempt and neglect."

Arnold was treated well by the British in the hope of encouraging other defections and was saluted by the English press. "The loss of such an experienced officer," one London paper declared, "must be severely felt by the Americans, and his known probity will make that cause appear very bad, which he could no longer support with honour."

But Arnold had brought nothing with him, no fort or body of men, and the cost of the foiled plot had been André's execution. Clinton cut Arnold's reward from £10,000 to 6,000 guineas and his rank from major general to that of brigadier—one of three appointed to lead the loyalist troops. Clinton also refused him a major command, in part because he didn't trust him, either in honor or disgrace. Arnold eventually put together a regiment in New York, made up almost entirely of deserters, that he called the American Legion.

Just then, New York was the right place in which to recruit his reprehensible troop. War had made it an unpleasant town. The trees along the streets had been cut down and the ground torn up for fortifications; many of the houses had been destroyed by successive fires. "Noisesome vapours arise from the mud left in the docks and slips at low water," wrote one visitor, "and unwholesome smells are occasioned by such a number of people being crowded together in so small a compass almost like herrings in a barrel, most of them very dirty and not a small number sick of some disease, the Itch, Pox, Fever, Flux, so that all together there is a complication of stinks, enough to drive a person . . . into a consumption in a space of twenty-four hours." A large proportion of the population was also made up of embittered refugees. And the criminal element among them was strong: "If any author had an inclination . . . to expose the vicious and unfeeling part of human nature, or the various arts, ways and means, that are used to pick up a living in this world, I recommend New York as a proper place to collect his characters."

Arnold was hanged and burned in effigy in various towns, and an image of him was paraded through the streets of Philadelphia in a wagon with a figure of the Devil sitting beside him holding a bag of gold. Not long after his defection, a captured American captain was brought before him and "Arnold asked him what he thought the Americans would do with him if they caught him. The captain at first declined to answer; but upon being repeatedly urged, said: 'Why, sir, if I must answer, you must excuse my telling you the plain truth. If my countrymen should catch you, I believe they would first cut off that lame leg which was wounded in the cause of freedom and virtue, and bury it with the honors of war; and afterwards hang the remainder of your body in gibbets, high.' "

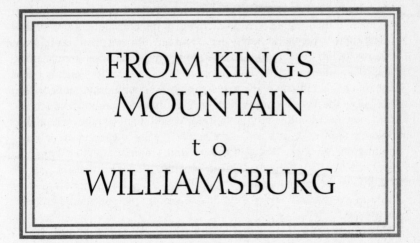

CHAPTER EIGHTEEN

FROM KINGS MOUNTAIN to WILLIAMSBURG

A FTER Cornwallis defeated Gates at the Battle of Camden, he had planned to march to Hillsboro, North Carolina, rally loyalists to his banner, and lay up provisions for the winter while coordinate operations were launched in the Chesapeake. In mid-October, Clinton sent General Alexander Leslie with a force of more than 2,000 men to invade the James estuary and occupy Portsmouth, which he did. Meanwhile, Cornwallis had also dispatched Major Patrick Ferguson to raise the royal standard in the border counties. Ferguson set out at once for Fort Ninety Six with 200 picked regulars and there established a training camp for Tory troops. "His camp," wrote a contemporary historian, "became at once the rendezvous of the desperate, the idle and vindictive, as well as of zealous loyalist youth." By the middle of June, he had a substantial contingent under his command.

From the Potomac to southern Georgia the British rode triumphant, and, except in forests and morasses, there was nowhere for a patriot to hide. Cornwallis offered clemency to all those willing to swear allegiance to the king, and many hastened to do so; others, though not the majority, retreated to the swamps and mountains of the interior and under Francis Marion (the "Swamp Fox"), Thomas Sumter (the "Carolina Gamecock"), Andrew Pickens, and other partisan leaders carried on guerrilla warfare against the occupation force. They lived in a bewildering landscape of land and water, mazelike canals, oxbow lakes, and tangled vines. Their attacking parties were sometimes as small as twenty men, seldom over a hundred, but the sudden and unanticipated fury of their attack and the swiftness of their flight were exasperating to the enemy.

Throughout the deep South there was anarchy and confusion, with loyalists and patriots murdering and plundering each other in retaliatory raids. The internecine warfare in South Carolina reached such a pitch that Nathanael Greene was moved to say, "The animosity between the Whigs and the Tories renders their situation truly deplorable. Some thousand have fallen in this way in this quarter, and the evil rages with more violence than ever. If a stop can not be put to these massacres, the country will be depopulated in a few months more, as neither Whig nor Tory can live." To General William Moultrie it seemed that the whole society was being shattered and brutalized: "A dark melancholy gloom appears everywhere and the morals of the people are almost entirely extirpated."

Many acquiesced or actively joined whichever side held sway. One Levi Smith, a South Carolina loyalist militia officer, for example, who was captured by patriots, was stripped, beaten, and otherwise abused in an effort to get him to renounce his allegiance. Arrangements were subsequently made to include him in a prisoner exchange when he was brought before General Greene, who had recently come into possession of captured documents showing that, before his capture, Smith had provided the British with military intelligence. "He asked me if I did not deserve death, as I was American born," Smith later remembered. "I told him that the province had been conquered [by the British] and that I had, of course, become a British subject." Greene, "taking into account his previous mistreatment," humanely paroled him to a nearby plantation to recuperate.

Patrick Ferguson marched his Tory battalion, on a fighting and recruiting expedition through North Carolina. His troop, made up of the King's American Regiment, the Loyal American Regiment, and the American Volunteers, in effect constituted the left wing of Cornwallis's army. Ferguson was an enterprising commander—tough, given to hard talk but decent, and a marksman of almost supernatural skill. A few years before, he had invented the first breech-loading rifle, which he could fire, with wonderful precision, seven times a minute. In an adventitious moment of the war, when all might have been changed, Washington himself, it may be remembered, had been at the mercy of this weapon just before the Battle of Brandywine.

If Ferguson's contingent could be checked or broken, Cornwallis might be forced to fall back upon Charleston, enabling the patriots to rally in his wake.

On the morning of September 25, some 840 stalwart and patriotic "over-mountain men," as they were called—among the wildest of the frontiersmen—assembled under their partisan leaders at Sycamore Shoals. Their horses were decked out in red-and-yellow trappings "of almost barbaric splendor" and the men themselves in hunting shirts of blue linen gaily decorated with tassels and fringe. Each man carried a blanket or knapsack on his back, a skillet fastened to the pommel of his saddle, and a buckskin shoulder pouch filled with parched corn. In addition to hunting knives, they carried the long Deckard rifle of the Kentucky frontier. Thus lightly encumbered, they could travel up to forty miles a day, and march and fight, it was said, for forty-eight hours without food or rest.

As they drew to within fifty miles or so of Ferguson's camp, they came to the base of Road Mountain, one of the loftiest of the Alleghenies, ascended a gap called Bright's Trace, and from there climbed to the summit, crowned with snow. The open tableland on the heights was large and flat, and there the men were drawn up into battalions and drilled. The atmosphere, nearly a mile above sea level, was so rare that "they could scarcely distinguish the report" of their own rifles when they fired.

A force of 550 men soon joined them, bringing their strength to nearly 1,400—still a thousand less than the number thought to be under Ferguson's command. Their officers told them, as all patriot troops seem to have been told before an engagement, "Don't fire till you see the whites of their eyes!"

For several weeks, Ferguson had been operating in the foothills of the mountains before crossing the border into North Carolina, about seventy miles west of Charlotte. Warning the local population of reprisals if they opposed him, at length, he came to Kings Mountain, a spur of the Blue Ridge range on the border between North and South Carolina, on October 6. Less a mountain than a plume of ground, it rose sixty feet above the surrounding countryside and had steep, forested slopes that culminated in a fortresslike escarpment of jagged rocks. Behind these rocks Ferguson had positioned his men, and had drawn all his supply wagons together to reinforce the most exposed point of his line. He wrote a dispatch to Cornwallis in which he said, "I have taken a post where I do not think I can be forced." And he assured his men it could be defended against "God Almighty and all the rebels out of hell." His position seemed nearly unassailable, though in fact he had far fewer men—about

1,100, including 150 British regulars—than the patriots thought. The regulars were armed with muskets and bayonets, the Tory militia with rifles and long butcher knives made to fit firmly into the muzzles of their guns.

After marching and riding all night through a drenching rain, the patriot forces came up to where Ferguson was ensconced at about three in the afternoon of October 7. They had traveled for thirty-six hours without rest, and some had gone without food for two days. Nevertheless, they paused only long enough to strap their blankets to their saddles and tether their horses among the trees. "Every man threw four or five balls in his mouth," recalled one young rifleman, James Collins, "to be in readiness to reload quick." Then they filed rapidly around the ridge and steadily advanced up the slope. "The shot of the enemy began to pass over us like hail. . . . I was soon in a profuse sweat," wrote Collins. "My lot happened to be in the center, where the severest part of the battle was fought." Although the heights gave Ferguson's men some advantage, the forested slopes, wrote a loyalist officer, "sheltered the [patriots] and enabled them to fight in their favorite manner. In fact, after driving in our pickets, they were able to advance . . . to the crest . . . in perfect safety, until they took post and opened an irregular but destructive fire." After twice being repulsed, the patriots prevailed on the third try, at which Ferguson's men, who were "falling very Fast," began to cry for quarter. But some of the patriots answered, "Tarleton's quarter!"—meaning no quarter, in recollection of the massacre at Waxhaw.

As was his custom, Ferguson had directed his men with a piercing silver whistle from above the fray. He had gone to the very front of the ridge to encourage his men, but "when the silver whistle ceased to sound and its gallant owner lay shot through the head upon the forest slope," wrote Theodore Roosevelt with unabashed admiration for him in *The Winning of the West,* "the fight was over, and there remained only the prisoners to be gathered and the dead collected."

The carnage on the crest had been great. "The dead lay in heaps on all sides," wrote Collins, "while the groans of the wounded were heard in every direction. I could not help turning away from the scene before me with horror, and, though exulting in victory, could not refrain from shedding tears. . . . On examining the dead body of their great chief [Ferguson], it appeared that almost fifty rifles must have been leveled at him at the same time. Seven rifle balls had passed through his body, both of his arms were broken, and his hat and clothing were literally shot to pieces." Two hundred twenty-five defenders lay dead upon that blood-stained hill; 185 more lay wounded; and all the rest, some 700, had fallen into American hands. American losses were 60 wounded and 28 killed.

The hardness, or rather insensibility, of the battle characterized its aftermath. Toward midnight, nine Tory field officers were court-martialed and hanged in retaliation for the recent torture and execution of forty-one patriots at Augusta and Fort Ninety Six. Nor was respect shown for the dead. "We proceeded to bury [them]," wrote Collins, "but it was badly done. They were thrown into convenient piles and covered with old logs, the bark of old trees and rocks." Before long, the whole area was overrun with packs of scavenging wolves so that "it was dangerous for anyone to be out at night for several miles around."

The battle at Kings Mountain marked the beginning of the end of British power in the colonies. "That glorious victory," said Jefferson, "was the joyful annunciation of that turn in the tide of success which terminated the Revolutionary War."

Cornwallis retreated south while awaiting reinforcements from Charleston by sea before resuming his North Carolina campaign. Meanwhile, Charlotte, North Carolina, which Cornwallis had evacuated, became the headquarters of General Nathanael Greene, who on October 14 was appointed to the southern command.

Greene had not been eager for the post. When word of his appointment arrived, he had just begun to settle in as commandant at West Point, where, upon replacing Arnold, he had been anticipating a restful winter with his wife. "My dear Angel, What I have been dreading has come to pass," he wrote to her when he realized he would have to leave before she arrived. "I am ordered away to another quarter. How unfriendly is war to domestic happiness." Greene rode into Charlotte on December 2. It was an awkward occasion, given the peremptory change of command. But it might have been more difficult than it was. According to Colonel Otho Williams, "A manly resignation marked the conduct of General Gates on the arrival of his successor, whom he received at headquarters with that liberal and gentlemanly air which was habitual to him. General Greene observed a plain, candid, respectful manner, neither betraying compassion nor the want of it—nothing like the pride of official consequence even *seemed*. In short, the officers who were present had an elegant lesson of propriety exhibited on a most delicate and interesting occasion."

Greene was a universal favorite among both officers and men. "His military abilities, his active spirit, his great resources when reduced to difficulties in the field, his having been quarter-master-general to the army under the commander-in-chief; all these qualities," wrote General William Moultrie, "combined together rendered him a proper officer to collect and to organize an army that was broken up and dispersed."

Awaiting Greene was a mostly militia force of fewer than 2,000 men.

It was not much of an army. Nor was the countryside ripe for recruitment, as the population throughout the Carolinas and much of Virginia had been dispirited by the enemy's conquests and the bitter partisan warfare that had erupted in their wake.

Greene's first care was to provide for his troops, his second to work out a strategy of cautious movements and protracted war. He had to hold the enemy in check along an extended front yet scrupulously avoid a major engagement with the superior British force. At the same time, to revive the spirits of his countrymen and troops, he must not seem to be merely in retreat. He must risk an occasional skirmish, confront the enemy's scouts and foraging parties, and fight, cripple, and beat him in detail.

Although Cornwallis underestimated some of the patriot generals, most notably Lafayette, whom he scornfully called "the boy," he made no such mistake with Greene. "Greene is as dangerous as Washington," he said. "He is vigilant, enterprising, and full of resources—there is but little hope of gaining any advantage over him. I never feel secure when encamped in his neighbourhood."

Small as his army was, Greene daringly divided it into two, leading one division into eastern South Carolina to the Cheraw Hills, about seventy miles to the British right, while sending the other under Daniel Morgan (the "Old Wagoner," called out of retirement and now a general), consisting of 400 Continentals, a few militia, and a corps of dragoons, southwestward across the Broad River, fifty miles or so to the British left.

This disposition gave patriots a rallying point in both the eastern and western parts of the Carolinas, facilitated the procurement of provisions, and aroused British fears for the safety of two British posts, Fort Ninety Six and Augusta. In response, Cornwallis dispatched Tarleton after Morgan with a thousand men, convinced that given the quality of the corps under Tarleton's command and his superior cavalry, he could not fail "of the most brilliant success."

On January 13, 1781, Morgan received the following note from Greene: "Colonel Tarleton is said to be on his way to pay you a visit. I doubt not but he will have a decent reception and proper dismission." Morgan began looking for tactical ground and halted at a place called "the Cowpens," named for a large stockyard or corral, with the Broad River at his back. On the face of it, it seemed a disastrous choice. Indeed, Tarleton, speaking of himself in the third person, said, "It is certainly as good a place for action as Lieutenant Colonel Tarleton could desire. America does not produce any more suitable to the nature of the troops under his command." When he came up to Morgan's position on the sixteenth, he was sure he had him trapped. Morgan, for his part, had no illusions about his vulnerabilities but, deploying his men in highly original formations, brilliantly turned them to account. To begin with, he knew his militia could not be counted on to fight. So he placed them in the very front lines to receive the first onslaught of the British attack. That might have been some kind of cruel folly, since they would certainly panic and run; but knowing they would do so anyway, he told them *not* to hold their ground! Instead, he told them to stand only until they could get off three good volleys at killing range and *then* to run—and he showed them exactly how to run around the left flank of the army so as to get behind it in time to re-form. Such a plan gave the militia courage, because not too much was being asked of them and because they could see that, if they did their part, they might survive. Moreover, Morgan rightly anticipated that their running would be misinterpreted by the enemy as a panic retreat. So behind the militia he placed his picked, or Continental, troops on a slight hill; and behind them, his cavalry, under Colonel William Washington, cousin of the commander in chief.

The night before the battle, according to one of the American soldiers, Morgan

> went among the volunteers, helped them fix their swords, joked with them about their sweethearts, told them to keep in good spirits, and the day would be ours. And long after I laid down, he was going about among the soldiers encouraging them and telling them that the old wagoner would crack his whip over Ben [Tarleton] in the morning, as sure as they lived.
>
> "Just hold up your heads, boys, three fires," he would say, "and you are free, and then when you return to your homes, how the old folks will bless you, and the girls kiss you for your gallant conduct!"
>
> I don't believe he slept a wink that night.

Tarleton attacked at sunrise in his usual dashing style. Morgan's raw militia fired three volleys as instructed, then began their retreat to safety in the rear. The British instantly spread out and rushed at the second line of Americans, intending to flank or envelop them on both sides. The latter, as also instructed in advance, fell back to the position of the cavalry while the cavalry circled round and attacked the British right flank. Meanwhile, the first line of militia, having re-formed, circled around the other way to attack the British left. The advancing British therefore faced the second, or picked, line of American troops, who fired straight on—"it seemed," wrote one American officer, "like one sheet of flame from right to left. Oh! it was beautiful!"—before charging with their bayonets. At the same time, Colonel Washington's cavalry descended upon the British "like a whirlwind. . . . The shock was so sudden and violent they could not stand it."

The British were overwhelmed. They "began to throw down their arms and surrender themselves," recalled a rifleman who had also fought at Kings Mountain. It was a scene scarcely witnessed before.

Upward of 500 of the British were taken prisoner and 100 killed. Two fieldpieces, 35 baggage wagons, and 800 stand of arms also fell into American hands. The American losses were 60 wounded and 12 killed. Only Tarleton himself and a handful of his dragoons escaped.

According to General Moultrie, then a prisoner of war on parole in Charleston, "This defeat . . . chagrined and disappointed the British officers and Tories exceedingly. . . . I saw them standing in the streets in small circles talking over the affair with very grave faces. . . . This great victory . . . changed the face of American affairs. . . . In two actions, soon after each other, the British lost about two thousand men. . . . The latter was of more serious consequence to Lord Cornwallis because it deprived him of nine hundred of his best troops."

Cornwallis tried to avenge it by going after Morgan himself. As Morgan hastened to rejoin Greene, Cornwallis raced to cut him off. Morgan beat him to the ford of the Catawba River, where Greene arrived on January 31. The two generals sat down together on a log for about twenty minutes to coordinate their plans, and early the next morning Cornwallis appeared and attempted to force his way across. But the main body of the Americans had already moved on, and Morgan's column was thirty miles away on a march to the Yadkin River by the time the British crossing was made. Cornwallis now put all his troops into light marching order, burned his baggage, and pushed forward through drenching rains, but as he came to the Yadkin, Morgan's men were already drawing up their boats on the other side.

The race went on, with Morgan's forces combining with Greene's. On February 9, 1781, Greene paused at Guilford Court House, where he had expected to meet up with reinforcements from Virginia under Steuben. But Steuben's troops were preoccupied with chasing Benedict Arnold, who had occupied Portsmouth on January 20 after raiding up the James River to Richmond. Greene brought his army across the Dan River into Virginia; Cornwallis marched back to Hillsboro, where he issued boastful proclamations announcing his conquest of the state.

Greene's main object had been to draw Cornwallis as far away from his base as possible, and in this he had succeeded. To prevent the British from consolidating their gains, he recrossed the Dan into North Carolina and eluded Cornwallis for three weeks, leading him in various directions and tempting him to a major battle that he never intended to fight. In so doing, he was playing for time until reinforcements could arrive. "Great God," Daniel Morgan had exclaimed on February 1, 1781, two weeks after his victory at Cowpens, "what is the reason we cant Have more men in the field—so many men in the country Nearby idle for want of employment." But at last the reinforcements came, 1,500 Continentals among them, increasing Greene's force to about 4,500, as compared to the 2,200 under his opponent's command. On March 15, Greene was back at Guilford Court House, ready to engage.

He knew better than to exaggerate his own strength. In fact, he wasn't entirely sure what it was. "The militia have flocked in from various quarters," he wrote Thomas Jefferson, then governor of Virginia, "but they come and go in such irregular bodies that I can make no calculations on the strength of my army or direct any future operations that can ensure me success. A force fluctuating in this manner can promise but slender hopes of success against an enemy regulated by discipline and made formidable by the superiority of their numbers [of regulars]. Hitherto I have been obliged to practice that by finesse, which I dare not attempt by force." Morgan (on leave due to illness) advised him in a letter, "If [the militia] fight, you beat Cornwallis, if not, he will beat you and perhaps cut your regulars to pieces.... Put the riflemen on the flanks. Put the militia in the centre, with some picked troops in their rear with orders to shoot down the first man that runs." For the most part, Greene followed Morgan's advice.

As Cornwallis marched to meet him, Greene disposed his army with the militia in front, Continentals in the rear. On both sides, these troops were flanked by riflemen and cavalry posted on a rise a mile and a half from where the courthouse stood. At 1:30 P.M., the British let loose a cannonade and advanced in three columns "in excellent order, at a smart run" toward the first American line. When they came to within forty yards of it, they paused, and, wrote one of their officers, "both parties surveyed each other for the moment with the most anxious suspense." Then, exhorted by their commanders—"Come on, my brave fusiliers!" —the British rushed on to face the American fire.

The North Carolina militia got off a single volley and then, to the "infinite distress and mortification" of their officers, "took to flight.... Every effort was made ... to stop this Unaccountable panic, for not a man of the corps had been killed or even wounded.... All was vain; so thoroughly confounded were these unhappy men that, throwing away arms, knapsacks, and even canteens, they rushed like a torrent headlong through the woods." The Virginians behind them proved more steady, but at length they too gave way as the hardened British regulars came on. On the flanks, however, the riflemen and cavalry held firm, and the third, or Continental, line likewise stood its ground. This obliged the British to swing to their right and left while their reserve moved into the center to press the attack.

By then, many of the Americans had posted themselves behind trees in the woods and, wrote a British officer, "did great execution" with "a galling fire." The British and American cavalry, infantry, militia, and regulars now all intermingled in a furious fight. "The slaughter was prodigious" wrote a participant, and very bloody and severe. The British turned the American right flank, but, according to Tarleton, "victory alternately presided over each arm," a situation that was intolerable to Cornwallis, who, in a desperate measure to break up the melee, fired his field guns into the midst of it, killing both friend and foe. The two armies disengaged in shock, and Greene at once ordered a retreat. Cornwallis had "won," he had kept the field, but it was a Pyrrhic victory. He had lost 800 men, including many of his best officers—twice the casualties suffered on the American side.

A few miles away, Greene took up a more advantageous position and again drew his forces up to fight. Cornwallis, however, declined, and the tables of the contest turned. Now Cornwallis began to retreat as Greene pursued.

The British general withdrew to Wilmington, the nearest seaport on the North Carolina coast, but instead of transferring his army to South Carolina by sea, as not only Greene but Sir Henry Clinton had expected, he marched northward into Virginia.

He explained his decision in a letter to Lord Germain from Wilmington on April 23:

If we are so unlucky as to suffer a severe blow in South Carolina, the spirit of revolt in that province would become very general, and the numerous rebels in this province be encouraged to be more than ever active and violent. This might enable General Greene to hem me in among the great rivers and by cutting off our subsistence render our arms useless. And to remain here for transports to carry us off . . . would lose our cavalry and be otherways . . . ruinous and disgraceful to Britain. . . . I have, therefore, under so many embarrassing circumstances (but looking upon Charleston as safe from any immediate attack from the rebels) resolved to take advantage of General Greene's having left the back part of Virginia open and march immediately into that province to attempt a junction with General Phillips.

General Phillips, he had just learned, had been sent with a considerable force into the Chesapeake to cooperate with him in any way he saw fit.

Cornwallis sent a copy of his letter to Clinton, adding, "It is very disagreeable to me to decide upon measures so very important and of such consequence to the general conduct of the war, without an opportunity of procuring your Excellency's directions or approbation; but the delay and difficulty of conveying letters, and the impossibility of waiting for answers render it indispensably necessary." To justify his departure from Clinton's orders, he later claimed, "I was most firmly persuaded that until Virginia was reduced, we could not hold the more southern provinces; and that after its reduction they would fall without much difficulty."

At the time, in fact, his haste lacked any clear purpose, and he was apparently at a loss as to what to do. At Wilmington, he had pondered the wreckage of his command. A few months before, it had been his opinion that "for the numbers there never was so fine an Army." But the Battle of Cowpens, the race to the Dan, and his costly victory at Guilford Court House had left it a stained and tattered band. In two and a half months, he had lost half his force, and the letter he wrote to Phillips about this time had a rather pathetic ring: "Now, my dear friend, what is our plan? Without one, we cannot succeed, and I assure you that I am quite tired of marching about the country in quest of adventures. If we mean an offensive war in America, we must abandon New York and bring our whole force into Virginia; we then have a stake to fight for and a successful battle may give us America. If our plan is defensive, mixed with desultory expeditions, let us quit the Carolinas (which cannot be held defensively while Virginia can be so easily armed against us) and stick to our salt pork at New York, sending now and then a detachment to steal tobacco, etc."

Such sarcasm could not make up for the plan they lacked. Meanwhile, Greene, having followed Cornwallis as far as Ramsay's Mills (and supposing he would embark for Charleston) turned south to strike against the British garrisons in South Carolina and Georgia before Cornwallis could come to their aid.

Greene had a plan. He wrote to Washington, "The enemy will be obliged to follow us, or give up their posts in that state. If the former takes place, it will draw the war out of this state [Virginia] and give it an opportunity to raise its proportion of men. If they leave their posts to fall, they must lose more there than they can gain here. If we continue in this state, the enemy will hold their possessions in both."

One of Greene's staff officers, who had recently distinguished himself in the Guilford Court House fight, was not satisfied with the proposed operations and asked Greene, by way of remonstrance, "What will you do, sir, in case Lord Cornwallis throws himself in your rear, and cuts off your communication with Virginia?" "I will punish his temerity," replied the general with great pleasantness, "by ordering you to charge him as you did at the battle of Guilford. But never fear, sir; his lordship has too much good sense ever again to risk his safety so far from the seaboard. He has just escaped ruin, and he knows it, and I am greatly mistaken in his character as an officer, if he has not the capacity to profit by experience."

VIRGINIA had been the scene of action for some time. Early in December 1780, Washington had alerted Thomas Jefferson that a British expedition had embarked for the South. Jefferson disregarded the possibility that its destination might be his state, but on the thirtieth twenty-seven sail—carrying 1,700 English and Hessian grenadiers, light infantrymen, and loyalist dragoons—entered the capes. Three days later, Benedict Arnold sailed up the James River and, overcoming token resistance, plundered Westover and Richmond. While this was going on, loyalist Lieutenant Colonel John Graves Simcoe had been detached to Westham, six miles upriver, where he destroyed a cannon foundry and sacked a public supply depot, including warehouses full of clothes. Simcoe and Arnold then withdrew to Portsmouth and on January 20 began to fortify it as a winter quarters, with every expectation of continuing their work of destruction in the spring.

More or less unscathed by the war so far, Virginia had been lulled into a false sense of security and was quite unprepared for the attack when it came. The best Virginia regulars were absent with Washington in the North; 3,000 had surrendered with Lincoln at Charleston; others were serving with Greene. Not much had been done to make up the deficiencies, and the militia that remained were short of arms.

Nevertheless, it was mortifying to Washington to see so inconsiderable a party committing such extensive depredations with impunity. He guessed that their principal object was to make a diversion in favor of Cornwallis. And in this he was right. Clinton hoped the raids would force Greene to withdraw to Virginia, easing pressure on the British in the Carolinas. But this Greene would not do. Nor would Washington have approved it. As he explained to Jefferson, who had appealed for help, the evils to be apprehended from Arnold's predatory incursions were not to be compared with the injury to the common cause and the danger to Virginia in particular which would result from the conquest of the states to the south. The survival of his own state, that is, depended on the survival of the Carolinas and Virginia's own immediate needs must be subordinate to the larger strategic goals.

Washington hoped to trap and capture Arnold, and to that end he dispatched about 1,200 of his light infantry under Lafayette. Washington's estimation of Lafayette's abilities was no longer in doubt. When a member of Congress criticized the appointment, Washington replied, "It is my opinion that the command of the troops cannot be in better hands than the Marquis's. He possesses uncommon military talents: is of a quick and sound military judgment; and besides these, he is of a very conciliating temper and perfectly sober—which are qualities that rarely combine in the same person. And were I to add that some men will gain as much experience in the course of three or four years as some others will in ten or a dozen, you cannot deny the fact and attack me on that ground." Meanwhile, a small French fleet had sailed from Newport to hem Arnold in by sea, but on March 16, it was intercepted and challenged near the entrance to the Chesapeake by an English fleet of comparable size, and the two fought to a draw. In the interim, Lafayette, having made his way by forced marches to the head of the Chesapeake, waited for the French vessels to carry his troops down the bay. When they failed to arrive, he crossed the bay in an open boat to Williamsburg, then the James River to York. But by April 8, he was back at the head of the Elk River in Maryland, where he received orders from Washington to return to Virginia to cooperate with General Greene.

As Lafayette marched toward Baltimore, his restive troops, mostly from New England (and therefore reluctant to risk their lives in a region so far from their own) began to desert. Lafayette hanged one as an example, then, to challenge the honor of the rest, announced that anyone wishing to leave was free to return to his unit in the North without risk of being charged; he himself, he said, would go forward, even if he had to march alone. From that moment on, "all desertions ceased" and his troops stood by him to a man.

Meanwhile, on March 26, a second British force had landed at the mouth of the James with 2,300 men under Major General William Phillips —presaging a more aggressive British southern campaign.

Lafayette hoped to secure Richmond before Arnold and Phillips could reach it and, starting from Baltimore on April 19, arrived by forced marches on the twenty-ninth, outracing the British by a day. Thereupon Phillips proceeded downriver to Jamestown Island, destroying ships, tobacco warehouses, and public stores in Chesterfield, Manchester, and Warwick before occupying Petersburg, which he turned into his base.

In the course of these marauding expeditions, one of the British contingents had ascended the Potomac River and menaced Washington's Mount Vernon estate. Lund Washington, its caretaker, met the flag the enemy sent onshore and saved the property from pillage by furnishing the vessel with supplies. George Washington was not pleased. "It would have been a less painful circumstance to me to have heard," he wrote Lund, "that in consequence of your noncompliance with their request they had burnt my house and laid my plantation in ruins. You ought to have considered yourself as my representative and should have reflected on the bad example of communicating with the enemy and making a voluntary offer of refreshments to them with a view to prevent a conflagration."

D u r i n g these same months, Washington had held his army in the vicinity of New York City, keeping guard over Clinton, who clung to his base. It had not been a comfortable time, being marked by numerous frustrations, including two mutinies in January among the troops. The first had taken place among the six regiments of the Pennsylvania Line, which had gone into winter quarters near Morristown, where all the familiar miseries of the past had been revived. General Wayne, who commanded them, was sympathetic to their plight:

> Poorly clothed, badly fed and worse paid, some of them not having received a paper dollar for near twelve months; exposed to winter's piercing cold, to drifting snows and chilling blasts, with no protection but old worn-out coats, tattered linen overalls and but one blanket between three men. In this situation the enemy begin to work upon their passions, and have found means to circulate some proclamations among them. . . . The Officers in general, as well as myself, find it necessary to stand for hours every day exposed to wind and weather among the poor naked fellows while they are working at their huts and redoubts, often assisting with our own hands in order to produce a conviction to their minds that we share, and more than share, every vicissitude in common with them; sometimes asking to participate their bread and water. The good effect of this conduct is very conspicuous and prevents their murmuring in public, but the delicate mind and eye of humanity are hurt, very much hurt, at their visible distress and private complainings.

Many of them had enlisted to serve for three years or the duration of the war—that is, as they understood it, for no more than three years and for less if the war should end sooner. But at the end of three years, when they sought their discharge, their officers, loath to lose such experienced soldiers, interpreted the terms of enlistment to mean three years or to the end of the war, should it continue for a *longer* time.

This perceived deceit was too much for them to take. On the evening of January 1, a great part of the line, noncommissioned officers included, turned out under arms, with six fieldpieces, and set out for Philadelphia to demand satisfaction from Congress. Congress, alarmed, dispatched a committee to meet them with a promise to hear out their complaints. Two emissaries from Clinton also arrived with offers of their own in an effort to take advantage of their disaffection. But the mutineers, as proof of their good faith, arrested the two men and turned them over to the army command. The two were tried as spies, found guilty, and hanged at the crossroads near Trenton. Afterward, in his report to Congress, General Sullivan expressed a decent respect and admiration for the disgruntled troops. "The whole progress of this affair except the first Tumult has been conducted on their part with a consistency, firmness and a degree of Policy mixed with candor," he wrote, "that must astonish every theorist on the nature of the American soldiery; and cover Sir Harry [Clinton] with Shame and Confusion." General Wayne, equally impressed, offered the mutineers amnesty, and Congress in turn granted their principal requests—in particular, that those who had already served three years be released from service and also paid in full.

Washington, though as sympathetic to the troops as Sullivan and Wayne, thought it had been a mistake to accommodate them while they were still under arms. And he predicted that other troops, with just as much justice, would follow their lead. Ten days later, his apprehensions were borne out. On the night of January 20, part of the Jersey Line stationed at Pompton marched out with their weapons and demanded the same concessions the Pennsylvanians had just obtained. Washington sent troops to compel the mutineers to unconditional submission and prohibited any negotiations until they laid down their arms. Upon their surrender, two of the ringleaders were executed by a firing squad. Dr. Thacher, who witnessed the proceedings, wrote, "It is most painful to reflect that circumstances should imperiously demand the infliction of capital punishment on soldiers who have more than a shadow of plea to extenuate their crime."

The strain of the mutinies—perhaps especially the apparent need to quell their spread by executions—had made Washington inordinately sensitive to any insubordinate act. Perhaps as a result, in mid-February he and Alexander Hamilton, then his aide-de-camp, had a brief falling-out. A few days before, Washington had written to General Sullivan in response to an inquiry as to whether Hamilton was qualified to head up a new department of finance. "I am unable to answer," replied Washington, "because I never entered upon a discussion with him, but this I can venture to advance, from a thorough knowledge of him, that there are few men to be found of his age who have more general knowledge than he possesses, and none whose soul is more firmly engaged in the cause or who exceeds him in probity and sterling virtue."

This was high praise from the general. By that time, Hamilton had been on Washington's staff for several years, and Washington had always treated him with marked attention and regard. But Hamilton was restless and looking for an excuse to go his own way. As he himself recounted the incident in a February 18 letter to General Schuyler, whose daughter he had recently married, "The general and I passed each other on the stairs. He told me he wanted to speak to me. I answered that I would wait on him immediately." Hamilton went downstairs to give Tench Tilghman, a fellow aide, a letter to be sent to the commissary. As he was about to go back up, he ran into Lafayette. They conversed together briefly; then Hamilton hurried up the stairs. As he entered Washington's room, Washington exclaimed angrily, "Colonel Hamilton, you have kept me waiting at the head of the stairs these ten minutes. I must tell you, sir, you treat me with disrespect!" "I am not conscious of it, sir," replied Hamilton, "but since you have thought it necessary to tell me so, we part." "Very well, sir," returned Washington, "if it be your choice." Hamilton insisted to Schuyler, "I sincerely believe my absence which gave so much umbrage did not last two minutes."

Before an hour had passed, Washington sent Tilghman to Hamilton to tell him he was sorry the outburst had occurred and that he was willing to forget it. In the end, Washington, who knew that Hamilton had always disliked the office of aide-de-camp, gave him an active command.

Washington's overall discouragement was great at this time. After 3,000 Hessians arrived from Europe to reinforce Clinton, he pleaded for reinforcements from the eastern states. With some embarrassment, he pointed out that the French had long expected to see more American troops enlist, especially since they were putting thousands of their own sons on the line, but instead had only seen the promising prospects for a major campaign "waste fruitlessly away. It will be no small degree of triumph to our enemies, and will have a pernicious influence upon our friends in Europe, should they find such a failure of resource or such a want of energy to draw it out that our boasted and extensive preparations end only in idle parade." In his military journal, he enumerated the many problems he still faced:

Instead of having magazines filled with provisions, we have a scanty pittance scattered here and there in the different States. Instead of having our arsenals well supplied with military stores, they are poorly provided. . . . Instead of having the regiments completed . . . scarce any state in the union has, at this hour, an eighth part of its quota in the field, and little prospect, that I can see, of ever getting more than half. In a word, instead of having everything in readiness to take the field, we have nothing; and instead of having the prospect of a glorious offensive campaign before us, we have a bewildered and gloomy defensive one, unless we should receive a powerful aid of ships, land troops, and money from our generous allies; and these, at present, are too contingent to build upon.

France also seemed to doubt the outcome of the struggle and proposed a truce through a third party that would have allowed each of the belligerents to retain possession of the territory it held. That would have enabled the British to keep New York, Long Island, Charleston, Savannah, much of Georgia and the Carolinas, as well as fortified posts in Maine and the Northwest. Russia and Austria both offered to mediate and invited France and Great Britain (but not the United States, which was supposedly represented by France) to Vienna for talks. The United States, however, refused to cooperate, and Great Britain rejected the mediation as foreign interference in its domestic affairs.

GREENE'S Carolina campaign promised a different denouement. In conjunction with partisan troops under Thomas Sumter, Andrew Pickens, Francis Marion, and others, he set out to take Camden and the other British posts. On April 7, he decamped from Ramsay's Mills, and on the nineteenth he took up a position on Hobkirk's Hill, about two miles to the north of Camden, where Lord Francis Rawdon, Cornwallis's second in command, was strongly entrenched with 1,500 men. Greene had about as many Continentals to oppose him, but most of his militia, as was their wont after battle, had gone home.

The British position was protected on the south and east by a river and a creek, and to the west and north by six redoubts. Greene encamped about a mile from the town, cut off Rawdon's supply line, and, by a process of attrition, obliged the British to yield on May 10. Over the next six weeks, Fort Watson, Fort Motte, Orangeburg, Georgetown, and other garrisoned forts (as well as Augusta, on June 5) fell into American hands. On July 3, Greene also took Fort Ninety Six.

. . .

O N E of the more celebrated junior officers of the Revolution, and one much involved in these actions was Major Henry "Light-Horse Harry" Lee, whose illustrious son, Robert E. Lee, would lead the Confederate armies in the Civil War. Lee had attended Princeton, where James Madison had been one of his classmates, and had originally planned to go to England to study law. The revolutionary turmoil prevented this, however, and in 1776 he was made a captain in a unit of Virginia dragoons. By April 1778, his reputation as an outstanding cavalry officer had earned him an independent command. As "Light-Horse Harry," he led a partisan legion skilled in sudden, quick attacks—a style that was of a piece with his personality, which was impetuous and bold. But he also had a streak of brutality in him which Washington, by a reasoned appeal to his better nature, tried to curb. "The measure you propose of putting deserters from our Army to immediate death," Washington wrote to him in response to one of his proposals, "would probably tend to discourage the practice. But it ought to be executed with caution and only when the fact is very clear and unequivocal. I think that that part of your proposal which respects cutting off their heads . . . had better be omitted. Examples however severe ought not to be attended with an appearance of inhumanity otherwise they give disgust and may excite resentment rather than terror."

Without waiting for approval, however, Lee gratified his impulse. He went out after and captured a company of men who had deserted and "at first," according to a member of his camp, "determined to put them all to death, but on consultation or debate agreed to kill only one out of every three." Afterward, he decapitated one of them and had the severed head paraded about his camp on a pole. Washington censured him for this and reiterated the guidelines his former letter had laid down.

On August 19, 1779, inspired by Wayne's attack at Stony Point, Lee had led the assault against the British positions at Paulus Hook, in New Jersey, but afterward fellow officers charged him with grave errors of command. A court-martial was convened and Lee was acquitted, but he never got out from under the shadow it cast. That made him unceasingly seethe with rage, and not even Nathanael Greene's patronage and confidence in his abilities could appease him. Lee thereafter complained incessantly about being overlooked for commendation or promotion and being shortchanged on supplies. An exasperated Greene once told him, "I have run every risk to favor your operations perhaps more than I ought; clearly so, if I had not my own reputation less at heart than the public service in general, and the glory of my friends in particular."

Promoted at last to lieutenant colonel, Lee was ordered in March 1780 to take his legion to the southern front in support of Greene's defense of the Carolinas and Georgia. There he fought in the Battle of Guilford Court House as commander of the American advance guard and took part in the assaults that reclaimed Forts Watson, Motte, and Granby in South Carolina as well as the city of Augusta.

Subsequently, however, he resigned his commission in a petulant letter to Greene. He spoke vaguely of persecution by his enemies and a general lack of acknowledgment for services rendered in the war. Claiming to be "disgusted with human nature," he even accused Greene of being among those who had denied him the recognition he deserved. To all this, Greene replied calmly, "Give yourself time to cool."

Lee quit anyway, not without disgrace.

T H E British last stand in the Carolinas came on September 8 at Eutaw Springs, even though, after four hours of hard fighting, the Americans lost the opportunity for a decisive victory by giving themselves up to plunder as the British fled their camp. "The tents were all standing," wrote an American colonel afterward, "and presented many objects to tempt a thirsty, naked and fatigued soldiery" who thought the rout complete. A counterattack disabused them of this, but the British were unable to bear their losses, which on this occasion amounted to almost half their men.

Greene's operations in the Carolinas were perhaps more brilliant than any other operation of the war. The British had defeated him in every fight yet had gained nothing by their victories. Each encounter wore their army down, and whatever ground they gained they could not hold. In the end, Greene managed to expel them from every post except Savannah and Charleston, which they held only by virtue of their naval power. Moreover, it is extraordinary what Greene had been able to do with a sometimes pitiful force. Of the condition of his men, he discreetly wrote at the time, "I have more embarrassments than it is proper to disclose to the world." Afterward, he confessed, "At the battle of Eutaw Springs, hundreds of my men were naked as they were born. The bare loins of many were galled by their cartridge-boxes, while a folded rag or a tuft of moss alone protected their shoulders from being chafed by their guns."

The day after the battle, a French fleet sailed into Chesapeake Bay in Virginia and the fate of the king's army in America was sealed.

• • •

CORNWALLIS in Virginia had been unable to achieve any of his strategic objectives, despite his apparent strength. From Wilmington, on the coast, he had set out for Petersburg on April 24 and, after a monthlong march, had assumed command of a combined army of 7,200 men on May 20. Against him were Lafayette, twenty-three miles away at Richmond with 3,000 Continentals and militia, and Steuben, southeast of Charlottesville, training 500 more.

In Virginia, Cornwallis and Lafayette proved agile opponents, and throughout the summer their armies crisscrossed the state, occasionally coming close enough to skirmish but without a major or decisive battle taking place. In their pursuit of each other, they covered more than a thousand miles. The British had two to three times as many men as the marquis, who was usually in retreat. But from time to time he would turn about, catch Cornwallis off-guard, and strike a deft, if retiring, blow—just enough to give the British pause.

"Were I to fight a battle," he explained to Washington, on May 24, "I should be cut to pieces, the militia dispersed, and the arms lost. Were I to decline fighting, the country would think itself given up. I am therefore determined to skirmish, but not to engage too far, and particularly to take care against their immense and excellent body of horse, whom the militia fear as they would so many wild beasts." Cornwallis had a veteran force of 4,500 regulars; Lafayette but 2,000 militia, 1,000 light infantry, and 40 dragoons. "I am not strong enough," he wrote sensibly, "even to be beaten." Learning on the twenty-seventh that the British general was advancing on Richmond, he evacuated that city and decamped to Fredericksburg.

"The boy cannot escape me," Cornwallis wrote to Clinton. But he did, retreating more rapidly than Cornwallis could pursue. Cornwallis tried to prevent him from effecting a junction with Wayne, who had started south with three regiments, or 1,000 troops, of the Pennsylvania Line; but on May 31, the latter crossed the Potomac and, without pausing, pushed directly north to the far bank of the North Anna River, leaving the British behind.

After Lafayette crossed the Rapidan River at Ely's Ford on June 4, Cornwallis paused, not wanting to repeat the mistake he had made in pursuing Greene by being drawn too far away from his base.

Meanwhile, on June 3, Tarleton led a raid on Charlottesville, where the Virginia legislature, under Jefferson, had convened to plan measures for the defense of the state. With 230 mounted troops, he nearly surprised and captured the entire Assembly, including Jefferson, who barely escaped. Indeed, had Tarleton not paused maliciously for three hours at the Louisa Court House to burn a number of wagons carrying clothing to Greene's army, the legislature would have fallen into his hands. But a lookout at the Cuckoo Tavern across the way sped ahead by a shortcut to give the alarm.

Patrick Henry, John Tyler, and Benjamin Harrison were among those to flee to the mountains, and an amusing story is told about their flight that illustrates in how much affection and esteem Patrick Henry was held:

> Late in the day, fatigued and eager for food and drink, they drew their horses up to the door of a small hut in the gorge of the hills and asked for refreshments. A rugged woman asked who they were; and when they replied that they were members of the legislature who had been forced to flee before Tarleton's cavalry, the old woman's eyes flashed with contempt. "Ride on, ye cowardly knaves," she said. "Here have my husband and sons just gone to Charlottesville to fight for ye, and you running away with all your might. Clear out—ye shall have nothing here."
>
> Tyler then tried his hand.
>
> "What would you say, my good woman, if I were to tell you that Patrick Henry fled with the rest of us?"
>
> "Patrick Henry? I would tell you there was not a word of truth in it. Patrick Henry would never do such a cowardly thing," she said, bristling.
>
> "But this is Mr. Henry," said Tyler, pointing to him.
>
> The old woman pulled nervously at her apron, looking her amazement.
>
> "Well, then," she said, "if that is Patrick Henry, it must be all right. Come in and ye shall have the best I have in the house."

Jefferson had also fled, and Cornwallis shamelessly plundered and pilfered his estate. His silver plate was taken, his buildings burned, his corn and tobacco crops destroyed. His cattle, sheep, and hogs were all killed to feed the British soldiers and his horses appropriated for British dragoons. The throats of the colts too young for service were cut. Thirty slaves were also taken—not to be freed but, in an early biological warfare experiment, to be exposed to smallpox in an effort to spread it to the American camp. Some years later, Jefferson declared that had the slaves been emancipated, Cornwallis "would have done right, but it was done to consign them to inevitable death from small pox and putrid fever then raging in his camp. This I knew afterwards to have been the fate of 27 of them. I never had news of the remaining three." These thirty were but a fraction of the general toll. In Jefferson's estimate, Cornwallis ultimately appropriated about 30,000 slaves in Virginia alone, "and of these about 27,000 died of the small pox and camp fever, and the rest were partly sent to the West Indies and exchanged for rum, sugar, coffee and fruits." If so, more blacks were directly or indirectly killed by the British between 1780 and 1781 alone than patriot soldiers in battle during the entire war.

Lafayette now turned to confront his pursuers. He crossed the North Anna River on the tenth, the South Anna River the following day. From there he made his way along a path through the woods toward Charlottesville, to maneuver himself between Cornwallis and the stores at the old Albemarle Court House, which Cornwallis had hoped to destroy.

The weather was hot, supplies were short, and the region through which the armies passed was almost uninhabited. "We frequently march whole days without seeing anything like a house except a log hut or two," one American soldier wrote home to his father. But the wilderness also had an enchantment all its own: "Our encampments were always chosen on the banks of a stream and were extremely picturesque," recalled a redcoat, "as we had no tents, and were obliged to construct wigwams of fresh boughs to keep off the rays of the sun during the day. At night the blazing fires which we made of the fence-rails illuminated the surrounding scenery, which, in this part of America, is of the most magnificent description."

Cornwallis was very anxious "to come up with the marquis," and the byword among his officers each evening as they parted was *"Proelium pugnatum est!"* ("Let the battle be fought!") But he was not to be gratified. As Cornwallis entered Richmond on the sixteenth, Lafayette pitched his camp about twenty miles to the northwest. Two days later, Steuben arrived with about 450 more soldiers, which brought the marquis's strength up to 5,200 men.

After plundering warehouses in Richmond and putting storehouses full of tobacco to the torch, Cornwallis began a march toward the coast on the twentieth. Lafayette moved into Richmond right behind him, less than a month after he had been obliged to evacuate it himself.

Although Lafayette's army was now substantial, his artillery, about eight fieldpieces, was not large, and his cavalry consisted of only 120 horse, half of them volunteers. Therefore, to convey the impression of large numbers, it was his policy to scatter this force on different roads. Detachments of Continentals and riflemen generally formed the advance, and the army never encamped wholly in one place. Organized in this way and always on the move, marching by night as often as by day, Lafayette followed the British down the peninsula.

"The enemy has been so kind as to retire before us," wrote a jubilant Lafayette to Washington on June 28. "Twice I gave them a chance of fighting (taking care not to engage them farther than I pleased) but they continued their retrograde motions. Our numbers are, I think, exaggerated to them, and our seeming boldness confirms the opinion."

Cornwallis came to Williamsburg, where he received an anxious letter from Clinton asking for 2,000 men to help bolster his New York garrison against an anticipated allied attack. Cornwallis decided to embark these troops from Portsmouth, a deepwater port, but before he let them go, he tried to lure Lafayette to destruction.

On the afternoon of July 6, at Green Spring, Cornwallis did everything he could to create the impression that almost his whole army had crossed the James River (en route to Portsmouth) and that only his rear guard remained. In fact only a company of rangers and the baggage train had been ferried over, while the bulk of his force concealed themselves behind swamps and high ground near the bank, where a wood screened them from view. The American vanguard under General Wayne approached and began to skirmish with the enemy; the British guard fell back slowly through the trees. "The very obstinacy" of their resistance, writes one historian, "excited Lafayette's suspicion." So rather than bring his entire army forward into the fight, he reinforced Wayne with one Continental detachment and one battalion of light infantry while prudently holding two other infantry battalions in reserve. Suddenly, the whole British army seemed to rise from the riverbank and threatened to overwhelm the American force. "It was a choice of difficulties," Wayne later remarked. "A sudden retreat might end in panic. To await the shock of the approaching enemy would be ruinous." Instead, he hurled his men forward and, coming to within seventy yards of the British line, stood and for fifteen minutes traded volley after volley of withering fire. His very boldness checked the British advance and allowed him in the end to effect a more orderly retreat. Meanwhile, Lafayette himself had ridden forward to give the order to withdraw. The Americans retired rapidly across a marsh, and though they suffered 145 casualties, dead and wounded, all things considered they had gotten off lightly, for the whole army might have been destroyed.

When Greene heard of the near escape, he wrote to Wayne, "It gives me great pleasure to hear of the success of my friends; but be a little careful and tread softly, for, depend upon it, you have a modern Hannibal to deal with in the person of Lord Cornwallis."

F O R years, Washington had hoped for money, troops, adequate arms, and ships, and when the time was ripe, they came.

Although Clinton had weakened his own position by sending several detachments south to Cornwallis, he still had 10,500 men in heavily fortified positions against the 3,500-man American army quartered around West Point. The French corps under Rochambeau encamped at Newport numbered about 4,000 and had "chafed bitterly at their year of inactivity," but without the assistance of a French fleet, an allied attack appeared unlikely to prevail. But now a large fleet, under the comte de Grasse, was on its way, and on May 21, Washington met with Rochambeau at Wethersfield, Connecticut, and together they laid out a plan for a combined attack on New York.

At the time, there was no particular discussion of a Virginia campaign. The conference reportedly closed with this exchange:

> Rochambeau: "Should the squadron from the West Indies arrive in these seas—an event which will probably be announced by a frigate beforehand —what operations will General Washington have in view, after a union of the French army with his own?"
>
> Washington: "It is thought advisable to form a junction of the French and American armies upon the North [Hudson] River as soon as possible, and move down to the vicinity of New York, to be ready to take advantage of any opportunity which the weakness of the enemy may afford. Should the West India fleet arrive upon the coast, the force thus combined may either proceed in the operation against New York, or may be directed against the enemy in some other quarter, as circumstances shall dictate."

Washington afterward summarized the conference in a letter to Greene: "Our affairs were very attentively considered in every point of view, and it was finally determined to make an attempt upon New York, with its present garrison, in preference to a southern operation, as we had not the decided command of the water.... I hope that one of these consequences will follow: either that the enemy will be expelled from the most valuable position which they hold upon the Continent, or be obliged to recall part of their force from the southward to defend it. Should the latter happen, you will be most essentially relieved by it."

Rochambeau returned to Newport; Washington remained in Wethersfield to write urgent letters to the governors of the New England states, asking for as many troops as they could send. "The enemy, counting upon our want of ability, or upon our want of energy," he told them in implied rebuke,

> have, by repeated detachments to the southward, reduced themselves in New York to a situation which invites us to take advantage of it; and should the lucky moment be lost, it is to be feared that they will, after subduing

the Southern States, raise a force in them sufficient to hold them, and return again to the northward with such a number of men as will render New York secure against any force which we can at this time raise or maintain. Our allies in this country expect and depend upon being supported by us in the attempt which we are about to make, and those in Europe will be astonished should we neglect the favorable opportunity which is now offered.

He also wrote to the French minister at Philadelphia, urging him to do what he could to see to it that Admiral de Grasse reached the American coast in time to cooperate in the plan.

By the evening of May 25, Washington was back at his headquarters at New Windsor on the Hudson and began to prepare his army for the siege. Troops were drilled; outlying Continental detachments were ordered to hold themselves in readiness; Congress was urged to new exertions. "We must not despair," he wrote. "The game is yet in our own hands; to play it well is all we have to do, and I trust the experience of error will enable us to act better in future. A cloud may yet pass over us, individuals may be ruined, and the country at large, or particular states, undergo temporary distress, but certain I am that it is in our power to bring the war to a happy conclusion."

Even as he wrote these words in June, they were coming true. He learned that the king of France had authorized a huge sum, 6 million livres, as "a new proof of his affection . . . independent of the four millions which the ministry have enabled Dr. Franklin to borrow for the service of the coming year," in the words of the French minister, Luzerne, and a dispatch from Lafayette revealed Cornwallis's new and more vulnerable position and retreat. On June 13, Rochambeau disclosed that the comte de Grasse, admiral of the French West Indies fleet, would arrive in American waters before summer's end. De Grasse's letter to his French compatriot, dated "at sea," March 29, also urged that if his fleet were to cooperate in some action, everything should be in readiness upon his arrival, as his stay on the coast would be short. Rochambeau replied by frigate with a review of the enemy's current position and the allied plan. However, he also suggested, whether at Washington's request or not, that de Grasse direct his course to the Chesapeake first, to give the Americans a strategic option there before proceeding to New York.

The French broke camp at Newport, where they had been stationed for eleven months, crossed by boat to Providence, and began their march toward the Hudson. Their vanguard reached Hartford on June 23, and by July 5, Rochambeau was with Washington at White Plains. The allied

American and French armies linked up on the eastern bank of the lower Hudson and threatened the enemy fortifications near King's Bridge, as well as Forts Tyron and Knyphausen at the northern end of Manhattan Island. Over the next three weeks, they continued to test Clinton's defenses and drew up plans for a siege.

Clinton, alarmed, tried to recall some of the troops he had assigned to Cornwallis, then reversed his order in a letter that reached Cornwallis at Portsmouth on July 20, just as they were about to embark. Instead, he directed Cornwallis to abandon Portsmouth and fortify Old Point Comfort as a naval station "for ships-of-the-line as well as frigates" on the coast. Cornwallis, however, found the latter unsuitable and decided instead to fortify Yorktown, a village on the Virginia peninsula.

On August 14, a message arrived from de Grasse, who had been refurbishing his fleet at Santo Domingo, that he was starting for the Chesapeake. Coincident with this, Washington received word from Lafayette that Cornwallis had ensconced himself at Yorktown, where he had deep water on three sides of him and a narrow neck in front. That made him eminently vulnerable to a naval blockade. Seizing opportunity by the forelock, Washington decided to move his army south.

The next day, August 15, he wrote to Lafayette, "By the time this reaches you, the Count de Grasse will either be in the Chesapeake or may be looked for every moment. . . . you will immediately take such a position as will best enable you to prevent [the] sudden retreat [of the enemy] through North Carolina, which I presume they will attempt the instant they perceive so formidable an armament."

Although Washington had been eager to lay siege to New York as late as August 1, he had also considered other possibilities, including a move to Virginia. Indeed, after Lafayette had earlier written Washington that he was eager to be a part of such an operation, the latter, on July 30, had counseled patience, suggesting he might turn out to be in the right place after all. Moreover, before he had learned of de Grasse's destination, Washington had already sounded out Robert Morris, the superintendent of finance, at Philadelphia, about the logistics of transporting his army to the South.

Washington's undetectably swift transfer of his forces from New York to Virginia was the largest and perhaps boldest movement of the war. It anticipated, and has justly been compared to, Napoleon's famous march from the English Channel to Bavaria in the Ulm campaign of 1805. Washington had already sent most of his light infantry and the whole Pennsylvania Line to oppose the British in Virginia and left a mere 5,500 or so Continentals and Connecticut state troops spread along a wide arc to bottle up the British, Hessian, and Tory troops in New York. It was therefore an act of great daring to pull 2,000 more Continentals out of their Hudson River positions for his celebrated march to the South.

On August 19, that march began. To deceive the enemy as to his real intentions, Washington disguised the movement as a thrust against New York through Staten Island to facilitate the entrance of the French fleet into Raritan Bay. Breaking camp at Dobbs Ferry, the army crossed the Hudson above at King's Ferry (about eight miles below Peekskill), marched southward in three columns by a circuitous route, and on the twenty-eighth converged at Chatham, where, to create the impression that the French were settling in for a siege, ovens were built for baking bread. This ruse worked long enough to get the armies safely on their way. Indeed, the plan was maintained with such "impenetrable secrecy," recalled Dr. Thacher, that until New Brunswick, New Jersey, was reached not even Washington's own officers had divined the true object of the campaign. But on the thirtieth, the army turned straight toward Trenton, and the goal of the march could no longer be concealed.

It now assumed a rapidity and determination consonant with its ambition, as the troops passed through Trenton on the thirty-first. When Washington found that not enough boats had been assembled on the Delaware to carry them all down to Wilmington, he pressed his advance by land rather than delay, sending his entrenching tools and artillery with two regiments by boat. The soldiers, relieved of their packs (carried on wagons behind), now proceeded almost at a run, leaving all the enemy posts behind. The Americans crossed the Delaware on September 1, a day ahead of the French, while Rochambeau and Washington went ahead to Philadelphia in advance of their troops.

As for Clinton, he afterward explained his predicament this way:

If I had as many reasons to believe that Mr. Washington would move his army into Virginia without a covering fleet as I had to think he would not, I could not have prevented his passing the Hudson under cover of his forts at Verplank's and Stoney Points. Nor (supposing I had boats properly manned) would it have been advisable to have landed at Elizabethtown, in the face of works which he might easily have occupied, as they were only seven miles from his camp at Chatham, whithout subjecting my army to be beat *en detail*. Nor could I, when informed of his march toward the Delaware, have passed any army in time to have made any impression upon him before he crossed that river.

In short, if one believes him, Clinton had been helpless to do anything at all.

At Philadelphia, Washington was met by a troop of light horse, and escorted into town. He stopped at the City Tavern, where others came to pay their respects, and later that afternoon dined with his suite, including Rochambeau and Knox, at the house of Robert Morris. There they drank toasts to the United States, to the kings of France and Spain, to the allied armies, and especially to the speedy arrival of de Grasse.

From Morris, Washington learned that on August 25 Colonel John Laurens had returned from aboard with the first substantial installment of the subsidy granted by the French king. Everything seemed to be falling into place.

In the evening there was "a general illumination" in Washington's honor as he strolled the streets of Philadelphia, surrounded by enthusiastic crowds. Two days later, on September 2, the troops came marching in. The weather had been warm and dry, and the Americans, in a line that extended for two miles, raised a cloud of dust "like a smothering snow-storm." Their step was slow and solemn, "regulated by the drum and fife," and each brigade was followed by field artillery and a baggage train. The officers were resplendent in smart, clean uniforms and mounted on elegantly caparisoned steeds.

On the following day, September 3, the French, in turn, came through on parade, in white uniforms faced with green, dressed "as elegantly as ever the soldiers of a garrison were on a day of review."

Cornwallis, oblivious to the developments around him, continued to fortify Yorktown as a naval station, while Lafayette, in conformity to Washington's instructions, took measures to cut off his retreat by land.

On September 3, the allied army, "with an amazing train of ordnance and military stores," crossed the Schuylkill River, passed through Wilmington, Delaware, and came to the head of the Elk River in Maryland on the sixth, having completed a march of two hundred miles in fifteen days. "It is extraordinary," noted one American officer, "that notwithstanding the Fatigue of such a long & rapid March, there is scarcely a sick man to be found." This was a revitalized army, determined to end the long and brutal war.

Washington left Philadelphia for the Head of Elk on the fifth, and as he passed through Chester that same afternoon, he learned of de Grasse's arrival in the Chesapeake Bay with twenty-eight ships of the line. "I never saw a man so thoroughly and openly delighted than General Washington," recalled the duc de Lauzun, a member of the French general staff, and in a congratulatory order issued to his army the next morning, Washington declared, "Nothing but want of exertion can possibly blast the pleasing prospect before us."

The expectation was tremendous. Benjamin Rush wrote to Gates on the fifth, "Before this reaches you, the fate of Great Britain and the repose of Europe will probably be determined in Chesapeake Bay."

At Philadelphia, French officers learned of de Grasse's arrival just as they were sitting down to a banquet, and before the banquet was over, a messenger arrived to announce that 3,000 troops had already landed under the marquis de Saint-Simon.

At the Head of Elk the main allied armies now paused to await the result of an engagement that developed between the British and French fleets near the mouth of Chesapeake Bay.

A T the beginning of the summer, the naval balance of power had been this: the English had a substantial fleet in the West Indies under Admirals George Rodney and Samuel Hood and a squadron of eight ships under Admirals Marriot Arbuthnot and Thomas Graves guarding New York. The French, likewise, had eight ships at Newport, Rhode Island, under the comte de Barras.

De Grasse's fleet—twenty-four ships of the line—had originally sailed from Brest on March 22 to protect French colonial interests in the West Indies. Toward the close of April, it had skirmished with a British fleet of equal size under Admiral Hood off Martinique, and at the beginning of May it had captured Tobago. De Grasse had then sailed to Cape Haitien, where he had found a frigate awaiting him with dispatches from Washington and Rochambeau. Deciding to direct his course to the Chesapeake, he had enlarged his fleet to twenty-eight sail of the line and six frigates and embarked 3,000 troops under the marquis de Saint-Simon.

In early May, Rodney had warned Arbuthnot at New York of the possible arrival of de Grasse's fleet and had promised every assistance in his power. Graves, succeeding Arbuthnot, sailed off to the north to reconnoiter Boston, unaccountably depriving the British positions of naval cooperation and defense. When Rodney, commanding in the West Indies, heard that de Grasse had repaired to Cape Haitien, he accurately read between the lines and promptly sent a second message to Graves, urging him to sail for the Chesapeake, to which he promised to bring his own squadron in the shortest possible time. This dispatch never arrived. The captain of the sloop of war which carried it, not finding Graves at New York, sailed off in search of him. Almost immediately, he encountered three American privateers and to escape them ran his vessel aground on Long Island. He sank part of his cargo and with it his dispatches, to prevent them from falling into American hands. Meanwhile,

Rodney had fallen ill and had sent Hood in his place to reinforce Graves and intercept de Grasse. Hood followed the French fleet northward up the coast but lost sight of it. Without realizing it, he had outsailed it, so that he looked into the Chesapeake before the French fleet had arrived. Nor was there a packet boat or frigate waiting for him there, as he might have expected, with word from Graves. So he sailed on to New York, where he assumed de Grasse must be. He arrived at Sandy Hook and there at last found Graves, who had just returned to New York and who, up until that moment, had known nothing of de Grasse's approach. At the news, Graves visibly trembled and rolled his eyes toward heaven as his mouth assumed a terrible grimace. Joining his ships to Hood's, he at once bore down to the Chesapeake. But they arrived too late: de Grasse was already there.

On September 5, the day Saint-Simon's troops landed at Jamestown Island, the two fleets hove in sight of each other and prepared for action. De Grasse, anxious to protect the comte de Barras's squadron, which was expected from Rhode Island, immediately slipped his cables and put to sea with twenty-four ships, leaving the remainder to blockade the York and James Rivers. Graves had twenty ships but fewer guns.

After a fierce fight of two hours, in which more than 300 men were killed and wounded on each side, the British ships withdrew. Graves lingered in the bay for four days, hoping to force another engagement on his terms, until the squadron of de Barras, which had sailed from Newport while Washington and Rochambeau were moving through New Jersey, appeared with eight ships of the line, four frigates, and eighteen transports. French naval power in the Chesapeake was now too powerful for Graves to oppose.

Had the British prevailed, Washington's march to Virginia would have been in vain. Moreover, his army, caught in its transports without a naval escort, might have been sunk or captured by the British fleet, making possible a British victory in the war. Instead, Graves returned to New York and de Grasse was left master of the bay.

F R O M the Head of Elk, the allied vanguard embarked unmolested down the bay in light transports, while the main body of the French and American troops, proceeding on to Baltimore and Annapolis, were conveyed to Williamsburg in frigates sent by de Grasse. The vanguard at once formed a junction with the troops under Saint-Simon and the marquis de Lafayette. Other troops under General Lincoln came on from Baltimore by land.

Meanwhile, Washington had ridden on ahead to Baltimore with Rochambeau, taking time to pause for three days at his home at Mount Vernon, which he had not seen in six years. Two days later, on September 14, he was at Lafayette's headquarters at Williamsburg, four days in advance of his army. Upon his arrival, he was greeted by parading troops and a twenty-one-gun salute; and in a demonstration of affection that astonished onlookers, he was embraced by Lafayette, who "caught the General round his body, hugged him as close as it was possible, and absolutely kissed him from ear to ear once or twice . . . with as much ardor as ever an absent lover kissed his mistress on his return." That night Washington was feted by the marquis de Saint-Simon, the future father of French socialism, who entertained him with operatic overtures played by a military band.

Cornwallis by now was aware of his perilous situation, but there was little he could do. Both the York and James Rivers had been blockaded, and Williamsburg transformed into an armed camp. There was no escape for him by land or sea. In truth, he could do nothing but hope for help from Clinton and strengthen his works at Yorktown (and at Gloucester Point opposite) against the inevitable, impending assault.

From Williamsburg, Washington wrote to Lincoln to hasten his march: "Every day we now lose is comparatively an age. As soon as it is in our power with safety, we ought to take our position near the enemy. Hurry on, then, my dear sir, with your troops on the wings of speed. The want of our men and stores is now all that retards our immediate operations. Lord Cornwallis is improving every moment to the best advantage, and every day that is given him to make his preparations may cost us many lives to encounter them."

By the twenty-sixth, the entire allied force—16,000 strong—was encamped near Williamsburg, and on September 28, 1781, the siege of Yorktown began.

CHAPTER NINETEEN

YORKTOWN

I N the early morning, under a fair sky, the troops marched out of
Williamsburg in two columns, American and French, along the great road
down the peninsula. They were lightly accoutred, ready for action, arms
shouldered, bayonets fixed. The day before, Washington had told them
that if the enemy tried to interdict them, they should rely on their bayonets to "prove the vanity of the boast which the British make of their
peculiar prowess in deciding battles with that weapon. The justice of
the cause in which we are engaged . . . must inspire every breast with
sentiments that are the presage of victory." When they came to within
six miles of Yorktown, the two columns diverged, and about noon they
pitched their respective camps about two miles from the enemy's position.

Cornwallis had been helpless to stop their advance. His pickets had
fallen back as soon as the combined columns appeared, and though a
few shots were fired, no one fell. Nevertheless, the allies were prepared
to deal with any attempted sortie from the town. Washington's brief order
that evening was: "The whole army, officers and soldiers, will lay on
their arms this night."

Yorktown had been fortified by Cornwallis, but not for a lengthy siege.
He had been asked by Clinton to turn it into a naval station with stout
defensive works, but he would never have chosen it for a major stand.

To begin with, the town stood on an embankment thirty or forty feet above the river but possessed no commanding features to oppose a land assault. There was a ravine that extended above the town from the river, with a creek lower down, and these two natural obstructions helped protect the British flanks. But between them and the town there was elevated ground. Cornwallis had surrounded it with a line of earthworks, including ten redoubts: two on the right, facing the river road to Williamsburg; three in back of the town; three on the left, commanding the river; and two others, known by the numbers "9" and "10," in advance of the rest on the left. There were also entrenchments at a mill near the head of Wormley Creek, and on the extreme right, beyond the ravine on the riverbank, was a large star-shaped fort known as the "Fusiliers' Redoubt," garrisoned by Royal Welsh Fusiliers. One projecting redoubt, called the Hornwork, commanded the road to Hampton.

Under the circumstances, Cornwallis had done rather well. Sixty-five cannon had been mounted on the fourteen batteries constructed along the line, but they were not of the largest caliber. The most powerful were eighteen-pounders, and to obtain these he had had to strip the British frigate *Charon,* anchored in the river, of her guns. The armed frigate *Guadeloupe* had been moored opposite the Fusiliers' Redoubt to help defend it, while across the river, which at that point was a mile wide, the village of Gloucester had been fortified with a line of entrenchments, four redoubts, and three batteries mounting nineteen guns. Other vessels had been drawn up to the shore, moored head and stern, and their sails cut up for tents. Steuben wrote to Greene, "Cornwallis is fortifying himself like a brave general who must fall."

The 16,000-man army that now began to test these defenses was made up of 9,000 Americans (of whom 5,500 were Continentals and 3,500 militia) and 7,000 French. The Americans, organized into three divisions of two brigades each under Generals Lincoln, Lafayette, and Steuben, formed the right wing of the allied army. The French under Rochambeau —with seven regiments of infantry (including three from the West Indies under Saint-Simon), a formidable 600-man artillery corps, and a legion of horse and foot—formed the left. General Knox commanded the Artillery Brigade, while the Corps of Sappers and Miners was under Louis Duportail, a French engineer who had entered the American service about the same time as Lafayette.

Benjamin Franklin afterward marveled not only that the French and American forces had been able to coalesce with such perfect timing "from different places by land and water, [to] form their junction punctually without the least regard for cross accidents of wind or weather or interruption from the enemy" but "that the [enemy] army which was their object should in the meantime have had the goodness to quit a situation from whence it might have escaped, and place itself in another from whence an escape was impossible."

Indeed, Clinton must now have wished he had not revoked his earlier order to recall some of his detachments, for inside Yorktown some 7,500 officers and men, as well as 800 or 900 marines—the elite of the king's army in America—lay trapped.

On September 29, the allied army spread out into permanent camps. These formed a semicircular line with each end resting on the York River. In the center was ground intersected by marshes, "running out in the shape of a bird's claw," whose rivulets united to form what was known as Beaverdam Creek. Bridged by a causeway, this creek was the dividing line of the allied army, with the American wing arrayed on the right, the French on the left.

No sooner had the allies assumed their siege positions than the British (to the astonishment of both French and American officers) quietly abandoned their outworks during the night. The allies had regarded the outworks as defensible—and worth defending to gain time for a relief force to arrive. Later, in an unseemly exchange of recriminations with Cornwallis, Sir Henry Clinton would criticize the latter's decision, while Cornwallis claimed that since Clinton had just informed him by dispatch that a mighty fleet of twenty-three ships of the line bearing 5,000 men would soon sail from New York to break the siege, he could better hold out by consolidating his inner line.

Indeed, Cornwallis had replied to Sir Henry's dispatch, "I have ventured these last two days to look General Washington's whole force in the face . . . and have the pleasure to assure your Excellency that there is but one wish throughout the army, which is that the enemy would advance. . . . I shall retire this night within the works, and have no doubt, if relief arrives in any reasonable time, York and Gloucester will be both in the possession of His Majesty's troops."

The British withdrawal had left a considerable extent of commanding ground which might have cost the allies "much labor and many lives to obtain by force," noted Dr. Thacher in his diary the following day, as well as two enclosed redoubts almost within point-blank shot of their principal works. The allies moved in at once to occupy the area, which also enabled them to take a closer measure of the defenses of the town. Small commanding knolls and ravines formerly protecting the British were now conveniently situated to give the allied entrenchments cover, and with other general officers and engineers, Washington rode out to make his own survey. He remained in full view until he had noted everything to his own satisfaction, as British cannon shot tore above him into the trees.

Although the siege was proceeding more expeditiously than he could have hoped, there was no time to waste. He called upon the troops' "unabating ardor" and declared, "The present moment offers, in prospect, the epoch which will decide American Independence, the glory and superiority of the allies. A vigorous use of the means in our power cannot but insure success. The passive conduct of the enemy argues his weakness and the uncertainty of his councils. The liberties of America, and the honor of the Allied Arms are in our hands."

Under fire, the Americans constructed two new redoubts in four days, and what had been Cornwallis's outer line of defense became Washington's advanced fortified position, extending from the ravine above to the head of Wormley Creek. Accompanied by an army chaplain named Evans, Washington reviewed this work while it was going on. At one point a shot struck the ground so near that it splattered the chaplain's hat with sand. Much agitated, he took it off and said, "See, here, General!" "Mr. Evans," replied Washington, "you had better carry that home and show it to your wife and children."

Meanwhile, to prevent escape or even foraging expeditions by the British on the Gloucester side, where their positions were defended by Tarleton's Legion and Simcoe's Queen's Rangers, Washington deployed across the river 1,800 infantry (mostly Virginia militia), 300 cavalry, and 800 French marines.

The French blockade was having its effect, and almost at once the British found themselves short of supplies. "We get terrible provisions now," complained one, "putrid meat and wormy biscuits that have spoiled on the ships. Many of the men have taken sick here with dysentery or the bloody flux and diarrhea. . . . Foul fever is spreading . . . we have had little rest day or night." They began to kill off their horses in great numbers—seven hundred in a week—and for days afterward the skinned and butchered carcasses were seen floating down the York.

Early in October, the British expelled from Yorktown several hundred blacks whom they had deliberately infected with smallpox in an attempt to precipitate an epidemic in the allied camp. This despicable stratagem failed, but it was clear that Cornwallis was willing to do anything to keep his own hopes alive. As Wayne put it, "His political and military character are now at stake—he has led the British king and ministry into a deception by assuring them of the subjugation of the Carolinas, and his maneuver into Virginia was a child of his own creation, which he will attempt to nourish at every risk and consequence. . . . I have for some time viewed him as a fiery meteor that displays a momentary lustre, then falls —to rise no more."

The siege proceeded along classic lines and, not incidentally, was the last in history of its kind. Exactly according to the rules laid down a century before by French marshal Sébastien de Vauban for investiture, the first of a series of parallel encircling trenches was opened by the allies "with drums beating and flags flying" about six hundred yards from the besieged fortifications, out of range of small-arms fire and grape and canister shot. The earth excavated from the parallels was thrown over fascines in front of the parallels to form parapets, and earthen artillery batteries were constructed and connected to the parallels by trenches. Meanwhile, saps, or smaller trenches protected by gabions, were dug in a manner that zigzagged toward the enemy's walls. To create these fascines, gabions, and other works, hundreds of American soldiers had been gathering wicker material in the woods. By October 5, they had fashioned more than two thousand fascines, six hundred gabions, and six thousand stakes. Meanwhile, siege guns had been landed from the French ships and heavy guns brought up from the James.

Steuben was the only officer in the American command who had been present at a scientific siege before. But he had all the experience in this vein that Washington could have wished, beginning with the siege of Prague, which he had witnessed as a volunteer at the age of fourteen, and ending as an aide to Frederick the Great, during the siege of Schweidnitz at the finale of the Seven Years' War. Now, in the trenches at Yorktown, he saw another great war drawing rapidly to a close.

On the night of the fifth, which was dark and rainy, the trenches were carefully marked out by laying laths of pinewood end to end in lines. It was extremely dangerous work, for by the laws of warfare sappers and miners were allowed no quarter if caught. One anxious soldier detailed to this service recalled that Washington himself came out and "talked familiarly with us a few minutes" while he examined the progress being made.

On the following night, the opening of the approaches was begun. Four thousand three hundred French and Americans, almost a third of the allied force, paraded at dusk and marched to the designated ground. As they came up, they were positioned at intervals along the line by the engineers. Washington struck a few blows with a pickax, that it might be said that "General Washington with his own hands first broke ground at the siege of Yorktown," and then the troops, standing ready, began their work with entrenching tools. The greatest silence prevailed. The soft, sandy ground was congenial to their task, and the night, too—dark and cloudy, with a gentle rain—favored the enterprise. Campfires had been built as a decoy far to the right beyond a marsh, and all night long British gunners directed their fire in that direction, with a fatuous thundering that covered the sound of the digging nearby. The stakes, gabions, and fascines had been previously brought forward, and the men made such rapid progress that by dawn they had dug themselves out of sight of the enemy's shot. At daybreak, with shouts of alarm, the British sentinels beheld a long embankment, two miles in extent, rising before their eyes.

About noon on the seventh, Lafayette's light infantry moved into the trenches and planted its standards on the parapet. One banner bore the inscription HAEC MANUS INIMICA TYRANNIS ("This company is an enemy to tyranny"). To make the parallel safe against sorties, four palisaded redoubts and five batteries were constructed at intervals along the line. All this was accomplished without much attempt on the part of the British to intervene. "The enemy seem embarrassed, confused, and indeterminate," remarked one Continental colonel, "their fire seems feeble to what might be expected, their works, too, are not formed on any regular plan, but thrown up in a hurry occasionally, and although we have not as yet fired one shot from a piece of artillery, they are as cautious as if the heaviest fire was kept up." The British, in fact, were already frantic and demoralized.

The allies now worked night and day to prepare the emplacements for the heavy guns and mortars of their siege train. By the afternoon of October 9, the first parallel had been completed and the bombardment of Yorktown could begin. About noon, an American flag was hoisted above a battery near the bank of the York River, and "I confess I felt a secret pride swell my heart," wrote one patriot soldier, "when I saw the 'star-spangled banner' waving majestically in the very faces of our implacable foes." Washington himself put the match to the first gun, and its firing was followed by a simultaneous and furious discharge of all the guns in the line. The whole French army stood and cheered for America as the muzzles flashed.

Cornwallis had turned the home of Thomas Nelson, who had succeeded Jefferson as governor of Virginia, into his headquarters. Nelson, a signer of the Declaration of Independence, had led three Virginia brigades, or 3,000 men, to Yorktown and, when the shelling of the town was about to begin, urged Washington to bombard his own house. And that is where Washington, with his experienced surveyor's eye, reputedly pointed the gun for the first (and singularly fatal) allied shot. Legend has it that the shell went right through a window and landed at the dinner table where some British officers, including the British commissary general, had just sat down to dine. The general was killed and several others wounded as it burst among their plates.

The allies had ninety-two cannon of varying caliber, including several twenty-four-pounders, in their arsenal, and about half of them were in place for the first cannonade. That cannonade continued through the night, and on the tenth two new batteries—the "Grand French Battery" on the left of the parallel and an American battery on the right—opened up. That evening French gunners also turned their ordnance, with red-hot shot, on the little squadron of English ships in the river and set the *Charon* and two transports alongside her ablaze. "The ships were enwrapped in a torrent of fire," wrote Dr. Thacher, "spreading with vivid brightness among the combustible rigging, and running with amazing rapidity to the tops of the several masts, while all around was thunder and lightning from our numerous cannon and mortars, and in the darkness of night, presented one of the most sublime and magnificent spectacles which can be imagined. Some of our shells, overreaching the town, were seen to fall into the river and, bursting, throw up columns of water like the spouting of the monsters of the deep." As the British artillery returned fire, the bombshells crossed one another's path in the air like fiery meteors with blazing tails. But by late afternoon on the eleventh, the allied bombardment was so formidable that the British were virtually unable to respond. Cornwallis wrote to Clinton, "Against so powerful an attack we cannot hope to make a very long resistance." And a young British lieutenant confided to his diary, "I now want words to express the dreadful situation of the garrison. . . . Upwards of a thousand shells were thrown into the works this night."

That evening, a second parallel of entrenchments was begun under Steuben's direction from three to five hundred yards in advance of the first, thus bringing both wings within storming distance of the British lines. As dusk fell, the parties moved out, carrying fascines, shovels, spades, grubbing hoes, and other tools, and by morning they had thrown up an entrenchment 750 yards long, $3\frac{1}{2}$ feet deep, and 7 feet wide. The British opened up with a desperate fire, but all their shot and shells, wrote one soldier, "[went] over our heads in a continual blaze the whole night." Meanwhile, a tremendous and incessant firing from the American and French batteries was kept up as Cornwallis ate his scanty meals in his smoke-blackened abode. He looked across the bay, hoping to see the ships of the British navy, but there was nothing on the horizon except the tall masts of the French fleet. Within a few days, he had moved out of the Nelson house and taken refuge in a kind of underground shelter or bunker which he had hastily built at the foot of the garden on the grounds.

By October 14, the second parallel had been largely completed, but before it could be made secure and extended to the river, the two outer British redoubts, 9 and 10, had to be seized. Two light infantry brigades —one American, under Alexander Hamilton (who had finally received a field command), the other French, under the baron de Viominel—were given the task. The work was to be done with the bayonet, and the two that evening were to undertake simultaneous attacks.

At eight o'clock, the signal—three successive shells—rose in a fiery train, their luminous arc appearing to join with Jupiter and Venus into a brilliant new constellation shining in the western sky. Hamilton's detachment advanced with muskets unloaded, bayonets fixed, hurrying on with such determination that they overran their sappers, who were hacking a path through the abatis in front of the redoubt. As they scaled the parapet, their watchword was "Rochambeau"—"a good one," noted one American, because it "sounded like 'Rush-on-boys' when pronounced quick." Within ten minutes they had overwhelmed the Hessian defenders, and with but few casualties of their own (eight killed and thirty wounded) the redoubt was in their hands. The French brigade was just as successful, but more costly (forty-six being killed and sixty-eight wounded) as the redoubt they charged was stoutly defended and its more formidable abatis took longer to cut through.

Washington stood watching these assaults through an embrasure of the main battery with Generals Knox and Lincoln by his side. His position was exposed, as one of his aides nervously remarked. "If you think so," said Washington, "you are at liberty to step back." Moments later, a musket ball ricocheted through the embrasure off a cannon and fell at Washington's feet.

No sooner were the redoubts taken than they were connected by trenches, mounted with howitzers, and included in the second parallel. From this forward position, a covert way and angling work now snaked to within 275 yards of Cornwallis's line. "My situation," wrote Cornwallis to Clinton, "becomes very critical. We dare not show a gun. . . . The safety of the place is therefore so precarious that I can not recommend that the fleet and army should run great risk in endeavoring to save us."

The increasingly strong position of the allies allowed Hamilton and Knox, during an inspection of Redoubt 10, to indulge in an academic dispute almost within view of the enemy. Washington had issued a general standing order that when a shell was seen, the soldiers might cry out, "A shell," but not, when a shot, "A shot," because a shell could be avoided but a shot could not. Therefore to shout "A shot" would only cause confusion and futile alarm. According to a soldier who witnessed the altercation, however, Hamilton evidently thought it "unsoldierlike" to shout, "A shell," while Knox contended that the order showed how much Washington "cared for the life of the men." The argument became heated when suddenly, "*spatl spatl* two shells fell and struck within the redoubt. Instantly the cry broke out on all sides, 'A shell! A shell!' " and everyone scrambled to get behind the blinds. Both Knox and Hamilton did so too, but Hamilton gripped Knox (a large man) from behind for greater cover. "Upon this Knox struggled to throw Hamilton off. . . . In two minutes the shells burst and threw their deadly missiles in all directions. It was now safe and soldierlike to stand out. 'Now,' says Knox, 'now what do you think, Mr. Hamilton, about crying 'shell'? But let me tell you not to make a breastwork of me again!' "

On the night of October 15, the British made a dashing but futile sortie at the second parallel, killing several gunners and spiking seven or eight cannon with bayonets. But by morning the guns were all action again.

On the night of the sixteenth, Cornwallis tried to escape. Abandoning his supplies and even his sick and wounded, he began to transfer his troops in sixteen boats to the opposite side of the York River at Gloucester Point. There he hoped to break through the allied guard with his whole force and by rapid marches to push northward to New York. But at midnight a storm arose, preventing the crossing of all the troops, and at dawn those who had managed to make it to the other side were called back to their old stations at the works.

Those works were now crumbling under the point-blank allied fire.

Every cannon and mortar in the allied arsenal had been brought into action, and the whole peninsula seemed to shake with their pounding, which soon leveled part of the British fortifications and completely silenced their guns.

And so, on October 17—the anniversary of Burgoyne's surrender at Saratoga and after a siege of thirteen days—the end came. At ten in the morning, a drummer in red mounted the enemy's hornwork and began to beat a parley. "As for being heard," wrote one American, "he might have played till doomsday; but he could readily be seen, and the cannonading stopped." Few doubted the meaning of his plaintive beat, and most even then divined that that solitary, forlorn figure of a drummer was tapping out an obsequy for British colonial power over the thirteen states.

A British officer soon came out waving a white handkerchief and approached the American lines. He was met, blindfolded, and conducted to their rear. There he asked Washington on behalf of Cornwallis for a suspension of hostilities for twenty-four hours while joint commissioners could be appointed to determine capitulation terms. Washington replied that he had "an ardent desire to spare the further effusion of blood" and was ready to listen to "such terms . . . as are admissible" but that he would like to have the British proposals in writing first and for that he would suspend the bombardment for two hours. Cornwallis complied and sent Washington the terms he proposed. These included an unacceptable provision allowing his troops to return to England on parole. Washington, mindful of the possibility that a British fleet might at any moment attempt to break the siege, replied with an ultimatum.

The next day, October 18, representatives of both camps met at a house located behind the allied lines, where the fourteen articles of capitulation were drawn up. These were submitted to Cornwallis on the morning of the nineteenth, accompanied by a note from Washington that he expected them to be signed by eleven o'clock. British troops would then be expected to march out to surrender their arms at two that afternoon. The post of Gloucester, falling with that of York, was to be delivered up on the same day.

The terms of capitulation were deliberately framed to match those exacted from General Lincoln at the surrender of Charleston the previous year. The British troops were to march out with arms shouldered, colors cased, and drums beating a British or German march (no mocking rendition of "Yankee Doodle" to be tolerated here) and to ground their arms at a place assigned. All military and artillery stores were to be delivered up, and all enemy troops were to be held as prisoners of war. The soldiers, however, were to be allowed to keep their personal effects and the officers their effects and sidearms. British doctors were also to be allowed to tend to their own sick and wounded. Tens of thousands of civilians—outnumbering even the great forces on display—gathered from throughout the surrounding countryside to witness the event. Everyone seemed to understand the solemnity of the occasion, and "universal silence and order prevailed."

In "recognition of so many reiterated and astonishing interpositions of Providence," morning service was performed in all the different divisions and brigades of the allied army, and at two o'clock the captive soldiers filed out of Yorktown. Sullen and dejected, they proceeded in a somewhat "careless and irregular" manner between the two victorious lines —the Americans on the right, the French on the left—formed for their reception, drums beating a British march. That march, according to tradition, was "The World Turned Upsidedown," which borrowed its tune from an earlier and more optimistic English ballad, "When the King Shall Enjoy His Own Again." But that he never would.

All eyes waited to behold Lord Cornwallis, but the celebrated general, claiming to be indisposed, failed to appear. He had looked Washington's "whole army in the face" but, when the defining moment came, couldn't bear to look them in the eye. It was rumored at the time that he had given himself up "entirely to vexation and despair." But what was more disgracefully obvious was that he had refused to ride forth at the head of his captured army, even though he had always appeared in splendid triumph at its head when it had been victorious in arms. Brigadier General Charles O'Hara, his deputy, was delegated to represent him, and at first, by error (or by design, so as not to acknowledge the event as an American triumph), he tried to surrender to the French. He presented his sword to Rochambeau, but Rochambeau refused it and pointed to Washington. Washington, unwilling to allow Cornwallis to compel him to accept surrender from a deputy, in turn directed O'Hara to General Lincoln, who conducted the British army into a spacious field, where, within a circle formed by French hussars, the troops were to ground their arms. A number of the soldiers reportedly threw them down onto the pile with resentful violence, in an attempt to prevent their future use.

Washington had been wise to prosecute the siege with such expedition, for even as these ceremonies were taking place, Sir Henry Clinton, with twenty-five ships of the line, two fifty-gun ships, and eight frigates, carrying 7,000 British troops, had sailed out of New York to Cornwallis's relief. Five days later, he entered the mouth of the Chesapeake, only to learn he was too late.

The day after the surrender, Cornwallis wrote to Clinton, "Sir,—I have the mortification to inform your excellency that I have been forced to give up the posts of York and Gloucester, and to surrender the troops under my command, by capitulation on the 19th instant, as prisoners of war to the combined forces of America and France." He then lost no time in shifting a measure of the blame:

> I never saw this post in a very favorable light; but when I found I was to be attacked in it, in so unprepared a state, by so powerful an army and artillery, nothing but the hopes of relief would have induced me to attempt its defence; or I would either have endeavored to escape to New York by rapid marches from the Gloucester side, immediately on the arrival of General Washington's troops at Williamsburg, or, I would, notwithstanding the disparity of numbers, have attacked them in the open field, where it might have been just possible that fortune would have favored the gallantry

of the handfull of troops under my command. But, being assured by your excellency's letters that every possible means would be tried by the navy and army to relieve us, I could not think myself at liberty to venture upon either of those desperate attempts; therefore, after remaining for two days in a strong position in front of this place, in hopes of being attacked, upon observing that the enemy were taking measures which could not fail of turning my left flank in a short time, and receiving on the second evening your letter of the 24th of September, that the relief would fall about the 5th of October, I withdrew within the works on the night of the 29th of September, hoping by the valor and firmness of the soldiers to protect the defence until you could arrive.

Under all these circumstances, I thought it would have been wanton and inhuman to the last degree to sacrifice the lives of this small body of gallant soldiers, who had ever behaved with so much fidelity and courage, by exposing them to an assault which, from the numbers and precautions of the enemy, could not fail to succeed. I therefore proposed to capitulate, and I have the honor to enclose to your excellency the copy of the correspondence between General Washington and me on that subject, and the terms of the capitulation agreed upon. I sincerely lament that better could not be obtained; but I have neglected nothing in my power to alleviate the misfortune and distress of both officers and soldiers.

A few days later, the British rank and file, together with some of their officers, were marched off to prison camps in Virginia and Maryland, while Cornwallis and his principal officers were entertained by their allied counterparts before being allowed to return to New York on parole.

In all, 7,247 officers and men and 840 British seamen had fallen into allied hands. Despite the magnitude of the confrontation and the forces involved, the casualties on both sides had been light: among the British, as reported by themselves, 156 killed, 326 wounded, and 1,500 reported as sick. The allied losses were 75 killed and 199 wounded. It had been an unexpectedly bloodless climax to a long and bloody war.

"Posterity will huzza for us," said Washington, implying that the victorious need not revel overmuch in their triumph as the memory of their deeds would never die.

At a banquet in a field tent, Cornwallis, in toasting Washington, wishfully remembered Trenton and Princeton as the greater victories: "When the illustrious part which your excellency has borne in the long and arduous contest becomes a matter of history, fame will gather your brightest laurels from the banks of the Delaware rather than those of the Chesapeake." But for America it was all of a piece.

Lieutenant Colonel Tench Tilghman, one of Washington's devoted aides, carried the "victory dispatch" to Congress in Philadelphia, where he arrived after midnight on October 24. One of the city watchmen, an elderly German, conducted him to the door of the president of Congress, then Thomas McKean of Delaware, who was roused at once from his bed. The watchman then continued his rounds, calling out, "Basht dree o'glock, und Gorn-wal-lis isht da-ken."

The victory appeared decisive. Congress met in the morning and upon hearing the news proceeded in a body to church for a special service of thanksgiving. Afterward, it resolved to erect a marble column at the site of the surrender. Medals and other honors were showered upon the allied general staff, and throughout the land people celebrated with bonfires, parades, ox roasts, and illuminations as "the completeness of the victory, its magnitude, its unexpectedness, in view of the slender prospect of such an event but a few weeks before, added zest to the general rejoicing." The president of Yale saluted Washington as "the deliverer" of his country, "the Defender of the Liberty and Rights of Humanity." In France, Louis XVI, upon hearing of the surrender, ordered a Te Deum to be sung in the Metropolitan Church in Paris, while the city administration directed that "all the bourgeois inhabitants" hang out lanterns in front of their homes. Shortly after the news reached Versailles, Benjamin Franklin attended a diplomatic dinner at which the French foreign minister toasted his king with champagne: "To his Majesty, Louis the Sixteenth, who, like the moon, fills the earth with a soft, benevolent glow." The British ambassador then rose and proclaimed, "To George the Third, who, like the sun at noonday, spreads his light and illumines the world." Whereupon Franklin stood up and reportedly said, "I cannot give you the sun or the moon, but I give you George Washington, General of the armies of the United States, who, like Joshua of old, commanded both the sun and the moon to stand still, and both obeyed."

In Great Britain, King George III was "in denial." Rather wishfully, he wrote to Lord North, on November 28, "I have no doubt when men are a little recovered of the shock felt by the bad news, and feel that if we recede no one can tell to what a degree the consequence of this country will be diminished, that they will then find the necessity of carrying on the war, though the mode of it may require alterations."

But Lord North had seen at once the writing on the wall. When he received word of the defeat at his residence in Downing Street, he took it, recalled Lord Germain, like "a ball in his breast." Pacing back and forth in a frenzy, his arms flung wide in despair, he exclaimed wildly, again and again, "Oh God! Oh God! It is over! It is all over!"

CHAPTER TWENTY

THE END

o f

THE BEGINNING

T H E American war is over," wrote Benjamin Rush after York-town, "but that is far from being the case with the American Revolution. On the contrary, nothing but the first act of the great drama is closed."

Washington left Yorktown on November 5 with a large retinue of American and French officers, proceeding first to Mount Vernon and then to Philadelphia, where, on the twenty-eighth, Congress presented him with two of the captured British flags.

But America dared not let her sword rust. North may have felt that it was all over, but Washington could not afford to make such an assumption.

At Yorktown, he had captured 7,247 soldiers, 840 seamen, 244 pieces of artillery, and thousands of small arms. But British forces still held New York; Wilmington, North Carolina; Savannah; and Charleston, and Washington expected at least another year of fighting. "My only apprehension (which I wish may be groundless)," he said shortly after the surrender, "is lest the late important success . . . should produce such a relaxation in the prosecution of the war, as will prolong the calamities." As for Yorktown, he preferred, rather modestly, to regard it as "an interesting event that may be productive of much good if properly improved."

Accordingly, he took steps to reinforce Greene in the South with 2,000 troops and won a commitment from Rochambeau to remain in the vicinity of Yorktown until the following spring. Meanwhile, the main American army embarked for the Head of Elk and returned north under General Lincoln to keep vigilant guard over the British in New York. Washington was unable to prevail upon de Grasse to collaborate in an attack on Charleston or Wilmington or to delay the departure of the French fleet to the West Indies, which enabled Britain to regain control of the seas. Under the circumstances, he reminded Congress, the more thoroughly America was prepared for war, the more leverage it would have in negotiations; but a contrary course would "expose us to the most disgraceful disasters." "My greatest fear," he told General Greene, "is that Congress will fall into a state of languor and relaxation." Thus he busied himself at Philadelphia all winter long to fill out the army's strength before returning to his troops at Newburgh, New York, on March 31, 1782.

Meanwhile, Cornwallis had been exchanged, and Benedict Arnold, having burned his hometown of New London, Connecticut, on September 6, in his last act of infamy in America, sailed with him to England. Throughout the voyage, Arnold endeavored to persuade Cornwallis that the war could still be won. In England, Arnold revived his family coat of arms with its lion crest, but in place of the old motto, "My Glory is on high," he chose (from an ode of Horace), *"Nil desperandum"* ("Never despair"). The remainder of his life was spent in an unsuccessful attempt to win respect and to acquire the great fortune that was his heart's true desire.

W A S H I N G T O N ' S stature at this time had never been greater, but he was uncomfortable with all the accolades. Among the few he seemed to enjoy were those he could dismiss lightly, such as the poetic tributes that came from Annie Boudinot, the wife of Elias Boudinot, his former commissary of prisoners and now a New Jersey congressman. She sent him verses she had composed on "Peace," "The Surrender of Cornwallis," and one she called "A Triumphal Ode to the Commander-in-Chief," with a note of apology for their deficiencies. Washington playfully replied:

You apply to me, my dear madam, for absolution, as though I was your father confessor, and as though you had committed a crime great in itself, yet of the venial class. You have reason good; for I find myself strangely disposed to be a very indulgent ghostly adviser upon this occasion, and notwithstanding "you are the most offending soul alive" (that is, if it is a crime to write elegant poetry), yet if you will come and dine with me on Thursday, and go through the proper course of penitence which shall be prescribed, I will strive hard to assist you in expiating these poetical trespasses on this side of purgatory.

Another writer on Washington's mind at the time was Thomas Paine. Paine was broke. During the Yorktown siege, he had written from Philadelphia to Colonel John Laurens at headquarters, "I went for your boots, the next day after you left town, but . . . I must borrow the money to pay for them. . . . I wish you had thought of me a little before you went away, and at least endeavored to put matters in a train that I might not have to reexperience what has already past."

Paine's personal financial embarrassment, which was chronic, was bound to become a matter of state concern. Paine understood this and wrote a remarkable letter of supplication to Washington couched in such terms as would oblige him to respond:

Second Street, opposite the Quaker Meeting House, Nov. 30th, 1781.

Sir,—As soon as I can suppose you to be a little at leisure from business and visits, I shall, with much pleasure, wait on you, to pay you my respects and congratulate you on the success you have most deservedly been blest with. I hope nothing in the perusal of this letter will add a care to the many that employ your mind; but as there is a satisfaction in speaking where one can be conceived and understood, I divulge to you the secret of my own situation; because I would wish to tell it to somebody, and as I do not want to make it public, I may not have a fairer opportunity.

It is seven years, *this day,* since I arrived in America, and tho' I consider them as the most honorary time of my life, they have nevertheless been the most inconvenient and even distressing. From an anxiety to support, as far as laid in my power, the reputation of the Cause of America, as well as the Cause itself, I declined the customary profits which authors are entitled to, and I have always continued to do so; yet I never thought (if I thought at all on the matter,) but that as I dealt generously and honorably by America, she would deal the same by me. But I have experienced the contrary—and it gives me much concern, not only on account of the inconvenience it has occasioned to me, but because it unpleasantly lessens my opinion of the character of a country which once appeared so fair, and it hurts my mind to see her so cold and inattentive to matters which affect her reputation.

Almost every body knows, not only in this country but in Europe, that I have been of service to her, and as far as the interest of the heart could carry a . . . man I have shared with her in the worst of her fortunes, yet so confused has been my private circumstances that for one summer I was obliged to hire myself as a common clerk to Owne Biddle of this city for my support: but this and many others of the like nature I have always endeavored to conceal, because to expose them would only serve to entail on her the reproach of being ungrateful, and might start an ill opinion of her honor and generosity in other countries, especially as there are pens enough abroad to spread and aggravate it. . . .

While it was every body's fate to suffer I chearfully suffered with them, but tho' the object of the country is now nearly established and her circumstances rising into prosperity, I feel myself left in a very unpleasant situation. Yet I am totally at a loss what to attribute it to; for wherever I go I find respect, and every body I meet treats me with friendship; all join in censuring the neglect and throwing blame on each other, so that their civility disarms me as much as their conduct distresses me. But in this situation I cannot go on, and as I have no inclination to differ with the Country or to tell the story of her neglect, it is my design to get to Europe, either to France or Holland. I have literary fame, and I am sure I cannot experience worse fortune than I have here. Besides a person who understood the affairs of America, and was capable and disposed to do her a kindness, might render her considerable service in Europe, where her situation is but imperfectly understood and much misrepresented by the publications which have appeared on that side the water, and tho' she has not behaved to me with any proportionate return of friendship, my wish for her prosperity is no ways abated, and I shall be very happy to see her character as fair as her cause.

This letter was written just six weeks after the capitulation at Yorktown, yet with all that was then on his mind, Washington graciously overlooked Paine's implied threat to publicize his own penury to America's discredit and tried to help. He suggested to Robert Morris, superintendent of finance, that some provision be made for Paine, and Morris told Paine that "something might turn up." Meanwhile, Morris had written to Robert Livingston about the matter, and the two met with Washington in Philadelphia on February 10, 1782, to see what could be done. Together, they decided that, given Paine's abilities, it would be "much for the interest of the United States" to engage him as a sort of unofficial state propagandist—"informing the people and rousing them into action"—at a salary of $800 per year to be paid out of a secret fund "not [to be] publicly avowed."

About a month later, while this scheme was pending, Paine invited Washington, who was still in Philadelphia, to dinner for a confidential tête-à-tête: "You will do me a great deal of pleasure, if you can make it convenient to yourself to spend a part of an evening at my apartments, and eat a few oysters or a crust of bread and cheese; for besides the favour you will do me, I want much to consult with you on a matter of public business, tho' of a secret nature, which I have already mentioned to Mr. Morris, whom I likewise intend to ask, as soon as yourself shall please to mention the evening when." Paine had in mind an official history of the Revolutionary War. But his invitation to partake of "a few oysters or a crust of bread and cheese" was also a deliberately pathetic touch.

O N April 12, 1782, a patriot militia captain, Josiah Huddy, was hanged by a band of Tories in New Jersey. Washington demanded that the British hand over the Tory officer responsible and, when he was not produced, retaliated by choosing by lot for execution a British officer of Huddy's rank. The lot fell upon Captain Charles Asgill, who had surrendered at Yorktown, even though, by Article 14 of the capitulation, he should have been exempted from any occasion for reprisal such as the one that had just transpired.

Washington went through agonies. He didn't want to execute Asgill, even though Huddy's murder had created a furor and Americans were crying out for blood. On June 5, he wrote to General Lincoln, looking for a way out: "Pray, let me know the opinions of the most sensible of those with whom you have conversed. Congress by their resolve has unanimously approved of my determination to retaliate. The army have advised it, and the country look for it. But how far is it justifiable upon an officer under the faith of a capitulation, if none other can be had is the question?" However, he said, if Asgill were simply allowed to go free, "the whole business [would] have the appearance of a farce."

Ultimately, an honorable solution was found by granting a formal request for clemency from France. Lady Asgill, the condemned captain's mother, had appealed directly to Marie-Antoinette, who in turn had appealed to the French foreign minister, Vergennes. Vergennes asked that the captain be released on the grounds that French arms had contributed to his capture. Washington, who abhorred capital punishment except in the greatest extremity, welcomed the reprieve, because the French request, so couched, could hardly be denied.

Meanwhile, in February 1782, a Whig government had come to power in England, intent on making peace. The king's hopes for a last military push had been rejected and a cessation of hostilities agreed upon by Parliament in March. Both sides appointed commissioners to treat for peace. Clinton was recalled, Germain was humiliated, and Sir Guy Carleton, whom Germain's petty spite had demoted in favor of the hapless

Burgoyne, was appointed to see to such arrangements as might bring the war to an honorable end. He arrived in New York in May, invested with extraordinary powers as "Commander-in-Chief of His Majesty's Forces between Nova Scotia and the Floridas."

Washington remained wary. When Carleton notified him on August 2 that peace negotiations had begun in Paris and that the British would recognize the independence of the United States at the outset, instead of making it the condition of a treaty, Washington thought it might be a ploy to undermine whatever military will the Americans had left: "From the former infatuation, duplicity and perverse system of British policy, I confess I am induced to doubt everything, to suspect everything." He therefore called for "increased exertion."

He also worried about a kind of postwar cynicism that seemed to be taking hold. In July, he wrote, "That spirit of freedom, which at the commencement of this contest would have gladly sacrificed every thing to the attainment of its object, has long since subsided, and every selfish passion has taken its place." As for the talks in Paris, "I have not so full a confidence in the success of the present negotiation for peace as some gentlemen entertain," he wrote on September 18. Nevertheless, he could not but be somewhat reassured as the British troops were withdrawn from their enclaves in stages—from Savannah in August, Charleston in December. By then, Rochambeau's army had marched north to reunite, in mid-September, with the American left wing at Verplanck's Point, below Peekskill. The British, however, would hold on to New York for almost another year.

Congress had instructed its plenipotentiaries in Paris to insist on the recognition of American independence but otherwise to follow the direction of the French. In fact, the last paragraph of the instructions had actually been dictated by the French ambassador to the United States: "You are to make the most candid and confidential communications, upon all subjects, to the ministers of our generous ally the king of France; to undertake nothing in the negotiations for peace or truce, without their knowledge and concurrence; and ultimately to govern yourselves by their advice and opinion." So indebted did Congress feel to France that it momentarily subordinated American national interest to French foreign policy. That policy, of course, was not only to thwart Great Britain, France's archenemy, but (with Spain, her chief ally) to keep the new United States from emerging as a great power. This was to be done by maintaining British power to the north and Spanish power to the south and west.

Wisely, the American plenipotentiaries, John Jay, John Adams, and Benjamin Franklin, disregarded their instructions.

• • •

T H O M A S Paine's plea for an annual stipend (and a modest one at that) had come at a time when the Department of Finance was under unparalleled strain. The coffers were empty, government salaries were in arrears, and fundamental prior commitments to the army and officer corps could not be met. Inflation continued to rise. Some relief came in September 1782, when John Adams arranged a loan of 5 million guilders (about £400,000) from Holland. More came when the king of France subsequently "remitted to us all the interest which he has paid for us," reported Edmund Randolph of Virginia, "or was due to him on loans to us, together with all the charges attending the Holland loan. Moreover, [he has] postponed the demand of the principal till one year after the war, and agreed to receive it then in twelve successive annual payments. These concessions amount to a very considerable reduction of the liquidated debt." Nevertheless, army pay was months in arrears, and since Congress was manifestly incapable of meeting its financial obligations— in particular, the promised pensions for officers serving to the end of the war—soldiers and officers alike faced the prospect of returning to civilian life without any security. The army's discontents continued to ferment until by spring the troops were again in an openly mutinous state.

The situation, perilous to the nascent republic, seemed almost to warrant martial law. Indeed, to obtain justice for themselves and others, some of the officers contemplated a military coup. The previous May, Washington had received an extraordinary letter from Colonel Lewis Nicola, the former commander of Fort Mifflin, who urged him to seize power with the army's help, enthrone himself as king or dictator, and establish a strong, stable government. To this unwanted communiqué, Washington administered a stern reproof: "With a mixture of great surprise and astonishment I have read [your proposal] which to me seems big with the greatest mischiefs that can befall my Country. If I am not deceived in myself, you could not have found a person to whom your schemes were more disagreeable. . . . Let me conjure you then, if you have any regard for your Country, for yourself or posterity, or respect for me, to banish these thoughts from your Mind, and never communicate, as from yourself, or any one else, a sentiment of like nature."

But mutinous views only increased in the intervening year, and after a long idle winter, during which the officer corps had had little to do but mull over its grievances, the situation came to a head. Some of the officers, as well as soldiers, were now owed as much as six years' back pay. Washington asked Congress whether it considered it just that they were about to return home.

goaded by a thousand stings of reflection on the past and of anticipation on the future, . . . turned into the world, soured by penury and what they call the ingratitude of the public, involved in debts, without one farthing of money to carry them home, after having spent the flowers of their days, and many of them their patrimonies, in establishing the freedom and independence of their country, and suffered everything human nature is capable of enduring on this side of death, without one thing to soothe their feelings or dispel the gloomy prospects, I cannot avoid apprehending that a train of evils will follow of a very serious and distressing nature.

Encamped in the wooded hills behind Newburgh, Washington's forces seethed with discontent. On January 1, 1783, three of their officers went to Philadelphia to petition Congress for redress of grievances. They submitted a request for back pay due and some assurance of the half pay for life promised in the fall of 1780. The officers also gave Congress the option of commuting the pension to six years' full pay, if it so desired. Congress, however, giving no assurances on either count, rejected this proposal. On February 5, the Department of Finance authorized one month's pay to the officers and soldiers on the hypothetical credit of bills drawn on loans still under negotiation from Holland and France. But this was a pathetically small amount considering what was owed. Meanwhile, appeals were also made to both General Knox of the Northern Army and General Greene in the South to use their troops to compel Congress to honor the pledges it had made. Both refused. Greene warned, memorably, "When soldiers advance without authority, who can halt them? We have many Claudiuses and Catilines in America, who may give a different direction to this business, than either you or I expect."

But the officer corps would not be pacified. At Newburgh, on March 10, 1783, an anonymous paper was circulated through the camp calling for a mass meeting of the officers to plan some kind of strong action against the government. Another document warned, "Suspect the man who would advise to more moderation and longer forebearance." Washington denounced the proposed proceedings as "irregular and disorderly" and called a meeting of his own for Saturday, March 15, at noon.

Washington, "sensibly agitated," faced a sullen and hostile crowd. He spoke of his long and devoted service and of how much feeling he had for the men. He counseled patience and explained that Congress, "despite the slowness inherent in deliberative bodies," would ultimately find some way to satisfy their demands. He also promised to do everything humanly possible himself on their behalf. In truth, he had always been their most eloquent advocate. As for the anonymous admonition about moderation and forbearance, how could the time for moderation be past? That would mean that

> reason is of no use to us. . . . Let me conjure you, in the name of our common country, as you value your own sacred honor, as you respect the rights of humanity and as you regard the military and national character of America, to express your utmost horror and detestation of the man who wishes, under any specious pretenses, to overturn the liberties of our country and who wickedly attempts to open the floodgates of civil discord and deluge our rising empire in blood. You will [thereby] give one more distinguished proof of unexampled patriotism and patient virtue rising superior to the pressure of the most complicated sufferings. And you will, by the dignity of your conduct, afford occasion for posterity to say, when speaking of the glorious example you have exhibited to mankind: "Had this day been wanting, the world had never seen the last stage of perfection to which human nature is capable of attaining."

It was, in its way, a magnificent homily and exhortation to virtue; yet the officers remained unmollified. Then, remembering that he had brought a letter with him from a sympathetic congressman, Washington took it out to read it, paused for a moment as though he were having difficulty making out the words, reached into his pocket again, and took out a pair of eyeglasses. Apologizing for the delay, he remarked quietly, "I have already grown gray in the service of my country. I am now going blind."

That completely personal, seemingly offhand remark—"so natural, so unaffected . . . as rendered it superior to the most studied oratory," wrote one major—recalled his audience to themselves. "It forced its way into the heart, and you might see sensibility moisten every eye." When he had finished, the officers thanked him, asked him to intercede on their behalf, and quietly left the hall.

Wrote Thomas Jefferson, "The moderation and virtue of a single character probably prevented this Revolution from being closed, as most others have been, by a subversion of that liberty it was intended to establish."

Washington was as good as his word. He wrote a vehement letter to the president of Congress warning that if the officers were "to grow old in poverty, wretchedness and contempt; if they are to wade through the vile mire of dependency and owe the miserable remnant of that life to charity which has hitherto been spent in honor; then shall I have learned what ingratitude is, then I shall have realized a tale which will embitter every moment of my future life." Congress responded by commuting the officers' pensions (originally to have been half pay for life) to a lump sum of five years' full pay.

O N March 23, the warship *Triumph,* belonging to the comte d'Estaing's squadron, docked at Philadelphia with a letter from the marquis de Lafayette to the president of Congress announcing that a peace treaty had been signed in Paris on January 20. On March 26, Washington was notified and immediately sent a copy of the dispatches to Governor George Clinton of New York. On the envelope, in large bold letters which he underlined, he wrote the word PEACE. Shortly thereafter, Sir Guy Carleton proclaimed a cessation of hostilities and Congress followed suit. At noon on April 19—eight years to the day after the first patriots had fallen on Lexington Green—the news was announced to the army. In saluting his troops, Washington echoed the spirit of the stirring language spoken before the Battle of Agincourt by Shakespeare's King Henry V: "happy, thrice happy, shall they be pronounced hereafter who have contributed anything, who have performed the meanest office in erecting this stupendous fabric of Freedom and Empire." By their sacrifices, he told them, they had protected "the rights of human nature" and established "an asylum for the poor and oppressed of all nations" irrespective of their religious creed. "Nothing now remains but for the actors of this mighty scene to preserve a perfect, unvarying consistency of character through the very last act, to close the drama with applause and to retire from the military theatre with the same approbation of angels and men which has crowned all their former virtuous actions."

On April 23, the army began to disband by furloughs; by October 18, Congress had discharged most from the ranks. Only a small force remained, with Washington at its head, to keep an eye on the British troops in New York. Washington longed for home and, in a letter sent to the governors of the thirteen states, spoke of "a retirement for which I never ceased to sigh" and in which he hoped "to pass the remainder of life in a state of undisturbed repose." He then went on to offer some political advice. Americans, he said, were now

sole lords and proprietors of a vast tract of continent comprehending all the various soils and climates of the world and abounding with all the necessaries and conveniences of life. . . . Heaven has crowned all other blessings, by giving a fairer opportunity for political happiness, than any other nation has been favored with. . . . This is the time of their political probation; this is the moment when the eyes of the whole world are turned upon them; this is the moment to establish or ruin their national character forever; this is the favorable moment to give such a tone to our federal government as will enable it to answer the ends of its institution; or this may be the ill-fated moment for relaxing the powers of the Union, annihilating the cement of the Confederation and exposing us to become the sport of European politics, which may play one state against another, to prevent their growing importance and to serve their own interested purposes. For, according to the system of policy the states shall adopt at this moment, they will stand or fall; and by their confirmation or lapse it is yet to be decided whether the Revolution must ultimately be considered as a blessing or a curse—a blessing or a curse, not to the present age alone, for with our fate will the destiny of unborn millions be involved.

He went on to list four requirements for the efflorescence of America as a great nation:

First. An indissoluble union of the states under one federal head. Secondly. A sacred regard to public justice (that is, the payment of debts). Thirdly. The adoption of a proper peace establishment (that is, an army and a navy). Fourthly. The prevalence of that pacific and friendly disposition among the people of the Union, which will influence them to forget their local prejudices and policies; to make those mutual concessions, which are requisite to the general prosperity; and, in some instances, to sacrifice their individual advantages to the interest of the community. These are the pillars on which the glorious future of our independency and national character must be supported.

Congress grumbled at "the unsolicited obtrusion of his advice," as Edmund Randolph put it in a letter to James Madison, even as it voted to erect a bronze equestrian statue of him in Roman dress with a truncheon in his right hand and a laurel wreath encircling his brow. On a marble pedestal, in bas-relief, were to be depicted the five great military events of the war in which he had personally led the command: the Siege of Boston, the Capture of the Hessians at Trenton, the Battle of Princeton, the Action at Monmouth, and the Surrender of Cornwallis at Yorktown. An inscription on the upper part of the pedestal was to read THE ILLUSTRI-OUS COMMANDER-IN-CHIEF OF THE ARMIES OF THE UNITED STATES OF AMERICA DURING THE WAR WHICH VINDICATED AND SECURED THEIR LIBERTY, SOVER-EIGNTY, AND INDEPENDENCE.

The statue, however, was never made.

• • •

T H E British troops were at last withdrawn from New York City on November 25. As they sailed away, a detachment from West Point, with Washington riding at its head, marched in. The soldiers proceeded down the Bowery to Broadway, then to the harbor to take possession of the battery. The king's ensign still flew over it, and it proved difficult to get the flag down, as the British, in a bit of parting spite, had removed the tackle and pulleys from the flagstaff and had greased the pole. But a sailor with a hammer and cleats made the ascent at last, and "Old Glory" rose to the thunder of salutes.

Washington and his principal officers were feted at an elaborate public dinner, and a few days later there was a tremendous display of fireworks on lower Broadway, near Bowling Green. It included a "Balloon of Serpents," a "Yew Tree of Brilliant Fire," and an "Illuminated Pyramid, with Archimedian Screws, a Globe and Vertical Sun," culminating in "Fame, Descending" and the firing of one hundred rockets high into the air.

Washington now prepared to depart for Congress to resign his command, and on December 4 he met with his ranking officers in the long room of Faunces Tavern at the corner of Broad and Pearl Streets. It was an utterly poignant scene of farewell worthy of Plato's *Apology*. The officers gathered at noon, and a few minutes later Washington entered. He poured himself a glass of wine, turned to them, and said, "With a heart full of love and gratitude, I now take leave of you. I most devoutly wish that your latter days may be as prosperous and happy as your former ones have been glorious and honorable." He paused, drained his glass, then added, "I cannot come to each of you to take my leave, but shall be obliged if each of you will come and take me by the hand." General Knox, who stood nearby, approached and grasped his hand and then, with much emotion, embraced him. Each officer in turn, in silence, did the same. "Such a scene of sorrow and weeping," recalled Lieutenant Colonel Benjamin Tallmadge, "I had never before witnessed, and hope I may never be called upon to witness again. . . . The simple thought that we were then about to part from the man who had conducted us through a long and bloody war, and under whose conduct the glory and independence of our country had been achieved, and that we should see his face no more in this world, seemed to me utterly insupportable."

Immediately thereafter, Washington himself, "suffused in tears," left the room and, passing through a corps of light infantry, walked silently on to Whitehall, where a barge was waiting to convey him across the Hudson to Paulus Hook. "We all followed," wrote one officer, "in mournful silence to the wharf."

Washington entered the barge, turned, took off his hat and waved it in a silent good-bye. The officers replied in the same manner and stood watching until his barge receded from sight.

Congress transferred itself from its temporary quarters at Princeton to Annapolis, Maryland, and Washington followed, through New Jersey, Pennsylvania, and Maryland, where the local legislatures bestowed their accolades. At Annapolis, at noon on December 23, he was ushered into the presence of Congress in the Senate Chamber of the old Maryland State House. The gallery and the floor of the hall were filled with spectators and various dignitaries, standing; the members of Congress sat in their seats. Washington entered, and took his seat in the chair appointed. After a brief pause the president of Congress, Thomas Mifflin, said, "Sir, the United States in Congress assembled, are prepared to receive your communications." Washington rose and delivered a short speech. His hand, holding the paper, shook visibly as he began, "Mr. President: The great events on which my resignation depended having at length taken place, I have now the honor of offering my sincere congratulations to Congress and of presenting myself before them to surrender into their hands the trust committed to me and to claim the indulgence of retiring from the service of my country." When he came to some lines he had written in affectionate tribute to his fellow officers, he was overcome with emotion and had to steady his text with both hands. When he had composed himself, he concluded, "Having now finished the work assigned me . . . I here offer my commission and take my leave of all the employments of public life."

The surrender of his sword was a momentous act, establishing a precedent for the subordination of military to civilian authority, no matter how great that military power was. And it was made all the more self-effacing as the president of Congress on that occasion was Thomas Mifflin, who four years before had tried, with Conway and others, to topple Washington from his command. In a sense, no one deserved to receive Washington's sword less, yet it was only Mifflin who lapsed in dignity as he thanked Washington on behalf of Congress in a statement written for him (since he had declined to write it himself) by Thomas Jefferson:

> Called upon by your country to defend its invaded rights, you accepted the sacred charge before it had formed alliances and while it was without funds, or a government to support you. You have conducted the great military contest with wisdom and fortitude, invariably regarding the rights of the civil power, through all the disasters and changes. You have, by the love and confidence of your fellow citizens, enabled them to display their

martial genius, and transmit their fame to posterity. You have persevered until these United States have been enabled, under a just Providence, to close the war in freedom, safety, and independence . . . but the glory of your virtues will not terminate with your military command—it will continue to animate remote ages. . . . And for you, we address to Him our earnest prayers that a life so beloved may be fostered with all His care; that your days may be happy, as they have been illustrious; and that He will finally give you that reward which this world will not give.

Instead of giving these words their due, he hurried through them in a flat, ungrateful monotone.

Before parting from Congress, Washington provided a full and meticulous accounting of his receipts and expenditures from the commencement of the war. These, written in his own hand and kept in the clearest, most accurate manner—each entry being accompanied by a statement of the occasion and object of the charge—amounted to £19,306. That included money expended for secret intelligence and a few incidental charges, such as Martha's expenses in coming to stay with him at Valley Forge. No one, in scrutinizing these accounts, could find a penny of padding or excess. Subsequently, it became apparent that he had devoted quite a bit of his own money to the cause, though this was a debt he neglected to claim. The only favor or reward he asked in retirement was that his letters be exempted from postage.

After dining with a few friends that evening, he and his wife departed the next morning with a small mounted escort for home. They came to their own door at Mount Vernon on Christmas Eve just as the sun was setting, the ridge of the distant hills catching fire.

O N January 14, 1784, the Treaty of Paris, which had officially been signed on September 3, 1783, was ratified by Congress, formally ending the Revolutionary War. Nevertheless, British garrisons lingered on in the strategic northwest strongholds of Niagara and Detroit until 1786—to protest American failure to honor the provisions regarding the loyalists (and the payment of prewar debts to British merchants) and (as tactical leverage) to exact a commercial treaty from the United States. Meanwhile, in February 1783, a separate peace treaty had been signed between England and France.

In the negotiations between the United States and England, there had been much wrangling, but eventually the principal issues between the two were settled and a new map of North America was drawn. In brief,

Britain abandoned much of the Great Lakes region and fixed the western boundary of the United States at the Mississippi River, tracing a line that generally followed the watershed between the Saint Lawrence River and the Atlantic coast.

The last item of contention concerned fishing rights off the Newfoundland coast. The British wanted the fishery to themselves. The Americans objected, and the English retreated step by step. On the last night of the negotiations, they held out for just one word. The Americans might have the "liberty," they said, but not the "right" to fish in those waters, as "the Word Right was an obnoxious Expression." "Upon this I rose up," recalled John Adams, "and said, Gentlemen, is there or can there be a clearer Right? . . . If Heaven in the Creation gave a Right, it is ours at least as much as yours. If Occupation, Use, and Possession give a Right, We have it as clearly as you. If War and Blood and Treasure give a Right, ours is as good as yours. . . . If then the Right cannot be denied, Why should it not be acknowledged?" Before this onslaught, the British resistance collapsed.

The fate of the loyalists, however, had been the hardest to resolve. The British had wanted them restored to their rights and property; the Americans denied them amnesty, but in the final document there was a tortured attempt to discriminate between the British- and American-born and between those who had and had not borne arms. The Americans made no promises, but Article V read, "It is agreed that the Congress shall earnestly recommend it to the legislatures of the respective states to provide for the restitution of all estates, rights, and properties which have been confiscated . . . and that persons . . . shall have free liberty to go into any part or parts of any of the thirteen of the United States and therein to remain twelve months unmolested in their endeavors to obtain restitution of such of their estates, rights, and properties as may have been confiscated." Article VI likewise recommended that no future "confiscations" or "prosecutions" of loyalists take place. But confiscations and prosecutions continued; loyalists returning from exile were frequently molested, and their chances of recovering their property were almost nil. They could, it is true, sue for reparations. But the American negotiators, in particular John Adams, who had proposed the article, had known very well how drawn-out the legal process could be. Permanent exile was therefore the price paid by most of those who had actively supported the Crown.

Not every patriot was happy about this. Though Washington had once said, in possibly his harshest pronouncement of the war, that the best thing the loyalists holed up in Boston with Howe could do was kill themselves, at war's end he was characteristically quick to forgive. In late April 1782, he had recommended to Congress that the seventy-five or more regiments of loyalists in British service be pardoned under certain conditions. And Alexander Hamilton deplored the numbers exiled—many of them prosperous, well educated, and industrious—as a loss to the community, comparable to the loss of talent and capacity occasioned by the Huguenot emigration from France. He wrote a series of newspaper articles under the name of "Phocion" (an Athenian leader given to espousing the views of those who differed with him), pointing out that Articles V and VI of the peace treaty enjoined the states to deal fairly with loyalist property: "Make it the interest of those citizens," he said, "who, during the Revolution were opposed to us, to be friends to the new government by affording them not only protection but a participation in its privileges, and they will undoubtedly become its friends."

Patrick Henry joined with Washington and Hamilton in urging, for the sake of the nation, that animosities toward the loyalists be laid aside. With regard to the return of loyalist refugees, he said:

> I feel no objection. . . . They have, to be sure, mistaken their own interests most wofully, and most wofully have they suffered the punishment due to their offence. But the relations which we bear to them and to their native country are now changed. Their king hath acknowledged our independence. The quarrel is over. Peace hath returned, and found us a free people. Let us have the magnanimity to lay aside our antipathies and prejudices, and consider the subject in a political light. . . . I have no fear of any mischief that they can do us. Afraid of them? What, sir, shall we, who have laid the proud British lion at our feet, now be afraid of his whelps?

Nevertheless, most of the loyalists who had actively collaborated with the British went into exile after the war. Some went to the Bahamas or the British West Indies, others to Canada or the British Isles. Canada received as many as forty-six thousand, including several thousand Indians and blacks, the British Isles about ten thousand, the British West Indies four thousand, the Bahamas two thousand, and so on; a few settled in Central America (present-day Honduras and Belize); and some loyalists of German extraction returned to the Rhine Valley. The situation of those who attempted to settle in east Florida was particularly pathetic, for they were almost immediately uprooted again by the return of Florida to Spain.

Some of the blacks were resold into slavery in the West Indies, but in

1783 Sir Guy Carleton, unlike Lord Dunmore a man of humanity and principle, insisted on evacuating 3,500 ex-slaves to Nova Scotia along with other loyalists. He did so even though blacks who had fought with the British or were runaway slaves were supposed to be returned to their masters. But he adopted the principle that when a slave reached the British lines he was free. Nevertheless, he did keep a careful list of them, with their names, descriptions, and to whom they had belonged, as a hedge against future compensation claims.

The exile of the loyalists led to the development of Canada. Although successive British ministries had seemed to share Voltaire's low opinion of the territory as *"quelques arpents de neige"* ("a few acres of snow"), the loyalist migration changed all that, as, by their settlement, Nova Scotia and parts of Ontario became wildernesses transformed. On April 27, 1783, some seven thousand exiles set sail from New York bound for Nova Scotia in the first stage of an evacuation that continued throughout the summer and fall.

They disembarked on a wild and lonely shore. The settlers had been given rations, clothes, and tools and a few hand gristmills for grinding wheat and corn, but they had to pound much of their grain between stones or even with cannonballs swung from saplings; and after the government's three-year allocation of supplies ran out, droughts and severe winters resulted in poor crops, followed, in southern Ontario, along the bay of Quinte, by the "hungry years."

Many survived by eating roots and wild plants or the bark of trees. Bran boiled in a bit of water was often the only meal they had. When a cow or an ox was accidentally killed, its bones were passed from house to house to be reboiled until they were white and dry as chalk.

Some loyalists in Canada actually dreamed of drawing the Republic back to the empire by the example of good government. Others hoped to bring the American Midwest under British control and to develop its economy from a Canadian base.

WASHINGTON'S first letter in retirement was to his friend Governor George Clinton of New York. "The scene is at last closed," he wrote. "I feel myself eased of a load of public care. I hope to spend the remainder of my days in cultivating the affections of good men and in the practice of the domestic Virtues."

In retirement, Washington devoted himself to animal husbandry, farming, the cultivation of his gardens; did his best to entertain and oblige the many friends and admirers who came to pay their respects or others seeking information or advice. "My manner of living," he wrote to a friend, "is plain, and I do not mean to be put out of it. A glass of wine and a bit of mutton are always ready, and such as will be content to partake of them are always welcome. Those who expect more will be disappointed." He was not infrequently importuned to sit for his portrait, and this at first annoyed but ultimately amused him. He wrote to Francis Hopkinson, "I am so hackneyed to the touches of the painters' pencil that I am altogether at their beck and sit 'like Patience on a monument' whilst they are delineating the lines of my face. It is a proof, among many others, of what habit and custom can accomplish. At first I was impatient. . . . Now no dray-horse moves more readily to his thill than I to the painter's chair."

However, he declined to write, or to encourage anyone else to write, a history of the Revolution and left it to Congress to decide when the official archives or even his own papers might be made available to the public. "I had rather glide gently down the stream of life," he explained, "leaving it to posterity to think and say what they please of me, than by any act of mine to have vanity or ostentation imputed to me."

He wrote to Lafayette, "At length, my dear Marquis, I am become a private citizen on the banks of the Potomac, and under the shadow of my own vine and my own fig tree, free from the bustle of the camp, and the busy scenes of public life. I have not only retired from all public employments, but I am retiring within myself, and shall be able to view the solitary walk and tread the paths of private life, with heartfelt satisfaction." To Lafayette's wife, he added, "I expect to glide gently down the stream of life till I am entombed in the mansion of my fathers." Urging them both to visit, he added, "You will see the plain manner in which we live, and meet with rustic civility; and you shall taste the simplicity of rural life. It will diversify the scene, and give you a higher relish for the gayeties of the court, when you return to Versailles."

Lafayette had sailed for France on December 23, 1781. In the entrance hall to his own home he had placed a large framed copy of the Declaration of Independence, with an empty space beside it. When someone asked what he was going to put there, he said, "The Declaration of French Rights." In the summer of 1784, he returned to America as Washington's guest. One day, traveling to Fredericksburg to pay his respects to Washington's mother, he found her in her garden, "clad in homespun garments, her head covered with a plain straw hat." They conversed awhile, and of course he praised her illustrious son. "I am not surprised at what George has done," she replied simply, "for he was always a good boy."

Lafayette often referred to himself, not inaptly, as Washington's "adopted son," and he named his own son after him, a compliment Washington especially savored since he had no offspring of his own. As Lafayette was about to embark again for France, Washington wrote to him, "In the moment of our separation, upon the road as I traveled, and every hour since, I have felt all that love, respect and attachment for you, with which length of years, close connection, and your merits have inspired me. I often asked myself, as our carriages separated, whether that was the last sight I ever should have of you? And though I wished to say No, my fears answered Yes. . . . I called to mind the days of my youth and found they had long since fled to return no more; that I was now descending the hill . . . but I will not repine, I have had my day."

Very soon, however, Washington discovered that his dreams of quiet retirement were not to be realized. He remained the central figure in the foundation of the young Republic, and the imploring eyes of the nation were soon turned toward him again as the one man capable of rescuing the ship of state.

T I M E S immediately after the war were hard. The economy was wracked by inflation; pensions were slow to be granted by Congress; veterans received little relief. One soldier who had been held as a prisoner of war recalled that public charity seemed to shrivel up at once. For the first time in American history, beggars abounded, and their supplications were met with "nothing but frowns."

Even heroes such as Steuben were at first victims of congressional neglect. Since he had failed to make a definite contract with Congress, being content at the time to accept its verbal assurances of compensation after the war, the august assembly demurred. And despite emphatic testimonials from Washington and other officers concerning his contribution to the cause, eight years passed before an annuity was voted him in reward.

Not all prisoners of war found their way home. One of the strangest tales was that of Israel Potter of Cranston, Rhode Island, who had run away from home at eighteen after a family dispute about a girlfriend and enlisted in a company of Minutemen in 1774. He had fought at Bunker Hill and during the siege of Boston served as a volunteer on one of the armed coastal sloops Washington delegated to interdict some of the supplies coming in to the British by sea. Sailing from Plymouth, however, he was captured by a British patrol and sent in chains to England, where he was held first at Portsmouth, then at nearby Spithead. He escaped, fled toward London, was recaptured, escaped again, hobbled eighty miles back toward the capital disguised as a cripple, was picked up en route on suspicion of being a deserter from the British navy, but a few days later freed himself from his handcuffs by sawing them across the grating of the window of his cell. With the bolt that held the cuffs together, he also managed to force the hasp and padlock securing the cell door. This time he succeeded in getting to London, where he lost himself in the crowd. Eventually, he was employed in Kew Gardens, the King's private preserve, and one day as he was graveling a walk, the king himself approached and asked him where he was from. "An American born, may it please Your Majesty," he said with candor, taking off his hat. "Ah!, an American," said the king good-naturedly, "a stubborn, a very stubborn people indeed! And what brought you to this country, and how long have you been here?" "The fate of war, Your Majesty—I was brought to this country a prisoner about eleven months since." Potter then boldly complained that he was afraid for his own safety, to which the king replied, "While you are here employed no one will trouble you." Sometime later, however, Potter was discharged. Thereafter, he was briefly recruited as a confidential agent by an American spy, sent to Paris with a message for Benjamin Franklin concealed in the heel of his boot, brought letters back, posed for a time as a farmer from Lincolnshire, and found work successively as a coachman, a brickmaker, and a mender of chairs. Years passed. He married a local girl, had several children, sank into poverty, and was cast into debtor's prison. He did not return to the United States until 1823, when he was almost eighty years old.

As for the infamous British prison ships, they were abandoned or destroyed. After a few remaining inmates were liberated from the *Jersey*'s black hull in 1783, the vessel was left to rot. It lay off the banks of Wallabout Bay between Manhattan and Long Island for several years, its moldering planks and timbers covered with thousands of names carved into the wood. Worms finally ate through her hull, and she slipped to the bottom of the bay.

No one knows how many perished on board the *Jersey* and her sister ships, but plausible estimates exceed ten thousand. "It is supposed," wrote one surviving inmate, Thomas Dring, "that more men perished on [the *Jersey*'s] decks than ever died in any other place of confinement on the face of the earth, in the same number of years." Time, decay, and the ebb and flow of the tides across the sands eventually revealed the remains of the multitudes who had been buried on the shore. In 1803, when the bank at the Wallabout was excavated for the construction of a navy yard, "a very great quantity of bones were collected." Five years later, they were reinterred in a solemn ceremony and the cornerstone of a monument laid "in the name of the Spirits of the Departed Free."

The king tried to find in the loss of the colonies a blessing in disguise: "I cannot conclude without mentioning how sensibly I feel the dismemberment of America from this Empire, and that I should be miserable indeed if I did not feel that no blame on that account can be laid at my door, and did I not know that knavery seems to be so much the striking feature of its inhabitants that it may not in the end be an evil that they become Aliens to this Kingdom." When John Adams, however, presented himself to the king as the first United States ambassador to England, the king said without rancor, "I wish you to believe, and that it may be understood in America that I have done nothing in the late contest but what I thought myself indispensably bound to do by the duty which I owed to my people. I will be very frank with you. I was the last to consent to the separation: but the separation having been made and having become inevitable, I have always said, as I say now, that I would be the first to meet the friendship of the United States of America as an independent power."

The British were already deeply involved in America's new economic life. A number of people had made money out of the war, and Boston, for example, was flooded with the new gentry, ready and anxious to take the place of the old social elite. "Fellows who would have cleaned my shoes five years ago," complained one scion of a venerable line, "now ride in chariots." The extravagant lifestyle that seemed to take over high society also appalled the likes of Samuel Adams, who blamed the luxuries on a conspiracy by Britain to deliberately infiltrate postwar American society with its decadent tastes. "The artful and insidious Cabinet of Britain," he declared one year after Yorktown, "have, in excess of their folly and lust for domination" set out to inundate the people with "a flood of their manufactures, and encouraging a commercial intercourse between us . . . by this trade they expect . . . to revive that foolish prediliction which we once had for British Manufactures and British manners."

Adams was not alone in these views. One independent observer, the young Venezuelan revolutionary Francisco de Miranda, who visited Boston in 1784, remarked, "Luxury, ostentation and a little vanity are the predominant figures in the character of those who now are called rich. Ten years ago a young man who wore silk stockings, breeches made of plain satin, and powdered his hair, had not need of anything else to forfeit his 'character' forever. Today, they have all this, and more." And he noted, a bit ominously, that "dignity and power" now seemed in

America to be given to property rather than to virtue, on which the integrity of a democratic republic must ultimately depend.

Of course, it had been the hope and policy of Britain to reconstitute its American relationship via binding economic ties. Britain looked to the development of the American interior as a market for British manufactures and investment, and Lord Shelbourne, the architect of the policy, even envisaged a sort of Atlantic alliance, including both economic union and a common foreign policy. After the preliminary Treaty of Paris was signed, a French diplomat remarked at an official party that the United States would become "the greatest empire in the world." "Yes, sir," said his British counterpart, "and they will *all* speak English, every one of 'em."

A F T E R the war, there was an inexorable, if tremendously conflicted, move toward a strong central government uniting the thirteen states. Under the Confederation, Congress had been unable to impose taxes or regulate currency, credit, or commerce; exercise full control over the military; or enforce any civil law. Its members had been nominated by state legislatures, not elected by the people; voted in state blocs; and could pass amendments only by a unanimous vote. Nevertheless, this tenuously constituted and impractical government had established relations (or alliances) with foreign powers, and had managed and financed a long and complex war through to its victorious end. But an increase in social unrest, a staggering national debt, and the separatist tendencies inherent in disunion—at a time when an American referring to his "country" still meant his own state—caused mounting alarm. Imperial union had departed; national unity had yet to take its place.

The Articles of Confederation were inadequate for the task. Adopted, after much misgiving and disputation in 1781, they had created a loose and weak federal organization that was unable to hold the separate states together by anything stronger than, in Washington's phrase, "a feeble thread." A national Constitutional Convention was called to meet in Philadelphia in May 1787 to address the crisis, and though Washington at first refused to be a delegate, he relented and was chosen president of the Convention on the fourteenth.

From the moment the war ended, Washington had worried that "local or state politics will interfere too much with that more liberal and extensive plan of government which wisdom and foresight, freed from the mist of prejudice, would dictate," as he had written to Lafayette in April 1783. At about the same time, he shared with another friend, William

Gordon, some of his convictions about government drawn from his war experience, during which the lack of such a cohesive force had continually jeopardized his army and the survival of the revolt:

> Certain I am that unless adequate powers are given to Congress for the general purposes of the Federal Union that we shall soon moulder into dust and become contemptible in the eyes of Europe, if we are not made the sport of her politics. . . . To suppose that the general concerns of this country can be directed by thirteen heads, or one head without competent powers, is a solecism, the bad effects of which every man who has had the practical knowledge to judge from that I have, is fully convinced of; though none perhaps has felt them in so forcible a degree. The People at large, and at a distance from the theatre of action, who only know that the machine was kept in motion and that they are at last arrived at the first object of their wishes, are satisfied with the event without investigating the slow progress to it or the expenses which have been incurred.

And in a letter to Benjamin Harrison he predicted that unless "the powers of Congress" were "enlarged, and made competent to all *general purposes,*" the Confederation would soon collapse and "anarchy and confusion" would ensue.

A S I D E from adequate authority, there was also the question of how best to moderate and balance the strong central powers. As John Adams had put it in his *Thoughts on Government* in 1775, a single-branch legislature was not a good model for popular government; there must be more on the legislative side than one assembly. "A people cannot be long free nor ever happy whose government is in one assembly," for a "single assembly is liable to all the vices, follies, and frailties of an individual; subject to fits of humor, starts of passion, flights of enthusiasm, partialities, or prejudice, and consequently productive of hasty results and absurd judgements." Nor, due to the same shortcomings, could it effectively exercise executive or judicial authority.

In a kindred spirit, Washington rose from his chair and warned the delegates against being swayed too directly by transient public opinion: "If to please the people we offer what we ourselves disapprove, how can we afterwards defend our work? Let us raise a standard to which the wise and honest can repair; the event is in the hands of God."

After much compromise and deliberation, the Constitutional Convention proposed a complex system of checks and balances in which, by a partial separation of interlocked powers, the executive, legislative, and judicial branches of government would all enjoy a measure of eminent domain. Congress was to be composed of two houses: a Senate, in which each state would have two members, and a House of Representatives, in which representation would be proportionate to the population of each state. The Congress as a whole was to have the power to tax, control the purse, and regulate interstate commerce and foreign trade. The executive power would reside in the person of a president, who would be elected indirectly (according to a kind of paradox) by direct popular vote and who would enjoy substantial control over the administrative apparatus of government, including the authority to veto legislation, though that veto could be overridden by a two-thirds vote of both the Senate and the House. Moreover, he and all of his subordinate officers would be subject to impeachment. Finally, the independence of the judiciary would be represented preeminently by a Supreme Court, which was to serve as the arbiter of all cases arising under the Constitution and bearing on fundamental rights. At the same time, the right of each state to self-government was to be uncontested with regard to all ordinary matters of legislation and administration.

The new Constitution, as it took shape, was not absolutely to Washington's liking, but in the end he went along with the majority. To Lafayette, he wrote, "It is the result of four months' deliberation. It is now a child of fortune, to be fostered by some and buffeted by others. What will be the general opinion or the reception of it is not for me to decide; nor shall I say anything for or against it. If it be good, I suppose it will work its way; if bad, it will recoil upon the framers." In due time, it was ratified by the requisite number of states, making them one nation; and in the spring of 1789, Washington, by the unanimous voice of the Electoral College, became the first president of the United States.

On the eve of his election, Washington observed to his private secretary, David Humphreys, "It is said that every man has his portion of ambition. I may have mine, I suppose, as well as the rest, but if I know my own heart, my ambition would not lead me into public life; my only ambition is to do my duty in this world as well as I am capable of performing it, and to merit the good opinion of all good men." Assuming the office with great misgiving and reluctance, he foresaw, he confided to General Knox, "an ocean of difficulties" for which he believed he lacked the "political skill." "Integrity and firmness are all I can promise," he concluded. "These, be the voyage long or short, shall never forsake me, although I may be deserted by all men."

On April 16, Washington left Mount Vernon and set out for his inauguration in New York, now the country's capital. Feted and saluted at

Georgetown, Baltimore, and other points along the way, he passed under triumphal arches on his way to Philadelphia, where thousands of citizens turned out in a tumultuous salute. From there he rode on to Trenton, under another arch and across a little bridge where "his way was strewn with flowers by thirteen young maidens, who chanted a song of welcome." At Elizabethtown, he was met by representatives of Congress, conveyed across the river to New York, and escorted through the streets to his new residence at 10 Cherry Street, near Franklin Square. On April 30, the day of his inauguration, he rose at sunrise, powdered his hair, and donned a dark brown suit with brass buttons embossed with eagles. Church bells were already ringing and a reverential throng had gathered before his house. After breakfast, he buckled on his dress sword, and at noon a delegation from Congress arrived to escort him to Federal Hall.

The ceremony took place in the open gallery or portico facing Wall Street, in the presence of a multitude of citizens, with the oath of office being administered by Robert R. Livingston, now chancellor of the state of New York. "Do you solemnly swear that you will faithfully execute the office of President of the United States and will, to the best of your ability, preserve, protect, and defend the Constitution of the United States?" Washington said, "I swear," and, lifting an open Bible which lay on a crimson cushion before him, exclaimed in a firm voice, "So help me, God!" The chancellor, turning to the people, said, "It is done!" and, in a loud voice, "Long live George Washington, President of the United States!"

The Stars and Stripes were raised on the cupola of Federal Hall, and thirteen guns boomed from the battery as Washington reentered the Senate chamber, took his seat on the dais, and, after all had resumed their places, rose to read his inaugural address.

In a deep, low, tremulous voice, he called on "that Almighty God who rules over the universe" to help the American people find "liberties and happiness" under "a government instituted by themselves" and urged a spirit of moderation in the years ahead. Always shy of public speaking, he moved his manuscript nervously from hand to hand, put several fingers of his left hand into his breeches pocket, and at one point, wrote an eyewitness, made a flourish with his right hand which "left a rather ungainly impression." His face, according to another, was "grave almost to sadness" throughout.

Afterward, Washington attended services at Saint Paul's Chapel before joining friends in the evening for a fireworks display. After it was all over, he wrote to a friend, "I greatly fear that my countrymen will expect too much from me."

Almost up to the last minute, Congress had fretted about what title to give him. Committees were appointed to consider the matter, that of the House reporting against anything august, that of the Senate proposing "His Highness, the President of the United States of America, and Protector of their Liberties." Various prominent civilians weighed in with "Most Honorable" or "Most Mightiness"; Washington himself preferred simply "President of the United States."

But as president, inevitably, he had to accept the special aura of a head of state. At the inaugural ball, attended by the president, the vice president, members of Congress with their families, officers of the army, and the ministers of France and Spain, each lady, passing the ticket taker, was presented with a fan made in Paris with an ivory frame containing a medallion portrait of Washington in profile.

In the first year of Washington's presidency, Congress adopted twelve amendments to the Constitution, of which ten were subsequently ratified by the states to form the Bill of Rights. In the ensuing years, the dimensions of the executive power would be clarified, giving the president more authority over the administrative system of the government, while the competition between Congress and the judiciary over the making of laws would be settled by Chief Justice John Marshall in his first great case, *Marbury* v. *Madison* (1803), which established the right of the Supreme Court to invalidate acts of Congress that conflicted with the Constitution. ("All those who have framed written constitutions contemplate them as forming the fundamental and paramount law of the nation," Marshall wrote, "and consequently the theory of every such government must be that an act of the legislature repugnant to the Constitution is void. . . . It is emphatically the province and duty of the judicial department to say what the law is.") In subsequent decisions, Marshall extended and consolidated the constitutional powers of the national government by subordinating the rights of states or corporations to the national will and by establishing the right of appeal, on constitutional issues, from state to federal courts.

Alexis de Tocqueville once said that the revolution had "contracted no alliance with the turbulent passion of anarchy." Not a single political murder was committed before the fighting began, and at the end of the struggle, no military coup or dictatorship subverted its ideals. Nor were there "bloodthirsty revolutionary tribunals," as one historian puts it, "to mete out 'justice' to dissenters or unseated administrators in years to follow. All the men who signed the Declaration of Independence died in bed."

If some angel did not ride in this whirlwind, what can we say?

O N the day the Declaration of Independence was signed, Benjamin Franklin, John Adams, and Thomas Jefferson were all appointed to a committee to devise a great seal for the new confederated states. Each proposed a device. Franklin, despite his deistic inclinations, had a biblical sense of destiny and believed in the providential hand of God; he proposed Moses lifting up his wand and dividing the Red Sea and the pharaoh in his chariot overwhelmed by the waters, with the motto "Rebellion to tyrants is obedience to God." Jefferson, acknowledging Providence, gave equal importance to the legal conceit of America's birth: on one side the Israelites in the wilderness, led by a cloud by day and a pillar of fire by night; on the reverse, Hengist and Horsa, the Saxon chiefs "from whom we claim the honor of being descended, and whose political principles and form of government we have assumed." Adams, for his part, proving the moralist, proposed "Hercules, as engraved by Gribeline . . . The Hero resting on his Clubb. Virtue pointing to her rugged Mountain, on one Hand, and perswading him to ascend. Sloth, glancing at her flowery Paths of Pleasure, wantonly reclining on the Ground, displaying the Charms both of her Eloquence and Person, to seduce him into Vice."

None of these was deemed satisfactory. A Swiss émigré artist, Pierre-Eugène du Simitière, was invited to contribute his own suggestions and came up with a democratic coat of arms that combined the emblems of various nations—Germany, England, Scotland, Ireland, Holland, and France—from which the American immigrants had come. This was not inappropriate: one third of the men who had signed the Declaration of Independence were of non-English stock.

Nevertheless, the design committee suspended its efforts until the end of the war. In 1782, William Barton of Philadelphia was asked by Congress to oversee a new design. He suggested a truncated pyramid with thirteen steps surmounted by the eye of Providence, set within a glory, with the motto *"Deo favente perennis"* ("God willing throughout the years"). Charles Thomson, the perennial secretary of Congress, replaced Barton's *"Deo favente"* with a motto borrowed from Virgil's *Aeneid*— *"Annuit coeptis"* ("God has nodded at the undertaking")—and another motto borrowed from Virgil's *Eclogues*—*"Novus ordo saeclorum"* ("A new order of the ages is born"). Barton accepted these changes but made the central image an eagle with an olive branch in one set of talons and a bundle of arrows gripped in the other, a shield of thirteen stripes, and a scroll inscribed *"E pluribus unum"* ("One from many") in its beak.

Above, a cloud enveloped a constellation of thirteen stars. According to the official gloss, as given by Thomson,

> The Constellation denotes a new State taking its place and rank among other sovereign powers. The Escutcheon is borne on the breast of an American Eagle without any other supporters, to denote that the United States of America ought to rely on their own Virtue. Reverse: The pyramid signifies Strength and Duration; The Eye over it & the Motto allude to the many signal interpositions of providence in favour of the American cause. The date underneath is that of the Declaration of Independence and the words under it signify the beginning of the new American Æra, which commences from that date.

On June 20, 1782, Congress adopted this design as the official seal of the United States.

W I L L I A M Barton is said to have come up with his winning design after a long afternoon of genteel drinking at a Philadelphia tavern. Whether true or not, there is a kind of poetic justice in the tale. "The tavern," Daniel Webster once remarked, "was the headquarters of the Revolution." It crops up everywhere in the story and, in a manner of speaking, forms its convivial common ground. It was, after all, the meetingplace of the community, where "the people" congregated and discussed the political issues that concerned them (among many other things), and where the Revolution, in a sense, began. But it was also an instrument of the struggle that was waged. The Boston Tea Party had been plotted at Boston's Green Dragon Tavern, and at Boston's Salutation other resistance schemes were hatched. At the Red Sabin Tavern in Providence, drink fortified those hoping to capture the British naval schooner *Gaspee* offshore; and after drilling on the town common or village green, Minutemen typically repaired to the local tavern, which served as their usual headquarters, for a few warming rounds of grog to end the day. After Lord Dunmore dissolved the Virginia Assembly in May 1774, its principal members reconvened in the Apollo Room of the Raleigh Tavern in Williamsburg. In New York, in response to the Stamp Act, merchants met at Burns's Tavern on Broadway to coordinate their boycott of British goods. In Philadelphia, delegates to the Congress often conducted business over drinks in their favorite taverns, and Thomas Jefferson is said to have written part of the Declaration of Independence at the city's Indian Queen. At the Tun Tavern, where the Naval Committee first met, wit, wisdom, and good cheer flowed with Jamaica rum. In June 1781, Banastre Tarleton's attempt to capture the Virginia Legislature had been foiled by a lookout at the Cuckoo Tavern in Louisa. Washington, of course, after quickly downing a glass of wine, had bid an emotional farewell to his devoted officer corps at Fraunces Tavern in New York. And so on. Even the first shot of the struggle—the first real "shot heard round the world"—may have been fired from an upper window in Buckman's Tavern overlooking the Lexington Green.

If the Revolution was, in a sense, conducted from the tavern, it may be said to have ended there as well. When the Treaty of Paris was proclaimed at Williamsburg in 1783, the order for the procession and celebration of the day read "From the Court House the Citizens are to proceed to the College [of William and Mary], and make proclamation at that Place, from whence they are to proceed to the Capitol and make proclamation there; and from thence proceed to the Raleigh [Tavern] & pass the rest of the Day."

NOTES
BIBLIOGRAPHY
INDEX

NOTES

For abbreviations used in the notes, and for full titles and other bibliographical information on books, articles, and other documents cited, the reader is referred to the Bibliography.

CHAPTER ONE: THE BEGINNING OF THE END

Page 18   "nearly all . . . France": Parkman, *Montcalm and Wolfe*, v. 1, p. 160.
19   "It happens that . . . another!": Forbes, *Paul Revere*, pp. 45–46.
20   "Crawled towards . . . gunpowder": Parkman, op. cit., p. 168.
20   "Rallied creditably . . . population": Bradley, op. cit., p. 39.
21   "Braddock might . . . Indians": Parkman, op. cit., p. 188.
21   "the slender . . . impression": Franklin, *Autobiography*, p. 241.
22   "We have . . . common sense": Quoted in Parkman, op. cit., p. 207.
22   "articles . . . necessity": Irving, *George Washington*, p. 59.
22   "General Braddock . . . scalped": Quoted in ibid., p. 65.
22   "I found . . . miles": Quoted in ibid., p. 61.
23   "as if . . . Park": Ibid., p. 67.
23   "When we . . . wild bears": Quoted in Parkman, op. cit., p. 222.
23   "it seemed . . . scalps": Quoted in ibid., p. 222.
23   "Who would . . . time": Quoted in Franklin, op. cit., p. 217.
23   "effacing every . . . corpse": Parkman, op. cit., p. 225.
23   "The dastardly . . . death": Quoted in ibid., p. 229.
24   "[this battle] . . . well founded": Quoted in Franklin, op. cit., p. 218.
24   "No road is safe": Quoted in Parkman, op. cit., p. 330.
24   "prisoners of . . . sex": Quoted in Boorstin, *Colonial Experience*, p. 56.
24   "The [Indians] . . . alive": Quoted in Parkman, op. cit., p. 330.
24   "The supplicating . . . ease": Quoted in Irving, op. cit., p. 86.
24   "an abominable . . . breathed": Quoted in Parkman, op. cit., p. 431.
25   "summer and winter . . . side: Ibid., p. 433.
26   "I know perfectly . . . want": Quoted in Davidson, *World in 1776*, p. 64.
27   "They run . . . peace": Ibid.
27   Great Britain shall . . . again: Ibid., p. 65.
28   "We retain nothing . . . sea": Ibid., p. 63.
28   Britannia, MISTRESS . . . arms: Quoted in Silverman, *Cultural History*, p. 51.
28   "God has . . . idolatry": Quoted in Parkman, op. cit., v. 2, p. 379.
29   "I console myself . . . tomb": Quoted in *Centennial of the Settlement of Upper Canada*, p. 25.
29   "The colonies will . . . chains": Quoted in Irving, op. cit., p. 108.
29   "If they could . . . oppression": Quoted in Parkman, op. cit., v. 2, p. 404.

CHAPTER TWO: THE COLONIAL WORLD

Page 30   "We have an old . . . can deny": Quoted in Japikse, *Selected Writings of Benjamin Franklin*, p. 70.
31   "Let us behave . . . veneration": Quoted in Brodie, *Thomas Jefferson*, p. 101.
31   "I love . . . prescribe": Ibid.
31   "in a triple . . . blood": Parkman, op. cit., v. 2, p. 413.
32   "Wee did bang . . . barne": Quoted in Earle, *Home Life in Colonial Days*, p. 381.
33   "surprisingly extensive . . . Monte Cristo": Wilson, *Barnaby's Travels*, p. 92.
33   "with the superfluities . . . life": Ibid.
33   "very loud . . . together": Quoted in Forbes, op. cit., p. 207.

33   *"greene . . . burnt"*: Quoted in Bridenbaugh, *Cities in the Wilderness*, p. 57.
34   *"straight as a string"*: Chase, *Letters of Barbé-Marbois*, p. 129.
34   *"where oftentimes . . . smoke"*: Bridenbaugh, *Gentleman's Progress*, p. 21.
34   *"Lanthorn . . . lights,"* etc.: Quoted in Earle, op. cit., p. 362.
35   *"a very strange . . . Colonies"*: Quoted in Bowen, *Most Dangerous Man in America*, p. 98.
35   *"Every Body . . . Parliament"*: Quoted in ibid., p. 141.
35   *"there would . . . England"*: Franklin, op. cit., p. 199.
36   *"very good . . . besides"*: Denton, *Brief Description of New-York*, p. 39.
36   *"Many are . . . cured"*: Ibid., p. 42.
36   *"There are . . . Disease"*: Ibid., p. 49.
36   *"Nature has . . . thrive there"*: Quoted in Boorstin, *Colonial Experience*, p. 75.
36   *"the most . . . Wig Wams"*: Quoted in Bridenbaugh, *Rebels and Gentlemen*, pp. 228–229.
36   *"and next . . . pay"*: *Narratives of Early Pennsylvania, West New Jersey, and Delaware*, p. 395n.
36   *"a full pail . . . goose"*: Quoted in Furnas, *Americans*, p. 171.
37   *"Every countryman . . . mown"*: Wilson, *Peter Kalm's Travels*, v. 1, p. 144.
37   *"in the back . . . estate"*: Quoted in Bailyn, *Voyagers to the West*, p. 23.
37   *"the prodigious . . . people"*: Ibid., p. 8.
37   *"repays a . . . generously"*: Chase, op. cit., pp. 120–121.
37   *"who was not . . . newspaper"*: Ibid., p. 126.
37   *"cheat . . . if they can"*: Bridenbaugh, *Gentleman's Progress*, p. 28.
37   *"care is taken . . . nor food"*: Chase, op. cit., p. 71.
37   *"the work of . . . humanity"*: Ibid., p. 129.
38   *"such as by . . . public good"*: Quoted in Boorstin, *Colonial Experience*, p. 101.
38   *"town meetings,"* etc.: Quoted in Davidson, op. cit., p. 326.
38   *"Each individual . . . lowest inhabitant"*: Ibid.
38   *"near equality of Wealth,"* etc.: Farish, *Journal & Letters of Philip Vickers Fithian*, p. 210.
38   *"No form . . . society"*: Chase, op. cit., p. 88.
38   *"Gentlemen . . . Domesticks"* and *"such amazing . . . property"*: Farish, op. cit., p. 211.
39   *"The house . . . of wood*: Ibid., p. xxxi.
39   *"They are assiduously . . . color"*: Chase, op. cit., p. 156.
39   *"It would seem . . . severity"*: Ibid., p. 157.
40   *'Twas mercy . . . Train*: Quoted in Farish, op. cit., p. 97.
40   *"very mixed . . . it bore"*: Bridenbaugh, *Gentleman's Progress*, p. 20.
41   *"the mass . . . realm"*: Bailyn, *The Peopling of British North America*, p. 9.
41   *"all the privileges . . . province"*: Wilson, op. cit., v. 1, p. 129.
42   *"whatever they lacked . . . mind"*: L. Wright, *The Atlantic Frontier*, p. 224.
42   *"good Musick . . . Clarinets, etc."*: Franklin, op. cit., p. 236.
42   *"the first Drudgery . . . cultivate"*: Best, *Benjamin Franklin on Education*, p. 99.
43   *"they were wretched . . . beggars"*: Franklin, op. cit., p. 24.
43   *arduous project . . . conduct*: Ibid., p. 123.
43   1. *Temperance* . . . Socrates.: Ibid., pp. 124–125.
44   *"which of all things I dreaded"*: Quoted in Van Doren, *Benjamin Franklin*, p. 91.
44   *"In its proper . . . that day"*: Franklin, op. cit., p. 125.
45   *"that by means . . . thunder"* and *"to stand . . . conductor"*: Quoted in Van Doren, op. cit., p. 104.
45   *"raised blemishes . . . corruption"*: Silverman, op. cit., p. 23.
45   *"Prick that hand . . . out"*: Quoted in ibid., p. 23.
46   *"a good ear . . . instruments"* and *"built in part . . . design"*: Quoted in ibid., p. 36.
46   *"a soft, warbling sound"*: Ibid., p. 35.
46   *"the finest Singing . . . me"*: Quoted in ibid., p. 195.
47   *"not a good . . . Boston"*: Quoted in Bowen, op. cit., p. 116.
48   *"The rules . . . victory"*: Ibid.
48   *"These libraries . . . in some degree"*: Quoted in Boorstin, *Colonial Experience*, p. 311.
49   *"active . . . honest"*: Earle, op. cit., p. 332.
49   *"In no country . . . science"*: Quoted in Boorstin, *Hidden History*, p. 73.
50   *"Gods, can"* and *"What pity is it"*: Silverman, op. cit., pp. 82–83.
50   *"lured people . . . of life"*: Ibid., p. 66.
50   *"Moral Dialogues . . . Virtue"*: Furnas, op. cit., p. 100.
50   *"whosoever shall . . . masques"*: Silverman, op. cit., p. 66.

51 *"the whole company . . . pipe,"* etc.: Bridenbaugh, *Gentleman's Progress,* p. 84.
51 *"half a foot . . . head":* Ibid., p. 92.
51 *"laugh'd and grinned . . . place":* Ibid., p. 140.
52 *"perform'd afoot . . . stars":* Quoted in Hawke, op. cit., p. 96.
52 *"that curiosity . . . everywhere":* Bridenbaugh, *Gentleman's Progress,* p. 99.
52 *"country rabble . . . lives":* Ibid.
52 *"Here the time . . . begotten":* Quoted in J. T. Adams, *Revolutionary New England,* p. 276.
52 OH, HOW . . . WORLD?: Quoted in Sellers, *Benedict Arnold,* p. 46.
52 *"a bell in every room":* Quoted in Earle, op. cit., p. 359.
53 *"as much liquor . . . South":* Adams, *Provincial Society,* p. 75.
53 *"laid a wager . . . dead":* R. Wright, *Early American Wags and Eccentrics,* p. 55.
53 *"joy of connoisseurs":* Ibid., p. 56.
54 *"in almost . . . Bell":* Ibid., p. 57.
54 *"does more mischief . . . their own":* Quoted in Hawke, op. cit., p. 79.
54 *"Strip and Go Naked":* Quoted in R. Wright, op. cit., p. 253.
54 *"a Breast of Milk":* Chase, op. cit., p. 190.
54 *"with small expense . . . Stone":* *Pennsylvania Gazette,* June 18, 1767.
54 *"one of the most . . . relief":* Quoted in Irving, op. cit., p. 61.
55 *"vanityes of the head"* and *"oyle of radishes":* Quoted in Earle, op. cit., p. 428.
55 *"Tis as easy . . . garden":* Bridenbaugh, *Gentleman's Progress,* p. 207.
56 *In the spring . . . of thee:* Quoted in Hawke, op. cit., p. 83.
56 *"The distinction . . . very well":* Quoted in Boorstin, *Colonial Experience,* p. 230.
57 *"a constant diet . . . provisions":* Bridenbaugh, *Gentleman's Progress,* p. 79.
58 *"free and affable . . . pritty":* Ibid., p. 146.
58 *"pritty, frank girls":* Ibid., p. 157.
58 *"If a young couple . . . automobile":* Forbes, op. cit., p. 57.
58 *"that to walk out . . . Dutch":* Bridenbaugh, *Gentleman's Progress,* p. 46.
58 *"One meets nobody . . . Bible:* Quoted in Sherrill, *French Memoirs of 18th Century America,* p. 260.
58 *"Merry and Vain,"* etc.: Quoted in R. Wright, op. cit., p. 279.
59 *"Primitive Zeal . . . parents":* Quoted in ibid., p. 249.
59 *"pray'rs read over,"* etc.: Quoted in Furnas, op. cit., p. 184.
59 *They thunder out . . . in their hearts:* Quoted in Boorstin, *Colonial Experience,* p. 135.
60 *"truly born again"* and *"this late remarkable season":* Quoted in Scott, *Settlers on the Eastern Shore,* p. 161.
60 *"I thought at first . . . souls:* Ibid., p. 145.
60 *"looked black . . . gone":* Ibid., pp. 145–146.
60 *"I emptied . . . dish":* Franklin, *Autobiography,* p. 118.
61 *"prepared them . . . war":* Scott, op. cit., p. 165.
61 *If an archangel . . . nearly related:* Dickinson, "Essay on the Constitutional Power of Great Britain," quoted in Brock, *Character of American History,* pp. 33–34.
62 *"not precise . . . is not":* Quoted in L. Wright, op. cit., p. 238.
62 *"dare not exercise,"* etc.: Bailyn, *Pamphlets,* p. 55.
62 *"The liberties . . . peace":* Ibid., p. 18.
62 *"the colonization . . . aims":* Ibid., p. 17.
63 *"the most unbounded,"* etc.: Ibid., pp. 56–57.
63 *"Liberty can no . . . pitch":* Ibid., p. 81.
63 *"A true . . . man":* C. Adams, *Familiar Letters,* p. 22.
64 *"the most perfect . . . happiness":* Bailyn, *Pamphlets,* p. 45.
64 *"I would rather be . . . no nation":* Quoted in Brown and Senior, *Victorious in Defeat,* p. 4.
64 *"surmounted by Ability . . . Nature":* Quoted in Chase, op. cit., p. 97.

CHAPTER THREE: KING, PARLIAMENT, AND INHERITED RIGHTS

Page 65 *"as to the tomb of their apostle":* Chase, op. cit., p. 110.
65 *"What do we mean . . . obligations":* J. Adams, Letter of February 13, 1818, to H. Niles, in *Works,* v. 10, 267.
66 *a regard to . . . damnation:* Bailyn, *Pamphlets,* pp. 58–59.
66 *"The forms of a free . . . incompatible":* Quoted in Conway, *Life of Thomas Paine,* v. 1, p. 279.
66 *"tenacious in the Opinion . . . Power":* Quoted in Calhoon, *Loyalist Perception,* p. 14.

67 *"answered in the main . . . liberty"*: Burke, "Observations on a Late State of the Nation," in Writings and Speeches, v. 2, p. 87.

67 *"the colonists met . . . and prayer"*: G. Smith, op. cit., p. 28.

67 *"If we in America . . . seas through"*: Quoted in G. Smith, *The United States*, p. 29.

67 *"after some fluctuation . . . rule"*: Ibid., p. 45.

67 *"tenacious of . . . king"*: Ibid.

68 *"a number equal . . . proportion"*: Quoted in Fiske, op. cit., p. 15.

68 *"and all their . . . years to come"*: Ibid.

69 *"hath sovereign . . . laws"*: Blackstone, *Laws of England*, Book I, Chapter 2, Sec. III, quoted in Brock, op. cit., p. 33.

69 *"was born . . . philosophical debate"*: Boorstin, *Hidden History*, p. 104.

69 *"burning down . . . egg"*: Quoted in W. Randall, *Benedict Arnold*, p. 47.

70 *"Our whole Wealth . . . Britain"*: Quoted in Bowen, op. cit., p. 144.

70 *"Our houses . . . employ"*: Bailyn, *Pamphlets*, p. 73.

70 *"by one year's war . . . sea"*: Quoted in Cutter, *Life of Israel Putnam*, p. 123.

71 *"in just subordination . . . kingdom"*: Quoted in Bailyn, *Voyagers*, p. 31.

71 *"absolutely irreconcileable . . . men"*: Quoted in E. Greene, *Foundation of American Nationality*, p. 406.

71 *"I am not set . . . raised"*: Quoted in Forbes, op. cit., p. 100.

72 *"as little inconvenient . . . possible"*: Ibid., p. 406.

72 *"other than such . . . bay"*: Bailyn, *Pamphlets*, p. 382.

72 *"Nothing is wanted . . . PLEASURE"*: Bailyn, *Pamphlets*, p. 63.

72 *"We might as well . . . candles"*: Quoted in Fiske, op. cit., p. 18.

72 Whereas, *the honorable . . . American freedom*: Tyler, *Patrick Henry*, pp. 70–71.

73 *"Caesar had . . . most of it!"*: Ibid., pp. 72–73.

73 *"I well remember . . . vociferated"*: Jefferson, *Writings of Thomas Jefferson*, v. 14, p. 169.

74 Henry *"spoke . . . wrote"*: Quoted in Bowers, *Young Jefferson*, p. 41.

74 *"indolent, dreamy . . . gift"*: Tyler, op. cit., p. 5.

74 *"A firm loyalty . . . tendency"*: Quoted in Van Doren, op. cit., p. 327.

75 *"people of all . . . denominations"*: Quoted in W. Randall, op. cit., p. 49.

75 *"The Stamp Act . . . disaffected"*: Quoted in Fiske, op. cit., p. 23.

75 *"It has been said . . . existed*: J. Adams, *Works*, v. 3, p. 450.

76 *The stamp act engrosses . . . industry*: Quoted in Irving, op. cit., p. 121.

77 *"that it is inseparable . . . colonists"*: Quoted in Brock, op. cit., p. 46.

77 *"It is inconsistent . . . sense"*: J. Adams, op. cit., p. 466.

77 *The [British] covenanted . . . Representatives*: Quoted in Forbes, op. cit., p. 374.

77 *"nine tenths of the people,"* etc.: Bailyn, *Pamphlets*, p. 95.

78 *"the Colonies . . . Disgust"*: Quoted in Calhoon, op. cit., p. 22.

78 *"Until now . . . them"*: Quoted in Morgan and Morgan, *Stamp Act Crisis*, p. 369.

78 *"a subject . . . free!"* Quoted in O'Brien, *Great Melody*, p. 106.

78 *"if I could . . . Englishmen"*: Beloff, *Debate on the Revolution*, p. 29.

78 *"When I proposed . . . emancipated?"*: Beloff, op. cit., p. 35.

78 *"rejoice . . . rest of us"*: Quoted in Bowers, op. cit., p. 59.

79 *"Let the Stamp Act . . . consent"*: Quoted in C. Bowen, op. cit., p. 207.

79 *"All colonies have . . . House"*: Ibid., p. 212.

79 *"It is said . . . protection*: Quoted in Brock, op. cit., p. 34n.

79 *"What was the temper . . . force of arms"*: Quoted in C. Bowen, op. cit., p. 220, and Irving, op. cit., p. 124.

80 *"An external tax . . . arguments"*: Bailyn, *Pamphlets*, p. 126.

81 *"fatal . . . demand"*: Quoted in *Handbook for the Exhibition Buildings*, p. 16.

81 *"composed every wave . . . calm"*: Quoted in Davidson, op. cit., p. 35.

81 *"to make laws . . . whatsoever"*: Bailyn, *Pamphlets*, p. 118.

81 *" 'I will, I will!' "*: Quoted in P. Smith, op. cit., p. 92.

82 *"A free people . . . terms"*: Morison, *Sources and Documents*, pp. 47–48.

82 *"We are asked . . . forever"*: Quoted in Fiske, op. cit., p. 50.

82 *"the colonists are . . . states"*: Quoted in Alden, *American Revolution*, p. 86.

83 *"the ships of . . . Powder and Ball"*: Quoted in Forbes, op. cit., p. 139.

83 *"to rescue . . . power"*: Ibid.

83 *COME join Hand in Hand . . . Name*: Quoted in Silverman, op. cit., p. 114.

83 *In freedom . . . give*: Quoted in P. Smith, *John Adams*, v. 1, p. 111.

83 *"a man . . . in accord"*: Quoted in P. Smith, op. cit., p. 114.

84 *"chief instigators . . . punishment"*: Ibid., p. 128.

84 *America, an immense . . . want of it*: Franklin, *Writings*, v. 5, pp. 21–22.
84 *"a new kind . . . for ever"*: Quoted in Van Doren, op. cit., p. 376.
84 *At a time when . . . pleasure*: Quoted in Irving, op. cit., p. 128.
85 *"It is somewhat . . . flow"*: Quoted in Hudleston, *Gentleman Johnny Burgoyne*, p. 55.
85 *"There was one thing . . . fire"*: Forbes, op. cit., p. 142.
86 *"Yankey war . . . burials"*: Ibid., pp. 142–143.
87 *"I had no . . . prefer"*: Quoted in Davidson, op. cit., p. 314.
87 *"a motley rabble . . . street"*: Quoted in Forbes, op. cit., p. 156.
87 *"behave . . . philosopher"*: Quoted in P. Smith, *John Adams*, p. 125.
87 *"the prints exhibited . . . fancy"*: Quoted in Davidson, op. cit., p. 314.
87 *"The properest time . . . our feet"*: Quoted in Irving, op. cit., p. 134.
87 *To effect this . . . our side*: Quoted in Fiske, op. cit., p. 61.
88 *"a deadness and vapidity"*: Quoted in Forbes, op. cit., p. 188.
88 *"mankind . . . interest"*: Quoted in Davidson, op. cit., p. 314.
89 *Any further . . . rising spirit*: Reed, *Life and Correspondence of Joseph Reed*, v. 1, pp. 54–55.
89 *"Friends! . . . administration"*: Quoted in P. Smith, *John Adams*, p. 146.
90 *"This meeting . . . country"*: Ibid., p. 147.
90 *"We wore . . . men"*: Quoted in Forbes, op. cit., p. 198.
90 *"there was a . . . Dorchester"*: Ibid., p. 199.
90 *"Not the least . . . person"*: Quoted in Davidson, op. cit., p. 314.
90 *"Well, boys . . . yet"*: Quoted in Forbes, op. cit., p. 200.
90 *"an act of . . . Britain"*: Quoted in Van Doren, op. cit., p. 452.
90 *"subject[ed] ourselves . . . servitude"*: Quoted in P. Smith, *John Adams*, p. 148.
90 *"There is a Dignity . . . History"*: Ibid., p. 148.
91 *"unwarrantable . . . proceedings"*: Quoted in G. Smith op. cit., p. 40.
91 *"We must master . . . alone"*: Quoted in Davidson, op. cit., p. 314.
91 *"You can't pursue . . . Trade of America?"*: Quoted in O'Brien, op. cit., p. 137.
91 *"Does it not appear . . . tests?"*: Quoted in Freeman, *George Washington*, v. 3, p. 360.
91 *"If Parliament . . . churches"*: Bailyn, *Pamphlets*, p. 158.
92 *"dismayed . . . severity"*: Quoted in P. Smith, op. cit., p. 153.
92 *"devoutly to implore . . . war"*: Quoted in Bowers, op. cit., p. 80.
93 *"in such terms . . . Parliament"*: Ibid.
93 *"If need be . . . Boston"*: Quoted in Fiske, *American Revolution*, v. 1, p. 103.
93 *"God be with . . . will"*: Quoted in Lossing, *Mary and Martha*, p. 129.
93 *"Yes; I foresee . . . him"*: Ibid.
93 *"all his just rights . . . divided us"*: Quoted in Tyler, op. cit., pp. 99–100.
94 *Did ever any kingdom . . . liberty*: C. Adams, op. cit., p. 25.
94 *"All America . . . but an American"*: Quoted in Irving, op. cit., p. 146.
94 *"we could not . . . worship"* and *"hear a prayer . . . country"*: C. Adams, op. cit., p. 37.
95 *"the united wisdom of North America"*: "Letter of Instructions to the Virginia Delegates," quoted in Tyler, op. cit., p. 99.
95 *"I wander alone . . . terrible"*: Quoted in Brodie, op. cit., p. 108.
95 *"There is in . . . venal herd"*: C. Adams, op. cit., p. 31.
95 *"implied lace ruffles . . . Greek"*: Forbes, op. cit., p. 56.
95 *"very sensible,"* etc., and *"clever . . . eye-stone"*: Quoted in Montross, op. cit., p. 132.
96 *"eats little . . . objects"*: Quoted in Bowers, op. cit., p. 107.
96 *"Whether it be . . . preserved"*: Forbes, op. cit., p. 26.
96 *"born and tempered . . . Britain"*: Quoted in Malone, *Story of the Declaration of Independence*, p. 111.
96 *"He had a fine . . . upon him"*: Quoted in Tyler, op. cit., pp. 296–297.
96 *"He is a soldier . . . prayers"*: *Virginia Magazine of History and Biography*, v. 15, p. 356.
96 *"look'd at the . . . telescope"*: Quoted in Ellis, "Friends at Twilight," p. 52.
97 *"My constitution is a glass bubble"*: Quoted in P. Smith, *John Adams*, p. 1102.
97 *"had corrupted . . . juices"*: Ibid., p. 35.
97 *"No virgin or matron,"* etc.: Butterfield, *Diary and Autobiography of John Adams*, v. 2, pp. 42–43.
97 *"a love of Books . . . ladies"*: Ibid., p. 24.
97 *"Oh! that I could . . . passion"*: Quoted in P. Smith, *John Adams*, p. 30.
97 *"to rise with the sun,"* etc.: Ibid., p. 31.
98 *"the universal spirit . . . introduced"*: C. Adams, op. cit., p. 13.
98 *"These tarrings and . . . discountenanced"*: Ibid., p. 20.
98 *"Aim at an exact . . . Bolinbroke"*: Quoted in Brodie, op. cit., p. 100.

98 "There are few people . . . company": Quoted in P. Smith, John Adams, p. 263.
99 "My religion is . . . I can": Adams, Works, v. 10, p. 170.
99 "probably fixed . . . placed": Quoted in Bowers, op. cit., p. 19.
99 "I heard . . . besides": Ibid., p. 21.
100 "everything is useful . . . virtue": Ibid., p. 24.
100 "in pleading . . . word": Ibid., p. 29.
100 "every case of value," etc.: Ibid., p. 32.
100 "up to the point . . . required": Quoted in Handbook for the Exhibition Buildings, p. 50.
101 "Americans wish . . . we all wish": Ibid., p. 93.
101 "Single acts . . . slavery": Ibid., p. 88.
101 "a settled, fixed . . . government": Bailyn, Pamphlets, p. 73.
101 "Those who are . . . slaves": Ibid., p. 141.
101 "I speak it . . . slaves": Quoted in Brodie, op. cit., p. 100.
101 "endeavoring by every . . . us": Ibid.
101 "How is it that . . . slaves?": Ibid.
101 "I should think . . . Americans": Ibid.
101 "The Negroes . . . words?": Quoted in Silverman, op. cit., p. 215.
101 "by the law . . . tyrant": Bailyn, Pamphlets, p. 144.
102 "those who are . . . others": Ibid., p. 149.
102 "I wish most sincerely . . . have": C. Adams, op. cit., p. 41.
102 "hung in chains" and "shrivelling . . . mummy": Forbes, op. cit., p. 39.
103 "The consequence . . . unanimously": C. Adams, op. cit., p. 45.
103 "we are unable . . . drink": Quoted in Bowers, op. cit., p. 118.
103 "I shall be killed . . . place": C. Adams, op. cit., p. 46.
103 "sinful feasts," etc.: Quoted in P. Smith, John Adams, p. 175.
103 "[We] go home . . . surprisingly": C. Adams, op. cit., p. 43.
103 "If we arrest . . . eternity": Quoted in Silverman, op. cit., p. 266.
103 "As men and . . . as possible": Quoted in W. Randall, op. cit., p. 144.
103 "The dye is now cast . . . retreat": The king to Lord North, September 11, 1774, quoted in Brock, op. cit., p. 34.
104 "This was one . . . her": Quoted in P. Smith, John Adams, p. 176.
104 "men of property . . . merchants": Quoted in Bowers, op. cit., p. 113.
104 "the colonies from . . . representation": Calhoon, op. cit., p. 76.
104 "Parliament ought not . . . Mother Country": Quoted in Calhoon, op. cit., p. 79.
104 "all the like . . . other": Quoted in P. Smith, John Adams, p. 178.
105 "When I consider . . . dead": Quoted in Calhoon, op. cit., p. 81.
105 "with a moderation . . . council": Quoted in Irving, op. cit., p. 150.
105 "They walked into . . . country": Bowers, op. cit., p. 63.
105 "You have been told . . . world: Quoted in Davidson, op. cit., p. 320.
106 "When your lordships . . . Philadelphia": Ibid.
106 "If you speak . . . floor": Quoted in Lossing, Mary and Martha, p. 130.
106 Permit me with . . . insecure: Quoted in Irving, op. cit., p. 152.
107 "resolves, declarations . . . England": Quoted in Tyler, op. cit., p. 123.
107 "After all, we must fight" and "raised his . . . mind!' ": Quoted in ibid., p. 125.
107 "It is surprising . . . here": Quoted in Irving, op. cit., p. 155.
107 "would in a . . . wish": Quoted in Van Doren, op. cit., p. 485.
107 "such a carnage . . . healed": Ibid.
108 "[Miss Howe] told me . . . minutes": Ibid., p. 503.
108 "He received me . . . times": Ibid.
108 "drunk or sober": Quoted in Conway, Life of Thomas Paine, p. 56.
108 "You might destroy . . . extremity": Quoted in Bowers, op. cit., p. 100.
108 "though on so . . . porter": Quoted in Van Doren, op. cit., p. 513.
109 "When I saw . . . power": Quoted in Bowers, op. cit., p. 104.
109 "We think ourselves . . . emergency": Quoted in Tyler, op. cit., p. 130.
109 "The first act . . . Georgia": Ibid.
109 "unless the banditti . . . Park": Ibid., pp. 130–131.
109 "Such militia . . . province": Ibid., p. 132.
109 "now arming . . . require": Ibid., p. 133.
110 "British guard stationed . . . give me death!: Ibid., p. 145.
110 "an unearthly fire," etc.: Ibid., p. 146.
110 "It was their . . . refused": Quoted in Handbook for the Exhibition Buildings, p. 75.

CHAPTER FOUR: REVOLT

Page 111   *"If you think . . . friends"*: Quoted in W. Randall, op. cit., p. 79.
111   *"To keep quiet . . . determination"*: Ibid., p. 80.
112   *"ringleaders . . . of the tea"*: Ibid.
112   *"expectation of . . . event"*: Martin, *Private Yankee Doodle,* p. 6.
112   *"Sam Adams writes . . . postage"*: Forbes, op. cit., p. 87.
112   *"as a demagogue . . . harangued"*: Bradley, *United Empire Loyalists,* p. 54.
113   *"eager to fix . . . come"*: Ibid., p. 243.
113   *"I asked him . . . way"*: Ibid.
113   *"10,000 regulars . . . alive"*: Ibid., p. 246.
114   *"still warm from her body"*: Ibid., p. 249.
115   *"The moon shone . . . me [off]"*: Ibid., p. 259.
115   *"I awaked the . . . Lexington"*: Ibid.
115   *"Noise! . . . are out"*: Wheeler, *Voices of 1776,* p. 5.
115   *"seised my bridle . . . dismount"*: Quoted in Forbes, op. cit., p. 262.
115   *"they threatened . . . out"*: Ibid.
115   *"claiming to be . . . have"*: Ibid., p. 475n.
116   *"Lay down . . . disperse!"*: Wheeler, op. cit., p. 6.
116   *"Stand your ground . . . here"*: Quoted in Fiske, op. cit., p. 122.
116   *"O! What . . . this!"*: Ibid.
117   *"good-naturedly"*: Forbes, op. cit., p. 270.
117   *"set out chairs . . . in"*: Ibid.
117   *By the rude . . . world*: Emerson, *Collected Poems,* p. 44.
117   *"raised himself . . . face"*: Ibid., p. 476n.
118   *"Such was the . . . men"*: Quoted in Davidson, op. cit., p. 321.
118   *"a grait many . . . bloddy"*: Quoted in Scheer and Rankin, *Rebels and Redcoats,* p. 35.
118   *"We were fired on . . . expended"*: Barker, *British in Boston,* p. 35.
118   *"their tongues hanging . . . chase"*: Quoted in Cutter, op. cit., p. 149.
119   *"If the retreat . . . off"*: Quoted in Irving, op. cit., p. 163.
119   *"some desperate attempt . . . do"*: Scheer and Rankin, op. cit., p. 47.
119   *"with drums beating . . . America' "* and *"to the rabble . . . direct"*: Wheeler, op. cit., p. 18.
120   *"Whoever looks upon . . . home"*: Scheer and Rankin, op. cit., p. 43.
120   *"The flame of . . . subdue"*: Ibid., p. 45.
120   *"The whole country . . . companies"*: Adlum, *Memoirs of the Life of John Adlum,* p. 4.
120   *"I was ploughing . . . succession"*: Martin, op. cit., p. 6.
120   *"pretty correct . . . contest"*: Ibid.
121   *"every man . . . arms"*: Scheer and Rankin, op. cit., p. 65.
121   *"made to resemble . . . tail"*: Ibid., p. 66.
121   *"great exactness"*: C. Adams, op. cit., p. 65.
121   *"nothing to preserve . . . bed"*: Scheer and Rankin op. cit., p. 67.
121   *"Hunting Shirts . . . Marksman"*: Quoted in Boorstin, *Colonial Experience,* p. 351.
121   *"We will show . . . proscriptions"*: Quoted in Fiske, op. cit., p. 133.
122   *"composed and grave . . . maintain it"*: C. Adams, op. cit., p. 83.
122   *"ten minutes at . . . themselves"*: Quoted in Van Doren, op. cit., p. 529.
122   *"Unhappy it is . . . choice?"*: Quoted in Irving, op. cit., p. 165.
122   *"There is among . . . aristocracy"*: Quoted in P. Smith, *John Adams,* p. 248.
122   *"were heard in,"* etc.: C. Adams, op. cit., p. 66.
123   *"motions and . . . etc."*: J. Adams, *Works,* v. 2, p. 415.
123   *"Hancock himself . . . mind"*: Ibid., p. 416.
123   *"What shall we do?"*: Ibid.
123   *"a gentleman whose . . . Union"*: Quoted in Irving, op. cit., p. 167.
124   *"with visible pleasure,"* etc.: J. Adams, *Works,* v. 2, p. 417.
124   *"But lest some unlucky event,"* etc.: Scheer and Rankin, op. cit., p. 71.
125   *"[Washington] is a Gent. . . . Calm"*: Quoted in Montross, op. cit., p. 74.
125   *"The modest, virtuous . . . colonies"*: Quoted in P. Smith, *John Adams,* p. 199.
125   *"You had prepared . . . face"*: C. Adams, op. cit., pp. 78–79.
126   *"My good friends . . . ourselves?"*: Quoted in Lossing, op. cit., pp. 3–4.
127   *"frankness and rural . . . refinement"*: Quoted in Irving, op. cit., p. 8.
127   *"one thread Bear . . . &c"*: Quoted in the *Encyclopaedia Britannica* (1988), v. 29, p. 717.

127 *"It is honorable . . . profitable"*: Ibid.
128 *"I am principled . . . species"*: Ibid., p. 719.
128 *"Of the mother . . . obeyed"*: Quoted in R. Smith, *Patriarch*, p. 4.
128 *"He is subject to . . . life"*: Ibid.
128 *"the kind of . . . self"*: Parkman, op. cit., pp. 333–334.
129 *"gave him throughout . . . accuracy"*: Irving, op. cit., p. 7.
129 *These are the things . . . soul*: Quoted in R. Smith, op. cit., p. 7.
130 *"That is too good for me"*: Quoted in Lossing, op. cit., p. 309.
130 *"I have several . . . arch"*: Quoted in R. Smith, op. cit., p. 6.
130 *"He learned early . . . road"*: Irving, op. cit., p. 9.
130 *"the most amiable . . . met"*: Quoted in Wharton, *Colonial Days and Dames*, p. 112.
131 *"He has a . . . reverence"*: Quoted in R. Smith, op. cit., p. xix.
131 *"Be easy and . . . command"*: Ibid., p. xx.
131 *"True friendship . . . appellation"*: Ibid.
131 *"brave and steady,"* etc.: *Handbook for the Exhibition Buildings*, p. 14.
131 *"he allways avoided . . . Engaged"*: Quoted in Silverman, op. cit., p. 317.
132 *"innate and unassuming . . . examination"*: Marshall, *Life of George Washington*, p. 99.
132 *"From the day . . . reputation"*: Quoted in R. Smith, op. cit., p. 13.
132 *"I am embarked . . . choice"*: Burnett, *Letters*, v. 1, p. 138.
132 *My Dearest: . . . fall*: Quoted in Freeman, op. cit., pp. 452–454.
133 *"remarkable dexterity . . . anywhere"*: C. Adams, op. cit., p. 61.
134 *"Oh that I . . . be"*: Ibid., p. 59.
134 *"Such is the . . . case"*: Ibid., p. 60.
134 *The business . . . men"*: Ibid., p. 85.
135 *"I, Peter Boles . . . America"*: Quoted in W. Randall, op. cit., p. 57.
135 *"Cruel, Wanton . . . Murders"*: Quoted in Sellers, op. cit., p. 16.
135 *"Good God, are . . . was"*: Ibid.
136 *"the best drilled . . . camp"*: Ibid., p. 24.
136 *"eighty pieces . . . onset"*: Quoted in W. Randall, op. cit., p. 86.
137 *"an original . . . admiration"*: Quoted in Orton, *Republic of Vermont*, p. 43.
137 *"In the name . . . Congress"*: Allen, *Narrative of Col. Ethan Allen's Captivity*, p. 15.
137 *"Give up . . . gentlemen"*: Quoted in Sellers, op. cit., p. 30.
137 *"The sun seemed . . . America"*: Allen, op. cit., p. 33.
137 *"plunder"*: Quoted in W. Randall, op. cit., p. 96.
137 *"Upon our briskly . . . against us"*: Wheeler, op. cit., p. 27.

CHAPTER FIVE: BOSTON

Page 139 *Behold the Cerberus . . . wow*: Quoted in Hudleston, op. cit., p. 52.
140 *"What! Ten . . . room"*: Quoted in Johnson, *Battles of the Revolutionary War*, p. 40.
140 *"condign punishment"*: Quoted in Irving, op. cit., p. 172.
140 *"fulness of Chastisement"*: Quoted in Silverman, op. cit., p. 277.
140 *"Who is that . . . men"*: Quoted in Hudleston, op. cit., p. 60.
140 *"These kept up . . . bombs"*: Wheeler, op. cit., p. 41.
141 *"He was so near . . . instantly"*: Ibid., p. 41.
141 *"little victuals . . . rum"*: Scheer and Rankin, op. cit., p. 56.
141 *"like unto . . . staged"*: Quoted in *Heroes of the American Revolution*, p. 224.
141 *"to be cool . . . eyes"*: Potter, *Life and Remarkable Adventures of Israel R. Potter*, p. 99.
141 *"Fire low . . . coats"*: Quoted in Cutter, op. cit., p. 173.
142 *"with great confidence . . . five"*: Scheer and Rankin, op. cit., p. 58.
142 *"So precise . . . killed"*: Wheeler, op. cit., p. 48.
142 *Now ensued . . . witness to*: Scheer and Rankin, op. cit., p. 59.
143 *"a moment . . . before"*: Ibid.
143 *"To be forced . . . all"*: Quoted in Hudleston, op. cit., p. 61.
143 *"There are few . . . berm"*: Wheeler, op. cit., p. 50.
143 *"The dead . . . fold"*: Quoted in Hudleston, op. cit., p. 61.
143 *"but upon the whole . . . price"*: Wheeler, op. cit., p. 53.
143 *"in triumph"*: C. Adams, op. cit., p. 91.
144 *"The rebels . . . be"*: Quoted in Davidson, op. cit., p. 321.
144 *"it seemed as . . . safe!"*: Quoted in Irving, op. cit., p. 175.

144 *The Continental . . . engaged:* Quoted in Urwin, *United States Infantry,* p. 14.
144 *"The rebels certainly . . . provisions":* Scheer and Rankin, op. cit., p. 46.
144 *"no man dared . . . street":* C. Adams, op. cit., p. 79.
144 *"to wipe his face . . . mutiny":* Ibid., p. 87.
145 *"but none . . . volunteers":* Irving, op. cit., p. 173.
145 *"frowned on all . . . soldiering":* Sellers, op. cit., p. 46.
145 *"an over-confidence . . . troops":* Morgan, *The New York Review of Books,* June 23, 1994, p. 38.
146 *"where the principles . . . detestable":* Reed, op. cit., p. 243.
146 *"there was a great . . . done":* Scheer and Rankin, op. cit., p. 83.
146 *"earnestly recommended . . . held:* Ford, *Journals,* v. 2, p. 111.
146 *They are the most . . . people:* Washington, *Writings* (Ford ed.), v. 3, p. 433.
147 *"I hope the people . . . degree":* C. Adams, op. cit., p. 66.
147 *"Pray tell me . . . continent":* J. Adams, *Works,* v. 1, p. 256.
147 *"My countrymen want . . . continent":* C. Adams, op. cit., p. 207.
147 *His Excellency . . . esteem:* Greene, *Life of Nathanael Greene,* v. 1, pp. 126–127.
148 *"rushing into the . . . throat":* Quoted in Irving, op. cit., p. 210.
148 *"contempt for . . . rusticity":* Silverman, op. cit., p. 290.
149 *We have a bold . . . Americay:* Quoted in Brodie, op. cit., pp. 107–108.
149 *No fop in arms . . . fair:* Quoted in Silverman, op. cit., p. 286.
150 *"We [have] nothing more . . . vigilant":* Wheeler, op. cit., p. 63.
150 *"His knowledge was . . . most":* Quoted in *Heroes,* p. 73.
151 *"My wife is daughter . . . you":* Quoted in Fiske, *Essays,* p. 59.
151 *"plain in . . . ugliness":* Quoted in Wharton, op. cit., p. 112.
151 *"remarkable partiality for dogs":* *Heroes,* p. 196.
151 *"lapped up . . . plates":* Fiske, *Essays,* p. 68.
152 *"determined that I . . . paw":* Quoted in Irving, op. cit., p. 208.
152 *"puppies":Heroes,* p. 197.
152 *"The whole Congress . . . oftener":* C. Adams, op. cit., p. 126.
152 *"My time was never . . . ones":* Burnett, *Letters,* v. 1, p. 156.
152 *"for the sole . . . world":* Quoted in Montross, op. cit., p. 109.
152 *"sink its . . . Congress":* Ford, *Journals,* v. 2, p. 221.
153 *"America is a . . . pace":* C. Adams, op. cit., p. 66.
153 *"Let us eat . . . us":* Ibid., p. 40.
153 *"Mr. Lee, Mr. Gadsen . . . qualities:* J. Adams, *Works,* v. 3, pp. 11–12.
154 *We are reduced . . . Slaves:* Ford, *Journals,* v. 2, pp. 129–130.
154 *"signal proof . . . country":* Quoted in Montross, op. cit., pp. 80–81.
154 *"against the supine . . . rights":* Bowers, op. cit., p. 119.
154 *"This measure . . . taste":* Ibid., p. 128.
154 *"else it would . . . effect":* Ibid.
154 *"We have . . . forever":* Quoted in Montross, op. cit., p. 81.
155 *"a piddling . . . doings":* Bowers, op. cit., p. 128.
155 *"As I was . . . War:* Ibid.
155 *Mr. Benj. Harrison . . . train:* Ibid., p. 129.
155 *"near enough . . . hand":* Ibid.
156 *"The authors and . . . empire":* Bailyn, *Pamphlets,* p. 88.
156 *"I am unalterably . . . doctrines":* Quoted in Bowers, op. cit., p. 129.
156 *"seemed to have . . . hand":* Quoted in Forbes, op. cit., p. 235.
157 *"Make use of . . . perish":* Quoted in Freeman, *Washington* (one-volume ed.), p. 240.
157 *"I stand . . . patriots":* French, *General Gage's Informers,* p. 195.
157 *"Who could have . . . crimes?":* Burnett, *Letters,* v. 1, pp. 225–226.
158 *"but 32 barrels":* Quoted in Forbes, op. cit., p. 301.
158 *"We live in . . . supply?":* C. Adams, op. cit., p. 63.
159 *"they fired one . . . fence!":* Scheer and Rankin, op. cit., p. 91.
159 *"notwithstanding the town . . . destroyed":* Ford, *Journals,* v. 3, p. 445.
159 *"an equal claim," etc.:* Quoted in Irving, op. cit., pp. 190–191.
160 *"a casualty . . . siege life":* Urwin, op. cit., p. 15.
160 *"retire into a chimney-corner":* Ibid., p. 214.
160 *"almost within . . . firesides":* Ibid.
160 *"After the last . . . another":* Washington, *Writings* (Fitzpatrick, ed.), v. 4, pp. 124–125.
160 *"Search the vast . . . everything:* Ibid., p. 211.

161 *"I have oftentimes . . . under:* Ibid., p. 212.
161 *"including sick . . . officers":* Quoted in Irving, op. cit., p. 224.
161 *"plying the Rivers . . . Negroes":* Quoted in Brodie, op. cit., p. 112.
161 *"that if 1,000 . . . themselves":* Ibid., p. 111.
162 *"If [Dunmore] is not . . . snowball":* Quoted in Irving, op. cit., p. 212.
162 *"Let the hospitality . . . idleness":* Quoted in Lossing, op. cit., p. 155.
162 *"are not in . . . few":* Ibid., p. 149.
163 *"I think my . . . resignation":* Quoted in Tyler, op. cit., p. 186.
163 *"We have plays . . . Garrick":* Scheer and Rankin, op. cit., p. 96.
163 *"where . . . Cabals":* Quoted in Silverman, op. cit., p. 292.
163 *"as an uncouth . . . sword":* Ibid., p. 292.
164 *dressed in the . . . tumult:* Willard, *Letters on the American Revolution,* p. 258.
164 *"I cannot help . . . leaders":* Ibid., p. 57.
164 *"the enterprise . . . dangerous":* Quoted in Irving, op. cit., p. 225.
165 *"where I shall . . . artillery":* Sparks, *Correspondence of the American Revolution,* v. 1, pp. 94–95.
165 *"the flash and . . . perceived":* Irving, op. cit., p. 227.
165 *"Perhaps there never . . . time":* Heath, *Memoirs,* p. 32.
165 *"My God! these . . . months":* C. Adams, op. cit., p. 141.
166 *"hauled off . . . front":* Trumball, *Autobiography,* p. 24.
166 *"gave the enemy . . . success":* Wheeler, op. cit., p. 104.
166 *"The more I think . . . blood":* C. Adams, op. cit., p. 143.
166 *"The army of . . . attempt":* Quoted in Irving, op. cit., p. 233.
167 *"My teeth are . . . ass":* Quoted in Silverman, op. cit., p. 295.

CHAPTER SIX: QUEBEC

Page 168 *"imbibed too much . . . Independence":* Quoted in Sellers, op. cit., p. 50.
169 *"to carry . . . of it":* Ibid., p. 42.
169 *"easy, graceful . . . army":* Scheer and Rankin, op. cit., p. 112.
169 *"a treacherous . . . morass":* Sellers, op. cit., p. 45.
169 *"Come then ye . . . prevail":* Quoted in Sellers, op. cit., p. 50.
169 *"Use all possible . . . depend":* Quoted in Freeman, *Washington* (one-volume ed.), p. 238.
170 *"Let me entreat . . . artillery":* Quoted in P. Smith, op. cit., p. 598.
170 *"We have been . . . swamp":* Scheer and Rankin, op. cit., p. 112.
170 *"Allen's misfortune . . . officers":* Washington, *Writings* (Fitzpatrick ed.), v. 4, p. 46.
170 *"active woodsmen . . . batteaux":* Quoted in Sellers, op. cit., p. 46.
170 *"beautiful boys . . . shoot":* Ibid., p. 47.
171 *"gave the idea . . . Belisarius":* Scheer and Rankin, op. cit., p. 117.
171 *"Golden Thighs":* W. Randall, op. cit., p. 151.
171 *"instantly devoured . . . fate":* Quoted in Roberts, *March to Quebec,* pp. 202–203.
171 *"were so weak . . . burst":* Quoted in Roberts, op. cit., p. 555.
171 *"We sat down . . . stars":* Ibid., p. 219.
172 *"a short . . . speech":* Quoted in Sellers, op. cit., p. 70.
172 *"His corps is . . . campaign":* Ibid.
173 *"drummed out of town":* Ibid., p. 72.
173 *"yet this example . . . generality":* Wheeler, op. cit., p. 78.
173 *"The [Americans] . . . them":* Quoted in Sellers, op. cit., p. 75.
174 *"a horrible . . . cannon":* Wheeler, op. cit., p. 81.
174 *"searching . . . souvenirs":* W. Randall, op. cit., p. 223.
174 *"We now . . . 'em":* Quoted in Sellers, op. cit., p. 87.
175 *"The merit of . . . arms":* Ibid., p. 87.
175 *"[Canada] must be . . . quick":* Quoted in Montross, op. cit., p. 108.
175 *"all the . . . Frontiers":* Ibid.
175 *"I have no . . . triumph":* Scheer and Rankin, op. cit., p. 128.
175 *"for God's sake . . . bring":* Ibid.
175 *"at a loss . . . officer":* Quoted in W. Randall, op. cit., p. 226.
175 *"thirty years . . . accomplishment":* Quoted in Sellers, op. cit., p. 93.
175 *"an old woman"* and *"I have . . . genius":* Ibid.
176 *"masterly acquaintance . . . Address":* Quoted in Montross, op. cit., p. 123.
176 *"to promote . . . Canada":* Quoted in W. Randall, op. cit., p. 229.

176 *"our army in . . . Army":* Burnett, *Letters,* v. 1, p. 476.
176 *"disheartened . . . mouth":* Quoted in Montross, op. cit., p. 166.
176 *"In the most belter . . . bands":* Senter, *Journal,* p. 33.
176 *"The junction of . . . country":* Quoted in W. Randall, op. cit., p. 236.
177 *My Dear General: . . . Arnold:* Quoted in Sellers, op. cit., p. 103.
178 *"and other . . . army":* Ibid., p. 101.
178 *"The warmth . . . time":* Ibid., p. 103.

Chapter Seven: The Declaration of Independence

Page 180 *These people show . . . government:* Gage, *Correspondence,* v. 2, pp. 686–687.
180 *"immediately follow . . . march":* Quoted in Cutter, op. cit., p. 208.
181 *"New York, in . . . beyond":* Quoted in Silverman, op. cit., p. 325.
181 *"All the mechanics . . . works":* Wheeler, op. cit., p. 117.
181 *"hurried about . . . post":* Ibid., p. 119.
182 *"They will knock . . . hour":* Ibid., p. 120.
182 *"we had a . . . us":* Ibid., p. 121.
183 *"the union between . . . blessings":* Quoted in Brock, op. cit., p. 59.
183 *"is become . . . exertions":* Ibid.
183 *"the execrable . . . want":* Quoted in Montross, op. cit., pp. 111–112.
184 *"die very fast":* C. Adams, op. cit., p. 74.
184 *"The information . . . Boston":* Quoted in Hudleston, op. cit., p. 56.
184 *"startled into . . . ground!":* Quoted in Dorson, op. cit., p. 20.
184 *"feared the Lord . . . dry":* Kirke, *Rear-Guard of the Revolution,* p. 148.
184 *"If no pacific . . . die":* Ibid., p. 148.
185 *"very well recommended . . . father":* Quoted in Conway, *Thomas Paine,* v. 1, p. 40.
185 *"naturally indolent . . . passions":* Ibid., p. 77n.
185 *"Your countenancing . . . increasing":* Ibid., pp. 40–41.
186 *"We conversed . . . with him":* Ibid., p. 41.
186 *"As extasy . . . entertaining":* Ibid., p. 45.
186 *"robbed of . . . America":* Ibid., p. 53.
186 *"The principal . . . coronation":* Ibid.
186 *Here lies . . . fall:* Ibid., p. 12.
186 *"I thought it . . . it":* Ibid., p. 56.
187 *"with an effect . . . paper":* Ibid., p. 61.
187 *"hitherto unknown . . . people":* Ibid., pp. 63–64.
187 *"a wonderful change . . . men":* Ibid., p. 78.
187 *"not the affair . . . now":* Paine, *Common Sense,* p. 82.
187 *"The cause of . . . paradise:* Ibid., p. 65.
187 *"A French bastard . . . it":* Ibid., p. 78.
188 *Male and female . . . lived:* Ibid., pp. 72–73.
188 *I have heard . . . Spain:* Ibid., pp. 83–84.
188 *Every thing . . . above:* Ibid., pp. 87, 90–91, 98.
189 *"Every natural . . . hold":* Quoted in Furnas, op. cit., p. 67.
189 *"He who wishes . . . alone":* Quoted in Mintz, *Gouverneur Morris,* p. 73.
189 *"sound doctrine . . . reasoning":* Quoted in Conway, op. cit., p. 62.
189 *"You ask . . . building up":* C. Adams, op. cit., p. 146.
189 *"without any . . . work":* Bailyn, *Pamphlets,* p. 181.
189 *"foam at the mouth":* Conway, op. cit., p. 293.
189 *"Where the plague . . . way":* Burnett, *Letters,* v. 1, p. 416.
190 *"[Independence] is . . . longer":* Quoted in Montross, op. cit., pp. 130–131.
190 *"Every post . . . it":* Burnett, *Letters,* v. 1, p. 460.
190 *That these United . . . approbation:* Burns, *Thomas Jefferson,* p. 38.
190 *"not yet . . . stem":* Quoted in Malone, op. cit., p. 60.
191 *"The natural . . . governments":* Quoted in Burnett, *Continental Congress,* p. 171.
191 *"render themselves . . . other":* Burnett, *Letters,* v. 1, p. 476.
191 *"The superior commerce . . . truths":* Quoted in Tyler, op. cit., p. 195.
191 *"split and divide . . . everything":* Ibid., p. 199.
192 *"The half of . . . dreadful":* Ibid.
192 *"to inquire . . . with them":* Quoted in Greene, *German Element,* pp. 102–103.
192 *"the breach . . . ever,"* etc.: Ibid., p. 104.

193 *"to satisfy . . . direction"*: Ibid., p. 105.
193 *"a general . . . without"*: Ibid., p. 106.
193 *"imbued with . . . time"*: Ibid., p. 114.
193 *"You will draw . . . doors"*: Quoted in Montross, op. cit., p. 170.
194 *"he was . . . information"*: Ibid., p. 117.
194 *"providing goods . . . country"*: Ibid., p. 118.
194 *"the people . . . persons"*: Quoted in Perkins, *France in the American Revolution*, p. 64.
194 *"veiled . . . Commerce"*: Ibid., p. 170.
195 *"that no . . . work"*: Ford, *Journals*, v. 5, p. 428.
195 *"In fact . . . together"*: Quoted in Bowers, op. cit., p. 146.
195 *"You should . . . meeting"*: Ibid., p. 148.
196 *"scratched . . . exercise"*: Bruns, *Thomas Jefferson*, p. 15.
196 *"delighted . . . oratory"*: Bowers, op. cit., p. 148.
196 *"too passionate . . . document"*: Quoted in Munves, *Thomas Jefferson and the Declaration of Independence*, p. 52.
196 *"We do not . . . subject"*: Burnett, *Letters*, v. 1, p. 401.
196 *"Mr. Harrison . . . adversaries"*: J. Adams, *Works*, v. 3, p. 35.
197 *"a Constitutional Whig . . . pattern"*: Bowers, op. cit., p. 120.
197 *"a rich casket . . . contains"*: Ibid.
197 *"He was . . . scruples"*: Ibid., p. 126.
197 *"had prepared . . . spirit"*: J. Adams, *Works*, v. 3, p. 54.
197 *"John Adams was . . . seats"*: Quoted in Shaw, *Character of John Adams*, p. 98.
198 *"fault-finding"* and *"declamation"*: Munves, op. cit., p. 77.
198 *When I was . . . subjoined*: Jefferson, *Writings*, v. 18, pp. 169–170.
199 *"foreign . . . destroy us"*: Quoted in Munves, op. cit., p. 91.
199 *"given the last . . . dignity"*: Ibid.
199 *"The pusillanimous . . . many,"* etc.: Ibid., v. 1, p. 19.
199 *"He [the king] . . . thither"*: Munves, op. cit., p. 87.
200 *"was struck out . . . others"*: Jefferson, *Writings* (Washington, ed.) v. 1, p. 19.
200 *"obliterated some . . . of it"*: Quoted in Bowers, op. cit., p. 154.
200 *"I wish sincerely . . . freemen"*: Ibid., p. 155.
200 *"a lofty . . . oratory"*: Silverman, op. cit., p. 318.
201 *"the rights essential . . . justice"*: Bailyn, *Pamphlets*, p. 108.
201 *"That all men . . . Safety"*: Quoted in Ellis, op. cit., p. 61.
201 *"[It] may all . . . before"*: Jefferson, *Writings of Thomas Jefferson*, v. 15, p. 462.
201 *"All honor . . . oppression"*: Quoted in Ellis, op. cit., p. 58.
202 *"started suddenly upright . . . it' "*: Burnett, *Letters*, v. 1, p. 537.
202 *"We must be . . . separately"*: Quoted in Van Doren, op. cit., p. 550.
202 *"I shall have . . . dead"*: Rush, *Letters*, v. 2, p. 1090.
202 *"God preserve . . . Storm?"*: Jefferson, *Papers*, v. 1, p. 468.
202 *"You will think . . . not"*: J. Adams, *Works*, v. 1, p. 231.
203 *Time has been . . . ago*: C. Adams, op. cit., p. 193.
203 *"celebrated . . . forevermore"*: Ibid., pp. 193–194.
203 *"The General hopes . . . country"*: Quoted in Cutter, op. cit., p. 221.
204 *"Perpetual itching . . . America"*: Quoted in McDowell, *Revolutionary War*, p. 91.
204 *"like a man . . . leprosy"*: Quoted in Montross, op. cit., p. 163.
204 *"Dickinson, Morris . . . union"*: Ibid.
204 *"The enemy are . . . me"*: Ibid.
205 *"Is it not . . . ones?"*: Ibid., p. 181.
205 *"No colony . . . herself"*: Quoted in Smith, op. cit., p. 281.
205 *"based upon . . . America"*: Ibid.

CHAPTER EIGHT: NEW YORK

Page 206 *"His coming . . . clouds"*: Quoted in Irving, op. cit., p. 267.
207 *"Of all . . . mercenaries"*: Quoted in Thomas, "'And When America Was Free,'" p. 175.
207 *"aid in restoring tranquillity"*: Fiske, *American Revolution*, v. 1, p. 202.
207 *"the etceteras . . . anything"*: Ibid., p. 203.
207 *"No doubt . . . found"*: Ibid., p. 204.
208 *"We resolve . . . paper"*: Burnett, *Letters*, v. 1, p. 455.
208 *"to prevail . . . harvests"*: Quoted in Bowers, op. cit., p. 160.

208 *"thought I . . . receding,"* etc.: Martin, op. cit., p. 16.
208 *"It made no . . . soon"*: Ibid., p. 15.
208 *"hard enough . . . rat"*: Ibid., p. 23.
209 *"the strangest . . . Crew"*: Tatum, *American Journal of Ambrose Serle*, p. 88.
209 *"such an entire . . . good"*: Ford, *Journals*, v. 5, p. 602.
210 *"Turks . . . Catholics"*: Quoted in Brown and Senior, op. cit., p. 124.
210 *"motley mob . . . jacktars"*: Quoted in Forbes, op. cit., p. 156.
210 *"the action . . . stream"*: Montross, op. cit., p. 134.
210 *"We have . . . resentment"*: Ibid., p. 135.
210 *"that the inhabitants . . . omission"*: Quoted in Montross, op. cit., p. 125.
211 *"a Test upon . . . operations"*: Ibid.
211 *"A universal . . . New England"*: Wheeler, op. cit., p. 126.
212 *"to admit . . . requisite,"* etc.: Quoted in Montross, op. cit., pp. 103–104.
213 *"The morning . . . sorrow"*: Vanderbilt, *Social History*, p. 370.
214 *"faithful . . . manservant"* and *"rushed . . . shout"*: Ibid.
214 *"all the Furniture . . . defaced"*: Quoted in Montross, op. cit., p. 168.
214 *"put all . . . resist"*: Wheeler, op. cit., p. 135.
214 *"to settle . . . encampments"*: Ibid., p. 137.
214 *"the atmosphere . . . too"*: Irving, op. cit., p. 273.
215 *"they could not . . . themselves"*: Fiske, *American Revolution*, v. 1, p. 211.
215 *"General Howe . . . dreadful"*: Wheeler, op. cit., p. 138.
215 *"It cannot . . . allied"*: Ibid.
215 *"to burn . . . full"*: Quoted in O'Brien, op. cit., p. 161.
215 *"Our situation . . . time"*: Wheeler, op. cit., p. 139.
215 *"for . . . mustard"*: Ibid.
216 *"to bear . . . make"*: C. Adams, op. cit., p. 223.
216 *"The window . . . colds' "*: J. Adams, *Works*, v. 3, pp. 75–76.
216 *"between lines . . . mutton"*: Ibid., pp. 77–78.
217 *"very favorably . . . crept in,"* etc.: Ibid., pp. 79–81.
217 *"His lordship . . . friends"*: Quoted in Van Doren, op. cit., p. 560.
217 *"produce more . . . men"*: Ibid., p. 561.
218 *"Britain, at the . . . America"*: Ibid., p. 535.
218 *"When an American . . . discussion?"*: Ibid., p. 561.
218 *"forces . . . force"*: Ibid.
218 *"in case be . . . same"*: Quoted in Montross, op. cit., p. 178.
219 *"Are these . . . America!"*: Quoted in Irving, op. cit., p. 280.
219 *"absolutely . . . away"*: Ibid.
219 *"The [Americans] had . . . filth"*: Bradley, *Journal of Nicholas Cresswell*, p. 245.
219 *"a misguided patriot"*: Quoted in Cutter, op. cit., p. 59.
219 *"that the rebels . . . firmness"*: Quoted in *Heroes*, p. 173.
220 *By your delay . . . endured*: Quoted in O'Brien, op. cit., p. 162.
221 *"Some suppose . . . army?"*: Quoted in Irving, op. cit., p. 285.
221 *"they left . . . fire"*: Wheeler, op. cit., p. 164.
221 *"I am wearied . . . expectation"*: Quoted in Conway, op. cit., p. 83.
222 *"All the shores . . . Equipage"*: Quoted in Silverman, op. cit., p. 327.
222 *"with all . . . war"*: Quoted in Irving, op. cit., p. 315.
222 *"I tremble . . . save it"*: Quoted in Conway, op. cit., p. 84.
223 *"pretended . . . increase disaffection"*: Quoted in Fiske, *Essays*, v. 1, p. 79.
223 *I do not mean . . . present*: Quoted in Irving, op. cit., p. 300.
223 *"O general! . . . importance"*: Ibid., p. 301.
224 *"Before the . . . insanity"*: Ibid., p. 303.
224 *"Affairs appear . . . treason"*: Ibid.
224 *"I lament . . . courage"*: Ibid., p. 307.
224 *"Dear Sir . . . to"*: Ibid.
225 *"I am in . . . Jerseys"*: Ibid., p. 318.
225 *"The ingenious . . . deficient"*: Quoted in Hudleston, op. cit., p. 180.
225 *"Here, sir . . . fire?"*: Wheeler, op. cit., p. 167.
225 *"with every . . . indignity"*: Quoted in Irving, op. cit., p. 324.
225 *"according to . . . war"*: Quoted in Montross, op. cit., p. 191.
226 *"Happy should I . . . not"*: Washington, *Writings* (Fitzpatrick, ed.), v. 5, p. 84.
226 *"I wish you . . . it?"*: Quoted in W. Randall, op. cit., p. 242.
226 *"A general . . . you"*: Ibid.

226 *"We have ordered . . . October":* Ibid.
227 *"With infinite . . . care":* Quoted in Sellers, op. cit., p. 110.
227 *"not an army . . . subordination":* Quoted in W. Randall, op. cit., p. 244.
227 *"We begin . . . us":* Quoted in Sellers, op. cit., p. 112.
227 *"with such . . . temerity":* Ibid., p. 118.
228 *"Great confusion . . . Satan":* Ibid., p. 130.
229 *"being entirely . . . service":* Quoted in Conway, op. cit., p. 84.
229 *"Ten days . . . army":* Quoted in Montross, op. cit., p. 193.
229 *"Our only dependence . . . up":* Quoted in Conway, op. cit., p. 84.
229 *"no lust . . . ploughshare":* Washington, *Writings* (Fitzpatrick ed.), v. 5, p. 114.
229 *"Congress never . . . posterity":* C. Adams, op. cit., p. 255.
230 *"safe from . . . bath":* Johnson, op. cit., p. 52.
230 *"Christmas-day . . . attempt":* Quoted in Conway, op. cit., p. 85.
230 *"These are . . . woman":* Paine, *The Crisis*, p. 1.
231 *"As I presented . . . the seal":* Quoted in Irving, op. cit., p. 331.
231 *"While Washington was . . . to Congress":* Ibid., p. 329.
231 *"stentorian lungs":* Wilkinson, *Memoirs*, v. 1, p. 188.
232 *"sparkled . . . storm":* Ibid.
232 *"What is . . . bayonet":* Quoted in Irving, op. cit., p. 173.
232 *" 'I don't know . . . tree' ":* Wilkinson, op. cit., v. 1, p. 189.
233 *"taking two . . . guns":* Ibid., p. 190.
233 *"Alle was . . . vorwerds!":* Quoted in Johnson, op. cit., p. 57.
234 *"on receipt . . . bounty":* Wilkinson, op. cit., v. 1, p. 191.
234 *"the troops should . . . repose":* Ibid., p. 192.
234 *"My Lord . . . morning!":* Ibid.
235 *"More effectually . . . enemy":* Ibid., p. 193.
235 *"The smoke . . . cloud":* Ibid., p. 195.
236 *"I understand . . . custody":* Quoted in Hudleston, op. cit., p. 87.
236 *"Britons ever . . . removed":* Ibid.
237 *"Since that time . . . placed":* Dring, *Recollections of the Jersey Prison-Ship*, p. 53.
237 *"the extraordinary . . . impunity":* Quoted in Irving, op. cit., p. 352.
237 *"a force of . . . them":* Bradley, *United Empire Loyalists*, p. 77.
238 *"give out . . . is":* Quoted in Cutter, op. cit., p. 276.
239 *"have been omitted . . . wanting":* Quoted in Sellers, op. cit., p. 142.
239 *"whether General . . . slight":* Quoted in W. Randall, op. cit., p. 328.
239 *Congress undoubtedly . . . intentions:* Quoted in Sellers, op. cit., p. 143.
240 *It is needless . . . in you:* Washington, *Writings* (Fitzpatrick ed.), v. 5, pp. 399–400.
241 *I know some . . . honour:* Quoted in Sellers, op. cit., p. 142.
241 *"I cannot . . . cleared":* Quoted in W. Randall, op. cit., p. 331.
241 *"chiefly down . . . long":* Sellers, op. cit., p. 145.
241 *"the town was . . . burnt":* Martin, op. cit., p. 63.
242 *"General Arnold's . . . ago":* Quoted in Sellers, op. cit., p. 150.
242 *"Money is this . . . country":* Quoted in W. Randall, op. cit., p. 334.
242 *"Conscious of . . . injured":* Quoted in Sellers, op. cit., p. 151.
242 *"I am wearied . . . nuts":* C. Adams, op. cit., p. 275.

CHAPTER NINE: SARATOGA

Page 244 *I John . . . rotten:* Quoted in Hudleston, op. cit., p. 11.
244 *"training men . . . stick":* Ibid.
244 *"the levities . . . life":* Ibid., p. 44.
244 *"I look upon . . . indulgence":* Ibid., p. 43.
244 *"For my part . . . step-mother":* Ibid.
245 *"two armies . . . half":* Ibid., p. 44.
245 *"the dirtiest . . . army":* Quoted in Urwin, op. cit., p. 12.
245 *"an extream . . . people":* Ibid.
245 *Everything here . . . through:* Quoted in Hudleston, op. cit., pp. 38–39.
246 *Accustomed to . . . infantry:* Ibid., p. 44.
246 *"General Carleton is . . . it":* Ibid., p. 167.
247 *"an intricate network . . . in Quebec":* Quoted in Calhoun, op. cit., p. 165.
247 *"hoped to bring . . . returned"* and *"Be not . . . parole":* Quoted in Hudleston, op. cit., p. 119.

248   "a runaway . . . Major": Ibid., p. 124.

248   "haversacks . . . queues": Ibid.

248   "he had upwards . . . time": Bradley, *Journal of Nicholas Cresswell*, p. 99.

248   "All the letters . . . you": Quoted in Hudleston, op. cit., p. 127.

248   "a paper handed . . . letter": Ibid., p. 135.

249   It is . . . easy prey: Thacher, *Military Journal*, p. 160.

249   "If the Government . . . Subordination": Quoted in Mika and Mika, *United Empire Loyalists*, p. 90.

249   Burgoyne, the King's . . . flew": Ibid., p. 156.

250   "to vindicate . . . Retreat": Ibid., p. 154.

251   "Where a goat . . . gun": Ibid., p. 157.

252   "We must away . . . one": Wilkinson, op. cit., p. 199.

252   "greatly distressed . . . fatigue": Thacher, op. cit., p. 175.

253   "I have beat . . . Americans": Quoted in Hudleston, op. cit., p. 157.

253   "I have the honor . . . amount": Quoted in Mika and Mika, op. cit., p. 94.

253   "How are all . . . away?" and "howsoever . . . exalted": C. Adams, op. cit., p. 285.

253   "I think we . . . unexpiated": Ibid., p. 292.

253   "The affair . . . conjecture": Quoted in Irving, op. cit., p. 374.

253   "The evacuation . . . again": Ibid., p. 377.

253   "they deemed . . . hands": Ibid., p. 386.

254   "I will venture . . . surmount": Quoted in Mintz, op. cit., p. 80.

254   "Ticonderoga reduced . . . operations": Quoted in Hudleston, op. cit., p. 163.

254   Though our affairs . . . anxiety: Quoted in Irving, op. cit., p. 390.

255   "I begin to . . . enemy": Ibid.

255   "I begin to . . . themselves": C. Adams, op. cit., p. 283.

255   "apparently so . . . power": Thacher, op. cit., p. 180.

255   "I trust you . . . command": Quoted in Irving, op. cit., p. 390.

255   "an active . . . officer": Ibid.

256   "it was with . . . length": Anburey, *Travels Through America*, v. 1, p. 233.

256   "The Indians . . . scalp": Thacher, op. cit., p. 199.

256   "a body of . . . extremities": Gage, op. cit., v. 1, p. 599.

257   "our brethren . . . Liberty": Ford, *Journals*, v. 3, p. 499.

257   "We need not . . . collect": Gage, op. cit., v. 1, p. 606.

257   "to take . . . America": Quoted in Hudleston, op. cit., p. 124.

257   "in order . . . importance": Burnett, *Letters*, v. 1, p. 466.

257   "After shaking . . . side' ": Quoted in Conway, op. cit., pp. 88–89.

258   "from the . . . lurk": Quoted in Mika and Mika, op. cit., p. 101.

258   "aged men . . . dead": Ibid.

258   "was just as . . . children' ": Quoted in O'Brien, op. cit., p. 17.

258   "We had sullied . . . fire-lock": Quoted in Hibbert, *Redcoats and Rebels*, p. 166.

258   "were much encouraged . . . anything": Ibid., p. 167.

258   "Were they left . . . prey": Quoted in Hudleston, op. cit., p. 162.

258   "a Negro man . . . them": Hibbert, op. cit., p. 172.

259   You mention . . . them: Quoted in Irving, op. cit., p. 391.

259   "selected from . . . fighting": Ibid., p. 394.

259   "try the . . . country": Quoted in Hudleston, op. cit., p. 166.

260   "Tonight our . . . widow!": Ibid., p. 204.

260   "Such an explosion . . . noise": Digby, *British Invasion from the North*, p. 274.

260   "207 dead . . . killed": Wheeler, op. cit., p. 204.

260   "a common . . . party": Quoted in Johnson, op. cit., p. 81.

260   "The New Hampshire . . . left": Quoted in Orton, op. cit., p. 71.

262   "The letter intended . . . sent": Quoted in Hudleston, op. cit., p. 116.

263   "Where the scourge . . . horses": Quoted in Bradley, *United Empire Loyalists*, p. 80.

264   "Our soldiers . . . way": C. Adams, op. cit., pp. 297–299.

264   "The officers drink . . . one' ": Ibid., pp. 305–307.

264   "1. Because there . . . Burgoyne": Ibid., p. 296.

265   "I could have . . . alone": Hargreaves, "The Man Who Almost Shot Washington," p. 64.

265   "You, sir . . . command": Quoted in *Heroes*, p. 34.

266   "in all . . . beheld": Quoted in Hibbert, op. cit., p. 159.

267   "had it in . . . morning": C. Adams, op. cit., p. 314.

267   "wrapping the whole . . . pall": Ketchum, *American Heritage Book of the American Revolution*, p. 99.

267 *"The enemy were . . . ground"*: Ibid., p. 73.
267 *"just returned . . . hour"*: Wheeler, op. cit., p. 229.
267 *"had we not . . . killed"*: Quoted in Johnson, op. cit., p. 67.
267 *"were not . . . Bayonets"*: Ibid.
267 *I met several . . . defeat:* Quoted in Conway, op. cit., p. 105.
268 *"Fortune smiled . . . us"*: Quoted in Irving, op. cit., p. 435.
268 *"Though the event . . . undertaking"*: Quoted in Johnson, p. 72.
268 *"the best designs . . . incidents"*: Quoted in Montross, op. cit., p. 212.
268 *"Don't bury . . . sons"*: Quoted in Wharton, op. cit., p. 178.
270 *"I perish . . . prince"*: Quoted in Greene, op. cit., p. 199.
270 *"were nothing . . . dirt"*: Martin, op. cit., p. 88.
270 *"waiting with impatience,"* etc.: Ibid., pp. 89–92.
271 *"I find daily . . . Howe"*: Wheeler, op. cit., p. 205.
271 *"Of the messengers . . . William"*: Ibid., p. 204.
271 *"When I wrote . . . operations"*: Quoted in Hudleston, op. cit., p. 175.
271 *"If you can . . . measure"*: Ibid., p. 178.
272 *"I am sensible . . . place"*: Quoted in Headley, op. cit., v. 2, p. 254.
272 *"I have done . . . labors"*: Quoted in W. Randall, op. cit., p. 351.
272 *"As Adjutant-General . . . wisdom"*: Sellers, op. cit., p. 108.
272 *"the wives . . . happen"* and *"The Americans . . . us"*: Riedesel, op. cit., p. 125.
273 *"who loved . . . he"*: Ibid., p. 128.
273 *"Britons never lose ground"*: Quoted in Riedesel, op. cit., p. 113.
273 *The British are . . . to?:* Quoted in Hibbert, op. cit., p. 184.
274 *"In this manner . . . sea"*: Wilkinson, op. cit., p. 225.
274 *"I was full . . . bowels"*: Riedesel, op. cit., p. 114.
275 *"as thick . . . scene"*: Quoted in Sellers, op. cit., p. 169.
275 *"no very great . . . day"*: Quoted in Hibbert, op. cit., p. 186.
275 *"To which I . . . Burgoyne"*: Quoted in Hudleston, op. cit., p. 191.
275 *"Many bodies . . . sand"*: Ibid., p. 192.
275 *"almost daily . . . lines"*: Wilkinson, op. cit., p. 229.
276 *Sir, Major . . . 1777:* Quoted in W. Randall, op. cit., p. 360.
276 *"condescend to acquaint . . . indignity"*: Ibid., p. 360.
276 *"Perhaps his despair . . . time"*: Quoted in Hudleston, op. cit., p. 185.
276 *Fort Montgomery . . . CLINTON:* Ibid., p. 193.
277 *"Could you . . . Albany?"*: Ibid., p. 194.
277 *"To my question . . . War!"*: Riedesel, op. cit., p. 116.
277 *"I returned . . . game'*: Wilkinson, op. cit., p. 235.
277 *"Do you see . . . die"*: Quoted in *Heroes,* p. 159.
277 *"You are singled . . . forbids it"*: Quoted in Irving, op. cit., p. 422.
277 *"I heard skirmishing . . . bowels"*: Riedesel, op. cit., p. 117.
278 *"It was very . . . freely"*: Wilkinson, op. cit., p. 240.
278 *"He was a bloody . . . him"*: Quoted in Johnson, op. cit., p. 81.
278 *"My chambermaid . . . other!' "*: Riedesel, op. cit., p. 121.
279 *"the greatest misery . . . prevailed"*: Ibid., p. 122.
279 *"everything was lost"*: Ibid., p. 124.
279 *"I laid myself . . . operation"*: p. 125.
279 *"hard toil . . . Gates:* Quoted in Mosely, *War in the North,* p. 233.
280 *"This article is . . . quarter"*: Morris, *Great Republic,* p. 214.
280 *"afterwards, the Americans . . . killed"*: Riedesel, op. cit., p. 133.
280 *"a great number . . . attachment"*: Silverman, op. cit., p. 331.
280 *"it was not . . . play"*: Ibid.
280 *"Not one . . . behold"*: Quoted in Davidson, op. cit., p. 324.
281 *"bestowed so much . . . warrior"*: Quoted in Morris, op. cit., p. 215.
281 *"General Gates . . . excellency' "*: Wilkinson, op. cit., p. 249.
281 *"extremely friendly . . . bread"*: Riedesel, op. cit., p. 134.
282 *Lieutenant General . . . Congress:* Quoted in Mosely, op. cit., p. 245.
282 *"General Gates . . . with"*: C. Adams, op. cit., p. 321.
282 *"Had the force . . . made"*: Quoted in Hudleston, op. cit., p. 257.
282 *"As soon as . . . number"*: Ibid.
283 *"Oh la! . . . Britainer"*: Anburey, op. cit., p. 250.
283 *"disrespectful by word . . . insult"*: Quoted in Hudleston, op. cit., p. 254.

283   *"The officers . . . broke":* Ibid., pp. 255–256.
284   *"That the embarkation . . . Congress":* Ford, *Journals,* v. 10, p. 30.
284   *"Unless great . . . Rebels?":* Quoted in Montross, op. cit., p. 220.
284   *"the news . . . stars":* Quoted in P. Smith, op. cit., p. 341.
284   *"a piece of . . . report":* Quoted in O'Brien, op. cit., p. 167.
284   *"delusive advantages . . . termination,"* etc.: Ibid.

CHAPTER TEN: VALLEY FORGE

Page 286   *"a strongly fortified place":* Quoted in Conway, op. cit., p. 109.
287   *"a dreary . . . provided":* Scheer and Rankin, op. cit., p. 304.
287   *"I will share . . . inconvenience":* Quoted in Lossing, op. cit., p. 167.
287   *"The General . . . now":* Ibid., p. 165.
287   *"The [soldiers] . . . together":* Quoted in Conway, op. cit., p. 110.
287   *"to discharge . . . camp":* Thacher, op. cit., p. 225.
287   *"Our prospect . . . persevere":* Martin, op. cit., p. 102.
288   *"by force . . . earth":* Ibid., p. 103.
288   *"upon a rock . . . it":* Ibid.
288   *"in their own . . . English":* C. Adams, op. cit., p. 323.
289   *"I do not . . . dissolve":* Quoted in Irving, op. cit., p. 451.
289   *"Since . . . quartermaster-general":* Ibid., p. 453.
289   as much as if . . . Calumny": Quoted in Preacher, *Song of Freedom,* p. 333.
289   *"Take an impartial . . . beam":* Quoted in Montross, op. cit., p. 215.
290   *"The powerful . . . depreciated":* Ibid., p. 225.
290   *"The Congress . . . discretion":* Ibid.
290   I am sick . . . spew: Waldo, "Diary," p. 306.
290   *"one of the . . . life!":* Ibid., p. 313.
291   *"For some days . . . desertion":* Washington, *Writings* (Fitzpatrick ed.), v. 10, p. 469.
291   *"No pay! . . . rum!":* Quoted in Freeman, *Washington* (one-volume ed.), p. 374.
291   *"framed, planked . . . fraised":* Irving, op. cit., p. 448.
292   *"Speculations . . . virtue":* Quoted in Bradley, *United Empire Loyalists,* p. 85.
292   *"The Love of . . . man?":* Quoted in Montross, op. cit., p. 225.
292   *"The Avarice . . . Peru":* Ibid.
292   *"to subsist . . . vicinity":* Ibid., p. 223.
292   *"delicacy . . . America":* Ibid.
292   *"Such procedures . . . afterward":* Quoted in Irving, op. cit., p. 454.
293   *"an instinct for renown":* Quoted in Woodward, *Lafayette,* p. 29.
293   *"The welfare . . . liberty":* Ibid., p. 33.
294   *"He [Lovell] . . . them' ":* Ibid., p. 13.
294   *"You cannot . . . language":* Quoted in Hudleston, op. cit., p. 133.
295   *"high birth . . . provinces":* Quoted in Perkins, *France in the American Revolution,* p. 177.
295   The Marquis . . . nation: Quoted in Woodward, op. cit., p. 17.
295   *"We are rather . . . France":* Ibid., p. 22.
295   *"I am here . . . teach":* Ibid.
296   What the designs . . . them: Ibid.
296   *"silent disposition"* and *"singular . . . age":* Quoted in Johnston, *Yorktown Campaign,* p. 32n.
296   *"I was deeply . . . Understanding":* Quoted in Mintz, op. cit., p. 89.
296   *"That inestimable . . . him":* Quoted in Woodward, op. cit., p. 52.
296   *"I am established . . . cordiality":* Quoted in Johnston, op. cit., p. 31.
296   *"Treat him . . . son":* Quoted in Woodward, op. cit., p. 50.
297   *"I do not . . . Court":* Ibid., p. 18.
297   *"the professor . . . age":* Greene, *The German Element,* p. 93.
298   *"There is . . . kind!":* Scheer and Rankin, op. cit., p. 296.
298   Upon so interesting . . . place: Washington, *Writings* (Fitzpatrick ed.), v. 9, p. 388.
299   By this opportunity . . . fact: Quoted in Irving, op. cit., p. 443.
299   *"We want you . . . breeches":* Ibid., p. 448.
299   *"This is only . . . Burgoyne":* Ibid., p. 445.
300   *"Many country . . . people":* Waldo, op. cit., pp. 312–313.
300   The Assembly . . . destroyed: Thacher, op. cit., p. 230.
301   You have saved . . . you: Quoted in Irving, op. cit., p. 446.

301   *"I have been . . . army"*: Burnett, *Letters,* v. 2, p. 263.
301   *"Congress will . . . savior"*: C. Adams, op. cit., pp. 322–323.
302   *"If you were lost . . . conquer"*: Quoted in Woodward, op. cit., p. 62.
302   *"I found . . . power"*: Ibid., p. 63.
302   *Sir: A letter . . . Washington:* Washington, *Writings* (Fitzpatrick ed.), v. 10, p. 29.
303   *I spoke my mind . . . you:* Scheer and Rankin, op. cit., p. 296.
303   *"The perplexity . . . guilt"*: Ibid.
303   *"If General Conway . . . appointment"*: Washington, *Writings* (Fitzpatrick ed.), v. 10, p. 249.
303   *"There is scarcely . . . pocket"*: Quoted in Irving, op. cit., p. 458.
303   *"As a public . . . sercret"*: Ibid.
304   *Your letter . . . mistaken"*: Washington, *Writings* (Fitzpatrick ed.), vol. 10, pp. 264–265.
304   *"The letter . . . purposes"*: Quoted in Irving, op. cit., p. 464.
304   *"The morning . . . resign"*: Ibid., p. 460.
304   *"We have only . . . country"*: Quoted in Tyler, op. cit., p. 244.
305   *"This man . . . you"*: Ibid., p. 250.
305   *"Were it necessary . . . faction"*: Washington, *Writings* (Fitzpatrick ed.), v. 10, pp. 440–441.
305   *"I was too . . . speak"*: Quoted in Irving, op. cit., p. 473.
306   *"acts of . . . falsehood"*: Quoted in Woodward, op. cit., p. 63.
306   *"Why do you not fire?,"* etc.: Quoted in *Heroes,* p. 128.
306   *"I have stopped . . . rate"*: Quoted in Woodward, op. cit., p. 64.
306   *"Sir, I find . . . CONWAY"*: Quoted in *Heroes,* p. 131.
306   *"I am as averse . . . injurious"*: Washington, *Writings* (Fitzpatrick ed.), v. 10 pp. 508–509.
307   *"But why should . . . error"*: Washington, *Writings* (Ford ed.), v. 6, pp. 353–354.
307   *I cannot precisely . . . themselves:* Quoted in Tyler, op. cit., p. 250.
307   *"I beg . . . Howe"*: Quoted in Lossing, op. cit., p. 175.
308   *"You can have . . . gentlemen"*: Scheer and Rankin, op. cit., p. 318.
308   *"proper allowances . . . for"*: Ibid., p. 319.
308   *Awake, awake . . . spear:* Quoted in Silverman, op. cit., p. 335.
308   *"a very handsome . . . reckless"*: Quoted in Callahan, p. 110.
309   *"illustrious courtesan"*: Jones, *History of New York,* v. 2, p. 86n.
309   *"Nothing seemed to . . . Loring"*: Ibid., v. 1, p. 351.
309   *Sir William . . . Loring:* Quoted in Silverman, op. cit., p. 336.
309   *"[Howe] shut . . . whore"*: Quoted in Hudleston, op. cit., p. 180.
309   *"a handsome . . . song"*: Palmer, *General von Steuben,* p. 88.
309   *"excellent . . . instant"*: Waldo, op. cit., p. 311.
309   *"a tall Indian . . . Italienne"*: Scheer and Rankin, op. cit., p. 310.
310   *"whole broadsides . . . arms"*: Moore, *Diary of the American Revolution,* p. 532.
310   *"he could . . . reorganize"*: Steele, op. cit., p. 37.
311   *"riot in . . . frivolities"*: Steele, *American Campaigns,* p. 37.
311   *"Although some . . . severity"*: Wheeler, op. cit., p. 263.
311   *"Sir William . . . commander"*: Quoted in Hudleston, op. cit., p. 66.
311   *"He had . . . conviviality"*: Ibid.
312   *"directed his men . . . one round"*: Urwin, op. cit., p. 26.
312   *"No one could . . . calculations"*: Bradley, *United Empire Loyalists,* p. 72.
312   *"No other . . . together as he did"*: Jones, op. cit., v. 1, p. 333.

CHAPTER ELEVEN: "NABOUR AGAINST NABOUR"

Page 314   *"Nabour was against Nabour"*: Quoted in Brown and Senior, op. cit., p. 19.
314   *"I was happy . . . Mind"*: Quoted in Smith, op. cit., p. 205.
315   *"O Lord . . . issue"*: Quoted in R. Wright, op. cit., p. 290.
315   *"O Lord . . . band"*: Ibid.
315   *"There are too . . . front"*: Ibid., p. 292.
316   *"that Great . . . rank"*: Ibid., p. 291.
316   *"to join in . . . tumults"*: Quoted in Calhoon, op. cit., p. 199.
316   *"were willing to sell . . . Pietist sects"*: Ibid.
316   *"upon what side . . . victory"*: Ibid.
317   *"the dawn of . . . Liberty"* and *"tyrant"*: Quoted in Brown and Senior, op. cit., p. 12.
317   *"blackest . . . war"*: Ibid., p. 5.
317   *"The Eyes . . . army"*: Ibid., p. 6.

317 *"My inducement . . . Order":* Ibid.
317 *"The most . . . characters":* Ibid.
317 *"The plot . . . Tea-Act":* Ibid.
318 *"the most ardent . . . colonies":* Ibid., p. 7.
318 *"a state of . . . security":* Quoted in Calhoon, op. cit., p. 135.
318 *"led down . . . rebellion":* Ibid.
318 *"The annals . . . rebellion":* Ibid.
318 *"we are . . . troops":* Quoted in Brown and Senior, op. cit., p. 12.
318 *"inclined to . . . and security":* Quoted in Calhoon, op. cit., p. 143.
319 *"either . . . first":* Quoted in Brown and Senior, op. cit., p. 12.
319 *"more concerned . . . administration":* Quoted in Calhoon, op. cit., p. 200.
319 *"infinitely more . . . force":* Quoted in Brown and Senior, op. cit., p. 12.
319 *"men struggled . . . blood":* Forbes, op. cit., p. 127.
319 *"their faces blacked . . . hands":* Ibid., p. 179.
319 *"as the enemies . . . liberty":* Quoted in Calhoon, op. cit., p. 195.
319 *"it would be futile,"* etc.: Ibid.
320 *"As My comfort . . . ask":* Ibid.
320 *"implore the . . . esteem":* Ibid.
320 *"a cleansing force":* Ibid.
320 *"anyone who . . . cause,":* Adlum, op. cit., pp. 6–9.
321 *"Well, Mr. Sower . . . sauce":* Quoted in Callahan, *Flight from the Republic,* p. 113.
322 *"She made no . . . sight":* Quoted in Dorson, op. cit., p. 107.
322 *"Pennsylvania . . . civil war":* Quoted in Calhoon, op. cit., p. 200.
322 *"he conceived . . . neutrality":* Ibid., p. 199.
322 *"No such state":* etc.: Ibid.
322 *"just and . . . British":* Quoted in Forbes, op. cit., p. 324.
322 *"to frustrate the . . . men":* Ford, *Journals,* v. 4, pp. 19–20.
322 *"confiscate . . . certificates":* Ibid., v. 19, p. 971.
323 *"One [person] . . . debts":* Quoted in Brown and Senior, op. cit., p. 16.
323 *"the infamous . . . theft":* Quoted in Cutter, op. cit., p. 262.
323 *"From every colony . . . lines":* Van Tyne, *Loyalists in the American Revolution,* p. 33.
323 *"It brings . . . property":* Bradley, *Journal of Nicholas Cresswell,* p. 244.
325 *"The rebellion . . . enterprise":* Quoted in Calhoon, op. cit., p. 158.

CHAPTER TWELVE: MONMOUTH

Page 326 *"mixed with . . . Parties":* Quoted in Martin, op. cit., p. 118n.
326 *"as the instrument . . . peoples":* Boorstin, op. cit., p. 356.
327 *"Our inn-keeper . . . colonels":* Quoted in Davidson, op. cit., p. 324.
327 *"Our Militia . . . authority":* Quoted in Boorstin, op. cit., p. 366.
327 *"The militia come in . . . moment":* Quoted in Bradley, *United Empire Loyalists,* p. 78.
327 *"patrolled the coastline . . . tide of the war":* Urwin, op. cit., p. 16.
327 *To place any . . . reigns:* Quoted in Cutter, op. cit., p. 260.
328 *"There was not . . . troops":* Martin, op. cit., p. 134.
328 *"I have labored . . . brigadiers?":* Quoted in Boorstin, op. cit., p. 367.
328 *"that all Troops . . . North America":* Quoted in Boorstin, *Colonial Experience,* p. 366.
329 *"Not an hour . . . precedence":* Ibid., p. 366.
329 *"If in all . . . both":* Ibid., p. 367.
329 *"desperate men . . . at war's end":* Urwin, op. cit., p. 34.
329 *"They were . . . slaves":* Urwin, op. cit., p. 32.
329 *"a noticeable . . . Line":* Urwin, op. cit., p. 32.
329 *"nearly hard . . . flints":* Martin, op. cit., p. 23.
329 *"Here, eat . . . soldier":* Ibid., p. 43.
329 *"Men may speculate . . . Interest":* Quoted in R. Smith, op. cit., p. 16.
329 *"To see men . . . paralleled":* Washington, *Writings* (Fitzpatrick ed.), v. 11, pp. 291–292.
330 *"Now it is . . . fight":* Quoted in Boorstin, *Colonial Experience,* p. 345.
330 *"on large open . . . rules":* Ibid., p. 347.
331 *"depended . . . it took":* Quoted in Urwin, op. cit., p. 26.
331 *"at least . . . hundred":* Adlum, op. cit., p. 54.
331 *"taking into . . . were fired":* Ibid.
331 *"to propel . . . line":* Urwin, op. cit., p. 26.

518 Notes

331 *"[The baron] appears . . . world"*: Quoted in Palmer, *General von Steuben*, p. 112.
332 *"is the Baron,"* etc.: Quoted in Van Doren, op. cit., p. 580.
332 *"My greatest ambition . . . you"*: Quoted in Palmer, op. cit., pp. 114–115.
332 *"I have no . . . pistols!"*: Ibid., p. 140.
332 *"Never before . . . idea"*: Quoted in Palmer, op. cit., p. 136.
334 *"The words company . . . book"*: Quoted in Woodward, op. cit., p. 56.
334 *"each colonel . . . own"*: Ibid.
334 *"My good . . . prejudices"*: Quoted in Palmer, op. cit., p. 157.
334 *"is not in . . . it' "*: Ibid.
335 *"To see a . . . men"*: Ibid., pp. 154–155.
335 *"when some . . . performed"*: Scheer and Rankin, op. cit., p. 308.
335 *"Ah, madam . . . was"*: Quoted in Greene, op. cit., p. 87.
336 *"utter confusion and dismay"*: Scheer and Rankin, op. cit., p. 312.
336 *"each regiment on its own parade"* and *"with as much . . . company"*: Quoted in Palmer, op. cit., p. 157.
336 *"till the pleasure . . . obvious"*: Ibid.
336 *"There is not . . . knot"*: Quoted in *Heroes*, p. 36.
337 *"urging him . . . his family"*: Quoted in P. Smith, op. cit., p. 286.
337 *"as if . . . brother"*: Boudinot, *Journal of Historical Recollections*, p. 77.
337 *"the next morning . . . that night"*: Ibid., pp. 77–78.
338 *"General Washington . . . guard"*: Ibid., p. 78.
338 *"confess their . . . people"*: Quoted in Montross, op. cit., p. 223.
338 *"swelling and . . . Schuylkill"*: Wheeler, op. cit., p. 260.
338 *"with loud huzzas . . . times"*: Scheer and Rankin, op. cit., p. 317.
338 *The day serene . . . there*: Ibid., p. 313.
339 *"I know that . . . never!"*: Quoted in Montross, op. cit., p. 231.
339 *"Be very sure . . . conjunction"*: Quoted in O'Brien, op. cit., p. 158.
339 *"All Europe . . . patience"*: Quoted in P. Smith, *John Adams*, v. 1, p. 323.
340 *"a dull melancholy . . . assembly"*: Quoted in O'Brien, op. cit., p. 170.
340 *"little passed . . . dismissed"*: Quoted in Hudleston, op. cit., p. 50.
341 *"as a . . . terms"*: Ford, *Journals*, v. 10, pp. 375–376.
341 *"lull you . . . designs"*: Ibid., v. 11, p. 475.
341 *"The subjugation . . . question"*: Quoted in Greene, op. cit., p. 148.
341 *"It is impossible . . . it"*: Quoted in Montross, op. cit., p. 239.
342 *"twenty-four black . . . ground"*: Quoted in Lossing, *The Two Spies*, p. 58.
342 *"The exhibition . . . consequence"*: Jones, op. cit., v. 2, p. 44.
343 *"Our Enemies . . . it"*: Serle, *American Journal*, p. 266.
343 *"to obstruct . . . designs"*: Quoted in Woodward, op. cit., p. 65.
343 *"You will . . . surprise"*: Ibid.
344 *"the rebels . . . take"*: Wheeler, op. cit., p. 294.
344 *"the primum . . . detachment"*: Scheer and Rankin, op. cit., p. 328.
344 *"when the front . . . off"*: Quoted in Johnson, op. cit., p. 93.
344 *"better . . . circumstances"*: Ibid.
345 *"did not need . . . stay"*: Martin, op. cit., p. 126.
345 *"individual units . . . themselves"*: Quoted in Johnson, op. cit., p. 96.
345 *"Tell the General . . . enough"*: Scheer and Rankin, op. cit., p. 329.
345 *"it was almost . . . breathe"*: Martin, op. cit., p. 126.
345 *"What is the meaning,"* etc.: Boller, *Presidential Anecdotes*, p. 11.
345 *"swore on . . . trees"*: Scheer and Rankin, op. cit., p. 331.
345 *"He remained . . . him"*: Martin, op. cit., p. 127.
346 *"amid the shouts . . . fight"*: Scheer and Rankin, op. cit., p. 331.
346 *"while in the . . . occupation"*: Ibid., p. 333.
346 *"Tell the Philadelphia . . . Monmouth"*: Quoted in Preacher, op. cit., p. 100.
347 *"It is not . . . [fact]"*: Quoted in Martin, op. cit., p. 134.
347 *"so much altered . . . waste"*: Scheer and Rankin, op. cit., p. 326.
347 *"it is agreed . . . prostitutes"*: Ibid., p. 327.
347 *"Here it is . . . taste"*: Quoted in W. Randall, op. cit., p. 418.
348 *"a noted . . . officer"*: Scheer and Rankin, op. cit., p. 327.
349 *"mere Adventurer . . . Grammar"*: Quoted in Mintz, op. cit., p. 120.
349 Camp, English-Town . . . Washington: Quoted in *Heroes*, pp. 191–192.
350 Head-quarters . . . *WASHINGTON*: Washington, *Writings* (Fitzpatrick ed.), vol. 12, pp. 132–133.

350   "You cannot afford . . . army," etc.: Quoted in *Heroes*, pp. 195–196.
351   "I desire . . . dead": Ibid., p. 199.
351   "Stand . . . grenadiers": Ibid., p. 196.

CHAPTER THIRTEEN: FROM NEWPORT TO STONY POINT

Page 356   "laughable . . . pattern": Wheeler, op. cit., p. 272.
357   "If the garrison . . . away": Quoted in Irving, op. cit., p. 487.
358   "Prudence dictates . . . matter": Washington, *Writings* (Fitzpatrick ed.), vol. 12, p. 369.
358   "afford a bealing . . . made": Quoted in Woodward, op. cit., p. 72.
358   "more than . . . allies": Quoted in Perkins, op. cit., p. x.
359   "I beared . . . slavery": Quoted in Brodie, op. cit., p. 127.
359   "We want . . . you": Ibid., p. 128.
359   "It was found . . . free": Quoted in Bowers, op. cit., p. 175.
359   "that no man . . . character": Ibid., p. 212.
360   "Almighty God . . . debate": Quoted in Brodie, op. cit., p. 129.
360   "unhappy disposition" and "prejudices and passions": Nagle, *Lees of Virginia*, p. 107.
360   "His countenance . . . wrong": Ibid.
360   "sick mind . . . insanity": Ibid., p. 109.
360   "indolent . . . needs": Perkins, op. cit., p. 449.
360   "The Life . . . bairs": Quoted in P. Smith, *John Adams*, v. 1, p. 377.
360   "obtain the . . . company": Ibid.
361   "The delights . . . please": C. Adams, op. cit., p. 329.
361   "If human . . . believe": Ibid., p. 330.
361   "character more beloved . . . age": Quoted in Van Doren, op. cit., p. 600.
361   "Our affairs . . . equivalent": Quoted in P. Smith, *John Adams*, v. 1, p. 388.
361   "on baving bis . . . sum": Quoted in Conway, op. cit., p. 146.
362   "The local . . . riches": Scheer and Rankin, op. cit., p. 356.
362   "the demon . . . fortune-making": Quoted in Nagle, op. cit., p. 110.
362   "Can we carry . . . forestallers": Washington, *Writings* (Fitzpatrick ed.), vol. 13, pp. 21–22.
362   "If I was . . . roused": Ibid., pp. 466–468.
363   "We bad a . . . frisk": Scheer and Rankin, op. cit., p. 358.
363   "We spend . . . army": Ibid.
363   "BY YOUR TYRANNY . . . empire": Quoted in Lossing, *Mary and Martha*, p. 181.
364   "THOSE WHO . . . FOREVER": Ibid., p. 182.
364   "to prevent . . . possible": Scheer and Rankin, op. cit., p. 360.
365   "as large . . . state": Wheeler, op. cit., p. 294.
365   "The British . . . treatment": Ibid.
365   "all the small . . . shore": Ibid., p. 295.
365   "Should America . . . indeed": Quoted in O'Brien, op. cit., p. 208.
365   "appeared . . . arms": Quoted in Forbes, op. cit., p. 355.
365   "a soldier with . . . them": Ibid.
365   "To attempt . . . conceived": Ibid.
366   "Should there be . . . belongs": Stillé, *Major-General Anthony Wayne*, p. 181.
366   "15 July . . . carnage": Ibid.
366   "guided . . . manner": Irving, op. cit., p. 501.
367   "Carry me . . . free": Wheeler, op. cit., p. 296.
367   Spurred on . . . thyself: Scheer and Rankin, op. cit., p. 363.
367   "The bumanity . . . killed": Quoted in Irving, op. cit., p. 502.
367   "a dry rag . . . meat": Quoted in Greene, *German Element*, p. 150.
368   "Large round . . . meals": Ibid.
368   "[Washington] received . . . nation: Chase, op. cit., pp. 113–114.
369   "The general . . . knowledge": Ibid., p. 114.
369   "came right . . . roar": Ibid., p. 115.
369   "Washington," be recalled . . . son' ": Ibid., p. 116.
370   "I have a . . . you": Washington, *Writings* (Fitzpatrick ed.), v. 16, p. 372.
370   Tell [your wife] . . . man: Ibid., pp. 375–376.

CHAPTER FOURTEEN: FROM SAVANNAH TO VINCENNES

Page 371   "all America . . . duty": Quoted in Johnston, op. cit., p. 18.
372   "vigorous campaign . . . enterprise": Quoted in Calhoon, op. cit., p. 158.

372 *"gallant to . . . another"*: Quoted in W. Randall, op. cit., p. 459.
372 *"I have thus . . . rebellion"*: Scheer and Rankin, op. cit., p. 392.
373 *"drove them . . . woods"*: Wheeler, op. cit., p. 286.
373 *"the capital . . . dark"*: Ibid., p. 287.
373 *"Never was . . . loss"*: Ibid.
373 *"and the French . . . submission"*: Quoted in Calhoon, op. cit., p. 158.
373 *"distressing . . . sufferings"*: Quoted in Calhoon, op. cit., p. 158.
373 *"the metropolis . . . follow"*: Ibid.
374 *"for a long . . . Shamokin"*: Quoted in P. Smith, *New Age Begins*, v. 2, p. 1157.
374 *the enemy . . . treated*: Wheeler, op. cit., p. 282.
375 *"The man who . . . unequal"*: Scheer and Rankin, op. cit., p. 351.
375 *"impetuosity . . . more"*: Quoted in Smith, *New Age Begins*, pp. 1163–1164.
375 *"merely overrun but destroyed"*: Scheer and Rankin, op. cit., p. 351.
375 *"like cutthroats, all"*: Quoted in Lossing, *Mary and Martha*, p. 185.
376 *"I cannot but . . . hardships"*: Quoted in Smith, *New Age Begins*, p. 1165.
376 *"very large . . . miles"*: Ibid., p. 1170.
377 *"so mad . . . spies"*: Scheer and Rankin, op. cit., p. 346.
377 *"Thus insensibly . . . before"*: Ibid.
378 *"One of them . . . thrown in"*: Ibid., p. 347.
378 *"spoke with . . . hands"*: Ibid.
379 *"Having been . . . shore"*: Wheeler, op. cit., p. 315.
379 *"was filled . . . dead"*: Scheer and Rankin, op. cit., p. 395.

Chapter Fifteen: Flamborough Head

Page 380 *"It is the . . . Continent"* and *"Why should . . . condit"*: Morison, *John Paul Jones*, p. 33.
381 *"for the protection . . . Colonies"*: Quoted in Morrison, op. cit., p. 34.
381 *"in action . . . fire"*: Quoted in Dorson, op. cit., p. 93.
382 *"That the inhabitants . . . Colonies"*: Ford, *Journals*, v. 4, p. 230.
382 *"so heavily . . . vessel"*: Morison, op. cit., p. 32.
382 *"Prizes are . . . afloat"*: C. Adams, op. cit., p. 208.
382 *"antique character"*: Quoted in Morison, op. cit., p. 41.
382 *"the Enemie's . . . destroy"*: Ibid.
383 *"which carried . . . tye"*: Fanning, *Memoirs*, p. 200.
383 *"What cutter . . . course"*: Ibid.
384 *"to Seize . . . destroy"*: Quoted in Morison, op. cit., p. 54.
384 *"the private . . . Fleet"*: Ibid., p. 65.
385 *"officered . . . Commission"*: Ibid., p. 109.
385 *"our Infant . . . relieved"*: Ibid., p. 92.
385 *"It appears . . . Ocean"*: Ibid., p. 94.
385 *"I fancy . . . booty"*: Ibid., p. 92.
386 *"made very . . . liquor"*: Ibid., p. xviii.
386 *"behaved . . . civility"*: Ibid.
386 *Tho' I have . . . bed*: Ibid., pp. 149–150.
387 *"to attack . . . Kingdom"*: Ibid., p. 134.
387 *"His voice . . . it"*: Ibid., p. 201.
387 *From the intrepid . . . skin*: Ibid., p. 278.
388 *"take a . . . Française"*: Ibid., p. 200.
388 *"Perhaps both . . . Comédie"*: Quoted in Smith, *John Adams*, v. 1, pp. 429–430.
388 *"with a little . . . palatable"*: Ibid., p. 203.
388 *"only . . . discharged"*: Ibid.
388 *"perfectly smooth . . . millpond"*: Ibid., p. 229.
388 *"What ship is . . . shot!"*: Ibid., p. 240.
389 *"The battle . . . it"*: Ibid., p. 230.
389 *"such that . . . touched"*: Ibid., p. 232.
389 *"lost his nerve"*: Morison, op. cit., p. 237.
389 *"It is with . . . neck!"*: Quoted in Fanning, op. cit., p. 47.
389 *"Sir, you have . . . it"*: Ibid.
390 *"Very well . . . us"*: Ibid., p. 48.
390 *"A person . . . consequences"*: Quoted in Morison, op. cit., p. 238.
390 *"to appall . . . heaven"*: Fanning, op. cit., p. 52.

390 *"Scarce anything . . . Bravery":* Quoted in Morison, op. cit., p. 250.
390 *"The cry of . . . strong":* Ibid., p. 250.
390 *"Judge if I . . . nation!":* Quoted in Woodward, op. cit., p. 79.
391 *"whatever share . . . us":* Quoted in Morison, op. cit., p. 188.

CHAPTER SIXTEEN: FROM MORRISTOWN TO CHARLESTON

Page 393 *"every kind . . . bay":* Quoted in Lossing, *Mary and Martha,* pp. 191–192.
393 *"We were . . . little dog":* Martin, op. cit., p. 368.
393 *"Yankees [are] . . . starch":* Ibid., p. 175.
393 *"I cherish . . . ages":* Quoted in Palmer, op. cit., p. 100.
393 *"upon a bare . . . snow":* Martin, op. cit., p. 170.
394 *"affable . . . War":* Quoted in Lossing, *Mary and Martha,* p. 150.
394 *"We expected . . . them":* Ibid., p. 193.
394 *"Certain I am . . . advantage:* Washington, *Writings* (Fitzpatrick ed.), v. 18, p. 453.
395 *"monopolizers, forestallers . . . ruin":* Ibid., v. 12, p. 383.
395 *"I assure you . . . sedition":* Quoted in Conway, op. cit., p. 157.
395 *"Their complaints are . . . true":* Thacher, op. cit., p. 285.
396 *"were brought . . . doom":* Ibid., p. 286.
396 *"He appeared . . . eternity:* Ibid., pp. 287–288.
396 *"I have almost . . . better":* Quoted in Irving, op. cit., p. 514.
396 *The present . . . persist:* Ibid., p. 515.
397 *"Britain's boasted . . . nation":* Quoted in Montross, op. cit., p. 310.
397 *"a very . . . Europe":* Scheer and Rankin, op. cit., pp. 390–391.
398 *"to hold . . . extremity":* Scheer and Rankin, op. cit., p. 397.
398 *"a tremendous . . . capitulated:* Moultrie, *Memoirs,* v. 2, pp. 96–97.
399 *"with the horrid . . . demons":* Scheer and Rankin, op. cit., p. 402.
399 *"perceiving that . . . life":* Ibid.
399 *"One hundred . . . forgot":* Wheeler, op. cit., p. 329.
400 *The conquest . . . submission:* Quoted in Calhoon, op. cit., p. 156.
401 *The series . . . heart:* Scheer and Rankin, op. cit., p. 404.
401 *"strong by nature . . . art":* Greene, *German Element,* p. 161.
401 *"We have . . . face":* Ibid.
402 *"The impetuosity . . . consternation":* Scheer and Rankin, op. cit., p. 407.
402 *"Was there ever . . . flight?":* Scheer and Rankin, op. cit., p. 410.
402 *"The victory is . . . here":* Ibid., p. 412.
403 *"I solemnly . . . over-powered":* Quoted in Boorstin, *Colonial Experience,* p. 369.
404 *"quite charmed . . . another":* Scheer and Rankin, op. cit., p. 378.
404 *"We could only . . . events":* Scheer and Rankin, op. cit., p. 379.
404 *"treason . . . dye":* Quoted in Irving, op. cit., p. 528.

CHAPTER SEVENTEEN: WEST POINT

Page 405 *"inveterate schemer":* Silverman, op. cit., p. 288.
405 *"for any deeds . . . superior":* Quoted in Sellers, op. cit., p. 93.
405 *"money . . . country":* Ibid., p. 135.
406 *April 8th . . . soul:* Ibid., p. 186.
406 *"Had I imagined . . . Bosom":* Ibid., pp. 190–191.
408 *"Scarcely one . . . fair one":* Ibid., p. 203.
408 *"a slim and . . . man":* Ibid.
408 *"Twenty times . . . soul":* Ibid., pp. 204–205.
410 *"You will take . . . other":* Quoted in W. Randall, op. cit., p. 418.
410 *"You must know . . . Presence":* Sellers, op. cit., p. 210.
410 *"to suppress . . . manners":* Ford, *Journals,* v. 12, p. 1001.
410 *"that the right . . . him":* Quoted in Sellers, op. cit., p. 209.
411 *"I wish . . . in":* Ibid., p. 216.
411 *"I little . . . coin":* Quoted in Montross, op. cit., p. 274.
411 *"to render . . . individuals":* Quoted in W. Randall, op. cit., p. 469.
411 *"no public . . . attempt":* Ibid., p. 454.
412 *"Accept a command . . . guineas":* Ibid., p. 473.
412 *"self-invited . . . presence":* Ibid., p. 470.

412 *Mr. President . . . service:* Ibid., p. 487.
413 *Our profession . . . country:* Washington, *Writings* (Fitzpatrick ed.), v. 18, p. 225.
414 *"I am convinced . . . it":* Quoted in W. Randall, op. cit., p. 505.
414 *"We make ourselves . . . glee":* Quoted in Sellers, op. cit., p. 232.
414 *"I shall be . . . secret":* Quoted in W. Randall, op. cit., p. 532.
415 *Why, soldiers . . . again:* Quoted in Sellers, op. cit., p. 233.
415 *"I found him . . . war":* Wheeler, op. cit., p. 344.
416 *"I hope . . . party,"* etc.: Scheer and Rankin, op. cit., p. 381.
416 *"You never saw . . . me!' ":* Quoted in W. Randall, op. cit., p. 554.
417 *"The impropriety . . . cause":* Ibid., p. 557.
417 *"he looked at . . . now?' ":* Sellers, op. cit., p. 242.
417 *"her clothing . . . face":* Ibid., p. 243.
417 *"The enemy . . . posts":* Quoted in Irving, op. cit., p. 528.
417 *"Transactions . . . discovered":* Ibid.
418 *Treason . . . dispute:* Washington, *Writings* (Fitzpatrick ed.), v. 20, pp. 95–96.
418 *On Board . . . Arnold:* Quoted in W. Randall, op. cit., p. 560.
419 *"became . . . fate":* Tallmadge, *Memoir,* p. 88.
419 *"staggered . . . resolution":* *Heroes,* p. 39.
419 *"Andre is either . . . free:* Ibid., p. 40.
420 *"Remember . . . blood":* Quoted in Sellers, op. cit., p. 245.
420 *"When the hour . . . arm:* Thacher, op. cit., pp. 222–223.
420 *"I am reconciled . . . pang' ":* Ibid., p. 223.
420 *"I pray you . . . man":* Ibid.
420 *"Andre has met . . . remorse":* Washington, *Writings* (Fitzpatrick ed.), v. 20, p. 173.
421 *"They may be . . . neglect":* Quoted in W. Randall, op. cit., p. 575.
421 *"The loss of . . . honour":* Quoted in Sellers, op. cit., p. 249.
421 *"Noisesome vapours . . . characters":* Bradley, *Journal of Nicholas Cresswell,* p. 245.
422 *"Arnold asked . . . high' ":* Wheeler, op. cit., p. 388.

CHAPTER EIGHTEEN: FROM KINGS MOUNTAIN TO WILLIAMSBURG

Page 423 *"His camp . . . youth":* Quoted in Kirke, op. cit., p. 194.
424 *"The animosity . . . live":* Ibid., p. 146.
424 *"A dark . . . extirpated":* Quoted in Calhoon, op. cit., p. 204.
424 *"He asked . . . subject":* Ibid., p. 135.
424 *"taking into . . . mistreatment":* Quoted in Calhoon, op. cit., p. 135.
425 *"they could . . . report":* Kirke, op. cit., p. 220.
425 *"I have taken . . . forced"* and *"God . . . bell":* Wheeler, op. cit., p. 355.
426 *"Every man . . . quick":* Collins, *Autobiography,* p. 52.
426 *"The shot of . . . fought":* Ibid.
426 *"sheltered the [patriots] . . . fire":* Ibid.
426 *"when the silver . . . collected":* Quoted in Bradley, *United Empire Loyalists,* p. 103.
426 *"The dead lay . . . pieces":* Ibid., p. 53.
427 *"We proceeded . . . around":* Collins, op. cit., p. 53.
427 *"That glorious . . . War":* Quoted in Kirke, op. cit., p. 274.
427 *"My dear Angel . . . happiness":* Scheer and Rankin, op. cit., p. 423.
427 *"A manly . . . occasion":* W. Johnson, op. cit., p. 510.
427 *"His military abilities . . . dispersed":* Moultrie, *Memoirs,* v. 2, p. 133.
428 *"Greene is . . . neighbourhood":* Quoted in *Heroes,* p. 34.
428 *"of the most brilliant success":* Wheeler, op. cit., p. 360.
428 *"Colonel Tarleton . . . dismission":* Scheer and Rankin, op. cit., p. 427.
428 *"It is certainly . . . command":* Ibid.
429 *went among . . . night:* Ibid., p. 428.
429 *"it seemed . . . beautiful!":* Ibid., p. 430.
430 *"like a whirlwind . . . stand it":* Collins, op. cit., p. 57.
430 *"began to . . . themselves":* Ibid.
430 *"This defeat . . . troops":* Wheeler, op. cit., p. 363.
431 *"Great God . . . employment":* Quoted in Boorstin, *Colonial Experience,* p. 369.
431 *"The militia have . . . force":* Scheer and Rankin, op. cit., p. 443.
431 *"If [the militia fight . . . runs":* Quoted in Boorstin, *Colonial Experience,* p. 369.
431 *"in excellent order,"* etc.: Scheer and Rankin, op. cit., p. 447.

431 *"took to ... woods"*: Lee, *Memoirs of the War,* p. 277.
432 *"did ... execution"* and *"a galling fire"*: Scheer and Rankin, op. cit., p. 448.
432 *"victory ... arm"*: Ibid., p. 449.
432 *If we are ... Phillips:* Ibid., p. 467.
433 *"It is very ... necessary"*: Ibid.
433 *"I was most ... difficulty"*: Wheeler, op. cit., p. 388.
433 *"for the ... Army"*: C. Johnson, op. cit., p. 112.
433 *"Now, my dear ... etc."*: Scheer and Rankin, op. cit., p. 469.
433 *"The enemy ... both"*: Sparks, *Correspondence of the American Revolution,* v. 3, p. 278.
434 *"What will you ... experience"*: Quoted in *Heroes,* p. 56.
435 *"It is my ... ground"*: Quoted in Woodward, op. cit., p. 89.
435 *"all desertions ceased"*: Johnston, *Yorktown Campaign,* p. 33.
436 *"It would have ... conflagration"*: Quoted in Irving, op. cit., p. 562.
436 *Poorly clothed ... complaining:* Quoted in ibid., p. 538.
437 *"The whole ... Confusion"*: Burnett, *Letters,* v. 5, p. 527.
437 *"It is most ... crime"*: Thacher, op. cit., p. 233.
438 *"I am unable ... virtue"*: Quoted in Irving, op. cit., p. 549.
438 *"The general and I,"* etc.: Ibid., p. 551, and Boller, *Presidential Anecdotes,* p. 12.
438 *"waste fruitlessly ... parade"*: Irving, op. cit., p. 564.
439 *Instead of ... upon:* Quoted in Johnston, op. cit., p. 72.
440 *"The measure you ... terror,"* etc.: Washington, *Writings* (Fitzpatrick ed.), v. 15, p. 388.
440 *"I have run ... particular"*: Quoted in Nagle, op. cit., p. 162.
441 *"Give yourself ... cool"*: Ibid., p. 163.
441 *"The tents ... soldiery"*: Scheer and Rankin, op. cit., p. 464.
441 *"I have more ... world"*: Quoted in *Heroes,* p. 67.
441 *"At the battle ... guns"*: Ibid.
442 *"Were I to ... beasts"*: Quoted in Woodward, op. cit., p. 92.
442 *"I am not ... beaten"*: Ibid.
442 *"The boy cannot ... me"*: Quoted in Johnston, op. cit., p. 39.
443 *Late in the ... house"*: Quoted in Bowers, op. cit., pp. 275–276.
443 *"would have done ... three"*: Quoted in Brodie, op. cit., p. 280.
443 *"and of ... fruits"*: Ibid.
444 *"We frequently ... but or two"*: Quoted in Johnston, op. cit., p. 53.
444 *"Our encampments ... description"*: Ibid., p. 53.
444 *"The enemy ... opinion"*: Quoted in C. Johnson, op. cit., p. 112.
445 *"The very ... suspicion"*: Quoted in Johnston, op. cit., p. 63.
445 *"It was ... ruinous"*: Ibid., p. 65.
445 *"It gives me ... Cornwallis"*: Ibid., p. 68.
446 *Rochambeau: ... dictate"*: Ibid., pp. 76–77.
446 *"Our affairs ... it"*: Ibid, pp 76–77n.
446 *"The enemy ... offered:* Ibid., p. 77.
447 *"We must not ... conclusion"*: Quoted in R. Smith, op. cit., p. 18.
447 *"a new ... year"*: F. Wharton, *Diplomatic Correspondence,* v. 4, p. 434.
448 *"By the time ... armament"*: Quoted in Irving, op. cit., p. 565.
449 *"impenetrable secrecy"*: Thacher, op. cit., p. 244.
449 *If I had ... river:* Quoted in Johnston, op. cit., p. 91.
450 *"like a ... snow-storm"* and *"regulated ... fife"*: Quoted in ibid., p. 93.
450 *"as elegantly ... review"*: Ibid.
450 *"It is ... found"*: Ibid., p. 173.
450 *"I never ... Washington"*: Ibid., p. 95.
450 *"Nothing but ... us"*: Ibid.
453 *"caught the ... return"*: Scheer and Rankin, op. cit., p. 476.
453 *"Every day ... them"*: Quoted in Irving, op. cit., p. 578.

CHAPTER NINETEEN: YORKTOWN

Page 454 *"prove the ... victory"*: Quoted in Johnston, op. cit., p. 105.
454 *"The whole ... night"*: Ibid., p. 106.
455 *"Cornwallis ... fall"*: Palmer, op. cit., p. 289.
455 *"from different ... impossible"*: Franklin, *Writings,* v. 8, p. 333.
456 *"I have ... troops"*: Quoted in Irving, op. cit., p. 580.

456 *"much labor . . . force"*: Wheeler, op. cit., p. 398.
457 *"unabating ardor . . . hands"*: Quoted in Johnston, op. cit., pp. 122–123.
457 *"See, here . . . children"*: Thacher, op. cit., p. 255.
457 *"We get . . . night"*: Wheeler, op. cit., p. 397.
457 *"His political . . . more"*: Quoted in Johnston, op. cit., p. 127.
458 *"talked familiarly . . . minutes"*: Martin, op. cit., p. 231.
458 *"General Washington . . . Yorktown"*: Ibid., p. 232.
459 *"The enemy seem . . . kept up"*: Quoted in Johnston, op. cit., p. 128.
459 *"I confess . . . foes"*: Martin, op. cit., p. 233.
460 *"The ships . . . deep"*: Thacher, op. cit., p. 339.
460 *"Against so . . . resistance"*: Quoted in Johnston, p. 130.
460 *"I now . . . night"*: Ibid.
460 *"[went] over . . . night"*: Ibid., p. 141n.
461 *"a good one . . . quick"*: Martin, op. cit., p. 234.
461 *"If you think . . . back"*: Thacher, op. cit., p. 341.
461 *"My situation . . . save us"*: Quoted in Johnson, op. cit. p. 122.
461 *"A shell,"* etc.: Scheer and Rankin, op. cit., p. 489.
463 *"an ardent . . . admissible"*: Ibid., p. 490.
463 *"universal silence . . . prevailed"*: Thacher, op. cit., p. 344.
463 *"recognition . . . Providence"*: Quoted in Irving, op. cit. p. 591.
463 *"careless and irregular"*: Ibid.
464 *"entirely to . . . despair"*: Ibid., p. 346.
464 *"Sir,— . . . soldiers:* Quoted in Johnston, pp. 181–183.
465 *"Posterity will . . . us"*: Quoted in R. Smith, op. cit., p. 18.
465 *"When the illustrious . . . Chesapeake"*: Quoted in Preacher, op. cit., p. 203.
466 *"Basht . . . da-ken"*: Quoted in Johnston, op. cit., p. 158.
466 *"the completeness . . . rejoicing"*: Ibid., p. 11.
466 *"To his Majesty . . . obeyed"*: Boller, op. cit., p. 13.
466 *"I have no . . . alterations"*: Quoted in Johnston, op. cit., p. 160.
466 *"a ball . . . over!"*: Wraxall, *Historical Memoirs*, p. 246.

CHAPTER TWENTY: THE END OF THE BEGINNING

Page 467 *"My only . . . calamities"*: Scheer and Rankin, op. cit., p. 497.
467 *"an interesting . . . improved"*: Quoted in Flexner, *George Washington*, p. 164.
468 *"expose us . . . disasters"*: Quoted in Freeman, *Washington* (one-volume ed.), p. 494.
468 *"My greatest . . . relaxation"*: Quoted in Silverman, op. cit., p. 410.
468 *You apply . . . purgatory:* Quoted in Wharton, op. cit., p. 114.
469 *"I went for . . . past"*: Quoted in Conway, *Thomas Paine*, p. 174.
469 *Second Street . . . cause:* Ibid., pp. 178–180.
470 *"much for . . . avowed"*: Ibid., p. 182.
470 *"You will do . . . when"*: Ibid., pp. 184–185.
471 *"Pray, let me . . . farce"*: Ibid., p. 186.
472 *"From the former . . . exertion"*: Quoted in Flexner, op. cit., p. 167.
472 *"That spirit . . . place"*: Quoted in Silverman, op. cit., p. 420.
472 *"I have not . . . entertain"*: Quoted in Conway, *Thomas Paine*, pp. 191–192.
472 *"You are to . . . opinion"*: Quoted in S. Shaw, *Journals of Major Samuel Shaw*, p. 107.
473 *"remitted to us . . . debt"*: Quoted in Montross, op. cit., p. 337.
473 *"With a mixture . . . nature"*: Quoted in Preacher, op. cit., p. 244.
474 *goaded by . . . nature:* Quoted in Flexner, op. cit., p. 167.
474 *"When soldiers advance . . . expect"*: Quoted in Mintz, op. cit., p. 160.
474 *"Suspect the man . . . forebearance"*: Quoted in Irving, op. cit., p. 602.
474 *"sensibly agitated,"* etc.: S. Shaw, op. cit., pp. 103–104.
475 *reason is of . . . attaining"*: Quoted in Flexner, op. cit., p. 174.
475 *"I have already . . . blind"*: S. Shaw, op. cit., p. 104.
475 *"so natural . . . eye"*: S. Shaw, op. cit., p. 104.
475 *"The moderation . . . establish"*: Quoted in Flexner, op. cit., p. 175.
475 *"to grow old . . . life"*: Ibid., p. 176.
476 *"happy, thrice happy,"* etc.: Ibid.
476 *"Nothing now . . . actions"*: Quoted in R. Smith, op. cit., p. 19.
476 *"a retirement for . . . repose"*: Quoted in Irving, op. cit., p. 612.

476 *sole lords . . . involved:* Quoted in Hendrick, *Bulwark of the Republic,* p. 19.
477 *"First. An . . . supported":* Ibid., p. 20.
477 *"the unsolicited . . . advice":* Ibid., p. 18.
477 *"THE ILLUSTRIOUS . . . INDEPENDENCE":* Lossing, *Mary and Martha,* p. 222n.
478 *"With a heart,"* etc.: Tallmadge, op. cit., pp. 95–98.
479 *"Mr. President: . . . life":* Washington, *Writings* (Fitzpatrick ed.), v. 27, pp. 284–285.
479 *Called upon by . . . give:* Quoted in Bowers, op. cit., p. 320.
481 *"the Word Right . . . acknowledged?":* Quoted in S. Shaw, op. cit., p. 179.
481 *"It is agreed . . . confiscated":* Otto, *Treaty of Paris,* pp. 21–22.
482 *"Make it the . . . friends":* Quoted in Callahan, *Flight from the Republic,* p. 138.
482 *I feel no . . . whelps?:* Quoted in Tyler, op. cit., pp. 290–291.
483 *"I feel myself . . . Virtues":* Quoted in Lossing, *Mary and Martha,* p. 231.
484 *"My manner of . . . disappointed":* Ibid., p. 233.
484 *"I am so hackneyed . . . chair":* Quoted in Irving, op. cit., p. 628.
484 *"I had rather glide . . . me":* Quoted in R. Smith, op. cit., p. xvi.
484 *"At length . . . satisfaction":* Quoted in Hendrick, op. cit., p. 12.
484 *"I expect to . . . Versailles":* Quoted in Lossing, *Mary and Martha,* p. 233.
484 *"The Declaration . . . Rights":* Quoted in Woodward, p. 132.
484 *"clad in . . . hat":* Quoted in Lossing, *Mary and Martha,* p. 64.
484 *"I am not . . . boy":* Ibid., p. 65.
485 *"In the moment . . . day":* Quoted Woodward, op. cit., p. 152.
485 *"nothing but frowns":* Quoted in Dorson, op. cit., p. 288.
486 *"An American born,"* etc.: Ibid., pp. 304–305.
486 *"It is supposed . . . years":* Ibid., p. 90.
486 *"a very great . . . collected":* Ibid., p. 91.
487 *"in the name . . . Free":* Ibid.
487 *"I cannot conclude . . . Kingdom":* Quoted in O'Brien, op. cit., p. 233.
487 *"I wish you . . . power":* Quoted in Davidson, op. cit., p. 322.
487 *"Fellows who . . . chariots":* Quoted in Forbes, op. cit., p. 366.
487 *"The artful and . . . manners":* Ibid.
487 *"Luxury, ostentation . . . more":* Ibid.
488 *"the greatest . . . 'em":* Quoted in Brown and Senior, op. cit., p. 27.
488 *"a feeble thread":* Quoted in Hendrick, op. cit., p. 17.
488 *"local or state . . . dictate":* Quoted in R. Smith, op. cit., p. 19.
489 *Certain I am . . . incurred:* Quoted in Hendrick, op. cit., p. 17.
489 *"A people cannot . . . judgements":* Quoted in P. Smith, op. cit., p. 246.
490 *"It is the result . . . framers":* Quoted in Lossing, *Mary and Martha,* pp. 255–256.
490 *"It is said . . . men":* Quoted in R. Smith, op. cit., p. 21.
490 *"an ocean of difficulties,"* etc.: Quoted in Lossing, *Mary and Martha,* pp. 256–257.
491 *"Do you solemnly swear,"* etc.: Ibid., p. 272.
491 *"I greatly fear . . . me":* Boller, *Presidential Anecdotes,* p. 20.
492 *"All those who . . . is":* Quoted in Brock, op. cit., p. 73n.
492 *"contracted no . . . anarchy":* Quoted in Davidson, op. cit., p. 325.
492 *"to mete out . . . bed":* Ibid.
493 *"Rebellion to tyrants,"* etc.: C. Adams, op. cit., p. 211.
494 *The Constellation denotes . . . date:* Quoted in Silverman, op. cit., p. 416.
494 *"The tavern . . . Revolution":* Quoted in R. Wright, op. cit., p. 49.
495 *"From the Court House . . . Day":* Quoted in *Handbook for the Exhibition Buildings,* p. 47.

BIBLIOGRAPHY

Abbott, W. W. "An Uncommon Awareness of Self: The Papers of George Washington." *Prologue* (National Archives publication), Spring 1989, pp. 1–15.

Adams, Charles Francis, ed. *Familiar Letters of John Adams and His Wife*. Boston, 1875.

Adams, James Truslow. *Provincial Society*. Boston, 1933.

———. *Revolutionary New England*. New York, 1930.

Adams, John. *The Works of John Adams*. 10 vols. Charles Francis Adams, ed. Boston, 1850–1856.

Adlum, John. *Memoirs of the Life of John Adlum*. Chicago, 1968.

Alden, John R. *A History of the American Revolution*. New York, 1969.

Allen, Ethan. *A Narrative of Colonel Ethan Allen's Captivity*. Burlington, Vt., 1846.

Anburey, Thomas. *Travels Through the Interior Parts of America*. 2 vols. Boston, 1923.

Bailyn, Bernard, ed. *Pamphlets of the American Revolution*. Vol. 1., *1750–1765*. Cambridge, Mass., 1965.

———. *The Peopling of British North America*. London, 1986.

———. *Voyagers to the West*. New York, 1987.

Barker, John. *The British in Boston*. Cambridge, Mass., 1924.

Bellamy, Francis R. *The Private Life of George Washington*. New York, 1951.

Beloff, M., ed. *The Debate on the American Revolution*. London, 1949.

Best, John Hardin, ed. *Benjamin Franklin on Education*. New York, 1962.

Best, Mary Agnes. *Thomas Paine*. London, n.d.

Boller, Paul F., Jr. "George Washington and Civilian Supremacy." *Southwest Review* 39 (Winter 1954), 16–21.

———. *Presidential Anecdotes*. New York, 1984.

Boorstin, Daniel J. *The Americans: The Colonial Experience*. New York, 1958.

———. *Hidden History*. New York, 1987.

Boudinot, Elias. *Journal of Historical Recollections*. Philadelphia, 1894.

Bowen, Catherine Drinker. *The Most Dangerous Man in America*. Boston, 1974.

Bowen, Francis. *The Life of Baron Steuben*. Vol. 9 of Jared Sparks, ed., *The Library of American Biography*. Boston, 1838.

Bowers, Claude G. *The Young Jefferson*. Boston, 1945.

Boyd, Thomas. *Light-Horse Harry Lee*. New York, 1931.

Bradley, A. G., ed. *The Journal of Nicholas Cresswell*. New York, 1928.

———. *The United Empire Loyalists*. London, 1932.

Bridenbaugh, Carl. *Cities in the Wilderness*. New York, 1955.

———. *Early Americans*. New York, 1960.

———, ed. *Gentleman's Progress: The Itinerarium of Dr. Alexander Hamilton, 1744*. Chapel Hill, 1948.

———. *Rebels and Gentlemen*. New York, 1942.

Brock, W. R. *The Character of American History*. New York, 1960.

Brodie, Fawn M. *Thomas Jefferson: An Intimate History*. New York, 1974.

Brown, Clarence Winthrop, ed. *The History of the Centennial Celebration of the Inauguration of George Washington as First President of the United States*. New York, 1892.

Brown, Wallace, and Hereward Senior. *Victorious in Defeat: The American Loyalists in Exile*. New York, 1984.

Bruns, Roger. *Thomas Jefferson*. New York, 1986.

Burke, Edmund, *Writings and Speeches*. Gen. Ed. Paul Langford. 8 vols. Oxford, 1973 to present.

Burnett, Edmund Cody. *The Continental Congress*. New York, 1941.

———, ed. *Letters of Members of the Continental Congress*. 8 vols. Washington, D.C., 1921–1936.

Butterfield, L. H., ed. *Diary and Autobiography of John Adams.* 2 vols. Cambridge, Mass., 1961.

Byrd, William, II. *William Byrd II's History of the Dividing Line Betwixt Virginia and North Carolina.* Raleigh, 1929.

Calhoon, Robert M. *The Loyalist Perception, and Other Essays.* Columbia, S.C., 1989.

Callahan, North. *Flight from the Republic: The Tories of the American Revolution.* New York, 1967.

———. *Henry Knox.* New York, 1958.

The Centennial of the Settlement of Upper Canada by the United Empire Loyalists, 1784–1884. Toronto, 1885.

Chase, Eugene Parker, ed. and trans. *Our Revolutionary Forefathers. The Letters of François, Marquis de Barbé-Marbois, 1779–1785.* New York, 1929.

Chastellux, Marquis de. *Travels in North America in the Years 1780, 1781 and 1782.* 2 vols. Philadelphia, 1812.

Collins, James P. *Autobiography of a Revolutionary Soldier.* Clinton, La., 1859.

Commager, Henry Steele, and Richard B. Morris. *The Spirit of Seventy-six.* 2 vols. New York, 1967.

Conway, Moncure D. *George Washington of Mount Vernon.* New York, 1888.

———. *The Life of Thomas Paine.* 2 vols. New York, 1892.

Crèvecoeur, St. John de. *Sketches of Eighteenth Century America.* 1925.

Custis, G. W. P. *Memoirs of Washington.* Chicago, 1859.

Cutter, William. *The Life of Israel Putnam.* Boston, 1846.

Davidson, Marshall B. *The Horizon History of the World in 1776.* New York, 1975.

DeGregorio, William A. *The Complete Book of U.S. Presidents.* New York, 1984.

Denton, Daniel. *A Brief Description of New-York: Formerly Called New-Netherlands.* London, 1670.

Dexter, Elizabeth W. *Colonial Women of Affairs.* Boston, 1924.

Digby, William. *The British Invasion from the North.* Albany, 1887.

Dorson, Richard M. *American Rebels: Narratives of the Patriots.* New York, 1953.

Dow, George Francis. *Arts and Crafts in New England.* Topsfield, Mass., 1927.

Drake, Francis. *Henry Knox.* Boston, 1873.

Dring, Thomas. *Recollections of the Jersey Prison-Ship.* Providence, 1929.

Earle, Alice Morse. *Home Life in Colonial Days.* Stockbridge, Mass., 1974.

Ellis, Joseph J. "Editing the 'Declaration.' " *Civilization,* July/August 1995, 58–63.

———. "Friends at Twilight." *American Heritage,* May/June 1993, 44–52.

Emerson, Ralph Waldo. *Collected Poems.* New York, 1921.

Fanning, Nathaniel. *The Memoirs of Nathaniel Fanning.* New York, 1912.

Farish, Hunter D., ed. *Journal & Letters of Philip Vickers Fithian, 1773–1774: A Plantation Tutor of the Old Dominion.* Williamsburg, Va., 1943.

Fiske, John. *The American Revolution.* 2 vols. Boston, 1901.

———. *Essays Historical and Literary.* 2 vols. London, 1903.

Flexner, James Thomas. *George Washington in the American Revolution.* Boston, 1967.

Forbes, Esther. *Paul Revere and the World He Lived In.* Cambridge, Mass., 1942.

Ford, Worthington Chauncey. *Inventory of the Contents of Mount Vernon, 1810.* Portland, 1909.

———, ed. *Journals of the Continental Congress.* 34 vols. Washington, D.C., 1904–1937.

Franklin, Benjamin. *Autobiography.* New York, 1968.

Freeman, Douglas Southall. *George Washington: A Biography.* 7 vols. New York, 1948–1957. Abridged to 1 vol. by Richard Harwell, New York, 1968.

French, Allen. *The Taking of Ticonderoga in 1775.* Cambridge, Mass., 1928.

———. *General Gage's Informers.* Ann Arbor, Mich., 1932.

Furnas, J. C. *The Americans.* New York, 1969.

Gage, Thomas. *The Correspondence of General Thomas Gage.* 2 vols. New Haven, Conn.: 1931–1933.

Gérard, Conrad-Alexandre. *Despatches and Instructions, 1778–1780.* John J. Meng, ed. Baltimore, 1939.

Gerlach, Don R. *Philip Schuyler and the American Revolution in New York, 1733–1777.* Lincoln, 1964.

Gordon, John Steele. "Land of the Free Trade." *American Heritage* 44, no. 4 (July/August 1993), 50–61.

Gottschalk, Louis. *Lafayette Joins the American Army.* Chicago, 1937.

Graeff, Arthur D. "Anecdotes Related in Pennsylvanian-German Almanacs." Part 2, *The American-German Review* 6 (June 1940), 33–45.

Graham, James. *The Life of General Daniel Morgan*. New York, 1856.

Greene, Evarts. *The Foundations of American Nationality*. Chicago, 1922.

Greene, George Washington. *The German Element in the War of Independence*. New York, 1876.

———. *The Life of Nathanael Greene*. 3 vols. New York, 1867–1871.

A Handbook for the Exhibition Buildings of Colonial Williamsburg. Williamsburg, Va., 1937.

Hargreaves, Reginald. "The Man Who Almost Shot Washington." *American Heritage,* December 1955, 62–65.

Hawke, David Freeman. *Everyday Life in Early America*. New York, 1988.

Headley, W. T. *Washington and His Generals*. 2 vols. New York, 1848.

Heath, William. *Memoirs of Major-General William Heath*. New York, 1901.

Hendrick, Burton J. *Bulwark of the Republic*. Boston, 1937.

Heroes of the American Revolution. Boston, 1855.

Hibbert, Christopher. *Redcoat and Rebels*. New York, 1990.

Higginbotham, Don. *The War of American Independence*. New York, 1971.

Hudleston, F. J. *Gentleman Johnny Burgoyne*. Garden City, N.Y., 1927.

Irving, Washington. *George Washington: A Biography*. Ed. and abridged by Charles Neider. New York, 1975.

Japikse, Carl, ed. *Selected Writings of Benjamin Franklin*. Columbus, Ohio, 1990.

Jefferson, Thomas. *The Papers of Thomas Jefferson*. Julian P. Boyd, ed. vols. 1 and 2. Princeton, N.J., 1950.

———. *Writings*. 9 vols. H. A. Washington, ed. New York, 1853–1854.

———. *The Writings of Thomas Jefferson*. 20 vols. Albert Ellery Bergh, ed. Washington, D.C., 1904–1905.

Jones, Thomas. *History of New York During the Revolutionary War*. 2 vols. New York, 1879.

Johnson, Curt. *The Battles of the Revolutionary War*. London, 1975.

Johnston, Henry P. *The Yorktown Campaign and the Surrender of Cornwallis, 1781*. New York, 1881.

Ketchum, Richard M., ed. *The American Heritage Book of the Revolution*. New York, 1974.

Kirke, Edmund. *The Rear-Guard of the Revolution*. New York, 1887.

Knight, Sarah Kemble. *The Journal of Madam Knight*. Boston, 1920.

Knollenberg, Bernhard. *Washington and the Revolution*. New York, 1942.

Lafayette, Marquis de. *Mémoires*. H. Fournier Aîné, ed. Leipzig, 1838.

Lancaster, Bruce. *The American Revolution*. Boston, 1971.

Larkin, David, June Sprigg, and James Johnson. *Colonial Design in the New World*. New York, 1988.

Lee, Henry. *Memoirs of the War*. New York, 1870.

Lewis, Taylor Biggs, Jr., and Joanne B. Young. *Christmas in Williamsburg*. New York, 1970.

Lossing, Benson J. *Field-book of the American Revolution*. 2 vols. New York, 1850.

———. *The Life of Philip Schuyler*. 2 vols. New York, 1872.

———. *Mary and Martha*. New York, 1886.

———. *The Two Spies: Nathan Hale and John André*. New York, 1886.

Maier, Pauline. *The Old Revolutionaries*. New York, 1980.

———. Review of Gordon Wood's *The Radicalism of the American Revolution, The New York Times Book Review*, March 1, 1992, p. 33.

Malone, Dumas. *The Story of the Declaration of Independence*. New York, 1954.

Marshall, John. *The Life of George Washington*. Philadelphia, 1807.

Martin, Joseph Plumb. *Private Yankee Doodle*. New York, 1962.

Mason, G. C. "African Slave Trade in Colonial Times," *American Historical Record*, vol. 1, 1872.

McDowell, Bart. *The Revolutionary War*. Washington, D.C., 1967.

Middlekauff, Robert. *The Glorious Cause*. New York, 1982.

Mika, Nick and Helma. *The United Empire Loyalists*. Belleville, Ont., 1976.

Miller, John C. *Origins of the American Revolution*. Boston, 1943.

Miller, Perry, and Thomas H. Johnson, eds. *The Puritans: A Sourcebook of Their Writings*. 2 vols. Boston, 1963.

Mintz, Max M. *Gouverneur Morris and the American Revolution*. Norman, Okla., 1970.

Montross, Lynn. *The Reluctant Rebels*. New York, 1950.

Moore, Frank, ed. *The Diary of the American Revolution*. Hartford, Conn., 1875.

Moreau de St.-Méry, Médéric. *American Journey*. Garden City, N.Y., 1947.

Morgan, Edmund S., and Helen M. Morgan. *The Stamp Act Crisis: Prologue to Revolution*. Chapel Hill, N.C., 1953.

Morison, Samuel Eliot. *John Paul Jones*. New York, 1959.

———, ed. *Sources and Documents Illustrating the American Revolution*. Oxford, England, 1923.

Morris, Charles, ed. *The Great Republic by the Master Historians*. New York, 1902.

Mosely, Jeremy. *The War in the North*. Bennington, Vt., 1890.

Moultrie, William. *Memoirs*. 2 vols. New York, 1802.

Munves, James. *Thomas Jefferson and the Declaration of Independence*. Washington, D.C., 1976.

Nagle, Paul C. *The Lees of Virginia*. New York, 1990.

Narratives of Early Pennsylvania, West New Jersey, and Delaware, 1630–1707. New York, 1912.

O'Brien, Conor Cruise. *The Great Melody*. Chicago, 1992.

Orton, Vrest. *Republic of Vermont*. Rutland, Vt., 1977.

Otto, Calvin P. *Treaty of Paris, 1783*. Bennington, Vt., 1976.

Paine, Thomas. *Common Sense*. New York, 1982.

———. *The Crisis*. New York, 1995.

Palmer, John McAuley. *General von Steuben*. New Haven, Conn., 1937.

Parkman, Francis. *Montcalm and Wolfe*. 2 vols. Cambridge, Mass., 1884.

Peckham, Howard H., ed. *Memoirs of the Life of John Adlum in the Revolutionary War*. Chicago, 1968.

Perkins, James Breck. *France in the American Revolution*. Boston, 1911.

Potter, Israel. *Life and Remarkable Adventures of Israel R. Potter*. Providence, 1824.

Preacher, Florence. *Song of Freedom*. Baltimore, 1899.

Purcell, L. Edward, and David F. Burg. *The World Almanac of the American Revolution*. New York, 1992.

Randall, Henry S. *The Life of Thomas Jefferson*. 3 vols. New York, 1858.

Randall, Willard Sterne. *Benedict Arnold: Patriot and Traitor*. New York, 1990.

Reed, William B. *Life and Correspondence of Joseph Reed*. 2 vols. Philadelphia, 1847.

Riedesel, Baroness von. *Letters and Journals Relating to the War of the American Revolution, and the Capture of the German Troops at Saratoga*. Translated by William L. Stone. Albany, 1867.

Roberts, Kenneth L. *March to Quebec*. New York, 1940.

Rochambeau, Marshal Count de. *Memoirs . . . Relative to the War of Independence*. Paris, 1838.

Rush, Benjamin. *Letters*. Lyman H. Butterfield, ed. 2 vols. Princeton, N.J., 1951.

Sabine, Lorenzo. *The American Loyalists*. Boston, 1847.

Sargent, Winthrop, ed. *Every Day Life in Massachusetts Bay Colony*. Boston, 1935.

Scheer, George F., and Hugh F. Rankin. *Rebels and Redcoats. The American Revolution Through the Eyes of Those Who Fought and Lived It*. New York, 1957.

Scott, James B. *The Declaration of Independence, The Articles of Confederation, The Constitution of the United States*. New York, 1917.

Scott, John Anthony. *Settlers on the Eastern Shore*. New York, 1967.

Sellers, Charles Coleman. *Benedict Arnold*. New York, 1930.

Senter, Isaac. *The Journal of Isaac Senter*. New York, 1969.

Serle, Ambrose. *American Journal*. San Marino, Calif., 1940.

Shaw, Peter. *The Character of John Adams*. Chapel Hill, N.C., 1976.

Shaw, Samuel. *The Journals of Major Shaw*. Boston, 1847.

Sherrill, C. H. *French Memoirs of 18th-Century America*. Boston, 1904.

Silverman, Kenneth. *A Cultural History of the American Revolution*. New York, 1987.

Simms, William Gilmore. *Nathanael Greene*. New York, 1858.

Smith, Goldwin. *The United States: An Outline of Political History*. New York, 1901.

Smith, Page. *John Adams*, Vol. 1, *1735–1784*. Garden City, N.Y., 1962.

———. *A New Age Begins*. 2 vols. New York, 1976.

Smith, Richard Norton. *Patriarch: George Washington and the New American Nation*. Boston, 1993.

Sparks, Jared, ed. *Correspondence of the American Revolution*. 4 vols. Boston, 1853.

———. *John Sullivan*. Boston, 1848.

Steele, Matthew Forney. *American Campaigns*. War Dept. Doc. No. 324, Office Chief of Staff. Harrisburg, Pa., 1943.

Stillé, Charles J. *Major-General Anthony Wayne and the Pennsylvania Line*. Philadelphia, 1893.

Stokesbury, James L. *A Short History of the American Revolution*. New York, 1991.

Stubenrauch, Bob. *Where Freedom Grew*. New York, 1858.

Tallmadge, Benjamin. *Memoir*. New York, 1970.

Tatum, Edward H., ed. *The American Journal of Ambrose Serle, Secretary to Lord Howe, 1776–1778*. San Marino, Calif., 1940.

Thacher, James. *Military Journal of the American Revolution*. Hartford, Conn., 1827.

Thane, Elswyth. *The Fighting Quaker: Nathanael Greene*. New York, 1972.

Thayer, Theodore. *Nathanael Green*. New York, 1960.

Thomas, Gordon K. "'And When America Was Free'": Thomas Paine and the English Romantics." *The Charles Lamb Bulletin, The Journal of the Charles Lamb Society,* New Series No. 69 (January 1990), 164–176.

Thornton, John Wingate, ed. *The Pulpit of the American Revolution*. New York, 1970.

Trevelyan, Sir George O. *The American Revolution*. 4 vols. New York, 1899–1907.

Trumbull, John. *Autobiography, Reminiscences and Letters*. New York, 1841.

Tuckerman, Bayard. *Lafayette*. 2 vols. New York, 1889.

———. *Life of General Philip Schuyler*. New York, 1905.

Turner, Larry. *Voyage of a Different Kind: The Associated Loyalists of Kingston and Adolphustown*. Belleville, Ont., 1984.

Tyler, Moses Coit. *Patrick Henry*. Boston, 1898.

Urwin, Gregory J. W. *The United States Infantry*. New York, 1991.

Valentine, Alan. *Lord Stirling*. New York, 1969.

Vanderbilt, Gertrude L. *Social History of Flatbush*. New York, 1900.

Van Doren, Carl. *Benjamin Franklin*. New York, 1938.

Van Tyne, Claude Halstead. *The Loyalists in the American Revolution*. New York, 1922.

Waldo, Albigence. "Diary," in *Pennsylvania Magazine of History and Biography* 21 (1897), 299–323.

Washington, George. *The Writings of George Washington*. John C. Fitzpatrick, ed. 39 vols. Washington, D.C., 1925.

———. *The Writings of George Washington*. Worthington Chauncey Ford, ed. 14 vols. New York, 1893.

Wector, Dixon. *Hero in America*. New York, 1941.

Wharton, Anne Hollingsworth. *Colonial Days and Dames*. Philadelphia, 1898.

Wheeler, Richard. *Voices of 1776*. New York, 1972.

Whitlock, Brand. *Lafayette*. 2 vols. New York, 1929.

Wilkinson, James. *Memoirs of My Own Times*. 3 vols. Philadelphia, 1816.

Willard, Margaret W., ed. *Letters on the American Revolution, 1774–1776*. Boston, 1825.

Wilson, Rufus R., ed. *Barnaby's Travels Through North America*. New York, 1904.

———, ed. *Peter Kalm's Travels in North America*. 2 vols. New York, 1937.

Wood, Gordon S. *The Creation of the American Republic, 1776–1787*. New York, 1969.

Woodward, W. E. *Lafayette*. New York, 1938.

Wraxall, Nathaniel W. *Historical Memoirs of My Own Time*. Philadelphia, 1845.

Wright, Louis B. *The Atlantic Frontier*. New York, 1947.

Wright, Richardson. *Early American Wags and Eccentrics from Colonial Times to the Civil War*. Philadelphia, 1939.

Young, Eleanor. *Forgotten Patriot: Robert Morris*. New York, 1950.

INDEX

Louis XVI, King of France, 193, 363–64,
447, 450, 466, 472, 473
Louisiana, 19, 390
Lovell, James, 294–95, 299–301
Loyal American Regiment, 324, 424
loyalists, 105, 209–11, 237, 313–25, 342,
371–72
in British forces, 261 (*see also specific
units*)
exile of, 481–83
Indian attack on, 256
in New Jersey, 238, 316, 321, 471
in New York, 210–11, 258, 313, 318,
319, 321–23, 396
and outbreak of war, 119–20
in Pennsylvania, 266, 316, 321, 322,
324
retribution against, 409–10
in South, 373–74, 423–24, 434
Lusk, George, 321
Lutherans, 41
Luzerne, César de la, 368, 404, 447
Lynch, William, 323

Mackenzie, Capt. Robert, 106
Madison, James, 440
Maier, Pauline, 112
Maine, 19, 32, 183
Arnold in, 169, 171
British in, 365
Manchester, duke of, 166
Marbury v. Madison (1803), 492
Maresquelle, Louis de, 159
Marie-Antoinette, Queen of France,
471
Marine Corps, 381
Marion, Francis, 400, 423, 439
Marshall, John, 100, 132, 298, 492
Martin, Joseph Plumb, 208
Martin, Josiah, 210
Martinique, 27, 192, 195
Maryland, 33, 53, 371, 435
British positions in, 179
colonial life in, 32, 33, 38, 39, 41
Continental Congress delegation of,
124, 154, 190, 292
events leading to Revolution in, 92
in French and Indian War, 24
legislature of, 479
loyalists in, 316, 324
mustering of troops in, 109, 110, 123

prisoners of war in, 465
stamp tax in, 71
Mason, George, 84, 95, 201, 362
Mason-Dixon Line, 39, 42
Massachusetts, 97, 108
Assembly, 66, 71, 75, 76, 83, 84, 111,
318
colonial life in, 32, 52
Committee of Public Safety, 114, 136,
156
Continental Congress delegation of,
95, 103–4, 107, 121–23, 133
and Declaration of Independence, 204
events leading to Revolution in, 76, 78,
82, 84, 91, 92
loyalists in, 320, 322
militia of, 255, 261, 326
mustering of troops in, 145
powder mills in, 159
Provincial Congress, 111, 112, 123,
145, 156, 158, 257
slave trade abolished in, 102
tradition of independence in, 67
see also Boston
Massachusetts Gazette, 155
Massachusetts Spy, 51, 317
Mather, Cotton, 46
Mathews, David, 211
Mayflower (ship), 32
Mayhew, Jonathan, 65, 66
Mayr, Gen. von, 332
McCrea, Jane, 256, 258
McKean, Thomas, 466
McPherson, Capt., 238
McWilliams, Maj., 304
medicine, colonial-era, 54–57
Melville, Herman, 90, 130
Melville, Thomas, 90
Mennonites, 40, 316, 320
Menotomy, Battle of, 118–19
mercenaries, German, *see* Hessians
Mercer, Fort, 269, 271
Mercer, Gen. Hugh, 235
Methodists, 101
Mexico, 390
Miami Indians, 376
Mifflin, Fort, 269–71
Mifflin, Thomas, 134, 239, 298, 336, 479–
480
militia system, 326–28
see also militia *under specific states*

FOR THE BEST IN PAPERBACKS, LOOK FOR THE

In every corner of the world, on every subject under the sun, Penguin represents quality and variety—the very best in publishing today.

For complete information about books available from Penguin—including Puffins, Penguin Classics, and Arkana—and how to order them, write to us at the appropriate address below. Please note that for copyright reasons the selection of books varies from country to country.

In the United Kingdom: Please write to *Dept. JC, Penguin Books Ltd, FREEPOST, West Drayton, Middlesex UB7 0BR.*

If you have any difficulty in obtaining a title, please send your order with the correct money, plus ten percent for postage and packaging, to *P.O. Box No. 11, West Drayton, Middlesex UB7 0BR*

In the United States: Please write to *Consumer Sales, Penguin USA, P.O. Box 999, Dept. 17109, Bergenfield, New Jersey 07621-0120.* VISA and MasterCard holders call 1-800-253-6476 to order all Penguin titles

In Canada: Please write to *Penguin Books Canada Ltd, 10 Alcorn Avenue, Suite 300, Toronto, Ontario M4V 3B2*

In Australia: Please write to *Penguin Books Australia Ltd, P.O. Box 257, Ringwood, Victoria 3134*

In New Zealand: Please write to *Penguin Books (NZ) Ltd, Private Bag 102902, North Shore Mail Centre, Auckland 10*

In India: Please write to *Penguin Books India Pvt Ltd, 706 Eros Apartments, 56 Nehru Place, New Delhi 110 019*

In the Netherlands: Please write to *Penguin Books Netherlands bv, Postbus 3507, NL-1001 AH Amsterdam*

In Germany: Please write to *Penguin Books Deutschland GmbH, Metzlerstrasse 26, 60594 Frankfurt am Main*

In Spain: Please write to *Penguin Books S. A., Bravo Murillo 19, 1° B, 28015 Madrid*

In Italy: Please write to *Penguin Italia s.r.l., Via Felice Casati 20, I-20124 Milano*

In France: Please write to *Penguin France S. A., 17 rue Lejeune, F–31000 Toulouse*

In Japan: Please write to *Penguin Books Japan, Ishikiribashi Building, 2–5–4, Suido, Bunkyo-ku, Tokyo 112*

In Greece: Please write to *Penguin Hellas Ltd, Dimocritou 3, GR–106 71 Athens*

In South Africa: Please write to *Longman Penguin Southern Africa (Pty) Ltd, Private Bag X08, Bertsham 2013*